FROM TUDOR TO STUART

FROM TUDOR TO STUART

THE REGIME CHANGE FROM ELIZABETH I TO JAMES I

SUSAN DORAN

OXFORD
UNIVERSITY PRESS

Great Clarendon Street, Oxford, OX2 6DP,
United Kingdom

Oxford University Press is a department of the University of Oxford.
It furthers the University's objective of excellence in research, scholarship,
and education by publishing worldwide. Oxford is a registered trade mark of
Oxford University Press in the UK and in certain other countries

© Susan Doran 2024

The moral rights of the author have been asserted

All rights reserved. No part of this publication may be reproduced, stored in
a retrieval system, or transmitted, in any form or by any means, without the
prior permission in writing of Oxford University Press, or as expressly permitted
by law, by licence or under terms agreed with the appropriate reprographics
rights organization. Enquiries concerning reproduction outside the scope of the
above should be sent to the Rights Department, Oxford University Press, at the
address above

You must not circulate this work in any other form
and you must impose this same condition on any acquirer

Published in the United States of America by Oxford University Press
198 Madison Avenue, New York, NY 10016, United States of America

British Library Cataloguing in Publication Data
Data available

Library of Congress Control Number: 2023947243

ISBN 978–0–19–875464–0

DOI: 10.1093/oso/9780198754640.001.0001

Printed and bound in the UK by
Clays Ltd, Elcograf S.p.A.

Links to third party websites are provided by Oxford in good faith and
for information only. Oxford disclaims any responsibility for the materials
contained in any third party website referenced in this work.

For Edie, Guy, and Hugo

Acknowledgements

In many respects, it was a foolhardy venture for me to embark on an entirely new period of research some eight years ago. But I had studied the Tudors for decades and felt the need for a fresh challenge. What was more, I had spent many years working on the Elizabethan succession question and wished to investigate what happened next. However, the early Stuart period was then outside my comfort zone, and I have been greatly indebted to friends and colleagues who have offered me advice and generously commented in depth on drafts of chapters. My deepest thanks go to Lori Anne Ferrell, Kenneth Fincham, Norman Jones, Brendan Kane, Anthony Milton, Steven Reid, Malcolm Smuts, Tracey Sowerby, and Andrew Thrush, all of whom gave me the benefit of their specialized knowledge, corrected errors, and made invaluable suggestions to improve the text. As always, Paulina Kewes raised stimulating ideas on our many walks together and generously passed on secondary literature that I might otherwise have missed. The book would have been poorer without her input. My husband Alan read the whole book and came up with ways of making it more accessible to a general reader. Of course, I take responsibility for any remaining errors.

I am immensely grateful to Jesus College and St Benet's Hall, Oxford, for providing me with research funding that enabled me to carry out archival research in Edinburgh and at the Folger Library in Washington, USA. I am also indebted to the Huntington Library, San Marino, California for granting me a short-term fellowship that allowed me to spend a month working in their archives. My thanks are equally due to the Governing Body of Jesus College which awarded me a generous grant to cover the cost of the illustrations.

Because of Covid some of my research had to be delayed or curtailed. It would have come to a complete halt without the scan and delivery service of the Bodleian Library and its extension of electronic access to many books. The helpfulness of the Bodleian staff is hugely appreciated, as is the assistance of archivists at the National Archives and National Library of Scotland.

Oxford University Press—especially Matthew Cotton—have been remarkably patient as well as generous in allowing the text to go well beyond the contracted word limit. Finally, I want to thank the external reader for supporting the project and the whole production team for bringing it to print.

Conventions

In quotations, I have kept the spellings as they appear in the manuscripts and printed sources used. But for easier reading, I have converted the j to i, i to j, u to v, vv to w where appropriate, both in the text and bibliography. I have modernized punctuation and modified capitalization in accordance with the book's conventions. Words abbreviated or compressed in the original texts are given in full.

Foreign place names and names of rulers are anglicized. The Netherlands refers to the geographical area of present-day Holland and Belgium. The United Provinces is the name used for the Northern Netherlands (present-day Holland) which had broken away from its Spanish ruler; the States General is its government. The Spanish or Habsburg Netherlands is the name for the southern provinces under the rule of Archdukes Albert and Isabella.

Because of his frequent change of titles, Sir Robert Cecil is called 'Cecil' throughout the book in the hope of avoiding confusion. All other nobles are referred to by their title at the point of the discussion. James VI and I's wife is here called 'Anna'—not 'Anne'—as this was the name she generally used and is now preferred by historians. The Union (capital u) refers to James's specific project to create a 'Great Britain'.

Many sources used here are now online. My references consequently do not always give the page references which are in the hard copies and instead provide either the document number or online references. This affects, for example, the referencing of the *Calendar of State Papers Venice* (*CSPVen*) and the *Journals of the House of Commons* (*CJ*). To prevent the book being impossibly long, I have minimized references; full details of works cited can be found in the bibliography.

Old Style dating (following the Julian Calendar) is used throughout the text. The year is assumed to start on 1 January, not 25 March, which was customary in this period.

To provide a rough indication of what the sums of money quoted might mean in today's currency, I have used the online National Archives Currency converter: 1270–2017.

Contents

List of Illustrations   xiii

Introduction   1

PART 1. SUCCESSION AND ACCESSION

1. The Queen Is Dead   9
2. A King in Waiting   35
3. Elizabeth's Legacy   73
4. Long Live the King   95
5. Conspiracy and Coronation   126
6. Three Royal Performances   154

PART 2. PEOPLE AND INSTITUTIONS

7. Queen Consort and Royal Children   185
8. Courts and Courtiers   216
9. Privy Council and Councillors   254
10. Parliament and its Members   284

PART 3. RELIGION AND POLITICS

11. Protestants and Puritans   321
12. Catholics and Recusants   353
13. Union and Empire   390
14. The Habsburgs and the Dutch   430

Conclusion   465

Appendix 1. James's English Privy Council 1603–12	477
Appendix 2. Lord Lieutenants 1603–12	479
Appendix 3. Installations of Knights of the Garter 1603–12	480
Abbreviations in Notes	481
Notes	483
Select Bibliography of Works Cited in Notes	557
Index	617

List of Illustrations

1. Elizabeth borne along in her funeral procession, British Library, Additional MS, 35324, fol. 37ᵛ © Wikipedia. — 21
2. Title page of Thomas Heywood, *The Second Part of Queene Elizabeth's Troubles* (London, 1606) © Folger Shakespeare Library, Washington DC. — 28
3. Locket with miniatures inside depicting James I and an ark, from the workshop of Nicholas Hilliard © Victoria and Albert Museum, London. — 33
4. James VI as a boy © National Trust Images. — 37
5. James's and Anna's marriage medal, GLAHM 38056 © The Hunterian, University of Glasgow. — 49
6. 'Ane Metaphoricall Invention of a Tragedie Called Phoenix', James VI's poem in *The Essayes of a Prentise in the Divine Art of Poesie*, sigs Gii–Iiiᵛ © The Huntington Library, San Marino, California. — 57
7. James VI of Scotland, 1595, by Adrian Vanson © National Galleries of Scotland, Edinburgh. — 70
8. James VI in the 'Atrium Heroicum' series by the printmaker Domenicus Custos (1602), British Museum BM1873,0510.2736 © Artokoloro/Alamy Stock Photo. — 71
9. Engraving of James, 1603, '*Maximo Applausu, Electus Rex*' © Harris Brisbane Dick Fund, 1917/Metropolitan Museum, New York City. — 102
10. The Londinium Arch at Fenchurch from Stephen Harrison, *The Arch's of Triumph Erected in Honor of the High and Mighty Prince. James the First of That Name* (1604) © The Trustees of the British Museum. — 171
11. The Dutch Arch at the Royal Exchange from Stephen Harrison, *The Arch's of Triumph Erected in Honor of the High and Mighty Prince. James the First of That Name* (1604) © British Library Board. All Rights Reserved/Bridgeman Images. — 173
12. The tombs of Mary and Sophia in Westminster Abbey © 2023 Dean and Chapter of Westminster. — 188
13. The 'Woburn Portrait' of Anna of Denmark by Marcus Gheeraerts the Younger, *c.*1611–14 Woburn Abbey/Wikipedia. — 198

14. Prince Henry and Sir John Harington by Robert Peake the Elder (1603) © Joseph Pulitzer Bequest, 1944, Metropolitan Museum of Art, New York City. 206
15. Miniature of Prince Henry by Isaac Oliver, Royal Collection, RCIN 420058 © His Majesty King Charles III 2023. 208
16. Title page of Robert Pricket, *The Jesuits Miracles, or New Popish Wonders* (1607) © The Huntington Library, San Marino, California. 371
17. A broadside on the Gunpowder Plot (1606), British Museum 1848,0911.451 © The Trustees of the British Museum. 376
18. 'The Papists' Powder Treason' © Lambeth Palace Library, London. 378
19. John Speed, *Theatre of the Empire of Great Britain* (1611). Reproduced with the permission of Special Collections, Leeds University Library, The Whitaker Collection, 9 fol. 422
20. The Somerset House Conference, 1604 © National Portrait Gallery, London. 441

Introduction

The succession issue dogged the Tudors. Both Henry VII and Henry VIII struggled unsuccessfully to produce a male heir and spare. In a vain attempt to provide a second son for Henry VII after the death of their eldest child, Prince Arthur, Elizabeth of York died from a post-partum infection at the age of thirty-seven. Henry VIII's quest for a male heir resulted in his rejection of his first wife, Katherine of Aragon, and the execution of his second, Anne Boleyn. The English Reformation was to exacerbate the problem since the heir by bloodline of the Protestant Edward VI and Elizabeth I were both Catholics: Mary I in 1553 and Mary, Queen of Scots, from 1558 until her execution in 1587. No wonder, then, that Elizabeth was bombarded with pleas to marry when she was young enough to bear a child, and that she faced similar urgent calls to name an heir right until her death. No wonder too that her single status provoked a debate about the succession regarding not only who should be the next monarch but also what laws and procedures should be followed to ensure a smooth transfer of power.

By 1603, James VI of Scotland had emerged as Elizabeth's most likely successor, but his title was by no means uncontested. In 1600, Thomas Wilson had identified twelve potential candidates who could follow Elizabeth as monarch, four of whom had a plausible title or at least backers: James VI of Scotland (the son of Mary, Queen of Scots); Isabella Clara Eugenia (daughter of Philip II of Spain who was co-ruler of the Spanish Netherlands with her husband the Archduke Albert of Austria); Edward, Lord Beauchamp (a direct descendant of Henry VII); and Arbella Stuart (James's English-born first cousin on his father's side).[1] Faced with these potential competitors, James directed his efforts to win over people of influence in England and build up allies abroad in case he might have to fight for the throne. Meanwhile, many in England feared a contested succession accompanied by foreign invasion and internal unrest.

Disputed successions were not unusual in early modern England and Europe. Henry VII had won the crown at the battle of Bosworth against the sitting king, Richard III, who was himself a usurper. Henry's granddaughter Mary I had had to raise an army to withstand the attempted coup of Lady Jane Grey which had been engineered by Edward VI and John Dudley, duke of Northumberland. Elizabeth herself had thought she might need to fight for the throne against a Catholic claimant, but in the event she underwent the easiest accession of all as English Catholics as well as Protestants rallied behind her straightaway.

On the Continent, the final decades of the sixteenth century saw several contested successions, all of which were more devastating than their English counterparts. The deaths of two childless kings—King Sebastian I in the battle of Alcácer Quibir in 1578 and his great-uncle King Henry I of natural causes in 1580—left the Portuguese succession open and the kingdom vulnerable to foreign conquest. And, indeed, Philip II took the throne in 1580 after his army swept aside the forces of Dom Antonio, prior of Crato, whom the Portuguese had already proclaimed king. Although the crisis in Portugal was short-lived, Dom Antonio remained a thorn in Philip's side until his death in 1595, especially on the occasions when he obtained English or French military aid. In France the late sixteenth-century succession crisis lasted longer and was more severe. The death of Henry III's younger brother in 1584 left the French king without direct heirs. This succession issue led to a renewal of civil war even before Henry III was assassinated in 1589. The conflict arose because the man with the best claim to the French throne by bloodline was a Protestant, Henry of Navarre, whom Catholics would rather fight than obey. Rejecting the rules of primogeniture, the Catholic League in France elected Charles, cardinal of Bourbon, as their king, and very soon foreign powers were drawn into the struggle: Elizabeth sent over several expeditions to help Navarre, now Henry IV, while Catholic resistance was bolstered by Spanish men and money. Even after Henry IV converted to Protestantism, the war did not end; instead, France and Spain slugged it out until the Treaty of Vervins was signed in 1598. Further afield, the death of Tsar Fyodor I of Russia in 1598 ended the old Muscovite ruling dynasty and resulted in civil war and foreign interventions, a period popularly known in English as the 'Time of Troubles'. Internal peace was only restored with the election of Michael Romanov in February 1613.

There was, therefore, very good cause for Elizabeth's subjects to fear that a similar disputed succession, with an attendant civil war and international intervention, might follow the queen's decease. Yet this nightmare scenario did not ultimately occur. As we shall see, James was proclaimed king immediately upon the queen's death and had a trouble-free progress from Scotland to London during which his new subjects heralded him as king with relief and joy. For that reason, historians have tended to look on James's succession as smooth and tranquil.[2] Yet, while there is no denying that domestic risings and foreign interventions were avoided in 1603 (or at least in England, more on Ireland later), James's accession was far less smooth than is often supposed. Part I of this book tells the story of the new king's bumpy ride to establish his authority and explains when, how, and why he became the unchallenged ruler of what was to become the new entity of Great Britain.

Once James took the throne, did he introduce any significant changes or was it simply business as usual? I address this question in Parts 2 and 3, enquiring how far the establishment of a new Stuart dynasty resulted in fresh personnel at the centre of power, alterations in monarchical institutions, shifts in political culture, and a different direction in governmental policies. In the early modern period, the accession of a new monarch often resulted in a variety of major changes at the national level. This was especially true in England after the death of Henry VIII in 1547 when each of his children altered the religious settlement and ecclesiastical institutions that they inherited. Their appointments to, and dismissals from, office largely reflected their religious outlook. Religious conservatives for example were ousted from Edward VI's privy council and Protestants came to hold posts in his privy chamber. After his death, first Mary and then Elizabeth brought people who shared their religion into their privy council and royal household while removing many of those who did not. Similarly, the Catholic presence in local government was reduced in 1547, restored over Mary's reign from 1553 to 1558, and then purged in stages over the course of Elizabeth's reign.[3] Given this historical precedent and the crown's control over all such appointments, there was an expectation that a comparable turnover of office holders might take place on Elizabeth's death, no matter who occupied the English throne. Nervousness on this score, in the words of the historian Paul Hammer, 'encouraged many officeholders to exploit their charges as fully as possible while they still could' during the 1590s, a mindset that led to the rampant corruption and burdensome exactions of the Elizabethan *fin de siècle*.[4]

As we shall see, the anxieties of displacement were for the most part unwarranted. Once James was proclaimed king, very few office holders at the centre and in the localities lost their posts. However, those who did were high profile, including Sir Walter Ralegh who was ejected as captain of the guard; Robert Cecil's older brother Thomas Cecil, Baron Burghley, who was forced to step down as president of the council of the north; and Sir John Fortescue who lost two offices, one in the household and the other in the exchequer. Furthermore, several prominent Elizabethans—again Ralegh, this time together with Henry Brooke, eleventh Baron Cobham, Thomas Grey, fifteenth Baron Grey of Wilton, and Henry Percy, ninth earl of Northumberland—not only lost their positions at court but also their liberty as they ended up in the Tower. Their dramatic falls are charted in several chapters of the book.

While leaving most office holders *in situ*, James added plentiful new men to their ranks. In 1603, the privy council pretty much doubled in size, largely filled by men who had already given valuable service to Elizabeth as soldiers, naval officers, or presidents of regional councils. Only one of the newcomers—Lord Henry Howard, soon to be earl of Northampton—had been a complete political outsider under Elizabeth. But five of the new privy councillors were Scots who had accompanied James from Edinburgh. Scots were also prominent in the court, occupying several key household offices and filling the new department of the bedchamber. When James went hunting away from London, his Scottish friends accompanied him while his English ministers normally stayed behind. The influence of Scottish courtiers—or perceived influence—had a major impact on political life and culture and is explored in Part 2 of this book, alongside some discussion of the most influential early Jacobean English privy councillors and courtiers.

The institutions that James inherited remained fundamentally intact. However, as will be seen—also in Part 2—the new king imposed his own stamp on the workings of the privy council, the structure and protocols of the court, and the proceedings of parliament. The importance of the presence of a queen consort and royal children in the royal palaces—for the first time in more than half a century—also had a major impact on the court, its culture, and its cost.

Expectations of policy changes were rife in 1603. To ensure support from all confessional groups, James had given Catholics hope that they could expect a considerable degree of toleration once he was king, while at the same time godly Protestants ('Puritans') were encouraged to believe that the king would remove what they saw as 'popish' ceremonies from the established prayer book used in English and Welsh churches. Also on the horizon were policies that had little popular support: peace with Spain looked likely, as did a union of James's two kingdoms. As for James's third kingdom, Ireland, it was uncertain how the king would react to the surrender of Hugh O'Neill, earl of Tyrone, who had just been defeated after a destructive nine-year war against England. Consequently, many in England expected not just dynastic change in 1603 but a more substantial regime change. Part 3 of this book provides a study of James's policies during the first decade of his reign, assessing their novelty, popularity (or otherwise), and impact.

The end point of this book is 1612, the year that saw the deaths of Robert Cecil, then earl of Salisbury, and Prince Henry, James's first-born son. Salisbury's death ended the era of Cecilian dominance in government and political life. He and his father William Cecil, Lord Burghley, had acted as principal secretary, lord treasurer, and master of the court of wards at one time or another under both Elizabeth and James. And although Salisbury's son, William, inherited his title, he was a political lightweight, and the mantle of power fell on others. The Jacobean era after 1612 saw James's favourites, first Robert Carr and then George Villiers, come to power, dominating patronage and influencing policy far more than Cecil had been able to do. At the same time competition for offices became more intense and factional infighting far more evident.

★ ★ ★

The Tudors—Henry VIII and Elizabeth I—have attracted a great deal of popular interest and media attention; James I and his wife Anna far less. Yet the king is an intriguing figure: as clever and witty as his predecessor and just as skilled in the arts of deception and *realpolitik*. Wrongly depicted as careless about his majesty, James too projected an image of legitimacy and power: court ceremonial, visual displays, and in his case his writings. His wife too is an interesting figure; born into the royal house of Denmark, her tastes were sophisticated and cosmopolitan, albeit expensive. The royal couple's relationship has too often been misunderstood, even traduced, because of James's reputation as a bisexual and Anna's supposed dislike of his male friendships. As shown here, James and Anna worked in a partnership for the most part during their early years in England and certainly until James allowed Carr the influence that had eluded him while Cecil and Henry were alive.

Jacobean court ceremony was as colourful as it had been under Elizabeth, while the early Jacobean drama in the playhouses as well as at court was more diverse and even richer. Arguably, Shakespeare wrote his best plays—*Macbeth*, *King Lear*, *The Tempest*—after 1603; even one version of *Hamlet* (the longer second quarto) was published after 1603 and reflected the accession of James. Other canonical authors were active in the early Jacobean period: Ben Jonson, John Donne, and Samuel Daniel. Finally, the events of James's early reign are themselves full of drama. Alright, there was no Spanish Armada, but there was a plot which had it been successful would have wiped out most of the royal family and political elite. Furthermore, in Ireland, the upheaval of the flight of the earls resulted in the plantations of Ulster, which has left a profound mark on the history of the island even until today. Similarly, the early Jacobean period saw the establishment of the first successful colony in America. So, this period of British history is as important as it is exciting, and I hope to have captured something of this in the following pages.

PART I

Succession and Accession

I

The Queen Is Dead

In early 1603, Elizabeth I seemed 'strong of constitucion'. She had always looked after her health, eating meats 'that susteyne and strengthen nature', not overindulging in good food or wine, and taking regular exercise—whether dancing, hunting, or walking briskly in her gardens. Early in February 1603, a Venetian diplomat Giovanni Scaramelli described her as being 'in perfect possession of all her senses' and in such good health that everyone in England hoped and believed that she still had years to live.[1]

Yet, despite her apparent physical health, there were reasons for concern. At sixty-nine years of age, Elizabeth was in her 'climactericall year' [a year usually calculated as a multiple of seven] which was thought to be particularly dangerous to an individual.[2] Furthermore, some courtiers found her forgetful and showing her age. In late 1602, her spirits had been low, and it was noticeable that she took no enjoyment in the Christmas revels.[3] About 16 January, she developed a cold, although she soon recovered and was well enough four days later to be entertained at the Charterhouse residence of Lord Thomas Howard of Walden. She then moved to Richmond Palace either to escape the extreme chill of Whitehall or possibly—or so it was said—because the astrologer Dr John Dee had forewarned her 'to beware of Whitehall'.[4]

At the end of February, the queen again felt unwell. This time, however, she sank into lethargy during the day and experienced wakefulness at night. Her temper was particularly bad, and she was often so 'impatient and testye' that only Sir Robert Cecil, her principal secretary over the previous decade, dared to come into her presence.[5] Initially, privy councillors and physicians believed that she was just suffering from a more intense form of melancholy for she had no obvious physical symptoms: 'she hath good appetite, hath nether cough nor fever, distemper, nor inordinate desire to drinke'.[6] Also she would say something like: 'I am not sick, I feele no payne, and yet

I pine away.'[7] For this reason, she rejected the advice of doctors and refused all medicines. In this phase of her illness, Cecil had high hopes that she would recover, especially since on some days 'her dullness vanishets, which was the only great signe of danger'.[8]

The queen's melancholy, observers thought, could be partially explained by the death on 20 February of 'her old acquentance' and beloved cousin Katherine, countess of Nottingham, but they noted that Elizabeth also expressed 'choler and grief' at the possibility of having to offer a pardon to the Irish rebel Hugh O'Neill, earl of Tyrone, and at the rumours that Arbella Stuart (another royal cousin) had been caught out seeking a marriage without permission. To make matters worse, the second anniversary on 9 March of the execution of Robert Devereux, second earl of Essex—whom Elizabeth had once greatly favoured—was a reminder of his betrayal and gave rise to the shedding of tears.[9]

The possible severity of the queen's illness was initially kept quiet in the hope that she would soon regain her spirits and health. Her privy councillors and others were simply told that she was sick with a cold or a degree of melancholy. But by 9 March, Cecil and others close to Elizabeth had to admit that the prospects were grave. Governmental business was coming to a standstill since she could no longer 'abide discourses of government and state' but preferred, instead, to hear 'old Canterbery tales'.[10] On that day, Cecil confessed to his agent in Scotland that the situation was potentially serious, and shortly afterwards the English privy council wrote to James VI, the queen's likely successor, with news of her condition.[11] On 11 March, her symptoms worsened. An abscess in her throat then burst, and 'her attendants were alarmed lest the blood should suffocate her or cause her to break a blood vessel'.[12] Although she survived this crisis, the abscess may have been a symptom of quinsy, complications arising from tonsillitis, which could be fatal without antibiotics.[13]

During this period, Elizabeth refused to go to bed—perhaps in denial of her illness or out of fear that 'yf she once lay downe she shold never rise'— and so she rested listlessly on cushions.[14] Elizabeth Southwell, one of her women attendants, later recalled that when Cecil had told the queen that she must take herself to bed: 'she smiled wonderfully contemning him, saing that the word "must" was not to be used to princes' and adding 'little man, little man yf your father [William Cecil, Lord Burghley] had lived, ye durst not have said so much, but thou knowest I must die and that maketh thee so presumtious'.[15] At last, on Sunday 20 March, Elizabeth was persuaded by her cousin and old friend Charles Howard, earl of Nottingham, to go to bed. Known to have influence over the queen, the widower had been summoned to court from his house of mourning for this very purpose and to cajole her into taking some broth. The doctors were by now alarmed, cautioning that the queen would likely fall into 'a dulnesse and a lethargie' before passing away.[16]

★ ★ ★

Even before the doctor's dire warning, the privy council recognized that Elizabeth's time was up and that it needed to act expeditiously to prevent a disputed succession. During her forty-four-year reign, the unmarried and childless queen had not only consistently refused to name an heir but also prevented parliament from passing a statute that would legitimate a successor. Consequently, the privy council was alert to the danger that several claimants might make a bid for the crown on her decease. The worst possible scenario was that a long and bloody civil war would erupt, possibly religious in nature with Catholics fighting against Protestants and with Spain and France intervening in support of their favoured candidate. Something similar had occurred in France on the death of Henry III in 1589 and resulted in a war of succession that lasted nearly a decade. So, there were good reasons for alarm. To prevent it happening in England, the privy council had to seize the initiative quickly. As precautionary measures, it directed sheriffs, justices of the peace, and lords in the localities to quell any rumours of the queen's illness, to keep an eye out for troublemakers, prevent unlawful assemblies, and arrest notorious Catholic recusants and anyone else thought dangerous. Simultaneously 'watches' were set up in London to detect signs of unrest.[17] To forestall an invasion, the privy council closed the ports and 'ordered the navie to be in redines against foren attempts'. Then, on Saturday 19 March, it summoned to court the lords and bishops who were 'neerest at hand' to discuss what else needed to be done in the event of the queen's impending death.[18]

At the meeting held on the 20th, the nobility was told to be ready to suppress any domestic turmoil and stand together behind a new monarch. Those present also discussed and agreed to procedures proposed by the privy council that were designed to ensure a smooth transition to a new dynasty. Since its authority would instantaneously cease on the queen's death, the privy council had to find a mechanism that would prevent a power vacuum with a corresponding paralysis of government developing before a new monarch was chosen and assumed power. To fill the void of an interregnum, they proposed that, on the queen's death, the present privy councillors would join with the nobility and other important men to create 'the universall and grand councell of the realme' and arrange the succession. Who the next monarch would be was apparently not discussed or announced, but 'all spake generallie' of James VI of Scotland 'to ther frendes privatelie'.[19] Later that day, the privy council sent out letters of reassurance to 'sondrie earles and barons', who could not attend the 'conference' because of their distance from London, the communication informing them of the queen's 'indisposition' and promising that the privy council would now and in the future do all it could to preserve 'the peace and welfare of the state' with their 'concurrence and consent'. Again, no name was mentioned for the succession.[20] Later that day or on the following morning, a proclamation was drafted that declared James's accession in the name of the nobility and other principal officers of the realm.[21]

Elizabeth's unwillingness to make provision for the succession—unique among English monarchs—harmed her reputation both at the time and among historians ever since. For a queen who purported to care for her subjects, it showed an acute insensitivity to their fears and forced them to live in uncertainty about the future political and religious direction of the realm. Her stance was understandable during the lifetime of James VI's mother Mary, Queen of Scots. Although Elizabeth favoured her title to be heir presumptive, as a Catholic she was unacceptable to most Protestants especially after her suspected involvement in various treasonous plots while a prisoner in England. The idea of naming James as heir while his mother was alive—a solution proposed by some of Elizabeth's subjects in the 1570s and early 1580s—was rejected, not least because it offended the hereditary dynastic principle that was so important to the English queen. However, after Mary's execution in February 1587, Elizabeth still refused to designate James her heir. This was all the more remarkable considering that he was officially her ally and had on numerous occasions shown his goodwill towards her. The reason for her silence was that neither she nor Burghley, her chief adviser, trusted the Scottish king despite his professions of friendship. James had a long record of deviousness and deceit. From the early 1580s, he had flirted with Elizabeth's enemies—the Scottish Catholics, the French Catholics, the pope, and Philip II of Spain—and so Elizabeth and Burghley used the undeclared succession as both a carrot and stick to keep him serving their interests.[22]

But did Elizabeth name James the rightful heir on her deathbed? According to one contemporary story, Cecil, Nottingham, and Sir Thomas Egerton (the lord keeper) had raised the question of the succession with her on the Tuesday before her death, at which time she answered: 'I told you my seat had been the seat of kings, and I will have no rascall to succeed mee: and who should succeed mee but a king'. Failing to understand, 'this darke speeche', the councillors asked for clarification, and Elizabeth then apparently said that she meant for King James, 'our cosen of Scotland'. When they asked for further elucidation, she replied: 'I praye you trouble mee no more, I'le have none but him.'[23] Seeing that the French ambassador and others were reporting that the queen was unable to speak over this period and in no fit state to make a will or declare her successor, this story lacks credibility and was almost certainly fabricated to bolster James's title to the English throne.[24] It went on, however, in a somewhat more plausible vein: the privy councillors returned the following afternoon and found Elizabeth 'in a manner speechles', but they still wanted confirmation of James's nomination. When they asked her to make some sign that she preferred him as her heir, she apparently heaved herself upwards in her bed, pulled her arms out, and 'held both her hands joyntly to geather over her head in manner of a crowne'.[25]

Sir Robert Carey, the queen's cousin, who was a bystander, described a similar scene, claiming that 'by putting her hand to her head, when the king of Scottes was named to succeed her, they all knew hee was the man she desired should reigne after her'.[26] Whether true or not, this story was spread immediately upon her death to justify the privy council and nobility's actions on behalf of James.[27] On 28 March, 'all the councell and divers of the nobilitie' wanted the king of France to know that on her sickbed Elizabeth had given 'her owne princely allowance and wished recommendacon' of James's title.[28] Some months later Cecil declared in the prerogative court of star chamber that 'her late Majestie in her laste sicknes devyse[d]' the crown 'by parolle' [word] to the king of Scotland.[29] Whether these accounts were believed or not is another matter.[30] But it is indicative that their authors lacked confidence in the legitimacy of their new king's title simply based on 'law' and hereditary right.

★ ★ ★

At three o'clock on the Wednesday afternoon before her death, Archbishop John Whitgift of Canterbury came to Elizabeth's bedside to pray with her and tend to 'her spiritual safety'. Needing his comfort, she held onto him several times to prevent him leaving, but eventually the old man—who was himself sick—had to depart, exhausted by the emotions of the occasion.[31] A little later, the queen's almoner and chaplain Anthony Watson, bishop of Chichester, arrived. He too tried to prepare his royal mistress for death. Both clerics 'rehearsed unto her the grounds of Christian faith' and begged her to make a Protestant confession and recommend her soul to God.[32] Most accounts of this deathbed scene portray the queen feeding upon the bishops' words, readily embracing death, and expressing beliefs that were in accordance with the theology of the Established Church. According to Carey who was present, when Watson 'examined her first of her faith', she answered all his questions 'by lifting up her eyes and holding up her hand' and 'gave testimony to us all of her Christian and comfortable end'.[33] Contemporary printed accounts told a similar story. Keen to show the dying queen fulfilling the Protestant ideal of a good death, they described her signalling her 'love unto the doctrine and glad tydings of salvation' and affirming her faith by lifting her eyes and hands up to heaven to testify her 'apprehension of God's mercy to her in Christ'.[34]

By contrast, some four years later, Elizabeth Southwell wrote an account which depicted her mistress's approach to death very differently. As a maid of honour, Southwell had attended upon the queen during her last illness but, later living abroad and a Catholic convert, she constructed a narrative that depicted a heretical queen destined for hellfire. In her text, Elizabeth was desperate not to die. To protect herself from death, wrote Southwell, the queen had worn a strangely marked gold coin as an amulet around her neck throughout her illness. When the prelates gathered around her towards the end, 'she was much offended' and angrily bade 'them be packing'. The bishops only returned to say prayers once the queen was 'past sense'.[35] This image of Elizabeth rejecting spiritual comfort conflicts with all other narratives of her last days and had a clear confessional purpose. Nonetheless, the consensus view of the queen's behaviour throughout March does offer some confirmation of Southwell's description of a woman fearful of death. The queen's failure to dictate a will also indicates that she did not embrace 'eternal life' quite as joyfully as credited in the published accounts.

Elizabeth expired between two and three o'clock on the morning of Thursday 24 March, the eve of the feast of the Annunciation of the Virgin Mary (known as Lady Day). The timing had a significance for those commentators who found meaning in correspondences. One chronicler noted that Thursday had been 'a fatal day to Henry the eyght, and all his posteritie' since each one had died on that day of the week.[36] The eve of Mary's Annunciation, meanwhile, seemed an apt day for the death of the 'Virgin Queen', especially as she had been born on 7 September, the eve of the feast of the Virgin Mary. Additionally, Lady Day was considered the start of spring since the vernal equinox begins around 20 March, a fact which James's eulogists exploited by portraying his accession as the beginning of a new and revitalized season and era.

There is considerable uncertainty about whether Elizabeth's corpse was disembowelled and embalmed before burial, as was normal practice for English monarchs in the sixteenth century.[37] The queen had explicitly ordered that it should remain intact—perhaps because she disliked the thought of male surgeons touching and cutting open her body. Certainly, her privy councillors issued an order meeting her wishes, and some contemporaries specifically stated that the dead queen was 'not opened' or 'embowelled'.[38] However, according to Southwell, privy councillors also gave surgeons a secret warrant to come and do the work.[39] It makes sense that embalming would take place to prevent the body decomposing; otherwise, the stench would have become noxious during the month before the burial. After embalming, the corpse was wrapped in cerecloth [linen coated with wax] and enclosed in a coffin lined with lead.[40]

Meanwhile, Elizabeth's privy councillors—who had in fact no official status now that the queen was dead—set about managing the succession. No time was lost. At about 9.00 a.m. on the morning of her decease, a deputation of lords took the proclamation announcing James I's accession to Whitehall, where Cecil solemnly read it aloud and affixed it to a post. From there, some three hundred men—heralds, the archbishop of Canterbury, earls, barons, three bishops, judges, and London's mayor and aldermen—processed to the City to the sound of trumpets and proclaimed the king at key sites.[41] The handwritten proclamation was then printed and distributed to the rest of the country.[42] On the same day, Whitgift wrote to all bishops enjoining them to 'cause publique thankes to bee given' both for the life of the late queen and that God had now placed in her stead a king of the same religious persuasion and 'endowed with such excellent qualities as hee is'.[43]

In obedience, sermons were immediately preached to eulogize the late queen, praise the new king, and instruct their hearers on how to react to the change. All of them called for the mourning of the queen's death to be tempered with joy at the peaceful accession of so worthy an heir.[44] How people did react was mixed. Some experienced her death as a 'great losse'.

According to one diarist, 'the sorrowe for hir Majestie's departure' went 'deep in many heartes', while a letter writer commented that amid the rejoicing at the settlement of the succession and proclamation of a new king there were 'meny wepyng' at her passing.[45] Nevertheless, others mourned little and were looking forward to an adult male king sitting on the throne for the first time since the death of Henry VIII in January 1547.[46] One clergy man even preached that 'England under an aged queene did seeme to waxe olde' but now under James would 'begin to flourish and to recover her youth againe'.[47] A small group of people who were delighted at the news of the queen's death was the immediate family and associates of the late earl of Essex. They could barely contain their joy at the change of regime. Essex's twelve-year-old son was brought to his mother at Essex House to celebrate, and Henry Wriothesley (the earl of Southampton before his attainder in 1601)—who had been imprisoned in the Tower since participating in his friend's abortive rising—'did much rejoce'.[48]

Overall, the immediate response in England was probably shock, even disbelief. After all, during the queen's illness, the privy council had taken measures to suppress rumours about its severity.[49] Some people had feared the worst and felt 'heavie, and much troubled' during her last week, praying to God both to preserve her life and safeguard the nation if she died.[50] Yet, despite the uncertainties and anxieties of mid-March, the news of her death came as 'a thunderclap' and—according to the pamphleteer and playwright Thomas Dekker—was greeted with astonishment that 'tooke away harte from millions', for they 'never understoode what that strange out landish word *Change* signified'.[51] Accompanying shock was fear: 'many men in the Citty', wrote another observer, were 'in armes and more affrayed then hurt' by the news, predicting 'confusion' and unrest as rival candidates battled to secure the throne. Armour and munitions were being stockpiled in London, and food prices immediately rose.[52] As the poet and preacher John Donne later remembered the mood: 'every one of you in the City were running up and down like ants with their eggs bigger then themselves, every man with his bags, to seek where to hide them safely'.[53] But great relief followed as soon as people realized that there would be no challenge to James's accession. By early April, correspondents were writing to their friends abroad: 'All things are very quiet here at this time, and the common people so well satisfied and so joyful as ever they were, hoping of a flourishing common wealth', with 'everye man following his owne ayfayres without the lest shewe of discontentment in the world'.[54] The theologian and poet Joseph Hall celebrated the change in mood with the lines:

> Then did I feare this earth should drenched lie
>   With purple streames in civil tumults shed…
> Yet God that thought forefended
>   That the world's course with her [Elizabeth] course was not ended.[55]

Or as Henry Chettle cheerfully announced:

> The sound of civille warre is heard no more
>   Each countenance is garnished with smiles.[56]

★ ★ ★

The Saturday night after the queen's decease, her coffin was conveyed on a black-draped barge lit by torches along the Thames to Whitehall Palace. There it was placed upon a bed of state in the withdrawing chamber 'all hung with mournings'. Following established custom, her late privy councillors and ladies of the privy chamber waited upon the queen during the day 'with the same ceremony' as if she had been alive, and at night six ladies maintained a vigil over the body.[57]

It did not take long before 'strange stories'—said to be the malicious gossip of Catholics—circulated in London. As reported in a contemporary letter by John Chamberlain, whose correspondence is an invaluable source for historians, these 'strange stories' were unspecific, but Southwell afterwards reported an extraordinary incident that may well have been one of the rumours heard by Chamberlain. In Southwell's account, the queen's corpse exploded during one night of the wake:

> it happened that her body brake the coffin with such a cracke, that it spleated the wood, lead, and cercloath, to the terror and astonishment of all that wer present, so that the next day the body had to be new trimed up.[58]

The only natural cause for such an extraordinary event would have been a build-up and eruption of gases in the queen's decomposing corpse. But this could not have occurred had Elizabeth been disembowelled and embalmed as Southwell had previously asserted. Elizabeth's exploding corpse was almost certainly a Catholic fantasy, a trope for the queen's moral and heretical corruption that could not be contained within her mortal remains. Catholics had told similar stories about Henry VIII's coffin cracking open and about poisonous vapours emanating from the corpse of the fiercely anti-Catholic Elizabethan, Sir Francis Walsingham.[59] When Elizabeth's coffin was dug up and examined in 1868, some damage was detected to the wooden outer case, but the corpse was found securely enclosed within its leaden shell; another indication that the tale of the exploding corpse was a myth.[60]

Elizabeth's funeral was next on the ceremonial agenda, and James was keen for it to be carried out with appropriate pomp and dignity:

> For that we do so much respect the dignitie to her appertayning, being not only successor to her in the kingdome, but so neere as we are of bloude, as we will not stande so much upon the ceremonies of our owne joy, but that we would have in that which concernith her all that to be done, which may most testefie the honnor we doe beare towards her memory.[61]

James also made clear that he wanted to observe the customs of his new realm in terms of both the funeral's timing and whether he was expected to attend. Because the English custom was that monarchs were not present at the obsequies of their predecessors, James agreed to wait outside London until they were over. He also allowed the former servants and principal officers of the late queen to watch over her body until after the funeral, even though it inconvenienced him not to have them come north and accompany him and his wife on their journey to the capital. Appearances were all important, and the king well understood the wisdom of showing his new subjects that, although a foreigner, he respected their traditions. Besides this, he wanted to display his close family relationship to the dead queen as it underlined his bloodline and title to the crown.[62] However, his decision to stay away from the funeral was misinterpreted in some quarters. When giving James's reason for absence, Scaramelli reported: 'they say he wishes to see her neither alive nor dead, for he can never expel from his memory the fact that his mother was put to death at the hands of the public executioner'.[63]

To organize the funeral, James appointed Thomas Lord Howard to act as lord chamberlain, replacing the incumbent Lord Hunsdon who was then seriously ill.[64] Howard and Cecil discussed together the arrangements and made most of the decisions themselves, since Elizabeth—unlike her Tudor predecessors—had left no directions about her funeral or place of burial (surely another sign that she did not embrace death willingly). By 12 April, it was known in London that the event would take place at Westminster Abbey on 28 April, the Thursday after Easter, 'with as much solemnitie as hath ben used to any former prince and that by the king's owne direction'. The details that had seeped out were that the late queen's closest kinswoman and only 'princess of the blood' Arbella Stuart would be the chief mourner, accompanied by two marchionesses and thirty baronesses, and that all the queen's erstwhile privy councillors and household officers would be in the funeral procession together with the greater part of the nobility.[65]

However, two problems quickly emerged. The first was that Arbella Stuart refused to attend, and a new chief mourner had to be found. Arbella, who had been confined to her grandmother's house in Derbyshire for much of Elizabeth's reign, was said to have commented that since 'her accesse to the queene (in hir life time) might not be permitted, she would not (after hir death) be brought upon the stage for a publick spectacle'.[66] The second difficulty was that the late date for the funeral affected the timing of the formal entry of the king and his wife into London. James had directed that Anna should leave Scotland within twenty days of his own departure, and he had also insisted that Elizabeth's former ladies should attend upon her at Berwick and escort her through their new kingdom. But, since Elizabeth's ladies could not leave for Berwick until after the funeral, Anna would be unable to leave Scotland until early May. Furthermore, since she was already a few months pregnant, it was expected that her journey southwards would be slow. The royal entry into London, consequently, had to be rescheduled.[67]

★ ★ ★

Elizabeth's funeral cortège was magnificent, on a far grander scale than that of her half-siblings. It cost a huge sum, something between £11,305 and £20,000 [c.£1.5 million–£3.75 million in today's currency]. In addition to fees paid for the attendance of 'the officers of armes', the privy council paid for over 12,000 yards of black cloth which was to be distributed to the men and women who walked in the long, orderly procession.[68] 'Never did the English nation behold so much black worne as there was at her funerall', wrote Dekker, though in fact more black cloth had been provided for Henry VIII's funeral.[69] Each participant had requested, or received, a quantity and quality of black cloth relative to his or her status. A few of the mourning cloaks were incredibly long: that of the French ambassador was at least six yards in length and had to be held up by a servant. The train of Helena, marchioness of Northampton, had to be borne by two countesses.[70] The marchioness at least had an excuse for such ostentation. As the senior noblewoman and long-time friend of the late queen, she was the chief female mourner. The chief male mourner was Whitgift, who during the service received 'the offering' and had 'the banners presented to him'.[71]

The predominant colour of the funeral procession was of course mourning black, but bright colours could be seen on the 'rich' copes worn by the gentlemen of the queen's chapel, the coats of arms decorating the heralds' outfits, and the standards borne aloft marking out the different segments of the procession. Over 3,000 mourners participated, walking in rows of fours or fives, and organized according to their status. All ranks were represented. Fifteen almsmen of Westminster and 266 poor women started the procession, and they were followed in turn by some 1,000 menial servants (men, women, and children), numerous household officers, the gentlemen and children from the royal chapel ('singing a mournful tune'), the royal chaplains, the aldermen and lord mayor of London, the lords of Elizabeth's council, the bishops, and the noblemen and their wives. Edward Seymour, fourth earl of Worcester, Elizabeth's last master of the horse, led a symbolic riderless horse known as 'the palfrie of honour' or 'palfrey of estate', which was followed by the principal female mourner, assisted by Elizabeth's cousins Nottingham and Thomas Sackville, Lord Buckhurst.[72]

Then came the centrepiece of the cortège: the coffin placed in an open chariot, which was drawn along by four horses draped in black velvet emblazoned with the arms of England and Ireland. As was traditional, the coffin was covered with purple velvet and on its top lay a full-size effigy of the crowned queen.[73] Dressed in her golden parliament robes and a cloak of red velvet and ermine, she held an orb and sceptre in each hand. Her face, painted from a death mask, was 'coloured so faithfully' and offered such 'a lively picture' that it seemed almost lifelike, especially as the eyes were open. As one poet versified:

> ...a man of judgement would have thought,
> Had he not knowne her dead (but seene her so
>   Tryumphant drawne in robes so richly wrought,
> Crowne on her head, in hand her scepter to).
>   At this rare sight he would have sworne and said,
> To parliament rides this sweet slumbring maide.[74]

In truth, it is doubtful that the spectators lining the streets could see the effigy as the view was pretty much blocked. Six noblemen held aloft the fringed black velvet canopy over the chariot, while twelve barons carrying bannerols walked on each side of it (see Figure 1).[75] Following the coffin came Elizabeth's gentlemen ushers holding their white rods, her gentlemen pensioners [bodyguards] with their poleaxes pointing downwards, and the women of the privy chamber and maids of honour. Bringing up the rear was the company of guards, led by their captain Sir Walter Ralegh, their halberds also pointing downwards.[76]

Figure 1. Elizabeth borne along in her funeral procession, British Library, Additional MS, 35324, fol. 37^v © Wikipedia.

The procession that moved slowly from Whitehall to Westminster Abbey was watched by 'multitudes', an estimated 200,000.[77] Londoners turned out in force: 'all sorts of people in their streetes, houses, windows, leads and gutters'.[78] When they beheld the coffin and royal effigy, they gave full rein to grief. According to Dekker: 'Her herse (as it was borne) semed to be an iland swimming in water, for round about it there rayned showers of teares.'[79] Stow's *Annales* also testified to the emotional atmosphere, the chronicler telling readers that when the queen's coffin passed by:

> there was such a general sighing, groning, and weeping, as the like hath not beene seene or knowne in the memory of man, neither doeth any history mention any people, time, or state, to make like lamentation for the death of their soveraigne.[80]

There is no reason to think that these emotions were fake, or the narratives fabricated. Elizabeth had ruled throughout the lifespan of most English men and women, many of whom might well have thought of her as a caring mother to her subjects and the source of stability for the realm. After all, this had been her image in the propaganda and panegyric of the previous decades. No wonder, then, that there was an outpouring of grief as her hearse passed by, but it was a grief intensified by fears for the future. Elizabeth's successor was not yet in London and, as Dekker noted, everyone was 'so pitifullie distracted by the horror of a change'.[81]

Compared to the funeral procession, the service in Westminster Abbey paled into insignificance. In the printed works commemorating the event, attention focused entirely upon the procession and the naturalistic quality of the queen's effigy.[82] Scaramelli, who as a Catholic had declined to attend the service, heard that 'little else was done except the chanting of two psalms in English and the delivery of a funeral oration'.[83] According to the barrister John Hawarde, the funeral service was performed 'with greate solemnities, as appeareth by a booke in printe', but no such book is now extant.[84] The oration, preached by the queen's chaplain and almoner Bishop Watson of Chichester, likewise, has not survived, and even though Whitgift told Dr Parry, another of the queen's chaplains, 'to make a kinde of funeral oracion... to be published', nothing of that kind exists today.[85]

However, neat notes on Watson's sermon have recently been found and deposited in the British Library. Taking as his biblical text the death of David in Chronicles 29:26–8, Watson compared Elizabeth to the biblical king, commending her 'invincible spirit' and 'extraordinarie magnanimitie' which was 'farr farr to exceed her weake & frayle sexe'. The queen's speech at Tilbury at the time of the Spanish Armada, pronounced Watson, had 'encouraged the souldyers to fighte in God's and her cause'. Her other speeches were equally impressive, whether her 'pithie answers unto divers and sondrye ambassadors' in different languages, or her 'politicke speeches' to her parliaments. Declaring 'how many blessings the land had enjoyed' during her reign, Watson claimed that she now left 'as peaceable and as settled an estate after her unto her successor as ever did [any] prince in this worlde'.[86]

Following precedent, the body was not interred at this time. The coffin was left under a canopied wooden hearse on display in the abbey, surrounded by heraldic banners.[87] The expectation was that it would remain there until the king arrived in London, since the corpse of a deceased monarch was a ritualized substitute for the presence of the new living king and created a symbolic sense of continuity. But, for once, James breached tradition by ordering that the burial should take place before his appearance in London.[88] Consequently, without any further public ceremony, in early May the body was laid to rest in the vault under the magnificent tomb of Henry VII and Elizabeth of York, the queen's paternal grandparents and founders of the Tudor dynasty. This was situated behind the altar in the centre of the Lady Chapel of Henry VII. The effigy then joined other royal statues in the abbey's store.

★ ★ ★

Poets and printers capitalized on the sense of mourning for the dead queen to produce for sale hundreds of commendatory laments that eulogized her.[89] Their authors tended to be poetasters or hacks, and people at the time noticed that the realm's prime poets did not put pen to paper to write about Elizabeth's passing.[90] Some later scholars have suggested that Shakespeare's sonnet 107 makes an oblique reference to Elizabeth's death in the lines:

> The mortal moon hath her eclipse endured
>   And the sad augurs mock their own presage;
> Incertainties now crown themselves assured
>   And peace proclaims olives of endless age.

But not all critics accept this reading.[91] In any event, Shakespeare wrote no full elegy to the dead queen, nor did George Chapman, Michael Drayton, or Ben Jonson. A contemporary writer described those men who failed to praise the departed queen in their haste to welcome James as 'Janus Scicophants' [two-faced sycophants] and 'flattering parasites'.[92] Drayton implicitly agreed for he later explained that on James's entry

> When cowardise had tyd up every tongue
>   And all stood stood silent, yet for him I sung.[93]

His meaning was that he and other poets had feared that expressing too much grief for Elizabeth's demise would not go down well with her successor and might close opportunities for future royal patronage. For this same reason, Samuel Daniel in his panegyric to the new king was at pains to explain that the sorrow expressed at Elizabeth's death was not special to her but on the contrary a sign of the loyalty and love shown by the English towards all their sovereigns and consequently augured well for James's own reign.[94]

The commemorative poems eulogizing Elizabeth took several forms: some were popular ballads and 'vulgar verse' which were intended to 'feed plebeian eyes'.[95] Others were pastoral elegies, using complex metrical forms and sophisticated literary devices, which were targeting a more elite readership. A number were single poems composed by one author, but the majority were pieces written by different men and assembled in anthologies, as were the Latin, Greek, and Hebrew tributes composed by university scholars.[96] Despite their differences, all the verses adopted the language, tone, and themes that had been commonplace in the panegyric literature of the queen's lifetime, in which praise centred on Elizabeth's unusual learning, facility with languages, piety, love of peace, and promotion of Protestantism. The epithets applied to her were just as recognizable. The dead queen was once more likened to biblical heroes (Moses, Samuel, David, Solomon, Josiah, Judith, Deborah, and Esther), pagan goddesses (Cynthia, Astraea, Pallas, and Diana), and classical figures (Dido and Caesar). As in her lifetime, attention was paid to what was seen as the providential nature of her rule, the myth that God had protected her first as a princess and later as queen of England. Largely engendered by the Protestant martyrologist John Foxe, the story of Elizabeth's escape from death at the hands of her half-sister or Catholic agents had circulated widely during her reign and was now repeated in the tributes made on her death. In the words of one anonymous poet:

> Thus, did the Lord from troubles many a one,
>   preserve and keepe her gratious Majestie.
> And with his hand did set her on her throne,
>   to be admired of all posteritie.
> That after ages might report and say,
>   Thus, deales the Lord with them that him obay.[97]

Similarly, Protestant sermons, ballads, poems, and chronicles had repeatedly recited how God had saved the queen from the 1569 rebellion of the northern earls, Catholic assassination attempts, and the 1588 Spanish Armada.[98] Now on her death, this narrative was retold, writers making much of her miraculous deliverance from Catholic foes and the fact that she had died of natural causes in her bed and not at their hands. John Hanson's poem, *Time is a Turne-coate*, was fairly typical in reminding readers

> How many treasons, direfull accidents,
>   Base-bred complots and experiments,
> Conspir'd her death; yet still preserv'd was she
>   By heav'ns eternall triple-unitie?
> How many striv'd to stop Elizae's breath?
>   Yet (to their shame) she died a living death.[99]

Another theme in 1603 was the peace and prosperity that England had enjoyed under the queen. The hardships of the long Spanish war were ignored, and instead her long reign was contrasted with the short one of her predecessor Mary, a period presented as a time of religious persecution, defeat in war, and Spanish tyranny. As one Latin scholar wrote (in translation):

> The Marian age, that day to be marked by welling tears.
>   Oh, how many funeral flames did she kindle with blood!
> But such violent power is unable to last for long.
>   The light of Eliza banished this darkness as it rose
> The darkness of error, and the profane laws of papism.[100]

Such sentiments had also been common currency during Elizabeth's reign.

Added to these standard representations of the queen were the traditional forms of praise constructed to memorialize individuals who had recently died. Within the conventions of commemorative Renaissance poetry and art, the fame of Elizabeth was said to triumph over her decease. One poet, for instance, called her 'the splendour of her country, the light of the age, the world's glory' who:

> Succumbed to death. But yet she will not die,
>   Since upon the lips of men,
> The name of Eliza will always fly.[101]

At the same time, proclaimed many poets, Elizabeth could now enjoy eternal life. 'Eliza lives, and rules in the heights of heaven', declared one, while another wrote:

> Who may call her dead, she who wholly survives
>   Dwelling in heaven, and ruling on her throne?[102]

And, in several epitaphs, authors exploited the date of Elizabeth's death to draw a comparison between the Virgin Queen and Virgin Mary. Within an anthology composed by Oxford scholars, Robert Chamberlayne's Latin verse pointed out that on the day before the Annunciation:

> when Christ descended into his mother's womb
>   His chaste daughter [Elizabeth] ascended into the bosom of the father.[103]

In a more extended parallel, the Oxford scholar Thomas Morton claimed to see no coincidence in the date of Mary's death, for:

> Mary and she were virgins. Mary was blessed,
>   And so was Beth, among the ranks of women.
> To one, a king was heir; the other was the king's heir.
>   This one carried God in her womb; that one, in her heart.
> In all other ways they were similar, indeed, almost twins,
>   But in this one condition they were not alike:
> This one lived as a pauper on earth, and now reigns among the stars;
>   That one was blessed both on earth, and in the skies above.[104]

Despite the elaborate praise, in every single elegy the dead queen had to share centre stage with her successor. The titles of many works said it all: *Queene Elizabeth's Losse, and King James his Welcome*; *Sorrowe's Joy*; *Weepe with Joy*, *Elizae's Memoriall, King James his Arrivall*; and *Threno-thriambeuticon* [a composition both mournful and triumphant]. In each one, the outpourings of grief at Elizabeth's death were followed by an outburst of joy at the accession of James. Even when titles referred only to the nation's loss, the new king was joyfully hailed towards the end of the poem or song. A frequent trope was that James was a second phoenix rising from the queen's 'warme cynders', the phoenix being a mythical bird that regenerated itself after it had been burnt to ashes as well as a motif employed by Elizabeth for much of her reign.[105] Poets also favoured images that compared Elizabeth to the moon and James to the sun or Elizabeth to winter and James to spring.[106] This homage to James was to be expected. Authors were both following the conventions of the elegiac genre, which insisted upon moderation, and more cynically seeking to ingratiate themselves with their new sovereign.[107]

Some writers seemed to be genuinely looking forward to better days under James. Making the contrast between a 'mayden-queene' and 'a manly king', they implicitly suggested improvement was on its way now that the gender of the monarch had returned to normality.[108] James, moreover, had two sons, not to mention a daughter, and so the continuity of his dynasty looked assured. Gone, it seemed, were the anxieties about the succession that had plagued the last century. Furthermore, hopes for reform both religious and secular were in the air now that the old conservative queen was in her grave. The Protestant minister Andrew Willet greeted James's accession with three works, each one articulating the theme that the religious reformation advanced by Elizabeth remained to be completed by James, who was the Joshua to her Moses, the Solomon to her David.[109] Nor were Protestants alone. Catholics hoped that the whole anti-papal Elizabethan regime would be swept away by the new king.[110] Expectations were high but also contradictory.

★ ★ ★

Elizabeth was not forgotten once James assumed power. The cultural memory of the queen lived on not just over the next few years but throughout the seventeenth century.[111] The physical sites of memory were evident for all to see: statues of the queen in public places; portraits still hanging in town halls, universities, and private homes; engravings and medals collected by her erstwhile subjects; even coins stamped with her head which were still in circulation. Additionally, books and pamphlets bearing her picture or name or containing her story continued to be printed. Some were new, but others were unrevised reprints of previous works, including Foxe's *Actes and*

Monuments with its new edition in 1610 and Richard Day's *A Booke of Christian Praiers* (also known as 'Queen Elizabeth's Prayer Book'), which went into a fourth edition in 1608 and reproduced the picture of Elizabeth at prayer as its frontispiece. The description of the late queen's 1559 coronation passage from the Tower to Whitehall was reprinted in two separate editions in 1604 about the time when James made his own royal entry into the City of London.[112] Sermons that had previously been delivered before Elizabeth were reprinted when they were thought to have a new relevance under James.[113] New chronicles added to her fame, as did Dekker's 'dolefull lines' about her death that were copied into seventeenth-century manuscript verse miscellanies and printed again in William Camden's *Remaines*:

> The queene was brought by water to WhiteHall
>   At every stroake the owers [oars] teares let fall
> More clung about the barge: fish under water
>   Wept out their eyes of pearle, and swom blind after.[114]

Within four years of her death, several plays featuring Elizabeth as a character opened on the London stage. The earliest one to fictionalize the dead queen was Thomas Heywood's *If You Know Not Me, You Know Nobody*, which had the subtitle *The Troubles of Queene Elizabeth*. First performed around 1604, it was a huge hit, proving as popular during the first half of the seventeenth century as any Shakespeare drama.[115] The plot was based on the well-known story in Foxe's *Actes and Monuments* that related the 'troubles' which Elizabeth had faced as a young pious Protestant princess during Mary's reign, and it ended with her pre-coronation regal entry into London and acceptance of homage from her officers of state.[116]

Thanks to its success, Heywood wrote a sequel, entitled somewhat unimaginatively *The Second Part of Queene Elizabeth's Troubles* (see Figure 2). Yet, here Elizabeth had a supporting rather than starring role, and the play itself—or at least its text—was something of a hybrid, as is evident from its title page.[117] As well as being a history play that dealt with Catholic plots against the queen and the construction of London's bourse, the piece was a city comedy featuring a haberdasher and pedlar. Elizabeth was dominant only in the play's later scenes when she emerged as the iconic Virgin Queen, favouring peace but triumphant in war against England's Catholic foes. Hearing of the launch of the Spanish Armada, she appears 'compleately armed', declaiming 'A mayden queene will be your generall'.[118] Like its prequel, *The Second Part* was an immediate success, its script revised and reprinted four times between 1606 and 1633.[119]

THE
SECOND PART OF
Queene *Elizabeths* troubles. Doctor *Paries* treasons : The building of the *Royall Exchange*, and the famous *Victorie in 1588*.

With the Humors of *Hobson* and *Tawny-coat*.

AT LONDON,
Printed for *Nathaniell Butter*.

Figure 2. Title page of Thomas Heywood, *The Second Part of Queene Elizabeth's Troubles* (London, 1606) © Folger Shakespeare Library, Washington DC.

Far less popular, yet still significant in the dramatic afterlife of Elizabeth, was Dekker's long—even tedious—allegorical play, *The Whore of Babylon*, which opened in 1606 not long after the discovery of the Gunpowder Plot. This deeply anti-Catholic piece centred its action on the numerous stratagems devised by the empress of Babylon and three allied kings to destroy the power of Titania, the queen of Fairyland. The play's last scenes showed Titania in full armour mobilizing land forces against Babylon and her victory over the empress's invasion fleet. But it ended with a warning since the disgraced and defeated empress swore revenge. The play's relevance was spelled out in the *Dramatis Personae*, which noted that the 'Faerie Queen' represented Elizabeth while the empress of Babylon—the titular whore—stood for the Roman Catholic Church. Since for Protestants, the 'Whore of Babylon', a figure in the biblical Book of Revelation, was construed as the 'Romish harlot' [the Church of Rome], this identification would have come as no surprise to spectators or readers. As for the other fictional characters in the play, some names punned those of actual men who had been executed for treason in the 1580s and 1590s: Doctor Paridel for William Parry; Campeius, a poor scholar, for the Jesuit Edmund Campion; and Lopus for Dr Lopez. There was also a pun on the name of Guy Fawkes within the play.

Many literary scholars and historians have viewed all three plays as early Jacobean expressions of nostalgia for the dead queen and a sign of disillusionment with her successor.[120] This interpretation is questionable. Let us take Heywood's first play. Given that there was a spate of history plays during the late Elizabethan and early Jacobean period, Heywood—who earned his living as a playwright—correctly anticipated that a production of *Elizabeth's Troubles* would appeal to London audiences who were then enjoying the genre and might also be attracted to a dramatization of Foxe's famous story.[121] There is no obvious critique of James in the play; on the contrary it ends with Elizabeth's hopeful utterance that 'the happy yssue that shall us succeed' will 'build' his rule on the bible, a hope that might have seemed realized in 1605 for by then James had embarked on the task of putting together a team of scholars to create a new and better translation of the English bible. Nor can the play be interpreted as an attack on James's recent peace with Spain, given that Philip II is portrayed as Elizabeth's protector against the villains of the piece, Queen Mary and the bishop of Winchester.

As for Heywood's sequel, it is likely that he incorporated the character of Elizabeth into his comedy simply to capitalize both on the first play's success and the anti-Catholicism engendered by the Gunpowder Plot.[122]

The sections involving the queen reflected the fevered atmosphere of post-plot London when sermons and polemical writings told the same stories about the menacing assaults of Catholics and the providential deliverances of Elizabeth and James from their malevolent attacks. Again, the play does not seem to be a critique of the peace-loving James since Elizabeth was characterized as a reluctant warrior, declaring in her last lines: 'We wish no warres, yet we must guard our owne', words that mirrored James's own sentiment in his well-known work *Basilikon Doron*.[123] Besides, like the prequel, the play is anti-Catholic rather than anti-Spanish. Only when the text was expanded and revised for a fourth edition in 1633 did a strong anti-Spanish sentiment surface.[124]

The Whore of Babylon was the most anti-Catholic of the three plays. As Dekker explained in the 1607 quarto edition, its purpose was to set forth 'the incomparable heroical vertues of our late queene in contrast to the inveterate malice, treasons, machinations underminings, & continual blody stratagems of the false Church of Rome'.[125] Nonetheless, it seems unlikely that Dekker was using the figure of a militant Protestant Elizabeth to shame James for inadequacy in confronting the Catholic threat.[126] The language of the play echoed contemporary rhetoric about Catholic treachery and, besides, harsh measures against recusants had already been introduced in parliament. What is more, in the third act, Dekker allowed a character (one of the empress's cardinals) to prophesy that:

> A second phoenix rise, of larger wing,
>   Of stronger talent, of more dreadfull beake.
> would drive away the birds taking shelter in the trees [denoting
>   Catholic conspirators].

In case readers of the play might miss the intended meaning, a marginal note in the script identified 'K. James' as the 'phoenix'.[127] Admittedly, Dekker might have been intending to spur James on to take a more militant stance for the cardinal extended the metaphor to add:

> ...perhaps his talent [talons]
> May be so bonie and so large of gripe,
>   That it may shake all Babilon.

But the tone was hardly critical.

Along with these plays, the Gunpowder Plot spawned a wide range of anti-Catholic material—sermons, poems, and polemic—that equally contributed to Elizabeth's afterlife. Their plaudits for the dead queen could put

James in the shade, as when John King, who had already written a eulogy of Elizabeth in 1603, lauded her in a Gunpowder anniversary sermon as: 'a Queene of Queenes, a paragon (whilest she lived) of mortal princes, the diamond in the ring of the monarches of the earth, the glorie of hir sexe, the pleasure of mankind, the miracle of the Christian, and the mark and scope even of the infidel world'. She was also an English Deborah presiding over the 1588 defeat of Catholic 'idolators'. All King had to say about James was that his accession was equally the work of God.[128]

It was in part to commemorate the Plot and remember Catholic treachery that early memorials of Elizabeth were commissioned for view in parish churches. The stained-glass window erected at St Mildred's Bread Street depicted the defeat of the Spanish Armada together with the Gunpowder Plot.[129] Similarly, two painted panels in St Faith's Church near King's Lynn, Norfolk, linked Elizabeth with the Plot: one showing her reviewing the troops at Tilbury after the Armada's defeat, the other the Gunpowder plotters.

★ ★ ★

The 1605 Gunpowder Plot possibly encouraged the erection of monuments to the late queen in other churches, but the main one erected over her tomb in Westminster Abbey was conceived beforehand.[130] Unlike her father and grandfather, Elizabeth had left no detailed instructions about its design. All she had said—or so Francis Bacon attested—was that she wanted it simple, with just a few lines recording her name, her virginity, the dates of her reign, the reformation of religion, and preservation of peace.[131] As a result, Cecil took responsibility for the project. Making sure the money was available, despite a shortage of cash, he explained: 'It doth my hart good to falsify the blynd prophesy that sayd none of King Henry the 8th's children shold ever be buried, with any memory'. Completed in 1606, the memorial cost £965, a relatively small sum by the standards of the day.[132] The carver was the French-born craftsman Maximilian Colt, who was brought to Cecil's attention by the serjeant painter, John de Critz.

The structure was conventional: it took a triumphal arch as its basic form, and a gilded and painted effigy of the queen in marble lay beneath on a raised panelled chest, which resembled a bier and was surrounded by ten columns. Latin inscriptions were carved in large letters on a pair of tablets at the east and west ends of the tomb. One of them summarized (or rather exaggerated) her achievements, listing the restoration of true religion, the restoration of the coinage after numerous debasements, vanquishing the

Spanish Armada, settling peace, quelling domestic rebellion, supporting France and the United Provinces, routing the Spanish in Ireland, enlarging the revenues of both universities, and finally enriching all England. The other inscription referred to Elizabeth's lineage and described her as: 'Mother of her country, a nursing-mother to religion and all liberal sciences, skilled in many languages, adorned with excellent endowments both of body and mind, and excellent for princely virtues beyond her sex.' It ended with a tribute to James, who was said to have 'devoutly and justly erected this monument to her whose virtues and kingdoms he inherits'—another exaggeration since it was Cecil who had initiated and supervised its construction. James's main concerns had been: first, that it would not cost too much; and second, that his own mother should also have a new tomb in the abbey.[133]

What is unusual and indeed controversial about Elizabeth's tomb was its siting. The late queen was disinterred from her original burial spot in the centre of the Lady Chapel and reburied in the north aisle on top of the unmarked grave of her childless half-sister Mary. No separate monument was devoted to England's first queen regnant; indeed, only the Latin inscription on a small panel at the base of the tomb—'Partners in throne and grave, here we sleep Elizabeth and Mary, sisters in hope of the Resurrection'— recorded Mary's presence beneath. What is more, while the childless Tudor queens were situated in this side-chapel—soon to be accompanied by the corpses and tombs of the king and queen's two infant daughters—James ensured in 1612 that his mother's cadaver was removed from its place in Peterborough Cathedral and reburied in the south aisle of the chapel alongside two of his female ancestors: his royal great-great-grandmother Margaret Beaufort (the mother of Henry VII) and his paternal grandmother Margaret, countess of Lennox (a granddaughter of Henry VII). The symbolism of this siting could hardly be missed: the infertile Tudors represented the past; the legitimate and fertile line of the Stuarts was the present and future.[134] James intended his own tomb to be placed in the central nave (where Elizabeth's had originally been), near those of Henry VII and Edward VI. And, indeed, on his death in 1625, he was laid in the vault beneath Henry VII's monument, but there is no inscription or statue marking his burial spot.

Well before his mother's reburial, in fact immediately after his coronation, James had chosen to honour Mary, Queen of Scots, publicly. In August 1603, he dispatched Sir William Dethick (the garter king of arms) to place 'a rich pall of velvet' embroidered with Mary's royal coat of arms on her unadorned tomb. Since Dethick had overseen Mary's low-key funeral in

1587, it was significant that he now had the role of according her the greatest respect as the king's mother. This Jacobean ceremony took place during divine service, attended by many knights, members of the gentry, and the bishop of Peterborough.[135]

James found other ways to ensure that commemorations of Elizabeth would remain understated, or even non-existent, after her funeral. No longer was her accession day marked, although 17 November had brought an end to Catholic rule in England.[136] In its place, a thanksgiving service for James's accession—the anniversary of her death—was officially held in all churches (the service being inserted into the new official prayer book of 1604), while at court the day was joyously celebrated with a tournament and banquet. James's birthday in June and coronation day in July were equally days of jubilation. Bells were rung in some parishes and cathedrals, and a special song was written for the coronation day in 1606.[137] While the

Figure 3. Locket with miniatures inside depicting James I and an ark, from the workshop of Nicholas Hilliard © Victoria and Albert Museum, London.

anniversary of the Spanish Armada now went unobserved, two new holy days were established to commemorate James's providential escape from death: not just the foiling of the Gunpowder Plot but the more questionable Gowrie Day assassination plot of 5 August 1600.[138]

At the same time as seeking to eclipse his predecessor, James was canny enough to exploit her memory when it suited him. It was not only that he had deep respect for monarchy but that he also wanted to reassure his new subjects that nothing significant had changed despite the fact that the king of a foreign country—a country that for many years had been England's enemy—was now sitting on the English throne. In this spirit, James consistently made positive references to the 'late queene of famous memory' and 'Our late deere sister Queene Elizabeth' in his speeches, proclamations, and letters. Keen to emphasize his dynastic continuity with her line, he retained the use of the Tudor rose (linked to the thistle) on coins and medals, and adopted a few of her other emblems, such as the ark painted on his locket that replicated the one on the cover of the late Elizabethan locket known as the Heneage Jewel (see Figure 3). Anna, too, chose at times to represent herself as a renewed Elizabeth, wearing similar clothes, sporting the same hairstyle, and assuming personas—Pallas and Oriana—favoured by the late queen.

★ ★ ★

Elizabeth's afterlife in the early Jacobean period was not 'nostalgia' for the dead queen, as too often claimed. Leaving aside the fact that 'nostalgia' is not a word that Jacobeans would have recognized, since it was not coined until the 1680s, 'nostalgia' implies a wistfulness and sentimentality which were generally lacking in remembrances of Elizabeth before 1613, not least because the actual memories of the queen were far less rosy.[139] Nor should the idealization of her person in commemorations be interpreted as an implicit critique of her successor. As will be seen in later chapters, criticisms of James were to take a different form during his first decade as king of England. Only after the deaths of Cecil and James's elder son Henry in 1612 did dissatisfaction with the king result in an appropriation of Elizabeth's memory as a weapon against him. James's seemingly pro-Spanish foreign and dynastic policies then caused Elizabeth—'the rod of Spain'—to be used as a device designed to spur him into a change of policy. In this activity, though, there was little in the way of nostalgia for a past age but rather frustration and anger with the present one.[140]

2

A King in Waiting

By 1603, James VI had been king for nearly forty years in Scotland, ruling as an adult for almost twenty-five. During that period, he accumulated political, social, and cultural skills which at times served him well as king of England.

Like Elizabeth, James had been born into a dysfunctional family. His parents were on such bad terms at his birth on 19 June 1566 that his father Henry Stuart, Lord Darnley, refused to attend his baptism the following December. Two months later Darnley was dead. He was murdered, so it was said, at the instigation of his wife Mary, Queen of Scots and her alleged lover James Hepburn, fourth earl of Bothwell. Also, like Elizabeth, James lost his mother at a very early age. The last time Mary saw her son was on 21 April 1567 when he was less than a year old. The following June, she was imprisoned in Lochleven Castle and forced to abdicate in favour of James. After a dramatic escape on 2 May 1568, she failed to retake her throne and fled to England, never to return to her country of birth.[1]

At thirteen months old, Charles James—as he was baptized—became James VI of Scotland. Proclaimed king on 24 July 1567, he was crowned in Stirling parish church five days later. On 22 August, his maternal uncle James Stewart, earl of Moray, was named regent. Not all the Scottish lords recognized the king's accession, however, and a civil war erupted after Moray was assassinated in January 1570. Five years of turmoil ensued before Mary's adherents were forced to admit defeat. Although rivalries remained among the Scottish nobles, the government under James's fourth regent— James Douglas, fourth earl of Morton—enjoyed a new stability that lasted five years.[2]

During the period of unrest and warfare, the young king was insulated from political life. His mother had initially placed him in the care of Sir Alexander Erskine of Gogar but a few months later removed him with his own household to Stirling Castle, an impregnable site, under the guardianship of John Erskine, first earl of Mar, and his wife Annabella. They supervised the boy's household until the earl's death in 1572. Then Erskine of Gogar (the uncle of the underage second earl of Mar) resumed the role as guardian along with the dowager countess. By some accounts, Annabella was distant and 'severe'. If so, James—unlike Elizabeth—had no consistently warm mother substitute.[3] Nonetheless, James may have felt some affection towards the countess as he addressed her as 'Lady Minny'.[4]

From the age of four, James began his formal education at Stirling in the company of aristocratic boys of about his own age, as was usual for a Scottish prince. Among them was John Erskine, the future earl of Mar, who later came to England with him. Until the king reached the age of fourteen, his tutors were Scotland's foremost scholar and poet, the elderly and fierce George Buchanan, together with the much younger and gentler Peter Young, a Calvinist who taught his royal charge religion.[5] They gave James a traditional liberal arts education with a dose of Calvinist theology. He learned Latin and Greek grammar, rhetoric, poetry, history, and moral philosophy together with bible study and Calvinist commentaries. The theological and moral lessons from these studies were designed to instil in him the classical virtues of moderation, self-discipline, and religious piety, so as to counteract the hereditary influence of his mother, whom Buchanan branded a wicked papist and adulterous murderer akin to Jezebel in the Hebrew Bible.[6]

Buchanan also endeavoured to transmit to James his theory of contractual kingship: the obligations of a king towards his subjects, and the people's right of resistance if he failed to rule justly. James's own position as the crowned king of Scotland while his mother was still alive was of course entirely dependent on this theory. By contrast, Young wanted to cultivate in his royal charge a bookish culture and a capacity for critical thought. Buchanan was a hard taskmaster, inclined to use the stick, whereas Young preferred to encourage James with gifts and games. It is not therefore surprising that James grew up terrified of the older tutor, but felt a strong affection for Young, who later accompanied him to England and became Prince Charles's tutor in 1604 and overseer of his household.[7] As we shall see, James also came to reject Buchanan's political ideas while retaining the basic theological teachings and reading culture imparted by Young. But that was for the future; as a child, James appeared to thrive on the demanding intellectual diet provided by Buchanan and proved a very able student. According to an English observer, James at the age of eight could spontaneously 'reade a

Figure 4. James VI as a boy © National Trust Images.

chapter of the bible out of Latin into French, and out of French after into English' far better than most men could.[8]

James's intelligence and studiousness compensated for his unprepossessing appearance. An early portrait shows a sweet child with his father's long and delicate face (see Figure 4). However, he grew up to be less attractive. From later portraits, he appears heavy lidded, narrow-mouthed, slender, and spindly legged. James also had a couple of physical disadvantages. His tongue was somewhat too large for his mouth, a disability that barely affected his speech but made it difficult for him to swallow and—according to one hostile witness—caused him to slobber, especially when drinking.[9] He also had poor muscular coordination and a weakness in the legs that led to a somewhat 'ungainly' way of walking. This probably explains why he preferred not to dance but was happy on horseback.[10] The muscular weakness may have been caused by rickets as a boy or a mild cerebral palsy. Whatever the cause, the slight disability was passed down to his youngest son Charles.

★ ★ ★

At eleven years old, James formally took on the duties of kingship. In March 1578, under pressure from rival noble factions, Morton resigned as regent, and James was declared of age although not yet deemed fit to rule alone. The boy's new role as an adult king was marked by his removal from Stirling to Holyroodhouse in late September 1579 and his royal entry into Edinburgh on Saturday 17 October, when he was greeted by the elaborate pageants and ceremonial that were traditional on such occasions. Over the next few years, he increasingly began to play a public role in government. However, his hold on power was tenuous. Between 1579 and 1585, he faced six attempted or successful coups from different factions within the nobility and confronted challenges to his authority from the Kirk. During this same period, Elizabeth and her government consistently intervened in Scottish political life to forward England's security interests, which were often contrary to those of the Scottish king.

Three months after Morton's enforced resignation, James and his noble councillors allowed the earl to re-enter the council. All seemed to work fairly harmoniously until September 1579, when James's cousin Esmé Stuart, sixth seigneur d'Aubigny, arrived in Scotland from France.[11] D'Aubigny was a handsome and cultured thirty-seven-year-old who immediately captivated the young king. Within a year, James granted the Frenchman lands, offices, and a noble title, first the earldom and in 1581 the dukedom of Lennox. Lennox took on the positions of lord great chamberlain (regulating access to the king) and first gentleman of the bedchamber in the royal household. Soon afterwards, he sat on the council. On the last day of 1580, his rival Morton was arrested and five months later executed on the charge that he had been involved in the murder of Darnley, a charge that at the same time exculpated James's mother.[12]

With Morton's fall, Lennox became pre-eminent in government. He clearly had James's confidence and affection, but the exact nature of that affection is a matter of dispute. One biographer has described it as 'first and foremost familial', James loving and trusting Lennox as a close cousin and father substitute.[13] Other scholars have seen the relationship as homoerotic or even homosexual, the first in a line of favourites whom James wanted to—or possibly did—bed.[14] That there was physical intimacy between the two men is undisputed. Famously, a hostile English official reported from Berwick that James 'in oppen sight of the people oftentymes will claspe him [Lennox] about the neck with his armes and kisse him'.[15] But, if Lennox and James were lovers, the Kirk and court were apparently unaware of it. The Kirk's main concern about Lennox was that he would entice James into Catholicism not carnal sin. When it did show unease that Lennox—and James's other leading minister, Captain James Stewart (later earl of Arran)—would introduce the king to 'carnall lust', the Kirk was evidently thinking about whores, swearing, and other ungodly behaviour.[16] As for the court, in a later memoir the diplomat and courtier Sir James referred to Lennox's 'gud qualites' and made no suggestion that there was anything sexual in his association with James.[17] My guess is that James was physically attracted to Lennox but that their relationship was sexually unconsummated.

The Kirk and Scottish Protestant lords were, anyway, more apprehensive about Lennox's politics and perceived religion than either his or James's sexuality. The favourite was thought to be pro-French and pro-Catholic and the promoter of a scheme to have Mary restored to the Scottish throne in joint sovereignty with her son. To end his primacy, pro-English Protestant lords—led by Mar and William Ruthven, first earl of Gowrie—mounted a coup known as the Ruthven Raid. On 22 August 1582, they seized James as he was returning from a month's hunting without Lennox in highland Perthshire and held him for six days in Gowrie's castle of Ruthven (now Huntingtower Castle) near Perth before taking him first to Stirling Castle and then Holyrood. Claiming to be rescuing the king from evil councillors, the 'Raiders' then banished Lennox from the kingdom and imprisoned Arran until December 1582. On Arran's release, he was denied access to the king; Lennox, meanwhile, died in France in May 1583. Over the next ten months, the 'Raiders' ran the country while James was kept a virtual prisoner. However, in June 1583, he escaped their clutches and resumed power with the aid of Arran.[18]

Over the next couple of years, James ruled with the anti-Presbyterian Arran at his side and gained almost total control over the nobility. The 'Raiders' were either systematically exiled or fled to England between September 1583 and January 1584. After they attempted an abortive coup, Gowrie was executed in May 1584. Having gained authority over his nobles, James sought to do the same over the Presbyterian ministers. That same month, his conflict with the Kirk culminated in the introduction of statutes in parliament, known to their critics as the 'Black Acts'. The measures abolished presbyteries, enhanced the episcopate, and established an English-style royal supremacy over the Kirk. Simultaneously, Jesuits slipped into Scotland, and one of them even participated in a disputation with eight ministers of the Kirk in front of the king.[19]

In November 1585, with English connivance, the Ruthven lords returned to Scotland and ousted Arran. Rather than seeking revenge, James prudently adopted a policy of reconciliation with the noble factions and the Kirk, a policy that resulted in greater political stability over the next eighteen years. Simultaneously, he tried to patch up his relations with Elizabeth, signing the Treaty of Berwick with her in 1586. As part of the agreement, he received an annual English pension that was crucial for his needs: all told, Elizabeth paid him over £58,000 [c. £8m in today's currency] until her death. But she refused to name him her heir.

Despite these successes, the king continued to have difficulties with his nobility, the Kirk, and the English queen. He confronted an armed noble force, led by George Gordon, sixth earl of Huntly, at Brig o'Dee near Aberdeen in April 1589 and was beset by violent challenges to his authority from Francis Stewart, fifth earl of Bothwell, during the early 1590s. Factional politics involving the powerful Catholic lords Huntly and Francis Hay, ninth earl of Errol, forced James to take up arms against them in 1594 and agree to their exile in 1595.[20] A murky 'conspiracy' in August 1600 led by Alexander Ruthven and his brother, the second earl of Gowrie, to kidnap the king was said to have resulted in an assassination attempt that was thwarted by members of the king's retinue.[21] Nonetheless, by 1603, James had tamed—or, in the case of Bothwell, exiled—the troublemakers among the nobility. Additionally, he had managed to induce the nobility to agree to legislation in 1598 which would end their violent blood feuds and bring their disputes before the royal courts, thereby reinforcing the position of the king as the source of justice.[22] James's policy, though, was not anti-noble. Like all European monarchs, he needed the nobility to enforce law and order in the localities and bring lustre to his court. For this reason, as well as his personal liking for Huntly, who was married to his beloved Lennox's daughter Henrietta, he allowed the earl and Errol to return to Scotland in June 1596, but only after they had submitted both to him and the Kirk.[23]

As for the Kirk, James made concessions while continuing his struggle to erode its independence. A statute of 1592 exemplified his approach.

The 'Golden Act', as it became known, overturned some of the 'Black Acts' and authorized the Presbyterian system of ecclesiastical government while retaining the principle of royal and parliamentary control over the Kirk. James also set to work to undermine the radicals in the Kirk. After a confrontation had almost led to an armed uprising in Edinburgh during December 1596, James used his influence and patronage both to boost the representation of moderates in the Kirk's General Assembly and to win round previously oppositional ministers.[24] His position strengthened, he then appointed five bishops between 1600 and 1603 and admitted two of them to his council in 1600 and 1602.[25]

After the difficulties of his minority, therefore, James had developed into an accomplished and effective adult ruler. His political manoeuvrings with the Kirk and nobility brought domestic peace to Scotland as did his policy of ensuring that his government was broadly based. Men suspected of 'popery', such as Alexander Seton of Fyvie, sat among his advisers alongside Protestants, such as John Lindsay of Balcarres, who was appointed lord keeper of the privy seal and secretary of state in 1596.[26] That is not to say that there were no political problems in Scotland, for the Kirk was on the defensive, royal finances in a muddle, while law and order remained precarious in the Highlands, borders, and Western Isles.[27] Nevertheless, overall, Scotland was in a relatively settled state at the time when James inherited the English crown.

The king was also successful in his foreign policy.[28] The terms of the Anglo-Scottish Treaty of Berwick had made him and Elizabeth formal allies but did not oblige either of them to enter the other's wars. As a result, he could and did remain at peace with Spain even after Philip II's 1588 invasion attempt upon England, a wise move since Scotland was vulnerable to assaults by sea and had few resources to fight. Yet James's studied neutrality did not make him an isolationist. On the contrary, he courted both Catholic and Protestant rulers: on the Catholic side, the pope, the Spanish king, the archdukes of the Spanish Netherlands, Henry IV of France, and the rulers of various Italian states. Among the Protestants, he built up friendly relations with the king of Denmark, the states general of the United Provinces, and the rulers of various North German territories. As at home, James manoeuvred to keep everyone on board: to Catholic powers he offered the prospect of his potential conversion; to Protestants he proposed an anti-papal alliance. When giving such conflicting assurances, he developed the techniques of misleading his audiences and developing a plausible deniability: so, while telling Elizabeth that he would never deal with her enemies, he secretly sent agents to Spain for informal discussions; and while allowing Scottish volunteers to serve alongside the Dutch in their war against Spain, he communicated warmly with the archdukes of the Spanish Netherlands. No wonder he developed a reputation for duplicity and untrustworthiness.

James's far-flung diplomatic efforts were effective in keeping Scotland at peace while much of Europe was plagued by wars. His communications with foreign powers also gave him an enhanced international profile, especially after his marriage to Anna informally allied him to the princes of Denmark and North Germany. Arguably, too, his diplomacy aided his bid for the English throne. His assurance to the Catholic powers that he was not their enemy and might even change his religion was a factor that led to their decision not to block his accession in 1603.

★ ★ ★

Like Elizabeth, James had no siblings and would have no direct successor unless he were to marry and his wife to bear an heir. Consequently, from the age of seventeen, he was on the marriage market. There was no question of James taking a Scottish bride. Scottish monarchs had a long history of marrying into the French and Danish royal families. Accordingly, the two main candidates were Catherine of Bourbon, the sister of Henry of Navarre (then the Huguenot heir to the French throne), and Elizabeth, the elder daughter of Frederick II of Denmark. Both women were Protestant and therefore acceptable to the Kirk and to the English queen, although she marginally preferred Catherine. James's mother was not consulted. The king's lack of political independence delayed matters, but in 1585 informal talks began with Denmark. They got nowhere, however, partly because Arran was hostile to this match. It was only after his fall that negotiations began in earnest. Even then, they were so slow and protracted that during their course Frederick arranged another marriage for his elder daughter.[29]

During the summer of 1587, Henry of Navarre sent the poet Guillaume de Salluste, Sieur Du Bartas, to Scotland to discuss James's possible match with Catherine. However, despite his deep admiration for Du Bartas and his nobles' support for a French marriage, the king decided to wed Frederick's younger daughter Anna. At first, he had been reluctant to consider her because he felt dishonoured by the Danish king's decision to marry the senior princess elsewhere.[30] However, Anna had distinct advantages over her rival. Catherine was eight years older than James, and her dowry would be insubstantial, whereas Anna was eight years younger, said to be a beauty, and the Danes offered a dowry of 150,000 Scottish pounds. Equally important, the Scottish towns, especially Edinburgh, backed a matrimonial alliance with Frederick. Scotland already had strong economic ties to Denmark and Norway (the two countries were united), and merchants hoped to gain further commercial advantages in the marriage treaty, such as the relief of tolls which Denmark extracted from ships passing through the Sound into the Baltic.[31]

In June 1588, a Scottish embassy, headed by George Keith, fourth earl marischal, departed for Denmark to negotiate and finalize a matrimonial treaty.[32] Frederick had died the previous April—delaying matters—and his widow Queen Sophia took the lead in the negotiations. After difficulties were sorted out—notably about the queen's dowry and the status of the Orkney and Shetland islands which both countries claimed—James and Anna's nuptials took place by proxy on 20 August 1589. Keith stood in for the bridegroom at the civil wedding and banquet, and he afterwards participated in a bedding ceremony (symbolically enacting the deferred consummation of the marriage), accompanied by twelve nobles from each realm carrying different coloured wedding torches.[33] In early September, the fourteen-year-old Anna set out for Scotland.

James had already begun preparations for his bride's arrival, there being much to do since the royal palaces needed repair and refurbishment. While waiting for Anna, he appeared to observers like 'a true lover... hau700f out of pacience with the wind and wether' and thinking 'everie daie a yere' until he saw his new wife.[34] Although the journey from Copenhagen to Leith should have taken about five days, there was still no news of the Danish ships by the beginning of the second week in October. James became quite frantic, commanding a 'publicke fast and praier' for Anna's safety. Shortly afterwards, he learned that a sudden storm had separated her ship from its naval convoy and driven it onto the coast of Norway.[35] So badly damaged was her vessel that it seemed she would have to postpone her sea journey until the spring. Hearing this, James immediately resolved to fetch Anna himself, but he kept this plan close to his chest as he knew that it would upset many of his subjects.[36]

At midnight on 22 October, James set sail, 'with five ships in company' and escorted by perhaps three hundred barons and gentlemen, including most of his chief officers of state. The privy council was to rule Scotland during his absence under the presidency of his nearest relative, the fifteen-year-old Ludovick, second duke of Lennox, Esmé's elder son who had been living in Scotland since 1583. Bothwell, admiral of Scotland, was appointed Lennox's lieutenant. The borders were to be run by a council led by another senior nobleman and kinsman, Lord John Hamilton.[37] James expected to be away for only three weeks or so, but it turned into an absence of more than six months. Yet, despite Lennox's youth and Bothwell's unpredictable loyalty, the realm suffered no serious disturbances during that time.[38]

James was not the first Scottish king to go abroad to bring back a bride: his maternal grandfather James V had spent nine months in France pursuing and marrying Madelaine, the daughter of Francis I. Nonetheless, many were startled at the king's decision to brave the Baltic winter seas and escort his bride to Scotland. Elizabeth and her ministers 'feared that some stirrs and trobles maye be moved in the kinge's absence', while the Scots were mainly worried that James might be shipwrecked at sea, leaving no clear heir to rule.[39] To his subjects, James downplayed the dangers of the voyage and ordered that 'no man grudge or murmor at these my proceadinges'.[40]

Why did James go on such a risky venture? In his explanation to his subjects, he referred to a political imperative, namely the need to consummate the marriage quickly and produce an heir for the good of his realm.[41] But, for the most part, he emphasized the chivalric nature of the enterprise, constructing it as the quest of a romantic hero, a persona which he had adopted in his love poems *Amatoria*, written in 1589 supposedly for Anna.[42] And, indeed, after his return, the journey was to be celebrated as a chivalric exploit in Scottish poems and later royal pageants.[43]

There may have been further motives for his venture. Almost certainly, James considered the immediate political objectives that might be garnered from the foreign trip. It would show the Scots that he could govern by pen, if and when he took the throne of England; and it would allow him to forge important personal contacts and connections abroad that could prove useful when he made his bid to succeed Elizabeth. In December, it was reported that his intention from the start had been to enter a 'confederation' with the Protestant German princes, and he set to work on this task once in Denmark.[44] At the same time, psychological considerations may have come into play. It seems likely that James yearned for some freedom and adventure after years of confinement, hard work, and political anxiety. Probably too, he wanted to seize an opportunity to prove and project his manhood both at home and abroad by bravely rescuing his wife marooned in Norway.

As he had been slow to wed and had no known mistresses, questions had evidently been raised about his masculinity. By showing an impatient and passionate desire to meet his wife, he could still any lurking suspicions that he suffered from 'inhabilitie' [impotency], as if he 'were a barron stock'.[45] Additionally, James was portraying himself as an independent adult ruler by taking 'this resolutioun onlie of myself as I am a trew prince'.[46]

James met Anna for the first time on 19 November 1589 in Oslo. It was a formal occasion and, according to a Danish account, the king wore a red velvet coat, appliquéd with gold, and a black velvet cloak, lined with sable; what Anna wore went unrecorded.[47] The couple spoke together for about thirty minutes, and the following morning James saw Anna again for a meal at her residence. On 23 November, they were wed in the great hall of the Old Bishop's Palace. James's chaplain David Lindsay delivered the sermon and conducted the service in French, a language they both understood and were to speak together until Anna learned Scottish English. Unable to return immediately to Scotland because of the frozen sea, the couple travelled by land to the magnificent Kronborg Castle near Elsinore in Denmark where they remained from January until the spring. Their stay was enjoyable for bridegroom and bride: Anna was cosseted by her family while James was royally entertained with hunting, heavy drinking, and trips to satisfy his intellectual curiosity. At Copenhagen, he attended the Royal Academy where he listened to a four-hour academic disputation. At Roskilde, he talked with the leading Danish theologian Niels Hemmingsen. Then, on 20 March 1590, he visited Uraniborg, the castle observatory of the famous astronomer and mathematician Tycho Brahe.[48] James was so impressed with the scholar that he afterwards composed a sonnet and two more poems 'on Ticho Brahe', commending him on understanding the workings of the planets and by extension the works of God.[49]

In Denmark, James also used the time to build up political connections with important members of Anna's family: her grandfather Ulrik, duke of Mecklenburg; her brothers the twelve-year-old Christian IV and Ulrik and Hans, dukes of Schleswig-Holstein; and Henry Julius, duke of Brunswick, who was soon to marry Anna's sister. Although James failed to persuade these men to sign a Protestant league for mutual defence or act as mediators to end the war between England and Spain, he did forge a bond with them that endured beyond his homecoming.[50] They corresponded, their ambassadors visited James on special occasions, and both Christian and Duke Ulrik of Holsten stayed with James and Anna in England.[51]

At last, on 21 April 1590, James and Anna left Denmark for Scotland. In advance of their departure James had sent out directives to ensure that the food and furnishings at Holyrood were sumptuous.[52] He wanted his new wife to be comfortable, but equally important he wanted to impress the Danish nobles who were accompanying her. James understood the importance of royal magnificence. In Denmark, he had given lavish gifts to Anna's family, including diamonds and rubies for her brother and mother.[53] Now, acting as host to the large Danish embassy accompanying Anna, he aimed to project an image of royal grandeur and sophistication to match that of his in-laws. But since the Scottish crown was relatively poor, he had to call upon his nobles, burghs, and even the English queen to help him out with money, materials, and provisions.[54] James also paid close attention to the ceremonials that would greet the royal party landing at Leith. His instructions included specifics about the decoration of the harbour, the firing of cannons from ships and castles, and the people who should attend.[55] He planned for a guard of two hundred footmen to be present, much to the annoyance of his nobility who feared it would be used to limit their 'free accesse' to the king, as was the practice in Denmark. Their concerns were evidently justified, for on his return to Holyrood James kept his chamber 'more private than before'.[56]

The royal couple disembarked at Leith late on Friday 1 May. The weather was hardly spring-like, as the coast was shrouded in a great mist, but nevertheless—as James had arranged—a large group of spectators were present to welcome their new queen. Scotland's principal noblemen—Lennox, Bothwell, and Hamilton—were the first to greet the king and queen, and they immediately escorted them towards the King's Hall (a royal house specially set up for them) along a walkway covered and decorated with tapestries and cloth of gold 'so that thair feit sould not tevitch [touch] the vare [very] earth'.[57] At the Hall, James's secretary James Elphinstone delivered a Latin oration of welcome, and from there they all went to church where Patrick Galloway offered thanks for their safe arrival in a sermon preached in English. After a few days, the royal party made its way to Holyrood, James on horseback and Anna sitting with her maids of honour in a 'chariot' drawn by eight horses. As they passed through each burgh, they were greeted with a volley of cannon fire.[58]

James had intended Anna's coronation and royal entry to occur the following Sunday, but they did not take place until two and a half weeks later. Unexpected disputes between James and the Kirk about the ceremonies had first to be resolved. To reinforce the doctrine of divine right monarchy, James insisted upon his royal consort being anointed, but the Presbyterian ministers refused to perform a ritual that they deemed a Catholic superstition borrowed from the Jews. The ministers also objected to the royal entry taking place on a Sunday because 'the pagions [pageants] and devises for th'entrie should partlie prophane the Saboth daie'.[59] In the end, a compromise was reached: the queen would be anointed in a coronation service on Sunday 17 May held in the royal chapel of Holyrood Abbey and not in St Giles Church, which was under the Kirk's control. The royal entry would take place the following Tuesday and so not desecrate the Sabbath.

Anna's coronation followed the pattern traditionally used for royal consorts in Scotland. However, some changes were made to the liturgy and royal oath to reflect the change in religion that had taken place since 1538, the date of the last coronation of a queen consort.[60] As to be expected of such an important royal event, no expense was spared. The abbey and palace of Holyrood were decorated magnificently with scarlet and green cloth hangings while the chairs and stools were covered with red, green, and white velvet, and decorated with gold. The four trumpeters' banners bearing the royal arms were specially designed for the occasion by the king's painter Adam Vanson. James spent nearly 2,950 Scottish pounds on clothing for ministers and courtiers; he himself wore purple velvet 'embrodered and furred with ermin' and a long train. Following tradition, Anna arrived at the church in her ordinary garments but, after the ceremony, changed into a coronation robe of purple velvet, embroidered with purple, white, and yellow silk and furred with ermine, a change of apparel denoting her political and spiritual transformation into a consecrated queen.[61] She would do the same at her English coronation in 1603.

The morning of the coronation, James created at least fifteen knights and ennobled his chancellor John Maitland, as Baron Thirlestane. During the ceremony, the Danish and English ambassadors received the honour of escorting Anna into the abbey. James's former guardian, the dowager countess of Mar, prepared her for the anointing. The Presbyterian minister Robert Bruce anointed her, but he attempted to disconnect the ritual from its Catholic roots in his oration. The king's closest relatives and heirs presumptive, Lennox and Hamilton, together with Thirlestone, participated in the crowning, although it was Bruce who placed the crown on her head. After Anna had received her regalia, the coronation oath was read out to her in French (the language she understood), and she showed her acquiescence by touching a bible with her right hand.[62] She then sat through a two-hundred-line congratulatory poem in Latin, commonly known as *Stephaniskion*, composed and recited by the Presbyterian theologian Andrew Melville, who had been given just two days to prepare it. Heralding the marriage as a step towards the future unification of England and Scotland, the poem so pleased the king that he ordered the royal printer Robert Waldegrave to publish it.[63] The ceremony ended with representatives of the estates giving homage to Anna, and James according her his royal blessing.

Like the coronation, Anna's royal entry into Edinburgh on 19 May was essentially traditional in its route, form, and pageantry.[64] So that his wife would be under the spotlight, the king absented himself, as had James V at the royal entry of his wife Mary of Guise. Following the precedent of previous entries of royal consorts, four of the town's burgesses carried a canopy above Anna who was seated in a carriage, 'very finely ornamented'. Her guard of honour comprised sixty young men with black masks and dressed as Moors, little different from the fifty youths in the same disguise who had attended upon Mary, Queen of Scots, at her royal entry in 1561. Along the route, Anna encountered conventional figures in pageants and interludes: the nine muses singing psalms, the four cardinal virtues uttering words of counsel, and classical representations of prosperity. As in other royal entries, at several points Anna was offered not only praise but also advice about her duties as wife and queen: a 'holy woman', for example, spoke of her responsibility to bear royal children. The final pageant represented her as the queen of Sheba (another foreign queen) who would learn wisdom at the feet of Solomon/James. Even the mechanical structure that greeted Anna at the outset was not novel: the device of a globe descending before the queen and opening to reveal a young boy had previously been used at the entries of both Mary of Guise and Mary, Queen of Scots. In another familiar action, the boy presented Anna with the keys of the city, a psalter, and a bible. The one departure from traditional entries of royal consorts was Anna's scheduled stop at the church of St Giles, where she heard a short sermon, yet this followed the pattern of James VI's own royal entry of 1579.

What Anna made of the event is anyone's guess. In the two surviving printed accounts, there is no description of her responses. All we know is that she could not possibly have understood the orations delivered to her since they were mainly in Latin—a language missing from her education—and that she lingered over and therefore presumably enjoyed the sweet singing of the psalms. As a lover of precious stones, she must have been delighted with the gift of a jewel, presented in a velvet box with her initial 'A' upon it and set with diamonds and other gems; it was said to have been worth 20,000 crowns.[65] That evening Anna dined with her husband and watched Scottish sword-dancing at Holyrood while the town was lit up with bonfires.

Anna's coronation and entry were commemorated in print in Scotland, Denmark, and England. A long poem written in Scottish English by John Burel had little to say about the new queen but provided a detailed description of the entry, indicating that the verse was possibly commissioned by the burghers of Edinburgh who had staged the event.[66] The Danish ambassador composed a Latin poem. In England, two ballads and two pamphlets went to press, though only one has survived.[67] Presumably the English were curious about the woman who might one day be their own queen.

If a marriage portrait was commissioned to mark the occasion, as would seem likely, it has disappeared; the earliest extant painting of the couple dates from 1594. But James did celebrate Anna's arrival and coronation with a medal. Medals were popular with Renaissance rulers owing to their association with the power and authority of ancient Roman emperors, and in some of them James is depicted wearing a laurel wreath in the guise of an emperor. Here on the obverse, he and Anna face each other, with a single crown hovering over both their heads; on the reverse, a lion rampant [the symbol of the Scottish crown] is in the centre, held up by two unicorns [Scotland's national animal] on each side. Below is the badge and collar of St Andrew, above a fleur-de-lys with a thistle surmounted by a crown. Around the edge is a motto of the Scottish monarchy, 'In Defence' (see Figure 5).

★ ★ ★

Figure 5. James's and Anna's marriage medal, GLAHM 38056 © The Hunterian, University of Glasgow.

It took nearly four years for Anna to fulfil her dynastic duty and produce an heir. After a series of miscarriages, the twenty-year-old queen delivered a son on 19 February 1594. Personally delighted at the birth of a boy, James also seized the opportunity to use the baptism for specific political ends. Over the previous few years, his authority had been undermined at home by the disloyalty and disruptive behaviour of Bothwell, while abroad his league with England was close to breaking point. Elizabeth was furious with him for failing to prosecute Scottish Catholic earls who had been plotting to help the Spanish king in his war against England, while James was furious with her for aiding Bothwell in retaliation.[68] Now, James designed the baptismal arrangements to demonstrate to the known world his control over his state, to mend bridges with Elizabeth, and promote his claim to the English throne on her death. His nobles were summoned and expected to turn out in force.[69] Invitations were also sent to foreign dignitaries: Anna's royal relatives in Denmark and Germany, Henry IV of France, and representatives from the United Provinces. Elizabeth was given the honour of acting as the infant's godmother. All but the French sent ambassadors to represent them, and everyone bestowed generous gifts on the prince; Elizabeth's was 'a fair cupboard of silver overguilt' and some decorated cups of gold, altogether thought to be worth £3,000.[70]

So that the event would be publicized widely in Scotland and England, James sponsored the printing in both Edinburgh and London of a thirty-page pamphlet describing the service and celebrations. Entitled *A True Reportarie of the Baptism of the Prince of Scotland*, its author was almost certainly the poet and Anna's secretary William Fowler, who also helped devise the baptismal entertainments. Versions of the pamphlet were anglicized for an English readership and constructed to make the king appear less foreign and impeccably Protestant.[71] As portrayed in *A True Reportarie*, the Scottish tournament and festivities mirrored those routinely held at the English royal court while the religious service was reassuringly Protestant. Furthermore, the oath taken by the newly knighted gentlemen included the pledge that they would defend the religion 'now presently preached within this realme'.[72]

Another publication celebrating the royal birth was a Latin poem *Principis Scoto-Britannorum Natalia* ['On the birth of the prince of the Scoto-Britons']. Written by Andrew Melville, the poem had two interrelated themes: the Stuarts' future right to the English throne and the downfall of Catholic Europe. The baby, wrote Melville, was 'destined to be king to both the celebrated Britons and the ancient Caledonians', and this would result not just in 'one Scoto-Britannic people' but also in 'Scoto-Britannic glory', for the united British nation would enter a Protestant league with Denmark and defeat the 'accursed pope' and the forces of Catholic Spain and Italy, 'the minions of the Antichrist'. James did not commission this work—as he had *A True Reportarie*—but, at Melville's request, he did allow it to be printed by the royal printer.[73] The poem was also published in Holland, and from there it reached England, provoking a protest from Elizabeth. She was apparently offended not so much because Melville treated James as her undoubted successor but rather because he named James 'king of all Brittayne in posession', whereas, in actual fact 'hir person is the greatest part of Brittayne and his the lesse'. Seeking to avoid a diplomatic incident, James claimed that he had not read the verses before authorizing their printing, an excuse that deceived no-one.[74]

Following Scottish tradition, the setting for the baptism of James's firstborn son was to be Stirling Castle. Accordingly, despite the considerable expense, James had the castle refurbished and the royal chapel—which had fallen into serious disrepair—rebuilt.[75] The new chapel was designed to associate James with Solomon and project the ideology of the divine right of kings. Its dimensions were the same as those given for Solomon's temple in the bible (1 Kings 6: 2 and Chronicles 3), while the raised platform inside at the west end (where the baby was to be baptized) corresponded to the area of the Holy of Holies in the temple.[76]

The rebuilding of the chapel is one explanation for the postponement of the baptism until late August. Another was the tardiness in London to sort out Elizabeth's representative. She initially chose George Clifford, third earl of Cumberland, as her proxy godparent, but ill-health first delayed and then prevented his attendance. Robert Radcliffe, fifth earl of Sussex, was his replacement, and James was prepared to wait for him to arrive. He was determined that Elizabeth's representative should be present at the baptism of his son, whom he hoped would be a future king of England.

The celebrations eventually began on Wednesday 28 August with a 'running at the ring', an equestrian game popular in the Scottish, English, and Continental courts. All the riders had *imprese* painted on pasteboard shields and wore allegorical costumes, as was common in Elizabethan tournaments. Three of the competitors wore the costumes of the Christian knights of Malta with a white cross on their tunics; three were dressed as Turks, 'verie gorgeouslie attired', and three as Amazons 'in women's attire, very sumptuously clad'. James was one of the Christian knights, and his *impresa* was a lion's head with open eyes, symbolizing fortitude and a vigilant head of state, together with the motto '*Timeat & primus & ultimus orbis*' [he strikes fear into those who are first and last in the world]. The *impresa* had a double significance: its motto implied that James would inherit the English throne and become the founder of a British empire since the Roman poet Ovid had applied the same phrase to Aeneas, the mythical founder of Rome; while the general tenor of the *impresa* countered Elizabeth's recent accusation that the king was showing timidity in his treatment of the Catholic earls.[77]

The baptismal service took place two days later during the Friday afternoon. Large numbers of the nobility attended as did the king, but not the queen as was customary. The six-month-old boy was named Frederick (after his late Danish grandfather) and Henry (after his paternal grandfather, English great-great grandfather, the king of France, and possibly even Henry VIII), but the correct order of the two forenames was not immediately clear, since the baptismal names that rang out in the chapel were 'Frederick Henry, Henry Frederick'.[78]

To honour Elizabeth, James had ensured that Sussex and her resident representative Robert Bowes were given prominent roles in the proceedings. Both were satisfied. Sussex reported home that: 'precedency was given to mee for her Majestie, and therby I did carrye the childe to and fro the church, wher all things were ordered and used with all rights for her Majestie's honor'.[79] Bowes, the more experienced observer, agreed but was somewhat perturbed by the Latin oration delivered by the officiant David Cunningham, bishop of Aberdeen. After going through the 'genealogyes, allyances, leagues, and amyties' contracted between the king and every one of the princes whose ambassadors were present, the bishop 'labored muche to make knowne howe this prince was...descended from these princes, namely [especially] from the kings of Englande'. However, the bishop just managed to avoid the dangerous territory of the prince's future claim to the throne of England and concluded, to Bowes's relief, with 'great prayse of her Majestie and her benifitts shewed to the king'.[80]

After the baptismal service came a ceremonial feast in the castle's great hall. Again, James set out to impress his important guests, this time with 'rare shewes and singular inventions' that were to entertain them between courses.[81] After the first course, there entered 'a *Black-Moore*, drawing (as it seemed to the beholders) a triumphall chariot' that contained 'all sorts of exquisite delicates and dainties, of pattisserie, frutages, and confections'.

Originally the organizers had wanted a live lion to pull the chariot, but the idea was dropped when it was decided that the wild animal might frighten the guests.[82] Distributing the desserts were six ladies: two represented Plenty and Fecundity (symbolizing Anna's success in delivering a prince); three stood for Faith, Concord, and Liberality (Roman public virtues) and the final one, Perseverance.

After the chariot departed, to the sound of trumpets there entered 'a most sumptuous, artificiall and well-proportioned ship', eighteen feet long and with a forty-foot mast, standing upon a colourful painted sea. The ship, decked with emblematic devices, contained two dozen people, including musicians. 'None could perceive what brought her in', and 'she made sayle till shee came to the table, discharging the ordinance in her stern by the way'. This ship, explained Fowler, alluded to James's chivalric quest, 'like a new Jason', to bring his queen home from Norway and was a device invented by the king.[83] But it also represented the ship of state which had James at its helm.[84] The ship's cargo, all sorts of sea food modelled in sugar, was then unloaded and served from crystal glass goblets while musicians played and sang. The banquet ended with an elaborate rendering of the 128th Psalm harmonized in seven parts, a hymn blessing those who walked in the way of the Lord (James as well as God). The ship then 'wayed anchor, made saile, and with noise of howboyes [oboes] and trumpets, retyred, and then discharged the rest of her ordinance, to the great admiration of the beholders'.[85] The evening's entertainment continued with yet another dessert and eventually ended at about 3.00 a.m.[86]

Despite the inventiveness, splendour, and expense of the occasion, a few scholars have suggested that it misfired.[87] We have already seen that the English were uneasy at the pointed references to James and Henry's future role as kings of Britain. Additionally, Presbyterian ministers not only 'mislyked' the king wearing the badge of a Catholic order of knights at the 'running of the ring' but also had concerns that a bishop was administering the sacrament of baptism, and even worse in Latin as well as Scots English. There were other causes for unease as well. Readers of Fowler's report might have wondered about the prowess of the king since they were told the winner of the equestrian game was not James but Lennox, who took the prize of 'a riche ring of diamonds' awarded by Anna. Fowler's readers might also have thought it odd, even laughable, that some aspects of the celebrations had to be cancelled. Although spectators were probably unaware of the omissions—certainly the English ambassadors made no mention of them in their reports home, but nor did they mention the splendid ship—Fowler spelled out for readers the changes in the arrangements. Three costumed Moors were supposed to have participated in the 'running at the ring' but failed to turn up; entertainments planned for the day before the baptism had to be abandoned because the craftsmen 'were employed in other businesse' and therefore had no time to complete the beasts that were required for the centrepiece. The story of the missing lion Fowler also reported, and it was translated into a comedic episode by Shakespeare in *A Midsummer Night's Dream* (written around 1595). When Bottom wants to play the part of a lion in the mechanicals' play, Quince vetoes it for fear he will frighten the ladies.[88]

James's handling of his marriage and the baptism of his eldest child makes clear that he understood the importance of royal ceremonials and pageantry well before he became king of England. It was only because of financial restraints that the baptisms of his four other children—Elizabeth's on 28 November 1596, Margaret's on 15 April 1599, Charles's on 23 December 1600, and Robert's on 2 May 1602—were far less opulent affairs.[89]

The English queen was the only foreign ruler to be invited to the baptism of James's first-born daughter, her namesake; but since her relations with James were then especially fraught, she sent neither a special ambassador nor gift. Bowes acted as her representative, and James gave him the honour of carrying the three-month-old baby into the chapel. Because it was a time of austerity, the celebrations were low-key: no special entertainments nor tilts, just a baptismal banquet with music at Holyroodhouse, attended by a small number of nobles and the 'balifs and cheif of Edinburgh'.[90] Held during a cold winter, there were also no outdoor processions. Nonetheless, every royal servant received a new livery, and the main palace rooms were smartened up for the celebrations.[91]

Margaret's baptism in the spring was celebrated with a 'running at the ring' and other sports as well as feasting and dancing. Anna's brother Ulrik attended but only because he happened to be in the country at the time.[92] Sadly, the princess died in August 1600 before her second birthday. Because James's second son Charles was sickly, his baptism took place just five weeks after his birth for fear he might not long survive. The ceremony was attended by the cream of Scottish nobility, the Huguenot leader, the prince of Rohan, and his brother Soubise. A procession took place from Holyroodhouse to the chapel; and Edinburgh Castle let off nine rounds of canon fire after the one-month-old child was ennobled with the titles duke of Albany, marquis of Ormond, earl of Ross, and Lord Ardmannoc.[93] The baptism of James's third son Robert was held in the kirk at Dunfermline in Fife as plague was lingering in Edinburgh. Originally, his brother Henry was to have been the godfather, and new clothes were ordered for him and Charles, but at the last minute the king decided that the children should not attend. This was probably because he wanted to use the occasion to solidify and display the recent reconciliation that he had achieved between two of his nobles by giving them the most prominent roles in the ceremony.[94] The banquet and triumph lasted for two days, but just a few weeks later the boy was dead. His burial in the abbey of Holyrood was private. Both the king and 'especially the queen' were reported as devastated by their loss.[95]

★ ★ ★

During his thirty years as an adult king of Scotland, James became confident in his use of staged spectacles to project his own authority, promote his diplomatic agenda, and publicize his right to the English succession. But his favourite form of self-promotion was through his own words. He could speak in public, apparently impromptu, for an hour at a time. In Scotland he gave orations before parliament, noble conventions, the Presbyterian General Assembly, and in the presence of the citizens of Edinburgh. Somewhat surprisingly his Scottish speeches were not disseminated in manuscript or print but they were commented upon by contemporaries and reported in seventeenth-century memoirs and histories. Speechifying became part of James's royal identity.[96]

James was also a recognized author of poetry, translations, scriptural commentaries, and political treatises. Most went into print, while a few circulated only in manuscript. The printed works were afterwards translated into Latin and other foreign languages for sale abroad. As a result, by the time that James inherited the English throne, he had built up a reputation as a poet and scholar among the educated elite of Europe.

James was not the only monarch to write poetry in the sixteenth century. Henry VIII, Mary, Queen of Scots, and Elizabeth all penned poems, but James was the first British monarch to have poems printed and put on sale. Emerging from turbulent minority rule in a land where the previous monarch had been deposed, he evidently felt the need to act out and demonstrate the command of language that in Renaissance Europe was thought to be an essential attribute of leadership. In this period, poetry—a power over words—signified an ability to rule.[97]

James's poems were first printed in *The Essayes of a Prentise in the Divine Art of Poesie*, a modest quarto book coming from the Edinburgh printing press of the Huguenot Thomas Vautrollier in 1584. Although James's name did not appear on the title page, his authorship was evident from the acrostic dedicatory poem spelling out JACOBUS SEXTUS and the opening epigrams which slowly revealed him. The book was an anthology of James's own verses accompanied by several translations of other poems and a short prose work on the 'reulis and cautelis [rules and cautions] to be observit and eschewit [eschewed]' in Scottish poetic practice. Some literary scholars have seen the prose work simply as a humanist text modelled on Joachim du Bellay's book of 1549 which defended and illustrated the French language.[98] But Richard McCabe has argued convincingly that, by laying down general rules for writing poetry, James was asserting his sovereignty and 'absolutist' tendencies.[99] More specifically, one of James's rules denounced verse libels, such as those that had defamed Lennox and earlier still his mother. The king had already condemned these libels in a proclamation of July 1583; here he claimed poetry should not meddle directly with grave matters of state since it limited poetic invention.[100]

In his translations, too, James was often making a political statement. This is most evident in 'Paraphrasticall Translation' of a passage from the *Pharsalia* of the Roman poet Lucan. Here James fashioned himself as Julius Caesar, asserted the divine right of kings, and denounced rebellion. To communicate his own political thinking, James manipulated the text to subvert the original meaning of the Lucan piece. In the last stanza, the Roman poet had endorsed rebellion, unsurprisingly perhaps as he had joined a conspiracy to depose the emperor Nero. But in his translation James pronounced rebellion to be an act of 'follie' because kings meet their subjects' needs through God's grace.[101]

Elsewhere, James put his Protestantism on show. One poem selected for translation was 'Uranie or Heavenlie Muse', originally created by the Huguenot Du Bartas in 1574, in which the eponymous Christian Muse calls on all poets to instruct people in the ways of God through scripture.[102] Another translated poem was the Calvinist Immanuel Tremellius' version of Psalm 104, in which James entreats God to inspire his 'spreit [spirit] and pen' to praise Him 'whose greatnes far surpass all'.[103]

One of James's own poems in the collection, the 'Phoenix', was a lament for Lennox's death. There, his erstwhile favourite is allegorized as the mythical bird cruelly pursued by 'ravening fowlis' [the 'Ruthven Raiders'] and forced to return homeward [to France] where the bird was 'bred' and came to die. The phoenix's rebirth—'this worme of phoenix ashe which grew'—was probably intended to signify Lennox's young son Ludovick whom James invited to Scotland and elevated to the dukedom of Lennox in his late father's place. To ensure that the allegory's meaning would be clear and to emphasize the tragedy of the phoenix's fate, the first page of the poem was laid out in the shape of a funeral urn, while an acrostic of Lennox's name ran along the edge of the facing leaf (see Figure 6).[104]

 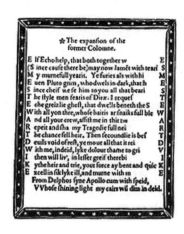

Figure 6. 'Ane Metaphoricall Invention of a Tragedie Called Phoenix', James VI's poem in *The Essayes of a Prentise in the Divine Art of Poesie*, sigs Gii–Iii[v] © The Huntington Library, San Marino, California.

The Essayes was not intended for Scottish readers alone. In addition to seeking to rebut his Scottish Presbyterian critics who in 1584 were branding him ungodly, James was wanting to display his religious credentials and merits to the English so that they would view him positively as their future king. Choosing Protestant authors to translate and a Huguenot printer for the anthology would, he evidently hoped, demonstrate how unfounded were English fears that he had been enticed by Lennox into the Catholic Church.[105] At the same time, James wanted his future subjects to be made aware of his scholarship, linguistic ability (after all Elizabeth was a known linguist), and mastery of the written word. For all these reasons, he ensured that specially bound copies of *The Essayes* were presented to Burghley and Henry Carey, Lord Hunsdon, the queen's first cousin who was then playing an important role in Anglo-Scottish politics. Plainer copies were sold in Vautrollier's shop in London.[106]

In February 1587, James sought a wider English readership for his poetry. On his own initiative, he contributed a sonnet to a volume of Latin verse commissioned to commemorate Sir Philip Sidney, then England's premier poet, who had died some five months earlier from a wound incurred while fighting for the Dutch in the battle of Zutphen. James offered his piece for inclusion at a very sensitive time in his relationship with Elizabeth, for she had ignored his pleas to waive his mother's death sentence just a few weeks previously. The appearance of his elegy in this anthology, James seemingly calculated, would signal to English readers his respect for their literary culture and militant Protestantism despite the treason and Catholicism of his mother. Its inclusion might thereby reassure them of his suitability to be their future king.[107] James's authorship was identified by the title '*Illustrisimi Scotorum Regis*', and his poem stood out as the only one in the collection to appear in both Latin and English.[108]

James's second collection of poetry was printed in 1591 with his name proudly displayed on the title page and a preface written by him as author. *His Majestie's Poeticall Exercises at Vacant Houres* again contained his translation of Du Bartas's works—this time *The Furies*—as well as his own poems. The most important of James's compositions was *The Lepanto*, an epic poem which he judged to be his masterpiece. This was in part because the genre was thought the highest form of literature, 'the best and most accomplished kinde of poetry'.[109] James had circulated the piece in manuscript around 1585, but he now wanted it printed to add lustre to his reputation as a poet-king.[110] It had its own title page and was later to be printed separately in its own edition.

Before *The Lepanto* reached the printed page, however, a problem became evident. The poem had originally been written during or just after the Arran years when James's relations with Protestants at home and abroad were deeply troubled. He was estranged from England and wooing both Catholic Spain and France; many of his Protestant nobles and Presbyterian ministers were in exile whereas Catholic noblemen and even Jesuits were being welcomed at his court. Reflecting this political circumstance, the poem had avoided anti-papal invective and applauded Don John of Austria, Philip II's illegitimate half-brother, who had led the Catholic forces to victory against the Turks in the 1571 naval battle of Lepanto. In 1591, however, the situation was transformed. James was then trying to work harmoniously with the Kirk and maintain the friendship of his English allies who were at war against Spain. He consequently felt the need to combat any suggestion that the poem had been penned 'in praise of a forraine papist bastard' (James's own words). Accordingly, he attached a preface to the poem that vehemently rejected such a reading. He was no 'hireling', he explained, employed to use his pen to commend any man—and certainly not a Catholic fighting on behalf of Spain—but, a king whose duty was not to withhold praise out of 'feare [or] favour' from anyone who deserved it. Besides, continued James, he had 'compiled this poëme as the exhortation to the persecuted' and intended Don John's defeat of the Turks to be read as an allegory for Protestants' struggles against Catholics since he had been moved to create the piece 'by the stirring uppe of the [Catholic] League and cruell persecution of the Protestants in all countries'.[111] This last explanation, though of questionable veracity, could be sustained because in the closing verses, the poet—through the voice of a chorus of angels—had exclaimed that since God had given such a victory to Catholics, how much more would He do for Protestants.

In 1591, James no doubt hoped the preface would reinforce the concluding Protestant tone of the poem and once again reassure English readers about his suitability to be their ally and king. To satisfy them further, two of the dedicatory poems at the beginning of the whole collection were composed by Protestant Englishmen: one by Henry Constable, who had been sent to Edinburgh around 1589 to bring greetings from the English court; the second by Henry Lok, whose patron may have been Hunsdon.[112] But what exactly was the message James intended to convey in the poem? Scholars disagree. For a few, in its call for Christian unity it displayed ecumenism, a principle—they maintain—that underlay James's religious policy both in Scotland and later on in England.[113] Rejecting this analysis, Astrud Stilma has argued that the poem was always more clearly Protestant and less conciliatory than is apparent at an immediate reading and that the 1591 preface was designed simply to protect the text from misinterpretations.[114] Other scholars contend, however, that the poem was deliberately ambiguous, revealing James's practical politics and political flexibility. In 1585, it invited different readings from people of different faiths and reflected his own unwillingness to come off the fence and commit unequivocally to either political Protestantism or Catholicism; in 1591, he hoped it would be read as a militantly Protestant piece.[115] This judgement is the one I find most plausible.

From the age of seventeen, James started to have some standing as a skilful writer of poetry. The writer and scholar Gabriel Harvey, who read *The Essayes* 'hot off the press' in February 1585, commented that James was 'a divine poet', while Henry Constable addressed a sonnet to James that paid tribute to his literary output.[116] Robert Allot, a literary compiler, included four extracts from James's translation of 'Uranie' in his anthology, *England's Parnassus*, which was printed in London in 1600.[117] But it was *The Lepanto* that won James most fame. It was widely read outside Scotland, with translations into French in 1591, Dutch in 1593, and Latin in 1604. It was read in England too, but presumably in its Scottish form because it was not anglicized until 1603. This poem did much to earn James the status he craved as a poet-king. One English scholar wrote in dire doggerel:

> The king of Scots now living is a poet,
>   As his *Lepanto*, and his *Furies* show it.[118]

By the time James succeeded to the English throne, he was acclaimed as 'a notable poet' who 'daily setteth out most learned poems, to the admiration of all his subjects'.[119] In 1603, Thomas Greene congratulated James for not only achieving the 'triple crowne' of rule over England, Scotland, and Ireland but also a 'triple crowne' of laurel, earned through his accomplishments as a poet. When a poet is 'commixed' with a king, exclaimed Greene in his tribute, 'he then is equall with a deitie'.[120] The next year, at James's entry into London, one of the panels on the triumphal arch erected by the Italians depicted the figure of Apollo, the patron god of poetry, pointing to 'the battell of Lepanto fought by the Turkes (of which his Majestie hath written a poem)'.[121]

Despite such public praise, contemporaries may not have rated James's poetry highly in private. Steven May has meticulously documented the absence of his poems in manuscript compilations, which suggests that they were not thought worth keeping and reading, although it needs to be remembered that James did not approve of the unofficial circulation of his poems.[122] After the king's death, moreover, his public reputation as a poet slipped badly. In the mid-seventeenth century, a jibe was levelled at Sir William Alexander that: 'He was born a poet and aimed to be a king. Therefore, would he have his royal title from King James, who was born a king and aimed to be a poet.'[123] Generally modern critics have also been unkind, describing James's poetry as second-rate and 'the work of a clever schoolboy'.[124] Today, the poems are largely valued for providing insights into the king's mind and politics.

★ ★ ★

James did not write only poetry; he also turned his hand to religious works. During the 1580s, he began a translation of the psalms and completed three short texts of biblical exegesis. One of them—*A Paraphrase upon the Revelation of the Apostle John*—remained in manuscript until 1616, but the two other scriptural commentaries were printed soon after they were completed: a meditation on the verses in the Book of Revelation dealing with the defeat of Satan (*Ane Fruitfull Meditatioun*, 1588); and a meditation on chapters from the First Book of Chronicles that described King David's removal of the ark of the covenant to Jerusalem (*Ane Meditatioun*, 1589). Both publications were part of James's attempts to shed his erstwhile notoriety as a Catholic sympathizer and create a new image as a committed and militant Protestant. They were endorsed in their prefaces by Patrick Galloway, one of the Presbyterian ministers who had fled to England in May 1584. Galloway also claimed credit for having had the meditations printed, although James was almost certainly behind this decision.[125]

In *Ane Fruitfull Meditatioun*, James affirmed his belief in the predestination of the elect, identified the pope with the Antichrist, described the Jesuits as the pope's 'maist pernicious vermine', and called upon Protestants everywhere to 'use lawfull resistance' and stand up as warriors for God's cause. In a marginal note, he made clear that this resistance was to be both 'spirituallie and bodelie'. He ended the work with an exhortation for readers to put their trust in God's promise 'to give us victorie' over the enemies of the true Church.[126] Later, as king of England, James acquired a reputation as a peacemaker; however, here—no doubt influenced by the English victory over the 1588 Spanish Armada—he was assuming a militant Protestant identity.

The following year, in *Ane Meditatioun*, James directly celebrated the Armada's defeat by comparing the Protestant victory of 1588 with that of David over the Philistines. But James treated the event as a British, not an English, victory. England was not named at all; instead, James deliberately referred to 'this ile' and spoke of its inhabitants as sharing the same religion and facing the same enemy, the 'haiteris [haters] of ye holie word'. At the same time, James had something to say about the present state of Scotland. Drawing an explicit parallel between David's kingship and his own, he maintained that just as the biblical king had brought the ark to Jerusalem with the help of the elders, the captains, and the priests of the Israelite tribes, so he, James, would continue to establish the Gospel in his realm with the help of the magistrates, nobility, and Kirk. In declaring 'David dois nathing in matteris apperteining to God without ye presence and speciall concurrence of Goddis ministeris apponitit to be spirituall rewlleris [rulers] in his Kirk', James was advertising his own readiness to co-operate with the Scottish Kirk in the service of religion as long as the Presbyterians acknowledged his royal supremacy.[127]

The meditations not only advanced James's own immediate political interests, they also served a more general political purpose. In interpreting scripture, James was asserting his special proximity to God and unique ability to discern the meaning of His Word. James likened the first meditation to a sermon; the frontispiece of the second declared him to be a 'sincere professour of the treuth', while its text compared him to the theocratic King David. In both works, therefore, James was implicitly articulating the divine right of kings. This underlying message explains why he had them both reprinted in 1603 and included in his complete works printed in 1616.[128]

Ane Fruitfull Meditatioun became one of the most widely disseminated of James's writings. The work was translated into French and published in the Huguenot centre of La Rochelle during an acute stage in the wars of religion; then, in 1596, it was translated into Latin and printed in Basel and Jena, to be reprinted in Halle in 1603.[129] Its popularity was partly because Revelation was a scriptural book that provoked debate throughout the Reformation period, but mainly because its call to militant Protestantism remained politically relevant for many years. *Ane Meditatioun* was read less abroad, probably because it seemed more rooted in a particular and temporary historical moment.

These writings, however, failed to convince everyone that James was now treading a godly path. Although Scottish Presbyterians initially praised the works, they soon used them as a weapon to expose his insincerity. When in May 1594 the minister John Ross criticized James's failure to prosecute the Catholic earls, Huntly and Errol, he denounced the king as a 'fine hypocrite', wished his 'words war fewar and his deidis war in greater number', and accused him of quoting scripture with more regard to 'his awin particular then the caus of God'.[130] The English queen and ministers, likewise, came to disbelieve James's declarations of Protestant zeal, whether in his compositions, letters, or speeches.[131] Reading of James's renewed promises to proceed against the Catholic earls at the end of May 1594, Cecil sarcastically wrote in the margin '*Credo in Deum*'.[132]

* * *

In the late 1590s, James turned away from the genres of poetry and biblical commentary towards more heavy-weight tomes: *Daemonologie* in 1597, *The Trew Law of Free Monarchies* in 1598, and *Basilikon Doron* in 1599. These are the writings (together with his *A Counterblaste to Tobacco* published in 1604) for which James is best known today. In all of them, he assumed the voice of the wise patriarch teaching his subjects how they should think and behave. In all of them, he used scriptural arguments and affirmed his divinely ordained royal authority. All three were intended to showcase him as an intellectual, an ideal philosopher-king.

James's interest in witches went back to at least 1589 when out of curiosity he participated in the examination of an accused witch in Aberdeen. The following year, witchcraft trials took place in Aberdeenshire and East Lothian: two women were hanged in Edinburgh; and an investigation began in North Berwick to root out witches.[133] Again out of intellectual curiosity, James summoned two of the accused from North Berwick before him for questioning about their claims to be using magic. To his surprise and alarm, one of them repeated 'the verye woordes' that he had spoken to his wife on their wedding night. Any prior scepticism immediately evaporated.[134] In subsequent interviews, another self-confessed witch—Agnes Thomson—confessed an attempt to shipwreck the king and queen by magic on their journey from Denmark. It had failed, she said, only because James's faith had 'prevailed above their ententions'. Further interrogations revealed several other assassination plots. All of them were said to have been the work of the magician Richard Graham at the instigation of powerful men at court, including Bothwell.[135] The king's role in these investigations and later trials was publicized in *Newes from Scotland*, a short pamphlet printed first in Edinburgh and then in London. The tract—thought to have been written by the Presbyterian minister James Carmichael—portrayed the king in a special relationship with God, one that protected him from the malign practices of witches.[136]

The North Berwick investigations sparked off the first great witchcraft panic in Scotland, and it was around then that James wrote a draft of *Daemonologie*.[137] Seven years later, a second witchcraft panic took hold in Scotland, and James again took an interest in the trials since they revealed further attempts on his life through witchcraft. However, Margaret Aitken—the 'Great Witch of Balwearie'—was soon exposed as a fraud, leading to critical voices being raised against witch-hunting. In this climate of scepticism, James elected to return to his draft and defend orthodox beliefs about demonology.[138] Designed to be read in England as well as Scotland, the work was anglicized in its spelling by the English printer Waldegrave, though admittedly not very well.

Daemonologie, explained James, was intended 'to resolve the doubting harts of many: both that such assaultes of Sathan are most certainly practized, and that the instrumentes thereof merits most severly to be punished'. Wanting his treatise to be 'the more plesaunt and facil' to read, James wrote it in the form of a dialogue between Philomathis [eager for knowledge] and Epistemon [learned] whose arguments proved conclusive. But since dialogue was the Socratic mode of debate dominant in humanist works, James was also parading his intellectual credentials before his readers by choosing this genre. The arguments he constructed in the text displayed his knowledge of Continental theories about devil worship and the witches' sabbath as well as the rationalist arguments against witchcraft laid down by the Englishman Reginald Scot. Equally, they propounded his own understanding of the power of kingship, for Epistemon pronounced that only a godly magistrate could successfully disempower the devil: 'For where God beginnes justlie to strike by his lawfull lieutennentes, it is not in the Deville's power to defraude or bereave him of the office, or effect of his powerfull and revenging scepter.'[139] In simpler words, the godly magistrate alone could effectively protect the state against the devil who might infect and elude lesser mortals.[140]

The following year, James published his first political text, *The Trew Law*, a 64-page octavo pamphlet that came out in the assumed name of 'C. Philopatris' [lover of his country]. We do not know if readers guessed the identity of the author, but it seems likely as the work was immediately republished in 1603 under the king's name. Here James countered the elective and contractual ideas of both the Protestant George Buchanan and the Jesuit Robert Persons.

In his writings, Buchanan had argued that all monarchies were elective, contractual, and limited.[141] As a corollary, he had defended resistance to kings and even single-handed tyrannicide. Persons (under the pseudonym R. Doleman) teasingly picked up on these ideas in *A Conference About the Next Succession* (printed in Antwerp 1594/95) where he argued that the English succession need not follow the hereditary principle because all monarchies were fundamentally elective. Since subjects were entitled to overthrow a tyrant—however strong his or her hereditary claim—they could prevent the succession of an heir apparent if that seemed to be in the interests of a commonwealth. Both polemicists appealed to history and natural law, but Buchanan was justifying Mary's deposition, whereas Persons was seeking James's exclusion from the English throne.

It was the publication of *A Conference* that prompted the king to write and publish *The Trew Law*, but his target was also Buchanan.[142] To refute the arguments of both men, James relied on scripture, history, and natural law. Based on his reading of the Book of Samuel, he argued that kings were divinely sanctioned, accountable only to God and therefore removable only by Him. Even when a ruler was initially elected, as was Saul, the transfer of sovereignty was complete, not limited, and permanent. Engaging with history, James argued that England and Scotland were free hereditary monarchies: the powers of the English king resulted from the conquest of William I of Normandy; those of the Scottish monarch were owed to the polity established peacefully by the fifth-century King Fergus. Kings preceded parliaments, and so 'kings were the authors and makers of the lawes, and not the lawes of the kings'.[143] It followed that kings were above the laws, and parliaments could not make laws in the absence of the king. Turning finally to natural law, James used conventional metaphors and analogies to prove royal authority and reject resistance theory: it was unnatural, even absurd, for a body/the body politic to cast off its head or for children/the people to resist the patriarchal authority of their father/king. Yet, despite its justification for unlimited monarchy, *The Trew Law* was not a blueprint for tyranny. James was keen to stress that monarchs should rule in the interests of the commonwealth. Again, employing the patriarchal image, he described the king as a loving father towards his children. He also argued that monarchs should endeavour to obey the law, not because they were obliged to but voluntarily of their own free will. Were princes to fall into wickedness, they would face the 'scourges' of divine justice.

There was actually very little in the book with which Elizabeth would have disagreed, except for the fact that James wrote the book at all. From numerous statements and actions, she evidently believed in the divine right of kings, but she never articulated any theory. Had she done so, she would have come up against rival theories—not just Buchanan's—that privileged common law. As with the succession, she wanted to suppress, not ignite, political debate.

Basilikon Doron was a very different kind of book. Essentially a manual for rulers, it was addressed to James's eldest son Henry, then only four years old, in the genre of advice literature. Initially printed in 1599 in a very limited edition of seven copies in quarto, it had possibly been penned during the winter of 1598–99 when a seriously ill James decided to leave a political testament for his heir.[144] Although the book's emphasis was on the responsibilities and duties of kings, it reflected the same ideas about kingship that had appeared in *The Trew Law*. Answering Persons's challenge to James's right to succeed in England, both works insisted that the institution of monarchy was appointed by God and a visible sign of His authority on earth. Although *Basilikon Doron* was intended to have a very limited circulation, it was soon leaked to Andrew Melville who drew up a list of eighteen objections to it. As a result, in a later edition of the book, James tempered his harsh words about Presbyterians. Nonetheless, he still described Puritans as 'very pestes in the Churche and common-weale... breathing nothing but sedition and calumnies'.[145]

All three books were known in England before James's accession.[146] However, only in 1603 was there a rush to read them. *Daemonologie* was printed in two London editions that year; there were at least four reprints of *The Trew Law*; but *Basilikon Doron* was the biggest seller, going through eight editions during James's first regnal year and published by different printers.[147] What is more, the latter was read and absorbed, not just purchased, judging by the phrases from it that were quoted in English poems, tracts, and sermons. The book was also translated into Dutch, French, German, Swedish, Hungarian, Welsh, and Latin, although the pope banned it in January 1606.[148] By contrast, *Daemonologie* was translated only into Dutch and Latin and *The Trew Law* was left untranslated, its message unpalatable to republics (like the United Provinces) and elected monarchies (like Sweden).[149]

★ ★ ★

As well as a writer, James was a patron of the arts. Scotland was far from a cultural backwater in 1567 when he became king, since its royal court had already embraced Renaissance scholarship, literature, and architecture and been open to foreign influences arriving from France, Italy, and the Netherlands.[150] James built on this foundation. Arguably, he did more to promote culture—especially poetry—in Scotland than ever Elizabeth did in England.

James's first efforts were directed towards music and poetry. Music had suffered a severe blow during the Reformation, and James sought to reestablish a musical culture at court. Under his patronage, the chapel royal again became a centre of fine music, especially after his appointment of the English violinist Thomas Hudson, 'a person of some account', as its master. The king also encouraged the return of Scottish musician-composers from his mother's court who had gone into exile; for example, the Catholic James Lauder, a composer of dance (the pavane) and song music, rejoined the Scottish court in 1588 after a period on the Continent. A group of permanent musicians were on the court payroll, and visiting instrumentalists also provided entertainment on occasion.[151]

Music was often conjoined with poetry, the art which James loved best, especially in the masques performed at the Scottish court. James had himself written a masque for the wedding of Lennox's daughter Henrietta to Huntly in 1588, and the costume records indicate that he performed in it too. He and Anna danced in interludes at other weddings despite the disapproval of the Kirk.[152] Freed from the Kirk after 1603 and with more money at her disposal, Anna—as we shall see—put on elaborate masques in which she and her ladies performed. James, however, preferred not to dance in England.[153]

Assuming the dual role of Apollo, the master-poet, and Maecenas, the patron, James gathered around him in the mid-1580s several poets, whom later critics (such as Helena Shire) labelled the 'Castalian band', a name derived from the spring 'Castalia' on Parnassus, the mountain sacred to Apollo. More recent scholars have, however, questioned whether any kind of band or poetic brotherhood existed at all.[154] Nonetheless, present at James's court were inventive poets seeking or receiving royal patronage. Inspired by Italian and French rhetorical and metaphorical poetry, these court poets experimented with metrical forms within a distinctively Middle Scots language; it took another generation before Scottish poets intentionally adopted southern English.

Perhaps the most influential poet was Alexander Montgomerie, who had been a friend of Lennox. James gave him the name of 'maister poet', and the title of the king's first volume of poetry implied that he was this master's apprentice. It was mainly to Montgomerie's poetry that James turned when offering examples of 'reulis and cautelis'. For a time, Montgomerie received a pension from the king, but he lost it during a short period abroad and then became involved in a bitter legal dispute.[155] His literary rival was briefly Sir Patrick Hume of Polwarth, who came to the king's attention as a poet in 1579 after composing *The Promine*, which celebrated James's initiation into the courtly exercise of hunting. Other works by Hume have not survived save for a co-authored poem with Montgomerie.[156] Hume's younger brother Alexander is known for his devotional verse, which was published in 1599, but he may have written courtly verse when younger, which has also not survived.[157] More significant a courtly poet was John Stewart of Baldynneis, who composed some thirty-three sonnets and translated an abridged version of Ariosto's popular *Orlando Furioso* (called *Roland Furious*), which preceded Sir John Harington's better-known translation of 1591.[158] Yet, despite writing poems that followed James's 'reulis' and flattered the king, there is no evidence that Stewart received any royal patronage.[159]

More successful as court poets were William Fowler and the Hudson brothers. Fowler (later the author of *The True Reportarie*) translated Petrarch's *Trionfi* (1587) and composed his own sonnets, while his surviving notebooks show a penchant for acrostic verse.[160] Thomas Hudson, a court musician, 'englished' Du Bartas's *La Judit*, which was printed as *The Historie of Judith in Forme of a Poeme* in 1584, while his brother Robert, also a violinist, wrote sonnets that circulated in manuscript. Their poems were often dedicated to James, Hudson giving the king credit for assigning him the task of translating *La Judit*.[161] They also contributed commendatory sonnets to James's first book of poetry. All three received pensions from the king, found employment in his household, and later came down to London with him.

By the mid-1590s, some new poets were making their mark on court culture. The best-known of them was the Irishman Walter Quinn, who arrived in Edinburgh in 1595 and had contacts with the poets clustered around the earl of Essex in England. He caught James's attention when he presented the king with a small book of adulatory verses in Latin, English, Italian, and French, one of which especially pleased James. Laying down the king's right to the English throne, it opened with the line 'A peerless pearl and prince claims Arthur's seat' [i.e. the English throne] and anagrammatized the king's full name (Charles James Stuart) to 'Claimes Arthur's Seat' and 'Ceass Letts, I am Arthur'. It was James's destiny, wrote Quinn on the king's behalf, 'to clayme my seat and throne/My kingdomes severed to rejoyne in one'. Quinn was quickly appointed a tutor to the king's children and, in 1600, wrote an elegy for Henry. After 1603, he followed the royal heir to England. In 1605, James ensured that Quinn's 'litle bowke of annagrames' was reissued.[162]

Although James favoured the written word in his patronage, he did not ignore the visual arts. He inherited the Flemish artist Arnold van Bronckhurst, who painted him and several members of the nobility in 1579, and he sufficiently liked his work to appoint him court painter for life in September 1581. Adrian Vanson, also from the Netherlands, came to James's attention the same year when the king commissioned him to paint two small portraits to be presented to the Calvinist theologian Theodore Beza. In 1584, Vanson succeeded Bronckhorst as the court's official painter, and, in 1594, James presented him with a medal which referred to him as 'our painter'. He stayed in that position until his death in 1602.[163]

One of Vanson's extant paintings of the king dates from about 1585 and may have been sent to Denmark as part of marriage diplomacy; a second half-length portrait shows James about ten years afterwards as a serious young man, wearing a satin doublet, embroidered in gold, and a cloak lined with ermine; his jewelled hat is encrusted with diamonds set in an A (for Anna) and a smaller H (for the newly born Henry); the top of a sword by his right arm is apparent in a smaller contemporary version of the painting.[164]

Two roundel portraits of James and Anna, attributed to Vanson and dated 1595, have also survived (see Figure 7). Again, James wears a bejewelled hat while the portrait of Anna shows her in a huge round ruff and adorned with pearls in her headdress round her neck and in her ears. Although both portraits testify to the couple's noble status, there are no symbols denoting their royal rank.

The artistic commissions of Anna and James were modest in their quantity and style, especially when compared to the paintings and miniatures they were later to commission in England. In part, this may have been the result of a suspicion of figurative art in Calvinist Scotland.[165] More likely, it was because the limited financial resources of the Scottish crown left little spare for employing first-rate artists. Lennox told the Venetian ambassador in July 1603 that he had previously been unable to send pictures of the royal family abroad 'for lack of artists in Scotland; now, however, I will not fail to send them'.[166]

Before 1603, the royal image was mainly disseminated through engravings created by artists and printers in Germany or the Netherlands. A few of the royal couple were freestanding, but others were plates in books containing portrait series of monarchs.[167] At this period in his life, James was not represented as a peacemaker; on the contrary, several portraits depict him in full armour or wearing a breastplate, garb which was thought appropriate for a king (see Figure 8).

Figure 7. James VI of Scotland, 1595, by Adrian Vanson © National Galleries of Scotland, Edinburgh.

The queen consort is sometimes shown alone with legends describing her royal heritage but there are also references to her success as a mother, and occasionally she is shown with her children. The inscriptions on the engravings were in Scots English, English, or Latin, reflecting their appeal in foreign countries and James's international standing.

A KING IN WAITING 71

Figure 8. James VI in the 'Atrium Heroicum' series by the printmaker Domenicus Custos (1602), British Museum BM1873,0510.2736; © Artokoloro/Alamy Stock Photo.

* * *

In a long poem of welcome addressed to James at Theobalds, in Hertfordshire, the English poet Samuel Daniel spoke of England's joy that its new king was already an experienced and successful ruler:

> Thou, borne a king, hast in thy state, indur'd
>   The sowre affronts of private discontent
> With subjects' broiles; and ever beene inur'd [accustomed]
>   To this great mystery of government:
> Whereby thy princely wisedome hath allur'd
>   A state to peace, left to thee turbulent.[168]

Yet, had Elizabeth died before 1596, few in her government would have agreed with these sentiments. During James's first eighteen years of adult rule, English observers repeatedly described Scotland as factional and unstable and its king as a figure lacking authority. On many occasions, Elizabeth herself berated James for weakness and negligence in ruling over his 'diseased state'.[169] However, from 1596 onwards, James took tough actions against his unruly Catholic noblemen, reached an accommodation with the troublesome Kirk, and eventually gained the respect of his future English subjects. So, although Daniel's praise was panegyric, calculated to earn the poet future royal patronage, the view that James had brought peace to a turbulent state was not thought wide of the mark when the poem was delivered and published in 1603.

Unusually, James was a political veteran when he became king of England. Indeed, he was the first king of England to have previously been a monarch elsewhere. His political battles and practices in Scotland inevitably affected his rule in his new realm. Having been attacked by radical Presbyterians in the Kirk, James would demand loyalty and obedience—indeed conformity— from all his English subjects. As in Scotland, he would maintain a broad-based government; his English privy council was to include Protestants and crypto-Catholics, Englishmen and Scots, and men from previously rival factions. In his Scottish speeches and writings, he had constructed himself as a father to his people and a physician to the body politic; he was to do the same in England and show himself open to reforms in the English Church and state. Additionally, James regularly repeated his articulation of the divine right of kings in both his pre- and post-1603 political writings. And, finally, James's favoured strategy of masking his intentions and hiding behind plausible deniability remained a constant feature of his style of rule, whether dealing with foreign princes or his English subjects. As we shall see in later chapters, James I of England differed little from James VI of Scotland.

3

Elizabeth's Legacy

The image of Elizabeth as the goddess Astraea ruling over a harmonious, peaceful, and prosperous realm was always far from the reality, but never more so than in her last decade. Although the queen continued to be eulogized, her subjects knew very well that a lot was wrong with her realm. It was even rumoured that she knew it too: one story circulating after her death was that she 'longed to see the ende of her dayes, for that too too [sic] manie abuses were crepte in to the state'.[1] Seventeen years of warfare, unfavourable economic conditions, and unpopular royal policies had taken their toll, creating a perfect storm of political tensions, social unrest, and religious unease. At her death, the queen left her successor a divided and disaffected realm.

In 1603, England was still at war against Spain. Hostilities had begun in 1585 when Elizabeth provocatively sent military troops to assist the Dutch in their rebellion against Philip II, the ruler of the Netherlands, and dispatched Sir Francis Drake to raid Spanish settlements in the Caribbean. War was never formally declared, and Elizabeth initially set modest objectives. She simply hoped that her aggressive actions would bring Philip to the negotiating table and to accept a settlement which allowed Dutch Protestants freedom of worship and Spanish troops to be withdrawn from northern Europe, from where they might launch an invasion of England.

The high point of the war for England was the defeat of the Spanish Armada in 1588, but the war dragged on afterwards with fewer victories and some costly failures. To combat Spain, Elizabeth sent troops to Portugal in 1589 (a spectacular failure), mounted campaigns in France from 1589 to 1593 (a moderate success), and retained an army in the Northern Netherlands which was continuing the fight against Spain. At sea, there were no major battles after 1588. English spirits lifted when Lord Admiral Howard (later earl of Nottingham) and Essex sacked and burned the Spanish town of

Cadiz in 1596, but otherwise naval attempts to defend England's shores and intercept the Iberian silver fleets could hardly be counted victories. Gales, not an English naval force, dispersed the Spanish Armadas of 1596 and 1597, while the 'Islands Voyage' of 1597 failed in its objective to establish a base in the Azores which would disrupt the passage of the silver fleets. After 1597, national naval expeditions came to an end. Instead, private captains, operating as privateers, holding letters of marque, led the naval war effort, harassing Spanish shipping, winning some valuable prizes, and sacking settlements in the West Indies.[2]

Nevertheless, by the turn of the century, the queen and certain of her councillors considered the danger from Spain to England's security and European Protestantism was less acute, even contained. The Protestant Henry IV had ousted Spanish troops from his territory and won the French throne after converting to Catholicism; and in 1598 he issued the edict of Nantes, which guaranteed a degree of toleration for his Protestant subjects. With France united under a strong king for the first time in ages, Spain would no longer have hegemony in western Europe. Even though Henry signed the Peace of Vervins with Spain in 1598, thereby withdrawing from his formal alliance with England and the Dutch, the king continued to work surreptitiously against Spanish interests in the Netherlands and Italy.

Meanwhile, the seven northern provinces of the Netherlands, which became known as the United Provinces, ruled by a states general, had thrown off Spanish rule and established a Calvinist Church in its midst. By 1600, Elizabeth's government had reason to be confident that the republic's defences and military leadership could now survive Spanish attempts at reconquest with very little English support. The ten provinces of the south remained Catholic but had been handed over to Philip II's daughter Infanta Isabella Clara Eugenia and her husband Archduke Albert of Austria, both of whom wanted peace with England. They were sovereign rulers and, as such, could send ambassadors abroad and defend their own interests, but their powers were restricted in foreign policy. Nonetheless, they put out peace feelers to Elizabeth, and exploratory negotiations began in Boulogne in 1600. But these talks soon collapsed, and the war had still not ended when James inherited the English throne.[3] Nor was peace desirable in everyone's eyes: on the contrary, it was a divisive issue and printed pamphlets entered the public domain putting the case for each side.[4]

After the failure of the Boulogne talks, Philip III decided to intervene in the Irish rebellion which had broken out in Ulster in 1594, spreading to

Connacht and Leinster in 1595 and Munster in 1598. The leaders of this Nine Years' War were Hugh O'Neill, earl of Tyrone, and his son-in-law Hugh O'Donnell, lord of Tyrconnell, who together used ambushes brilliantly to cut down English troops, which anyway struggled with the unfamiliar terrain of bogs and woodland. The most humiliating defeat for the English came in August 1598 when some 2,000 soldiers, including the marshal of Ireland, were killed in an encounter with O'Neill's men at Yellow Ford in County Armagh. The next year, Elizabeth sent Essex over to Ireland with 17,000 men, but his expedition proved an expensive failure. He lost a third of his army to camp diseases and was in no shape to attack Ulster as the queen demanded. Disobeying instructions, he signed a six-week truce with O'Neill, an initiative that brought an end to his career but not the Irish rebellion.[5]

The tide turned in Ireland when Charles Blount, eighth Baron Mountjoy, took over the English command in 1600. Within months, he restored English morale, changed their military tactics, and introduced a wide range of reforms. By the end of 1601, he had brought order to much of the island. However, Mountjoy's hard-fought campaign was hugely expensive for the English government and devastating for the Irish people. The line of fortresses he established, the scorched-earth warfare he initiated, and the debasement of the Irish currency enacted by the English government in May 1601 created famine and economic turmoil.[6] The English government had feared that Spain would take advantage of this period of Irish unrest and send troops to aid O'Neill, but it was only in October 1601 that a Spanish force of about 4,000 men landed at Kinsale on the southern coast of Ireland. Diverted from his assault on Ulster, Mountjoy marched south to besiege the garrison, and O'Neill too turned towards Munster to join his new allies. On Christmas Eve, O'Neill attacked Mountjoy's smaller force a few miles from Kinsale with disastrous results for the Irish. O'Neill's army was routed, and he withdrew with its rump back to Ulster. The Spanish quickly surrendered, but it took another fifteen months—until six days after Elizabeth's death—before O'Neill eventually capitulated. The realm of Ireland which James inherited in March 1603 was therefore submissive but also on its knees.

Elizabeth's total expenditure on warfare amounted to something like £4.5 million. The Irish campaigns alone, it has been estimated, accounted for an astronomical £1,845,696.[7] Such costs obviously could not be met from the crown's ordinary income of about £300,000 a year. Short-term loans from the City of London, forced loans, and sales of crown lands to the value of at least half a million pounds made up some of the shortfall, while taxpayers had to cough up much of the rest.[8]

Multiple parliamentary subsidies (a direct tax on individuals) and fifteenths (a fixed rate tax on counties) were levied almost every year during the 1590s, raising an estimated £100,000 per annum, nearly three times as much as had been demanded twenty years previously. The financial burden did not stop there. Additional sums had to be levied to equip soldiers and ships, while the crown requisitioned provisions and carriages at fixed (usually lower than market) prices to supply both its household and military forces, a practice known as purveyance. These demands at a local level may have added another 50 per cent to the tax bill of the government. Unsurprisingly, all the crown's expedients were unpopular, but purveyance was especially hated, described in a 1592 'discourse' as 'hurtfull to many and odious to all'.[9] Cries were also heard that the burden was heaviest on the poor, and undoubtedly the worst affected were smaller farmers since poultry and cattle were seized from their landholdings on a regular basis.[10] Gentlemen and nobles usually secured exemptions from purveyance, either legally or through bribery, and were consequently less directly affected, but they too resented the intrusion of purveyors into their counties. Members of parliament, therefore, introduced parliamentary bills to curb abuses, but Elizabeth consistently refused to permit such legislation because it would encroach upon her prerogative. As a substitute, Lord Treasurer Burghley introduced his own reforms. These did not end complaints, not least because purveyors continued to pocket sums which should have been directed towards the royal household. Taking note, Elizabeth ordered an investigation, but she died before it got off the ground, and it took no time at all before James made matters worse because of the increased size of his royal household and extensive travelling.[11]

As far as the country's economy was concerned, the war had a less adverse effect than might be expected. Certainly, trade with the Netherlands and Germany was sometimes disrupted, causing temporary unemployment in large ports like London or cloth-manufacturing towns such as Colchester and Gloucester. Nonetheless, the profitable pre-war Anglo-Iberian trade did not cease altogether, despite its official suspension in 1585, but went on illicitly because it was to the advantage of Spain as well as England. Trade also expanded in the Eastern Mediterranean. During the 1590s, the Levant Company, which had been established in 1581, exported some £60,000 worth of cloth, and imported a wide range of luxury goods worth twice as much. That being said, there were some long-standing weaknesses in the economy: the country was too reliant on imports for luxury manufactured goods and too dependent on broadcloths for exports.[12]

★ ★ ★

The greatest setback for the economy after the outbreak of the Spanish war arose from a series of terrible harvests, perhaps the worse sequence of the whole century. Owing to wet summers, the crops of 1594 and 1595 were inadequate and those of 1596 and 1597 catastrophic. The result was dearth, the contemporary term for dearness of food, as the scarcity of grain drove up the price of all other foodstuffs. Furthermore, since a greater proportion of people's incomes had now to be spent on food, demand for all other goods declined, leading to unemployment in the manufacturing and retailing sectors. The domestic cloth trade was hit especially hard.[13] The effect inevitably was severe hardship for many families and a growth in the number of the poor or destitute. In some regions, people died of starvation, especially if they were old, very young, or migrants. Many others suffered from malnutrition which made them susceptible to the normal diseases of the period. Those who had enough to eat suffered a dramatic drop in their standard of living since real wages could not keep up with prices.

Even before these harvest failures, there had been a steady rise in the cost of food. A rapid growth in England's population (probably a 35 per cent increase over Elizabeth's reign) had already raised prices and depressed real wages. But four harvest failures in a row resulted in the price of flour tripling in London and elsewhere. To make matters worse, real wages dropped by another 22 per cent or so during the 1590s.[14] As if this was not enough, England was hit by episodes of plague. Heavily populated London had the worst outbreaks (in 1592–93 and 1597). Each time, the mortality rate was horribly high, especially in the poorer suburbs of the City; the epidemic of 1593, for example, killed over 21,000 Londoners. Other areas suffered too. The plague of 1597 left thousands dead in Kendal, Penrith, and Carlisle in the northwest of England.[15]

★ ★ ★

High prices caused food riots in many rural areas. A first cluster had occurred in 1586; a second arose during the dearth of 1595–97. The rioters were mainly landless artisans or agricultural labourers—and often their womenfolk—who were just about economically self-sufficient in good times but sank into destitution at times of dearth. Protesting the export of grain to markets outside their region, the hungry rioters attacked carts or barges carrying the foodstuffs and seized the cargo for themselves. A woman from Essex joined a food seizure 'because she could not have corn in the market' yet certain Flemish ships were preparing to transport it overseas; another from Somerset was heard to say that 'they were as good to be slain in the marketplace as starve in their own houses'.[16]

A further cause of protest and riot was enclosure. The practice of landowners fencing in common land to create large open pastures for sheep was not new to the late Elizabethan age; nor was the enclosure of forests to exploit their timber or improve hunting expeditions. But the pressure on resources had intensified during the queen's reign because of population growth, while the effects of enclosure were felt more keenly during periods of economic hardship such as the 1590s. Objections to enclosure were often brought to local courts, the litigation being paid for out of a common purse. But sometimes desperation at the loss of rights to pasture or fuel, especially at times of grain shortages and high prices, spilled over into the direct action of destroying hedges. In Middlesex, for example, twenty-nine women in 1589 were brought before the courts for tearing up hedges that had been newly planted to enclose Enfield Chase, an enclosure that threatened common rights to wood for fuel. In Heckington in Lincolnshire, six men armed 'with dyvers weapons' broke down hedges and ditches and put to pasture some sixty or more head of cattle there. Enclosure was very much a live issue during the war years and, when litigation failed, the commons used 'weapons of the weak' to resist wealthy landowners.[17]

Not all protests and disturbances were in the countryside. In London, there were numerous riots, some arising spontaneously, others more organized. Among the latter was the protest in late 1592 of some three hundred discharged seamen who assembled at Paul's Cross 'with the sounde of a dromme' and marched towards Hampton Court to claim arrears of pay from the queen. The most serious unrest occurred in 1595 when at least thirteen riots broke out in just one month. Southwark was the scene of food riots when a group of apprentices protested the price of fish on 12 June and the price of butter the next day. Soon afterwards the leaders of the apprentices joined forces with discharged soldiers to co-ordinate further actions, and a large crowd surrounded the lord mayor's dwelling and threatened him with death. Then, on Sunday 29 June, about a thousand apprentices together with ex-soldiers converged on Tower Hill, possibly with the intention of breaking open the armoury and rescuing prisoners.[18] It was the largest uprising in the City for nearly eighty years, and several days passed before order was restored. Subsequently, five of the rioters were convicted of treason and hanged, drawn, and quartered on Tower Hill.

Judging from court records, many other people spoke seditious words and even fantasized about rebellion in protests about high prices and enclosure. The best-known incident was in Oxfordshire in 1596 when four men planned a full-scale armed rising to protest both enclosure and the high price of grain. It came to nothing, as only about a dozen or so men turned up for the action and soon dispersed, but two of the leaders were executed.[19]

Unsurprisingly these signs of unrest alarmed the government and local authorities. They were also disturbed by an increase in vagrancy, which meant hungry beggars taking to the streets, moving into towns when the harvest failed, and often committing petty crime. To prevent riots, members of parliament and local authorities pressed for prices to be controlled, relief to be given to the poor, and corn distributed at times of dearth. But local magistrates also saw the need to discipline the migrant poor more strictly, and vagrants were rounded up, whipped, and sometimes imprisoned.[20]

Although the economic downturns and plague were thought outside government control, many people (of all social groups) blamed Elizabeth's extended use of monopolies for some of the high prices. Monopolies had originally been privileges granted by a monarch to allow the grantee the sole right to enjoy *new* inventions or trades, but from the late 1580s onwards an increasing number covered old industries and were given as rewards to courtiers. Sir Walter Ralegh, for example, held a monopoly to license taverns and to mine tin. Price rises on a range of goods in common use were attributed to monopolists' personal greed as well as their control of the market. Lobbied in 1597 and 1601 to speak out against holders of monopolies, members of the house of commons loudly attacked them as 'bloodsuckers' and came close to challenging the crown's right to issue any patent at all.[21] Under pressure, Elizabeth revoked patents on certain commodities and referred others to the common law as a test of their validity. But like purveyance, the grievance remained at the forefront of many people's minds at her death.[22]

★ ★ ★

Naturally, landowners fared much better in the face of inflation and bad harvests than did tenant farmers, landless labourers, or urban apprentices.

Landowners who farmed a substantial part of their own estates benefited from the rise in grain prices and the decrease in the cost of agricultural labour. Those who let out some or most of their land often found ways of converting customary tenures to leaseholds of fixed tenures, which allowed them to charge higher rents and entry fines at the beginning of a new lease. They showed off their increased wealth by building mansions in the English countryside. Upwardly mobile yeomen extended their houses, purchased more material goods, and sent their sons to grammar schools and universities. Many merchants were also doing well, especially those engaged in importing luxury goods from outside Europe. Their wealth was evident from 'their great provision of tapestry, Turkey work, pewter, brass, fine linen, and thereto costly cupboards of plate' which they put on display in their homes.[23]

Nonetheless, wealthy landowners had their own grievances that were surfacing in the 1590s. Resentment was growing against the monarch's right—as a feudal overlord—to administer the estates of minors, widows, and 'idiots' and to pocket their yearly revenues in a system known as wardship. Because the crown often sold these rights of wardship or dispensed them as favours, complaints were made that Elizabeth's master of the court of wards (who supervised the administration of wardships) sold them to raise cash 'as men do horse and other cattell'. Purchasers of wardships who were supposed to act as guardians, protecting the minors and their property, were accused of asset-stripping, wastage, and fraud. Guardians were also criticized for arranging unsuitable marriages for their wards: 'a thinge verie uncivill and unchristian which hath byn the cause of manie unkynde and unhappie matches'.[24] On his accession, therefore, James was immediately greeted with calls for the reform or abolition of wardship.[25]

Nobles and landed gentlemen also felt aggrieved that the flow of royal patronage had dried up during the war years, which meant that many of them were left unrewarded for their service to the crown. Always parsimonious, Elizabeth was positively stingy during the latter part of her reign. As Robert Cecil explained to a disappointed suitor in 1602: 'her Majesty's mynd is not soe apt to give as before her warrs'.[26] Her leading subjects were not best pleased. A number saw Elizabeth's failure to reward her soldiers and nobles as part of a bigger problem: her dependence on a small clique of courtiers and councillors, notably the Cecils and their friends, to the detriment, even exclusion, of Essex and his military associates. Their discontent expressed itself in criticisms of the court as corrupt, self-seeking, and degenerate; it exploded in the Essex rising of February 1601. Although Elizabeth added a couple more nobles to the privy council after 1601, those who remained deprived of honours and recompense for their service hoped for better days once she was dead. One of these was Henry Percy, ninth earl of Northumberland, who told James that:

> The nobilitie are unsatisfied that places of honor are not given them...that her majestie is percimonius [parsimonious] and sloe to reliefe their wants.... They repyne that the state value them not at that rate thay prise themselves worthy of; nether is there many in this ranke.[27]

Readers of James's book, *Basilikon Doron*, had reason to hope for better times since he wrote there that it was a monarch's duty to choose 'men of the noblest blood that may bee' for his servants and to 'use true liberalitie in rewarding the good'.[28]

★ ★ ★

On the religious front, superficially all was well. The 1559 Protestant settlement had had more than forty years to bed down in the parishes, and by Elizabeth's death few people had clear memories of the religious confusions, upheavals, and changes that had occurred during the reigns of Henry VIII, Edward VI, and Mary. Although the laity may not have understood the subtleties of the Church's theology, they were now used to participating in English services, hearing readings from an English bible, and listening to regular sermons. By 1603, only about 1.5 per cent of the population (about 40,000) admitted their Catholicism by regularly refusing to attend parish services and paying recusancy fines; and even these men and women professed to be loyal to the crown despite the 1570 papal bull of excommunication.

Unquestionably, then, Elizabeth left a predominantly Protestant realm to her heir. Yet Catholicism had not been destroyed. Despite heavy fines, the number of recusants held firm, even grew, during the 1580s and 1590s, largely due to the pastoral work of missionary priests, trained in seminaries or Jesuit colleges abroad. Although their numbers were relatively small, recusants nonetheless appeared a grave threat to the secular and ecclesiastical authorities, not least because they came disproportionately from noble and gentry families. In truth, most recusants could be trusted to keep the peace. By 1600 they had recognized that the restoration of their Church by foreign invasion or internal rebellion was an unrealistic prospect, and their immediate objective was to secure some form of religious toleration by political means. Their expectations that this might be achieved under

Elizabeth were dashed, however, when a royal proclamation of November 1602 not only reiterated the ban on Catholic priests but also denied rumours that the queen had ever intended 'to grant toleration of two religions within our realme'.[29] Consequently, recusants sat tight to await the succession of a new monarch who might be more sympathetic to their Church.

Equally worrying for the Elizabethan Church and state, still more people—perhaps as many as a quarter of the total population—self-identified as Catholics. These 'church papists', as Protestants insultingly labelled them, occasionally attended parish church services to avoid fines, but they stayed away from communion, sometimes left before the sermon, and practised their religion secretly in their homes. If they had no access to Catholic priests, they prayed using rosaries or Catholic devotional books. The Elizabethan regime was well aware of their presence, hated them as an obstacle to the establishment of a godly realm, and feared them as a potential threat, for it was axiomatic in the sixteenth century that religious unity was essential for political and social order, not to mention God's favour towards the realm.[30]

Social, familial, and political networks bound together many Catholic families, but tensions were nonetheless present within their communities. Bad feeling sometimes existed between those who put their lives at risk by outward show of their faith and those who tried to play it safe. Of more political significance was the bitter conflict between the Jesuits and secular priests [those not in religious orders], both integral to the Catholic mission in England. The rift between them first emerged in 1594 when a Jesuit inmate tried to impose a rule over all the captured priests interned in Wisbech Castle on the island of Ely. It flared up again in 1598 when the seculars opposed the papal appointment of the Jesuit George Blackwood as an archpriest with authority over the whole English mission. The seculars and their lay friends then formally appealed to Rome against Blackwell, so earning the name 'appellants'. In cahoots with the English government, the appellants circulated anti-Jesuit books that branded the order pro-Spanish and politically subversive.[31]

It was not only rivalry that divided the Catholic mission. Politically, the seculars and Jesuits were at odds. The Jesuit Robert Persons was responsible for an influential book promoting elective monarchy and the succession of Infanta Isabella to the English throne, whereas the appellants supported the accession of James as the heir to Mary, Queen of Scots. Furthermore, the appellants saw themselves as English loyalists, prepared to do a deal with

England's Protestant regime in return for a measure of toleration, whereas Jesuits were usually more hard-line, upholding political resistance and a non-compromising spirituality.[32] Although Jesuits as well as appellants were to parade their loyalty to the new monarch in 1603, the breach between them was not healed and immediately created difficulties for the new regime.

The Protestant community was also far from united. In the 1590s, theologians at the University of Cambridge fell into a dispute over predestination, a central plank in the Calvinist doctrines which then dominated the English Church. Embedded in article 17 of the thirty-nine articles of faith, predestinarian beliefs laid down that God had preordained some people to salvation, irrespective of their merits. However, a handful of churchmen had begun in the 1580s to question this doctrine or at least some of its implications. One of them was Peter Baro, the holder of the Lady Margaret chair of divinity at Cambridge since 1574, who thought election [salvation] and reprobation [damnation] were conditional not absolute. Apparently, spoiling for a fight with Baro, the regius professor of divinity William Whitaker denounced all those who denied predestinarian theology in a public lecture of early 1595. Baro, though, did not rise to the bait. However, a young scholar, William Barrett, went on the counterattack and delivered an anti-Calvinist sermon in the university church, a provocation that resulted in the heads of houses disciplining him. Barrett then appealed to Archbishop Whitgift for an adjudication. To settle the doctrines in dispute, Whitgift issued the Lambeth articles, nine propositions that set out his and other bishops' position on predestination. They affirmed 'double predestination', the belief that God had 'from eternity' predestined some people to salvation and condemned others to damnation. They also stated that neither an individual's faith nor good works could affect predestination, which was the result solely of 'the will of the good pleasure of God'; and finally, they affirmed that the elect were 'assured' of salvation and could not fall from grace.[33]

Instead of settling the Cambridge dispute, as Whitgift had hoped, the articles ignited it. Baro challenged them in a sermon of January 1596, partly on the grounds that predestination limited the benefit of Christ's death only to the elect. The university authorities came down hard on him, and, later that year, he lost his chair. Although the Calvinists had scored a significant victory, the Lambeth articles did not become the official doctrine of the Church as they would have liked. Considering predestination 'a matter tender and dangerous to weak, ignorant minds' and 'unfit that the same should any ways be publicly dealt with, either in sermons or disputations', the queen blocked the publication of the Lambeth articles and rejected any attempt to have them affixed to the existing thirty-nine articles as part of the official statement of faith for the Church of England.[34]

Nor was the debate over. A few theologians continued to speak out against hard-line predestinarian doctrines. In 1599, John Overall, the new regius professor, clashed with the Cambridge authorities by maintaining that Christ died for 'every singular man' and that the salvation of the truly justified was conditional upon their repentance for sin.[35] That same year, Lancelot Andrewes—who was later to become one of James's favourite preachers—made a still stronger critique of Calvinist predestinarian theology. In a sermon on Cain and Abel (Genesis 4:1–18) at St Giles Cripplegate, he interpreted God's refusal to accept Cain's sacrifice, the consequent murder of his brother Abel, and God's curse upon Cain as the consequence of Cain's own wilful rebellion against the light, and not of his status as a predestined reprobate.[36]

As important as they were, these theological debates were nothing like as divisive as the conflict within the Elizabethan Church between, on the one hand, 'conformists' (those who upheld, even embraced, the Elizabethan prayer book) and, on the other, Puritans and Presbyterians who criticized it. Although historians have long agonized over the definition of 'Puritan'— some eschewing the label altogether—the nomenclature is useful and legitimate, not least because late Elizabethans and Jacobeans used the term themselves, albeit pejoratively.[37] As one scholar has aptly and succinctly explained: 'Jacobean churchmen, like Jacobean theatre audiences, knew a puritan when they saw one.'[38]

Churchmen understood that Puritans were those Protestant ministers who strongly objected to wearing clerical dress (a square clerical cap and white linen surplice) and carrying out certain rites and ceremonies in the prayer book, such as kneeling at communion and making the sign of the cross at baptism.[39] More moderate Puritans thought such matters were 'indifferent' but disliked them as reminiscent of popery; the more radical, however, rejected and wrote polemics against the 'massinge garment' and 'popish' ceremonies, berating them as unscriptural and ungodly. When the queen would not permit any changes to the prayer book that would meet their objections, Puritans argued passionately that 'popish rags' and ceremonies should not be imposed on Protestant ministers with tender consciences. For a time, bishops closed their eyes to departures from legal practice, but once Whitgift had been appointed archbishop of Canterbury in 1583, the Church mounted a 'subscription' campaign designed to impose conformity. The strategy was to compel non-conforming ministers to swear that the prayer book contained nothing contrary to the Word of God and then to abide by their oath. The most recalcitrant Puritans who refused to subscribe were supposed to be suspended from the ministry until they did, and persistent offenders were to be deprived of their livings. Despite this draconian clampdown on non-conforming ministers, clerics not considered troublemakers were often protected by sympathetic bishops or lay friends in high places and so kept their livings. As a result, notwithstanding their discontents, the godly—as they preferred to call themselves—chose to stay within the Church of England in the belief that, although flawed, it retained its spiritual integrity. However, their Protestant opponents treated them as if they were a disruptive, disloyal sect.

In 1590, nine leading Puritans were brought before the ecclesiastical court of high commission, and several of them ended up in jail or were forced into exile, usually in Scotland. One controversial tool used by the court was the *ex officio* oath, which compelled those summoned before it to answer any question truthfully, no matter how self-incriminatory it might be, even before they were accused of a crime. Consequently, a general question, such as 'Have you recently committed a transgression?', could expose the deponent to punishment or perjury. Refusal to take the oath would result in penalties for contempt of court as well as a conviction for the crime under investigation. The use of this oath against non-conforming ministers set off a bitter debate about its legality, as opponents claimed it violated the common-law principle that no-one was 'bound to betray himself' and was bringing the practices of the Spanish Inquisition into England.[40]

Puritans were not just clerics. Within their own communities, they were recognized as 'hotter sorts of Protestants', men and women who led an intensely spiritual life centred around Sabbath observance, gadding to sermons, reading godly books, writing meditations, psalm-singing, fasting, and rejecting earthly vanities. Although their values were not fundamentally different from those of other Protestants, their religious zeal and lifestyles often distinguished them from their neighbours. And indeed, the 'godly' or 'Puritans' often embraced these cultural differences and the antagonisms they generated: 'Whosoever, will live godly in Christ Jesus', preached the Puritan minister Stephen Denison, 'must suffer persecution, as the apostle speaketh.'[41] Godly attempts to pull down maypoles, ban church ales, or end wakes held once a year to commemorate local saints' days could result in public ridicule of the perpetrators and sometimes acts of violence. Local communities also resisted godly endeavours to promote or curtail sports and music on the Sabbath.[42] Over time, these godly men and women came to be characterized negatively in the popular imagination, and stock characters of Puritans appeared in late Elizabethan plays as sanctimonious hypocrites or killjoys. One such figure was Malvolio. Described as 'some kind of Puritan' in Shakespeare's *Twelfth Night*, he nonetheless dresses up in yellow hose and dances before Countess Olivia in the hope of an upwardly mobile marriage.

English Presbyterians were those Puritans who, in addition to leading an enthusiastic devotional life and objecting to the prayer book, rejected the system of episcopacy. In its place, they wanted a form of church governance that would be close to the fourfold ministry operating in Calvinist Geneva and the other 'best reformed churches' abroad: doctors interpreting and teaching doctrine; elders who were laypeople in charge of discipline; ministers or pastors taking services and preaching; and deacons caring for the poor. Because of their wish to overturn the clerical hierarchy, Presbyterians were thought politically and socially subversive, a danger to the state as well as the Church. Such a view was reinforced by the satirical pamphlets, known as the 'Marprelate Tracts' of 1588 and 1589, which lampooned bishops and appealed to a popular readership by using colloquial, sometimes scurrilous prose. As few conformists made any distinction between Puritans and Presbyterians, the 'godly' were very often all tarred with the same brush. As one Puritan complained, by 1601 'puritans were trounced and traduced as troublers of the state'.[43]

The 'Marprelate Tracts' resulted in a backlash. Their publication provoked the bishop of London, Richard Bancroft, to mount an operation against Presbyterians, putting their leaders on trial, seeking out and closing their underground presses, and promoting a print campaign. The anti-Martinist propaganda demonized all Puritans in sermons, proclamations, and pamphlets, and it was at this time that the burlesques of Puritans appeared on stage.[44] By the mid-1590s English Presbyterians—never large in number— were in retreat. Nonetheless, Presbyterians as well as Puritans were ready to spring into action once a new monarch sat on the throne. With high hopes of a king who had been brought up in the Presbyterian Kirk of Scotland, they swiftly prepared a petitioning onslaught on Elizabeth's death to bring about change.

★ ★ ★

The death of Elizabeth seemed an ideal opportunity for the many disaffected to seek remedy. On hearing reports of the regime change, gentlemen and women rushed north with requests for personal advancement and the redress of individual injustices. Those quick off the mark hoped to ingratiate themselves through demonstrations of loyalty and personal interactions with the new monarch. Those who stayed at home sent their petitions for honour, office, and privileges either to the king directly or to important courtiers in the hope that they would intercede with James. Although no-one knew for certain who would have the greatest influence in the future, from the outset men and women petitioned Cecil, Lord Henry Howard, and Lord Thomas Howard to forward their suits.[45] Both the English and Scots, one observer commented, 'never ceased to devise and solicit suits to his majesty'.[46] Unsurprisingly, within a couple of months, James was overwhelmed by the extent of such petitions, 'some seeking rewardes for service, some easement of greevance, some graces of other kindes'.[47]

James did not only receive personal suits; also directed to him were petitions that addressed the country's ills. Expectations were unrealistically high that as a new broom he would sweep away old abuses and corruptions in the system. One short verse entitled 'Howe England maye be reformed' ended with the lines:

Might some newe officer amend old disorder?
   Yes: one good Stewarte will set all in order.[48]

Although soliciting a new monarch to attend to long-standing public grievances was hardly novel, it does appear that the wave of requests and complaints greeting James during his first regnal year—in sermons, speeches, literary works, or formal petitions—was unusual. This circumstance was in part a measure of the problems Elizabeth had left to her successor. As explained by one anonymous petitioner, people targeted him with petitions because they were unwilling to tolerate any longer the burdens which they had borne under Elizabeth: 'people did for Saloman [i.e. Elizabeth] that they should not doe for Rehoboam' [Solomon's successor, namely James]. The same petitioner also warned James to heed their appeals for otherwise he might end up like Rehoboam, a king who encountered rebellion, civil war, and the eventual division of the Israelite kingdom because he had disregarded the petitions he had received on his accession.[49]

Additionally, James may have been assailed with so many 'complaints' because of the reception of *Basilikon Doron*, which had been published immediately upon his accession. Since James had expressed there a king's duty to rule justly and fairly, acting as a physician to his country's ills, readers felt encouraged to resort to petitions which drew his attention to 'the agues [a deadly disease], which keepe lowe this great body, whereof your Majestie is the sound-head'.[50] Furthermore, James himself initially encouraged petitioning. In a proclamation issued on 7 May 1603, he told his subjects to 'resort to us or our councell by way of humble petition' and to do so 'in lawfull and decent maner without numbers, without clamor, or any other kind of disorder'.[51] It was only when he came to believe that some of the petitioning amounted to a co-ordinated conspiracy to effect radical change that James issued another proclamation in October condemning and prohibiting those who had gathered the names of 'multitudes of vulgar persons' as signatories, a course which was 'unlawfull and doe favour of tumult, sedition, and violence'.[52]

Unsurprisingly, many of the petitioners and speechmakers complained about wartime taxation and burdens. As one of them told the king: 'Your subjectes have bene of late yeres chardged with manie subsideis, and tenths. And withoute all doubte the commons are pooer and indebted. They desier some ease.'[53] Shortly before James's first parliament, a poet implored the king to introduce no new taxes although loyally acknowledging his right to levy them:

> Next, for the common-wealth (as is begun)
>   Take off oppressions from the subjects' backe,
> And to the commons do not always runne
>   For every thing that common-wealth doth lacke,
> For so poore subjects still shall go to wracke,
>   And yet must subjects Caesar's duties pay:
> No faithfull subiect will thereof say nay.[54]

Monopolies and purveyance were likewise pinpointed as serious burdens that needed relief; the former many people wanted abolished, the latter reformed. In the preface to a printed sermon, the dean of Chichester urged the king: 'thou must scourge out all monopolye-mongers, and such like monsters out of thy common-weale: as Christ did those money-changers out of his church'.[55] A 'poor man's petition', delivered to James by a gentleman, similarly called for monopolies to be cut out of the commonwealth.[56] As for purveyance, the author of a 'memorial' listing 'thinges grievous and offensive to the commonwealth' demanded that a financial penalty be imposed on wrongdoers who illegally seized the cattle, grain, poultry, and other victuals of 'poore farmers', so to end their 'extortion and violent dealing'.[57] Reforms in wardship were also solicited. Essentially, landlords wanted its abolition and for mothers or the next of kin to have the guardianship of a fatherless child. In order that the crown's revenue would not be adversely affected, a proposal was made that a yearly sum be paid to the king by all those who held land from him.[58]

Petitioners and preachers were highly critical of the crown's officers, and not just purveyors and monopolists; an assortment of royal officials and their practices came under fire. One petitioner called for an end to the sale of offices, especially in the exchequer and customs house, and for the disbandment of lord lieutenants and their deputies since they were unnecessary in peacetime and had abused the prince's service. At least two petitions attacked the 'plurality of offices'; one 'named and shamed' Cecil, Ralegh, and Egerton among the offenders; the other pleaded: 'Let no man have more than one office, especially in law and in the court.'[59] In addition to general petitions, nearly thirty individual ones of 1603–04 complained of the delay in securing justice, false imprisonment, and unfair verdicts. 'Lett there be noe suche delayes nor craftie proceedings in lawe, and lett lawyers have moderate fees. A pox take the covetous atturney and the merciles lawier', spat out one petitioner.[60] In fact there is no evidence that the late Elizabethan law courts were prone to excessive fees or delays, but perhaps because people were increasingly using the courts to resolve disputes, there was more widespread frustration at the price and pace of judicial proceedings.[61] Then again, complaints about the high cost and slow speed of legal procedures were hardly new, and lawyers have been the butt of criticism in most periods of history.[62]

When it came to socio-economic issues, appeals were made to James in both personal and general terms. Some petitioners called for fair treatment to be given to the discharged and maimed soldiers filling the ranks of the poor as a matter of principle, while individual petitions from soldiers seeking alms were also addressed to the king.[63] During James's progress to London, fenmen crossing the marshes on stilts in Northamptonshire presented in person their petition objecting to the high rents and enclosure imposed by their local landowner Lady Hatton (Cecil's niece and wife of Sir Edward Coke).[64] In addition to many similar ones complaining about rackrenting or enclosing landowners, other tenants petitioned that they had been wrongly dispossessed of their copyhold land or that their crops had been despoiled by rabbits kept by a local gentleman.[65] Petitions were sometimes encouraged by local office holders to forestall or end protests, as when the earl of Cumberland encouraged the commons of Enfield Chase to draft a petition to the king instead of continuing their direct action aimed at protecting their communal rights to wood in the royal forest.[66] During his first eighteen months in England, the king received some sixty petitions of this sort.[67]

Meanwhile, in 1604, Francis Trigge, a minister in Lincolnshire, made a 'humble suite' in print beseeching the king to cure the 'canker' of enclosure.[68] Trigge hoped for success, or so he claimed, because of James's 'godly and golden saying' to his son in *Basilikon Doron* that 'hee should bee the poore man's king', and he fashioned his moral and practical arguments to make the king take notice. On the title page of Trigge's tract was a line from Proverbs 14:28: 'In the multitude of the people is the honour of a king, and for the want of people, commeth the destruction of the prince.' This maxim summarized the argument in the text where Trigge maintained that the conversion of arable land to pasture resulted in the depopulation of villages that not only impoverished but also worked against the interests of the king: 'It dishonoreth also your Majesty and weakeneth your Highnesse power.'[69]

Petitions detailing abuses in the commonwealth usually had something to say about the state of the Church. A lack of preachers was the most common complaint, one that was made by conformists as well as Puritans. The 'poor man's petition', for example, asked for 'good preachers' to be placed in every parish, but also requested 'an uniformitie and true religion without disturbance of papists or puritains'.[70] Conformist clergy made the same point. Andrew Willet wanted well-trained ministers and preachers but not those (like Puritans) who 'varie from their text' or 'meddle with matters of state'.[71] Less specifically, Robert Fletcher, a former servant to Elizabeth, uttered a prayer (in print) that God would:

> inspire the hart of our king to looke into the ruines of the Church and common-weale of England, that as her late Majestie like David had conceived to build the Temple, &c., so his Majesty like Salomon may fully finish and effect the same.[72]

As already mentioned, Puritans were organizing their own petitioning campaign. The organizers—probably the two Presbyterians Stephen Egerton and Arthur Hildersham—sent around recommendations to sympathetic ministers and laypeople for tactics to be followed. In order 'to avoyde the suspition of conspiracie', they proposed that only a few people should sign each petition and that the wording should be varied. Petitioners were advised to list abuses in the Church yet be moderate in the remedies advocated. It would be fine to supplicate for the removal of ignorant, idle, and non-resident clergy but important not to 'expresslie desire the removing of bishops'. To supplement the petitioning campaign, it was suggested that godly ministers deliver sermons and prayers to kindle parishioners' desire for reformation and encourage them to present their own petitions. They were also to contact friends at court who would promote the cause.[73] The plan was to deliver the petitions not only to the king but also to the parliament which everyone expected would soon be called.

The Puritan petitions that were sent from many counties did vary somewhat in their wording though not much in their substance. One from Northamptonshire asked that 'the present state of our Church may be further reformed in all thinges needful' according to God's holy words and laws and 'agreeably to th'example of other reformed Churches' in discipline and doctrine. The petition from Oxfordshire, however, preferred to leave out that line as too radical, and simply asked that 'the present state of our Church may be further reformed in all thinges needful' according to God's holy words and laws. To be more explicit, it pleaded that the Church might be 'disburdened of insufficient ministers, nonresidencie, and pluralities' and that the godly's 'yoke' might be lightened by the removal of both 'ceremonies that seeme superstitious' and the *ex officio* power of the ecclesiastical courts.[74]

The most famous petition was the Millenary Petition, so called because it claimed to have the 'consent' of more than a thousand ministers and laypeople. Presented to James on his way to London, probably in April 1603, it detailed four areas where reform was needed. In worship, it requested the stricter observance of the Sabbath, the abolition of the cross in baptism, the end of confirmations as superfluous, and the removal of the clerical cap and surplice. To reform the personnel in the ministry, it urged that only suitably qualified preachers be given livings and non-residency be prohibited. For 'church livings and maintenance', it demanded that pluralism be ended and that all income from tithes would go to maintain a preaching clergy. Finally, concerning discipline, it petitioned that excommunication should be administered only by pastors and not for trifling matters and that the *ex officio* oath be used more sparingly. Like others, the authors used James's own language in *Basilikon Doron* in calling the king a physician 'to heal these diseases'.[75]

The Puritan petitions alarmed the ecclesiastical authorities and several privy councillors. Not deceived by the different phrasing in the petitions, they correctly suspected a co-ordinated campaign. The petitioners, they thought, were employing tactics 'to avoyde suspicion of conspiracy, not to avoyde conspiracye'; they were working for 'the people to be styrred for reformacon' by preaching and praying; and they were using lawyers to draft bills to be presented in the next parliament. Moreover, the reformation they sought included the removal of bishops even though this objective was not expressly stated in their petitions.[76]

After a new wave of petitioning in Sussex during the late summer, Thomas Sackville, Lord Buckhurst, warned the king of the 'seditious and daungerous precedings of thes Puritans', and the privy council ordered Bishop Watson of Chichester and a number of local gentlemen to arrest and examine those involved.[77] The investigations revealed that in some parish churches 'gathered multitudes helde conventicles and therein hatched and bredd theise petitions'; the number of signatories on the three Sussex petitions scrutinized were as many as 1,325; and their signatures had been procured in churches 'whear the petition was redd unto the people', and 'mutche by private solicitation, sometymes by a constable, and at one time by an officer or sergiant', which made them appear officially sanctioned. Worse still, from Buckhurst's perspective, the Puritan organizers believed that they could count on friends at court to further their objectives; the two named were Patrick Galloway, the king's chaplain, and Lewis Pickering.[78]

Catholics, too, hoped to gain the ear of the king. Most of them were not really expecting any instant reversion to Roman Catholicism, but many did anticipate that James would introduce a measure of toleration. One anonymous Catholic told a friend that he believed 'the benignity of his [James's] nature, fresh memorie of his late mother', and 'the securitie of his estate and person' would induce him to have 'compassion' to the 'many thousands' who had hitherto suffered for their religion.[79] Another reason for optimism might have been the conversion of Anna to Catholicism in the 1590s, although this was not widely known in England. But, perhaps most important of all, James had declared shortly before his accession that he would not persecute any Catholic 'that will be quiet and give but an outward obedience to the law', nor would he fail 'to advance any of them that will by good service worthily deserve it'. He had written to that effect to the earl of Northumberland, and the secular priest William Watson had interpreted similar statements made to him while in Scotland as a commitment to toleration.[80] Whether because of their hopes or the need to distance themselves from the Jesuits who had rejected James's claim to the throne,

Catholics ostentatiously expressed their joy at his accession. A few, such as Sir Griffin Markham, sped north to express their loyalty before the king. Others, like the Northamptonshire recusant Sir Thomas Tresham, rushed to proclaim James as king in their own localities and welcomed him enthusiastically when he progressed through their shires.[81] Somewhat recklessly an English priest made his way into the king's presence at one of his stopping places and tried to preach before him, but he was arrested and sent to London.[82]

No sooner had James succeeded to the throne than Catholics—like Puritans—started a petitioning campaign to plead for a change in established policy. They had been advised to use loyalist discourse as their tactic and present their best face before the king. Those delivering a petition were to be influential figures of 'knowne merite' to the king and his mother, not anyone who had originally opposed his accession, and their spokespersons were to dissociate themselves from disloyal and treacherous Catholics.[83] For the most part, the petitioners followed this advice, and their demands were not excessive.[84]

Catholic petitions for toleration, however, provoked a storm. Protestant magistrates were quick to warn James not just of Catholic plotting and words of disloyalty but also that the number of recusants was growing fast in their localities. Catholics, they alleged, were coming out of the woodwork, 'beinge incoraged therto by the hopes which playnely they say they have ether of the alteration or tolleration of relygyon'.[85] Tobie Matthew, bishop of Durham, told Cecil of 'meetinges and devises of papistes' where their leaders tried 'to persuade men and women yea and children in a greate longe schedule of parchement to subscribe their names to a supplicacon to be presented' to the king.[86] Protestants took to print, begging James to 'tolerate no papists to live and to blaspheme our God with idolatrie and false worship'.[87] Citing an Old Testament precedent, one preacher made clear that toleration was against God's will: 'David expelled the Jebusites, not admitting contrarie religion in Hierusalem: And it is no doubt, but that God will so direct our David's heart, that religion shall be sincerely professed among us, without any mixture or toleration.'[88]

★ ★ ★

The petitioning campaigns of 1603, which reflected deep dissatisfaction with the late Elizabethan regime, were unsettling and divisive. They created uncertainty because James seemed to be taking the petitions seriously;

they were divisive because not everyone wanted to see the reforms in Church and state that the petitioners proposed. Whilst there was probably a consensus that the commonwealth was sick and needed healing, there was disagreement about the medicine to be applied.

In early 1603, James was keen to present himself as a physician, a reformer willing to listen to his new subjects' grievances and ready to act on them.[89] But during his first decade as king of England he was to find it difficult, if not impossible, to introduce major reforms in the state, not least because of the vested interests of people who were doing well out of the corruptions and injustices in the system. Furthermore, the crown's finances were deeply embedded in the practices of wardship and purveyance which were under attack. As for the Church, it was impossible to satisfy everyone. The petitions of Puritans and Catholics were not just incompatible but generally thought dangerous and condemned by many of the leading bishops and ministers who remained in power. James began his reign confronting Elizabeth's legacy with a will to 'to bee the great servant of the common-wealthe'.[90] But, as we shall see, the many subjects who greeted his accession with hope for change were to be disappointed.

4

Long Live the King

Around midnight on Saturday 26 March 1603, James VI was called from his bed at Holyrood Palace to receive an unexpected visitor. A dirty and dishevelled Sir Robert Carey had just arrived from London with news of Elizabeth's death. In hope of future advancement, Carey had wanted to be the first to inform James of his accession. Disobeying an order of Elizabeth's privy councillors that he and others stay at court 'till their pleasures were further known', he had slipped away during the morning of 24 March and ridden at breakneck speed towards Scotland. Only a nasty fall from his horse about sixty miles from Edinburgh slowed him down. Even so, Carey covered some four hundred miles in about three days.[1] It was not his first visit to the Scottish court; he had met with James as Elizabeth's official envoy on several previous occasions, his most difficult mission being to explain the reasons for the execution of Mary, Queen of Scots.

At Holyrood, Carey was immediately ushered into the king's chamber. Falling on his knees before James, Carey 'saluted' him by his new title of 'king of England, Scotland, France, and Ireland'. Carey obviously carried no official documents with him; instead, he handed over to James a sapphire ring 'from a faire lady' as evidence that he was telling the truth. This token satisfied James, allegedly because many years earlier his envoy Sir James Fullerton had given the ring to Carey's sister Philadelphia, Lady Scrope, with instructions that she should return it on the death of the English queen.[2]

Carey's news hardly came as a surprise. James's friends and agents at the English court had kept him apprised of Elizabeth's illness, and her privy council sent him the draft proclamation which announced Elizabeth's death and his own accession.[3] Among his informants was Cecil who had been secretly in correspondence with the king for more than two years. Other covert correspondents were the crypto-Catholics Northumberland and Lord Henry Howard. These three men had formed an informal alliance to ensure that James would secure the throne after Elizabeth's death. In 1601, Cecil had persuaded James to stop agitating to be named heir apparent and cease building a party of support in England. Instead, the Scottish king should bide his time, trusting in 'a choice election of a feaw'.[4] In other words, Cecil pledged to arrange the transfer of power on the queen's death in James's interest.

Cecil was as good as his word.[5] During Elizabeth's last illness, he sprang into action. Working with other members of the privy council, he arranged for the nobility to attend court and participate in some form of assembly of notables which would consent to and bring about James's accession. As seen in chapter 1, their meeting took place on 20 March, and shortly afterwards, the draft proclamation was dispatched to the Scottish king for his approval. Finding it so perfect a piece of music that he could 'alter no nots [notes] in so agreeable ane harmonie', James was satisfied that his accession would be stage-managed in London.[6] He therefore felt confident that he could enter England immediately upon the queen's death, not as a conqueror but as a man of peace and the 'righteous heir of England'.[7]

Immediately upon Elizabeth's death, all seemed in place for the smooth transition of power. The nobility, three bishops, the lord mayor of London, and other men of note gathered at Richmond to sign the proclamation announcing the queen's death and James's accession.[8] Yet, in reality, these signatories had no legal authority to act during an interregnum and certainly not to choose a new monarch. To overcome this constitutional difficulty, the proclamation implied that there *was* no interregnum by presenting James as a hereditary—not an elected—monarch, the queen's natural heir, who had instantaneously succeeded to the throne on her decease. Its wording emphasized James's descent from Henry VII and Elizabeth of York and upheld his 'manifest and undoubted' right to take the crown. The signatories, the text claimed, were doing 'nothing so much as to make it knowen to all persons, who it is that by law, by lineall succession, and undoubted right is now become the onely souveraigne lord and king'.[9]

At the same time, the signatories wanted the realm to believe that there was no dissenting opinion: James's right, they maintained, was accepted 'with one full voyce and consent of tongue and heart'.[10] When the proclamation was relayed to other parts of the country, the heralds similarly announced that peers, bishops, Elizabeth's late councillors, the City of London, and 'multitudes of the commonaltie' had already proclaimed James king 'with general consent and acclamation'.[11] The admitted objective behind all these proceedings was to resolve and acknowledge the succession swiftly in order to forestall the 'pernicious designes' of the state's enemies, and to 'endevor for the preservation of peace and tranquillite'.[12]

In truth, James's right was by no means as clear-cut as the proclamation stated. Henry VIII's will of December 1546—authorized by a 1544 parliamentary statute—had implicitly excluded the descendants of his elder sister Margaret (James's great-grandmother) from the succession by prioritizing the family line of Henry's younger sister Mary. So, according to statute, James was not Elizabeth's lawful heir at all. Furthermore, the question remained open as to whether foreigners were barred from taking the English throne. Protestants who had objected to the succession of Mary, Queen of Scots, had argued that common law banned aliens from inheriting English land or property and that a 1351 statute of Edward III had applied this rule to the succession. The Stuarts and their proponents, however, had dismissed these legal arguments by contending that common-law rules of inheritance did not apply to monarchs. God, they said, ruled the inheritance of crowns and, besides, the monarchy was 'a corporation' that continued in perpetuity and therefore was not subject to the same laws as private inheritance. English history, they maintained, supported this interpretation as it was littered with examples of foreign-born kings.[13]

After Mary's execution, another legal obstacle to James's right reared its head: heirs could not inherit the property or titles of attainted traitors. Elizabeth had tried to reassure James that this prohibition would not apply in his case, while others pointed out that Henry VII had been attainted as a traitor before assuming the throne. But James did not cease to worry that the condemnation of his mother might provide opponents of his succession with yet another excuse to exclude him. And James believed that there were many opponents: men and women who would balk at having a Scot as their king. After all, the two nations had often been at war; the two realms had different institutions; and anti-Scottish sentiment was strong in English popular culture. There was good reason, then, for James to suppose that the English might prefer a monarch from their own nation.[14]

The two English-born candidates who had the best lineal claim were Edward, Lord Beauchamp (the elder son of the late Katherine Grey, a granddaughter of Henry VIII's younger sister) and Arbella Stuart (James's English-born first cousin and another grandchild of Margaret Tudor). However, Elizabeth had ensured that neither of them could build up a political following. Beauchamp had been bastardized at his birth in 1562 because his parents could not prove the validity of their marriage, and afterwards the queen consistently refused to permit his legitimation. Arbella, born in 1575, was effectively banished to Derbyshire in 1588 under the supervision of her maternal grandmother Bess of Hardwick. Both potential pretenders, moreover, had pretty much ruined their credibility as future monarchs. Beauchamp had defied his father Edward, earl of Hertford, in marrying a gentlewoman of relatively low social status and, anyway, showed no inclination to be a future king. As for Arbella, after a failed attempt to elope in late 1602, she was thought unstable, refusing to eat and drink, and revealing 'little reason in most of her doings'.[15] Other possible English claimants in 1603 were George Hastings, fourth earl of Huntingdon, and his grandson, sixteen-year-old Henry, Lord Hastings, whose lineage could be traced back to Edward III. The third earl, a nobleman with powerful connections, had long been considered a potential Protestant heir, but he had died in 1595, leaving an impoverished estate and politically weak successor. During the queen's last sickness, an unnamed peer spoke secretly after dinner to another nobleman about the prospect of the young Hastings being sent to France from where he could build up a 'partye' which would challenge James's title.[16] But, there was zero support for such a reckless and divisive scheme.

The claimant who came to head the list of potential rivals was not in fact English but Spanish. She was Isabella Clara Eugenia, infanta of Castile, daughter of Philip II, and from 1598 co-ruler of the Spanish Netherlands with her new husband Archduke Albert of Austria. The Jesuit Robert Persons had commended her title in his succession tract, *A Conference*, based on her Lancastrian descent from John of Gaunt and Edmund Crouchback, her Catholicism, and for 'reasons of state'.[17]

Since Isabella's father had intervened militarily—albeit unsuccessfully—in France during the early 1590s to prevent the Protestant Henry IV from becoming king, James had every reason to suspect that his heir, Philip III, might mount an invasion to put his Catholic sister on the throne of England. Furthermore, since England was still at war against Spain, it would obviously be in Philip's political interests to arrange the accession of a close Habsburg relative. Two years before Elizabeth's death, Philip *did* decide to back Isabella as heir, but fortunately for James she and her husband were totally opposed to any such project. The archdukes preferred to consolidate their hold on the Spanish Netherlands and develop friendly relations with the Scottish king. Just as important, Philip also learned that Isabella's claim would be opposed by Pope Clement VIII and Henry IV (now safely ensconced on the French throne and a Catholic convert to boot), since they both had no wish to see any extension of Spanish power in Europe. To avoid hostilities with France, Philip renounced Isabella's claim, and in the summer of 1602 he 'declared himself ready to support any candidate whom the pope should think most helpful'. However, the Catholic powers could not agree on a foreign candidate acceptable to them all. In February 1603, Philip decided to identify and champion a Catholic of English blood, but by then it was too late.[18]

Consequently, by March 1603, James was effectively the last credible heir standing. Yet Elizabeth's privy councillors could still not be certain that his title would not be challenged. During the queen's last days, a close eye was kept on Beauchamp and Arbella. Although there were no reports of preparations for an armada, five ships due to voyage from England southwards were ordered to stay 'on the coaste for defence of the kingdom against any attempte which ill affected neighbors mighte attempte'.[19] In the event, all was quiet. Despite rumours that Beauchamp was 'up in armes and some say 10,000 strong', he and his powerful family immediately gave their allegiance to James.[20] The archdukes too promptly recognized James's accession and arranged to send over an envoy to discuss a peace treaty with the new king. In these circumstances, Philip was powerless to act, even had he wanted to.

★ ★ ★

Nonetheless, James's title was plainly dubious. Surely for this reason, the mayor and aldermen of London introduced an unusual ritual when the proclamation was brought to the City. At Ludgate, they barred the city gates and refused entry to the lords and heralds with the words: 'if you will proclayme any kynge but he that is righte indeede, you shall not come in'. Since Robert Lee, the lord mayor, had signed the proclamation, he and the aldermen already knew who was named king in it. It was hardly necessary for him to make such a demand. It was equally unnecessary for the lord mayor to announce his contentment when the lords replied they were to proclaim James or to require 'a pleadge' that the lords meant to do as they said.[21] The City authorities chose this public performance which emphasized James's legitimacy to counter the fact that he was not the direct heir by statute nor of the queen's body. A similar ritual was carried out at the Tower.

The many printed works that hailed James's accession also reveal the questionable nature of his right to the throne. Robert Fletcher, an ex-servant of the dead queen, claimed that he was prompted to write in defence of James's accession because he had heard 'some to dispute of his Majestie's just and most lawfull title'.[22] Preachers, songsters, and poets, similarly, wanted to silence potential objections by clarifying James's position. However, they did not all tell the same story about why James was the rightful king.

Whatever the genre, most authors affirmed the Scottish king's 'propinquity of blood' to justify his royal title. In a determination to reject any notion that James was anything other than a hereditary king, the preacher Leonell Sharpe declared in a sermon of 28 March that James would be the king of England even without the proclamation declaring his title: 'for it is he that gives force to the proclamation and not the proclamation right to him which he received from God, by his true discent and lineall succession of royall blood'. Sharpe also downplayed the importance of the queen's nomination, stating that it worked only 'to add to the king's right'.[23] Many others equally focused on James's 'true discent', emphasizing that his paternal and maternal bloodlines from the English-born Henry VII and Elizabeth of York were sufficient evidence of his dynastic right, especially since his grandmother Margaret was 'borne and bred in this lande'.[24]

Some writers went back further than James's Tudor pedigree. One balladeer spent ten verses on tracing James's descent from John of Gaunt, while the antiquarian and poet Sir George Buck drew a genealogical chart that tracked 'His Majestie's title from the Saxon kings'.[25] In more general terms, Fletcher thanked God for sending 'us a prince of our English tribe extracted from the loines of our most famous kings and queenes'.[26] Unsurprisingly, most of these Protestant works omitted reference to either of James's two parents, for that would remind readers of his Catholic forebears and Scottish heritage.[27]

A few men, however, presented James as an elected, rather than a hereditary, monarch. The most radical of these was the Puritan Miles Mosse. In a sermon of 5 April, he compared James's accession to the election of an early king of Rome, Numa Pompilius. Since Pompilius had been a Sabine and not a Roman, the comparison made by Mosse was especially apt. Like Pompilius, implied Mosse, James had been chosen to bring together two previously warring peoples. But in any case, added Mosse, the new king's personal qualities made him the best choice: he had received a 'holy and vertuous education'; his government in Scotland was known to have been 'peaceable and mercifull'; and he and his nobles offered a 'holie example' of true religion.[28]

Some Protestants avoided constitutional issues altogether and described James's right purely in providential terms. As Thomas Jackson was keen to remind readers, 'there are none advaunced to place of rule and government, but by the Lord'.[29] And, in this case, the speed and ease of the regime change proved that God's 'holy hand' was at work, organizing events so all would turn out well.[30] Likewise, in his panegyric to James, Samuel Daniel intoned that God had:

> Held other states imbroyld, whose envie might
>   Have fostred factions to impugne thy right

thereby allowing James to take the throne with ease.[31]

What was more, like Elizabeth, explained many writers, James had throughout his life enjoyed the protection and favour of divine mercy. Addressing the king in a dedication to his printed book, Andrew Willet told him that the Lord 'in your infancie from many perils most providently preserved you and in your former raigne miraculously delivered you, and now to a most flourishing kingdome most honourably advaunced you'.[32] It was an honourable advancement that benefited England as well as the king, explained another clergyman, for James was the right man for the job:

> Heaven loves this countrey and doth grace it thus,
>   In sending one like *Salomon* to us.[33]

The hope was that he would be like the biblical King Solomon who built on the work of his predecessor David by defending true religion and reforming religious practice.

Meanwhile, a fair number of writers hedged their bets and offered a range of justifications for James's accession. One example is the poet Anthony Nixon who thanked a providential God for guiding

> our nobles' hearts with one accord
>   The worthiest prince in Europe to elect

but also listed James's 'worthy princely ancestors' and named him 'next heire to the crowne'.[34] Similarly, an anonymous balladeer began with lauding the new king's lineage from King Henry VII, but then wrote of Elizabeth's nomination:

> All her state she hath assignd
>   to our noble King James

and finally moved on to sing of his election:

> The nobles of this our land,
> > faithfully: faithfully:
> Have set to their willing hands,
> > All in deare love.
> Giving him his lawfull right.[35]

Figure 9. Engraving of James, 1603, '*Maximo Applausu, Electus Rex*' © Harris Brisbane Dick Fund, 1917/Metropolitan Museum, New York City.

In view of this confusion at home, it is hardly surprising that foreigners too were unsure what to make of James's right to the English throne. Overall, they treated the new king as an elected monarch: the news of 'his election' was related in Spain; and an engraving of the new king of England, printed in Antwerp, contained the inscription '*Maximo Applausu, Electus Rex*', which both embodied and publicized the same interpretation of James's constitutional position (see Figure 9).[36] The French ambassador reported the 'election and nomination of the king of Scotland' as Elizabeth's successor, yet added in the same dispatch: 'his title is most legitimate and is supported by the good opinion the English have of his character, by the fact that he has sons, and because he is already versed in government'.[37]

★ ★ ★

Despite all the contradictory claims and constitutional uncertainties, the management of James's accession in London was remarkably efficient and unproblematic, even something of an anticlimax. The corporation ensured that wine flowed freely to toast the king's health, traditional bonfires were lit, and bells rung to celebrate the king's accession. And Londoners appeared to go along happily with the new situation, no-one challenging either the king's title or the constitutional process by which he had been proclaimed. Printing presses went into overdrive, pouring out texts that highlighted his right to the throne, praised his kingly qualities, and welcomed him to his new realm. James's own writings were newly printed and widely purchased. The anticipated internal protests and disturbances simply did not arise. The well-informed letter writer John Chamberlain was correct in his judgement that: 'the counsaile have dealt very providently and bejond [beyond] that that was to be expected or hoped for, in so sodain an accident'.[38] By acting quickly and ensuring the participation of representatives of the political nation, James's rule was recognized throughout the capital, and no-one there openly questioned the legitimacy of either the political act or the named heir.

By contrast, the immediate reactions to James's accession outside London reveal considerable uncertainty about its legality and anxiety about the future. When Carey announced the regime change at the towns he passed on his way to Edinburgh, local officers wanted authorization from London before agreeing to proclaim James as their king. Elsewhere, mayors and aldermen did not trust word of mouth or letters and refused to publicize

James's accession until a printed proclamation had arrived.[39] It was not that these men doubted the news of the queen's death; they were just unsure about James's natural right to the throne.[40]

But it took a while for the proclamation to be announced in the regions: at best a couple of days, at worst a week. The king was proclaimed at Leicester on Saturday 26 March; Bristol and Chelmsford on Monday the 28th; Chesterfield on the 29th; Falmouth on the 30th; and Dunwich in Suffolk the 31st.[41] Some smaller communities had to wait still longer to obtain the official news. The leading gentlemen of Norfolk, for example, delayed proclaiming James in a few towns until 1 or 2 April, presumably market days when villagers would be present.[42] Uncertainty therefore prevailed for anything up to a week in places where the proclamation was slower to arrive than rumours or unaccredited messengers.

Even when the proclamation was safely in their possession, some prominent men in the localities continued to hold concerns about its legality and feared that there might be a repetition of the 1553 crisis when the proclamation of Lady Jane Grey (who had challenged Queen Mary to the throne) had been proved invalid. After the mayor of Chester had read out the printed proclamation on Sunday the 27th, he heard 'ydle reportes conceaved uppon doubte of the aucthority of the sayd proclamation', and he had to request 'letters from their lordshipps subscribed with ther owne hands' to satisfy those doubters.[43] In Swaffham in Norfolk, a JP waited until he had obtained a second proclamation which was signed by three lords whose names had not appeared on the original text because of their absence from court.[44]

★   ★   ★

In Ireland, Catholic towns in the southern provinces were even slower to recognize James as king. The news of his accession reached Dublin on 5 April and trickled south well before the towns there received official notification from Dublin or London. But when urban leaders were commanded around the 11th to proclaim James as king, a number prevaricated. In Cork, for example, the mayor and recorder [senior judge] refused to issue a proclamation until 16 April on the grounds that they had no authority to do so without official word from London. Just as the memory of 1553 had made English towns wary of proclaiming James, the officials at Cork said their reluctance stemmed from their memory of the late 1480s and early 1490s when towns in Ireland had recognized the imposters Lambert Simnel and Perkin Warbeck as their rightful king.[45] However, this justification was almost certainly not the whole story. Although most Irish—both Protestants and Catholics—evidently received the news of James's accession 'with generall applause and satisfaction', there was some opposition in the towns of Munster and Leinster.[46] In Cork, one man was later accused of 'maintaining of the infanta's title', while in Waterford, a few Catholics 'resisted and abused' the local officials publishing the proclamation and did not spare to exclaim: 'Wee will not have a Scott to be our king.'[47]

Yet despite these instances of hostility to James, most Irish Catholics did favour him as Elizabeth's successor, for they hoped that he would be 'pleased to lett them have the libertie of their conscience'.[48] His friendship with Catholics in Scotland and cultivation of them in England had not gone unnoticed in Ireland. Catholic optimism can be best seen in two Irish language poems written immediately upon James's accession, one by Eochaidh Ó Eodhasa declaring: 'The brilliant sun has lit up, King James is the dispersal of all mist.' The other by Eoghan Ruadh Mac an Bhaird called James the 'spouse' of Ireland, which was an ancient trope in Irish political thinking and traditions, signifying that he was the lawful king who would bring peace and prosperity to the land.[49] James's genealogy also brought the Gaelic Irish comfort. Neither Welsh nor English like the Tudors, he was believed to have descended from Fergus, the first king of Ireland, on his mother's side and Core, the fifth-century king of Munster, on his father's. As such, James would not act as a foreign conqueror but would be sympathetic to their religion and culture, or so the Gaelic Irish who were Catholics wanted to believe.[50]

In hope or expectation of a new policy of toleration, many Catholics in the towns of Munster and Leinster came out in force to give public expression to their faith. Reclaiming public spaces for the exercise of their religion, priests publicly celebrated masses and led large religious processions along the urban streets. Images of saints were restored to churches, and Protestant bibles and prayer books torn up or destroyed. These open acts of Catholic piety occurred during the second half of April, which that year coincided with the holy weeks before Easter when Christian fervour was at its height.[51] On Good Friday, the people of Cork came out on the streets whipping themselves and carrying the cross.[52] The purpose of this disobedience and unrest, wrote Mountjoy, was 'only to declare there [sic] religion to his Majesty and the world', and they were doing so at 'that tyme between two raignes, wherin they suppose it lawfull or lesse daungerous'. Because James had not yet been crowned, Catholics claimed their conduct was 'no breach of his Majestie's lawes nor disturbance of his quiett'.[53] Taking advantage of the power vacuum left on Elizabeth's death, they were both anticipating a change in religion and seeking to propel the new regime into accepting it.

Even more disturbing for Mountjoy, the corporation at Cork launched an assault on the ring of fortresses that surrounded the city. Political grievances, not just religious ones, led to this act of rebellion. In his role as president of Munster, Sir George Carew—then in England, so creating a further power vacuum—had been curtailing the privileges and prestige of the towns under his jurisdiction, and the corporations of Cork and Waterford took the opportunity of the queen's death and Carew's absence to make their protest.[54]

'Now it is open war on all sides', thought the English authorities.[55] Unable to allow this simmering revolt to get out of hand, Mountjoy took an army of some 5,000 men down south in May to restore order. Many towns submitted, but at Waterford the citizens produced a charter of King John, which they claimed allowed them to refuse his troops entry. Allegedly, Mountjoy replied that 'he would cut King John's charter in pieces with King James's sword'.[56] Equally quickly, Mountjoy also overcame Cork's attempts to deny him entry.

★ ★ ★

Meanwhile in Scotland, James himself had to wait several days before receiving formal notification of his accession. Beset by rumours of conspiracies, the men in charge at Whitehall had taken nothing for granted, and it was not until the late evening of 24 March that they felt sufficiently confident to inform James of his successful installation. Early the next morning, Sir Charles Percy (Northumberland's brother) and Thomas Somerset (a son of Edward Somerset, fourth earl of Worcester) were dispatched to deliver a letter to the king and 'intreate his Majestie's cominge heather'. In the letter, they were highly critical of Carey for prematurely rushing north before they had quelled potential opposition and securely established 'your Majestie's right heere', but they could now inform James that his rightful succession had been proclaimed in London 'with an infinite applausing of your people'.[57]

Quite possibly the slight delay in sending the letter to James was also because a dispute had surfaced within the assembly of lords and ex-councillors about what message it should contain. Thomas, Lord Grey of Wilton, seconded by Sir John Fortescue, had apparently proposed that 'articles might be sent to the kinge for the preservation of the libertys and foundamentall laws of the kingdoms', which James would have to accept as a condition of his accession.[58] As the majority present wanted to avoid any such hint that James was an elected (not a hereditary) king, the proposition was in the end quashed. But that such a recommendation was proposed in the first place is revealing, for it expressed concerns within the governing elite that a foreign king might trample over England's laws, rights, and customs.

The accredited messengers did not reach Holyrood until 29 March, but James had not waited for this official communication before assuming his role as the English king. The day after Carey's arrival, he wrote to Elizabeth's ex-privy councillors and Cecil, empowering them to stay in office and warning them to expect his representative 'by whome you shall understand more amply of owr mynd'. At the same time, he directed the English garrison towns of Carlisle and Berwick, as well as the City of London, to continue in their good governance 'till our pleasure be known to you'.[59]

At last, on Thursday 31 March, James was declared king of his new realm to a fanfare of trumpets at the Market Cross of Edinburgh. As in England, bonfires, feasting, and 'merriment' marked the occasion. Shortly afterwards, James summoned those members of the nobility and privy council who might 'best be spared' from affairs in London and their own estates to attend upon him as he travelled towards his new capital. His thinking was that, if the realm's leading men were not witnessed welcoming and escorting him into his new realm, he might seem a foreign conqueror rather than the rightful king.[60] He need not have worried! Droves of Englishmen of rank were already riding north in search of favour and patronage. Chamberlain wryly noted that these men were acting as if 'preferment were a goale to be got by footmanship' and 'first come, first served'.[61] In fact, so many people were making their way towards Edinburgh that James had to issue another proclamation which ordered his new subjects to remain at home until his arrival in London, when he would be glad to see them. Now he was concerned that the absence of prominent landowners in their counties 'might breede disorder' and hamper 'the settling' of the state.[62]

As another tactic to prevent a power vacuum and consequent unrest developing in England before his arrival in its capital, James told English councillors and peers that he had no wish to 'change the ancient servants of the late queene'; and on 5 April he issued a proclamation confirming that all her office holders were to retain their accustomed authority 'untill his Majestie's pleasure bee further knowen'.[63] But, if James thought that his message would reassure the servants of the late queen that they would not be ousted under the new regime, he was mistaken. According to Scaramelli, the announcement caused unease because its wording implied that officers would stay in place 'only during the royal pleasure' and 'till the king's coming to London'.[64] Even more disconcerting, a dramatic change of personnel seemed to be in the offing. During the first week of April, James ordered the release of Henry Wriothesley, the attainted earl of Southampton, and Sir Henry Neville (both friends of Essex) from the Tower of London and told them to join him en route to London.[65] As far as James was concerned, the executed earl was a martyr to his cause, having taken up arms in 1601 to protect his right to the succession against a pro-Spanish 'faction' led by Henry, Lord Cobham, and Sir Walter Ralegh.[66] These early pardons, together with James's favour to others associated with Essex during April and May, gave the late earl's enemies reason to fear that they might well be sidelined or even dismissed in the near future.[67]

During his last couple of weeks in Scotland, James made ready for his progress to London. His English councillors and nobles had expected him to travel by sea and fitted out eight or ten ships to transport him safely. James, however, was eager to show himself to his new subjects and decided to progress in state by land.[68] To make a regal impression, he ordered fine new clothes, including one set made of purple velvet (the colour signifying both royalty and mourning), which was trimmed with ermine (the fur of nobility).[69] He also purchased five horses and had coaches prepared for the ride. As the costs mounted, he was forced to beg and borrow to pay the bills. The town of Edinburgh had to fork out 10,000 marks [£6,600], a sum which the citizens were told could not be refused at such a 'necessary tyme'.[70]

Before leaving for England, James set down arrangements for the government of Scotland during his absence. He decided not to appoint a regent but to give a council 'ample commission' to deal with the day-to-day administration of the realm. When it came to policy, he planned to rule 'by pen', issuing directives from London to the council sitting in Edinburgh.[71] He aimed, he claimed, to come back regularly to Scotland, and indeed made a public pledge at church on 3 April to visit 'everie three yeere at the least, or ofter'.[72] In fact, fourteen years were to pass before his return, and then his month-long stay from May to June 1617 turned out to be his last reappearance in the country of his birth.

Before his departure, James also gave thought to the care of his two sons, who would not immediately accompany him to England. He wrote a letter of farewell to ten-year-old Henry, who was to remain for the time being in Stirling Castle, and he formalized the care of Charles under the guardianship of his trusted friend Alexander Seton, Lord Fyvie.[73] As far as we know, James did not write to his middle child, the six-year-old Elizabeth, who was then residing in Linlithgow Castle under the tutelage of the Catholic Lady Livingston.[74] James intended that she and Henry would soon make the journey south, while Charles, who was not yet three and somewhat sickly, would not be moved until he grew older and stronger.

The English also needed to prepare for James's 400-mile journey south. Post horses had to be supplied to transport the king and his retinue; residences needed to be found where the royal party could stay; and entertainments arranged to greet it. Leading subjects were determined to communicate their delight at his accession by putting on an impressive display of loyalty and welcome.[75] Cecil's older half-brother, the second Lord Burghley, took charge of the arrangements in the north, and set in motion preparations for a fine show. The costs were to be borne partly by the individual and corporate hosts and partly from English coffers. To keep the expenses down, the council wanted James to avoid too much spectacle, but he would have none of it. He insisted, for example, that he should enter York—'a place of so much note in these partes' and 'the second citie' of his kingdom—in a 'publicke' manner with full pomp and solemnity to fit with his honour.[76] Burghley therefore sent orders for the city to put on as grand a reception as 'shorteness of the tyme' would allow and to arrange for the clergy to meet the king 'with all the pompe that maie be', and especially that he 'shalbe received into the cathedrall mynstere, under the estate of a canapie, and withall other ceremonies that this place can yield'.[77]

★ ★ ★

On Tuesday 5 April, James left Holyrood accompanied by 'multitudes' of Scottish nobles and gentlemen. He took his leave of Anna, fondly kissing her farewell 'in the full eye of all his subjects'.[78] As James departed, 'there was great lamentation and mourning among the commons for lose [loss] of the daylie sight of ther blessit prince'.[79] That night he stayed at Dunglass Castle, the house of Alexander, Lord Home, and the following day he crossed into England where he was met by the northern border lords and officials. These men 'having been employed by the queen [Elizabeth] in service upon the northern borders and given cause of offense to the king in former times, did then in humble manner present themselves before him'. James responded graciously. After 'plainely' showing his dislike of their former conduct, 'he comforted them againe, assuring them that their offences past were remitted, saying merrely: "It is not for the king of England to reveng the injuryes done to the king of Scotland." '[80]

James's first step into England was at the garrison town of Berwick-upon-Tweed, which had long been contested between England and Scotland. Situated on the north side of the river which marked the boundary between the two realms, it was a place of such strategic importance that James had already made sure of a smooth royal entry by directing his representative (Robert Stewart, the abbot of Holyrood) to accept the allegiance of its mayor and military governor on his behalf on 28 March. When James arrived a week later, the town had a strong incentive to flaunt its fidelity and provide a warm reception. After all, Berwick's officers and garrisons had been until then responsible for defending the border against the Scots.[81] Furthermore, its civic officers felt the need to make amends for a dire first impression, as they had not instantly and delightedly proclaimed James's accession when Carey passed through the town on his way to Edinburgh but had tarried until an official announcement arrived from London. They now wanted to forestall James reacting to this slight by not renewing their charter and privileges.[82] No wonder then that Berwick's recorder delivered an effusive oration acknowledging James as the 'rightful king' of England and 'absolute monarche of all the Bryttishe and landes', emphasizing his 'juste title and faire descente', and expressing delight at the 'happie beginning of a most perfecte and powrefull union of lions' [of England and Scotland].[83] The town's efforts to please proved successful, and in the printed narrative of James's journey south much was made of the joyous reception of a Scottish king coming in peace to an English town 'that many a 100 years hath bin a town of the enemie'.[84]

An impressive salute of cannons greeted James when he arrived on Berwick's outskirts in the late afternoon of Wednesday 6 April. The volleys were described as so great that 'all the ground thereabout trembled as in an earthquake', and they wrapped 'the town in a mantle of smoke' that made the fortress seem like 'an enchanted castle'. Silence then descended as the royal party reached the town gates, and the king received the town's keys only to return them to the gentleman porter of the garrison in a long-established ritual signifying the bond between a king and his subjects. 'For this his esspeciall service', the porter was immediately knighted. Next, the mayor and aldermen received James 'with no small signes of joy and such signes of triumph as the brevitie of time for prepatation [preparation] would admit'.[85]

Once the civic ceremonies were completed, James went into the parish church to give thanks to God 'for the benefites bestowed upon him'.[86] The preacher was Bishop Tobie Matthew of Durham who was well known as a past opponent of the Stuart succession. The bishop had wisely decided to attend upon the king in all haste to make reparation. In his sermon, he 'tendered his duty in all humility, craving pardon for his opposicion heretofore, with promise of faythfull service'.[87] James, he now accepted, was a worthy heir to Elizabeth for he 'was bourne in the same isle, discended of the same royall bloud, speaking the same toung, professing the same faith adorned'.[88] Equally wisely, James chose not to hold a grudge. He dined with the bishop that evening, heard him preach again at Newcastle and Durham, and promised to restore to him 'divers things taken from the bishoppricke', including Durham House on the Strand in London, which was then the residence of Sir Walter Ralegh.[89] Yet, despite his delicate situation, Matthew did not refrain from speaking his mind to the king. In a later sermon at Newcastle, he warned James against protecting English Catholics, taking as his text 2 Chronicles 15:2: 'The Lord is with you, while ye be with him...if ye forsake him, he wil forsake you.'[90]

James remained in Berwick for a further full day and morning, during which time he inspected the town's fortifications and rewarded its soldiers with 'rich and bounteous rewards'. His generosity was well received, as was his unexpected discharge of a shot of cannon while on the town walls. Commenting that it was to show 'how he loved and respected the art-militarie', he probably intended to exhibit his manliness as a positive contrast to the gender of his predecessor. Apparently, it went down well with the men.[91]

From Berwick, James crossed the River Tweed and covered around thirty-seven miles in four hours—which was very good going on horseback—to reach Carey's house at Widdrington. On the way, he took a detour to pay respects to a soldier 'blind with age', a gesture that was said to endear him to his new subjects.[92] At Widdrington Park, the king took time for his favourite recreation, hunting deer, before lodging there for the night.[93]

These first few days set the pattern for the remainder of the journey south. James made a ceremonial entry into the principal cities—Newcastle, Durham, York, Doncaster—where, in a feudal display of service and reward, he received their keys, regalia, and a purse full of gold and in return confirmed the privileges which the citizens had enjoyed under Elizabeth. In every city, he listened to civic orations and attended services at the central church. Deliberately displaying royal clemency, he emptied the jails of all their prisoners, except those accused or convicted of murder, treason, or Catholic recusancy. Showing magnanimity, he heard petitions and created knights. As he entered each new shire, the leading nobles and gentlemen greeted him, joined his retinue, offered him hospitality in their homes, and hunted with him in their parks.

Despite James's earlier order that his new subjects should not head north, the royal entourage was every day 'encreasing by the numbers of noblemen and gentlemen from the south parts', who were coming to offer him their allegiance and 'rejoyce at his sight'.[94] The incentive to head north arose out of apprehension that there might be few rewards left for those who stayed behind, since news of the king's 'bountifull beginnings' had reached London early on.[95] However, aware that such a large retinue imposed a heavy burden on the country and raised the cost of provisions, James issued a second order commanding that all men, other than named friends and some councillors, should remain in their homes.[96]

Among those whom James invited to join him were his key supporters and advisers, Cecil and Lord Henry Howard.[97] One person he had no wish to see was Ralegh, whom Cecil and Howard had been defaming for years. Conscious that he was going to be excluded from the king's inner circle, Ralegh ignored Cecil's attempt to stop him travelling northwards from his home in the West Country.[98] It was a mistake. His interview with James—which took place at Burghley House in Lincolnshire—was brief and unfriendly. According to one contemporary observer, Ralegh 'hath taken no greate roote here' and was sent on his way. A later story—possibly apocryphal—claimed that James had punned on seeing him: 'on my soule, mon, I have heard rawly of thee'.[99] Whatever the truth, on 8 May Ralegh was summoned before the privy council and dismissed from the office of captain of the guard to be replaced by Sir Thomas Erskine, who had fulfilled the same role in Scotland. Ralegh also lost his lord lieutenancy of Cornwall, lucrative monopolies, and Durham House.[100]

Howard left London suddenly and met James at Newcastle around 12 April.[101] Cecil joined them at York nearly a week later. Delayed a day or so because his 'owne fatte horses begann to fayle' him, Cecil arrived after midnight on 18 April, thereby missing the king's magnificent royal entry into the city.[102] Even before discussing matters with these two men who would soon become his chief advisers, James had already started making some significant decisions of his own. Wanting to end the emergency arrangement of the nobility working closely with privy councillors in London, he determined that the lords should return to their estates and leave the privy councillors to manage the realm alone. Concurrently, on 5 April, he boosted the number of nobles on the privy council with the appointment of two earls (Cumberland and Northumberland) and two barons (Mountjoy and Thomas, Lord Howard of Walden).[103] These promotions came as little surprise, as the king had already intimated that he intended to 'augment' the Elizabethan privy council with 'noble and worthy persons'.[104] And, indeed, all four were worthy of elevation. Northumberland was a pre-eminent peer, while the others had served in Elizabeth's wars against Spain or in Ireland.

Immediately after sorting out the privy council, James issued to it a stream of instructions on a wide range of topics: minting a new coinage, summoning a parliament, and dispatching soldiers to the English garrisons in the Netherlands. It is likely that Henry Howard advised the king at their meeting in Newcastle on some of these matters.[105] James also sent blank warrants signed by him to Cecil so that his instructions could be put into action immediately.[106] Nevertheless, James's absence from the capital created 'inconveniences' (as Cecil put it) and hampered the smooth running of the administration.[107]

At his meetings with Cecil in York, James discussed urgent matters of state, including the military situation in the Netherlands.[108] The two men also concentrated on ceremonial issues, specifically the arrangements for Elizabeth's funeral and James's coronation. Together they took several important decisions. In accordance with Cecil's advice, it was agreed that James would slow down his progress to London and arrive after the funeral. Concerning the coronation, James told Cecil that he wished his wife to be crowned alongside him. Given his desire for full dynastic union, he needed Anna to have the same status in England as she had in Scotland. Furthermore, a joint coronation with a queen who was visibly pregnant would emphasize the dynastic security which the English could now enjoy in contrast to their experience under Elizabeth. The date chosen for the coronation was 25 July, the feast of St James the Apostle, after whom the king was named, and a day close to the thirty-fifth anniversary of his accession in Scotland. The timetable for Anna's progress south was also determined at this meeting: she would set out from Edinburgh about 14 May and arrive four days later at

Berwick, where the late queen's attendants would join her. The royal party would then travel south at a leisurely pace because of Anna's pregnancy and reach London about 1 July.[109] Once these arrangements were made, Cecil departed for London not to see the king again until receiving him at Theobalds.

From York, James continued in the same manner, stopping at large towns and visiting the country seats of important figures. On this leg of the journey, he stayed in some of the most impressive houses belonging to the English nobility: Worksop Manor in Nottinghamshire (the grand house of Gilbert Talbot, seventh earl of Shrewsbury); Belvoir Castle (the ancestral home of Roger Manners, fifth earl of Rutland), Burghley House in Lincolnshire (the mansion of Cecil's half-brother), and Theobalds in Hertfordshire (Cecil's majestic house inherited from his father). Their owners entertained James with fine hunting, rich food on silver dishes, and entertainments such as the 'most excellent soule-ravishing musique' played to him at Worksop.[110] The magnificence of these houses and the opulent hospitality he received may well have given James a false impression about the wealth of his new realm.[111]

★ ★ ★

The printed accounts of the royal journey inevitably present the king in the best possible light. In all of them James comes across as pious, gracious, affable, and accessible. There is no sign of him being a remote figure who, in striking contrast to his predecessor, participated only grudgingly in public performances, as later commented.[112] Contemporary accounts showed James to have been ready and willing to engage in public performances that would please his subjects. When offered a coach to ride through York, for example, James 'graciously answered, I will have no coach, for the people are desirous to see a king, and so they shall, for they shall aswell see his body as his face', and so he walked to church.[113] Similarly, during his visit to Theobalds, he 'had not staied above an houre in his chamber, but hearing the multitude throng so fast into the uppermost court' to catch a view of him, 'hee showed himselfe openly, out of his chamber window, by the space of halfe an houre together'.[114]

Nonetheless, criticisms of James were voiced before he reached London. Those remaining in the capital or their own counties noticed and disliked his bounty on route, not just because they were not the recipients but also because of the expense: 'It is sayde your Majestie giveth much', yet 'your coffers are sayde not to be so full' that they should be emptied, wrote one complainant.[115] Although cheap by comparison, James's liberal bestowal of knighthoods also provoked hostile comment. Around 237 men were knighted on the progress from Edinburgh, about the same number as Elizabeth had created throughout her 45-year reign, and another 669 were dubbed knights before four months were out. The gentlemen promoted were obviously well satisfied, but many others grumbled that the order was being diluted, even debased; Francis Bacon, for example, came to call a knighthood an 'allmost prostituted title'.[116] Even those who had wanted the order to expand believed that it should be reserved for men of good birth, wealth, civil worth, or martial valour, and they detected that too many of James's new knights were unworthy of the honour. These new knights, moaned another critic, were 'a skumm of suche as it wolde make a man sycke to thinke of them'.[117] Even worse, it was widely believed that many of them had 'payd well for ther honor', the going price for the kickback being £30 or £50.[118] And, since James's Scottish companions were usually the brokers of the bribes, they were blamed for an unacceptable corruption, one that many believed was seeping into the body politic for the first time. Two years later, in the anti-Scottish satire, *Eastward Ho*, a character speaking with a heavy Scottish brogue referred to the debauched Sir Petronel Flash as 'one of my thirty-pound knights'.[119]

Another early expression of disapproval was over James's failure to observe English custom in a matter of law. On 5 May, the Venetian ambassador reported from London that 'a great number of cut purses and other criminals' had been summarily executed on James's 'royal warrant alone', and 'on one occasion sixteen were hanged at a time, including two gentlemen'.[120] A little later, the author of the semi-official account of James's progress cut the number to one, a cutpurse who had been thieving in Newark-upon-Trent.[121] In Scotland, punishment without trial was permitted in certain cases where the criminal had been caught red-handed, but this lack of judicial procedure flew in the face of English principles of justice, so was disliked and censured.[122] One wit commented on hearing the news: ''tis strangely done: now if the wynde blowethe thus, why may not a man be tryed before he hathe offended?'[123] In a sermon before the king at the Charterhouse on 10 May, Thomas Blague, the dean of Rochester, called upon the king to temper mercy with justice, colourfully warning him that 'extremity of law is open injustice. He that blowes his nose too hard, wrings out blood'.[124] Probably no coincidence, the next month, Anthony Rudd, bishop of St David's, preached before the king on the value of mercy and cautioned against 'all crueltie in execution of justice'.[125] It is unknown whether complainants thought James was behaving as a potential tyrant or as an ignorant foreigner; either way, they were troubled.

James's love of the hazardous sport of hunting also caused unease. An accident when he fell from his horse in Lincolnshire and 'very daungerously bruised his arm' was a reminder that his devotion to riding and hunting could prove fatal, leaving England with a minor on the throne.[126] Cecil was keen to stop 'all bruits and rumours' spreading about the incident and tried to reassure everyone that 'it is no more then may befall any other great and extreame ryder, as he is, at least once every month'.[127] But concerns continued. James's health was thought at risk if again he had a fall or hunted in the cold during the winter months, both of which were to happen frequently.[128] By 1605, the king's love of the sport was denounced as 'immoderate', even obsessive, while complaints arose over the damage caused to crops when huntsmen galloped over arable land.[129]

★ ★ ★

James held his first privy council meeting at Theobalds on 3 May. Sworn in as new members were five Scots, all long-standing friends and servants of the king: his cousin Lennox; his childhood companion Mar; the lord treasurer of Scotland, Sir George Home; the Scottish secretary of state, James Elphinstone; and the lawyer, Edward Bruce, Lord Kinloss. At the same time, one Englishman—Lord Henry Howard—was selected to add to the four appointed in early April.[130] On 11 May, James added two English barons to the privy council: Burghley and Zouche. Both already held important offices, Burghley then acting as lord president of the council of the north—a position he was soon to lose—and Zouche who was to remain as president of the council of the marches of Wales.

While at Theobalds, James tackled some of the grievances that had been conveyed to him in the many petitions delivered once his accession was officially announced. On 4 May, he appointed a committee of privy councillors 'to take knowledge and consider of all monopolies and grants that are offensive to the subjects of this realm', so that he could abolish those that were 'grievous and burdensome' to his subjects. Not waiting for the outcome, he signed a proclamation three days later that suspended nearly all the monopolies granted by Elizabeth. Additionally it ordered purveyors to execute their office 'without any maner of oppression, grievance or wrong to be done to any our loving subjects'. In the same document, James ordered all lawyers not to 'extort or take any undue or excessive fees' and insisted that sports, plays, and pastimes be banned on Sundays, a sabbatarian measure Elizabeth had vetoed in the 1584 parliament. He wanted to proceed quickly, he explained, to reciprocate his subjects' loyalty and recognition of his right to the throne and 'make manifest to our people, how willing we are now, and will be ready hereafter, to be as forward in requiting their love, as they have bin in expressing it'.[131]

On Saturday 7 May, James rode the twelve miles from Theobalds to London. At Stamford Hill, three miles from the City, he was met by the mayor and aldermen, dressed smartly in their new liveries, and some five hundred principal citizens, all riding on horseback and wearing velvet coats and golden chains.[132] It was quite a spectacle. Richard Martin, a lawyer of the Middle Temple, delivered the oration of welcome on behalf of the sheriffs of London and Middlesex. Because few of those present could actually hear his speech due to the roar of the huge crowd, it was not included in the printed narratives of James's progress.[133] However, it was thought of sufficient importance to be printed separately (with the king's approval) and copied out in many private commonplace books.[134] Martin began conventionally enough, reminding his audience of the late queen's virtues before turning to praise James, 'the bright starr of the north'. In the style of early modern encomia, he then added a note of counsel, warning the king against flatterers and drawing his attention to the many ills in society that required redress.[135] The king's response, as ever, was cordial and positive, raising hopes that matters would improve under his watch.

James's next stop was the Charterhouse in Smithfield's, the residence of Thomas, Lord Howard de Walden. Along the route, 'multitudes' of people watched the royal procession from 'highways, fields, medowes, closes, and on trees'. The plan had been for the royal entourage to hear the singing of the orphan children from Christ's Hospital, who had been 'orderly placed' by the Charterhouse, but the crowds pushed them aside, and 'the shouts and clamours were so great that one could scarce heare another speake'.[136] What James made of the disorder is unreported, but the fracas may help explain why he was later more cautious in making public appearances.

James lodged at the Charterhouse for three nights and was treated there to 'many rare and extraordinary bankets [banquets]'.[137] On Tuesday 10 May, he heard a Lenten sermon on Psalm 1:1–2, delivered by Thomas Blague who used the text and occasion to caution the king against walking 'in the counsell of the ungodly' and promise 'that so long as the law of God is his counseller, all things shall prosper with him'. As already mentioned, the preacher also advised James to temper justice with mercy.[138]

At last, on Wednesday 11 May, James moved to the Tower. Because of an outbreak of plague, he did not follow the ceremonial route through the City that Elizabeth had taken on her arrival from Hatfield to London in November 1558. Nor was he greeted by a pageant devised for the occasion by Thomas Dekker.[139] Instead, he rode quietly through Aldersgate to Whitehall where he took the royal barge to the Tower. He was saluted on landing by the loud discharge of cannon fire. At his coming up the stairs, a gentleman usher presented him with the sword of honour, which James gave to Lennox who bore it before him as they entered. James stayed in the Tower for a few days before travelling by barge to Greenwich.

Over the next few weeks, James stayed away from the City and Whitehall because plague was spreading in London. Greenwich Palace became his main base while he awaited Anna's arrival. His intention was that they should meet near Windsor and enter the town together for the order of the garter ceremonies. In the meantime, 'to his just contentment', he found time to 'see his howses, castells, forests, and chases within 20 miles of London' and enjoy the good hunting in the neighbouring parklands.[140] But he did not neglect public business, writing letters, meeting foreign ambassadors, and issuing proclamations.[141] The most politically significant proclamation was the one in which James declared the union of the two kingdoms of England and Scotland.[142] His most important diplomatic action was to negotiate a treaty of alliance with France, which was signed at Hampton Court soon after the coronation.[143]

James's most pressing problem at this time was how to deal with the tide of suits and petitions directed towards him. It was not only that he was drowning under their weight; he was also making mistakes in granting an office to one person that he had already promised to another.[144] To solve the problem, he instructed six privy councillors to sit weekly to hear suits and answer them within a fortnight. To prevent duplication, he agreed not to draw up any grants without their warrant.[145] However, James could not stop intervening. When, for example, he learned that his privy councillors had failed to respond within a month to a petition for patronage, he recommended its acceptance and added that if the councillors found the exact terms 'inconvenient' to grant, they should work out 'other fit meane, wherby his Majestie's gracious disposition and liberality may be extended upon this gentleman'. Occasionally, too, he intervened in a judicial dispute under pressure from a private petitioner.[146] James never got on top of the paperwork related to patronage, but in 1603 his micro-management and duplications were a novelty that generated muddle.

★ ★ ★

Anna's departure from Scotland did not go according to plan. James had ordered her to leave without the royal children, but she had other ideas. She had long resented her enforced separation from Henry, who from his birth in 1594 had been placed in Stirling Castle under the care of the earl of Mar and his family. Now that Mar was in London with James, Anna was resolved to take custody of her son and bring him with her to England, even though it was against James's express will. Her disobedience could well have been prompted by a letter from Henry that pleaded for her presence in the absence of his father and expressed his 'great greif and displeasure' that they had been kept apart.[147]

On 5 May, Anna left Edinburgh, taking with her Patrick Stewart, earl of Orkney, and a few of her own servants. After stopping briefly at Linlithgow to see her daughter, she arrived at Stirling on the 7th and demanded the surrender of Henry. Mar's wife and son—then in charge of the young prince—refused point-blank to hand him over to Anna without the direct permission of the king.[148] An angry confrontation ensued, and the queen became 'so insensed, as falling into a feaver', she miscarried.[149]

Immediately informed of this unexpected and alarming development, James sent Mar to Stirling 'with full commission' to bring Anna and the prince to England. Anna, however, refused to accompany Mar, whom she distrusted and disliked. Asked to resolve the dispute, the Scottish council was at a loss, not wanting to offend the king but also fearing to exacerbate the rage of the queen who was 'in extremeitie off seikness and disease'.[150] To make matters worse, some noblemen had gathered outside Stirling Castle, and the lord chancellor of Scotland John Graham, third earl of Montrose, warned the king that the dispute could well divide the Scottish nobility and cause 'ane greitar sturre in this cuntry' than any that had been seen for years.[151] To avoid Scotland descending into factional chaos during his absence, James prudently gave way. He sent Lennox to Anna with a conciliatory letter, four jewels, and a commission to escort her and Henry to England.[152] Anna was still not satisfied. She insisted that James revoke his earlier commission to Mar for otherwise she would not leave with Lennox. To break the deadlock James reluctantly agreed, and on 23 May Mar was formally discharged from 'his keeping' of the prince. Lennox now became Henry's temporary guardian, and Anna was given unlimited access to her son.[153] It was an important victory for the queen.

It took Anna several days to recover from the miscarriage, and she waited until Friday 27 May before journeying back to Edinburgh with Henry.[154] After spending a long weekend quietly in Holyrood Palace, she and her son shared a coach on their way to the main church in Edinburgh, where 'great was the confluence of people flocking to see the prince'. After this triumphant entrance into the city, mother and son heard a sermon in St Giles and then returned to Holyrood. The next day, Wednesday 1 June, Anna, Henry, and their large entourage started the trip towards London, some two weeks later than originally scheduled.[155] The queen had originally intended that her daughter would leave with them, but the princess had some mild sickness and had to stay behind a day. She caught up with her family at Berwick.[156]

In the royal party were Lennox, other Scottish noblemen, and a few English ladies who had not served Elizabeth and so were not needed at her funeral. These women had set off north, ahead of the official escort party, in order to gain some advantage in the search for patronage. Among them were Lucy, countess of Bedford, her mother Lady Anne Harington, and her paternal aunt, the widowed Lady Sara Hastings. For financial reasons, this family unit was desperate for a place in the queen's household, especially the countess whose husband had been implicated in Essex's 1601 rising and punished with a huge fine of £10,000. Lady Hastings was to be disappointed, but within a week or so in the queen's company the two other women achieved their objective. The countess was given a position in Anna's privy chamber, and Lady Harington shared charge of the young Elizabeth with the privy council's choice of governess, Frances, countess of Kildare (the wife of Lord Cobham, who retained her first husband's title).[157] Furthermore, on 21 June, Lucy's husband Edward was freed from paying the £3,000 still owing to the crown from his fine.[158]

At Berwick, Anna met the six ladies whom the privy council had chosen to act as her official escort. The royal party—now about ninety-five people— set off for London on 7 June, following closely James's itinerary two months previously.[159] The queen and her daughter travelled in a closed coach drawn by four horses, while Henry rode on horseback. Given the state of the roads, their progress was remarkably fast. They took only five days to cover the distance from Berwick to York. On the way, Anna received the same 'loving, duteous, and honorable' welcome as had earlier been proffered to James, and she gave 'great contentment to the world in her fashio[ns] and courteous behavior to the people'.[160] In certain respects, she appeared to share the same persona as the late queen.

Not all went smoothly, however. Within the royal party, some 'quarrels' erupted between the Scottish and English courtiers which threatened disorder. Apparently, two of them exchanged blows 'uppon a quarrel', and in addition the earls of Sussex and Argyll 'were at hard wordes'.[161] To prevent Anglo-Scottish disputes and rivalries getting out of hand, Lennox, Shrewsbury, and Cumberland formally ordered that everyone should 'carrie themselves peaceably and decentlie, forbearinge altogether to give anie occasion of quarrel or disturbance of the quiet'. Any disagreements that did arise were to be referred to the three nobles, who would try to arbitrate impartially.[162]

The royal party deviated from the intended route only in the Midlands. Accepting an invitation from the earl of Huntingdon, Anna agreed to visit his house at Ashby-de-la-Zouch in Leicestershire. As with other lords, Huntingdon hoped this gift of hospitality would be reciprocated later by James in the form of patronage. Perhaps too, he wanted to allay any concerns that he might have designs on the throne because of his royal descent. From Ashby, the queen made a grand entry into the county town of Leicester and afterwards moved on to spend the night at Dingley Hall in Northamptonshire, the house of Sir Edward Griffin. At this point, Elizabeth had become so weary from the journey that she was sent with a sizeable retinue to rest at Combe Abbey in Warwickshire, the home of Lady Harington, before travelling to Windsor where the royal family would unite.

The queen and Henry, meanwhile, proceeded on their ceremonial route to Althorp, the moated house of the Northamptonshire landowner Sir Robert Spencer, reputedly the richest man in England. By this time, the royal party had swollen to over two hundred. On entering Althorp's grounds in the early evening of Saturday 25 June—a day later than anticipated—the arrivals were treated to a pastoral entertainment composed by the poet and playwright Ben Jonson. Jonson had struggled to obtain commissions at Elizabeth's court and now seized the opportunity to present himself as an imaginative producer of masques to a potential new royal patron.[163]

Expecting the piece to be performed on Midsummer's Night (the 24th), a time associated with enchantment and fairies, Jonson set the masque in a fairy woodland. The entertainment began with musicians, concealed in thickets, providing 'excellent soft music'. Then a satyr and Queen Mab, with fairies and elves in her train, welcomed the royal family to England with speeches, songs, gifts of a jewel, and the presentation of a deer which was killed 'even in the sight of her Majesty'. Anna was hailed as the new Oriana (a poetic name previously used for Queen Elizabeth) who will 'exceed whom she succeeds, our late Diana' (another goddess associated with the late queen). Elsewhere in the pastime Jonson was critical of Elizabeth when a satyr gave a mock warning that James's courtiers were going to need more than the flattery employed at her court to secure favour.[164] James's abhorrence of flattery was known to Jonson since the king had condemned it in *Basilikon Doron*. So, the satyr's lines seemed especially apt, as Jonson looked forward to a brighter future.[165]

On the Sunday and Monday mornings, the royal party rested. After lunch on Monday Jonson had another entertainment in store before their departure, but it was disrupted by the din of the crowd. The leader of a troupe of clowns was supposed to implore the queen and Henry to stay in residence at Althorp (a conventional literary device to flatter royal visitors), but the man's voice was drowned out by the noise created by 'the throng of the country that came in'. Similarly, the final oration praising the queen and prince that Jonson had planned to be delivered by a youth, accompanied by 'divers gentlemen's younger sons', had to be abandoned. Jonson, though, made sure his work was not wasted. When the text of the Althorp entertainment was published the following year, it contained the speeches that had been inaudible or cut in performance.[166] Despite the glitches, Anna was evidently pleased with the entertainments, for Jonson received the court patronage he craved.

Two days after departing Althorp, Anna arrived at the home of Sir George Fermor at Easton Neston, also in Northamptonshire. There, on 28 June, she was reunited with the king. Impatient to see his wife and son, James had not waited at Windsor as originally arranged but came to meet them at Fermor's house. Two days later, he escorted them towards Windsor. At the town, Elizabeth entered first. Seated in a litter, she was attended by thirty horsemen, and greeted with trumpets and 'other formalities as well as the best'. The vast procession of the king, queen, and Henry followed but passed quickly into the castle. Unusually, all was quiet on the streets. With the warmer weather, the plague was raging in London, and there were rumours that the disease was spreading to the towns nearby. Few, therefore, were prepared to risk a mortal illness by mingling in a large crowd to see royalty.[167]

During the royal family's residence at Windsor, the feast of St George was 'performed with much solemnity'. The ceremony surrounding the chivalric order of the garter was normally held on the feast day (23 April), but that year it was postponed until early July so that Henry could be installed in person as a knight of the garter. James had already received the garter *in absentia* in 1590. However, the opportunity for a grand occasion was lost. Because of the danger of infection, James was reluctant to invite many people to attend the celebrations and indeed 'by his wyll would have none at all'. In the end, it was agreed that some forty or fifty would be present.[168]

Together with the prince, four other noblemen were admitted to the order on 2 July: two Scots—Lennox and Mar—and two Englishmen—Wriothesley (that is, Southampton) and William Herbert, third earl of Pembroke. Pembroke had been exiled from the court in 1601 after abandoning his pregnant mistress Mary Fitton, but on hearing the news of Elizabeth's death he hurried north to offer James homage and accompany him to London. Like so many of the nobles and gentlemen who joined James's entourage, he secured the favour he desired.

Excluded from this male chivalric ceremony, Anna participated in her own ritual. 'The same time, the great ladies of England...came to the court to perform their homage unto her highnesse.' One by one, they knelt before her and kissed her hand.[169] The day after the new knights' installation, the king processed with all the members of the order to St George's Chapel for the Sunday service and then back through the castle grounds to the great hall, where they dined in public. Anna was again not present, which some said was because of her hatred of Mar. The Scottish Presbyterian ministers who did attend the festivities were disgusted by them. As far as they were concerned, a ceremony that had associations with a saint stank of the pope, especially as the rituals were so elaborate.[170]

On the Monday, the king and prince absented themselves while the knights of the garter paid their final respects to Queen Elizabeth. As the order's head, her insignia were offered up at the chapel altar: her two cousins Nottingham and Buckhurst held the banner of her arms; Cumberland and Shrewsbury bore the sword; and Northumberland and Worcester carried the helmet.[171]

This sombre ceremony marked the last formal mourning for the dead queen. James had already told his wife, courtiers, and ambassadors to put aside their black mourning clothes, a command that a French envoy found disrespectful to the late queen.[172] James had also ordered that Elizabeth's coffin be interred and the effigy removed before his arrival in London. Clearly the king chose to follow the convention that demanded only a brief and restrained period of grieving for the departed.[173] At the same time, he was making a political statement, namely that the transitional stage between the two reigns was over. Now that he was physically present in the capital, he saw no need for any symbols relating to the previous monarch to remain on show. Likewise, after the queen's funeral, he had ordered that his own coat of arms replace hers in parish churches.[174] His subjects, he now demanded, should put aside any lingering grief and immediately show joy at the prospect of his coronation. In this spirit, the stanza of one ballad urged:

> Now English-men leave off your griefe,
>   for noble James bringes us reliefe:
> Pull mourning fethers from your head,
>   and flourish now in yellow and red.[175]

★ ★ ★

By the beginning of July, James's English subjects had cause to be joyful for his accession had been managed brilliantly. Thanks to the pre-planned arrangements put in place by Elizabeth's privy council and nobility, he was recognized in England as king with barely a protest, and the immediate power vacuum was filled with speed and order. Foreign rulers mounted no challenge; on the contrary they rushed to send him their ambassadors. The printing presses poured out texts—panegyrics, sermons, poems, and books—highlighting his right to the throne, commending his kingly qualities, and welcoming him to his new realm.[176] James's own writings, freshly printed and widely purchased, were much admired. James too played his part in this success. His own progress towards London was, for the most part, a public relations triumph, while the journey of his family nearly two months later reinforced good will towards the new dynasty. The new king had listened to the advice of Cecil and Henry Howard and—despite a few miscalculations—avoided actions that might gravely offend English sensibilities.

Yet the smoothness of the accession should not be exaggerated. As already seen, people were not entirely sure about the nature of James's right to the throne. Additionally, although everyone was relieved that civil unrest had been avoided (at least in England), there were still doubts about James's suitability to be their king. Tresham heard 'no applause' when he proclaimed the king at Northampton. Indeed, the puritan town preacher Robert Catelin was heard to carp that James should be recognized as king only if he proved 'sound in religion'.[177] Others were more concerned about James's nationality than his religion. One farm labourer from Hertfordshire, for example, was indicted in the summer for saying he was ready to take up arms to prevent a Scot wearing the crown of England, while a labourer from Sussex was hauled before the magistrates for maintaining that Henry VIII had sworn to his nobles that 'no forrayne prynce should inheritt the crowne'.[178] They were not alone.[179] The plague, which was disrupting the plans for the coronation, could, moreover, be interpreted as a bad omen for the new reign. But, more ominously, even before James's coronation, plots began to be uncovered that revealed a layer of discontent with the new regime and involved not just the usual suspects of Jesuits but Catholics previously known for their political loyalty together with Protestant knights and barons. To this last element of disquiet, I now turn.

5

Conspiracy and Coronation

In late June and early July, James's new government learned of several conspiracies against the king. As most contemporaries understood it, there were:

> two severall treasons sett on foote at once, the one was called the 'by' and the other the 'mayne'. The 'by' was the surprising of the king's person, and the other the murthering of the king and his children, which they call the 'mayne'.[1]

The Bye Plot—which earned its name because it was thought the less serious—was the first of the treasons to be discovered. It was the brainchild of two English Catholics, a priest and a layman, who had both been loyal under Elizabeth.[2]

The priest was William Watson.[3] Because he was an 'appellant' who was a self-declared enemy of the Jesuits, he had been given considerable freedom of movement in late Elizabethan England and even been encouraged by Bishop Richard Bancroft of London to write tracts attacking their shared adversary.[4] Like other secular priests, Watson had long approved of James's succession, expecting the king to grant freedom of worship to English Catholics once he became their king. Shortly before Elizabeth's death, Watson went to Edinburgh and pledged Catholic support in any disputed succession if James promised to grant toleration. Afterwards, Watson claimed that James gave such an undertaking, although most likely (as was his wont) all the king did was make a vague promise.[5] Trusting and inflating James's words, Watson felt bitterly betrayed once James took the throne. He received only 'disgusts' when he met the king in England for James apparently turned to a nobleman and said: 'Na, na, gud fayth, wee's not neede the papists now.'[6] Furthermore, during his first few months on the English throne, James showed no sign of allowing freedom of worship but on the contrary exiled some twenty priests then held prisoner in English jails.

The Catholic layman who helped Watson devise the Bye Plot was the veteran soldier Sir Griffin Markham. He had financed Watson's journey to Edinburgh—providing him with £10 and a horse—in the hope that the future king would remember Catholic offers of service and repeal the Elizabethan penal laws. Markham had also anticipated some personal rewards. From his perspective, he deserved royal favour since his mother had shown 'affection' to Mary, Queen of Scots, while he himself was an early backer of James's accession. Additionally, he had been a companion in arms of the late earl of Essex both in Normandy and Ireland, and other 'Essexians' had already benefited considerably from their association with the executed earl. However, Markham was to be deeply disappointed. In early June, James denied him a reversion of offices in Nottinghamshire that were then held by his father and vital for his own local prestige and future finances.[7] Adding insult to injury, the reversions were granted to the earl of Rutland, whose uncle had shown 'inveterate mallice' to Markham's family.[8] Since Markham was unable to gain access to the king, he had every reason to suppose that his exclusion from royal patronage would be permanent.

In brief, Watson and Markham's plan was to raise a Catholic force of about a hundred men which would capture the king at Greenwich, or at Hanworth on the way to Windsor if he 'gave them the slip there'. They would then hold him prisoner in either the Tower or Dover Castle until he guaranteed religious toleration, removed all anti-Catholic individuals from positions of power, and elevated their Catholic friends to governmental posts.[9] Although many historians have ridiculed the plot as absurd, it was following a mode of political action that had achieved some success in Scotland during the 1580s.[10] The plan also made sense to Catholics who had been exposed to the belief that evil councillors rather than the monarch were to blame for their persecution.[11] They therefore could imagine that the king would accept their demands once he was separated from the men who had been Elizabeth's privy councillors and responsible for implementing the harsh penal laws against priests and recusants.

Watson and Markham convinced themselves and their fellow-travelling conspirators that they would not be committing treason since the planned operation was timed to take place before the king's coronation. This meant, they claimed later, that James was not 'our crowned and annoynted souveraigne' and hence was owed no allegiance.[12] The proposed date for the abduction was Midsummer (24 June) 1603, a 'collar day' when dignitaries—wearing their golden chains and insignia—attended court. Since Lord Keeper

Egerton would obviously be present, the kidnappers could seize the great seal in his charge and assume royal authority until James met their demands.[13] Ultimately, the project had to be abandoned, partly because of disagreements among the conspirators and partly because an insufficient number of armed Catholics turned up to carry through the 'action'.[14]

The government learned of the plot by a circuitous route. Another of the conspirators, the Catholic poet and polemicist Anthony Copley, leaked the plan to his sister Margaret Gage, who in turn relayed it to George Blackwell, the Jesuit archpriest of all the Catholic clergy in England. She, or possibly Markham, may have additionally revealed the plot to the Jesuit John Gerard, who likewise informed the archpriest. Blackwell then passed on the intelligence to Francis Barnaby, a secular priest, who was imprisoned in The Clink [a jail in London]. Seemingly, Blackwell fully expected and encouraged Barnaby to reveal all to Bancroft.[15] Surprising as it seems, Blackwell was prepared to inform on his fellow Catholics for two reasons. First, both Copley and Watson were well-known adversaries of the Jesuits and neither accepted the archpriest's authority. Second, Blackwell was eager to demonstrate the loyalty of the Jesuits in order to distance the English congregation from Persons, the archenemy in print of James's accession.[16]

Notified about a possible conspiracy, the government acted promptly, issuing a proclamation for Copley's arrest on 2 July. When his sister refused to harbour him, the fugitive surrendered and was brought to the Tower within a few days. Examined by Bancroft and several other commissioners, he signed his first confession on 12 July and a second two days afterwards. Rumours hit the streets of London that Copley had been 'latelie upon the racke' [tortured], and indeed the commissioners told Cecil that they had 'taken great paynes' and used 'great labor to get matter from him'. However, they denied any use of 'torture or threateninge', and to highlight this claim the prisoner's confession was entitled 'a free and voluntary declaration'.[17] In his statements, Copley tried to save his skin by minimizing his own role in the conspiracy and stressing his loyalty to the king. Nonetheless, the outline of his narrative was borne out later by the other players in the plot.

Copley stated that he had been suborned by Watson. At some time in mid-June, the priest had enticed him into taking 'a forme of an othe… concerning some accon [action]' that would persuade the king to repeal or suspend the penal laws against Catholics. The action first mentioned by Watson was non-violent. Catholics would encounter the king at some leisure activity and present their petition to him. Only if this plan failed would they seize the king and some noblemen. What would happen next, conceded Copley, was left vague, even in dispute:

> I for my part not knowing yet dyrectly what it [the action] might be, save that Mr Watson talked muche about our displaceng of privie counsellors, cutting of of heads and getting the broade seal into his hands, whereat I greatly marvayled and held the discourse idle, I opposing my speeche really against all bloodshedd.

Watson, continued Copley, raised the possibility of deposing the king and advancing an unnamed other: 'whoe, by so great an obligacon from Catholiques, would he and his lyne abyde firme Catholique to the lyne's ende'. But, to this treason Copley would not agree. When, at a subsequent meeting, Watson spoke of Arbella Stuart as a replacement for James, Copley equally 'gainsayd [it] bothe in regard of hir voyd title and also hir religion'.[18]

It soon became evident to the conspirators that they could not raise a sufficient force of Catholics to capture the king. Watson therefore proposed to Copley that they should make use of 'Protestants or what so ever malcontents'. Following the priest's instructions, Copley contacted Markham and the Protestant Thomas, Lord Grey of Wilton, who was known to be a seriously disaffected courtier. Other men Copley named as part of the conspiracy were a young Cornishman Nicholas Kendall, another 'secular' priest William Clarke, George Brooke, the brother of Henry, Lord Cobham, and Cobham himself. Copley also suggested that three Catholic barons—Lords Windsor, Chandos, and Dudley—were 'disaffected and also in tearmes to be soone in action, especially Catholicke'.[19]

Although the threat to the state did not seem great at this stage and everyone at court was preoccupied with preparations for the coronation, Copley's revelations could hardly be ignored. Kendall was immediately brought in for questioning, and on 13 July warrants were issued for the arrests of Markham, Watson, Grey, Cobham, and Brooke.[20] A proclamation for the arrest of Clarke and Watson was published three days later. No move, though, was made to apprehend the other three Catholic lords identified by Copley. Very likely the government wanted to check them out informally before arresting such powerful figures.

Fearing capture, Markham fled to his home county of Nottinghamshire. But he could not be found when the sheriff arrived at his house at Beskwood on 16 July. Shortly afterwards, he decided the game was up and handed himself in.[21] Watson and Clarke remained on the loose until the second week of August despite a proclamation calling for their arrest and describing their appearance.[22] The other men quickly found themselves in the government's hands. Brooke was captured at his estranged wife's house in London on 14 July and placed with Bancroft at Fulham before ending up in the Tower five days later. Grey was initially detained at Sheen in the custody of Sir Thomas Gorges but committed to the Tower on 18 July. Cobham was held for questioning at his house in Blackfriars until sent to the Tower, also on the 18th.[23]

Why Cobham, Grey, and Brooke should have become involved in Catholic plots is not immediately obvious. For a start, all three were Protestants, and two of them were barons of the realm from an ancient noble lineage. Cobham was esteemed as a knight of the garter and was one of the ten or so wealthiest noblemen in England. Additionally, he still held the important office of warden of the Cinque Ports, responsible for oversight of seven ports and adjacent land along the coast of Kent and Sussex. The twenty-seven-year-old Grey held no major civil office but had been a loyal soldier serving with Essex in Ireland and was wounded fighting for the Dutch against Spain. He was, moreover, known as a Puritan and enjoyed some powerful connections. Brooke, as the youngest son of four, had most reason to be discontented with his lot, but he had married well (the Lady Burgh), inherited money from his maternal aunt, and received patronage from Cecil, who had been happily married to his sister Elizabeth until her death in 1597.[24]

Nevertheless, the queen's death threatened all their positions. Cobham feared a loss of honour and influence in the belief that the king's 'good opinion of him' was being 'in many ways assaulted' by 'accusations and malitious practis'. And he was right. Both Cecil and Lord Henry Howard had spoken ill of the baron to James well before 1603 with the result that the new king received Cobham very coolly at their first meeting and excluded him from the new promotions to the privy council.[25] James's evident affection for the Essexians was another source of anxiety since Cobham was considered one of those responsible for the earl's downfall. So, although the baron retained his office (unlike his friend Ralegh), he felt—by his own admission—'discontentment' with his own situation.[26] Nor was he quiet about it for he was heard to curse Cecil, calling him a 'traitor'.[27]

Grey was likewise disgruntled. In his case, it was James's display of benevolence towards Southampton that was particularly galling. The two noblemen had been enemies since their time together as soldiers in Ireland,

and at the end of June 1603 they 'renewed old quarrels' and had a public spat before Anna that led the council to condemn them both to a spell in the Tower. Although James pardoned them, Grey still felt aggrieved, complaining 'of Sowthampton's grace and his disgrace and that the Lord Cecill had forsaken him'. To Brooke, Grey confessed his desire not only to take revenge on Southampton but also to bring about 'reformacon of manie things'. Additionally, Grey spoke to Cobham of his dislike of 'the carryadg of the Scottishmen', and it may be that their presence at court also goaded him into conspiracy.[28]

As for Brooke, he was said to have been tempted into treason when James granted the mastership of St Cross's hospital at Winchester to a Scottish favourite, the mastership being a lucrative office which Brooke believed Elizabeth had promised him.[29] But Brooke consistently denied treason and defended his actions by insisting that his and Grey's involvement in the plot was simply the means to infiltrate the existing Catholic conspiracy. Everything 'he hath don hath ben by warrant from the kinge', maintained Brooke, and 'he and the Lord Gray do rather deserve thanks and favor for diverting and breaking the plott then to be imprisoned'.[30] But, if Brooke was a government agent, he was a remarkably inefficient one for at no point did he inform the king or privy councillors of any conspiracies or impending 'action'. It also needs to be remembered that it was not uncommon for men arrested as traitors to claim that they had intended to trap and betray the other conspirators.

Cobham's first recorded examination evidently took place on 16 July. All we know about it is that he then said very little and refused 'to set his hand' to the cursory statement he did make. He simply denied any knowledge of a petition to be handed to the king and of a project for 'the surprising of the king or the court, or to remove anie counsellors'. He also denied agreeing to give a passport to Markham once the plot had been discovered so that the traitor could leave the country on his authority as lord warden.[31] Given the specific nature of his answers, clearly one of the other alleged conspirators had already made these accusations.

On 17 July, Brooke set down some 'answers and assertions' which contradicted his brother's terse account. According to Brooke's testimony, Cobham 'knewe yt [the action] was broken of and manner how yt was broken of' and had indeed promised Markham a passport although had not ultimately given him one.[32] In this same confession, Brooke was outspoken and specific about the role of Grey: he implicated the baron directly in the attempt to kidnap the king and hold the Tower. Indeed, Brooke took full responsibility for recruiting Grey and confessed that the two men 'tooke securitie out of another for service', in other words pledged loyalty to each other. During the action, Grey was supposed to provide a hundred men to take the Tower. However, Brooke insisted, their purpose was not to further a Catholic plot but rather 'to make a counterpeaze [counterpoise] the better to staie it'. Grey, claimed Brooke, either intended to betray the Catholics at the last minute or else thought to take control of events after the king was in his hands.[33] Presumably, Grey was himself questioned about these allegations, but his depositions are missing, possibly because he admitted nothing. For the moment, the government's case against him depended upon the testimonies of the other Bye conspirators and not his own confessions.[34]

At Cobham's examination of 17 July, he was asked about his relationship with Arbella Stuart. Again, he denied any wrongdoing. All he would divulge was that they had exchanged courtesies: his kinwoman Frances Kyrby, who attended upon Arbella, had told him that her mistress 'would be glad to be acquainted with his lordship, to whom he aunswered that she wer a lady of great bloudde and he would be gladde to do her any servyce'. Cobham also conceded that he had written to Arbella, but 'only as a matter of curtesy', and she had replied in the same vein. However, as he had burned her letter to him—suspicious in itself—he could not produce it to corroborate his statement. His interrogators now insisted that he sign his answers, but he refused, 'thinking that being a baron of the realm...he is not bownd to do it'.[35]

At this stage, Cobham may have thought he was in the clear, but over the next few days he became implicated in a separate, and still more serious, treason, which became known as the Main Plot. Further questioning of Brooke on 18 July revealed that Cobham had solicited vast sums of money from Spain and France. The intermediary with Spain was said to have been Charles de Ligne, the prince count of Arenberg, who was then in England as the envoy of the archdukes of the Spanish Netherlands to bring an end to the war. Letters, said Brooke, had passed between Arenberg and Cobham touching the 'procuring' from Spain of some 500,000–600,000 crowns which were to be used 'to assiste and furnishe a second action for the surprise of his Majesty'.[36] That Cobham had communications with Arenberg was no secret, but these interactions were now presented in a new and damning light.[37] Brooke similarly represented Cobham's dealings with Arbella as treacherous. He alleged his brother had instructed her to write to several powerful Catholics abroad, including Arenberg and Philip III, 'to favire and assiste her titele' to the English throne.[38] When questioned the same day about his relationships with Arenberg and Arbella, Cobham maintained they were innocent, but Brooke's testimony was enough to send him to the Tower.[39]

★ ★ ★

As yet Ralegh's name had been mentioned only in passing. Brooke had simply said that he was 'a fitt man to be of the action' as were the Lords Chandos, Dudley, and Windsor.[40] Nevertheless, Ralegh needed watching because he was close to Cobham and known to be seriously disgruntled after his dismissal as captain of the guard, eviction from Durham House, and loss of lucrative monopolies. Taking no chances, the privy council summoned him before them to answer questions. A case against him, however, began to be built on 18 July when Copley admitted that Watson had told him of a plot by a Spanish 'partie' which included 'the betrayeng a parte of the navie into Sir Walter Raleigh, his hands'.[41] As a result, Ralegh was placed under house arrest in the charge of Sir Thomas Bodley at Fulham.[42]

No record has survived of Ralegh's answers to questioning at that time. We must rely on other texts, including the trial documents, to piece together his statements. Initially, Ralegh 'cleered' Cobham 'in all thinges', or at least that was what he wrote in a letter smuggled out to his friend.[43] But, shortly after Copley's testimony of the 18th, Ralegh provided information that could be used against Cobham. In a letter to Cecil—which has not survived so we cannot be certain of its actual wording—Ralegh wrote that Cobham was seen visiting Arenberg's agent Matthew La Renzi in London. Ralegh then added that the privy council should keep an eye on Renzi: 'for that in likelihood if any thing were in bruing [brewing] he must neede have a hand in yt'.[44] Why Ralegh passed on this observation and opinion can only be guessed at: presumably he was keen to present himself as a co-operative witness with nothing to hide; perhaps too, he thought he was adding nothing to the information already held by councillors. After all, why else would Cobham be in the Tower?

Ralegh's letter proved to be what he later called his 'utter ruin'. On 20 July, Cobham was questioned about receiving the promise of a huge sum from Arenberg for nefarious purposes and was shown the section of Ralegh's letter relating to Renzi (Cecil 'hidd the rest'). Ignorant of his brother's betrayal, Cobham—'conceyving that Ralegh had particularly informed against him all he knew'—broke into a 'passion' and called his one-time intimate a 'wretch and traitor, iterating the same three or fowre tymes' and swearing many oaths against him. Cobham then offered to make a full and true confession. Admitting high treason, he affirmed that he and Ralegh had done a deal with Arenberg. Their plan was that Cobham would travel first to Brussels for accreditation and then voyage to Spain, where he would receive 500,000 or 600,000 crowns from Philip III. On his return, he would meet with Ralegh at his residence in Jersey—Ralegh still held the governorship of the island—and the two conspirators would 'thereupon resolve what was to be done' to distribute the money and exploit 'the discontentment of the people'. Ralegh, claimed Cobham, was not only a key player in this conspiracy but he [Cobham] would never have 'entered into this course but by his instigacon'.[45] Although readily admitting treason, Cobham denied any plan to replace James with Arbella. Whatever his discontents and earliest thoughts, 'God is my wittnes', he declared, 'when I sawe her [Arbella], I resolved never to hazard my estat for her'.[46]

Thanks to Cobham's testimony, Ralegh was conveyed to the Tower.[47] It was his second time as a prisoner there. In 1592, he had spent a few months in the government fortress as punishment for secretly marrying Elizabeth Throckmorton, the queen's maid of honour. This time, however, he knew his situation was far graver: he 'standeth styll uppon his inocencye', wrote his custodian, 'but with a mynde the moste dejected that ever I sawe'.[48] At this crucial point, the interrogations had to be suspended for a few days as attention turned to the joint coronation of James and Anna.

★ ★ ★

James was exceptional in being a husband at the time of his coronation. For over three hundred years, English monarchs had been either single or widowed when crowned. The last joint coronation of both king and queen consort was that of Edward I and Eleanor of Castile, way back in 1274. As already explained, James had insisted upon his wife's coronation in England so that her status would be the same in both his realms, thereby creating another area of constitutional unity. There was no good reason for anyone in England to refuse.

Coronations were usually magnificent affairs but this one ended up relatively modest. Because the plague was raging in London, James was forced to draft two proclamations in early July downplaying the event: one urged people not to attend; the other announced the postponement of 'all shewe of state and pompe accustomed by our progenitors, which is not of necessitie to be done within the church'.[49] This meant that the arrangements for the traditional royal procession from the Tower to Westminster Abbey had to be abandoned, and the five triumphal arches already erected in the City in preparation for the pageants were unavoidably left to rot.[50] The new plan was for the royal party to travel from Whitehall Palace to the abbey in barges. The lines of a contemporary poem gave expression to London's disappointment:

> Thousands of treasure hath her bounty wasted
>   In honour of her king to welcome him:
> But woe is she, that honour is not tasted,
>   For royall James on silver Thames doth swim.[51]

To prevent Londoners who might be infectious from attending the service, guards was placed at the gates of London while access from the City to Westminster by water was prohibited on pain of death.[52] James simultaneously took steps to thwart insurrection. No doubt alarmed at the opposition to his rule exposed by the Bye and Main conspiracies, he ordered some five hundred guards to be positioned around Westminster and a levy of trained bands to be raised in Surrey 'for preventing of any sedicion or tumult to interrupt that solempnitie'.[53]

Among those absent from the coronation were the king's children since both had already moved to Oatlands, the royal palace in Surrey, to protect their health.[54] Nonetheless, most of the nobility and leading gentry risked infection to attend. James wanted them present to give him public homage and confirm their acceptance of his legitimacy. They wanted to be there so as not to miss out on the honours he would dispense. Nor did the crowds stay away: according to a German observer, 'all places and streets' around Westminster Abbey were so crowded with onlookers that 'one could not move for the multitude'.[55]

In the days preceding the coronation, James created several new titles of nobility and an extraordinary number of knights. On 21 July, two barons were promoted to earldoms: Howard of Waldon became earl of Suffolk; and Mountjoy was made earl of Devonshire. Additionally, the king restored Southampton to his previous earldom. On the same day, eight knights became barons.[56] As for knighthoods, James had decided that all landowners worth £40 a year were entitled to the honour, and, on Saturday 23 July, hundreds of men attended upon the king in the garden at Whitehall Palace to receive it.[57] The next day, James's liberality was again exhibited when he created sixty-two knights of the bath, more than twice as many as the twenty-seven installed by Henry VIII on the eve of his coronation and five times as many as the eleven dubbed by Elizabeth.[58] This ceremony was a more public event. The knights rode 'honorably' from St James to the court at Whitehall where—in their distinctive outfits of long purple robes and plumed hats—'they made shew with their squires and pages about the tilt-yarde'.[59] They then entered the palace for a more private ceremony although not the ancient ritual of being knighted while naked in the bath.

That evening, the king was given time for contemplation and prayers while Westminster Abbey was made ready for the ceremony. On Monday morning, the king and queen went in their brand-new gilded barges from Whitehall to Westminster pier, followed by members of the court in their own vessels.[60] After landing, the royal party processed to the west door of the Abbey in a regal display watched by 'a greate assemblie'.[61] Two Italians, Scaramelli and Giovanni degli Effetti, were in the crowd and each provided a detailed description of the procession in a letter home.

First to appear were the twelve heralds who wore open tabards displaying the arms of the four kingdoms. Behind them came the representatives of livery companies and officials of the City, the mayor in the rear followed by 'drums and trumpets sounding' and the officers of justice. Next in line were the knights of the bath, about thirty barons, and twenty earls. After them, the king could be seen walking under a canopy of purple silk supported by four silver rods, topped with silver bells, each rod carried by a baron of the Cinque Ports (the warden Cobham was of course in the Tower). James was robed in crimson velvet and ermine like the earls, but 'the crown on his bonnet was a little larger'. His gentlemen courtiers, with vests of crimson velvet reaching to their knees, were close behind. Then came his bodyguard and the gentlemen pensioners 'in scarlet, carrying weapons erect, with velvet handles'.[62]

The queen's party followed on. In an inverse to the king's retinue, those of highest rank came first, followed by those of lesser importance. Among the former were twelve countesses in robes of crimson velvet, lined with ermine, 'no ornaments, hair done up, and small crowns on their heads'. Anna, wearing a similar long robe of crimson velvet lined with ermine, walked under a canopy like that held over her husband. Her hair hung loose, as was traditional for a queen at her coronation, and on her head was a jewelled circlet of gold, set with diamonds, rubies, sapphires, emeralds, and pearls.[63] Behind her were about ten members of her court, likewise dressed in crimson velvet, and the king's guards. The cost of the procession—the robes, rich cloths, and liveries of the nobility and officers as well as all other items—was borne by the crown and amounted to nearly £20,000 (c. £3 million in today's currency). The robes for James alone came to £2,172 with another £1,996 spent on those for Anna.[64]

At the west door of Westminster Abbey, the king was met by the elderly archbishop of Canterbury and two senior bishops, Tobie Matthew of Durham and John Still of Bath and Wells.[65] They led the king inside to the sound of a musical hymn or anthem. Walking on red cloth through the nave to the choir, the king then mounted a raised platform, a 'stage' covered with crimson cloth, to the right of the 'altar' (the south side). He sat down on a 'throne of estate'.[66] Shortly afterwards, Anna entered and took her seat on a throne, placed a little lower than James's, to the left of the 'altar'. Then the service began.

The service in 1603 followed closely the rites prescribed in the fourteenth-century *Liber Regalis*.[67] This was the Latin order of service for coronations, known as the 'fourth recension' because it incorporated the fourth major revision since the Norman Conquest. James's respect for the traditional form was deliberate. Participating in England's long-established coronation rituals was essential for his legitimation and—equally important—demonstrated his commitment to English customs.[68] Despite this continuity, the service was the first ever rendered in English, and the new wording was not in places a literal translation of the Latin since it had to be in accordance with Protestant teachings.[69] So, when James was anointed, the English phrasing toned down the sacramental dimension of the ritual and the material nature of God's grace. When taking his oath, the king swore to uphold 'the true profession of the Gospel established in this kingdom', meaning Elizabeth's religious settlement of 1559. And of course, James took communion in both kinds [wine as well as bread] as customary in all Protestant Churches.[70]

Other significant modifications were introduced for political reasons. Traditionally monarchs swore to uphold the laws '*quas vulgus elegerit*' ['which the people had chosen'], but this phrase was translated into English as 'the laws the people have', so eliminating any suggestion that the people might play some role in making law.[71] Another amendment came at the moment when the archbishop would traditionally present the monarch to representatives of 'the people' for acclamation, 'inquiring their will and consent'. Because James was determined that this acclamation should not be construed as an election or in any sense conditional, he decided upon a form of words that denoted his position as 'the rightfull inheritour of the crowne' without any need for his people's consent.[72] Whitgift followed tradition in presenting the king to the assembled crowd at the four points of the compass, but he spoke novel lines in that they required 'the people' merely 'to make acknowledgement of their allegiance to his Majesty' with no mention of consent. Those present, 'signifieng their willingness', cried out in one voice 'Yea, yea, God save King James'.[73]

Writing about the coronation nearly two decades later, James explained his thinking about this part of the ceremony: 'a monarchie or hereditary kingdome cannot justly be denied to the lawfull successor, what ever the affections of the people bee; yet it is a great signe of the blessing of God, when he enters in it with the willing applause of his subjects'.[74] Nonetheless, not everyone in the audience appreciated the subtlety of the English formula: a lawyer from the Inner Temple who attended the ceremony, presumably in one of the noble retinues, certainly missed the point when he noted that the ceremony was designed 'to shewe the cause of that solemne assembly of the state of the common wealth to elect their king'.[75]

The acclamation over, the choir sang an anthem. Then the king and queen stood up and made the traditional first offering, each in turn placing on the altar a 'pallium' [royal mantle] and '*libra auri*' [a pound of gold]. Once they had returned to their seats, it was time for the sermon. The preacher was Thomas Bilson, bishop of Winchester, who had previously written two important and lengthy treatises against Catholicism and Presbyterianism. He was also a strong advocate of divine right kingship, maintaining in one of his tracts that: 'Princes are placed by God, and so not to be displaced by men.'[76] He was therefore a safe pair of hands to deliver a sermon on such an occasion, when it was customary for the Church to convey its views on the guiding principles that a new monarch ought to adopt.

For his text Bilson used verse 1 of Romans 13 which enjoined: 'the powers that are, are ordained of God'.[77] Appropriate for a coronation sermon, the verse also provided a perfect starting point for Bilson to reiterate his views on divine right monarchy and episcopacy, views he knew would go down well with James. Bilson began by drawing upon the theory of the king's two bodies [the distinction between a monarch's natural body and political office]. Circulated widely while Elizabeth was queen to justify female rule, it was now used in support of divine right monarchy:

Since then princes can not be gods by nature, being framed of the same mettall and in the same moulde that others are, it foloweth directly, they are gods by office; ruling, judging, and punishing in God's steede and so deserving God's name heere on earth.

The regalia used in the coronation, Bilson continued, symbolized this truth:

To princes then, as partakers with Christ in the power, honour, and justice of his kingdome heere on earth, are allowed of God a sword in signe of power, a crowne in shew of glory, a scepter for a token of direction, a throne for a seate of justice and judgement, and inunction [holy oil] as a pledge of outward protection, and inward infusion of grace.

Because kings were Christ's representative on earth, said Bilson, it was evident that their subjects were obliged to love them, obey their laws, pay their taxes, and submit to their authority. Bilson even insinuated that kings had the right to exact tribute [taxes] without parliamentary consent.

Kings had duties too, but Bilson explained that he would go into them more briefly: 'because I speake before a religious and learned king, who both by penne and practise these many yeeres hath witnessed to the world, how well acquainted he is with Christian and godly government'. And, indeed, in *Basilikon Doron*, James had devoted one chapter to a king's duties towards God and another discussing those arising from his office. Nonetheless, Bilson reminded James of three key duties. The first towards God required him to ensure preachers were 'maintained' and to protect the Church against its enemies, implicitly both Catholics and Presbyterians. The second was the exercise of 'moderation towards his subjects', so that they enjoyed 'publike and private peace' and were conserved from 'all hostilitie, miserie, and injurie'. The duty here was also to repress 'the unbrideled lusts of man's corruption' and to act against 'adulteries, incests, rapes, robberies, perjuries, conspiracies, witchcrafts, murders, rebellions, treasons, and such like hainous and impious enormities'. The king's third duty was 'the execution of just judgement'. Like God—the supreme judge—a king 'must heare indifferently, discerne wisely, and pronounce uprightly'.

But what if kings failed to uphold their duties or acted in ungodly ways? Then, said Bilson, 'we must reverence their power, but refuse their willes'. Refusal did not mean armed resistance. Bilson spelled out: 'Yet must wee not reject their yoke with violence, but rather endure their swordes with patience.' Reinforcing this point, he asserted elsewhere in the sermon that only God could remove the right to rule from a king and that papists had fallen into 'sin' in calling for the deposition of monarchs.

After the sermon, the king took the coronation oath. In response to ritualized questions from the archbishop, he swore in Latin, English, and French: to keep the laws and customs granted by his predecessors; 'to keepe peace and godly agreement' to God, the Church, the clergy, and people; to cause law, justice, and 'discretion in mercye and truth to bee executed' in all his judgements; and to respect and defend the privileges of the commons. In James's mind, he was swearing the oath to God and not to his subjects, and so it was *not* a political contract with his people that limited royal power. On the contrary, the oath was entirely compatible with divine right monarchy.

The anointing of the king—the spiritual climax of the coronation service—further strengthened royal claims to divine right. The anointing of Old Testament kings of Israel acted as precedent and authority for a rite that was generally believed to confer divine authority on monarchs and transform them into quasi-priestly figures. It was thanks to this sacred rite that monarchs were understood to have the miraculous power of curing scrofula [a bacterial infection] through their touch. In the post-Reformation world, however, such beliefs were controversial, and many Protestants—especially Scottish Presbyterians—rejected them as superstitious. James too dismissed as superstitious all notions about the miraculous powers of kings, but at the same time he understood that the ancient rituals of anointing and the king's touch enhanced royal authority and bolstered divine right kingship.[78] So, after some deliberation, he carried out the king's touch in England, but used words—'The king touches, may God heal thee'—that disclaimed the occurrence of any miracle and implied instead that God listened to kings more than to the sick when they called on Him to heal.[79]

The anointing ritual was especially theatrical. First, James's overgarments were removed, leaving him in a vest and hose of white satin. The loops in his vest were then untied and openings revealed to allow the chrism, a mixture of oil, balsam, and perfume, to touch his body. Kneeling before the archbishop, he was anointed in five places to represent the five wounds of Christ: the palms of his hands, his breast, the skin between the shoulders, his elbows, and the crown of his head.[80] Another novelty was that Whitgift did not make the form of the cross when touching James's skin, a sign many Protestants abhorred as 'popish'. Finally, Whitgift placed a linen coif over James's hair which he was to wear for seven days to keep the holy oil intact. The choir meanwhile sang 'the third anthem'.

The investiture followed next, a ceremony carried out by the dean of Westminster and an appointed earl. Dean Lancelot Andrewes dressed James in the robes and regalia of Edward the Confessor: a mantle of state; a long vest of crimson velvet lined with white; over it, a royal tunic woven with images in gold on the front and back; hose; and sandals. An earl chosen by the king tied on golden spurs (an emblem of knighthood and chivalry) and 'girt' the sword (a symbol of justice) around him. James was now ready to be crowned. He was led to the gilded coronation chair, which housed the famous stone of Scone (said to have been where the Patriarch Jacob had rested and seen the angels), taken from the Scots in battle. Whitgift then placed the crown of Edward the Confessor on his head. Made of gold and encrusted with precious stones, it was so heavy that two bishops had to hold on to it. After this, Whitgift blessed the coronation ring and placed it on the fourth finger of the king's left hand, an act that symbolized the king's marriage to his nation.

Donning linen gloves, James made an offering at the 'altar' of his sword, which was immediately redeemed by an earl who would soon afterwards carry it before the king in the procession leaving the abbey. James was then given a rod surmounted with a dove (emblematic of his role as governor of the Church) and a sceptre with a cross. Holding these, he was led again to St Edward's throne while the choir sang *Te deum laudamus*. There, he received fealty and homage from the prelates and great men of the realm. On their knees before the king, they kissed his hand and touched his crown as a gesture 'promising for ever to support it'. At this point, Pembroke introduced an irreverent note into the proceedings. According to Scaramelli, this 'handsome youth, who is always with the king and always joking with him, actually kissed his Majesty's face, whereupon the king laughed and gave him a little cuff'.[81]

The ceremonial for Anna's coronation came next. It was relatively short as the acclamation was omitted, and she was anointed in only two places—the head and breast. Like her husband, she opened her undergarment so that the oil could touch her skin and afterwards had a linen coif placed on her head and a ring on her finger.[82] She was then crowned and handed a sceptre in her right hand and an ivory rod in her left. Supported by the two bishops, she passed by the king's throne and bowed to him before returning to her own seat.

Finally came the Protestant communion service. Several Catholic ambassadors left at this moment. The queen—who was a covert Catholic convert—stayed but she would not approach the 'altar'. Rejecting James's earlier efforts to persuade her to participate in the service, she remained sitting on her throne while the king received the bread and wine from the hands of the archbishop. Husband and wife then withdrew to private chambers where he exchanged King Edward's crown for a lighter one and they both removed their regalia. After taking refreshments, they processed to the barges which conveyed them to the palace of Whitehall.

★ ★ ★

The coronation over, the interrogations of the prisoners in the Tower resumed and became the main preoccupation of the government for several weeks. Cobham had now calmed down and, on 29 July, he retracted his accusation against Ralegh. But Ralegh had grown so emotional and despairing that he attempted to stab himself in the heart with a kitchen knife while at dinner.[83] In a letter to his wife, Ralegh wrote that he sought death not because he was guilty but because: 'I am nowe made an enimie and traytour by the word of an unworthie man.' But far from proving his innocence, this attempt at suicide—an act deemed ungodly in itself—was thought to confirm not only his guilt but also earlier accusations that he was an atheist. Accordingly, the king ordered a preacher to attend Ralegh's next interrogation, for a man of God might teach the prisoner that 'it is his sole that he must wond and not his boddy'.[84]

Over the next week, the authorities interrogated the original conspirators again as well as a wider group of individuals. Grey's role was now revealed as pivotal in the Bye Plot: 'Lord Gray undertook to call leaders and soldiers owte of the Lowe Countries' to add to the men raised in England for the 'surprise'; and he and Markham were to be 'the chiefe actors' in kidnapping the king at Greenwich. That a coup was intended was now in no doubt. The interrogators were told that Watson had drafted a proclamation to be released on the king's capture and that he and the other chief conspirators had discussed plans for establishing a new government: Watson was to become lord chancellor, Markham secretary of state, Brooke lord treasurer, and Grey master of the horse and earl marshal. The relationship between the Bye and Main Plots also became clearer. Cobham, the government learned, 'was no particular actor nor contriver' in the Bye conspiracy but just hoped that 'one of these surprises would have happened in the meantime to save his labour'. However, if Brooke, Markham, and their friends failed, he intended his own action to put Arbella on the throne (despite his protestations to the contrary).[85] As yet, though, no further evidence was dug up concerning Ralegh: 'the proufes are not yet soe clear as wold be required in soe great and so foule cases'.[86]

★ ★ ★

The capture of Watson and Clarke in August 1603 resulted in a new round of interrogations and testimonies. The priests' statements somewhat muddied the water. For one thing, they spoke at length of a projected armed rising by the Jesuits and the 'Spanish faccon' against the king, and it was not entirely clear at first if this was the same as the plot involving Cobham. Only in later testimonies did Watson explicitly finger Cobham and Ralegh as members of the Spanish faction working with the Jesuits to kill the king and his heirs.[87] Second, the priests explained that their own scheming was intended to 'rescue' the king from the Jesuits and to request toleration for loyal Catholics, presumably as a reward.[88] Third, they referred to yet another plot, this one devised by Grey and the Puritans, which they had foiled by bringing the baron into their own scheme.[89]

At the same time, Watson admitted his own conspiracy was more than a simple rescue effort. He meant 'for the kinge to be taken... and kept in stronge hould' until he had granted their requests, as had sometimes happened in Scotland. His aim was to separate the king from 'evil councillors', who would be imprisoned in the Tower. This kind of action, claimed Watson, had precedents in English history and was not just Scottish practice:

> in former times when the common wealth was pestered and the souveraigne misled by evell counsellors, the lords and commonalty often rose in armes to suppresse suche insolencye, yea sometimes with imprisonment of their soveraigns, and all this upon a moste loyall minde in some.

Such an action, he pleaded, was not designed to harm the king but on the contrary to 'keepe him safe until justice wer don' upon those who were his enemies, whether Jesuits or 'evil councillors'. It was 'lawfull' because it would take place 'before the coronacon or the parlyement time', when James's title would be acknowledged 'by positive lawes or rather custome, and the bond of homage, feaulty, and allegiance'. Nonetheless, Watson evidently realized that this justification was tenuous, for—as he readily confessed—he had not always mentioned seizing the king's person when recruiting Catholics to the action. Consequently, some Catholics thought he simply wanted them to turn up in strength to demonstrate in support of a petitioning campaign to secure toleration, while others believed their armed presence was needed to protect the king from a Jesuit-inspired coup.[90]

On 23 August, Watson confessed to knowing of Cobham's treasonable dealings. Brooke—his co-conspirator in the Bye Plot—had told him not only that Cobham had 'to deale or had delt for' a large pension to be paid by Philip III to Arbella but also that the baron was plotting to murder the whole royal family. Cobham, said Watson, had pronounced:

> nothing was to be don well untill the kinge and his cubbs (to use his words delivered unto me by Mr Brooke) were all to be taken away; and that the Lady Arbella were a fitt matche for my L. Gray whoe might come to be our kinge by that meanes.

In a later testimony, Watson amplified this accusation—which became crucial for the crown's case against Cobham. Watson then made the famous statement that ultimately defined the plots. He had learned from Brooke that Cobham had said:

> those thinges that were plotted by his brother and the rest (which was the preestes' treasons) were but toyes and that they shott but at the bye, but he and Sir Walter Rawleigh shott at the mayne, which was to take away the king and his cubbes.[91]

When confronted with these new accusations, Cobham was evasive. He confessed that he had spoken 'discontentedly and unadvisedly' to his brother and others but could 'not answere to' his actual words. He admitted proposing a match with Arbella to Grey, but 'remembreth not what the Lord Gray further answered'. He also 'utterly' denied offering a pension to Arbella and disclaimed any knowledge of 'the practise of the surprising of the kinge'. The money he was to receive from Arenberg, he claimed, was intended only to advance peace negotiations between England and Spain. Once again, he excused Ralegh of any wrongdoing. However, he admitted that Ralegh had given him a book against James's title that he had passed on to his brother. When questioned about the book, Ralegh said it disputed the title not of James but of his mother.[92]

Arbella was not placed under arrest but she was asked about her communications with the Brooke brothers. While she admitted hearing a 'motion' from George that she should send out letters 'for the advancement of her title', she maintained she had 'made but a scoffe' at it.[93] She also handed to the king a letter which Cobham had sent her. It was said that the letter had been left unopened and that 'this act of loyalty has saved her now'.[94] Partly to keep her under surveillance but also to give her no cause for grievance, Arbella was summoned to court in early August 1603 and thereafter treated as a member of the royal family, granted in September a yearly pension of £800 for life, four times as much as the one she had previously received from Elizabeth.[95] Then, during Raleigh's trial in November, Arbella was publicly exonerated. Cecil told the court that she had played no part in the conspiracy and there was no 'spott or blemish' on 'her faith and fidelitie' to the king.[96]

Arenberg was quizzed too. In an interview with James, he acknowledged that he had promised Cobham 30,000 *escudos* if peace were to be concluded with Spain but was as surprised as everyone else about the revelation of the plots.[97] James chose to believe him; Habsburg involvement would have obstructed attempts to sign the peace treaty he desired. For this reason, Cobham was made to affirm that Arenberg thought the money was to be distributed only 'for the furtherance of the peace between England and Spaine' and not for any sinister purposes.[98]

★ ★ ★

Towards the end of August, the government had all it needed to draw up indictments against the conspirators, which were presented at Staines on 21 August.[99] Eleven men were accused under two charges: one concerned the Bye Plot (involving Grey, Watson, Clarke, Markham, Copley, Brooke and three other Catholics: Bartholomew Brookesby, Sir Edward Parham, and John Scudamore); the other dealt with the Main (involving Cobham and Ralegh). Sir Edward Coke—who as attorney general was to be the leading prosecutor—thought there was a third treason, that of Grey, but no separate indictment was made for this crime.[100] During interrogations, more than forty other men had been implicated in the conspiracies but were let off with a warning because they either were thought minnows or else had powerful kin or patrons.

There had been some doubt as to whether Ralegh would face a trial or, if tried, be found guilty, because it was 'sayd that the proofes are not so pregnant' against him. In the end, he too was indicted. The authorities argued that Cobham's retraction of his accusation against Ralegh 'came not from a cleere hart' and therefore a court should decide the truth.[101] Since treason cases almost always ended in a conviction, this argument was specious. The reality was that either the government truly believed him guilty or else Cecil and the Howards wanted him permanently out of the way so that there was no chance of him using his famed wit and charm to worm himself later into royal favour.

The arraignments and trials took place at Winchester because the weekly death toll from the plague remained high in both London and Reading.[102]

The two barons were escorted separately to the town a few days ahead of the commoners who arrived on the night of 12 November.[103] All the legal proceedings took place before a jury in the great hall of the castle 'where King Arthur and his 24 knights have some tymes kept the rownd table'.[104] The non-noble Bye conspirators were arraigned and tried, first—on Tuesday 15th—and the barons and Ralegh were tried separately although named as 'confederats' in the lesser plot. As a 'Main' plotter and commoner, Ralegh was tried alone before a jury on the 17th, while the two barons—as lords of the realm—appeared before thirty-one peers on the 22nd. As in all treason trials, no lawyers represented the accused, and there were restrictions on the form of defence allowed.[105]

At the first arraignment, the seven defendants made their excuses.[106] Only one was acquitted. Sir Edward Parham successfully pleaded that he was 'onely drawne in by the priestes as an assistant withowt knowing the purpose'. He had been recruited, he said, 'to defend the king's person' from an assault by Grey and other Puritans; and after swearing an oath of secrecy and fidelity to 'advance' the Catholic cause, he had never again heard from Watson or any other plotter. Surprisingly, Cecil spoke up for Parham, which caused 'a great and extraordinary applause in divers of the hearers'.[107] The acquittal was totally unexpected; the last time it had happened in a treason trial was half a century earlier.[108]

The other defendants were not so lucky. Watson made a poor impression on the court and was roundly condemned as the instigator who 'drew all the rest into these treasons'. One observer described him as obstinate, ill spoken, and 'of meane presence' and 'slow speeche'. Clarke was thought to be of 'a milder spiritt' and his treason 'not altogether so fowle as having bene no great contriver'. Nonetheless, he too was condemned to death.[109] So was Brookesby, who had confessed to copying out Watson's oath and proclamation as well as promising to participate in the action to seize the king, although he denied any murderous intent.[110] As for Brooke, the prosecutor swept aside his defence that he had been acting on the orders of the king, arguing:

> It is true that imediatly upon the queen's death he had given the king some strange advertisements (which since proved frivolous) that some conspiracy should be in hand against him, with offer of his service in the discovery. The king imbraced the offer. Since that time, he having long speeche with the king, he touched not that string at all, but onely spake of his owne private busines. So, as it is likely that Brooke made this offer to the king that under the pretence he might act his designe of treason with more safety.[111]

Unlike Brooke, Markham made few excuses. He confessed his intention to surprise the king and 'acknowledged his faute' very penitently but denied any intention to spill blood. Although his testimony was challenged on several points, he made such a favourable impression that many men felt pity for him, including Cecil who was said to have wept 'aboundantly' during his testimony. Markham had written to him before the trial expressing 'harty contrition for what is past' and begging his mediation with the king. At the trial, Markham was admired for carrying himself 'lyke a man', especially when he stated his readiness to die if not pardoned.[112] Observers were not quite sure what to make of Copley. One considered him ingenuous; another described him as 'a man of a whynynge speech, but a shrewd invention and resolution'. Most perspicacious was Gilbert Freville who pointed out that Copley 'used few words that daie, but his declaravon [declaration] was extraordinarily well pennd', implying perhaps that he had been coached in his statements.[113] Despite sympathy for several of the prisoners, all bar Parham were convicted and condemned to death. It is hard to see how the outcome could have been any different.

★ ★ ★

Two days later, Ralegh was arraigned and brought to trial before the same jury.[114] The charges against him dealt chiefly with details of the plot to kill the king and 'advaunce Arbella Steuart to the crowne', but he was additionally accused of writing a book 'against the just title of the king' which he had given to Cobham 'for the better effecting of their trayterous purposes'.[115] The prosecution case was largely dependent on Cobham's evidence; all else was hearsay or guilt by association. Knowing this, Ralegh had smuggled a letter to Cobham before the trial, imploring him to retract his accusations and clear his name: 'You knowe in your soule, that you never acquainted me with your Spanishe imagination...you knowe that you offered me the monie *bona fide* for the peace.' For a while it looked as if his pleas were effective. Cobham told the lieutenant of the Tower on 24 October that he wished to clear Ralegh, and on 4 November he responded to Ralegh's letter with the words: 'I will avowe I knowe no maner of practise you ever had against the kynge or the state, so God have mercy on my soule as this is true.'[116]

Ralegh's trial aroused great interest: it was well attended, and its proceedings were fully noted by bystanders as well as written up later in commonplace books.[117] Almost all tell similar stories about the weakness of the crown case and the skill of the defendant.[118]

The prosecution struggled to bring a clear-cut case against Ralegh. Much rested on his acknowledged discontent, Coke forming the 'syllogissme' that Ralegh was discontented, discontented men plot treason, ergo Ralegh was a traitor. The most compelling 'proof' against Ralegh was of course Cobham's angry outburst of 20 July. Although most legal authorities took the view that two witnesses were necessary to prove a charge of treason, justices during the trial claimed that one witness was sufficient in common law.[119] Meanwhile, Coke argued that, even if the two-witness principle was usual practice, it could be overruled here because Ralegh had taken it into account when plotting his treason: 'Raleighe in his Macchiavellian policy hath made a sanctuary for treason [in that] he might talke with none but Cobham, because one witness cannot condemne.'[120] That Cobham did not appear in person to deliver his own testimony—and had anyway changed his story several times—also severely weakened the crown's case. In Cobham's absence, the prosecution brought in some third-party witnesses, including an English sea captain who swore that he had heard on the docks in Lisbon that Ralegh and Cobham would prevent the king being crowned. No wonder then that one observer at the trial commented: 'I am bente to saie I did not heare any kind of proofe to make him [Ralegh] guilty', while another remarked: 'the main evidence was Cobham's accusation which, all things considered, was no more to be weighed than the barking of a dog'.[121] Perhaps for this reason Coke fell back on the tactic of insulting the prisoner—calling him an atheist, odious man, and Machiavellian.

Furthermore, Ralegh conducted his own defence brilliantly. Among many telling arguments, he pointed out that Cobham was not 'such a babe' as Coke made out and did not need to be propelled into treason by his friend; that he [Ralegh] had a long history of being anti-Spanish and had recently written a treatise for the king that gave reasons against peace with Spain.[122] He admitted that Cobham had offered him money from Spain, but asserted that: 'The offer is nothing, for the offer made to me was before Count Arumbr [Arenberg] comeng. The offer made unto the others was after.' Furthermore, he never knew of offers to Grey or Markham but only to privy councillors.[123]

Ralegh's worst moment in the trial came towards its very end when Coke unexpectedly produced a deposition which Cobham had made the previous day and which contained three new accusations against his 'co-conspirator'.[124] First, he alleged that Ralegh had intended to take an annual pension of £1,500 from Spain to do 'God knowes what service'; second, that he had passed on intelligence to Arenberg; and third, that he was the instigator of Cobham's own communications with the count.[125] Presumably, Cobham had provided this new account as a last-ditch attempt to avoid execution. His wife Lady Kildare had been urging him for months to save himself and take 'not the yueke [yoke] of others' burdens'.[126] And, as Ralegh desperately exclaimed, Cobham believed that 'there was no waye to save his life but to accuse me'.[127]

Amazed at what he understandably called Cobham's perfidy, Ralegh then pulled out from his pocket Cobham's letter of 4 November that exonerated him. Nonetheless, he was forced to admit that he had indeed been offered a Spanish pension 'for intelligence' after James's accession, although he denied that he had initiated the offer.[128] Leaving aside the damage done by this last-minute drama, observers were generally impressed with Ralegh's handling of his defence and commented favourably on his 'wit, learning, courage, and judgment'.[129] The effect was that:

> most of his audience when he came to the barr detested him: but when he departed there were few that did not pity him and admire him for his sufficiency, thoughe they did not love him because of the difference betweene his word and deed.[130]

In other words, the audience admired Ralegh's performance, thought the crown case against him was weak, yet still believed him guilty. The reason for this was Ralegh's reputation as an untrustworthy courtier, an unpopular monopolist, the destroyer of Essex, and a notorious liar (his name mockingly being punned as 'Raw Lye').[131] He was such an unpopular figure that crowds had gathered on the streets to jeer—even attack him with 'tobacco pipes, stones, and myre [mud]'—when he travelled from the Tower to Winchester.[132] The pipes were an allusion to the story that Ralegh had blown tobacco smoke into Essex's face as he went to his execution. Satirical rhymes were read and recited that applauded his 'tumbling downe', derided his treason, and labelled him a 'mischievous machiavell'.[133] Given this, it is not surprising that the jury declined to believe his protestations of innocence and 'without pause' convicted him. As Dudley Carleton commented, had it not been 'for an ill name, half hangd in th'opinion of all men', he would have been acquitted.[134]

After hearing the guilty verdict, Ralegh reasserted his innocence and made a final request that, if a royal pardon was not forthcoming, then 'Cobham might die first'. Perhaps he hoped Cobham would tell the truth on the scaffold. Ralegh's thoughts about the trial and the lack of justice he received can be deduced from a poem, 'Pilgrimage', that has been attributed to him. Said to have written the poem 'at the point of death', the poet expressed the hope that he would receive true justice in heaven:

> Where noe corrupted voyces brawl
>   Noe conscience molten into gold
> Noe forg'd accuser bought or sold;
>   No cause defer'd or vaine spent journy
> For there Christ is the king's attorney.[135]

Was Ralegh guilty of treason? One legal historian has asserted: 'The trial record leaves doubts about Ralegh's guilt; the historical record leaves doubts about his innocence.' Most political historians agree.[136] Nonetheless, in my view, it is highly improbable that Ralegh plotted with Cobham an overt act of treason, namely to raise the country in rebellion and aid a Spanish invasion to put Arbella on the throne. He was not desperate enough to risk his neck on such a wild venture and, besides, he had no liking of Spain. The worst that can be said of him is that he spoke intemperately with Cobham, that he knew of Cobham's dealings to secure pensions from Arenberg, and that he was prepared to take Spanish bribes (as indeed were many Jacobeans, including Cecil).

★ ★ ★

Cobham was brought to the bar on Friday 25 November, a few days later than first arranged to allow more questioning beforehand. Cobham had tried to prepare his defence by consulting lawyers about the scope of the treason laws and the one-witness principle that Ralegh had told him about. But, as soon as the government learned of his inquiries, Cecil and the lord chancellor put a stop to them.[137] By the end of October, therefore, Cobham had become utterly despondent about his chances of escaping the death penalty. When asking his wife to intercede for him, he accepted the hopelessness of his case: 'whatsoever you plead for me must be for mercy, other refuge I have none'.[138]

There is no transcript of Cobham's trial, and so we are obliged to piece together what we can from draft speeches, letters, and other documents.[139] In the draft of the speech he intended to make, the baron denied his own treason, saying that he had never favoured 'the compassing or imagining of the death of the kynge or his roiall issue' nor considered 'setting up'

Lady Arbella. His brother's testimony to the contrary, he said, was so false that it was obvious 'howe longe he hath thirsted after my deathe'. Besides, he added, Brooke could not be trusted as he had made his wife's sister pregnant, a true if somewhat irrelevant charge of incest. At the same time, Cobham admitted his discontents, reaffirmed his old accusations against Ralegh, and inserted a new one. Ralegh, he now alleged, 'mooved to sollicite Arenbergh to persuade the king of Spaine to send an army into Mylford Haven' in Wales. He ended by requesting mercy from the king, attempting 'to draw on favour that the king's father was his godfather, and that his own father had suffered imprisonment for the king's mother'. Throughout the trial, Cobham was a sorry spectacle, appearing fearful, and trembling before his peers. Unimpressed with his testimony, they took half an hour to find him guilty as charged.

Grey gave a more spirited and sympathetic performance. His trial began at 8.00 a.m., and he 'spake effectually' for many hours. While humbly acknowledging the offence of planning to raise a force of a hundred men, including some foreigners, he disclaimed any evil purpose. His defence was that he intended only to present the king with a petition and needed such a large force to make a mark. He had not revealed his conferences with Markham and Brooke, he explained, initially because he had been 'ignorant of any resolution for surprise or violence' against the king and afterwards because he 'could produce or prove so little'. And he had withdrawn from the action once he realized 'many papists' were involved. His offence, he concluded, should not be considered treason since 'it was but a verball matter and never tooke effect'.[140]

Grey also pleaded to be given a fair trial. He was 'full of doubt' that he would receive one, not only because justice was so rare in treason cases but also because some of the peers—he was no doubt thinking about Southampton and his friends—might want his destruction. He therefore reminded the judges that they would eventually have to justify their condemnation of an innocent man before God. He ended with no plea for mercy, just reminding the court of the many services he and his family had performed for their monarchs and country.[141]

The response to Grey's impassioned speech was mixed. Some felt 'a great compassion' for 'the gallant yong lord', but Ellesmere 'condemned his maner much, terming it Lucifer's pride', while the lords sitting in judgement disliked his speech 'because he disputed with them against theyr lawes'. As for Southampton, he said nothing until the peers retired to make their judgement but then spoke out against his old adversary.[142] Nonetheless, Grey aroused sufficient sympathy for the judges to take their time before sentencing him to death.

Given the evidence of all the other conspirators, Grey was surely guilty of treason. He was involved in the early stages of a planned coup—if not against the king, then one to remove his councillors—and he only thought better of it when the realization struck him that a successful 'surprise' would be in the interests of the Catholics whom he hated. Yet, even before the trial, commentators thought that 'Lord Grey will most move compassion', and shortly afterwards Cecil referred to him as a 'poore nobleman' who had been duped by the Catholics.[143]

★ ★ ★

Although brought to a satisfactory conclusion, the Bye and Main Plots were deeply embarrassing for James. Foreign rulers had been told that there had been no opposition 'in word or deed' to his accession and it enjoyed the 'generall consent and applause' of all Englishmen, everyone rushing 'to yeald him their most willing obedience'.[144] Similarly, at his coronation, the recognition and acclamation of his new subjects played a central role in the proceedings. Yet it had become evident that not all Englishmen had welcomed his rule and that early on some were planning to replace him with Arbella. Worse still, these conspirators were not just Catholic outsiders but included veteran soldiers, respected gentlemen, and two barons, one of whom held high office. Dozens more were implicated in the Bye conspiracy though not brought to trial. To undo the damage, Cecil was at pains to reassure foreign rulers (through his ambassadors) that James and Anna were every day experiencing the sympathy and affections of their subjects.[145]

Following the discovery of the plots, the government became acutely sensitive to words and behaviour that might indicate disaffection or sedition. On hearing that some 'wicked persons' from Somerset had spoken 'cursedlie' and spread malicious and false rumours about Buckhurst, Cecil, and Nottingham, the privy council wrote letters to 'all the judges of the land to take order at their several assizes for the punishing such as do libell and spread and raise slaunderouse reports of privie councillors'.[146] In September 1603, the privy council began to investigate an unofficial report that had been referred to Lord Kinloss and Sir David Foulis in early April about 'an opposytion' to James's title mouthed by an unnamed nobleman and passed on by the earl of Lincoln to Sir John Peyton shortly before

Elizabeth's death. At the time, the story had been ignored because the nobleman (an earl) had signed the accession proclamation, but in September both Peyton and Lincoln were questioned about these conversations.[147] Aware of the prevailing mood of suspicion, local officials referred to the privy council any case in which potentially seditious words had been written or spoken. A few of them sounded serious.[148] But others were trivial. That the mayor of Chichester bothered to report and send the depositions of several witnesses to the drunken ramblings of a 'very poore cobbler' is a sign of the government's political nervousness.[149]

The coronation had been important in restoring royal authority, but James still needed to do more to enhance his personal standing and political authority. This was not an entirely new situation for him: as king of Scotland, he had faced many noble rebellions and attempted coups. There—as seen in chapter 2—royal ceremonial and performances had often played an important role in the restoration of his power and authority. As we shall see in the next chapter, James took the same path in England in the months after the Winchester trials.

6

Three Royal Performances

'A king is as one set on a stage, whose smallest actions and gestures, all the people gazingly doe behold', wrote James in *Basilikon Doron*.[1] He was far from alone in making this observation. Comparing monarchs to actors was common in Renaissance Europe. Michel de Montaigne observed that 'to act and play the king' was one of the most difficult professions in the world; and Queen Elizabeth spoke of princes 'set on stages in the sight and view of all the world duly observed'.[2] While the public gaze could cause problems for royalty, it also offered opportunities. Princes were able to exploit performance and theatricality to imprint their legitimacy, publicize their authority, and persuade subjects of the validity of their policies.

During his first year as king of England, James self-consciously performed on the stage of state. As he well knew, each of his appearances was watched avidly by subjects attracted to royal charisma or keen to read political meanings into his words, actions, and gestures. Although this attention sometimes irked him, as he had little private life, he fully appreciated the political value of spectacles in which he had the starring role. This is evident from his performances during the progress to London in the spring of 1603 and at the coronation that followed in July. Over the next few months, however, the plague obliged James to withdraw from crowds. To avoid infection, he spent his time in private houses away from the public gaze. It was during this period of quarantine that he acquired a reputation for inaccessibility and 'a kinde of kinglie negligence' towards crowds.[3] However, once the plague subsided, James reappeared. During the remainder of his first regnal year, he gave three major public performances, all of which reflected not only English conventions and rituals but also his own distinctive style and character. The first performance was *in absentia* at the executions of three of the Bye and Main plotters; the second was at a conference James had summoned at Hampton Court to settle differences between the English bishops and their critics; and the third was the magnificent royal entry into London on the eve of the opening of his first parliament. All three were observed not just by actual witnesses to the events but also by readers of the printed accounts describing them. Although their authors were of course fashioning the king according to their own agendas, we can nevertheless appreciate that James's performative powers—although often compared unfavourably with those of his predecessor—were far from ineffective.[4]

★ ★ ★

To display impartiality the king had kept his distance from the treason trials taking place at Winchester. During October and November 1603, he resided at Wilton, the grand house belonging to Pembroke, which was about thirty miles away.[5] Many privy councillors and some courtiers attended the trials, as either commissioners or peers sitting in judgement, and even more turned up as bystanders. As soon as the sentences were announced, James summoned before him those councillors who had been present so that he could hear first-hand their impressions of the proceedings. He was especially interested in learning about the prisoners' demeanours at the bar, presumably to assess the extent of their guilt and remorse, which he needed to consider when deciding if he should perform the royal prerogative of clemency.[6]

James understood the political value of dispensing mercy. Like most well-educated men in early modern Britain, he would have read *De Clementia*, the key text on mercy, composed by the Roman philosopher and playwright Seneca the younger to instruct the Emperor Nero. Seneca had advised that the judicious use of clemency endeared a ruler to his subjects and enhanced his authority by displaying both his power and self-restraint. In *Basilikon Doron*, James had expressed a similar pragmatic approach to the grant of pardons, recommending that kings who were secure on their throne should 'mixe justice with mercie, punishing or sparing' depending on the intention and past behaviour of the wrongdoer. However, at the same time James warned that clemency was inadvisable when a king first assumed power. His own experience in Scotland had taught him that mercy did not always result in his subjects' obedience and love: 'I by the contrary found the disorder of the countrie and the losse of my thankes to be all my reward.' James therefore counselled that a king should apply 'the severitie of justice' until he was completely secure on the throne.[7]

What would James do now he was in England? Did he need to apply 'the severitie of justice' to gain the respect of his new subjects; or did he feel sufficiently secure that he could demonstrate the clemency associated with both wise kingship and sacral power? No one was quite sure. At least one man believed the two barons found guilty would receive a pardon; there were also rumours that Markham would be spared; and Copley, it was thought, might be reprieved 'for the service he did in discoursing of his knowledge' once in the Tower.[8] No-one expected the Catholic priests to be saved, and so it was.

The priests' execution was set for Tuesday 29 November. As was customary, they made final speeches. Both admitted their treason and regretted all past behaviour towards the Jesuits. Clarke added that he had not intended to act against a lawful prince and indeed had written 'of obedience to princes'. When the sheriff 'willed them to acknowledge' that they died for their treason and not their faith, Clarke answered that was true, but because they were priests 'theire falte was the more aggravated, and there death the sooner procured'.[9] As common traitors, they were to be hanged, drawn, and quartered, an excruciating death unless the hangman made sure they were dead or unconscious when he cut them down from the gibbet. Their hangman showed no pity. Both men were alive—and Clarke even spoke—at the time of their disembowelment. Afterwards, to act as a deterrent, their quartered bodies were nailed onto the gates at Winchester and their heads impaled on the first tower of the castle.[10]

Unlike the priests, George Brooke had hoped for royal clemency, though few—if any—initially thought he deserved it. He begged for mercy by appealing to James's high notions of kingship, telling him that kings could act like God in saving a sinner from deserved punishment:

> Amonge the saincts of God there are none so glorious as they that have fallen and are returned. Imitate Him then (gracious soveraigne) whose place you hold upon earth and reject not his true repentance whose offence was of frailty, not of malice.[11]

But the king chose not to intervene, and the date for Brooke's execution was fixed for 5 December. The only concession was that, as the son of a lord, he would be beheaded and spared the painful and degrading death meted out to commoners. For that purpose, a new scaffold was set up on Winchester castle green.

The day before the execution, Bishop Watson came to the prisoner's cell to hear his confession, give him communion, and offer spiritual comfort. At this meeting—presumably during confession—Brooke retracted the fatal charge he had made against his brother. Cobham, he now admitted, had never actually talked about killing 'the fox and his cubbs', although 'somewhat was spoken to lyk sence'.[12] Brooke similarly withdrew the accusations he had made against two men associated with Arbella (George Carew and Sir Henry Brounker, who had been questioned but not indicted); his words, he said, were but 'a jest'.[13] Brooke then reasserted his own innocence and with such conviction that Watson believed he was telling the truth.

Consequently, the execution did not go well for the government. Standing beside the condemned man on the scaffold, as 'his ghostly father', the bishop made an extraordinary speech, implying that the authorities were killing an innocent man. He spoke of Brooke's offences as 'errors' rather than 'capitall crimes', said that his sins were not as great as had been traduced, and affirmed that the 'God of truth and time' would ultimately reveal the truth.[14] Facing immediate death, Brooke 'died penitently'. Although he publicly cleared Cobham of using the 'odyous words' concerning 'the fox and cubbs', he 'constantly persisted' in his other accusations against his brother. The crowd seemed uneasy about the justice of the punishment. When Brooke's severed head was held up before the crowd, only the executioner and sheriff cried out 'God save the king'.[15]

Like Brooke, all the remaining prisoners—except for Grey—kept requesting pardons, either directly from the king or through intermediaries. Cobham and Markham were penning messages as late as 6 December, Cobham's hopes no doubt boosted by his brother's statement on the scaffold that seemed to exonerate him. Ralegh alone thought there was little chance of a reprieve and spent his last days clearing up his business affairs and making provision for his wife and son.[16] Meanwhile, men and women at court were petitioning the king, though not all of them to save the prisoners' lives. Although the privy councillors advised James to show mercy as well as severity at the beginning of his reign, others 'drew in hard the other way'. Among the latter was one of the king's Scottish chaplains, Patrick Galloway, who preached a sermon so strongly against 'remissness and moderation of justice' as if clemency 'were one of the seaven deadly sinnes'.[17] James ordered them all to desist from mediating in this cause since mercy was his prerogative alone, and he let everyone know he would be the final judge in his own good time.[18]

While awaiting their executions, the prisoners were visited, as was customary, by clerics who were supposed to help them make their peace with God. The Puritan Grey had his own minister and spent his days in great devotions with 'a careles regard' of dying. The king and privy council, however, appointed several spiritual advisers to go to Cobham and Ralegh in the hope that the condemned men would bare their souls and confess the truth about their role in the Main Plot. Bilson, one of those named, admitted that his task was 'both touching their preparation and readynes to die' and 'for the reconciling of such contrarie confessions and denyalls'.[19] But neither man would budge from previous testimonies. Ralegh 'with as great shew of synceritie for any evill meanyng agenst the king, offereth to gage his lyffe with the denyall of all, save geving patient eare to the Lord Cobham's unwise and lavishe projects'.[20] The spiritual adviser who was sent to Cobham found him in a terrible state: he 'powred out into my bosome, not without a streame of salte teares, his bitter mones [moans] and complaynts, how miserablie he was ruined and undone by the lewd complotments of an unnaturall brother and a treacherous frend (they are his owne termes)'. At the same time, Cobham stuck to the same narrative about Ralegh as he had given at his trial and in his last deposition.[21] While avowing that he never meant ill to the king or his children, he affirmed that his charges against Ralegh were true.[22]

On 5 December, James signed the warrants ordering the executions of Markham, Grey, and Cobham, and they reached the high sheriff of Hampshire (Sir Benjamin Tichborne) on the 7th.[23] The executions were due to take place in that sequence before 10 a.m. on Friday the 9th. Because the king was still wanting to learn the truth about Ralegh's role, he postponed signing the warrant for his execution, preferring to wait until he had heard if Cobham on the scaffold would 'make good his accusation' when preparing to face his maker.[24]

On the appointed morning, it was freezing and pouring with rain. A 'fowler' day could hardly have been selected or one 'fitter for such a tragedy', wrote Dudley Carleton who was present at the executions.[25] Yet, to everyone's surprise, a drama closer to a comedy than a tragedy unfolded, with the king as the offstage star performer. First Markham was brought to the scaffold. He complained that he had been 'deluded with hopes' of a reprieve and was therefore unprepared for death. But he did not lack resolution and rejected a napkin proffered by a friend to cover his eyes with the words: 'he would look upon death without blushing'. As he went to lay his head on the block, the sheriff was suddenly taken aside by one of James's Scottish grooms of the bedchamber (John Gibb) who was amid the crowd, unbeknownst to anyone there. Surreptitiously, Gibb handed over a document to the sheriff and passed on a whispered message. Seeming to ignore the interruption, Tichborne announced that since Markham was so ill prepared he should have two hours' respite. The condemned man was then led into the great hall.

Grey came next to the scaffold, supported on each side by two of his best friends. He had 'such gaitie and cheere in his countenance that he seemed a dapper yong bridegroom'. He fell to his knees by the block and prayed with his preacher, expressing 'the fervour and zeale of his religious spirit' and making a confession that God knew his fault was far from the greatest, yet he acknowledged his heart to be faulty. This went on for an hour. In the middle of his prayer for the king, he was interrupted by the sheriff who said he had just received an order that Cobham was to go before him. An astonished Grey was then escorted into the castle.

Out came Cobham, who recited some short prayers, said a few words craving pardon, and reiterated that 'he tooke it uppon the hope of his sole's resurrection' that all he had said about Ralegh was true. But before he could place his head on the block, Grey and Markham were each brought out separately. The three men looked in bemusement at each other: 'like men beheaded and met again in the other world'. Now, wrote Carleton, 'all th'actors' being together on the stage 'as th'use is at the end of a play', the sheriff made a short speech announcing the king's mercy in giving them their lives. It was a *deus ex machina*, if ever there was one! Overwhelmed, Cobham, 'holding his hand to heaven, applauded this incomparable mercie'; Grey broke into sobs and protested 'his zeale and desire to redeeme his fault, by any meanes of satisfaction'; and Markham 'did nothing but admire and pray'. The onlookers applauded with great fervour and spontaneously cried out 'God save the king'.

This last-minute reprieve was entirely James's own decision; at any rate, Cecil reported that he and the other privy councillors had been kept in the dark until the morning of the 9th.[26] It is likely that James chose such a theatrical method to save the condemned men as a means of highlighting his supreme authority. Probably too, he also wanted to hear what the convicted traitors, especially Cobham, would have to say on the scaffold. Certainly, this was how some interpreted it. The king wanted total secrecy, wrote one chronicler, 'to the end that each of them severally should prepare to breath out their last breath, with a true confession of their secret consciences'.[27] But why did James give the reprieve at all? His official reasons were set down in the warrant which was later printed:

in regaird that this is the first yeere of our raigne, in this kingdome, and that never king was so farre obleishid to his people, as we have bene to this, by our entrie heere with so hairtie and generall an applause of all sorts.

Among those welcoming him, he added, were 'the kinne, friendis, and allies' of the condemned men, all of whom had readily accepted the verdict of death and continued to show him obedience and loyalty.[28] James's act was, therefore, presented as a gift of reciprocity. Moreover, since he felt secure—or so he declared—that he had the loyalty of 'his people', he had no need to fear that the reprieves would be construed as weakness and exploited by enemies. Perhaps most important, though unstated, James recognized that his reign would get off to an even shakier start if it began with the executions of prominent English gentlemen and nobles. Almost certainly he had been told that the executions of the Catholic priests and Brooke had been greeted with a lack of enthusiasm, and it was obviously vital to avoid creating martyrs; the lionization of the executed Essex was likely a consideration here. Whatever his motivation, the stay of execution was a public relations triumph.[29] So that the king's performance of clemency would be widely known to his new subjects, a short book was immediately printed. It took the form of a letter from a witness at Winchester to a friend in London, detailing the scene, and included a copy of the royal warrant suspending the execution.[30] The story was then circulated in Speed's *History of Great Britaine*.

James's clemency was soon extended to the condemned men waiting in the wings. Brookesby was pardoned, set free, and disappeared from history. Copley was likewise pardoned and banished from the realm; and Markham was banished but never pardoned. Ralegh, Cobham, and Grey were not so lucky; all three were returned to the Tower and remained prisoners there for most of their remaining lives. Undoubtedly, this was because their enemies at court used their influence with the king to counter petitions for their release. Furthermore, suspicions aired against Cobham and Ralegh at the time of the Gunpowder Treason did not assist their cause.[31]

Admittedly life in the Tower was not terribly harsh since each of the prisoners had a suite of rooms lined with their books and was permitted regular visitors. Nonetheless, they and their families undoubtedly suffered. Grey died in the Tower in 1614; because of ill health, Cobham was released in the summer of 1617 to die in January 1619 an impoverished and broken man. Ralegh was let out in March 1616, but only because he promised to find James a gold mine in Guiana at a time when the king was in desperate need of money. However, the voyage was catastrophic. No gold mine was found, and James was furious when Ralegh's companions burned a Spanish settlement. To appease the Spaniards, James had Ralegh imprisoned on his return and revived the death sentence of 1603. On the scaffold, Ralegh defended his conduct in a brilliant 45-minute speech that was reprinted many times and led to his later representation as a victim to James's pro-Spanish policies.[32] Ralegh's 'good death' on 29 October 1618 was remembered far longer than James's earlier act of mercy and was one of the circumstances that badly damaged the king's historical reputation. But that was in the future; at the end of 1603, there was only delight and wonder at James's reprieves.

★ ★ ★

James's second public performance was in person. Shortly after the court's Christmas revels had ended, he presided over and participated in a three-day conference which discussed the state of the English Church. As already seen, during the previous year Puritans had presented James with numerous petitions detailing their grievances, criticizing the Elizabethan prayer book, and calling for reforms 'in all things needful'. Initially, James was impressed that 'persons of good sort' from 'many places' had drawn up these petitions telling of 'scandals' in the Church. Accordingly, he told Whitgift that 'we cannot but give some credit to them' and revealed his determination to introduce reforms that might assist the maintenance of a preaching ministry. His first thought was to press the universities to restore to the clergy 'impropriated tithes', payments which they were receiving as lay patrons of particular benefices, but Whitgift and other interested parties dissuaded James from this action.[33] Still taking the criticisms in the petitions seriously, the king decided to preside over a conference of bishops and godly ministers that would investigate the complaints and propose reforms where needed. James's role as chair or mediator would have the additional benefit of stamping his authority on his newly inherited English Church.[34]

The Hampton Court Conference was originally scheduled for 1 November 1603, but plague necessitated its postponement until the following January. Before it was to meet, the Puritans kept up their pressure by organizing a new barrage of petitions. But this campaign backfired badly as the king—encouraged by his bishops—deemed their campaign subversive and dangerous.[35] In October, James demanded an end to the petitioning, which he had learned was proceeding in 'an unlawfull and factious manner'. At the same time, he asserted his resolution to preserve the Established Church, 'reforming onely the abuses which we shall apparantly finde prooved'.[36] So, the prospects did not look good for Puritans even before the conference convened. Nevertheless, Puritan leaders still hoped that James would listen to their point of view as he had not cancelled the conference even though Bilson was reportedly urging him not to confer with 'men of so meane place and quality'.[37]

* * *

Aspects of the proceedings at Hampton Court were written up in letters, 'notes', and 'advertisements', some of which were later circulated.[38] But it was a printed quarto book of around one hundred pages written by William Barlow, dean of Chester, that provided the fullest report and was most widely read. Three editions of Barlow's book were printed in 1604 and reprints in 1605, 1625, and 1638.[39] Barlow's account was certainly partisan, commissioned as it was by Whitgift and reflecting the episcopal position; consequently, it has been criticized as deeply flawed.[40] Nonetheless, one of the godly participants accepted large chunks of Barlow's narrative as fundamentally accurate, and it probably did not stray far from the truth.[41] Accurate or not, it was largely from Barlow's narrative that James's image at the conference was forged. There he is presented as a knowledgeable theologian, caring monarch, and judicious supreme governor of the Church of England. To modern readers, though, James's chairmanship appears less impressive, looking 'idiosyncratic' at best and opinionated at worst.[42]

The conference opened at 9.00 a.m. on Thursday 12 January 1604, when invited representatives of bishops, deans, and godly ministers, together with nine of James's privy councillors, gathered in the presence chamber at Hampton Court. The king then told the assembly to return the following Saturday for a meeting in the privy chamber. As instructed, they all arrived on the 14th, but only the nine bishops and six deans were permitted to remain and participate in the day's discussions. At around 11.00 a.m., the king swept in and sat on his chair, 'removed forward from the cloth of state a prettie distance'. By this gesture, James retained his majesty but signified that he was to participate in the discussions and not act simply as an arbiter; and indeed, unlike moderators in university debates, he entered the fray as a disputant and held centre stage throughout the proceedings.

From this spot, James delivered an hour-long speech that explained the context and purpose of the assembly. The conference, said James, 'was no novell devise'; on the contrary, he was following the precedent of 'all Christian princes'—including his immediate English predecessors—who at the beginning of their reigns had taken 'the first course for the establishing of the Church, both for doctrine and policie'. In his case, he added, he was in the happier position of finding 'no cause so much to alter', and he thanked God ('at which wordes hee put off his hat') for bringing him into 'the promised land, where religion was purely professed'. Nevertheless, he added, some changes might be necessary. Comparing the institution of the Church to the human body, he acknowledged that 'corruptions might insensibly grow' and that a physician was sometimes needed to effect a cure:

> his purpose therefore was, like a good physition, to examine and trie the complaintes, and fully to remove the occasions thereof if they prove scandalous, or to cure them if they were daungerous, or if but frivolous, yet to take knowledge of them, thereby to cast a sop into Cerberus his mouth, that hee may never barke againe.[43]

Having reassured his divines that the fundamentals of the Church were to remain intact, James laid out the three main areas of Puritan complaint: certain words and rituals in the prayer book; errors and abuses in excommunication; and the reformation in Ireland.[44] James also drew attention to concerns of his own that he wanted tackled. These included the rite of confirmation, the signing of the cross in baptism, the 'dumbe ministerie', the ecclesiastical courts, and private baptisms. The latter he found especially obnoxious as they were usually administered by midwives to ensure that a sickly baby received the sacrament before dying. But, said James, 'hee had as live an ape, as a woman should baptise his childe'.[45] The subject was so important to him that, according to one account (not Barlow's), he disputed with the bishops on it for 'three hours at least'.[46] Throughout the session, James treated the divines with the utmost respect and approved their explanations so that, by the end, it seemed clear that any future amendments to the 1559 prayer book were likely to be minor.[47] The churchmen present were consequently both delighted and admiring of the king's 'theologicall and juridicail discourses'.[48]

At the next session, on Monday the 16th, it was the turn of the Puritan clergy to present their case. James would only allow two bishops to be present as spokesmen, and Whitgift chose Bancroft of London and Bilson of Winchester. But deans and theologians attended as did nearly thirty Puritan ministers and many lay people as observers.[49] Henry was there too, sitting on a stool beside his father. James began by summarizing the speech he had previously delivered to the bishops, and he then handed the floor to the Oxford theologian, Dr John Reynolds, who was 'the foreman' of the Puritans. On his knees before the king, Reynolds raised 'godly' concerns touching the prayer book, purity of doctrine, pastoral provision, and ecclesiastical discipline. While he spoke, James would brook no interruptions and silenced the fiery Bancroft who tried to stop Reynolds having his say on the basis that he was a schismatic and 'schismatics are not to be heard when they speak against bishops'.[50] James had already told the bishops that 'if he shoold refuse to hear them [the Puritans], they might justly give out agaynst him that he was an unjust king'.[51]

Nonetheless, James frequently made his own interjections, and during the discussion about baptism he took over the floor. Although this was inappropriate for a moderator, Barlow deemed it proper for the king since 'none present were able, with quicker conceit to understand, with a more singular dexteritie to refute, with a more judicious resolution to determine, then his Majestie'.[52] Yet, if one observer is to be believed, James's language was not always academic and moderate: according to James Harrington's recollection, the king 'rather usede upbraidinges than argumente', and 'the spirit was rather foule mouthede'.[53]

James also held forth during the discussion surrounding purity of doctrine. When a dispute arose between Reynolds and Overall (now dean of St Paul's) over the nature of predestination, James delivered a long speech giving his own views on the question as to whether the elect could fall from grace after committing a grievous sin. In brief (which he was not), James took a conventional Calvinist position—although not one accepted by hardliners—that those whom God had predestined for salvation would inevitably repent their sins and hence would not fall from grace:

> for although predestination, and election dependeth not upon any qualities, actions, or works of man, which be mutable; but upon God his eternall and immutable decree and purpose: yet such is the necessitie of repentance, after knowne sinnes committed, as that, without it there could not be either reconciliation with God, or remission of those sinnes.[54]

Later in the reign, the disagreements about the nature of predestination, which had emerged in the 1590s, were to grow intense, but at Hampton Court James's Calvinist position provoked little controversy.[55]

Although Barlow claimed that James kept 'an even hand' throughout the proceedings, the king usually appeared on the side of the bishops. During the debate about confirmation—in which Reynolds spoke against bishops confirming children—James interjected with the now famous aphorism 'no bishop, no king'. He then announced that 'hee meant not to take that from the bishops, which they had so long retained', and they should continue confirming parishioners.[56] When Reynolds protested against the line in the wedding service that read 'With my body I thee worship', James explained that the word 'worship' in England meant only 'honour' and added with a smile: 'if you had a good wife your selfe, you would thinke, all the honour and worshippe you could doe her were well bestowed'.[57] Reynolds was again James's butt when he complained about English rites and ceremonies that smacked of popery. James then retorted merrily: 'they used to weare hose and shooes in popery, therefore, you shall, now, go barefoote?'[58] But James was less merry when, towards the end of the day, Reynolds spoke in favour of synods comprising bishops and presbyters to settle theological disputes. The word 'presbyter' smacked to James of Presbyterianism, even though Reynolds was simply using it to signify an assembly of ministers or priests. At that moment, the king solemnly turned towards the bishops, saluted them by putting his hand to his hat, and declared: 'if once you were out and they in place, I knowe what would become of my supremacie. No bishop, no king, as before I sayd.'[59]

James's outburst resulted from his fraught experiences as king of Scotland. At various points during this second day of the conference, he drew contrasts between England and Scotland to the advantage of his new realm. Here, he said, 'grave, learned and reverend men' advised him, and there 'beardlesse boyes would brave him to his face'.[60] Scotland, he associated with a dangerous Presbyterianism, England with an episcopacy that bolstered royal power. Although all those present before him were content that bishops could wear caps, 'I shall tell you, if you should walke in one streete in Scotland, with such a cap on your head, if I were not with you, you shoulde bee stoned to death with your cap.'[61] While James's retorts may have partly been intended to sweet-talk his English subjects, they were also a measure of his bitterness towards the Kirk, which for decades had tried to constrain his authority.

James's performance, on this second day, pleased not only the bishops but also many privy councillors. Ellesmere was heard to say as he left the chamber: 'I have often hearde and read, that *Rex est mixta persona cum sacerdote* (a legal maxim referring to a king's sacral authority) but I never saw the truth thereof, till this day.'[62] Had the king heard him, he would have been delighted for these words echoed his own in *Basilikon Doron*, where he claimed that 'a king is not *mere laicus*'.[63]

On 18 January, the final day of the conference, James met again with the bishops, deans, and privy councillors, initially without the Puritan representatives but with some ecclesiastical lawyers now present. He explained to them what he had hoped to achieve in the conference: first, some small changes to the wording of the liturgy; second, 'contriving, howe thinges might be best done, without appearance of alteration' (presumably, because extensive change would be a propaganda coup for both Catholics and Presbyterians); and third, to ensure that 'each man may doe his dutie in his place'.[64] The first two purposes were achieved since the bishops had agreed to some minor amendments to the prayer book. For the third to be accomplished, his subjects had to do their duty by obeying his orders to conform.

Following this, the main topic for discussion was 'subscription' and Whitgift's policy of suspending or dismissing ministers who would not swear that the prayer book was in accordance with God's Word. Listening carefully to the case for subscription, James upheld it as the route to a harmonious Church. He went on to endorse the ecclesiastical court of high commission's use of the *ex officio* oath, which was so unpopular with the 'godly'.[65] Whitgift was naturally delighted, exclaiming that 'his Majestie spake by the speciall assistance of God's spirite'.[66] Nonetheless, the bishops did not have it all their own way, as James called for some reforms to be made to the practices of high commission and excommunication, some of which were later implemented. Additionally, he accepted the Puritans' appeal for a new, more accurate, translation of the bible.

When Reynolds and his three associates were brought in, James told them the decisions reached. After some quibbling on their part, James 'shut up all with a most pithy exhortation to both sides for unity'. Everyone agreed, but Reynolds's colleague Laurence Chaderton, master of Emmanuel College, Cambridge, who until then had been 'as mute as any fyshe', suddenly spoke up. He wanted the revised prayer book not to be enforced in parts of his native Lancashire (a region where both 'popery' and 'Puritanism' were strong), for if non-conforming ministers were deprived of their livings, only the Catholics would benefit. Ever reasonable, James answered that 'it was not his purpose', nor that of his bishops, 'to inforce those things, without fatherly admonitions, conferences, and perswasions'. If these non-conforming ministers were 'quiet of disposition, honest of life, and diligent in their calling', they would be given some leeway. But when Bancroft protested that every Puritan minister throughout England would make the same request, James responded that ministers would have only a short time to be persuaded to use the prayer book; if they still refused, they would be deprived. 'Finally, they [the Puritan representatives] joyntly promised, to bee quiet and obedient, now they knew it to be the kinge's mind, to have it so. His Majestie's gracious conclusion was so piercing, as that it fetched teares, from some, on both sides.'[67]

James himself was elated with his performance at the conference. 'We have kept such a revell with the Puritans, here this two days, as was never heard the like', he wrote gleefully in a letter sent to Scotland. He had 'peppered thaime [the Puritans] so soundlie as yee have done the papists thaire', and they had 'fled me so from argument to argument, without ever answering me directly'.[68]

With royal approval, Barlow's text emphasized the vindication of the bishops' understanding of scripture and the lack of significant change in church policy under James. Nevertheless, James wanted his subjects to view him as a reformer, and so he ensured that lists of agreed improvements were circulated in both England and Scotland. He felt a particular need to satisfy the Kirk that he had tackled the 'grosse corruptions' in the English Church, and so in a 'slender' account of the conference, written by Galloway but revised by James, the Kirk was assured of the king's 'resolutioun for reformatioun' and received 'a note of suche things as sall be reformed' in doctrine, the prayer book, discipline, the ministry, and education. At the same time, the matter of subscription was played down. However, the Kirk was neither fooled nor satisfied. Recognizing that James's account was 'different from the narratioun extant in print', it later expressed its disappointment with the outcome and consequent solidarity with its Puritan brethren.[69]

★ ★ ★

After the conference, James remained at Hampton Court until early February, when he rode 'with a selected company' towards Royston in Cambridgeshire for a few days of hunting and hawking before returning to London via Theobalds.[70] By then plans were afoot for another public performance, James's royal entry into the City on 15 March and the opening of parliament four days afterwards.[71] Taken together, these two occasions were to be the king's last major performance of his first regnal year in England.

The royal entry—a procession from the Tower towards Westminster—became the subject of four books.[72] Gilbert Dugdale produced a brief narrative from the perspective of a spectator; Ben Jonson and Thomas Dekker, the two main dramatists of the day, gave accounts of their own individual contributions to the entertainment; and Stephen Harrison, self-styled joiner and architect, provided a description—with illustrations by William Kip—of the triumphal arches lining the route which he helped to construct.[73] The publication of four different tracts about one ceremony was unusual, resulting in part from a bitter professional rivalry between Jonson and Dekker. Additionally, Harrison was keen to advertise his ingenuity while Dugdale, a pamphleteer from Chester, was possibly seeking royal patronage. Of these publications Dekker's was the most popular.[74] Cheaper than Harrison's and fuller than the other two, it was immediately snapped up, going into a second London edition in 1604.[75] Readers gained from it a far better sense of the whole spectacle than onlookers and participants could possibly have received on the day. They also had access to the speeches—three of them translated from Latin into English—which had been drowned out by the noise of the roaring crowd.

James's entry was understood as the 'residue of the solemnities of his coronation'.[76] Since the late fourteenth century, it had been normal practice for a procession to travel on the eve of the coronation through the City from the Tower to Westminster, along which route London craft guilds set up elaborate pageants. However, as already explained, James's pre-arranged coronation procession was abandoned because of the plague. Now that the epidemic had abated, both the king and his subjects were keen to resurrect the procession. Just before the opening of parliament seemed ideal timing. The royal entry would provide James's subjects with an entertaining spectacle and an opportunity to see their new 'foreign' monarch, while the occasion allowed the leading citizens of London to exhibit their status and importance. The king too recognized the value of the ceremony. It would display royal charisma, confirm his popularity, and demonstrate the loyalty of the political elite to the crown.[77] Furthermore, because the civic authorities had almost certainly consulted the court when planning the pageants, it was possible for the king to project his chosen royal image on the proceedings and promote the policies he intended to pursue. Indeed, to make sure all was in hand just as he wanted it, James and Anna went privately to spy out the staging at the Royal Exchange a few days beforehand.[78]

The official arrival of the royal party at the Tower took place on the evening of Monday 12 March. The king, queen, and Henry were transported by barge from Whitehall, and 'on landing they could only climb the stairs with difficulty, owing to the crowd which had gathered to see their Majesties'.[79] That evening, William Hubbock delivered a Latin oration before them. It was a sermon calculated to appeal to James and was later printed in English at 'his highnesse's special allowance'. Hubbock spoke of James's legitimacy as king through both his 'great grandfathers' and the 'divine decree'. Totally ignoring the recent plots, Hubbock declared that James had come to the throne universally acclaimed without any dissent or 'stirring of weapon'. Using classical imagery, he called James 'our Caesar'; drawing on biblical imagery, he praised James as a King David because of their comparable learning, religious writings, and uniting of two kingdoms (in David's case, the northern and southern kingdoms of Israel and Judah). The union of England and Scotland, preached Hubbock, was natural, since the two realms were like twins, and the work of God. Ending on a note of counsel, he called upon the king to plant the Gospel throughout his lands, rule with justice, and 'ease the lowe estate of the poore'.[80]

On the 13th, James created a new batch of knights and elevated Buckhurst to the earldom of Dorset and Lord Henry Howard to the earldom of Northampton. That day and the next, the royal family stayed in the Tower, enjoying 'the usual sports' as well as a water and firework display put on at the expense of the Cinque Ports. James was especially pleased with the latter, exclaiming that the love of his subjects was 'unquenchable' just like 'the wilde fire'.[81]

At about eleven o'clock on the Thursday morning (15 March), the procession through London began. James was preceded by all the magistrates of the City, the court functionaries, bishops and archbishops, the nobility, and knights, all 'superbly apparelled and clad in silk of gold, with pearl embroideries; a right royal show'. The prince was on horseback, ten paces ahead of his father, who rode on a small white horse (a jennet) under a canopy.[82] The queen, dressed in white, followed, seated 'in her chariott' [an open litter] drawn by two white mules. Arbella came next in a coach alongside Anne, dowager countess of Arundel (widow of Philip Howard), and followed by about seventy ladies on horseback. More than 1,000 people participated in the long and colourful procession, the cost of which was well over £36,000.[83] There were hordes of spectators too. The streets had to be railed off to 'keepe backe the violent pressing of the multitudes of people' who were watching from scaffolds and windows (with their glass removed) along the route. Each of the London craft guilds, in their ceremonial livery, stood together behind rails, draped in blue cloth and beneath heraldic banners bearing its coat of arms.[84]

The 1604 royal entry differed significantly from Elizabeth's coronation procession of January 1559. These contrasts would have been apparent to anyone who bought and read a copy of the newly reprinted book which described her earlier royal passage through London.[85] The allegories and iconography of 1604 were complex and sophisticated, far closer to the late Elizabethan style of panegyric than to that of 1559. James's 1604 entry was also more professional. The City employed well-known dramatists to write the pageants and practising actors from three playing companies to perform them. Another distinctive feature was that James's entry imitated a classical Roman triumph [a celebration to honour military exploits and imperial power]. Triumphal arches marked the spots where the pageants were staged, and the king was received as a Roman emperor. This motif offered fewer opportunities for citizens to recommend or provide counsel, which had been a key feature and theme of the 1559 pageants. Rather than presenting the commonwealth as a mixed monarchy and focusing on a monarch's need for counsel, the allegories of 1604 gave expression to James's own exalted vision of divine-right monarchy, even quoting from the recently published *Basilikon Doron*. Whereas in 1559 the pageants contained religious motifs, urging the new Deborah to install true religion [Protestantism] at home and fight idolatry [Catholicism] abroad, all but one of the 1604 pageants presented James as a figure of peace whose divine mission was to unite the English and Scottish crowns into a new imperial British monarchy. As we shall see, the Dutch arch was the only one to depict James as a militant Protestant. Finally, the hubbub from the crowd was so intense that verbal interjections from the king proved difficult, if not impossible. Whether because of this practical constraint or as a matter of personal preference, James—in contrast to Elizabeth—did not interact with the performers. He, consequently, appeared as a passive listener to the speeches and entertainments, a pose that reinforced his majesty and distance from his subjects.[86]

★ ★ ★

The seven triumphal arches stationed along the route were grandiose and elaborate, close to the style that had appeared on the Continent as part of the entry rituals for Renaissance monarchs visiting their major cities. Several had musicians' galleries and elevated stages where living actors mingled with carved plaster statues. Five of them were created out of wood and plaster by the major English craft guilds, and the remaining two by the Italian and Dutch merchants operating in London. James stopped before each one to look more closely at the devices, listen to the speeches, and enjoy the music, but viewers—including the well-educated king—really needed a guidebook or book of emblems to do them justice as their iconography was so complex.

Figure 10. The Londinium Arch at Fenchurch, in which London sits atop a dual arch and at the bottom are *Genius Urbis* flanked by the 'Councell of the City' and the 'Warlike force of the city', from Stephen Harrison, *The Arch's of Triumph Erected in Honor of the High and Mighty Prince. James the First of That Name* (1604) © The Trustees of the British Museum.

The first arch was at Fenchurch, the point where the procession entered the City (see Figure 10). Designed by Jonson, two themes dominated its iconography and the speeches of the two actors in the pageant performed there. The first was London's longevity, historical importance, and love for the king. The second was the divinely ordained union of England and Scotland. The figure of a 'richly attyr'd' woman representing 'The Brittayne Monarchy' was placed on the central façade below the roof; and hanging above her throne were the crowns and coats of arms of England and Scotland (those of France and Ireland were displayed less prominently on each side). On the figure's lap was a small globe inscribed with words that read in translation: 'The world of Britain, divided from the world.'

As James drew near the arch, a curtain of silk, painted like a thick cloud, was instantly drawn to reveal the central area and an inscription in praise of the king. The conceit was that James's presence was like the sun, dispersing the clouds that had hung over London since Elizabeth's death. The music stopped, and the speeches began. Genius (the spirit of the city, played by the famous actor Edward Alleyn) stepped forth and, in a verse dialogue with a boy actor playing the River Thames, gave London's thanks for the arrival of a British monarch who was a descendant of Brutus, the mythical founder and first king of Britain.[87] The English, went on Genius, were welcoming not just a new king but a 'Godlike race' of kings that would shelter Britain beneath its spreading 'branches' and 'knit with every shore/ In bonds of marriage'. Turning to Anna, Genius lauded her as 'daughter, sister, wife of several kings', and mother of a future one, and he conveyed England's hope that she would act as a 'good advocate' for the City by assuming the role of intercessor which queen consorts had traditionally executed.[88]

Though the assembled crowd had wished the royal procession might tarry longer at Fenchurch, the train moved slowly to the sound of music through the arch into the City and towards Gracious (today's Gracechurch) Street.[89] There, the Italian merchants had erected their own triumphal arch, which hailed James as an emperor, a writer, and philosopher king. On a large panel at the top was painted an enthroned Henry VII in his imperial robes, handing a sceptre to James, his legitimate heir, seated like an emperor on horseback. The inscription to the painting reads *Hic Vir, Hic Est* [This is the man, this is he], words that announced the appearance of Emperor Augustus in the 'Parade of Heroes' in Virgil's *Aeneid*. Other paintings and inscriptions on the arch alluded to James's writings, especially *Basilikon Doron*, and elevated him as '*regi musarum gloriosiss*' [the most glorious king of

Figure 11. The Dutch Arch at the Royal Exchange from Stephen Harrison, *The Arch's of Triumph Erected in Honor of the High and Mighty Prince. James the First of That Name* (1604) © British Library Board. All Rights Reserved/Bridgeman Images.

the muses]. The only speech delivered at this arch was in Latin. Flattering the king for his achievements, it borrowed a phrase from *Basilikon Doron* in declaring how subjects are blessed in places where a philosopher rules. As the king rode through the arch, an attempt was made to place a wreath of laurel—a symbol of victory and achievement—on his head.[90]

The third arch, erected at the Royal Exchange, was still more monumental and elaborate. Paid for by a committee of the London Dutch Church, it was three storeys high and so wide 'that it swallowed up the whole street'.[91] The investment of Dutch merchants in such a grandiose structure was undoubtedly thought worthwhile because of the strong rumours that James intended to make peace with their enemy, the Habsburgs. To convey the message that James should not abandon them, the arch was rich in symbols that gave thanks for England's long-term support in the war against Spain and reminded James of the value of the existing treaty of alliance between England and the United Provinces (see Figure 11).

A Latin inscription expressed the importance of preserving the existing '*Amicitia*' between the two peoples, as did another Latin tag, translated as 'Things honest endure'. Just over the opening of the arch, there was a painting of a phoenix, the emblem James had inherited from Elizabeth and used here to signify the hope of a continuity in their foreign policies. James's figure, moreover, was positioned prominently above four godly kings—David and Josiah from the Hebrew Bible; Lucius (the legendary king, said to have introduced Christianity to Britain); and Edward VI (the Tudor boy king who had established the first fully Protestant Church in England). This was a motif designed to show that James was their embodiment with the same duty to promote and sustain true religion, implicitly in the Netherlands as well as England. The seventeen damsels below represented the seventeen provinces of the Netherlands.

On the other side of the arch—which James would only see if he looked back—there were figures of Dutch merchants at trade and men, women, and children at their crafts. The Dutch, the decoration implied, were valuable economic partners in the Anglo-Dutch alliance. Whatever James thought of this arch's perhaps unwelcome message, he appeared to appreciate its immense structure and aesthetic decoration as he dallied there a while. As the king passed, a boy addressed him in Latin. Referring to James as a providential king, the child praised his virtues and adherence to religion, justice, and fortitude. Then he made a direct plea for the continuation of English support against Spain, saying the Dutch had been:

nurst and brought up in the tender bosome of a princely mother, Eliza. The love which we once dedicated to her (as a mother) doubly do we vowe it to thee, our soveraigne and father, intreating wee may bee sheltred under thy wings now, as under hers.[92]

However, James probably did not hear this speech as the pressure of time forced him to ride quickly by while the boy was still speaking.

Until then, Anna's presence had been acknowledged only slightly; but now, close to St Mildred's Church at the Poultry, nine trumpets and a kettle drum 'did very sprightly and actively sound the Danish march' to 'delight' her 'with her owne country musicke'.[93] At Soper Lane, the royal train encountered another remarkable arch, a majestic structure topped by a minaret and flanked by oriental towers. Dekker gave the arch the name of 'Nova Faelix Arabia' [New Happy Arabia]. This was an allusion to 'Arabia Britannica', the mythical home of the phoenix, and hence was a symbol for the mythic regeneration of Britain under its own phoenix. The two key figures on the arch were a veiled 'Arabia Britannica', wearing an imperial crown, and Fame with a trumpet in her hand. Other allegorical figures included the 'heavily drooping' five senses, the sleeping Detraction and Oblivion, the three Graces, and finally Love, Justice, and Peace. As the king approached, his presence seemed to bring all miraculously to life: Fame sounded her trumpet; the other wilting figures became reanimated; and wine suddenly poured forth 'very plenteously' into a basin called 'the Fount of Vertue'. A boy chorister explained the meaning of the pageant to James:

> Thou being that sacred phoenix that doest rise
>   From th'ashes of the first: beames from thine eyes
> So vertually shyning, that they bring,
>   To England new Arabia, a new spring:
> For joy whereof, nimphes, sences, houres, and Fame,
>   Eccho loud hymmes, to his imperiall name.

When he finished, two more boy choristers 'delivered in sweet and ravishing voyces' a song that praised London for spending a day courting the king rather than pursuing its usual commerce.[94]

At the Cheapside Cross (where James's accession had first been proclaimed the previous March), London's recorder—surrounded by the City's dignitaries—delivered an oration to his 'high imperiall Majestie'. A year ago, he said, the king had been acclaimed at that spot by all and now he came both as a bridegroom married to his kingdom and, together with his son Henry, as 'conquerors of hartes'. To mark the City's love and loyalty towards the royal family, he presented each of them with a small cup of gold—symbols, he said, of the 'golden reign' to come.[95]

Just beyond the cross, James was escorted by a pastoral figure Sylvanus to the fifth arch, called the 'Hortus Emporiae' [Garden of Plenty]. It had three domes covered in fruits and flowers, and on its top stood the figure of Fortune. Beneath her sat Peace and Plenty, Roman deities associated with fertility, the nine muses, and the seven liberal arts.[96] Since a garden was a familiar trope for England, the meaning was clear: under James's benevolent rule, the realm's prosperity and arts were destined to flourish. This point was underlined by the address of Vertumnus, the god of plants and trees, who offered the garden of state to James 'to be disposed after his royal pleasure'. James stayed longer at this spectacle, 'giving both good allowance to the song and musick, and liberally bestowing his eye on the workemanship of the place'.[97]

As the king advanced towards St Paul's, choristers sang out an anthem from the battlements and one of the scholars of the school delivered a Latin oration of welcome. Then at the Conduit, in Fleet Street, James saw the sixth arch, called 'Cozmoz Neoz' or 'New World'. Its novelty was that over the entrance was a mechanical 'engine' in the form of a globe and, as James approached, the globe was 'seene to moove...turned about by foure persons' who represented the four elements of Earth, Water, Air, and Fire. When the open part of the globe came into James's view, he could see in its hollow all the estates of his realm, in proper rank, from nobility to ploughman. At the very top of the structure, the figure of Astreae sat 'aloft, as being newly descended from heaven', an allusion to the legend that she had left the earth when the iron age destroyed virtue in men and would only return when a new golden age was at hand. Elsewhere, in tiers were decked figures of Fortuna and the Virtues. The figure of Envy, 'attirde all in blacke', loomed 'in a darke and obscure place'.

To explain this complex iconography, the actor William Bourne, in the guise of Zeal, stepped forth to say:

> The populous globe of this our English Ile
>   Seemed to move backward, at the funerall pile,
> Of her dead female Majestie.

But, since the arrival of the king, 'our globe is drawne in a right line agen', the four elements follow their natural order, and 'Envie's infectious eyes have lost their sight'. Zeal also praised James as the new Brutus, who had united four kingdoms, and as a monarch so full of virtue that Astreae who had fled England immediately upon Elizabeth's death now returned to usher in a golden age.[98]

The final arch, situated at Temple Bar on the western border of the City, has been justifiably called 'a towering mass of classical scholarship', since it was densely inscribed with quotations from Roman sources as well as Latin phrases invented by its creator Ben Jonson.[99] The structure supposedly represented the Temple of Janus, the Roman god of new beginnings. Janus' face was displayed at the highest point, just above a huge royal coat of arms, thereby implying that James and the four-faced god were similar in seeing all parts of the world and filling it with their majesty. One Latin inscription referred to Janus—and implicitly to James—as having the guardianship of the universe in his hands alone.[100]

Inside the temple were figures representing pairs of opposites: Mars submitting to Peace and Wealth; Tumult lying at the feet of Quiet; Liberty triumphing over Servitude; Safety over Danger; and Felicity over Unhappiness. All the devices explicitly signified the restoration of a golden age, as evoked in the *Aeneid*. Furthermore, James was proclaimed as a 'second Augustus'. Following the central theme of Jonson's first arch, his second one imagined London as the centre of a new Roman Empire. Mimicking the tag that appeared on public buildings in Classical Rome (SPQR), Jonson had the initials SPQL (standing for the senate and people of London) prominently placed on the arch. Another link with the first arch was evident when Edward Alleyn reappeared as the 'Genius of the City' to conclude the proceedings, his speech reiterating the theme of new beginnings.[101]

After James passed through this final arch, its doors closed behind him to denote the royal departure from the City. Now in the Strand, James passed through a rainbow and was hailed by a figure representing Electra, daughter of Atlas and mother of Harmonia. Announcing that she had stopped mourning the fall of ancient Troy and the plague in new Troy [England], she acclaimed the arrival of a new Augustus who would bring 'lasting glory' to the state. Once again, Jonson's themes of new beginnings and imperial rule prevailed.[102]

Despite the splendour of the procession and ingenuity of the pageants, the printed accounts occasionally hint that the king disappointed the spectators—or at any rate the authors of the pageants—when he failed to linger at the arches or interact with the players. But, given that the whole procession took about six hours from start to finish and that the hubbub throughout was tremendous, it is hard to see how James could have taken longer or played a more active role. Nevertheless, the king does seem to have assumed the persona of a distant, aloof presence. Dugdale makes no mention of him acknowledging the crowds in a stark contrast with his description of Anna, who 'did all the way so humbly and with mildenes salute her subjects, never leaving to bend her body to them...that women and men...wept with joy'. Even nine-year-old Henry was described 'smiling as over-joyde' and saluting the crowds 'with many a bende [bow]'.[103] The pageants presented the king as a godlike emperor, and this was a role he apparently performed to perfection. Whether or not this image of monarchy created unease among some of the more politically conscious members of the crowd or readers of the pamphlets is unrecorded. Did it seem to presage an age of absolute monarchy, or was it simply viewed as just an extension of the exaggerated panegyric of the late Elizabethan years?

Four days later, on 19 March, James, accompanied by Henry, made his state entry into parliament, once again performing on a stage before his subjects. The long procession rode from Whitehall to Westminster Abbey, where the bishop of Durham preached a sermon, and afterwards to the nearby parliament house in the Old Palace of Westminster. Visually, the procession was less magnificent than the royal entry, but it was still impressive. James wore his parliamentary robes, his nobility wore scarlet, and 'there were many fine liveries, different from those worn at the entry'. Nor did Londoners seem fatigued with royal spectacle; on the contrary they thronged 'to behold' the king, and many of them clamoured to enter the upper house to hear his opening speech before the lords and commons.[104] A speech from the monarch on such an occasion was unusual since the lord keeper or lord chancellor had been the crown's mouthpiece at the opening and closure of parliaments under Elizabeth.

Unfortunately, James was unaware of the exact ceremonial procedure for the occasion and delivered his oration 'before there was any notice given', which resulted in about a tenth of the commons, summoned from their house, missing it altogether. Regardless of the mishap, James was said to have made 'an excellent speech'.[105] Owing to its importance, James repeated it the next day.[106] Indeed, he thought his oration important enough to warrant printing.[107] His subjects evidently agreed as the printed version ran into four editions in 1604.

James spoke for about an hour, setting out his vision for England and his relationship with his subjects. In many respects, he restated the themes of both his oration towards the end of the Hampton Court Conference and the iconography of the royal entry, for he signalled his legitimacy and emphasized the peace, harmony, and unity that would now follow his accession.[108] However, unlike the writers of the pageants, he extolled the virtue of 'plainnesse' of speech and the avoidance of all ambiguity, desiring his message to come over loud and clear.

James began by stressing his 'birthright and lineall descent to the kingdom' and thanking his English subjects for their joyful and speedy reception of him as their 'undoubted and lawfull king and governor'. He would show his 'thankfulnes' by his actions, he said: first, by making peace 'with all forreine neighbours', which would encourage trade and bring security; and, second, by ensuring peace within the realm. Comparing himself to his ancestor Henry VII, who had united the warring houses of Lancaster and York, James pronounced that he too would generate internal peace. Of still greater importance, he would now unite the 'two ancient and famous kingdomes' of England and Scotland. A Union, he asserted, would make the whole stronger than its constituent parts, just as England was stronger than the 'seven little kingdomes, besides Wales' that had preceded it. A Union was essential for dynastic reasons too. He was wedded to the whole island as a husband to a wife and could not be a polygamist and wedded to two wives. Citing words from the wedding ceremony, he pronounced: 'What God hath conjoined then, let no man separate.' James went on to assure listeners that he, their head, was 'of the same religion that the body is of' and declared his wish that the two Christian confessions—Roman Catholicism and Protestantism—'might meete in the middest' and secure 'a generall Christian union in religion'. For this he required conformity to the prayer book from 'Puritaines', who after all did 'not so farre differ from us in points of religion as in their confused forme of policie and paritie', and demanded first loyalty and ultimately conversion from 'papists'. In the meantime, he would rationalize the penal code against recusants, a promise striking dismay into his Protestant subjects. Finally, he enjoined the parliament to bring in 'good laws', but not too many.[109]

Although there is no evidence of hostility from listeners to James's speech, he was soon to face opposition in parliament to his proposal for Union and call for religious unity around the prayer book. Listeners may also have been disconcerted—even alarmed—by the tone of the speech, especially when he said he was married to the realm. Although this phrase repeated a trope commonly used by his predecessor, the different gender of the two monarchs gave James's words another, perhaps more sinister, meaning. As a woman, Elizabeth was emphasizing the love and devotion she felt for her realm, which was like that owed by a wife to her husband. But, in patriarchal England, when James uttered that 'I am the husband, and all the whole isle is my lawfull wife', it implied that the country owed him obedience just as a wife did her husband.

★ ★ ★

These early performances of James reached a wide audience through printed books. Shortly afterwards, they were also re-imagined by two of the most gifted creative writers of his reign. Ben Jonson drew inspiration from James's performances in the two royal processions of March to compose his *Panegyric on the Happy Entrance of James... to his First High Session of Parliament*. Although the title of the poem related to James's entry to parliament, the poet referred to the earlier royal entry into London and used much of the imagery that he had employed in the iconography of the arches. In Jonson's piece, James is a Roman emperor moving silently in a triumphal procession past subjects who either 'amazed stood', struck dumb in wonder at his presence, or else:

> Cry out from tops of houses, thinking noise
> The fittest herald to proclaim true joys.

Recalling the Fenchurch arch, Jonson compared James to the sun, his rays reaching 'every nook and angle of his realm', clearing away sin and error. Then, through the voice of the goddess Themis [the personification of justice], Jonson played back to James the advice given in *Basilikon Doron*, which related to the divine right of kings and a king's obligations to his subjects, and had been a theme of the arch at Gracechurch Street. Themis ends her oration saying how fortunate his subjects were to have so 'deare a father', a saviour of the state, and a king who would sweep away the corruptions in the Church and state that had bedded down under his predecessor. It was an image that reproduced James's own self-image. The poem concluded with the Latin tag *'solus rex et poeta non quotannis nascitur'* [only kings and poets are born not made], a classical proverb which lauded Jonson as much as the poet king James.[110]

Shakespeare's *Measure for Measure* (1604) less obviously re-imagined James's performances, but arguably the play drew some of its inspiration from all three of them.[111] Duke Vincentio sees himself as a king of souls, a role James played out in the printed version of the Hampton Court

Conference and his first parliamentary speech, when expressing his concern for the spiritual welfare of his subjects. The play, moreover, ends with the reprieve of a series of capital sentences: the magistrate (Angelo) does not bring the felon (Claudio) to his deserved death on the scaffold, while Barnardine, the convicted and self-confessed murderer in the play, is pardoned. It is hard to believe that the politically informed among the play's first audiences would not have drawn parallels with James's own theatrical display of mercy the previous year. But the play has no happy ending: Angelo prefers death to marriage with Mariana; and Isabella is famously silent when the duke proposes. The trope of harmony through marriage was thereby subverted, and, instead of suggesting a new beginning, the ending sees a return to the old—unsatisfactory—order. The duke returns to power, while Angelo and Lucio return to their discarded lovers in enforced marriages. Shakespeare's vision of power and politics is as pessimistic in tone as Jonson's is optimistic. Seemingly, there were two contrasting responses to James's early performances.

PART 2

People and Institutions

7

Queen Consort and Royal Children

Anna was the first queen consort in England for more than half a century. The previous one had been Katherine Parr, married to Henry VIII in 1543, while the last one to have been crowned was Henry's second wife Anne Boleyn in 1533. Mary's husband Philip of Spain was king consort from 1554 to 1558, but he had been denied a coronation and anyway spent much of their married life abroad.

Anna had, of course, already played the role of queen consort in Scotland for more than a decade and fulfilled its primary function, that of delivering healthy children, preferably males. Admittedly, her younger son Charles seemed frail, but Henry was strong, healthy, and much admired for his manly qualities. Elizabeth was also a boon. Considered quite a beauty, she would be valuable as a potential marriage partner for a foreign prince in negotiations for a diplomatic alliance.[1] Anna, moreover, was expected to bear still more children, since she was still only twenty-eight years old on James's accession.

From the moment she arrived in England, Anna was associated with fertility and fruitfulness. Her progress to London with two of her children by her side paraded her success as a mother and provided a welcome contrast to the late queen, whose barrenness had given rise to political uncertainty. In the panegyrics that lauded the new dynasty, Anna earned praise as 'a royal fruitfull lady' who had borne 'such hopefull issue' that the succession was now assured.[2] And so it continued. Shortly after the discovery of the 1605 Gunpowder Plot, Anna was described by one as 'a fruitfull vine about the king's house' and by another as 'great in birth, greater in her marriage, but to all posterity greatest in the blessed fruit of her womb'.[3] Appositely, the biblical models associated with her were Leah and Rachel (the wives of Jacob) and Ruth (the Moabite), all of them women who had left their own country to become matriarchs of Israel.[4]

Anna seemed content with her representation as the progenitor of a royal line and source of the new family tree. Her secretary, the poet William Fowler, played on her name and title—'*Anna Britannorum Regina*'—to produce the anagram '*In anno regnantum arbor*' as the title of a verse that went on:

> Freshe budding bloomie trie [tree]
>   From Anna faire which springs
> Grove [grow] on blist birth with leafes and fruit
>   From branche to branche in kings.[5]

And on display in her London residence was 'a green palm tree'; 'in the upper part, the branches growing through a golden crown', and underneath Latin lines written in 'gilt letters' that compared her to an ever-growing tree.[6] Drawing on this image, Henry Peacham in his book of 'heroical devices' gave Anna the emblem of a tree bearing the fruit of 'H', 'E', and 'C'.[7]

Anna gave birth to two more daughters in England—Mary, named after James's mother, and Sophia after her own—and she may have been pregnant again in 1607 but miscarried.[8] Born on 8 April 1605, Mary was baptized during the late afternoon of Sunday 5 May in the chapel royal at Greenwich Palace. Her godparents were of the highest rank: a princess of the royal blood (Arbella Stuart); a senior woman peer (the countess of Northumberland); James's cousin Ludovick, earl of Lennox; and Anna's brother Ulrik, duke of Holstein, who happened to be visiting England at the time. It was a glittering occasion, comprising a service, banquet, and tournament attended by members of the English and Scottish nobility.[9] Throughout the kingdom, prayers of thanksgiving were ordered for Anna's safe delivery.[10]

Excited at the arrival of a first child born in England—though disappointed it was a girl—James chose to mark the happy occasion by creating three earls, a viscount, and four barons. The earls were Cecil (then Lord Cranborne), who was elevated to the earldom of Salisbury; his brother Thomas, Lord Burghley, now made earl of Exeter; and Philip Herbert, who became earl of Montgomery. On the day of the baptism, James presented Anna with a new set of jewels, a gift to show her honour and maybe mask his regret at the sex of their newborn.[11] A month later, the baby was placed in the charge of Sir Thomas Knyvett and his wife Elizabeth at their house in Stanwell, Middlesex.

Plans were put in place to celebrate Sophia's birth in like fashion, but she survived only one day in June 1606. When her death looked imminent, she was baptized privately in the queen's house at Greenwich. Her corpse was immediately conveyed to Westminster Abbey in a funeral barge and buried in Henry VII's chapel after a low-key funeral attended by most of James's privy councillors and 'many other great lords and ladyes, all clad in blacke but not in murninge weedes'.[12] Nine months later, James commissioned his master carver Maximilian Colt to make a suitable monument for the baby.[13]

Fifteen months on (16 September 1607), Mary died at the age of two years and five months from a severe chest infection.[14] Although Anna had been resilient at the loss of Sophia, she was grief-stricken at Mary's death. She immediately called for an autopsy to ascertain that the toddler had not been poisoned and requested that a decent sum be spent on the funeral.[15] James, who was hunting at Theobalds when he heard the news, continued with the chase and refused to return to Hampton Court to comfort Anna. His seeming indifference was not caused by heartlessness. James always had difficulty in dealing with his wife's emotions and, besides, sought solace for his own sorrow in physical activity. He left it to Cecil to console Anna and persuade her against holding a funeral, not because of the expense, James explained, but so that 'this beryal [burial] maye nott be a second greffe [grief]'.[16] The internment took place 'without any pompe' in Westminster Abbey, the king's councillors in attendance. The sermon, which commended the child's ready acceptance of death in a true Christian fashion, was afterwards printed to commemorate the young princess.[17] Colt was again commissioned to design a monument.

The monuments of the two Stuart princesses can still be seen in Westminster Abbey (see Figure 12). Sophia's shows the baby tucked up in a cradle, draped in black mourning cloth embellished with gold, her doll-like face turned upwards to heaven and her eyes closed. Mary's presents a toddler in adult mourning dress, who reclines on her left arm and whose feet rest upon a lion. Weeping cherubs sit at the corners of the marble base. Each princess is identified as a daughter of the king and queen in a Latin inscription, and the royal Stuart coat of arms is prominent on their tombs. Positioned near the recently completed tomb of Elizabeth, the siting again contrasted the fecundity of James and Anna with the barrenness of his Tudor predecessor.

The sorrow Anna experienced at the death of her daughter was nothing compared to her anguish at the decease of her eldest child. Unexpectedly, on 6 November 1612, eighteen-year-old Henry died after a short illness, now thought to have been typhoid fever.[18] His death took everyone by

Figure 12. The tombs of Mary and Sophia in Westminster Abbey © 2023 Dean and Chapter of Westminster.

surprise because he had always been robust and athletic. His whole family was inconsolable, and his parents went into seclusion until well into Christmas. While the king re-emerged in January to resume the New Year revels, Anna remained in mourning and re-appeared only for her daughter's wedding in February. Both Henry's siblings were also devastated for they had greatly admired their elder brother, corresponded with him regularly, and met together whenever they could.[19]

A tragic bereavement for his family, Henry's death was experienced as a cruel blow for the nation. The prince had been a popular figure since 1603. As a child, he had been much admired when accompanying his parents at court festivities, on progresses, and to other public events. As a man—from the age of sixteen—he had presided over a dazzling court in his own palaces at Richmond and St James. At the same time, he became associated with a political programme based on a martial Protestantism which had fervent support from the courtiers, soldiers, and others who were dismayed at the pacific policies of James.[20] Furthermore, Puritans apparently nurtured hopes that his successor would take the Church in a new direction; a rhyme ran 'in the mouthes of many' that:

> King Henry the Eyght
>   Puld down abbeyes and celles

The next of that name,
    Shall downe with bishops and belles.[21]

Henry's funeral was magnificent, matching that of Elizabeth some ten years previously. As customary, his parents did not attend; his brother Charles was the official chief mourner. Afterwards, some fifty memorial publications responded to his death, even more than those produced to eulogize the late queen.[22] Yet no monument was erected to honour him; and, somewhat ironically, the proud Protestant prince was buried in the vault beneath the grand tomb of his Catholic grandmother Mary, Queen of Scots, in Westminster Abbey. The Venetian ambassador Antonio Foscarini recorded that 'a rich tomb of marble and porphyry' was being prepared, but it was never realized.[23] Was the omission because of a lack of money, or did James not want a memorial which might expose the fragility of his line?

Certainly, the heir's death aroused immediate alarms about the succession, a problem which Anna's fruitfulness had until then laid to rest. At thirty-eight, the queen was most unlikely to bear another son; the risks were too high for a woman of her age even if she and James resumed their sexual relations, which had apparently been suspended after Anna's last miscarriage. To make matters worse, James himself was sick that year, and his sole male heir Charles was disappointingly delicate. On his arrival at the English court in August 1604, the three-year-old Charles had appeared a poor specimen: 'the weakest and sparest chylde of his yeares that ever I sawe', wrote one observer, 'weak in his joints and especially his ankles'.[24] Not only could Charles barely walk or talk, but he seemed so sickly that no-one wanted to be appointed his guardian in case he should die in their charge. In the event, Sir Robert Carey's wife Elizabeth, a lady-in-waiting to Anna, was appointed 'keeper' of the child in February 1605. It was largely owing to her care that James's draconian remedies for his son's disabilities were not applied: the king had wanted the string under the child's tongue to be cut and iron boots to be put on his feet 'to strengthen his sinews and joints'.[25] Thanks to Carey's nurturing, Charles flourished and by early 1608 was observed to be 'the joy of the king, the queen, and all the court'.[26] Nonetheless, in 1612, he still did not seem to be royal material, even were he to live long enough to succeed.

If Charles died childless, James's daughter was next in line, but, in November 1612, she was due to wed a foreign prince—Elector Palatine Frederick V—and any children born outside England might be excluded from the throne as foreigners. Then James's line would come to an end, and his two kingdoms split apart, ruled by different monarchs. Most likely, Lennox would be the successor in Scotland, while Arbella Stuart and her husband William Seymour (another descendant of Henry VII) might be co-monarchs in England.[27] To counter this possibility, James introduced a bill into his next parliament that would naturalize any children born to Elizabeth and securely place his daughter and her offspring in the succession after Charles and his line.[28] This was a dramatic, even potentially dangerous, U-turn for James. Giving parliament a role in deciding and declaring the future succession undermined the principle of the monarch's hereditary, indefeasible right which was so important to him. The succession bill passed both houses in April 1614, but never came into law because the assembly (known as the Addled Parliament) was dissolved without any legislation being enacted. A new succession bill was not reintroduced into James's next parliament, held in 1621, for by then circumstances had changed. Charles had become more robust and looked likely to marry and bear heirs; Arbella had died in 1615; while Elizabeth and her five children were expected to return to England since the Spaniards had booted her husband out of the Palatinate in 1620. The hereditary principle, therefore, remained intact, at least until 1649 when Charles I was executed. After this aberration, hereditary right was again waived in 1688 when the Protestant William and Mary displaced the Catholic James II, and then once more in 1701 when the Act of Settlement prevented Catholics from inheriting the crown, effectively disqualifying the male heirs of James II. This left Elizabeth's grandchild George to succeed to the English throne in 1714 as the first of the Hanoverians.

★ ★ ★

In addition to producing royal children, queen consorts—like all early-modern wives—were expected to be obedient to their husband and act in a subordinate role as his helpmate. This demand was doubly necessary for a queen consort because she owed her royal husband obedience both as a wife and as a subject. James had made clear his own expectations in *Basilikon Doron*, telling his son: 'ye are the head, shee is your body: it is your office to command, and hers to obey'. A queen consort, he went on, should eschew political power and stand aloof from politicking at court, and the prince should never allow his future wife to 'meddle with the politicke government of the commonweale'.[29]

James's counsel was no doubt influenced by his experience of Anna as queen consort in Scotland. There she had entered into a bitter feud with

James's lord chancellor John Maitland and Henry's guardian the earl of Mar.[30] That being said, James held a low opinion—even misogynistic view—of women, as evidenced by his equating queens regnant with minors, tyrants, and 'simple kings' and by his well-known aphorism: 'It hath like operation to make women learned as to make foxes tame, which toucheth them onely to steale more cunningly.'[31] Anna had been given a sound education in Denmark, but she was nowhere near as learned as James, and her lack of fluent Latin gave him a superior edge that he liked to display.[32]

Although Anna had frequently tussled with the king in Scotland, she accepted conventional patriarchal assumptions about a woman's subordinate role. Observers of her conduct in Scotland judged that she 'was nott mynded... to move or do any thing that maye offend the king' and was 'content to obey his wil', even when it flew in the face of her own wishes.[33] In England, she also took account of the king's will and rarely contravened his orders. Nonetheless, her new reign began with two high-profile acts of self-assertion and disobedience.

As we have already seen, Anna went against James's wishes when she took custody of Henry in April 1603. She defied the king further by refusing to communicate with Mar, whom James had dispatched to Stirling to deal with the difficult situation.[34] In her letter to James at that time, Anna apologized for the pain she had caused him by her outbreak of temper, begged him to 'give noe credit to fals reportes' about the incident, and drew attention to her own faltering health, no doubt in order to win his sympathy and forgiveness. In a handwritten postscript, she added: 'My hairt, for Godde's saik tak na cair nor anger, for it will renew ma payne an displesour.'[35] James's response was barely reassuring. He reminded her that she enjoyed the 'love and respecte' which 'by the law of God and nature I ought to do to my wyfe and mother of my children', but that she depended entirely on him for her honour and position. Knowing that she took deep pride in her status as the daughter and sister of a king, he stated categorically that it was as his wife, not as a king's daughter, that she was the 'partaker' of his 'honoure' and 'other fortunes'. He also cautioned her against interfering with his directions and questioning 'an honest and wise servant for his true service to me', namely Mar. Nonetheless, he gave way to what he called her 'wilfulness', and at their reunion in England he showed little sign of anger or irritation.[36]

Anna's second act of disobedience was when she refused to take communion during the coronation service in Westminster Abbey, as her husband had wished.[37] Almost certainly her refusal was the result of her conversion to Catholicism during the 1590s.[38] Yet, apart from this one incident in July 1603, Anna's public practice of her religion was consistently discreet. In England, she attended Protestant services regularly and was publicly churched according to English prayer-book rites after the births of her daughters. Her Danish Protestant chaplain Johann Seringius remained in her household, and there is no record of any permanent Catholic confessor attending upon her.[39] Listening to sermons with her husband, she was known to commend personally at least one Protestant preacher whom she liked.[40] Visitors to her apartments would see no devotional objects nor pictures that were obviously Catholic in the public rooms.[41] Unlike her Catholic successor, Henrietta Maria, Anna did not trumpet her religion and make it part of her identity. Furthermore, English Protestants never forgot that Anna was targeted to die alongside her husband and son in the Gunpowder Plot.[42] For these reasons, Anna's religion never became a political issue in England.

If anything, Anna's Catholicism proved useful rather than embarrassing for James. Knowing full well about her conversion, he exploited it for his own ends before and after 1603. Endeavouring to win the support of the Catholic powers for his succession to the English throne, he spoke freely of Anna's change in religion to their representatives and insinuated that he might follow her example. Anna likewise flaunted her religion as bait at that time. In 1601, when seeking Pope Clement VIII's backing for James's succession, she drew attention to her own covert Catholicism by requesting absolution for attending 'the rites of heretics' that she and other Catholics were 'compelled to endure'.[43] After 1603, Anna's Catholicism was an open secret among many foreign ambassadors although seemingly not among all English privy councillors.[44] Again, James and Anna used it for political advantage. When negotiating the Anglo-Spanish treaty of 1604, James was eager to emphasize that his wife was a Catholic in the hope that it would encourage the Habsburgs to trust that he would not continue the Elizabethan persecutions, which were a barrier to peace.[45] In the later pursuit of a Spanish or Savoyard wife for Henry, Anna again identified herself as a Catholic, although by then the pope and other Catholic rulers doubted her commitment or sincerity.[46]

Several scholars have contended that, soon after her arrival in England, Anna became estranged from her husband and went her own way by maintaining her own household outside James's court and following an independent lifestyle. This breach they put down to the couple's lack of shared interests and James's intimacy with male courtiers.[47] However, there is little evidence of any discord before 1612, though admittedly rumours were occasionally heard that there was 'some displeasure' between them that might lead to a separation.[48] While true that Anna had her own London residence, this practice was customary for royal consorts. Henry VIII's queens had owned Baynard Castle on the Thames. However, since this palace was held by Pembroke in 1603 and unavailable for Anna's use, she was assigned Somerset House on the Strand, which had previously housed foreign embassies. Known as Denmark House, it was to become her principal royal residence once extensive and expensive reconstructions had been completed in 1613.[49] Until then, Anna spent most time at Hampton Court or Greenwich Palace and removed to Whitehall for state occasions. While also true that James was frequently away on protracted hunting trips, Anna usually met him on his return at Theobalds or Hampton Court. The couple usually spent May and June in each other's company at Greenwich, went on progresses together in the summer months, and attended Christmas revels at Whitehall. After 1611, they also met up at Oatlands Palace in Surrey, the Henrician palace gifted to Anna by James that year.[50] After Anna took up full-time residence in Denmark House around early 1617, she and James continued to attend a variety of court functions together and travel jointly on royal progresses. Of course, their time together was essential to court ceremonial and could hardly be avoided without critical comments, but they did share some interests. Anna was a keen huntress, if not in her husband's league, and they both enjoyed playing cards and games.[51]

Just as important, Anna and James had no conspicuous disagreements before the deaths of Henry and Cecil in 1612. Anna had strong preferences in foreign policy, but they were generally in accord with her husband's own views. They both favoured a policy of rapprochement with the Habsburgs; and, provided that the financial terms were right, James was perfectly happy to negotiate a Catholic match for Henry, which Anna more fervently desired. Following gender norms, Anna did not generally vent her views publicly on these or other issues and sometimes even professed 'indifference' about matters of state.[52] Nonetheless, she made her opinions obvious. When she met Arenberg privately during his mission to persuade James to sign a peace treaty with the Habsburgs, she not only wore a miniature portrait of the Infanta Isabella (a gift brought by Arenberg) but stated publicly that the women's 'friendship was as indissoluble as a knot and as strong as a rock'.[53] Similarly, Anna revealed her views through court etiquette. By personally inviting the Spanish ambassador Juan de Tassis, count of Villamediana, to her court masque in January 1604, she again displayed her support for a peace treaty.[54] Later, in 1607, she showed her disapproval of the Dutch quest for a defensive treaty by refusing to grant access to their special ambassadors and absenting herself from their farewell dinner at the Merchant Tailors' Hall in the City, a grand feast and entertainment which the king and Henry attended.[55] More generally, it was noticed whenever she chose to dance with the Spanish ambassador or slighted ambassadors from France, Venice, or the United Provinces.[56]

Pretty much everyone was aware of Anna's pro-Spanish feelings. Yet, in line with James's inclinations, Anna did not neglect the French. When French ambassadors and their families left England in 1606 and 1609, Anna complimented them with gifts of farewell.[57] She also maintained a warm correspondence with Henry IV's wife, Marie de' Medici, exchanges of letters between queens consort being important elements in early modern diplomacy.[58] Immediately upon the conclusion of the Anglo-Spanish treaty, Anna wrote to Marie, who in turn responded graciously, expressing the desire 'to nourish and increase their mutual amite'.[59] After this, Anna wrote regularly to Marie, one time explaining that her letters were a sign of affection and not a 'simple salutation'. Additionally, Anna made sure that Marie received a fine portrait of her as another mark of friendship and goodwill.[60]

When it came to domestic arrangements, there was likewise no conflict between king and queen. Anna was content with James's decision that Charles should remain in Dunfermline until August 1604 when he was brought down to England and put in the charge of Lady Carey. Likewise, she had no concerns about her daughter being placed in the Harington household after Lady Kildare left her post as governess. And she raised no objections to Sir Thomas Chaloner's appointment as Henry's governor, no doubt because she had access to the boy whenever he stayed in one of the London palaces or joined his parents on royal progress. It is true she initially disliked James's choice of husband for her daughter—after all, Frederick was neither a king nor a Catholic—but she made no fuss about it, possibly because her brother favoured the match. Besides, by the time of the wedding, she seemed genuinely fond of her new son-in-law.[61]

The royal couple also had no disputes about the composition of the queen's privy chamber and household.[62] Anna accepted that the king—advised by Cecil—would have final oversight of appointments, and she made no protest on the rare occasions that James intervened to override her preferences. In the spring of 1603, at the king's command, she let go of the Scottish courtier Mr Kennedy, who was her first choice for the post of chamberlain, and she allowed Lady Audrey Walsingham to be foisted upon her as the guardian and keeper of her robes. It ended up a good choice as shortly afterwards Walsingham became a close friend.[63]

Anna's easy relations with James during these years owed a great deal to the rapport she enjoyed with his principal secretary. Unlike the dislike she had felt for Maitland and Mar in Scotland, she was genuinely fond of Cecil. They exchanged tokens, and he was the only male courtier who was allowed 'to comfort the queen' after the death of her daughter Mary. When he was mortally ill in 1612, although thought to be recovering, Anna visited him 'every second day'.[64] In his post as lord high steward of her estates and a member of her council, Cecil worked in Anna's interests, and she bowed to his decisions in matters of patronage. Cecil also operated as a bridge between king and queen, each using him to convey their wishes and personal messages to the other. When Anna was slandered by some 'knave', James asked Cecil to go with Dunbar to tell the queen what had happened and that he knew the story of her adultery was groundless.[65]

After the deaths of Cecil in May and Henry in November 1612, Anna found herself more isolated from James. The couple did not seek to comfort each other when their adored son died but, on the contrary, kept apart 'for fear to refresh the sense of the wound and each to aggrandise the other's grief in their mutuall lamentations'.[66] Although Cecil's death was not an emotional blow to either of them, it brought James further under the influence of Robert Carr (soon to become earl of Somerset), a Scot whom Anna distrusted and detested. As a result, she aligned herself with Carr's enemies seeking to replace him with George Villiers (later duke of Buckingham), the first time Anna entered factional politics in England.[67] Even then, we should be wary about exaggerating the differences between the royal couple. In the summer of 1613, while the queen was shooting deer at Theobalds, she 'mistooke her marke' and killed the king's 'most principall and special hound':

> at which he stormed exceedingly a while, but after he knew who did yt, he was sore pacified and with much kindness wisht her not to be troubled with yt, for he shold love her never the worse, and the next day sent her a diamond worth £2,000 as a legacie from his dead dogge: love and kindness increases dayly between them and yt is thought they were never in better termes.[68]

Later that year, James settled on Anna the palace of Greenwich, much to the annoyance of Northampton who was in possession of the lodge.[69] Four years later, the royal couple were on sufficiently good terms that James appointed her to the six-person council that was to rule England while he returned to Scotland.

* * *

Far from being an oppositional figure at court, Anna worked as James's 'helpmate' or representative during their early years together in England. In January 1605, he addressed complaints about his absences in the countryside by instructing privy councillors to assemble once a week 'in such places as our deerest wife shall kepe her courte', as this would lend a royal aura and hence authority to conciliar proceedings.[70] Additionally, the queen hosted ambassadors in her apartments, participated in ritualized gift exchanges with foreign rulers or their representatives, and staged royal entertainments. Her activities added to the king's efforts to forge close diplomatic relationships with Continental powers.

Anna was also important in the politics of display. Historians used to censure her for the heavy expenditure on clothes and jewellery. But, thanks to a better understanding of the importance of material culture, scholars today are far less critical. They appreciate that Anna's clothes and jewels were an indispensable component of magnificence, the display of majesty, wealth, and stylishness essential to a Renaissance court. Since James normally preferred to dress modestly, in accordance with the rules that he had laid down in *Basilikon Doron*, it was usually left to Anna to maintain the glitter that had been a feature of Elizabeth's court.[71] Onlookers were expected to be impressed, and they often were, relating Anna's appearance and the cost of the jewels to correspondents. At the wedding of her daughter in February 1613, admittedly a special occasion, the queen looked resplendent in a white satin gown and adorned with jewels: in her hair were 'a great number of pear-shaped pearls, the largest and most beautiful there are in the world; and there were diamonds all over her person, so that she was ablaze'.[72]

Despite her Scottish wardrobe and the clothes inherited from the late queen, the cost of Anna's wardrobe soon outstripped that of Elizabeth, whose own garments had been ornate and opulent. Indeed, the expense was so great that Anna's income from her dower could not cover the cost, and James frequently had to bale her out when she fell into debt for huge sums with London 'artificers'.[73] In her wardrobe, Anna made a conscious effort to dress in accordance with English fashions of the 1590s. She replaced the high-necked garments and ruffs worn in Scotland with the standing collars and lower necklines fashionable at the late Elizabethan court and wore the farthingale, even though the wide-hooped skirt was starting to go out of fashion in England. Perhaps Anna was seeking to signify continuity with Elizabeth, and perhaps she was also asserting her Danish identity and relationship with her sisters married to German princes, for the farthingale remained popular in the royal courts of northern Europe.[74]

Like all royalty, Anna favoured expensive fabrics—satin, taffeta, silks—all highly decorated with lace or embroidered in gold, silver, and coloured silks. The colours she tended to wear for formal occasions were white and crimson, which had also been favourites of Elizabeth. Also, like Elizabeth, she chose figurative emblems for embroidery designs—stars, suns, clouds, flies, birds, half-moons, feathers, fountains, esses, flowers, and butterflies—motifs that carried symbolic meanings.[75] The peacock feathers embroidered on Anna's dress in the Woburn portrait, for instance, signified her royal status since the bird represented Juno, queen of the Roman gods (see Figure 13).[76]

Again, like Elizabeth and other queens, Anna loved jewellery: she had over four hundred pieces for her own use in 1606, although not all had been purchased. Some items were inherited while others were gifts. Nonetheless, between 1605 and 1615, Anna paid over £42,000 [some £5.6 million in today's money] to her main jeweller, the Scot George Heriot, still owing him nearly £11,000 in unpaid bills at the time the accounts were drawn up. Other jewellers—notably the German Sir John Spillman and Englishman Sir William Herrick—likewise received thousands of pounds in remuneration. Many of the bills were paid from Anna's personal dower income, but at times the money came from James's privy purse or the exchequer, either when she had overspent or when the items purchased were for diplomatic gifts.[77]

Some of the payments were for repairs, but most were for the purchase of new pieces or the refiguration of old ones to make them more fashionable and reflect her own taste; Anna much preferred flowers, insects, and birds to the classical and mythological subjects liked by Elizabeth.[78] Nonetheless, Anna's choice of jewels could be equally symbolic. The anchor hanging below her collar, seen in a miniature by Isaac Oliver, represented the Christian symbol of hope; the diamond crossbow bodkin she wore in her hair was an expression of her love of hunting as well as a symbol of the power of reasoning over brute strength. Often, Anna wore jewelled letters,

Figure 13. The 'Woburn Portrait' of Anna of Denmark by Marcus Gheeraerts the Younger, *c.*1611–14 Woburn Abbey/Wikipedia.

a traditional fashion in Denmark, and her favourites were the initials 'S' and 'C' standing for her mother Sophie and brother Christian IV. Not only sentiment and familial devotion prompted this choice; the initials displayed the royal heritage in which she took such pride.[79] Jewels Anna purchased were not only worn; they were also set in picture frames, used to decorate ornate cups, or 'garnish' silver dog collars.[80]

Other jewels bought by Anna were tendered to ambassadors or members of foreign courts as part of customary gift exchanges. The queen would often supplement James's own presentations (usually plate and a chain, and sometimes a portrait) with fine jewellery that had added value as a personal gift.[81] Shortly after James had negotiated the end to the Anglo-Spanish war, Anna presented a jewel (then worth £260, now about £36,000) to Arenberg and gave lockets containing miniature portraits of herself and James in a jewelled case (then worth £1,000, now about £138,000) to Juan Fernández de Velasco, the fifth duke of Frías and constable of Castile, together with a necklace set with rich pearls for his wife.[82] This was an exceptional gift for an exceptional occasion; most often, Anna's present to a favoured ambassador was a simple diamond ring, sometimes containing a portrait of her and James, while miniatures set in jewelled cases were sent to foreign royals.[83]

Anna's gift-giving was naturally reciprocated. Foreign princes, their wives, and ambassadors gave jewels, paintings, and horses to the queen. In certain—though rare—circumstances the presents were immensely valuable. To mark the signing of the 1604 Anglo-Spanish peace, Anna received from the constable of Castile a gold cross embellished with 260 diamonds, costing £1,087 in English currency, three pendants set with diamonds, costing £3,250, and a dragon-shaped crystal cup, costing £111, from which James's health was drunk at the banquet held in Whitehall to celebrate the ratification of the peace treaty.[84] It was the munificence of these gifts that prompted the presentation of the queen's expensive gifts to the constable at his departure. Even so, Anna did very well out of the exchange.

Anna frequently put the gifts she received on display. She was painted several times wearing a brooch in the form of a crowned initial C4, a present from her brother Christian, while portraits of her foreign family members—presumably gifts—were hung in the great gallery at Denmark House. Part of formal diplomatic exchanges, these were exhibited to flatter the donor, exhibit Anna's own royal connections, and demonstrate the close relations between Britain and foreign courts.[85] Few gifts were offered outside this formal pattern of exchange. However, in late 1603, the pope sent Anna a semi-private gift of a relic of the true cross, four rosaries, and other devotional items in the false belief that she had requested some sacred objects and in the misplaced hope that it would encourage her to use her influence with James on behalf of fellow Catholics. Attached to one of the rosaries was a plenary indulgence for anyone who prayed daily over the period of a month for the restoration of the Catholic faith in England and the conversion of the king.[86] All these objects were banned by law from England, and the indulgence was an affront to England's religion and the royal supremacy. They were 'returned back again *sub silentio*' by the king.[87] Now that he was successfully seated on the throne of anti-papal England, he could not allow his wife to have a semi-independent relationship with Rome which broke English laws and challenged his patriarchal authority.[88]

★ ★ ★

During the medieval and early modern periods, queens consort acted as intercessors with reigning kings, often being used as an invaluable conduit to request mercy from royal justice. The model here was Esther in the Hebrew Bible, who had successfully pleaded with her husband King Ahasueras [Xerxes] to spare the Jews from the destruction planned by the evil counsellor Haman. A more recent exemplar was Katherine of Aragon who (in drama at least) successfully interceded for subjects taxed to the point of rebellion and unsuccessfully pleaded for the life of the earl of Buckingham charged with treason.[89] Anna was expected to perform this same mode of intercession. When on progress at Bristol in 1613, she viewed at the docks a staged sea battle between Christians and Turks that ended with a Christian victory and Turkish captives who:

> ...brought before her Grace on bended knees did crave
> For mercy, which her Majestie with pardon freely gave.[90]

Yet Anna rarely played this role in real life. As far as we know, she made no attempt to secure pardons for the subjects who participated in the 1607 wave of protests against enclosure, known as the Midlands Rising. Nor did she help imprisoned fellow Catholics despite requests from foreign rulers who thought she might be a co-religionist. The wife of the archduke's ambassador to England begged more than once for her to intercede and secure the liberty of ten priests, but these woman-to-woman communications made no discernible impression.[91] Nonetheless, there are a few extant letters that show Anna intervening to promote the suits of individuals, some of whom were Catholics. In June 1604, she wrote to Cecil of her 'desire' that he would look favourably at a case in star chamber of a gentleman who had entertained her the previous year in Yorkshire.[92] In August 1606, she recommended Anthony Standen, her Catholic 'servant', to her kinswoman Christina of Lorraine, the grand duchess of Tuscany. James had licensed Standen to travel abroad after a spell in the Tower. However, the duchess may have done little for him since he saw out his days in Rome.[93]

On the rare occasions when Anna interceded on behalf of a high-profile individual in serious trouble with the king, she greatly annoyed her husband and usually got nowhere. Her attempt to protect Lord Balmerino, who was put on trial in 1609 for allegedly forging the king's name on a letter to the pope, was met with a stern reprimand: 'If she did medle in a thing thus belonging to my honour, it mighte well harme her self but it wolde never move me.'[94] When Anna tried again, she did so indirectly. This time, 'on ner [one near] to the quen's majestie' wrote to Dunbar, who was then in Edinburgh, stating that, if Balmerino died, 'the quen would kerp itt in her hartt' and blame the earl and the king 'so longe as she levitt [lived] in this world'; and, according to Balmerino, out of respect for the queen, Dunbar did speak up for him.[95] Balmerino was reprieved, but it is unlikely that James saved him simply to please Anna.[96] Around the same time, Anna's old friend Henrietta, marchioness of Huntly, 'sent a special messenger to the queen to beg her Majesty to intercede on behalf of the marquis, her husband, who was in prison on account of his religion'. Again, James refused to listen to his wife's appeals. He drafted the answer to Henrietta 'in the queen's name', saying that 'she could not offer any opposition to the royal orders on this point, but would rather do all she could to see that they [his orders] were carried out and confirmed'.[97] Anna was equally unsuccessful in her attempts to help Arbella Stuart after her abortive elopement and spare the life of Ralegh in 1618.[98] Evidently, James did not respect his consort's role to beg for clemency but rather damned it as an attempt to undermine his orders.

Another form of intercession expected of a queen consort was the promotion of policies dear to her heart and in the public interest. Anne Boleyn and Katherine Parr, for example, had achieved fame in Foxe's *Actes and Monuments* as godly sponsors of evangelical reform. In the case of Anna, English Catholics hoped that she would press her husband to allow religious toleration. They were soon to be disappointed. During her progress to London in 1603, 'many ladyes' came out of Lancashire and other counties in the north to petition her to urge upon the king 'toleration of relygyon', but Anna's apparent lack of interest and definite unwillingness to act possibly discouraged further appeals.[99] In the expectation that she might have an influence on her son as well as her husband, Anna received a petition exhorting her to persuade both men to invest in the promotion of overseas discoveries and settlements. As it ended up in Cecil's papers, she likely handed it on to Henry who had a livelier interest in colonial exploration and settlement.[100] Otherwise, the queen was mainly left alone.

Finally, a queen consort was expected to bestow patronage on her friends and servants, indeed anyone in her favour.[101] Unlike other married women, she was a *femme sole* in law, owning lands that were part of her jointure. It was a privileged position that gave her not only an independent income but also—theoretically at least—the right of presentation to certain offices and benefices on her lands. Anna had two jointures, a Scottish one (which included the lands and castles in Dunfermline, Falkland, and Leith) bringing in an annual income of around £6,755 sterling (£950,000 in today's currency); and a jointure in England which was based on that of Katherine of Aragon and brought in another £6,376 a year in 1603.[102] By act of parliament, Anna was given the power to make leases of all her manors, and with her own household Anna could also offer people positions at court.[103] Unsurprisingly, then, ambitious women dashed north on hearing of James's accession with the intent of obtaining places in her service. By the time that she arrived at Windsor, her women had been appointed but there was still 'great sute' amongst men 'for place and ofice abowt her'.[104]

However, it soon became clear that Cecil—rather than Anna—was the patron with power. His approval was needed for all the early appointments to her household; and later on he had to authorize her grants of land and confirm her nominations to office.[105] When promoting a suit to her husband, Anna almost always did so with Cecil's 'privity and allowance'.[106] So, although it was said that Sir Thomas Parry obtained the reversion of an office 'by the queene's favor', Anna's success was only possible because of Parry's friendship with Cecil.[107] When she did attempt to use her influence in the interests of a suitor, she was ineffectual if her wishes did not correspond to those of the secretary.[108] Anna's consistent success as a patron only came in the field of the arts where she commissioned dramatists, musicians, portraitists, and architects of her own choice.

★ ★ ★

The importance of Anna's—and later Henry's—patronage of the arts in enhancing the reputation of the king and the Stuart courts should not be underestimated. Anna's role here was analogous to that of queen consorts on the Continent, and she carried it off brilliantly. The art form most associated with her, both at the time and since, was the masque, a theatrical performance combining poetry, song, and dance for a private audience. Masques had been staged at Elizabeth's court, but Anna's productions were very different. For a start, they were more formal, elaborate, and expensive than anything seen before. Even more important, for the first time ever, the performers included women—usually the queen and eleven ladies—most of whom were the wives of courtiers.[109] Men and boys had the speaking and singing roles, but the women were costumed, mimed their parts, and danced by themselves before they selected partners for the dance at the masque's conclusion. Although new to England, the ladies of Philip II and III's courts in Spain promoted masques, while in France Marie de' Medici commissioned and choreographed theatrical productions, known as *grands ballets*, in which she and aristocratic women danced before the court.[110] In all, Anna performed in seven masques at the Jacobean court, six of which are discussed in the next chapter.

Once he reached adulthood, Henry too was a patron of masques. The year of the sixteen-year-old's investiture as prince of Wales and earl of Chester, he commissioned and participated in two masques: on 6 January 1610, the 'Barriers', a combined tournament and masque to mark his coming of age; and the following January *Oberon: The Faery Prince*, an extravaganza written by Ben Jonson, designed by Inigo Jones, with music supplied by Henry's music tutor Alfonso Ferrabosco II.[111]

Sharing his mother's aesthetic tastes, Henry followed Anna in promoting the Italianate and French styles of architecture and garden design, which she had first encountered during her childhood in Denmark and Norway. Both royals commissioned architects who planned the integration of house and gardens so that each one was viewed as the extension of the other, a characteristic of Continental royal palaces. For their gardens, moreover, both chose to introduce elaborate and magnificent water features that were common in Italy and Denmark.

At Somerset House, in 1609, Anna ordered the layout of the grounds before the building was remodelled so that an integration would be possible. She first commissioned a new terraced privy garden to be situated to the east of the house, which was based on French geometrical designs that had originated in Italy. A little later, an orangery was planted and housed, another innovative development for English gardens but fashionable in France. Then, probably in 1610, Anna employed the French engineer Salomon de Caus to devise and execute a vast grotto fountain of Mount Parnassus in the garden. Shortly afterwards, de Caus designed for her a gilded fountain of a river goddess for Greenwich Palace.[112]

Henry followed suit. In 1610, he hired the Florentine court architect and engineer Constantino de' Servi to create a similar Italian-style garden at

Richmond, with fountains, grottoes, ponds, a hippodrome, and a gigantic statue of Neptune. But as de' Servi arrived later than expected, the prince brought de Caus into his household. The garden plan devised by de' Servi had envisaged two main spaces: a smaller area containing heraldic elements for festive performances against the backdrop of the older Tudor buildings; and a larger garden containing Roman monuments, which was classical in atmosphere. However, Henry's death put paid to the execution of the plans.[113] It is worth noting that James's interest in gardens was different in kind: his approach seems to have been largely utilitarian, confined to establishing mulberry plantations for the purpose of developing a silk industry in England.[114] Nonetheless, he was prepared to support his wife's endeavours by covering the cost from the crown's revenues.

When it came to the design of the actual buildings, Anna again turned to Continental models. She introduced classical elements into Somerset House, which transformed the old-fashioned Tudor mansion into an *avant garde* Italianate palace, and she reorientated its state apartments so that they would overlook the gardens, not a dull courtyard.[115] Henry was not a builder on that scale, but he too planned internal alterations in the Italianate style for his palaces. Towards the end of his life, Inigo Jones was employed as surveyor of his works.[116]

Fortunately for the public coffers, James did not share his wife's and son's enthusiasm for expensive and expansive architectural projects. Like Elizabeth, he commissioned no major building works. But then he had no need to. In 1607, Anna acquired Cecil's palatial house, gardens, and parks of Theobalds in Hertfordshire, to which James made some small internal improvements, and which became his favourite royal property in the country. Otherwise, he confined himself to refurbishing new apartments in existing palaces for his queen, overhauling the kitchens at Hampton Court as well as commissioning new accommodation for his hunting lodges.[117] In 1606, he did feel the need to replace 'the old rotten, sleight builded, banquetting house', constructed for his predecessor at Whitehall, but the new edifice was purely functional, not stylish. And James noticeably disliked certain of its features, such as the 'pillars which are sett up before the windowes', so he probably felt no regret when the building burned down in 1619.[118] It was then that Inigo Jones designed the elegant, classical banqueting house that graces Whitehall today.

For her new palaces, Anna assembled furnishings, carpets, and hangings, many embroidered with her initials. She put on display her collection of paintings: portraits of extended family and other European monarchs; biblical scenes (mainly New Testament); interiors (such as a Dutch kitchen); landscapes; and pictures of ordinary people (for instance, 'a picture of an old woman gapinge').[119] Henry too was an enthusiastic collector of art. He used Sir Edward Conway, governor of Brill, to purchase works for him from the Netherlands and Sir Henry Wotton, the resident ambassador in Venice, as his agent there.[120] The Venetian ambassador noted that, once prince of Wales, Henry paid 'special attention' to filling a new picture gallery at St James with 'very fine pictures, ancient and modern, the larger part brought out of Venice'.[121] Although Anna and Henry were more avid art collectors than James, the king too instructed diplomats working in Venice and Brussels to purchase works of art to add to the royal collection.[122]

When it came to commissioning painters for her own portrait, Anna initially accepted her husband's lead. During her first decade in England, she relied on the Flemish John de Critz, who had been active at Elizabeth's court in the 1590s and was appointed a serjeant painter shortly after James's accession.[123] He and his workshop painted at least nine full-length or three-quarter-length portraits of Anna as well as portraits of James and Henry, some of which were sent to foreign rulers.[124] Whether by her choice or his, de Critz depicted Anna in a pose similar to that preferred by Elizabeth: both standing close to a throne, without royal insignia, turning slightly towards their right, decked in pearls, and with emblematic flowers and creatures sewn into their gowns. Naturally, Anna was not portrayed with emblems of virginity, as the older Elizabeth had been; indeed, it is very probable that these early portraits of Anna were hung and viewed as companion pieces to those of James.

Around 1611, Anna chose her own portraitists whose works were more adventurous. By then, she had employed Inigo Jones to rebuild and refurbish Greenwich Palace, again in the fashionable Italianate style, and the portraits she commissioned were undoubtedly intended for her new houses. In the 'Woburn Portrait', painted by Marcus Gheeraerts the Younger sometime after 1611, Anna stands before a classical arch with a garden beyond (see Figure 13); one by Paul van Somer a little later shows her hunting in the countryside.

Another portraitist of Anna and her children was the Englishman Robert Peake. In 1607, James appointed him serjeant-painter alongside de Critz, but, in 1610, he may have become Henry's official portraitist.[125] Peake's style was flat, static, and decorative without the spatial depth of fashionable European works, but he produced a couple of novel portraits of Henry as a boy. His 1603 painting shows the prince in movement, sheathing a sword after killing a deer in the pose of a Roman hero (see Figure 14). Almost certainly the portrait was originally commissioned by John, Baron Harington of Exton, whose son was also in the scene, and was intended as a companion piece for Peake's portrait of the prince's sister, bearing the same date.

Figure 14. Prince Henry and Sir John Harington by Robert Peake the Elder (1603) © Joseph Pulitzer Bequest, 1944, Metropolitan Museum of Art, New York City.

Northampton is thought to have commissioned Peake's equally unusual full-size portrait of the young prince in armour and on horseback, his sword aloft, followed by Father Time holding Henry's lance and helmet.[126]

For miniatures, Anna was again more adventurous than her husband. James retained Elizabeth's limner Nicholas Hilliard and employed him to paint Anna and the royal children as well as himself. Between 1603 and 1618, Hilliard was responsible for at least fifteen miniature portraits of James, five of Anna, two of Henry, three of Charles, and one each of Elizabeth and her husband.[127] But Anna much preferred to use Isaac Oliver, whom she appointed her household limner in 1604 or 1605, and there survive about a dozen of his portraits of the queen consort. Oliver's elegant and naturalistic style was then popular at Continental courts, whereas Hilliard—who rejected the use of *chiaroscuro* and depended heavily on line for his effects— was beginning to look somewhat old-fashioned.[128] From 1608, Henry also became Oliver's patron, and, after 1610, the limner was attached to his household at St James's Palace. Oliver's exquisite miniature of Henry in gilt armour against a background of an encampment represented the prince as a chivalric champion just as he appeared in the 'Barriers' of the same year (see Figure 15).

As well as commissioning and buying paintings, Anna and Henry started to fill their new palaces with collections of objects, a practice that was common among Renaissance princes. For her palaces, the queen amassed sets of chessmen and boards, mechanical clocks, chests and cabinets, porcelain, and statuary.[129] The prince filled his new gallery at St James with sculptures, coins, medals, engraved gems, and curiosities.[130] James appears more alive to the value of commissioning medals than of collecting them: these included silver coronation medals for his and Anna's coronation (the first time an English coronation was marked in this way) and a medal to commemorate the Anglo-Spanish peace of 1604.[131]

Like many nobles, the royal family were patrons of musicians, taking instrumentalists and singers into their independent households. Anna had learned to play on stringed instruments in Denmark under the tutelage of Thomas Robinson but may not have played much in England, preferring to listen.[132] She appreciated the Italianate style and introduced foreign players of the lute and viol into her household. One of her musicians was John Maria Lugario, who had previously been employed at the court of Mantua, and, on his departure in 1612, she took on four Danish musicians (a gift from Christian IV) who had been trained in Italy.[133] Ferrabosco usually contributed the music for Jonson's masques, although whether he was her

Figure 15. Miniature of Prince Henry by Isaac Oliver, Royal Collection, RCIN 420058. Royal Collection Trust © His Majesty King Charles III 2023.

choice or the dramatist's is unknown. However, judging from dedications, Anna was not a noted patron of individual musicians. Her old music tutor Robinson sought patronage not from her but from James in 1603 and afterwards Cecil.[134] The earliest piece of music dedicated to her—John Dowland's *Lachrimae or Seaven Teares*—had originally been intended for

Queen Elizabeth in 1603.[135] Despite the dedication, Dowland obtained no place in Anna's household on his permanent return to England from Christian IV's court in 1606, although this may be because he left Denmark under something of a cloud. The talented lutenist remained in private service until he secured an appointment in the 'king's musick' in October 1612.[136] The Scottish musician Tobias Hume received some small payments from Anna for his music, but his dedicatory letter to her (attached to the flyleaf of a second collection of compositions) reeks of desperation for patronage: 'I doe in all humylitie beseech your majestie that you woulde be pleased to hear this musicke by mee; having excellent instruments to performe itt.'[137] What is more, Anna evidently did not like the pieces sufficiently, as Hume had to look elsewhere for a patron. The 1607 printed version of his *Poeticall Musicke* was dedicated to the earl of Arundel.[138] The last piece of music known to have been dedicated to Anna before 1612 was a theory of musical intervals and compositions written by Salomon de Caus, who was better known as her garden designer. In his dedication to Anna, de Caus referred to her love of music but explained that he was not looking for musical patronage; if she was pleased with his 'small labour', he wrote, it would encourage him to publish a treatise on the building of hydraulic machines.[139]

Henry too enjoyed music. His household accounts reveal that he installed a 'great organ' in St James, and presumably employed someone to play it; the same year he purchased instruments and songbooks for 'a singing boye'.[140] As with his house and gardens, he was experimental and Continental in his tastes, bringing an Italianate repertory into his household. The prince played music as well. The viol player and composer Ferrabosco was his teacher while Thomas Giles instructed him to dance in the French fashion, after the death of Nicholas Villiard in 1605.[141]

Because it was the king's decision to bring all aristocratic theatrical companies under royal patronage, James, Anna, and all three children were given their own companies of players. In practice, their patronage seems to have been in name rather than deed for they did not choose or vet their company's repertory. But the royal licence protected the men in the companies from the vagabondage laws that imposed punishments on travelling players.

Anna was the official patron of two theatrical companies: the 'Queen's Servants' formed in 1603 from the earl of Worcester's men; and the 'Children of the Chapel' renamed and relicensed as 'Children of the Queen's Revels' in 1604.[142] This latter company, based in the Blackfriars playhouse, put on several controversial plays that got its playwrights into trouble. The first was Samuel Daniel's history play *Philotas*, performed at court in 1604, which seemed to be referencing the downfall of the earl of Essex and portraying Cecil as the devious counsellor Craterus. Daniel—then in great favour with Anna—was hauled before the privy council but was let off with a warning probably through the influence of his other patron Charles, earl of Devonshire, although possibly Anna too intervened on his behalf.[143] More seriously, in 1605, *Eastward Ho* aroused James's 'high displeasure' and 'indignation' for its offensive treatment of the Scots. Two of its three authors—George Chapman and Ben Jonson—were briefly imprisoned, but as far as we can tell, the men did not call upon Anna to intercede.[144] Moreover, when released, they gave thanks to Lord Chamberlain Suffolk, not the queen.[145] John Day's *The Isle of Gulls* performed in February 1606 was the last straw for the company, as it cleverly satirized the court, Cecil, and the Scots.[146] There was 'much speech' at court about the play, and punishment this time not only meant the imprisonment of the leading actors but also resulted in the loss of the royal patent and transfer of the company's lease of Blackfriars theatre to the 'King's Men' in 1608. Royal displeasure did not last long, however. In 1610, the company received another royal patent and continued performances without incident.[147] Some literary scholars have suggested that Anna enjoyed the plays that mocked her husband; however, it is extremely unlikely that she had any say in the company's repertoire or foreknowledge of the plays' content.[148] Anyway, after 1606, she seems to have withdrawn her patronage from the company.[149]

Samuel Daniel had been appointed the licenser of the Children of the Revels [responsible for licensing the company's plays for performance at court] in 1604, but he sold his post the next year and later entered Anna's household as a groom of her privy chamber, a position that gave him the leisure to write for the queen and other courtly patrons.[150] Another groom was the renowned linguist John Florio, who had likewise been introduced to Anna by Lucy, countess of Bedford.[151] Florio became Anna's Italian secretary and was also tasked with tutoring the young royals in Italian and French. In gratitude for her 'protection and patronage', Florio renamed the 1611 edition and expanded version of his Italian–English dictionary *Queen Anna's New World of Words* and, in 1613, he dedicated the second edition of his translation of Montaigne's essays to her with a poem praising her magnanimity and virtue.[152] For the important post of secretary—ranked fourth in order of precedence in her household—Anna favoured Scottish literati:

the post was first held by Fowler, whom she had brought with her from Scotland and, in 1611, by the poet Sir Robert Ayton. Ayton had been a groom of the James's privy chamber and saw himself as a courtier rather than a poet. His Latin and English verses were, nonetheless, appreciated by other courtiers and turned into songs.[153]

★ ★ ★

While Anna and Henry had similar cultural tastes, they differed radically in their religion and European sympathies. As already seen, Anna was a crypto-Catholic and pro-Habsburg, whereas Henry was surrounded and educated by Protestants suspicious of Spain. His long-serving tutor Adam Newton was Presbyterian, while his governor Chaloner was a steadfast Protestant who had served under Elizabeth in the Netherlands and France against Spain.[154]

The differences between Henry and his mother came to the fore when he was old enough to have a say in his marriage. Anna had always been keen on a Spanish bride for her son and, during the 1604 peace negotiations, gave Philip III's ambassadors encouragement to pursue such a match. In the discussions that intermittently followed over the next few years, Anna continued her support while James kept his options open and Henry—as far as we know—kept quiet.[155] However, once he came of age in 1610, Henry's opinions could not be ignored, and there was a greater urgency in settling his future. By then, moreover, the fourteen-year-old Elizabeth was thought ready to enter the marriage market; that summer, the king of Sweden requested her hand for his son.[156]

During 1611, several foreign courts made bids for James's two elder children. In March, an ambassador arrived from Duke Charles Emmanuel I of Savoy with instructions to propose a marriage between his heir Victor Amadeus, prince of Piedmont, and Elizabeth 'with insinuation, likewise' that the duke would favour a marriage between Henry and his eldest daughter. At the very same time, Philip III intimated that he would welcome an English husband for the Infanta Anna, and in late spring James sent John Digby, the future earl of Bristol, as ambassador to Spain with instructions to request her hand for his son. However, Philip swiftly withdrew from the offer because he had already agreed on a Franco-Spanish double marriage which would see her married to Louis XIII of France. Philip could now only propose one of his younger daughters for the English prince, a substitution James found insulting. Adding injury to insult, Philip then spoke of the need to obtain papal permission before going forward, even implying that Henry would need to convert.[157]

In any case, Henry had no wish to marry a Spanish princess and far preferred to take a German Protestant bride. But this was ruled out on pragmatic grounds after a match was agreed in the spring of 1611 between Elizabeth and the Elector-Palatine Frederick V, a leader of the Protestant Union of German states. Another German Protestant dynastic alliance would add nothing to England's security, nor would it offer a large dowry. The remaining choices lay between the daughter of the Catholic duke of Savoy and the sister of the grand duke of Tuscany.[158] Because the Savoyard girl was a niece of Philip III, Anna preferred this match and ignored the appeals of the duchess of Tuscany who vainly tried to win her over on the basis of some distant dynastic connection between their families. Although in February 1611, the Venetian ambassador Marc' Antonio Correr relayed that Anna favoured the Tuscan match 'more than any other', his successor Antonio Foscarini reported in April 1612: 'The queen hates this match; she cannot endure to hear it spoken of and does all she can to alienate the mind of the prince, who is in fact opposed to it.'[159] Some leading members of the prince's household (including Chaloner), together with Cecil, did favour a Tuscan marriage while the archbishop of Canterbury George Abbot spoke out against the Savoy match because the duke had several times attacked Calvinist Geneva.[160] In fact, by 1612, the duke had not only abandoned his claims to Geneva but was also coming into conflict with Spain because of Savoy's expansionist ambitions in northern Italy.[161]

James wanted the marriage which would provide the larger dowry and help him out of his financial hole. Nevertheless, he was prepared to allow his son some choice. As he told Cecil: 'the prince owre sonn was now by God's grace advaunced to so much rypenesse of age and judgment as we could not denie him the freedome of his owne choice when he should be disposed to intertayne any motions of that kinde'.[162] However, Henry desired neither match: he 'comanded' Ralegh to write against a marriage with the Savoyard and Sir Charles Cornwallis (treasurer of his household) to present his negative views on the Tuscan proposal.[163] Nevertheless, negotiations with both princes trickled on.

Then in May 1612, a new offer arrived for the prince. The duke of Bouillon arrived in England that month to propose a marriage between James's son and Christine, the six-year-old sister of Louis XIII of France. Louis's mother, the French regent Marie de' Medici, wanted to counterbalance the recently arranged Franco-Spanish dynastic alliance with an English marriage, while Bouillon—a Huguenot—was looking to counteract Habsburg influence in both France and England.[164] This match was tempting for James: first, it could provide some security if his alliance with Philip III—then under severe strain—fell apart. Second, it was financially advantageous: the duke of Savoy had offered a dowry of 700,000 crowns (£210,000), but the French now upped it to 800,000 crowns (£240,000).[165] Again, James wanted Henry to have his say. On 29 July, he asked his son to set down in writing his opinions about the two suits. In his answer, Henry left the decision to his father but expressed his readiness to marry a Catholic on condition that she practised her religion only 'in her most private and secret chamber'. Henry also noted that a French marriage would 'give the greatest contentment and satisfaction to the general body of Protestants abroad', implying that it met with his approval.[166] He was probably correct in this assessment. Ralegh's pamphlet objecting to the Savoy match had promoted a French one, and it was widely copied and circulated.[167] Had Henry not died in 1612, a French marriage might well have been the outcome, overriding Anna's wishes, just as the marriage of her daughter to Frederick was initially not her will.

★ ★ ★

The arrival in England of a queen consort and her children had both political and cultural significance. On the positive side, the question of the succession that had dominated the Tudor period disappeared, or at least it did until the mini-crisis that temporarily followed Henry's death. For years, the prince had accompanied his father on public occasions, whether at formal meetings of ambassadors, sitting alongside him at meetings with privy councillors and MPs, or joining him on summer progresses. Until 1612, therefore, James's subjects had the reassurance that his heir would be well prepared for rule on his eventual accession.

For the most part, Anna kept out of the political limelight, yet she too played an important supportive role in political life. When the king was hunting in the countryside, she provided a valuable royal presence in London: she met ambassadors in his absence, and the council assembled in her house. She frequently agreed to become the godparent of courtiers' children, and she hosted the weddings of some of her ladies at Somerset House.[168] Her royal pedigree, moreover, contributed to James's prestige at home and abroad. Her lineage was proudly displayed on contemporary genealogies; and her coat of arms and that of her family were painted and carved on surfaces throughout her houses.[169] The visits of her brothers (Christian IV and Ulrik) and nephew (Frederick Ulrik, duke of Brunswick) signalled James's international worth to fellow rulers. At the same time, Anna avoided entanglement in disputes between family members. During the Cleves succession crisis of 1609 and 1610, members of her wider family took opposing stands, Christian IV supporting one candidate and Anna's brother-in-law the duke of Saxony supporting another. Wisely, Anna did not take sides and left policy to James.[170]

Also on the positive side, the presence of a royal family was beneficial to the crown because of the opportunities it offered for celebratory functions— baptisms, investitures, and a marriage—that enhanced the grandeur and splendour of monarchy both at court and in the provinces. On St George's Day 1610, for example, Henry's investiture occasioned the performance of the pageant 'Chester's Triumph in Honor of her Prince' in the Cheshire town.[171] Furthermore, a young and good-looking royal family was more glamourous than the elderly figure of Elizabeth who could not hide her wrinkled skin and rotting teeth during the last years of her life. And since the conduct of Anna and her children was dignified, it brought esteem to a court which intermittently appeared disorderly. Henry built up a reputation as a morally principled young man while Anna was viewed as 'chaste and rich in virtue'.[172] Although more in the background, Princess Elizabeth was noted as a beauty and 'most graceful in dancing and all her other actions' during her appearances at court. And, of course, her wedding made a huge splash.[173]

On the negative side, the expenditure of the royal household rocketed. The total cost of the wardrobe during the first five years of James's reign was set at £83,900, which contrasted sharply with the £21,300 spent in the last five years of Elizabeth's reign.[174] By the end of 1604, the privy council was growing concerned about the increase and suggesting royal discipline while, after the Christmas revels of 1604–05, 'ordinary people' were complaining about the 'wastfull and idle expence' in the court, especially as the 'the dett of the state' was 'so great'.[175] It was not only clothes, jewels, and the everyday expenses of three courts that ate away at the crown's revenues. Vast sums were paid out for extraordinary events such as Anna's lying in before child-birth (amounting to £15,593), the funerals of the royal children, and the wedding of Princess Elizabeth (which cost an astounding £93,293).[176] The price tag for reconstructing Somerset House was greater than anything seen since Henry VIII's reign: over £34,500 (well over £4 million in today's money), and Anna paid out an additional small fortune on decorations, furnishings, and equipment; these sums of money came from crown revenues, not the queen's dower.[177] The total spending on Anna's six masques (under £20,000) was relatively small in comparison, though certainly open to complaint. Yet few criticisms were levelled against the queen; rather, it was the king who got the blame. As a patriarch, he held responsibility for curbing his wife's spending and setting his household in order, and at this he had dismally failed.

8

Courts and Courtiers

The court in early modern Europe was both a place and a milieu.[1] It was the space surrounding monarchs, whether they were peripatetic or based in a capital city, as well as the environment in which they lived. Elite men and women who were granted regular access to these spaces can be considered courtiers; those who attended rarely were courtiers only during their visits to the royal palaces. Menial servants who worked in the royal household below stairs were not courtiers at all because they were excluded from the courtly environment.[2] Nor were the royal dramatists, players, and artists who did not reside at court, although they did help create its cultural milieu.[3]

The boundary between the court and the world outside was porous.[4] When on progress, members of the court interacted with local people; throughout the year, courtiers had webs of connections in urban and rural areas where they possessed estates, houses, and local offices. Consequently, they often behaved as intermediaries between regional gentry and privy councillors or household officers. Culture, news, and fashions spread easily in both directions. Plays which began life in the court were later performed in London theatres and sometimes went on provincial tours; plays successful in London were adapted for the court. Musicians, dramatists, and artists who were employed at court spent time working, even living, in aristocratic or gentry households in the country and in London.

As was true for all European capitals, the presence of the court in London accounted for much of its prosperity and growth. Together with the port, the court was the largest employer in the metropolis. Courtiers' lifestyles provided work for the City's manufacturers and craftsmen while, from 1609, retailing flourished with the opening of the New Exchange (an elegant indoor market, soon renamed Britain's Bourse), which offered courtiers high quality shopping opportunities along the Strand—the fashionable street linking Whitehall to the City. Also along the Strand, courtiers were building new townhouses or redeveloping older mansions, thereby providing yet another source of employment for builders and artisans.[5]

★ ★ ★

James's palaces, like those of his Tudor predecessors, were largely located on the River Thames around London. Housing administrative offices, the main common law courts, and star chamber was Whitehall Palace, a sprawling riverside building acquired and reconstructed by Henry VIII near the old Palace of Westminster. Further up the Thames, Hampton Court was the site where the court normally convened for the Christmas revels and assembled after James's summer progress. Anna was there more often than her husband, but Greenwich was the palace most associated with the queen. Even before James gifted it to her in 1616, she used it independently and chose to have her confinements there.[6]

Inside royal palaces, the space was organized to meet the needs of the royal household and routines of court life. Below stairs were the work rooms—the kitchens, laundries, cellars, and stores—which had originally been under the supervision of the lord steward, the second most important household officer. However, with one brief exception, the office of steward was left vacant during Elizabeth's reign, and his functions devolved on the treasurer and comptroller of the household who sat with clerks on what was called the Board of Green Cloth.[7] This practice was to continue under James. The stables and grounds outside were the responsibility of the master of the horse, the next great household officer. He inevitably had close and regular proximity to any monarch who enjoyed riding and hunting, as did both Elizabeth and James.

Above stairs were the public and private apartments. The large chambers were used primarily for public ceremonials and formal entertainments. The smaller rooms had restricted access and were places where the monarch retreated away from the public eye. The lord chamberlain had complete charge of running 'above stairs' (bar the privy chamber under Elizabeth), which meant managing the staff, arranging all the official ceremonials, staging grand entertainments, and regulating access to the king.[8] Another vital officer, though without the same status, was the master of the revels. Accountable to the lord chamberlain, he headed the 'revels office', whose function was to put on the theatrical entertainments at court. Shortly after his accession, James created a new household officer, 'master of the ceremonies'. Common on the Continent, this court official had charge of receiving and entertaining foreign dignitaries, especially ambassadors, a duty which under Elizabeth had been performed randomly by some or other nobleman.[9] The first incumbent appointed in 1605 was Sir Lewis Lewkenor. He had been carrying out the function informally before then and remained in post until 1627.[10]

With the arrival of a married king who had young children, changes inevitably occurred in the space of the court. Elizabeth had been a solitary royal, requiring only one court and household throughout her long reign. Females mainly staffed her private rooms: the privy chamber, a withdrawing chamber, and her bedchamber.[11] On James's accession, two households immediately came into operation. The king's was largely peripatetic and dominated by his 'hunting crew'. Staffed largely by women, Anna's was based initially in her own apartments in Whitehall, Hampton Court, and Greenwich Palace until she took up residence in Denmark House in the Strand.[12] Early in the reign, the royal children were raised in aristocratic households with their own tutors, grooms, and pages until Elizabeth was established at Kew Palace shortly after the Gunpowder Plot and Henry at St James and Richmond Palaces in 1610.[13] As seen in the previous chapter, this extension of the single royal court cost the crown dear, but it also offered greater openings for painters, poets, musicians, and dramatists.

This was not the only change under James. In a move that had major political consequences, the king downgraded the role of the privy chamber and transferred its functions to the bedchamber, a new department established by royal ordinance in 1603 with its own regulations. Presided over by a 'groom of the stool', the bedchamber was manned by gentlemen, grooms, and pages, almost all of whom were Scots.[14] The institutional innovation came as a surprise for it had been widely anticipated that members of James's privy chamber would retain the same status and fulfil the same functions as they had under Elizabeth, except that now of course all the personnel would be male. Many of those who had travelled north on James's accession were in pursuit of a position there.

Almost certainly, James and Cecil had agreed in York that the privy chamber would contain an identical number of English and Scottish gentlemen.[15] Accordingly, when he arrived at the Tower in May 1603, James swore two dozen Scots and the same number of Englishmen as gentlemen of the privy chamber. They were divided into four groups of gentlemen (six English and six Scots), each to be on duty for three months.[16] From the king's point of view, the equal partition would signal and advance the Anglo-Scottish Union; from Cecil's, it would prevent the Scots dominating access to and influence with the king.[17] However, James immediately performed a sleight of hand in instituting the new more exclusive department of the bedchamber, filled in 1603 entirely by Scots. The bedchamber—not the privy chamber—became the institutionalized private space where the king would withdraw and relax. By contrast, the privy chamber was transformed into a semi-public space for more formal dining and audiences with officials.[18] Yet, even here, James would not permit nobles or privy councillors to enter 'without being summoned', as they had been in the 'habit of doing during the last reign'.[19] The restriction, he explained, was because: 'wee doe find our selfs greatly pressed with the extraordinary company that come into our privy chamber...which course is both troublesome to us and the ready way to make all greatnes contemptible, when no difference is made between persons'.[20] Only a handful of named earls and gentlemen were given right of access; the remainder had to wait until the king granted them an audience. The lord chamberlain and gentlemen ushers were given the responsibility of ousting and punishing any transgressors.[21]

Why did this change occur? According to Neil Cuddy—who was the first historian to detect and appreciate the importance of this development—James had been used to a more open court in Scotland, where there was 'a lack of distinction between public and private'. When he encountered a totally different style of court in England, one 'designed for the preservation and manipulation of distance', he merged the two types to create 'a hybrid'. The privy chamber was to be open to privy councillors and nobility, as had occurred in the Scottish equivalent, whereas the bedchamber was to be the private preserve of the king and his intimates. However, as I have just explained, the English privy chamber like the bedchamber was far from open to all nobles or councillors. Furthermore, the more recent work of Amy Juhala on the Scottish royal household also raises questions about this explanation. She has pointed out that, shortly after his marriage to Anna, James had curtailed and controlled access to his chamber, bedchamber, and closet. Before 1590, Scottish courtiers had been known to walk in upon the king unannounced, even to the extent of seeing him in a state of undress. Once married, James understood the value of private apartments and created a clear distinction between private and public spaces in his Scottish palaces.[22] A better explanation for the creation of the bedchamber is that James wanted to keep his loyal Scottish friends close to him in England.

As he wrote in *Basilikon Doron*: 'bee carefull ever to preferre the gentilest natured and trustiest, to the inwardest offices about you; especially in your chalmer [chamber]'.[23]

The new arrangement had profound consequences and was ultimately a political error since the influence of the bedchamber Scots was deeply resented and for good reason. Thanks to their proximity to the king, many of them acquired the most lucrative gifts from him. A paper drawn up in 1610 reveals that bedchamber Scots had by then received £10,614 [c.£1.5m today] in annual pensions, £88,280 [c.£12m] in ready cash, and £133,100 [c.£18m] in old debts.[24] These Scots also acted as patronage brokers, doing favours for English suitors who had no direct access to the king, but often at a price. We have already seen how they sold knighthoods in 1603; later, they took backhanders after baronetcies were created and purchased. Another kind of corrupt practice is revealed in a letter of 1611 from the earl of Lincoln in which he bitterly complained that he had disbursed 'great summes of money' as well as horses and 'other chardges' to an unnamed gentleman of the bedchamber (a nobleman) in order to procure an order signed by James for his release from the Fleet prison. Lincoln had in addition paid out money to yet another Scot to secure the intercession of the bedchamber man.[25] Of course, it was not only the Scots who operated in this fashion, but, as they were outsiders, their conduct was more heavily criticized.

Some Scots were also brought into the lower echelons of the household, taking up positions that were highly sought after and could be sold for a sizeable sum. Fourteen of Elizabeth's household officers were replaced with Scots in 1603 while at least five others kept their posts but were given a Scot as a partner.[26] More Scots would have liked positions, but the privy council advised James against displacing too many of Elizabeth's servants and so he let go some of the men who had escorted him to England. Disappointed though they were, they received promises of pensions as compensation.[27]

★ ★ ★

The bedchamber Scots' right of access to the king did not automatically translate into influence and rich rewards.[28] For that to happen, it was necessary for them to develop a strong personal relationship with James. During the first decade of the reign, we can identify seven Scots who became closest to him, three of whom—Lennox, Home, and Carr—also joined the privy council before 1612. The remainder held no formal governmental positions but functioned as the king's personal servants with forays into public service. None of them controlled the sign manual, which applied the king's signature to grants, charters, or warrants authorizing payments of monies.[29]

The first gentleman of the bedchamber was Ludovick Stuart, second duke of Lennox, James's close friend and nearest kinsman, who had held the same office in Scotland. Born in France in 1574 and naturalized an English citizen by act of parliament in 1604, Lennox was considered a Scot since he had arrived at James's court at the age of nine. He was one of the first Scots to be appointed to the English privy council and—as will be seen in later chapters—was not just a token figure. James relied on him for help with Scottish affairs and used him as a special envoy to France.

As a courtier, Lennox was very close to James, 'always near his person'.[30] He had apartments in Whitehall Palace and regularly joined the royal hunting party outside London.[31] Sharing the king's love of the chase, he was praised 'as excellent as any prince in Christendome' in its art.[32] Lennox excelled at other feats of horsemanship as well. At Henry's baptism in 1594, he had won first prize at 'running at the ring', and in England he demonstrated his prowess at equestrian sports, although admittedly he rarely seems to have won.[33] At the Accession Day tournament of 1606, he attracted attention only because he 'exceeded all in feathers'.[34] Tournaments at early modern courts also included foot combat at the barriers, and Lennox was noted as a leading participant in these kinds of events too. He was one of two 'chieftains' and on the winning side at the barriers held to celebrate the Essex–Howard wedding in January 1606.[35] In June the same year, he performed as one of four 'assured champions' who issued a high-profile challenge to fight at the barriers in a tournament scheduled for that summer to celebrate the birth of the king's third daughter and the state visit of his brother-in-law, the king of Denmark.[36] In the event, the tournament was cancelled because of the newly born princess's death, but Lennox did participate in the prestigious barriers held during the Twelfth Night celebrations of 1610 that marked Henry's entry into adulthood.[37] Given that it was risky for a king to participate in tournaments, whether on foot or on horseback—Henry VIII of England had been badly injured when falling from a horse and Henry II of France was accidentally killed by a lance in his eye—James rarely entered the fray, and Lennox may have been acting unofficially as his proxy.

Lennox was not only a chivalric figure; he also had a keen interest in drama and poetry. In his previous office of high chamberlain in Scotland, he had been occupied with court entertainments and acted as a patron of poets and other writers.[38] In England, his opportunities for literary patronage were fewer since the lord chamberlain, the master of the revels, and the master of the ceremonies were responsible for court entertainments. Nonetheless, Lennox commissioned and performed in masques at court, sometimes offering parallel or rival entertainments to those staged by Anna. Outside the court, he sponsored a theatrical company and troupe of trumpeters which toured the provinces together. Furthermore, the poet and dramatist George Chapman—and quite possibly others—benefited from his patronage. Lennox was one of those who came to Chapman's aid when, in 1608, his play *The Conspiracy and Tragedy of Byron* gravely offended the French ambassador with whom Lennox was friendly.[39]

Lennox got on well with English courtiers on a day-to-day basis, but many noblemen refused 'to concur' when James planned, in 1613, to make him duke of Richmond—a title usually bestowed upon a king's son or 'those of the blood royal'.[40] Almost certainly, the English earls disliked the precedence (as an English duke) that the Scot would enjoy in court ceremonials, but perhaps too they feared that James intended to foist his second cousin onto the English throne if Charles died childless. To avoid contention, James raised Lennox only to the earldom of Richmond, in October 1613, and waited another ten years before promoting him to become a duke. Before then, Lennox was granted manors in England and land in Ireland.[41] Married three times but without sons, his heir was his younger brother Esmé, Lord Aubigny.[42] Aubigny was another gentleman of the bedchamber, a fine horseman and patron of the arts; for a time, Ben Jonson resided in his household.[43] Likewise not by birth a Scot since he had lived in France before 1603, Aubigny too was generally viewed as such.

Resembling Lennox, Sir George Home of Spott—soon to become earl of Dunbar—was a gentleman of the bedchamber who was also a privy councillor.[44] But he had more political clout than Lennox and even rivalled Cecil in influence. Home had been a prominent member of James's Scottish court since 1584 and master of the gardrop [wardrobe] from 1590 with ultimate responsibility for preparing, repairing, and keeping the accounts of the expensive garments and furnishings used by the monarch. In 1603, he was given the equivalent offices—keeper of the great wardrobe and gentleman of the robes—in England, thereby replacing the Elizabethan office holder Sir John Fortescue, who was not best pleased. The king went on to appoint Home as chancellor of the exchequer, again replacing the unfortunate

Fortescue.[45] Finally, James showed his trust in Home by making him the keeper of the privy purse, the office which gave him access to a stamp of the king's signature. Here he supplanted Henry Seckford.[46] At the same time, Home remained lord treasurer of Scotland, although he now exercised his authority through deputies. So, uniquely, he held offices in the royal households and governments of both James's realms, a mark of his friendship with the king but also of the royal desire for a united Britain. Unsurprisingly, Home grew wealthy from royal favour.

Unlike Lennox, Home was less the accomplished courtier. In 1607, the Venetian ambassador Molin thought him 'ungracious, ungrateful to his friends, incapable of winning friends, lacking in all the qualities which make a man beloved'. Indeed, Molin could not understand why the fifty-year-old courtier had ever risen to such prominence.[47] However, it was almost certainly because of his intelligence, energy, and loyalty. It was said Dunbar enjoyed James's 'entire confidence and was alone the partner of his most intimate secrets'.[48] Certainly, James depended upon him for advice about the proposed British Union, the 'great contract', and Scottish affairs. Indeed, one historian believes that the collapse of Cecil's plan of 1610 ('the great contract') to improve royal finances was due to Home's influence, though I doubt this.[49] James was also very fond of him. When Home died, the king 'bewailed him tenderly and spent the whole day of his death in bed'.[50]

A bedchamber Scot without governmental office was Sir Roger Aston, James's master huntsman and falconer.[51] Originally from Cheshire—so legally an Englishman—Aston was raised in Scotland and came to serve James's parents and paternal grandfather before he entered the royal household around 1578. Of value as a diplomat as well as a huntsman, Aston built up a close relationship with Elizabethan privy councillors during the 1580s and 1590s.[52] James, however, never questioned his loyalty. On Elizabeth's death, he sent Aston to London to prepare for his reception, knighted him, and brought him into the bedchamber.[53] Aston's responsibilities grew when, in 1605, he became joint keeper of the great wardrobe with Home and took sole control of this office the following year. Though Aston was never appointed a privy councillor, James relied upon him heavily, especially in parliament where he worked on the king's behalf in the commons.[54] The rewards he received were considerable but not astounding. 'In consideracon of service', he obtained numerous grants and leases of land in various counties of England and also gained monopolies and other licences.[55] But he did not get the extra-large handouts James rendered to several other bedchamber men. On 1 February 1611, four others were granted £8,000 each whereas Aston received only £2,000.[56]

Three Scottish gentlemen of the bedchamber who did become rich on royal gifts were Sir Thomas Erskine, Sir James Hay, and Sir John Ramsay. Erskine, a cousin of the earl of Mar, had been the king's companion from childhood and was made a gentleman of the Scottish bedchamber in 1585. In August 1600, he helped protect James against the would-be assassins of the Gowrie conspiracy, a service the king never forgot. Accompanying his master into England, Erskine immediately supplanted Ralegh as the captain of the royal bodyguard and, in 1604, was promoted to become groom of the stool. Close to Cecil, Erskine was one of the secretary's conduits to direct messages to James.[57] Additionally, Erskine sometimes assumed a more public role at court; for example, James ordered him to meet the constable of Castile 'at his first arrival at London'.[58] Perhaps the Scot's reputation as 'well affected' to the Catholic religion made him especially suited for the task.[59]

Although Erskine had previously sat on the Scottish council, he was not made a privy councillor in England for several years, but it did not take long before he rose into the ranks of the nobility, becoming Lord Fenton in 1604 and Viscount Fenton in 1606. Nevertheless, it took more than a decade for him to be created an earl (earl of Kellie). By that time, he had been appointed a privy councillor, married an Englishwoman (Elizabeth Pierrepont, widow of Sir Edward Norris), and received land in Bedfordshire and Ampthill, where he was already steward.[60]

Sir James Hay, who was born into a Scottish gentry family around 1580, was another fine horseman who like Lennox participated in tournaments as well as the hunt. He was noted too as a graceful dancer and a man of great charm and affability. Unacquainted with James in Scotland—presumably because he was then studying in France—Hay was made a gentleman of the bedchamber in October 1603, allegedly at the behest of the queen.[61] His excellent French proving useful, he was sent to the French court in March 1604 to convey James's condolences to Henry IV on the death of his sister, a diplomatic mission he performed with a 'grace and comely caryadge' that was 'exceedingly wel liked and commended of al sorts'.[62] However, it cost the king the outrageous sum of £6,000 [c.£827,265 in today's currency].[63] Hay continued to be a big spender, and his extravagance became notorious. Tales were spread about the lavish banquets he hosted, and—according to legend—he invented the notorious double-supper at which guests were shown a sumptuous meal of cold dishes only to have them ritually discarded as insufficiently generous and then replaced with a fresh spread of hot dishes.[64] True or not, this story articulated the perceived wastefulness of James's court and the profligacy of his Scottish courtiers.

Hay was one of the first Scots to take an English bride. He knew that intermarriage was dear to the king's heart and, besides, he needed a rich wife to sustain his lifestyle at court. The girl he chose was Honora Denny, a child heiress and Cecil's great-niece; her father Sir Edward, moreover, was a friend of the Howards. So, at a stroke, this marriage would bring Hay a sizeable income and several powerful patrons. Delighted by his choice, the king paid off Hay's debts, granted him several English manors, and made him a baron for life, although without the right to sit in the English parliament. For agreeing to the marriage, Sir Edward was likewise created a baron and forgiven a debt of £3,000 to the crown. In December 1605, Hay was promoted to replace Home as master of the robes; and the following year, he was given the reversion on the office of master of the great wardrobe, which he assumed on Aston's death in 1612.[65]

Hay's wedding to Honora took place in early 1607 when the bride came of age.[66] But, even after obtaining her dowry, Hay needed and continued to be given rich royal gifts, including the king paying off his debts.[67] One historian estimates that Hay acquired and spent some £400,000 during his career at the English court.[68] Yet, in spite of this evidence of royal favour, Hay was kept out of the privy council until 1617. Instead, he served as an active courtier, attending on the king, participating in tilts, and welcoming important guests on James's behalf.[69]

Sir John Ramsay, who entered James's English bedchamber in 1603, was another significant beneficiary of royal favour. He began his court career as a page in James's Scottish household and rose to favour after the Gowrie conspiracy when he stabbed its leader to death. In explicit recognition of this service, James ennobled him, in June 1606, as Viscount Haddington and Lord Ramsay of Barns and gave him lands worth £1,000 a year.[70] Like Hay, Ramsay was not a wealthy man and needed James's largesse to survive at the English court. For this reason, he recurrently obtained one-off payments of money, annual pensions, and profitable grants of land from the king.[71] At his marriage in February 1608 to Elizabeth Radcliffe (eldest daughter of the earl of Sussex), James gave the couple a pension of £600 a year for life with the message that 'he wisht them as much joy and comfort all theyre life, as he received that day he [Haddington] delivered him from the daunger of Gowry'.[72] Around that time, James also paid off Haddington's debts of

£7,200.[73] Yet, in truth, the viscount was of less value to the king than either Hay or Erskine because, unlike them, he spoke no foreign language. Nevertheless, James appreciated his loyalty and company as part of his hunting crew.[74]

Fond as James was of these Scottish gentlemen, none of them held as strong a hold on his affections as Robert Carr (Kerr in the Scots spelling) came to have after 1607. Before that year, Philip Herbert, the younger brother of the earl of Pembroke, came nearest to earning the title of favourite. He was the only Englishman to be given a position in the bedchamber before 1615, and titles, offices, and money were heaped upon him.[75] He joined the king on his hunting trips, and, when Sir Thomas Lake was absent, it was Herbert who stood in for him as secretary, a responsibility he did not enjoy.[76] Herbert much preferred the role of courtier, and his interactions with the king were affectionate, bantering, even flirtatious. When James was feeling low, Herbert was the courtier who tried to make him merry.[77] However, the feelings James revealed towards Carr were in a different league. Some historians think that king and favourite were lovers, but it is impossible to know from this distance.[78] At the time, though, their relationship was not viewed as sexually scandalous, unlike James's later intimacy with George Villiers, duke of Buckingham.[79]

Carr had been brought up in the royal household in Scotland on the death of his father, an ardent supporter of James's mother. He had afterwards followed the king to England as one of Home's pages.[80] Seemingly, James noticed Carr only at an Accession Day tilt, in March 1607, when he fell from his horse while dismounting to present a shield and impresa to the king. Shocked by the accident, James brought the invalid into the royal apartments so that his own physicians could nurse Carr's broken leg. Attracted to the youth's looks and charm, James frequently visited him, sometimes for an hour or more. Once he had fully recovered, James kept him close and 'took the pains himself to teach him the Latin tongue'. Before the end of the year, Carr was knighted, sworn in as a gentleman of the bedchamber, and described as a 'new favourite'.[81] He had constant access to the king, sleeping in his bedchamber, and hearing his secrets.[82] As Suffolk dryly commented, Carr had better reason 'to speak well of his own horse' that threw him than of the 'king's roan jennet' which visitors to the court were expected to admire.[83]

James showered lands and money upon Carr, together with more personal gifts such as a miniature portrait set in a gold frame studded with diamonds.[84] Carr also attracted funds by brokering deals for suitors. But he wanted power as well as riches. Schooled by his long-time friend and present mentor, the Englishman Thomas Overbury, Carr forged a network of connections at James's court which included both his own clients and powerful men who could carry through services for him.[85] Aware of the king's intense feelings for the new favourite, both Cecil and Northampton were careful to demonstrate that they were furthering his interests. In late 1608, for instance, Cecil recommended to James that Ralegh's house and estate of Sherborne in Dorset should be granted to the young man, and Northampton acquiesced graciously in the decision even though he wanted Sherborne for himself.[86] Even after learning that Carr had been using his influence to sabotage the 'great contract' in 1610, Cecil continued to show him outward cordiality, granting favours that Carr requested. But the power balance had undoubtedly shifted.[87]

Home's death in January 1611 propelled Carr directly onto the political stage. He then took over the position of lord high treasurer of Scotland, his first public office. Created baron of Winwick and Viscount Rochester on 25 March 1611, he became the first Scot to be given a seat in the house of lords. In May, he was installed a knight of the garter and, just before Cecil's death, he entered the privy council. By this time, he was deeply unpopular. Unsurprisingly, the 'Englishe lords' resented his elevation, but it was reported that the Scots' discontentment was 'much more'.[88] As for Anna, she despised both him and his sidekick Overbury so greatly that, in June 1611, she tried to have the latter banished permanently from court.[89] Carr's only known friend at court was Pembroke, a man who was later to become a powerful enemy.[90] Nonetheless, with the affection of the king so evident, Carr seemed an impregnable figure.

Despite the upward trajectory of Carr's political career, it was only after the deaths of Cecil and Henry that James allowed him to monopolize patronage. Filling both the political vacuum and James's emotional needs, Carr became the king's acting secretary, although Lake carried out some minor duties. The distribution of royal bounty was then placed almost entirely in the favourite's hands, and he was recognized as the '*primum mobile*' of the court.[91] Men scrambled for his patronage while Northampton consulted him on matters of policy and used him to present his ideas to the king.[92] When, in 1613, Carr (then earl of Somerset) decided to marry Frances—Northampton's great-niece—the Howard–Carr relationship solidified into a political alliance that opened up a new intense factionalism at court.[93]

★ ★ ★

The Scots soon settled into the traditional pattern of successful courtiers over the ages. As intimates of the king, they became personally rich, wielded considerable patronage, built up estates, and entered the English peerage. Those with male heirs gained a landed patrimony and title which their families would enjoy for generations. Since they were newcomers and foreigners, their good fortune was deeply resented. From the very first, the English grumbled bitterly about the influx of Scots into the bedchamber. According to Scaramelli, Elizabeth's ex-privy councillors were 'charged with having sold England to the Scots' by allowing the foreigners to monopolize the bedchamber.[94] The French ambassador, meanwhile, noted that Cecil was held particularly responsible for this ruinous situation. He was thought to have advised James to impose 'cette tirannie sur eux' [this tyranny upon them] because the Scots were his friends, and their promotion would allow him to maintain his pre-eminence.[95]

Anti-Scottish sentiment was not confined to the court. Some people vented their spleen against the Scots in composing and transmitting libels and songs, which were 'every where posted'.[96] One typical song compared the Scots unfavourably to English beggars, with a verse alluding to the promotions and favours they enjoyed. Its ending was all too predictable:

> Our noble King James, Lord ever defend
>   And all Scottish beggars soone home againe send
> A gallope a gallope.[97]

The Scots were also lampooned on the London stage. As already mentioned, both *Eastward Ho* and *The Isle of Gulls* mocked them, the latter being particularly offensive. Based upon Sir Philip Sidney's epic poem *Arcadia*, the drama was set in a corrupt court presided over by Duke Basilius (a pun on James's *Basilicon Doron*), a ruler who loved hunting, spent profligately, and had an effeminate favourite. Very likely, in performance the 'duke' was called the 'king' (a title later censored) and the actors playing Basilius and his courtiers simulated a Scottish accent.[98] Other London plays, though less obviously satires of James's court, similarly contained hostile allusions to the Scots, if only in asides. In one scene of John Marston's rollicking comedy *Dutch Courtesan*, performed in 1605, the anti-hero Cocledemoy assumed the role of a Scottish barber-surgeon with the name of Andrew Shark, who claimed (in another obvious pun) to have been 'shaving' the court for 'this two year'.[99] In 1608, an unnamed 'comedy' that played at Blackfriars 'made fun of the new fashion found in Scotland' and caused the author 'to run off in fear of losing his life'.[100] Although these dramas were building on long-held English prejudices, they were now topical and reflected present-day grievances against Scottish courtiers.[101]

Resentment at James's liberality towards the Scots at court extended into the parliamentary debates about the Union and especially the proposal that all Scots should automatically become naturalized Britons. Although constitutional issues were more important considerations, dislike of the measure was also founded on fear that—if it went through—still more Scots would descend upon the English court and receive honours, offices, and financial rewards from the king.[102] James tried to reassure members of the commons that he understood their 'disquiet' and they had nothing to worry about.[103] To match his deeds with his words, he planned to avoid appointing Scots to any place if there was 'any Inglishe man that douse ame [aim] at it'.[104] Yet few were reassured. Protests about James's liberality towards the Scots continued well after Union was off the parliamentary agenda. In 1610, Sir John Holles complained of the Scottish monopoly of James and begged the king that 'his bedchamber may be shared as well to those of our nation as to them'. As worthy as the Scots might be, he said, 'I wish equality that they should not seem to be the children of the family and we the servants.' At the same time, Holles blamed the crown's increasing financial difficulties on the Scots at court: 'by the reception of the other nation, the head is too heavy for this small body of England'.[105]

★ ★ ★

James's royal court was of course not the only one in town. As already seen, Anna and Henry had their own households and courtiers, creating what historians have called a 'polycentric world'.[106] The three courts, however, were not sites of faction and rival power blocs.[107] On the contrary, the personnel of each royal household had a web of remarkably frictionless connections across all three courts. For a start, James's right-hand man Cecil was lord high steward of Anna's household and very close to her ladies of the privy chamber, indeed so close that, according to gossip, two of them—Katherine, countess of Suffolk, and Lady Walsingham—were his mistresses.[108] Cecil also had friends and clients in Henry's independent household, notably Chaloner (who became the prince's chamberlain) and George More (Henry's treasurer and receiver-general). Lucy, countess of Bedford (lady of the queen's bedchamber), provided another nexus of cross-court relationships. Members of her maternal family had places in the households of Henry and Elizabeth. Similarly, Anna's master of the horse (Sir Thomas Seymour) was the son of James's (the earl of Worcester).[109] Some courtiers in the different royal households, moreover, had shared financial and commercial interests: for example, when in 1609 the East India Company admitted non-merchant 'favorers', they included nobles such as Cecil and Southampton, and lesser courtiers such as James's cofferer, Henry's keeper of St James, and one of Anna's gentlemen of the privy chamber.[110]

Unlike James's bedchamber, Scots did not dominate Anna's privy apartments. She had as many English ladies-in-waiting as foreign, and those born outside England came originally from Denmark, France, and Italy as well as Scotland. The Scots with greatest access to the queen were Jane Drummond (later Lady Roxburgh), Anne Hay, and Anna Livingstone, all of them Catholics who had served her in Scotland. The intimates who were English included Bedford, Walsingham, Penelope Rich (until December 1605), and the countess of Suffolk (who had charge of Anna's jewels until about 1608 when she left the queen's service), all but Suffolk committed Protestants.[111] Of these, only Drummond and Suffolk seem to have involved themselves in national politics. Agents and ambassadors from the Habsburgs showered the two women with jewels and pensions in the misguided hope that they would promote Habsburg interests.[112] Otherwise, Anna's women focused their ambitions upon furthering the interests of their own families, but not in any factional sense for they co-operated with each other and with men in the other courts.[113]

The most visible men in Anna's household were English. Her lord chamberlain Sir Robert Sidney (later Viscount Lisle) had been a disgruntled friend of Essex and effectively exiled in the United Provinces as governor of Flushing during Elizabeth's later years. However, after 1603, he achieved the status at court he craved as well as a corresponding boost to his finances, so on the whole he was contented with his lot, leaving aside frequent grumblings to his wife.[114] Only after Cecil's death did Sidney enter factional politics, when his hatred of Northampton and Carr could no longer be contained.[115] Anna's vice-chamberlain Sir George (later Baron) Carew, a long-time friend of Cecil, also played no oppositional role at this time and indeed assisted James in parliament as best he could.[116] Only Southampton, master of the queen's game, may have been disaffected. Although a recipient of James's generosity, allowed access to the king's privy chamber, and given precedence at many important royal events, he had probably expected a place on the privy council.[117] Furthermore, while he was away from court fulfilling official responsibilities as governor of the Isle of Wight and a lord lieutenant of Hampshire, he had to use Cecil as a mediator and patron, an expedient that was no doubt galling given his earlier dislike of the man. Yet, regardless of the lack of intimacy between the two, there is no evidence that the earl stirred a pot against Cecil at court. Nor is there clear evidence that, before 1614, Southampton spoke out in parliament against royal policies such as peace with Spain or even the Union.[118]

Henry's household was likewise not a site of factional politics. In 1603, the twelve-year-old prince was settled at Nonsuch (the home of John, Lord Lumley) under Chaloner's guardianship, a man long trusted by James as well as a friend of Ellesmere and Cecil.[119] These three men chose the prince's officers, servants, and chaplains. Paid for by the king, the household was ultimately under his control until 1610. Cecil actively helped with the prince's political education while Chaloner was instrumental in developing his cultural tastes.[120]

Members of Henry's household came from all parts of James's kingdoms, but the most important posts were held by Scots, most of whom had already served the prince in Stirling: the classical scholar Adam Newton (Henry's tutor and secretary); the noted poet Sir David Murray of Gorthy (the sole gentleman of the bedchamber, master of the wardrobe, and later groom of the stool and keeper of his privy purse); and David Foulis (cofferer of the wardrobe). One of his chaplains, Lewis Bayly, was a Welshman, and the prince's music master and assistant tutor was the Irish poet Walter Quin. Also, within the household were several English boys of about the prince's age, selected to be his companions: Robert, third earl of Essex; Lady Bedford's young brother John Harington of Exton; and Cecil's only son William.[121]

As Henry grew into adolescence, he understandably hankered after an independent household. For this to happen, he had to have an income of his own from landed estates, but the alienation of royal properties would adversely affect James's own income. For this reason, the king tried to delay his son's entry into adulthood. When the fifteen-year-old prince requested his own base in London, James suggested that he evict Southampton and Pembroke from their lodgings in the royal palaces on his visits to court, a proposal that was displeasing to both Henry and the earls.[122] Not to be thwarted, Henry commissioned research into historic investitures of previous princes of Wales that could be used as precedents for his own elevation and independence. By the end of 1609, James gave way. The following June, parliament installed Henry as Prince of Wales, and he set up his own court in the palaces of St James and Richmond.[123]

Henry's new court reflected the militantly Protestant and cultured image that he had already been fashioning with his coterie of companions. First, it was self-consciously male and martial. No ladies attended, and any man who married was liable for dismissal. Then, his household officers tended to be men experienced in warfare: the new comptroller, for example, was Sir John Holles, a veteran soldier and member of the band of gentleman pensioners. English officers based in the Netherlands communicated directly with the prince from abroad and helped him acquire the military intelligence that he flaunted before foreign ambassadors.[124] Henry was also known to be an enthusiast for the navy. In 1610, he accompanied his cousin, the visiting prince of Brunswick, to see new ships being built in the royal dockyards, and it was even rumoured that he aspired to replace Nottingham as lord admiral.[125]

Henry equally intended his palaces to be stylish centres of the arts. As seen in the previous chapter, he planned the reconstruction of Richmond Palace and gardens. At St James, he commissioned Inigo Jones to construct a new library and picture gallery where his newly acquired collection of books and paintings would be displayed. The library was initially filled with the vast number of books that he had inherited in 1609 from Lord Lumley. Over the next few years, this nucleus was augmented with volumes that were either gifts or purchases, many—but not all—on military subjects. Significantly, Henry ensured that they were all expensively bound with his initials and arms stamped upon the cover, thereby contributing to his self-image as a patron of scholarship.[126] In charge of supervising and cataloguing the collection was the king's own librarian Patrick Young, the son of James's old tutor Peter Young; also engaged to work in the library was Abraham van der Doort, previously the antiquary of Emperor Rudolph II.[127]

The Protestant zeal of Henry's household was obvious at the time. His servants had to attend religious services and were expected to take monthly communion; indeed, anyone who failed to take communion at Easter and Christmas was threatened with dismissal. Swearing (as it was blasphemy) was prohibited, and transgressors were made to pay a fine into an alms box for the poor. The poor were also to receive food every morning outside the palace gates as an act of Christian charity.[128] Henry's chaplains were noted Calvinists whose sermons offered an unadulterated diet of predestinarian theology and anti-Catholic militant Protestantism.[129] Consequently, Protestant authors of devotional works and religious controversy were attracted to the prince, and a few received his patronage.[130]

Henry's court is commonly portrayed as dissimilar from—even oppositional to—his father's.[131] Its militant Protestantism and chivalric values were supposedly at odds with James's desire to be represented as a *Rex Pacificus*, while its strict Calvinist tone ostensibly ran counter to the more freewheeling atmosphere of the king's court. There were certainly differences and even tensions between father and son. Nonetheless, the contrasts between them and between their courts were of emphasis rather than substance.[132]

Henry's martial interests barely conflicted with James's preference for peace. As Scottish king, James had argued in *Basilikon Doron* that princes needed to be ready to fight in defence of their realm, and as king of England he revealed himself to be no appeaser.[133] Nor was James averse to a martial image. His first great seal depicted him in armour on horseback with his sword aloft, while the silver crown and gold sovereign minted 1603–04 showed him again in armour and with the legend '*Exurgat deus dissipentur inimici*' ['Let God arise, let his enemies be scattered'] from the opening line of Psalm 68. On later coins and in many engravings, James appears in armour.[134] At the same time, Henry's militarism should not be exaggerated. In a dialogue about the merits of war or peace, he reputedly backed the arguments for peace that cited examples from history and propounded aphorisms such as 'one peace outgoes for worth innumerable triumphs'.[135]

The cultural focus of each court equally reveals no *kulturkampf*. It was not only Henry's court that valued the forms and ceremonies of chivalry. The order of the garter celebrations were important at James's court, and both father and son proudly wore the badge of the greater St George on special occasions and for their portraits.[136] Tournaments were a regular feature of life at James's court, and the king favoured men, such as the Herbert brothers, who performed well in them. Although James rarely took part himself, he accepted his son's challenge to tilt at the ring during the carnival festivities of 1609 and participated in 'running at the ring' with Henry and the young prince of Brunswick in April 1610.[137]

When it came to the religious temperature of the two courts, the contrast was stronger. Not all of James's preachers were Calvinists, and his courtiers were consequently exposed to a much wider range of doctrinal positions than were Henry's. Furthermore, some of James's courtiers and councillors were crypto-Catholics, staying away from communion without obvious penalty. On Easter Day 1605, 'there was some noise at court' because James had 'let it be known that he desired each of his councillors and his gentlemen to take communion with him; and had ordered a list of those who abstained to be drawn up'. Unsurprisingly, most Catholics stayed away from court that day, and the list was drawn up, but nothing noteworthy followed.[138] Yet again, the divergence should not be overstated. James loved sermons and increased their number and regularity at his court. While sermons under Elizabeth had been heard only on Sundays (except during Lent or on holy days), from 1603 a weekly Tuesday sermon was instituted in the chapel royal, following the pattern in Scotland after the Gowrie affair. Then, after the Gunpowder Plot, Thursday morning sermons were introduced. By the time that Henry had his own household, anti-Catholic sermons were preached in both households because the king was then engaged in a polemical battle against the pope and Jesuits.[139] One final point, Henry was no Malvolio; like his father and mother, he and his courtiers enjoyed plays, masques, music, tennis, hunting, and gambling—just not on the Sabbath.

★ ★ ★

Under James, the full calendar of courtly rituals and festivities that had existed under Elizabeth was maintained. Additionally, the king introduced several new feast days into the royal schedule and nation's celebrations: Accession Day, the king's birthday in June, coronation day in July, Gowrie Day on 5 August, and Gunpowder Plot Day on 5 November. As with holy days at court, they were all observed with a grand procession in the morning to the chapel royal, where a thanksgiving service and sermon was heard. The preacher on these mornings was usually the lord almoner, who, from 1605 to 1619, was James's favourite preacher Lancelot Andrewes, bishop of Chichester. In the afternoon, secular entertainments took over. Whenever Accession Day fell outside Easter, tilts and 'running at the ring' were staged, often with 'great pomp and beauty', and watched by members of the public.[140] Tilting also took place on Gowrie Day if James was in London, although usually he was on progress. Then courtiers, councillors, and ambassadors would ride out to show him their respects. On Gowrie Day in 1611, for example, they and the royal children joined James at Salisbury where fireworks were part of the celebrations 'by way of rejoicing for the king's safety'.[141] On the few occasions when privy councillors had to remain at Whitehall on Gowrie Day, they held 'a very solemn feast' in the royal palace 'where there were so many healths' to the king and royal family.[142]

Festivals surrounding the order of the garter were also important events in the royal calendar. On the feast day of St George (celebrated on 23 April unless it coincided with Easter week), when new knights were elected, there normally occurred a royal procession to Windsor, a service in St George's Chapel, and a grand banquet.[143] This made a contrast with the feast day's observance from 1567 to 1602, when Elizabeth had headed a procession usually to the chapel royal at Whitehall or sometimes Greenwich.[144]

The actual installation of the knights under James took place whenever was deemed convenient. Although the king did not always participate, he was naturally there for the 1611 investiture of his younger son Charles and favourite Carr. The day before the ceremony, the knights rode in a long and colourful procession from London to Windsor. The next morning, cheered on by a large crowd, the procession reassembled and moved through the town towards St George's Chapel where a private service was held together with the investiture of the knights. Afterwards, a ceremonial feast took place in the great hall of the castle, at which the king sat alone on a dais while the knights ate together below.[145]

Although the beginning of the year was officially Lady Day (25 March), James and his courtiers continued to mark 1 January by performing the traditional ceremony of the New Year's gift exchange. Few gift rolls or lists have survived for James's reign, but it is evident that the formal ritual, so important under Elizabeth, continued after 1603. James's gifts, like those of his predecessor, were always a carefully calibrated amount of plate that accorded with the recipient's rank and status. There were some changes, however. Whereas Elizabeth had often received personal pieces of jewellery or clothing, the gifts for James from senior nobles and bishops were standardized sums of money. It was left to knights and gentlemen to proffer more personal gifts, such as drinking glasses, rings, or confections.[146] Another difference was that far fewer gifts were directed by noblewomen to James than had been to Elizabeth.[147] Probably, the women gave their gifts to Anna instead. Although the queen consort's gift exchanges are not recorded on the extant lists, letters indicate that they too occurred at New Year, albeit more informally.[148] Likewise, the royal children gave gifts at this season— from monies provided by the king—and again this was likely a more unceremonious affair.[149] James frequently gave jewels to his family members at the New Year.[150] Henry's gift to his father was normally an oration or speech in Latin.[151]

Valentine's Day was another opportunity for gift exchange at court. On 13 February, the eve of the saint's day, gentlemen—including members of the royal family—put their names in a ballot box for each lady to draw out a name. The selected man then kissed the woman (only her hand in the case of the queen), became her companion for the next day, and gave her a Valentine's gift.[152] In 1604, the French ambassador joined the ritual—or at least in part—for he bestowed 'very fayre and rich presents' on the queen, prince, and several lords and ladies on that day.[153] In 1609, the ritual apparently took a slightly different form. The king and his male courtiers, who were hunting at Royston, drew out the names of their Valentines on 9 February.[154]

The winter season was the traditional time for festivities at court. Elizabeth's revels had commenced on St Stephen's Day (26 December) and continued for twelve days with a few days of entertainments over Shrovetide in February. James, however, extended the revels season to fill the period between All Saints' Day (1 November) and Shrovetide. During the Christmas season (from 24 December until 6 January) the palace was bursting with lords, ladies, foreign guests, and lesser courtiers who 'turn their minds to festivities and pleasures'.[155] Since theatrical productions were a mainstay of the revels, the longer season resulted in the performance of far more plays at James's court than had been customary under Elizabeth. Almost every evening of the twelve days of Christmas, plays were performed by candlelight after supper, starting around 9.00 p.m. and commonly lasting until 1.00 a.m. During intermissions, the audience would be treated to a small meal of rich food and drink.[156] During the 1607–08 season, John Chamberlain observed that there were plays 'all the holy-dayes' and the king even wanted one on Christmas night. When the lords told him 'yt was not the fashion', James answered 'what do you tell me of the fashion, I will mak yt a fashion'.[157] The 1611–12 season was particularly extended, with many visits by a range of players between 31 October and 26 April; this expansion was because the king's older children commissioned performers on their own account and watched them in the company of their own smaller group of courtiers.[158]

Masques became a vital part of the winter entertainments, and during James's first decade in England the most elaborate—and expensive—were associated with the queen. Anna's first masque was staged privately at Winchester in October 1603. With little time to prepare and no recourse to the revels' office or the great wardrobe for costumes and props, it made a poor impression. One English observer thought it 'a gallant masque', but the French ambassador—the only ambassador known to have attended—scorned the production as a cheap rustic masquerade.[159] Gossip had it that the masque was scandalous, no doubt because of the participation of the queen and her ladies.[160]

To dispel notions that the new English court was culturally backward or financially impoverished, it was put about that the queen intended to stage a magnificent masque during the coming Christmas season, a time when envoys were expected from Spain, France, Poland, Tuscany, and Savoy to congratulate the king formally on his accession.[161] Determined to impress all these foreign guests, James and Anna arranged splendid banquets and elaborate entertainments, including 'manie plaies and daunces with swords'.[162] Three masques were to take place over a period of eight days, in itself an unusual occurrence as there had been no Christmas masque at court since 1583.

Anna's masque was to be held on Twelfth Night, the high point of the revels. She had begun preparations several months earlier, hiring Samuel Daniel as the writer, James Kirton to construct the sets, and a variety of tailors and embroiderers to create headdresses and adapt robes in the late queen's wardrobe for the costumes.[163] Even before the performance began, word was out that Anna's masque was of 'more import' than the one sponsored by Lennox held on New Year's Day. For this reason, the French ambassador Christophe de Harlay, count of Beaumont, was desperate to see it and complained bitterly when denied entry because he had already attended Lennox's masque. His fury knew no bounds on learning that the Spanish count of Villamediana, who was in London to negotiate the Anglo-Spanish peace, had been given a seat at the more prestigious event. It was impossible for both ambassadors to attend, because the French traditionally had precedence over the Spanish at the English court, and at this moment the royal couple wanted to honour Villamediana. To avoid offending the French, some of James's councillors suggested cancelling Anna's masque altogether, but 'the king answered that the queen's will was his will and, as she had gone with it this far, he wanted it to be performed in the presence of those whom she chose'. To avoid a serious diplomatic incident, James did postpone Anna's masque for two days until Sunday 8 January. This allowed Beaumont to dine publicly with the king and queen on Twelfth Night, the concluding evening and acme of the Christmas revels.[164]

Known as *The Vision of Twelve Goddesses*, Anna's masque was designed as a tribute to James. Its purpose, explained Daniel in the authorized printed version, was to represent the benefits of his rule, notably the 'delights of peace' which were 'in their season'—a reference of course to the impending Anglo-Habsburg negotiations. The peace theme was a deliberate message for Villamediana. Before its performance, Anna had let the ambassador know 'through third parties' that she wanted him to see it, and she clearly hoped that he would interpret the narrative (or rather that his translator would, since the count knew little English) as a sign that the king was in favour of a peace treaty. Others in the audience seemingly picked up her meaning: at any rate, Daniel complained that the masque was subjected to 'captious censurers' and 'sinister interpretation', most likely from those who favoured a continuation of the war.[165]

The masque began in darkness with the figure of Night coming beneath the earth to the cave of her son Sleep who brought forth a dream vision. Summoned by Iris (the messenger of the gods), the three Graces 'in silver robes with white torches' led a procession of twelve goddesses who descended in threes from a mountain. Between 'every ranke of goddesses' there marched three torchbearers, 'their heads and robes all dect with starres'. Converging on the Temple of Peace, they presented their attributes as gifts and 'faire blessings' to the king and realm. After dancing 'their own measures' [a slow and stately dance], they stepped down to claim a dancing partner from men in the audience, which brought the masque to a close.[166] Their choice of partner, presumably pre-arranged, was keenly noted by observers as it marked out the elite within the court.

Anna's role and costume were designed to attract attention, establish her pre-eminence in the masque, and construct an image for herself at court. She played the part of the virgin goddess Pallas rather than Juno, the queen consort of Jupiter. In this masque, Pallas was the most important of all the goddesses, described by Iris as 'the all-directing Pallas, the glorious patronesse of this mightie monarchy'. By starring as Pallas, the youthful Anna could also appear as the legitimate successor to (and improvement on) the elderly Elizabeth, who had frequently been represented as the goddess of wisdom. Anna's appropriation of Elizabeth's role was also evident from her costume since it was widely known that the new queen had raided the old queen's wardrobe.[167] Additionally, Anna made sure that she stood out from her fellow goddesses. While they wore long and loose 'mantles and petticotes', her dress was so shockingly short (wrote Dudley Carleton disapprovingly) that 'we might see a woeman had both feete and legs, which I never knew before'. On her feet, she wore 'a paire of buskins sett with rich stones', and her helmet like her clothes were 'full of jewells'. Finally, the choreography favoured the queen: all the women danced well, wrote Carleton, 'but of all for goode grace and goode footemanship, Pallas bare the bell away'.[168]

Despite mixed reactions to the 1604 masque and conciliar anxieties about its cost, Anna was determined to produce another one the following year.

This time working with Ben Jonson and Inigo Jones, she commissioned the *Masque of Blackness* for a performance on Twelfth Night 1605 at Whitehall. Possibly, she had learned about the mumming [a masked mime] in black faces that had been part of the masque at Christian IV's coronation and decided to bring the Danish form of entertainment to the English court.[169] At any rate, she told Jonson of her wish to dress up with her ladies as 'black mores'.[170]

This masque created even more of a sensation than had the *Twelve Goddesses*. Again, the queen and her ladies were performers, but this time Anna was six months pregnant; the dresses were still more daring; and the female masquers had their faces and bodies painted black instead of wearing the black masks, gloves, and leggings customarily used to impersonate Africans. Audience reactions were again mixed. The Venetian ambassador called the masque 'very beautiful and sumptuous', whereas Carleton dismissed the painted women as 'a very lothsome sight' and found their costumes to be 'too lighte and curtizan like' [courtesan-like]. All commentators were astonished at the cost of the production—rumoured to have been more than £4,000 (well over £500,000 in today's currency)—owing to the spectacular sets and the jewel-encrusted costumes.[171] The money should have come out of the queen's dower but was actually paid for by the crown as it was 'for honor to the king' and, besides, Anna was already in serious debt.[172]

Jonson took responsibility for devising the narrative of the masque. The speakers (male actors) told how the twelve daughters (played by female masquers) of River Niger travelled from Ethiopia in a quest to be 'blanched' [made white]. They passed over 'black' countries before reaching 'Albion the fair' [England], newly named Britannia, a 'blest isle':

> For were the world, with all his wealth, a ring,
>   Britania (whose new name makes all tongues sing)
> Might be a diamant worthy to inchase it,
>   Rul'd by a sunne that to this height doth grace it.

The 'new name' of 'Britannia' drew attention to James's new title of 'king of Great Britain' which had been announced in a proclamation just eleven weeks previously.[173] In Britannia, away from the scorching African sun, the nymphs were to gain beauty, stability, and wisdom:

> Their beauties shalbe scorch'd no more:
>   This *sunne* is temperate, and refines
> All things, on which his radiance shines.[174]

The 'sun' was of course both the person of the king as well as the superior climate of Britain.

By today's standards, the masque was unquestionably racist.[175] But was it also proto-feminist? Several scholars have interpreted Anna's initiative and performance in her masques as an act of transgressive self-assertion: a deliberate attempt to subvert patriarchal expectations about women's dress and conduct.[176] After all, the women were parading themselves before men in gauze-like material that allowed the audience to see their arms and legs, forbidden territory! Taking the role of Euphoris, a fertility nymph, Anna highlighted her pregnancy, placed herself at the centre of the masque, and drew all eyes towards her and away from the king. Yet, if 'transgressive self-assertion' was indeed Anna's purpose, it is surprising that James showed no sign of disapproval, nor stopped her from taking to the stage again, nor censored the texts of this and her other masques when they were printed. On the contrary, he had allowed Anna's masque to go ahead in 1604 notwithstanding the diplomatic incident it provoked; he paid for all her masques and allowed them to become a feature—albeit irregular—of court life until 1611, the year of her last performance.

When placed within its political and cultural context, the *Masque of Blackness* appears less shocking. It was the highlight of an unusual set of 'feasting, revelling, and munificence' during that Christmas. Not an evening passed without the staging of 'some lovely play', including two by Shakespeare. The wedding of James's favourite courtier Sir Philip Herbert and Lady Susan de Vere (Cecil's niece and Anna's lady-in-waiting) was celebrated on the 27th with a 'very lovely and well-devised' masque (now lost), performed by an exclusively male cast. The conclusion of Christmas, moreover, saw an important royal event: on Twelfth Night, five-year-old Charles was invested as duke of York 'with much ceremonye and magnificence'.[177] In the presence of Henry, Anna's brother Ulrik, the archbishop of Canterbury, several privy councillors, and other prominent English and Scottish noblemen, a sword was girded round his waist, a 'circlet of gold' placed on his head, and a charter presented to him in the palace of Westminster.[178] In tune with the day's joyful proceedings, Anna's masque that evening fêted the Stuart monarchy: the splendour of its moving sets and sparkling costumes was a sign of the crown's wealth and power; Anna's fertility was on display; James was glorified as the powerful and radiant sun; and the Union was applauded for creating this 'blest isle' of Britain. Furthermore, the voyage of African nymphs to Britannia 'rul'd by a sunne' could well have been read as a parallel with the journey of the queen of Sheba to Jerusalem, ruled by Solomon. Far from being subversive, Anna's 1605 masque served her husband well by contributing to royal ceremonial, legitimation, and majesty.

Anna danced in four more masques before her retirement. She missed out on the Christmas seasons of 1605–06 and 1606–07, likely because of its potential cost at a time when the court was burdened with the expenses involved in the birth of two princesses and the visits of her two brothers. It was, therefore, not until January 1608 that Anna sponsored Jonson's sequel to the *Masque of Blackness*, named the *Masque of Beauty*. This entertainment should have taken place on Twelfth Night in James's new banqueting house at Whitehall but was delayed a few days. Rumour was that the postponement was 'by reason all thinges are not redy', but really it was because the queen's invitations to the masque were again creating a diplomatic row, which this time could not be resolved satisfactorily despite interventions by Lennox, Cecil, and the king.[179]

Anna had personally invited the resident Spanish ambassador (Don Pedro de Zúñiga) to the masque as her guest, and she refused point-blank to allow Antoine Le Fevre de la Boderie, the French ambassador, to attend as well because he would have precedence over the Spaniard. Once again, Anna was intent on showing special favour to Spain, but this time her purpose was to forward matrimonial negotiations between Henry and the daughter or niece of Philip III. Indeed, to signal her support for an Anglo-Spanish match, she chose to wear in the masque the jewelled collar decorated with the initials 'P' and 'M' that Philip II had given to Mary I, his Tudor bride.[180] The attempts made to mollify de la Boderie with an invitation from the king to a private dinner met with no success. In the ambassador's opinion: 'there was no comparison between a dinner given to me by the king and the honour that the Spanish ambassador would receive by attending the ballet [masque]; that one was a private event and the other a solemn and public spectacle'. Everyone would know he had been excluded, and the king of France would therefore be dishonoured. Like diplomats throughout Europe, de la Boderie had to defend his prince's precedence in a foreign court. He therefore declined James's invitation.[181] Yet Anna's masque went on with the approval of her husband and the exclusion of the French ambassador for James again felt the need to maintain good relations with Spain.[182] Enjoying his small victory over the French, the Spanish ambassador publicly invited all the female participants and their partners to a subsequent feast 'with permission from the queen'.[183]

The diplomatic spat was resumed during the Christmas revels of 1609. With Henry IV's approval, de la Boderie let it be known that he had been so insulted by his exclusion the previous year that he intended to leave the kingdom were he not invited to the queen's masque this time round. Recognizing that 'the French hath ben so longe and so much neglected, that yt is doubted more wold not be well indured', James had to avoid offending Henry IV again.[184] But at court over Christmas was a Spanish envoy, Don Ferdinand de Girone, who as special ambassador would have to take precedence over de la Boderie if both were invited to the masque. To resolve the problem, king and council suggested a deferral of the masque's performance, originally scheduled for Twelfth Night in the expectation that de Girone would by then have departed. Anna played her part in seeking to pacify the French: she agreed to the postponement of her masque to Candlemas (2 February), avoided issuing invitations to the Spanish diplomats, and privately apologized to de la Boderie's wife about what had happened. Luckily, de Girone headed off on 1 February, and de la Boderie was mollified when he received his invitation.[185]

Anna's masque was Jonson's *Masque of Queens* in which her ladies were each cast as a warrior queen of literary and historical fame. Significantly, Queen Elizabeth was missing. Effectively, her place was taken by Anna, who played herself for the first time in a masque. Seated at the top of a pyramid, she was 'Bel-Anna...queen of the ocean', the embodiment of all the others' virtues and hence 'the worthiest queen'. The masque was innovative in that it introduced the 'anti-masque' into the dramatic genre, and according to Jonson this device was Anna's idea. For the 'anti-masque', professional players took on the roles of twelve witches or hags who in their grotesque movements, frenzied dancing, and demonic singing were the antithesis of the twelve statuesque and graceful women who took the stage once the witches were swept away by the figure of 'Heroique Virtue'. These witches can best be read as symbolizing the forces of treason that were rendered impotent by the virtue of the Stuart monarchy, a message designed to appeal to James, the author of *Daemonologie*.[186]

De la Boderie did not notice the innovation in the masque, simply describing it as 'very ornate' and 'more beautiful than ingenious', but he did appreciate the royal family's efforts to shower him with honours that evening. He had supper with the king in the company of the two princes while his wife supped with the princess. During the masque, he was seated next to the king who engaged him in conversation 'almost continually' the whole evening. During one of the interludes—'of which there were too many and quite lamentable'—the queen went up to his wife and gave her 'a thousand demonstrations of affection'. A little later, Charles took his young daughter as a dancing partner. De la Boderie was delighted to report home that the favour he received trumped that shown to Zúñiga the previous year.[187]

Anna's next masque, *Tethys' Festival*—written by Samuel Daniel and designed by Inigo Jones—was part of the many festivities surrounding the installation of Henry as prince of Wales on 4 June 1610. To mark his entry into adulthood and public life, the ceremonial year opened on Twelfth Night with a special tournament and masque, called the 'Barriers'. A week earlier, the prince had appeared 'strangely attired' before the whole court and delivered a challenge 'to all knights of Great Britain' in the assumed name of Meliades. The name, 'an ancient title due to the first borne of Scotland', was also an anagram of *Miles a Deo* [soldier of God], and had an Arthurian resonance given that Meliades was the lover of the Lady of the Lake. On the day of the tournament, a Jonson–Jones masque was staged which picked up on the Arthurian theme. It began with the 'Lady of the Lake' comparing 'the glories of this place' favourably with the court of the legendary King Arthur, acclaiming James as Arthur's successor and applauding the reinvigoration of chivalric values at his court.[188] But, in place of the dance that typically closed a masque, there followed a series of choreographed combats at the barriers. The next day, the forty assailants came in their livery to Whitehall to invite and escort the king and queen to a banquet and play at St James's Palace hosted by the prince.[189]

The most intensive celebrations were organized for the week of the investiture. On 31 May, Henry travelled from Richmond to Whitehall by water in preference to riding the distance on horseback, possibly because of fears for his safety in view of Henry IV's assassination earlier that month. The multitude of boats and streamers on the Thames offered a colourful parade for spectators and an opportunity for an elaborate river pageant as entertainment. The investiture took place on Monday 4 June before parliament in the presence of ambassadors, foreign guests, the nobility of all Britain, the lord mayor of London, and representatives of the guilds. That evening, the celebrations concluded with a mock sea battle on the Thames and fireworks. Anna's masque was staged in the banqueting house on the evening of the following day.[190]

The masque picked up the river theme and was very much a family affair. For the first time, the two younger royals participated on stage:

thirteen-year-old Elizabeth appeared as the 'lovely nymph' of the 'stately Thames', one of thirteen who represented the rivers of England; ten-year-old Charles played Zephirus, the west wind, who was accompanied by twelve 'little ladies', the daughters of earls or barons. Anna herself played imperious Tethys, queen of the ocean and wife of Neptune, the 'monarch of Oceanus'. Henry sat as the most prestigious spectator alongside his father, both of whom were presented with gifts from Anna during the performance: James received Neptune's trident; Henry was given a sword and scarf. The direct involvement of the royal family in the masque highlighted its principal theme: the strength, security, and glory of Britain under the Stuart dynasty. The Stuarts' legitimacy was communicated through references to the Tudors and the Welsh harbour of Milford Haven, where Henry VII had landed in 1485 before the battle of Bosworth. The sea and land imagery evoked the creation of a united Britain, as did Henry's scarf which was embroidered with a map of the island. In the concluding scene, the nymphs placed urns containing flowers before a 'Tree of Victory' set up on the right side of James's throne, while a songster explained that they wished 'an everlasting spring/ Of glory, to the Ocean's king'.[191] At the same time, the masque contained a personal message for Henry: he should be content with Stuart power over Great Britain and give up any thoughts of far-ranging military adventures abroad.[192]

The last masque in which Anna performed was due to be staged on Twelfth Night 1611. However, this new Jonson–Jones production was postponed until 3 February because James wanted it to be the centrepiece of entertainments before an extraordinary ambassador due to arrive from France to sign a treaty between the two realms. The lack of contemporary comment suggests it excited neither anticipation of the event nor appreciation of the production, while the text of the masque was not published until five years later in a folio of Jonson's works. Less money was poured into it, and the court may have been jaded after so many festivities. Nonetheless, Anna did not intend *Love Freed from Ignorance and Folly* to be her final masque. She and her ladies had been rehearsing another for the following Christmas, but it was cancelled out of respect for the Spanish king whose queen consort had just died.[193] After that, given Henry's death, Anna probably lost enthusiasm for production and performance.

Anna, Henry, and Lennox were not the only patrons of court masques. During the Christmas season, others commissioned dazzling ones to celebrate their family weddings held at court. On Sunday 5 January 1606, Jonson's allegorical masque 'Hymenaei' [marriage rites] was performed at the nuptials of Suffolk's second daughter Frances (then aged about thirteen) to Essex (aged about fourteen). Songs in the masque linked the matrimonial union to the political Union then under consideration in parliament.[194] Ever the self-publicist, Jonson made sure that the text was printed, but it was Inigo Jones's sets—including a seemingly floating globe from which eight masquers (representing the four humours and four affections) descended—rather than the poet's words that impressed viewers. Again, women participated in the masque; dressed in crimson, with white heron plumes in their hair, they were 'so rich in jewels upon their heades as was most glorious'.[195]

On Twelfth Night 1607, it was the turn of the poet and lyricist Thomas Campion to produce a wedding masque, his first at court. Celebrating the nuptials of Hay and Honora Denny, Campion employed imagery that praised the Union, again the main political concern of the day.[196] Ironically, despite its theme of Anglo-Scottish unity, all but one of the performers were English. The set, doubtless designed by Inigo Jones, was as usual ambitious. It included a night scene with flying bats and owls, and a golden tree dancing to music—or rather the tree would have danced had the mechanism not proved faulty. On Shrove Tuesday (9 February) 1608, Haddington's wedding to Elizabeth Radcliffe was celebrated with yet another Jonson–Jones production, 'a singular brave maske of Englishe and Scotts' that thrilled the audience with moving parts, such as the clouds breaking open to reveal Venus descending in a chariot drawn by doves and swans.[197] In 1613, Campion was chosen to provide the libretti of two more wedding masques: one for the wedding of Princess Elizabeth, the other for Frances Howard's second marriage.

These masques—individually and collectively—created a new masque culture at court. They were more imaginative and expensive than anything that had been staged under the Tudors, and they projected the cultural sophistication of the Jacobean court onto an international stage. Although James never performed in them, each production physically centred around his presence as he was seated directly opposite the vanishing point of the backdrop. Not exactly propaganda, they lauded the king, enhanced his majesty, and celebrated his political projects.[198]

★ ★ ★

The winter season came to an end at Shrovetide, a week which James usually spent in one of the London palaces.[199] Then followed Lent when the court refrained from eating flesh and listened more attentively to the sermons which were preached on Fridays as well as the three other days of the week.[200] After Palm Sunday, James normally spent Holy Week in Whitehall or Greenwich and marked Maundy Thursday with the customary distribution of alms and washing the feet of the poor. Also, during Holy Week he touched the sick to cure them of the 'king's evil' [scrofula].[201] The Easter weekend was a time of solemnity and sermons, but the entertainment on the Tuesday afterwards included bear and bull baiting as well as the customary sermon.[202]

Although James spent the best part of the year hunting in the country, he followed the practice of his predecessor in going on progress during the summer months from July or August to mid-September. Like Elizabeth, he would stay at the homes of county nobles and gentry, many of whom were the sheriffs or JPs responsible for local government. But unlike her, he tended to return to the same houses and towns.[203] James also went further afield than had Elizabeth: reaching the Isle of Wight in the south and Derbyshire in the Midlands.

James's hosts outbid themselves to provide luxurious accommodation, lavish food, and lively entertainments for their monarch. Wherever the royal party went, it was exposed to a constant stream of dinners, dances, speeches, poems, masques, and plays—some pleasurable, others frankly tedious for them and us. Hunting was inevitably a major focus of the progress—summer was after all the stag hunting season—but James also made time for more ceremonial engagements such as royal entries into towns and visits to the two universities where he could be seen and fêted. The importance of the public (even if only the elite) having sight of the king at these times is evident from the lord chamberlain's reaction to the arrangements at Christ Church, Oxford, where James was due to watch a series of Latin plays in August 1605. The king had been assigned the best place for viewing the performance, but Suffolk was 'much troubled' that its position meant that 'the auditory could see but his cheek only'. As a result, the seating had to be changed. It might actually have been better had the king not been seen since he nodded off in boredom during one of the plays and expressed his displeasure during another.[204]

Anna accompanied James throughout six of his summer progresses before 1612 and was present for part of the journeys on two more. In 1605, and again between 1608 and 1612, the royal couple were joined by Henry and, in 1611, by Elizabeth. The local nobility and gentry flocked to attend upon them on progress, creating a court 'crowded and much fuller' than in

London.[205] Ambassadors and privy councillors joined for a few days or more. Consequently, there could be as many as 1,000 people in the royal train. However, in response to Cecil's economy drive at court in 1608 and conscious of the burden on the counties that had to provide provisions, James curtailed the progress's duration and size of his retinue that summer.[206]

Like Elizabeth, James also paid visits closer to home, honouring his subjects with his presence. To mention a few: on May Day 1604, he and Anna were treated to dinner and outdoors entertainment when visiting the house of Sir William Cornwallis in Highgate.[207] In the summer of 1607, James and Henry attended two civic functions held in the City.[208] The next year, the royal couple, both sons, and the court joined Cecil for 'a sumptuous banquet' in his house on the Strand to mark his appointment as lord treasurer.[209]

On progress, James played the role of the listening monarch, accepting petitions graciously and giving thanks for gifts. It is often said that he disliked crowds but, if so, he put aside his true feelings to behave like a monarch and mix with his subjects. Similarly, the common impression that James was timorous and terrified of assassination is belied by his willingness to risk attack when riding on horseback through urban areas while on progress.

★ ★ ★

In 1606, James's progress was delayed because of the arrival of his brother-in-law Christian IV. The visit seems to have been somewhat last-minute for James was out hunting at Oatlands when the Danes landed at Gravesend on 16 July, and it was only the day after their appearance that James issued an order for his leading nobles to come to court to give Christian a grand welcome.[210] As the party was expected to stay for a least a month, a tournament was quickly organized for 25 August.[211] It was the first time a reigning monarch had come to England since 1522 and, despite the short notice, James was determined to impress Christian and repay the hospitality he had himself received in Denmark sixteen years previously.

Public interest in Christian's visit was considerable. Three prose pamphlets and a long English poem were sold in London to describe and publicize the event. One pamphlet was translated into German for publication in Hamburg, and several Latin poems were printed for an international readership.[212] Told of the Danes' arrival, Londoners gathered at Tilbury to marvel at their flotilla of eight vessels, especially the massive and ornate flagship the *Trekoner* [Three Crowns], while crowds lined the riverbanks to watch English barges row the two kings, Henry, and numerous courtiers towards

Greenwich. Wherever the two kings travelled afterwards, the roads were clogged with 'multitudes' of people keen to watch the royal processions.[213]

At Gravesend, Christian was welcomed by Lennox, sent by James as his advance representative. The next day, James and Henry arrived to escort Christian to Greenwich where Anna was in residence recovering from her recent confinement and the death of Sophia. The summer weather and plague in London influenced the itinerary thereafter. Little time was spent in Whitehall, and the royal party mainly visited the palaces along the Thames, passed four nights in Cecil's grand house at Theobalds in Hertfordshire, and set off for a short trip to Windsor.

During his first week, Christian went hunting every day with James while every evening he was invited to 'royally superabundant' feasts. The second week began at Theobalds, five days that cost Cecil over £1,000.[214] In addition to further feasts and hunting, the party was treated to 'manie verie learned, delicate, and significant showes and devises' by Jonson and Jones, the meanings of which eluded many of the spectators. Christian—who did not understand English—had an interpreter who was likewise baffled. On Monday 28 July, the court moved back to Greenwich for yet more hunting, feasting, and 'other private delights', until all was ready for the royal entry into London.[215]

On Thursday 31 July, the two kings with their grand retinues set off from the Tower to ride along the customary ceremonial route towards the City's western gateway. Huge crowds turned out to watch behind rails. 'The ceremony was a magnificent and noble one, both on account of the great gathering of personages, the richness of their robes, and the trappings of their horses.' To display their equality in status and fraternal relationship, neither king 'wore any insignia of royalty, but were both in private dress and both alike'.[216] As usual on these occasions, the City fathers offered allegorical pageants, speeches, songs, and gifts to their royal guests; and, as to be expected, the themes of the day were the 'like splendor' of the two kings and the 'concord' between the two realms. The royal party eventually reached Whitehall 'where dismounting about seaven of the clocke in the evening, they feasted and reposed themselves there all that night'.[217]

The following day, accompanied by a few English noblemen, Christian made a private tour of the City. Afterwards, he joined James at the Tower where he was given sight of the jewel house, mint, royal wardrobe, and armoury.[218] The remainder of the trip was again spent away from Whitehall in a variety of palaces. On Sunday 3 August, Anna was churched at Greenwich and from then on devoted more time to her brother. Two days later, on Gowrie Day, 'many of the nobilitie and courtiers, shewed both manhood and skill' at a tilt in which Christian, 'armed very rich and mounted on a most stately courser', ran first against William, Lord Howard of Effingham, and then the earl of Arundel, honours being even.[219] But, at a match of the 'running at the ring', Christian outplayed James 'which putt him into no small impatiencies'.[220] Plays were also performed at court, and quite possibly one of them was Shakespeare's *Hamlet*.[221] Shortly before Christian's departure, earlier than expected, the court travelled to Windsor where he was installed as a knight of the garter.[222] Returning to Gravesend, he was brought to Chatham to admire twenty-two vessels of the royal navy that 'were sett owt in theyr best equipage'. The two kings, Anna, and Henry together with their councillors then dined on the galleon, the *Elizabeth Jonas*, 'wondrously adorned with cloth of gold'. At last, on board his own flagship on 11 August, there was a final farewell 'with drinck and gunshott' and an exchange of gifts before Christian set off the next day.[223]

This final reception ended on a sour note. Because James did not wish to stay too long on board, he assigned Nottingham to keep an eye on the time. Accordingly, the admiral 'purposely advaunced [his watch] some ii houwers' to give James an excuse to leave early. At two o'clock, James asked the time, and Nottingham duly replied that it was four o'clock and the moment to disembark. Christian, however, naturally maintained that it was still only two o'clock, and he raised two fingers to Nottingham. Mistaking the gesture, the earl thought that Christian was giving him a 'sin of the horns', which signified a cuckold, and 'tooke some secret dislike at the manner hereof'. His pregnant wife, who was not actually present, took still greater offence when she learned of the occurrence, and she sent a letter complaining bitterly of 'the great wronge the king of the Danes hath done me'.[224] Her sensitivity was acute because of the ridicule she and her husband had endured owing to the nearly forty-year age gap between them. Christian in turn complained to James about the countess, who was promptly banned from the English court. When she attempted to return, Anna rebuffed her. Nottingham, though, was protected from the queen's anger as she thought him an old man who deserved respect.[225]

Even without this embarrassing incident, the visit was not a great success.[226] James had put on a fine display before the powerful king of Denmark, but his brother-in-law had too often outshone him. In their gift exchange, the monarchs proved equal in terms of the value of the gifts, but Christian's were more inventive. Aside from the usual jewels, portraits, and plate, he gave a sword and a fighting ship to Henry and a 'beautiful and well-contrived firework' to James. Taking the form of a cube upon which stood a lion, with a chain in his hand which fettered eight vices, the firework burned and crackled for about forty-five minutes when lit.[227] In equestrian sports, James also came out second best. Dudley Carleton discreetly commented upon Christian's 'good hap' in never missing in the contest of 'running at the ring' and upon James's 'ill luck scarce ever to come neere it'.[228] Even worse, an anonymous letter was read at court that urged James to follow 'the example of his brother-in-law, the king of Denmark' who 'for his prowess at the joust has won golden opinions'.[229] The efforts to amuse Christian at the chase backfired since he took 'small pleasure' in hunting and found fault with it as a sport.[230] Indeed, Christian became so bored that he decided to leave several weeks earlier than originally planned.[231] As a result, the visit to the University of Oxford had to be cancelled, no doubt causing disappointment since its chancellor had put together a collection of Latin verses, written by ninety-eight members of the university. The compendium, consequently, had to be sent to court for presentation.[232]

Just as problematic for public relations, Christian was a critic not only of the hunting but also of his brother-in-law. On a personal note, he upbraided James for his neglect of the queen whom he found not looking well.[233] On political matters, he was heard expressing surprise that James did not support his merchants against Spanish attempts to exclude them from Atlantic trade.[234] Almost certainly, Christian had come to England to persuade James to join a Protestant league against the pope and Habsburg powers.[235] But, although the two monarchs agreed that the danger from papal power was a threat to 'all Christian princes', the Danish king returned home empty-handed.[236]

Nor did the two nations get on well. According to the French ambassador, the English courtiers despised the Danes as coarse while the Danes found the English very arrogant.[237] The few surviving letters written by Englishmen about the visit bear out his opinion: Carleton thought little of the gifts distributed by the Danish king; and Sir James Harington famously and hyperbolically described how the drinking habits of the Danes lured English men and women into unruly and disgusting conduct. During a feast at Theobalds, he remembered, Christian passed out from drunkenness and the male and female guests were too inebriated to walk or talk, a number vomiting in the hall.[238] Even one of the sanitized printed accounts of the visit hinted that the English hosts 'would have esteemed it more barbarous to have refused drinke, then disgrace to bee drunke'.[239]

★ ★ ★

The debauched behaviour during Christian's visit—a far cry from the decorum of Elizabeth's day (as Harington explicitly pointed out)—was not the everyday experience of life at James's court, though admittedly disorderly conduct was occasionally observed.[240] Usually, customary rituals surrounding informal dining were observed, and instrumental music was played at formal feasts to add to their grandeur.[241] On special occasions, James would pull out the stops to create an impression of great decorum and magnificence. When, for example, in 1610, an extraordinary Venetian envoy was presented to the king in the great chamber, he was greeted with 'a magnificent spectacle': 'At the door we were met by the great chamberlain, who preceded us, holding a long wand in his hand—the sign of his office. We passed between two rows of the great ladies and gentlemen of the court, all richly dressed and covered with jewels.' The royal family were seated together on a dais while the officers of the crown and other leading gentlemen sat 'each in his rank of pre-eminence and in seemly order' below.[242] Nor was this uncommon; when a special ambassador arrived from France in May 1612, the Venetian ambassador commented that the 'grandeur of this court was set forth that day, as they know how'.[243]

The three Jacobean courts were more international than Elizabeth's had been. Foreign ambassadors and visitors reached out to James on his accession, and James reached out to them as the reign progressed.[244] Anna's relatives arrived at the court with large retinues for short visits, although it was an overlong one in the case of her brother Ulrik who was asked to go home. At the same time, the culture of the court was becoming increasingly cosmopolitan, as patrons within the royal family and outside were attracted to Continental styles of painting, architecture, and music, especially though not exclusively Italian.

Despite, these positive aspects, many English commentators found certain aspects of the early Jacobean court novel and deplorable, whether the presence of Scots in the palaces' inner sanctums, women on the stage in masques, the extravagance of court life, or the perceived inaccessibility of the king. Over time, they became used to the British dimension of the court, especially after 1611 when many Scots returned home and after 1615 when Englishmen entered the privy chamber as grooms and gentlemen.[245] Possibly, courtiers also became accustomed to the participation of women in masques, since fewer criticisms are evident after the *Masque of Blackness*, or perhaps their appearance in the later masques was statelier and consequently thought less scandalous. However, the profligacy of the court continued to be a cause of concern and complaint. Although the crown's income increased after 1603, thanks to impositions, customs farming, and a revival of trade, it could not keep up with the ordinary expenditure of James's household: calculated at £64,000 in 1603, it soared to £90,800 in 1607.[246] In desperation, the privy council urged 'providence' and begged James in 1609 to curtail the number of his servants whose actual 'use' was questionable but whose residence at court was funded out of the royal purse. Such a reduction, they contended, would not limit royal magnificence for the king could still retain servants to serve him personally 'in a noble and generous fashion' and to 'adorne' his court. Simultaneously, the council wanted James to limit his 'liberality' and 'bounty'. Again, their recommendation was for him to show greater discrimination. The king, they advised, should weigh up men's 'merritts and reward in an even balance together'.[247] Some retrenchment did occur, and court expenses were brought down to £81,200 in 1612, an outlay still considerably more than that under Elizabeth and certainly far more than the crown could afford. Besides, it rose again after Cecil's death.[248] The results were crown debt, loans from London merchants, and calls for parliamentary subsidies, which revealed the parlous state of royal finances to the political nation.[249]

As presented here, the inaccessibility of James should not be exaggerated. Nonetheless, it is true that he tended to be unapproachable while hunting; he might then have a few lords with him for company, but otherwise he did not like to be disturbed while at his favourite sport.[250] Additionally, when residing in his palaces, James spent parts of his day in the bedchamber or privy chamber where access was strictly limited except by invitation. From the start, his inaccessibility aroused critical comment. In the summer of 1604, John Burges was warning the king of 'the generall murmuring and complaints, which every man hears' that 'you grace not your people, you speak not to them, you look not at them, you bless them not and therefore say they you love them not'.[251] James did not take the criticism well, and Burges was imprisoned for his frankness. This did not stop Robert Wakeman, in 1605, from urging the king to give 'easie accesses and audience unto all that came to speake with him' and warning him against the 'caterpillers' of courts' and 'cursed Machiavels' who persuade kings 'to keepe themselves always from the accesse of their subjects as the next way to make them great'. Wakeman evaded censure only because he larded his sermon with flattery and asserted the divine right of kings.[252] Matters did not improve, especially as the Gunpowder Plot and assassination of Henry IV made James wary of public interactions.

Although James was less approachable than his predecessor had been, his court was at least as visible to his subjects. Leaving aside gossip communicated orally and in correspondence, the court was revealed to many people in performance and print. Early Jacobean playwrights focused on the court more closely than had their Elizabethan counterparts, and audiences lapped up political dramas featuring an imagined courtly life. Readers purchased the texts of these plays, masques, and other court entertainments.[253] Unfortunately for James, these portrayals were usually uncomplimentary. Not only did dramas like the *Isle of Gulls* satirize his court remorselessly but other less obviously topical plays revealed the unsavoury political and social intrigues of fictive Renaissance courts that could be applied to contemporary England. Jonson's tragedies *Sejanus His Fall* (performed 1603–04, printed 1605) and *Catiline* (1611) depicted a court where deceit, sycophancy, and corruption prospered. At the same time, verse libels which scoffed at courtiers and even the king flourished in the early seventeenth century and became embedded in popular culture by the 1620s, even though they largely circulated in manuscript. So, although critiques of court life and courtiers were hardly novel, new targets for ridicule emerged under James and came to be transmitted in a wider range of media to the public.[254]

9

Privy Council and Councillors

'The council spares the king the trouble of governing, and not only do all subjects transact their business with it, but foreign representatives as well, and one might say it was the very ears, body, and voice of the king.'[1] Molin's assessment of the function of the English privy council, in 1607, was spot on. From at least the Elizabethan period, the monarch ruled, but the privy council governed the realm. As the monarch's 'voice', it held discussions with ambassadors from abroad and issued orders and regulations on the monarch's behalf to local officials. It also used its voice to advise the monarch, although under James its recommendations were given on paper rather than by mouth when the king was absent from his London palaces.

As the monarch's 'ears', the privy council was a major point of contact from the localities to the crown. It heard complaints from subjects about a broad range of perceived injustices, from monopolies or acts of piracy to unfair personal treatment by another individual. Additionally, local officials wrote to the privy council seeking advice on a huge variety of problems, both big and small, and passed on information about matters of interest, especially observations concerning the state's security.

As the 'body' of the monarch, the council was the location of patronage, which itself was the lifeblood of the state. With no properly paid bureaucracy nor police, the monarch had to dispense grants, pensions, honours, and privileges to secure the co-operation of his or her officials in governing the realm, both at the centre and in the regions. Most minor requests ended up at the council table or were handled by the principal secretary. The monarch became involved only in special cases when posts were important or the monarch had a personal relationship with a suitor or where there were rival claims involving high-ranking patrons.[2]

Finally, the privy council had a judicial function, unmentioned by Molin. Twice a week during the law term, its members joined with the chief justices of the realm to operate as a legal court hearing criminal cases and disputes that allegedly involved violence. It was then known as the court of star chamber, supposedly named after the painted roof of the chamber in which it sat. Both private plaintiffs and the crown's attorney general initiated the cases. The total number filed varied each year, but there were about 700 in Elizabeth's last year, dropping to an average of 358 under James.[3]

In Scotland, the privy council had similar administrative and judicial functions. During the reigns of Mary and James VI, the institution had grown in importance, meeting regularly, acquiring a corporate identity, and widening its competence. Its members included officers of state who acted as virtual department heads in the state's administration. During the 1580s, moreover, temporary subcommittees of the council—usually known as commissions—were appointed to help manage the increasing volume of business. James's Scottish council was therefore well able to provide a stable administrative and authoritative base in Edinburgh when the king was away, both briefly in Denmark and long-term in England.[4]

In 1603, James expected his English privy council to take on even more responsibilities than they had fulfilled under the late queen. Importing the institutional feature of commissions into England, he devolved responsibility 'for the examination of anie reporte to us of all sutes for matters of our bounty' to a 'commission' of six privy councillors that was essentially a subcommittee of the privy council. The members were originally directed to meet weekly but ended up, in December 1604, assigning an additional day to deal with the many suitors.[5] Furthermore, because he travelled more frequently than had Elizabeth, James required the English privy council to carry out business without him while he was away from the capital. As a result, some significant changes occurred in both the pattern of council meetings and conciliar interactions with the monarch.

Although Elizabeth had rarely attended council meetings, they took place in the royal palaces where she and her court were residing, and councillors could be consulted as necessary. When she was on summer progress, the most important councillors normally travelled with her to other parts of the realm, and her principal secretary was on hand to confer about correspondence received or matters raised in council.[6] Business therefore continued uninterrupted. By contrast, James spent weeks on end throughout the year away from the privy council and his principal secretary. As we have already seen, he went hunting in all seasons whether at his new lodges at Royston in Hertfordshire and Newmarket in Suffolk, or in the parks of favoured courtiers. When totted up, the time James spent at his favourite recreation amounted to about six months each year.

From the start of the reign, James made it clear that the privy council would have to get along without him in their management of the realm during his hunting trips.[7] Since he was not receptive to receiving dispatches about routine matters while at his sport, the privy councillors in Whitehall were left to deal with an enormous number of different issues without much—if indeed any—discussion with the king. Coming within their remit were negotiations with merchants, complaints about piracy, petitions to redress perceived injustices, requests for grants, the overview of the royal finances, and more besides. Given this, the nature of royal interactions with privy councillors was transformed. Instead of having regular face-to-face conversations with the monarch, Cecil and other privy councillors had to communicate with James by letter while he was away. Even then, the letters Cecil sent and received often went through intermediaries who acted as a sort of triage. Initially, Worcester assumed this role, as he was the one English privy councillor who attended upon the king while he was hunting.[8] Another intermediary was Aston, the king's chief huntsman, but increasingly Cecil's main correspondent was Sir Thomas Lake, one of the clerks of the signet, who was not made a privy councillor until 1616.

Initially, privy councillors were worried about this situation and warned the king that his absences both diminished their authority and affected the council board's procedures. James, however, refused to limit the sport that he claimed was vital for his health and well-being. He promised to return to London if his presence was required for the good of the realm but directed that such recalls should be rare:

> if my continuall presence in London be so necessarie, as my absence for my healthe makis the counsaillouris to be without autoritie or respecte, one worde shall bring me home and make me worke till my breath worke out, if that be the greattest well for the kingdome; but I can not thinke that course so neidfull if ye make not mountainis of moldehills [molehills].[9]

For routine matters, the privy council had to get on without him. But, to enhance its authority and ensure that its business was conducted more conveniently, he instructed the body, in early 1605, to meet once a week in Anna's apartments at Whitehall during his times away.[10] Justifying this new arrangement, James playfully told Cecil and 'his fellowis' that this meant little had changed since the days of Elizabeth, seeing that 'ye have gottin the gyding againe of a feminine courte in the olde fashion'.[11] But of course, everything had changed. Moreover, as already observed in the previous chapter, privy councillors no longer had automatic right of access to the king even when they were in the same residence. They had to be invited into James's private apartments.

By 1605, James seemed to realize that he might need his privy council to confer with him in person while he was in the countryside. When planning the construction of a new hunting lodge at Ampthill House in Bedfordshire, he instructed that provision be made for rooms that could accommodate some dozen privy councillors who might need to stay for urgent meetings.[12] However, the house was never built, and the other hunting lodges were not extensive enough to house a sizeable part of the council.

Consequently, James was forced to return to London for consultations. However, he did so only when he considered that his presence was vital, and he kept the visits as short as possible. In December 1605, for instance, he rushed back to Whitehall from Royston 'but to retorn within 2 dayes' in order to deliberate with his council about provisions for the Union; towards the end of that same month, he returned again 'in haste' to discuss what to do about Puritan troublemakers.[13] In January 1611, he attended a council meeting to consult with its members about the prorogation of the parliament then in session, but left for Royston within the shortest space of time.[14] To speed up journeys, James paid for the repair of highways and the erection of new bridges between London and Royston, and Newmarket.[15] James also begrudged delaying hunting for state business in London. In 1604, for example, the Venetian ambassador—a great source of gossip—reported that James was ready for a trip to Royston, but the commissioners working on the Union project 'remonstrated with him, and so he stayed, though against his will'.[16]

While hunting in the countryside, James was not idle. During the evenings or days off, he dealt with the paperwork sent via Worcester or Lake. On one occasion, he jokingly told Cecil that the number of letters he had written that evening rivalled the number of hares he had killed 'all this tyme'.[17] James did not just sign off documents drafted by his secretary; he read them through carefully, especially those he considered important, and he would revise the wording of drafts whenever he thought it necessary. In June 1604, for example, he extended the preamble of a bill to be submitted before parliament in order to provide a further reason for its introduction.[18] Another time, he made changes, not because he was dissatisfied with the content but in order to improve the style of a document. Amending a draft relating to the projected naturalization of Scots, James explained that he had made modifications because he 'thought there was some superfluity' in the original text: Lake passed on to Cecil that: 'the substance he [the king] takes no exception to, but prayeth to be excused for playing the secretary'.[19] Sometimes, James set down the agenda for council meetings that met in his absence.[20] When privy councillors sat together or had conferences with ambassadors, he demanded a full report and grew impatient at delays.[21] Likewise, he demanded speedy implementation of his orders and instructions: 'This is as much to say as that he think much you have not don yet', wrote Cecil in the margin of a letter in which Lake had listed the king's directives that needed completion by the time he returned from hunting.[22]

The government therefore continued to function normally during James's many absences. However, its efficiency was often impaired. The posts were slow, and papers were occasionally lost in transit or failed to be posted.[23] Other times, deliberations and decisions were put on hold because James wanted neither his recreation to be interrupted nor 'to begin or ende businesse in haste'.[24] Occasionally, petitions directed to the king or privy council could fall between the two stools. When, in January 1605, merchants from the Levant Company wanted to protest about the imposition of custom duties on currants, they first petitioned the privy council; then, on being told that they should resort to the king, they rode to Huntingdon where they delivered their petition to him, only to be told by James that their request was a subject for his privy councillors. Clearly irritated by the unexpected interruption to his sport, James directed Lake to tell his privy council:

> that if anie such aunsweare was given them [the merchants] that they should resort to his highness, he marvayled why he was not certefied thereof that he might be armed against their coming who otherwise being surprised by them might perhaps have made some other aunsweare then were fitting.[25]

Also, confusingly, James intervened in matters of patronage that he had supposedly left to the privy council. In May 1605, members wrote to him with the plea that he should refer all suitors to them, promising to treat them 'with courtesy and despatch'.[26] On this matter, it was not just a problem of blurred boundaries. Away from his council, James showed a largesse that needed to be curbed.

James's recurring periods outside London created a more general unease as well. Complaints were heard that his absences put power in the hands of his ministers, notably Cecil. As early as November 1604, Molin reported that libels were appearing in London, which accused

> the king of attending to nothing but his pleasures, especially to the chase, and of leaving all government entirely in the hands of his ministers, as though he had come to the throne for nothing else than to go a-hunting; warning him, too, that unless he changes he will bring himself and the kingdom as well down to the ground.[27]

Matters had not improved eighteen months on, when another Venetian ambassador related that James's 'perpetual occupation with country pursuits' was creating such discontent that 'there was affixed to the door of the privy chamber a general complaint of the king, alleging that his excessive kindness leaves his subjects a prey to the cupidity of his ministers'.[28] Had James been in London, the thinking went, he would have reined in his councillors' abuses of power. This perception encouraged both the trope of the 'evil councillor' and growing accusations of ministerial corruption that found expression in the libels written on Cecil's death.[29]

★ ★ ★

Like Elizabeth before him, James was advised to take counsel, and the privy council was one of the natural vehicles for this.[30] Like his predecessor, James declared in many proclamations that he was acting on conciliar advice. Yet, in his case, he was playing lip service to this expectation for he did not really see the privy council as the main advisory body for dealing with matters of state. He had written little about the king's need or duty to work with a council in *Basilikon Doron* and *Trew Law*; and in Scotland he listened to individual ministers and consulted more broadly through the institutions of conventions and estates rather than his privy council.[31] Once king of England, he rarely seems to have called upon the English privy council as a whole to discuss and advise on policy. He much preferred to listen to the opinions of individuals such as Cecil or Dunbar.[32] In this respect, he differed from Elizabeth whose privy council had met regularly to discuss foreign policy, security issues, and other matters of state, even though it is true that she too relied for advice upon individual privy councillors and courtiers.[33] Admittedly, we may be missing evidence for the privy council's role in giving counsel because its official registers, covering the years between 1602 and 1 May 1613, were burned in a major fire at Whitehall in 1619. Nevertheless, from other documents it does appear that James used his privy council to execute rather than help make policy.[34]

On certain matters, James considered his privy council lacked the expertise to give counsel. Although the realm's three leading law officers sat on its board, James chose to confer with a wider bench of judges—either alone or alongside the privy council—on issues concerning his prerogative. In November 1608, for instance, all but one of the Westminster judges were summoned to advise upon the jurisdiction of the prerogative court of Wales. At the meeting Ellesmere told them:

> the matter proposed was to bee consulted on by the kinge and his councell as a matter of state and that the kinge had his privy councell consistinge of the lords, ther present, and that the judges were alsoe of his counsel and to give theire councell when they are called thereunto and sworne to doe that aswell as to the administracon of justice.[35]

It so happened that James barely listened to the judges' opinion on this occasion but set out his own position on the prerogative court which he expected them to follow.

Privy councillors did offer advice, either individually or as a body and sometimes unsolicited, in the form of policy papers.[36] They took risks in doing so for the king could lose his temper when hearing or reading unwelcome news or advice. James also held the body of the privy council responsible when things did not go his way. Poor conciliar advice, James maintained, had been the cause of his bad relations with parliament. When he first came to England, claimed James in 1621, he knew not its laws and customs and had depended upon 'the old councillors that I found, which the old queen had left', but they had often misdirected him.[37] The privy council, he maintained, had failed to explain to him properly the issues involved in the election dispute of 1604 in Buckinghamshire when he had intervened using his royal prerogative to the fury of MPs.[38] The privy council, bemoaned James, had also not advised him properly about his project to unite his two kingdoms; 'representing the achievement of the Union as an easy affair', they had 'committed him to a labyrinth' in which his honour was involved and no way through was found.[39] James's criticisms may have been fair in the first case, but it is hard to see how the privy council could have diverted him from the cause of Union. On matters dear to his heart or in which he felt his prerogative was involved, James went his own way or listened to the more congenial voices in his bedchamber.

★ ★ ★

In the absence of a professional civil service, James was as reliant on the privy council to govern the country as Elizabeth had been. Like her, he used it to maintain contact with the localities and put pressure on local gentlemen to comply with royal orders and pay their taxes. To do this successfully, privy councillors had to hold local offices and develop relationships with regional power structures, both urban elites and county gentry. Understanding this, James continued the practice of appointing privy councillors as high stewards in corporate towns. Additionally, any privy councillor who was especially associated with a town usually assumed responsibility for government orders directed to that urban centre. Towns benefited too from a close relationship with one or more privy councillors for they could call upon these men at the heart of government to look after their interests. The mayor and aldermen of Hull, for example, sought the assistance of Cecil, the town's lord steward, regarding the restitution of ships confiscated by Christian IV of Denmark after earlier pleas for justice went unheeded.[40] Under Elizabeth, a few leading councillors—Leicester, Burghley, and Essex—had amassed most of the urban high stewardships, but between 1603 and 1612, some twelve privy councillors were appointed to these positions, although Cecil held the lion's share. Among them were lesser councillors like William, Lord Knollys, who had taken on Banbury by 1608 and held Abingdon in 1610, Oxford in 1611, and afterwards Reading.[41]

In the counties, leading privy councillors were usually named lord lieutenants of shires in which they normally held large landholdings. On his accession, James was advised to abolish the office as 'unnecessary and inconvenient' now that peace was on the horizon since JPs could carry out the duties of keeping order and holding musters for a county militia.[42] James, however, wanted the lieutenancies to operate as another point of contact between the centre and localities. He and the privy council recognized that they were a valuable organ for a governmental presence in the counties.[43] They could also keep the militia up to the mark in training and equipment to tackle emergencies, whether risings or invasions, and be an early port of call if there was any local unrest.[44] At the same time, James realized the dangers of concentrating too much provincial power in the hands of any one nobleman. For this reason, when Northampton was appointed as the new lord warden of the Cinque Ports with considerable patronage in Kent, James gave the county's lord lieutenancy to Edward, Lord Wotton.

Giving lieutenancies to privy councillors represented a distinct change from the 1590s. Then, the council was too small and fully engaged with the war to take on yet another responsibility, so Elizabeth tended to leave vacant lord lieutenancies unfilled and allowed deputy lieutenants to run military affairs under the title of muster commissioners. Under James, by contrast, the lord lieutenancy became a permanent feature of local government in most shires, even though it was not yet normal for each county to have its own individual lord lieutenant. Privy councillors were appointed to a significant number of the sixteen vacant posts that were filled after Elizabeth's death [see Appendix 2]. But, since the councillors were usually absent from their counties at court, James extended the provision for deputy lieutenants and depended upon them to do the job of organizing musters. The king retained as deputies the same local men who had served during the last years of Elizabeth's reign, thereby maintaining continuity.[45]

Justices of the peace were the other major governmental presence in the counties, bearing the main burden of local government just as they had under Elizabeth.[46] Each commission of the peace included two to four members of the privy council. The lord chancellor selected the rest, wherever possible from among the eminent men of a county: local nobles, gentlemen, and clergy. However, there were not always enough of these families to provide the thirty or more JPs needed for each county. Then, lawyers and esquires (lesser gentry) were also recruited to sit on the bench. The justices met every three months at the quarter sessions to try all criminal cases except felonies and be given the ever-increasing responsibilities for collecting taxes, controlling the poor, imposing religious conformity, keeping the peace, and implementing any further orders of the privy council. At the quarter sessions, they met with other county and parish officers to consult about local needs and concerns. There, they could also draw up petitions for parliament or lobby their MPs to present county grievances. Not all JPs, however, showed up: in Hertfordshire and Essex, for example, merely one-quarter to one-third were present at any given quarter session. Instead, a small working group of knights, esquires, and distinguished lawyers attended and handled the bulk of routine administration. Because of the creation of so many knighthoods, the percentage of knights as JPs increased under James.[47]

Their swelling workload had resulted in extra meetings taking place in some counties under Elizabeth, and, in 1605, the privy council regularized this practice by issuing a new set of orders that advised JPs to meet more often in what became known as petty sessions. There, they dealt with routine matters: overseeing poor relief, pursuing vagrants and beggars, licensing and suppressing alehouses, and organizing bridge and highway repairs.[48]

But not all were diligent in carrying out their responsibilities, and, in 1609, the privy council ordered the commissions of the peace to select every year some three or four or more JPs from their number who could be counted upon to execute governmental directions and 'reporte to his Majestie of ther indevores'.[49]

Towards the end of the 1610 parliament, James delivered a paper to the house of commons accusing JPs of neglecting their duties. First, he complained of their tendency to take up residency in London or nearby towns 'whereby the government and peace of the country which they ought cheifely to regard is neglected, hospitalytie decayed, and infinite disorders increased'. Then he gave a list of their failures, which included permitting 'tipling houses' to multiply, neglecting 'watches and wards' in towns, and failing to enforce laws and regulations.[50] While James's complaints might well have been justified, he was likely taking the opportunity to shame MPs, many of whom were also JPs, at a time when they seemed to be presenting endless grievances to him, not just about government finances but also about defects in the commonwealth.

Among their duties, JPs were expected to keep an eye out for troublemakers and intervene quickly if serious disorder threatened by either negotiating with the leaders or arresting them. If disturbances got out of hand, they had to call upon the lord lieutenant to raise the militia either to frighten assembled crowds or to use force to restore order. This happened in the Midlands during late spring and early summer of 1607.

On 29 May 1607, the privy council wrote to the high sheriffs and JPs of the counties of Leicestershire, Huntingdonshire, Worcestershire, Gloucestershire, and Derbyshire to authorize them to suppress people who 'had gathered together to pull downe inclosures', if necessary with arms.[51] The next day, the king issued a proclamation commanding the same men to use force against the protesters 'if admonitions and other lawfull meanes doe not serve to reduce them to their dueties'. James also promised to make enquiries into unlawful enclosures once peace was restored.[52] Since the rioters claimed that they were taking direct action 'to acquaint his Majestie' about the abuse of enclosure, James had every hope that the crowd would disperse with his promise of possible reform.[53]

In Northamptonshire, however, things turned ugly. About one thousand 'fellowes', who termed themselves 'levelers', gathered at Newton in Rockingham Forest, three miles north of Kettering, to dig out the hedges and fences of a local landlord. The county militia, under the command of the lord lieutenant Thomas Cecil, earl of Exeter, was called out but showed 'great backwardnes' in coming forward, probably because of its sympathy with the assembled crowd. To fill the gap, the local gentry (one of them a deputy lieutenant, the Puritan Sir Edward Montagu) put together a makeshift force of cavalry and infantry from their own household servants and clients. On 8 June, they confronted the protestors and twice read out another royal proclamation. Again, James insisted on 'all severity' and 'sharp remedies' against the rioters 'for their heinous treasons as well by our armes as lawes'.[54] When the crowd would not disperse, the force charged. At first, the assembly stood firm and 'fought desperatelie', but at the second charge they scattered, leaving forty or fifty slain.[55] It was the middle of June before all seemed quiet.[56]

Shocked by the rising, James issued another proclamation that justified his repression, absolved his government from the causes of the unrest, and promised reform. The enclosures, he asserted, had been made 'before we had taken the scepter of this government into our possession', and he was 'not minded that the offences of a few (though justly provoking our royall indignation) shall alter our gracious disposition to give reliefe in this case'.[57] Shortly afterwards, he offered a pardon to 'offendours' who submitted themselves before the lieutenant, deputy lieutenant, or sheriff in their county. Some 143 persons from fifteen towns came forward to plead a pardon by the end of September.[58] But the men captured at Newton were put on trial, and a number were executed, their quartered bodies displayed at Northampton, Oundle, and other local towns in accordance with the normal punishment for rebellion.[59]

It was left to the privy council to carry through the promise to investigate illegal enclosures that the king had made in his proclamation of 28 May. They no doubt lacked enthusiasm for the task since many of them, including Cecil, were themselves enclosers. James was, however, insistent: 'because he saith that nothing more despleaseth him then when his people are promised remedye and gett it not'. 'The execution', explained Cecil wearily to his colleagues, 'is the lyfe of all councells.'[60] So, the privy councillors set up commissions of inquiry to investigate the extent of illegal enclosures in the seven Midland counties thought to be affected, and, in February 1608, landlords named in the returns of the commission were prosecuted in star chamber.[61]

★ ★ ★

While the change of monarch did not result in any major change in the privy council's role in governance, its personnel did change under James. Under Elizabeth, the council had varied in size, with twenty members at the start of the reign and a mere fourteen at the end. Her final council board was too small for James's liking, and he was determined to add more of the 'ancient nobilitie' as well as some of his Scottish subjects to the existing membership. At the same time, however, he wanted the council's size to be manageable 'to keepe our affaires either from discoverie or disorder' [leaks or internal conflicts]. So, although he knew that many of his new subjects would be disappointed by their exclusion, he swore only twenty-four men into the council plus the two secretaries, one for England and one 'especially for Scottish affaires' [see Appendix 1].[62] James hoped the number would eventually decrease through deaths, but in fact it started to rise after 1615. Many members, though, rarely attended meetings, and an inner group of councillors usually managed the business in hand.[63] As under Elizabeth, letters from the privy council could be signed by fewer than ten members, sometimes as few as five.[64]

The proportion of noblemen on the privy council was augmented under James. All the new members were barons or earls, while three of Elizabeth's ex-councillors were promoted to baronies during James's first regnal year. This noble dominance followed the pattern in Scotland, but it had the disadvantage of leaving only two privy councillors without a noble title who could sit in the house of commons when it met.[65] Before 1603, senior privy councillors were used there to facilitate the passage of government legislation, restrain critical speakers, and smother unwelcome bills. In the queen's last parliament of 1601, five privy councillors, including Cecil, had managed to contain the vocal complaints about monopolies and ensure the passage of a very large subsidy bill. As we shall see in chapter 10, the lack of privy councillors in the early Jacobean house of commons made it more difficult for the government to expedite business and restrain unruly speeches.

The most important man on the privy council was the principal secretary. After some hesitation, James kept Cecil in this post to maintain continuity and reward a loyal supporter, but he soon came to value his secretary's extraordinary abilities and dedication to the job.[66] For ten years under Elizabeth, Cecil had been a tireless royal servant and, after his father's death in 1598, he was the linchpin of the privy council with remarkably wide-ranging responsibilities: like his father, he concerned himself with foreign affairs, Ireland, finance, justice, law and order, security, intelligence, and the Church.

He assumed the same role under James. Many correspondents addressed letters to Cecil as if he were the council; others wrote to the council as if it were the institutional extension of Cecil.[67] 'More then a president, [he] was alpha and omega in councell', observed a colleague, and he had 'solie managed all foren affaires especially Ireland'.[68] Indeed, as far as Irish affairs were concerned, after Devonshire's death in April 1606, Cecil supervised them so closely that other members of the privy council were often unaware of the details and decisions.[69] When it came to international relations, Cecil selected and oversaw the network of English representatives abroad. He had no time to write to them with news as often as they would have liked, but he expected them to keep him regularly informed and implement his instructions. James often ribbed Cecil, if somewhat heavy-handedly, for being all work and no play: while he was in his 'paradise of pleasure', commented the king, Cecil was stuck in London, sitting 'by the fyre, quhen [when] all the goode houndis are daylie running on the feildis' and 'frying in the paines of purgatorie for my service'.[70] In truth, though, Cecil would have found hunting in all weathers more hellish than working by the fire.

As principal secretary, Cecil gave the king advice, but normally it was about offering solutions to problems rather than devising policy objectives. James had his own strong views about the direction of policy, and simply relied on Cecil to find ways to implement his wishes: whether obtaining parliamentary acceptance of the Union, negotiating peace terms with Spain, or finding new revenue streams. James knew that Cecil had doubts about several of his projects and decisions—notably the Union—but trusted that his secretary would do whatever he commanded. And Cecil assured him that was the case.[71]

As if Cecil had not enough to do as secretary, James added to his portfolio in 1608 by appointing him lord treasurer on the death of the earl of Dorset. Cecil had already put his mind to finding answers to the crown's financial difficulties, so it was not a surprising choice. But it was unprecedented that one man should hold these two key offices of state as well as act as master of the court of wards. Of course, Cecil had deputies, clerks, and private secretaries for specific duties, which relieved him of much labour. Thomas Wilson, for example, managed the network of intelligencers working abroad, while Cecil's many clerical assistants provided him with summaries of incoming reports and wrote a fair proportion of his letters.[72] Further easing the burden, courtiers in the bedchamber were given charge of James's private correspondence.[73] Nonetheless, the excessive workload contributed to Cecil's ill health, which frequently laid him low.[74]

Cecil wore himself to the bone, especially in his attempt to balance the royal accounts by trying to curb James's expenditure and gifts to favourites. In 1608, he succeeded in persuading the king to accept a 'book of bounty'—a list of what suitors could and could not expect to receive. This restricted James's generosity and prevented the bestowal of major gifts, such as crown lands and customs that would diminish royal revenues. Building on this measure, in 1609, Cecil entailed a substantial proportion of crown lands so that James could not gift them, and he tried to buy back some land already given away. However, the 'book' did not include gifts of cash, and James handed out money liberally: between October and December 1610 alone, the exchequer paid out £36,000 in gifts to courtiers; and the yearly sum paid out as 'free gifts' reached a high point of £78,791 [over £10.5 million today] in 1611.[75]

Cecil was more successful in finding ways to safeguard or improve royal revenue streams. Between 1603 and 1610, he increased the king's income from the court of wards by 91 per cent and built on Dorset's work to augment James's total annual income. For a short time, the royal debt was significantly reduced, but the cost of Henry's separate household and James's seeming inability to curtail his expenditure meant the deficit between income and expenditure soon rose again.[76] To deal with the pressing problem, in 1610 Cecil attempted (and failed) to get parliament to agree to a 'great contract' in which the king would receive an immediate lump sum to eliminate the debt and obtain a fixed annual parliamentary grant in exchange for his renunciation of purveyance and wardship.[77] After the 'contract' was dropped, Cecil—desperate for cash—accepted the need to introduce a sale of honours, which had been proposed by Sir Francis Bacon and Sir Robert Cotton among others. In 1611, Cecil shaped a new project to create and sell a new title of baronet, each one going for £1,095; the eighty-eight creations that year brought more than £96,000 into the exchequer.[78] Around the same time, James was persuaded that his gift-giving had to be further restrained, and he agreed to have a version of the 'book of bounty' printed so that suitors would be discouraged from seeking new pensions and monopolies from him.[79] Unfortunately, neither king nor courtiers abided by it.

Cecil was not just a bureaucrat managing the royal finances. He was also of value to James as an experienced and skilful negotiator. At the peace conference held at Somerset House in 1604 to bring an end to the war with Spain, Cecil was the main spokesman for England.[80] It was in gratitude for this service that James elevated him to the barony of Cranborne. Cecil also proved adept at managing routine diplomatic relationships, building up an especially good rapport with ambassadors from the Italian states. On the home front, he usually knew how to handle the king and proved able to mediate successfully between him and his critics. According to one report, after the common lawyers—led by Sir Edward Coke—challenged the powers and authority of the ecclesiastical court of high commission, 'had not my lord threasurer, most humbly on his knee, used many good words to pacifie his Majestie and to excuse that which had been spoken, it was thought his highnes wolde have ben muche more offended'.[81]

However, as we shall see in the next chapter, Cecil was far less accomplished in bringing together the king and the opponents of royal policies in parliament, even those who were his clients. Consequently, at times, his relationship with James came under severe strain, and Cecil had to find courtly ways to pacify him. Andrew Thrush has convincingly suggested that Cecil made the offer to exchange the palatial Theobalds for several modest properties, including Hatfield in Hertfordshire, belonging to Anna in order to recover the king's good will after the particularly disastrous parliamentary session of May 1607.[82] Similarly, when his 'great contract' looked close to collapse in parliament, Cecil presented Anna with an expensive set of hangings; and when Cecil failed to obtain any supply at all in that parliamentary session, he assigned to James all his profits as master of the court of wards.[83]

Despite these significant policy setbacks, James valued Cecil's service to the end.[84] Unlike Henry VIII, but like Elizabeth, the king remained loyal to ministers even when they failed him. But was he fond of the man? Like Elizabeth, James gave nicknames to all his ministers, and Cecil was his 'little beagle' or 'little cankered beagle', epithets that reflected the king's love of hunting and drew attention to his servant's small stature [a beagle is a small hunting dog]. For less obvious reasons James occasionally called Cecil 'Thom Derry', or 'a monkee monger', or 'parrot monger', the latter two the sobriquets that his minister hated most.[85] Nonetheless, Cecil was not one of the king's intimates. He had no right of automatic entry into his master's privy lodgings even when the king was in Whitehall where Cecil had apartments. James's teasing aside, their meetings tended to be formal audiences rather than friendly conversations.[86] It is true that James grew alarmed when Cecil fell seriously ill in February 1612. As on similar occasions, he then visited his 'little beagle' daily and gave 'charge to the physicians upon their heads to be carefull of him and commanded all men for four days to forbear to speak to his lordship upon any business'. During the worst of Cecil's malady, Anna and Henry visited him daily too. Yet, when Cecil died, James did not seem emotionally touched, merely concerned about how to replace his irreplaceable minister.[87] On his side, Cecil tended to be stiff with the king, as indeed he had been with Elizabeth. Only rarely did he sign himself off as James's 'faithful beagle', and then it was to remind the king of his tireless work pursuing the royal wishes.[88] Nevertheless, Cecil usually tried to introduce a light tone to his dispatches to James in the knowledge that the king liked to be entertained as much as informed. Other than that, Cecil treated the royal family with the utmost respect and deference.

Cecil was well recompensed for his service. First made a baron, then a viscount, and finally an earl, he received higher honours than had his father. The monetary fruits of office were colossal. Although his official salaries brought in paltry sums, he became rich on the many perks of office. The farm of customs on imported silks, for example, brought him an estimated yearly sum of £7,000 [about £1 million in today's money] by 1612. Like other ministers, he received presents (bribes?) from suitors as well. From all this income, Cecil was able to spend lavishly on building projects, whether Cranborne which was totally rebuilt, his house in the Strand, or the mansion constructed at Hatfield which alone cost nearly £39,000.[89]

When, in December 1611, Cecil was taken seriously ill with what was possibly terminal cancer, he had to hand over the day-to-day running of the treasury to Sir Julius Caesar, the chancellor of the exchequer. The following spring, Cecil was clearly dying. He seemed resigned, allegedly saying: 'Ease and pleasures quake to heare of death, but my lyfe full of cares, and miseries desires to be dissolved.'[90] Although this could be taken as a conventional Christian sentiment, he had undoubtedly found the 'cares' of office utterly gruelling under James. His death was greeted with vicious attacks from those envious of his wealth and influence as well as those who continued to blame him for Essex's disgrace and execution. He was labelled Machiavellian, corrupt, lascivious, and as crippled in his mind as in his body. Catholics too considered Cecil a bitter enemy, albeit unfairly.[91] Only a few—mainly those men with whom he had worked—acknowledged his worth and saw that his loss had 'strangely altered the motion of our kingdom', and not for the better.[92]

★ ★ ★

Cecil's predecessor as lord treasurer was Thomas Sackville who, as Lord Buckhurst, had been appointed to the office in 1598. The king retained him in 1603 and created him earl of Dorset the following year. Dorset had the unenviable task of keeping royal finances afloat at a time when the king's expenses were high while his income was coming in 'but pecemele' and 'with grete difficulty'.[93] Yet Dorset had considerable success in improving royal revenues. In 1604, he updated the valuations of customs in line with inflation and, ignoring outcries in parliament, he also placed tariffs (impositions) on new imports such as currants. The collection of customs was made more efficient after he established the 'great farm of the customs' in December 1604, a measure which consolidated the rights to collect almost all the kingdom's duties into a single concession. A syndicate of London merchants won the bid and became wealthy from its profits, but the crown benefited too. The merchants paid the king a rent of £112,000 a year, which was raised in 1606 to £120,000, and they kept the surplus. Simultaneously, Dorset attempted to improve the rental income from the crown's estates which had suffered from neglect over the previous twenty-five years. However, his meticulous and costly land surveys brought little in the way of profit, since the tenants on the larger crown estates tenaciously defended their low rents and security of tenure. Cecil therefore dropped the initiative in 1609. Nonetheless, by the time of Dorset's death in 1608, the crown's ordinary revenue had risen by about £100,000 [nearly £13.5 million today] to around £366,000.[94] Concerning expenditure, Dorset—aided by the privy council—tried to persuade the king to resist the requests of suitors, which was costing the crown dearly. Councillors understood that 'the greatest and wisest princes' had to 'maintaine their people's love and service', but present circumstances meant that restraint was imperative both to avoid debt and to persuade parliament to grant supply.[95]

Despite his vigorous and valiant attempts at reform, Dorset acquired a reputation for corruption and incompetence. James dismissed such allegations as seditious when they reached his ears in 1603, but on Dorset's death they resurfaced.[96] The magnificence of the earl's renovated stately home at Knole in Kent no doubt encouraged allegations of dishonesty, but they were unfair. Dorset was no more 'corrupt' than anyone else; nor did he need to be, for he was extremely wealthy in his own right. It was largely his income from land, not the spoils of office, that financed the rebuilding of Knole.[97] The accusation of incompetence was also undeserved. The earl worked tirelessly on numerous fronts: sitting on commissions, devising financial reforms, as well as overseeing the exchequer. Like Cecil, he became worn out. Aged seventy-one or seventy-two, he dropped dead at the council table on the afternoon of 19 April 1608. In his will, he showed his charitable disposition, bequeathing £1,000 to build a public granary at Lewes, with a further £2,000 to stock it against times of scarcity or hardship.[98]

Another Elizabethan whom James retained on the privy council in 1603 was the sixty-three-year-old Sir Thomas Egerton. The bastard son of a Cheshire gentleman, Egerton had risen to high office under Elizabeth thanks to his command of the law: she appointed him solicitor general in 1581, attorney general in 1592, master of the rolls in 1594, and lord keeper of the great seal two years afterwards. In 1600, Egerton took the dowager countess of Derby as his third wife, a marriage that improved his stature but diminished his happiness.[99] Although reappointed to the council in 1603, Egerton had to resign the mastership of the rolls to Kinloss and his local office as chamberlain of Chester to William, sixth earl of Derby, both losses severe blows to his pocket and prestige. In compensation, he was soon afterwards advanced into the peerage as Baron Ellesmere and named lord chancellor, which was a promotion in name rather than substance. For several years, he complained bitterly that he had had lost out in James's early distribution of patronage.[100] But Ellesmere often found something to grumble about, whether it was overwork, ill health (like many others he suffered from gout and the stone), or inadequate recognition of his service.[101] He even moaned that his chamber at Whitehall was 'in a remote corner farre from all accesse', ignoring the fact that he had the right of residence at York House in the Strand, which had been leased to the keepers of the great seal since 1558.[102]

Keeper of the great seal, Ellesmere dealt with a huge amount of paperwork. As England's leading law officer, his chief judicial functions lay in presiding over the courts of star chamber and chancery, giving opinions over controversial legal problems, and serving as the crown's speaker in the house of lords. Almost always, he supported the king's position on questions of policy, as when he came out strongly in favour of the Union and naturalization of Scots. Equally, he upheld the royal prerogative when it came under fire. He protected the prerogative courts (star chamber, chancery, the council of Wales, and the ecclesiastical court of high commission), which were increasingly attacked by MPs and common lawyers, and he objected to 'writs of prohibition', a legal instrument issued to transfer cases from the prerogative courts to the court of the common pleas.[103] By the same token, Ellesmere defended the king's right to issue proclamations, a prerogative sometimes criticized for overriding statute. In his private notes, he endorsed the king's right to use his prerogative to 'restreyne the libertie of his subjectes in thinges that are agaynst the commen weal. And what is agaynst the commenweale, the king and his counsell are to judge and determyne.'[104] Conservative in these judgements and in his belief that 'innovations are dangerous', Ellesmere nonetheless accepted the need for reforms provided that they were grounded in precedent.[105] On this basis, he recommended improvements to the cost of justice and the quality of lawyers and put forward plans to codify statutes—refining some and repealing others.[106]

Another elderly Elizabethan on the privy council was the lord high admiral and England's premier peer Charles Howard, earl of Nottingham. His office was secure in 1603 because he had been in secret correspondence with the Scottish king for about a year, probably at the instigation of Cecil who realized that the admiral's support was vital in case Philip III decided to invade England on Elizabeth's death.[107] Already well past his prime in 1603, Nottingham only stepped down from office in 1618 when he was over eighty. Doubtless, he retained his place because James could not afford to alienate a powerful member of the Howard family.[108] Nonetheless, their relationship was often under strain. At the very start of the reign, Nottingham was slow to implement James's order to stop the plunder of Spanish shipping, now deemed piracy, because as lord admiral he obtained a share of the spoils. Furious with him, James was heard to say in October 1603: 'By God I'll hang the pirates with my own hands, and my lord admiral as well.'[109]

On the other hand, Nottingham delighted the king when he became one of the first Englishmen to marry a Scot—the king's young cousin and queen's lady-in-waiting Lady Margaret Stewart. Anna thought the match hilarious because of the age gap between bride and groom, but she soon became annoyed that the new countess was adopting too many airs. The king, though, was so pleased at this early instance of Anglo-Scottish intermarriage that he granted Nottingham land, a pension, and the lucrative wine monopoly previously held by Ralegh.[110] Perhaps because of Nottingham's misgivings about an Anglo-Spanish peace, James appointed him a commissioner at the Somerset House Conference. It might bring the earl onside as well as demonstrate to other opponents that any negotiated treaty would not sacrifice English interests. Afterwards Nottingham was given the honour of heading the spectacular embassy sent to Spain in May 1604 to witness the ratification of the peace treaty.[111]

A few years later, the earl enjoyed further royal support when he was exposed as a negligent administrator of the navy and his client

Sir Robert Mansell was suspected of embezzling some £14,000 during his four years as treasurer of the navy board. It was said of the lord admiral's supervision of the navy: 'much water passed by the mill, whereof the miller was ignorant'. Given his administrative incompetence in dealing with his own private affairs, this might be true. More likely, though, the admiral had some knowledge of the abuses under his watch but, benefiting from them, looked away.[112]

In his early fifties, Edward Somerset, fourth earl of Worcester, was the ex-Elizabethan privy councillor who had greatest access to the king. He had originally met James and Anna in 1590 when Elizabeth sent him to Scotland as her representative to congratulate the couple on their marriage. He had then made a good impression on James and was subsequently selected to assume temporarily the role of earl marshal—the highest heraldic office—in time for the coronation.[113] The king also confirmed him in his position as master of the horse, the household post granted to him in 1601 after the execution of the previous holder Essex. In command of the royal stables, Worcester accompanied James on his hunting trips, the only privy councillor to do so regularly. This role Worcester came to find exhausting for he had to ride with the hunting party all day and work all night, answering letters and sending information to the privy councillors left in London about James's mood and responses to their messages.[114] In 1612, he received an extra household appointment when he succeeded Cecil as high steward of the queen's revenues, a reward for his long-term close relationship with Anna: four of his daughters consistently had roles in her masques; his wife was a lady in her household, and his younger son Thomas served as her master of the horse. In 1616, he surrendered his office of master of the horse to George Villiers but was well compensated with an annuity of £1,500 a year.[115]

Elizabeth supposedly described Worcester as 'reconciling the irreconcilable: a stiff papist with a good subject'.[116] This portrayal of the earl is not strictly true. Yes, his wife was a committed Catholic, his daughters married into Catholic families, and he allowed the Jesuit Robert Jones to make Raglan Castle a centre for the Welsh mission. Additionally, his secretary, William Sterrell, was almost certainly the Catholic spy who went under the name of 'Anthony Rivers'.[117] Yet Worcester was no recusant and in that sense no 'stiff papist'; he attended Protestant services and possibly even took communion. The Catholic community thought him too great a careerist to be of much use to them.[118] Loyal and outwardly conformist, he was therefore

Elizabeth's and James's kind of Catholic. Chosen by James to suppress Catholic riots, impose conformity on recusants, and interrogate the Catholic conspirators of the Gunpowder Plot, Worcester was a valuable public relations asset, demonstrating to foreign and English Catholics the broadmindedness and fairness of the Jacobean regime.

★ ★ ★

Notwithstanding his deliberate efforts at continuity, James added six Englishmen to the privy council in 1603, most of whom had been political outsiders under Elizabeth. Although it is a commonplace that Essexians entered the privy council on James's accession, not one of the new members had been a close associate of the earl of Essex at the time of his rising. Moreover, before 1612, James kept out of office the earls of Southampton, Rutland, and Bedford who had been Essex's companions in 1601. Nevertheless, some of those appointed had been Essex's kin or friends before his ruin. Northumberland was his brother-in-law; Devonshire had been a loyal friend until 1600 and remained the long-term lover—and eventually husband—of his sister Lady Penelope Rich; and Northampton had been part of Essex's coterie until 1600. Two of the remainder—Suffolk and Cumberland—had served with Essex against Spain but were also close to Cecil. Burghley of course was Cecil's half-brother. James chose these men largely because they had actively supported his claim to the throne. Possibly, too, his aim was to appear inclusive and avoid resentments that might lead to a resurgence of faction within the political elite. However, there is no evidence that he saw the Howards as a counterweight to the Cecils. On the contrary, as James well knew, the Howards had enjoyed a friendly relationship with Cecil for several years before his accession.

Two of the new privy councillors died early in the reign, but their deaths did not leave gaping holes in the privy council. When Cumberland expired at the end of October 1605 at the age of forty-seven, it was said that 'the body of the council is no whit weakened thereby'.[119] This judgement was somewhat unfair. Cumberland had been very useful to James as a major landowner in the north with powerful connections on the border. Lord lieutenant in the three most northern English counties, he helped subdue the raiding clans and built up a stronger Clifford presence in the north-west borderlands which benefited the crown.[120] His role in London politics, though, was less significant.

Devonshire, who died in April 1606 aged about forty-three, had been a valued privy councillor until just before his death, especially in offering advice on Ireland. But his controversial and technically illegal marriage in December 1605 to Lady Penelope created a public scandal which looked likely to end his political career anyway. She had been given an ecclesiastical divorce from Robert, third Lord Rich, on grounds of her long-term adultery with Devonshire, but this gave her no right to remarry. When planning the earl's funeral at Westminster Abbey, the heralds queried whether her arms should be impaled with his [placed side by side in the same shield], thereby bringing into question the lawfulness of their marriage.[121]

Northumberland disappeared from the privy council at the end of 1605, but for a different reason. Born in 1564, he was the scion of the long-established northern Percy family whose loyalty to the crown could never be taken for granted. The previous two earls had both been adherents of Mary, Queen of Scots: his uncle was beheaded in 1572 after raising rebellion in the north; and his father died of a gunshot wound—possibly self-inflicted—while incarcerated in the Tower in 1585 on suspicion of complicity in a French plot to release Mary. Although also a Catholic, the ninth earl seemed loyal to Elizabeth. Fighting against Spain in the Netherlands, he was made a knight of the garter in 1593 in appreciation of his service. Nonetheless, because of his family connections and power in the north, the queen treated him as an outsider, 'as it were banished from court'.[122] Looking to the future, he joined the secret correspondence with James in 1602 and received his reward the next year when he entered the privy council and became captain of the gentlemen pensioners. However, he was not one of the council's inner circle: for instance, he played no role in the negotiations for peace with Spain. In any event, his role as a privy councillor ended at the time of the Gunpowder Plot. Thinking the earl was privy to the treason, because his cousin and estate manager Thomas Percy was a leading conspirator, James deprived him of his offices and kept him in the Tower for fifteen years.[123]

Like the Percies, many members of the Howard family were tainted with disloyalty to the crown but, unlike Northumberland, their loyalty to James was never in doubt. Northampton's poet father (Henry, earl of Surrey) had been executed for treason in January 1547; his elder brother and Suffolk's father (Thomas, duke of Norfolk) went to the executioner's block in June 1572; and his nephew and Suffolk's elder brother (Philip Howard, thirteenth or twentieth earl of Arundel) was also condemned to death as a traitor but died in the Tower in 1595 after eleven years' imprisonment.

Along with his older brother, Northampton had been a supporter of Mary, Queen of Scots; and like his nephew Philip, he was a Catholic. However, he had been cautious and canny enough to evade a trial and death sentence during Elizabeth's reign despite suspicions of conspiracy and five short stays in custody. During his periods of liberty, he remained on the margins of the court, dependent on the charity of family members, including Nottingham whom he later came to despise. Then, during the early 1590s, he came into Essex's orbit and his fortunes changed. Treating him as a key adviser and close intimate, the earl brought him into the queen's presence in 1597, obtained for him an annual pension of £200, and helped his nephew Thomas gain royal favour. But, perhaps aware of Essex's impetuousness and concerned that his patron might lose the queen's trust, Henry was careful not to alienate Burghley and Cecil. His astuteness paid off, and he was able to transfer his loyalties fully to Cecil after the earl's fall from power in 1600. Furthermore, after Essex's rising, he used his relationship with the Scottish king—begun through Essex—to benefit Cecil as well as himself. Convincing James that Cecil would support his succession, Howard paved the way for the secretary's secret correspondence with the Scottish king. Together the two men planned the transition of power to James on Elizabeth's death.[124]

James's accession lifted Henry Howard from the wings onto centre stage as he gained noble title, high office, wealth, and power. As already seen, in 1603, the sixty-three-year-old gained a place on the privy council and replaced Cobham as lord warden of the Cinque Ports. The following spring, he entered the nobility and, in 1605, he was installed as a knight of the garter. In 1608, when Cecil was made lord treasurer, he took over Cecil's office of lord privy seal, 'a post of great prestige and profit'.[125] So that he had an income to match his offices, 'in consideracon of service' James granted him a share of the Howard estates confiscated by the crown on the attainders of Norfolk and Arundel.[126]

Before assuming office, Howard had to take the oath of supremacy (which called the king supreme governor of the English Church), and to keep his posts he attended Protestant services. But few, if any, were convinced of his sincerity. Libellers called him a 'great archpapist' who 'is nowe perswaded to the Church to goe'. James teased him for believing in the Catholic doctrine of transubstantiation when he asked him to explain how 'he thinkes a priest can both make a god and eate a god'.[127] As with Worcester, it suited the king to have a conforming Catholic held in high esteem on the privy council since it displayed to the world the heights that loyal Catholics could reach. Furthermore, Northampton was extremely useful in this capacity: he stood out publicly against militant Catholicism and, thanks to his contacts, could keep a close eye on the Catholic community.[128] Other Catholics benefited from the earl's elevation; his biographer Linda Levy Peck has identified perhaps as many as 25 per cent of his many court clients as recusants or Catholic sympathizers.[129]

An unpopular figure, Northampton was described by contemporaries as a fawning courtier and corrupt minister, smears which were not far off the mark.[130] Ben Jonson thought him a hypocrite after he accused the playwright of 'poperie', an accusation that had led Jonson to be brought before the privy council; no doubt others thought the same.[131] Like most people in royal service, Northampton lined his own pockets. At his death in 1614, his estate was valued at the colossal sum of around £80,000 [nearly £11 million in today's currency]. From his landed estate and the spoils of office, he financed the construction of a magnificent house on the Strand and filled it with household goods valued at £8,150 at his death.[132]

At the same time, Northampton was a committed public servant who worked energetically to reform the finances and administration of the realm. Putting together a brains trust of scholars, merchants, and office holders, he instructed them to investigate abuses and recommend ways to improve the efficiency and probity of the household, the college of arms, and the navy.[133] Little, however, came of his endeavours. In October 1605, the earl gave the king 'a very juste account of this daie's labor wholly spent about the reformation of his house [household], the flawes and excesses of which are infinit'.[134] A few scandalous purveyors were brought to book, but no long-term solution was set in place to improve the household's efficiency and cut its expense. The earl's efforts to reform the navy similarly resulted in no substantial change. To improve its readiness against a possible Spanish invasion, Northampton was appointed, in April 1608, to head a commission of inquiry into its 'abuses and disorders'. Sitting on the commission for a year, Northampton's client Sir Robert Cotton compiled a damming dossier about the corruptions and inefficiencies that existed, details of which were presented to James at Greenwich over the course of three days in June 1609. After 'graciously' receiving the report, James gave the senior navy officers a lecture, but 'seeing the authority of and regard for the high admiral' was 'great', he pardoned the men who were fingered for corruption.[135] Northampton had no regard for the admiral at all, so the king's refusal to remove him and implement reforms to staunch the corruption was galling on several counts.

Northampton liked to create the fiction that he maintained a special relationship with James, continuing a secret correspondence with him after his accession. Using the ubiquitous hunting metaphor, Northampton claimed that his letters to James were 'a praye [prey]which many hunte after', even the trusted grooms of his bedchamber, and he urged him to 'burn them with his owne hande'.[136] As part of this special relationship, Northampton did not let the king forget that he had been a loyal adherent of his mother, the only English privy councillor for whom that was true. While Cecil took responsibility for erecting the tomb of Elizabeth, it was Northampton who had a hand in designing the Scottish queen's new tomb in Westminster Abbey; he also wrote the epitaph and elegy inscribed upon it.[137]

What James thought of Northampton is hard to gauge. He respected the earl's diligence and admired his brain, for he was a brilliant scholar and orator. Not only did Northampton commonly entertain the king at table 'with discourse' but also James regularly used him to present the crown's case in trials and in parliament.[138] Even so, the king saw through his minister's obsequious flattery and disliked the spiteful tongue that was every so often exposed.[139] When gravely ill in the summer of 1606, Northampton 'was not once visited by the king', whereas at about the same time Cecil received a royal visit and kind messages even though the secretary had merely 'a distemper upon a heat'.[140] Nevertheless, writing to the earl directly, James would sometimes address him with the formal 'right trusty and right well beloved cousin and counsellor' or the more intimate 'My faithful 3' (three being the code number used by Northampton in their secret correspondence before 1603), which denoted trust and confidentiality.[141] James also gave Northampton personal tokens; the earl treasured a ruby which James had sent him 'out of Scotland as his first token'; in England, James presented him with a 'George of gold enamilled' which was 'garnished' with forty diamonds, and a purple velvet garter 'garnished with smale rubies and smale dyamonds' and trimmed with lace.[142]

Northampton's nephew Thomas, earl of Suffolk, was brought up a Protestant and, unlike his half-brother Philip, never converted to Catholicism, although his wife Katherine was suspected of Catholic sympathies. Under Elizabeth, he was created a baron and admitted to the order of the garter for serving the regime loyally as an admiral of the fleet. Nonetheless, the queen did not give him high political office. Very likely, he was drawn into his uncle's secret correspondence with James during the last years of her reign for otherwise it is hard to explain why James favoured the forty-one-year-old so greatly in 1603.[143] Thomas had acted as lord chamberlain during the Elizabethan holder's terminal illness, and James not only later confirmed him in that household office but also promoted him to an earldom and brought him onto the privy council. Suffolk also received, in 1603, many of the properties that had been forfeited to the crown on the attainders of his father and half-brother.[144] James often called him 'honest Thomas', which now seems ironic as Suffolk fell from power after accusations of corruption. Another nickname seems to draw attention to his size—'big' or 'fat' chamberlain—but portraits show the earl of average build, so perhaps James was referring to another kind of worldly appetite, such as avarice.[145]

Irrespective of his higher office, Suffolk was the junior partner of the Howards for Northampton's patronage extended more widely. Nevertheless, the future seemed to lie with Suffolk. He was the younger man with at least eleven children, most of whom reached adulthood, whereas Northampton never married and died without a direct heir in 1614. Ambitious patriarch that he was, Suffolk arranged marriages for his children that would advance his career as well as their fortunes. In December 1605, his nineteen-year-old daughter Elizabeth wed the sixty-one-year-old William, Lord Knollys, who was treasurer of the household. The following January, Suffolk married his fifteen-year-old daughter Frances to Essex, who was thought to be a rising star at court. That same year, he followed the king's wishes for Anglo-Scottish marriages by betrothing his heir Theophilus to Dunbar's daughter, then a child of six. In 1608, he cemented his relationship with Cecil by wedding his youngest daughter Catherine to Cecil's only son William.

However, like the protagonist in a moral fairy tale, Suffolk came to a bad end. He managed to survive the domestic disaster of his daughter Frances's divorce, remarriage, and imprisonment in 1616, but he could not survive the enmity of James's new favourite, George Villiers. Thanks to Villiers, the earl and his wife were found guilty in 1619 of taking bribes and misappropriating royal monies on a grand scale during Suffolk's term as lord treasurer. They escaped a long sentence in prison, but he lost office and their debts brought them close to financial ruin.[146]

James brought five Scots into the privy council in 1603, much to the dismay of James's English councillors.[147] Even more disconcerting was the appointment of Home and Kinloss to become chancellor of the exchequer and master of the rolls respectively. As to be expected, the previous holders felt aggrieved, but they were not alone. Others complained that the Scots were 'ignorante of our lawes and customes' and thus unsuited to holding these pivotal positions.[148] It is possible that James had also intended to make a Scot a second secretary of state who would work alongside Cecil but, if so, nothing came of the proposal because of English objections.[149] A second keeper of the council chamber (the officer who controlled access) *was* put in place—another Scot, Alexander Douglas.[150]

Of the new Scottish privy councillors, James Elphinstone spent little time in England and returned to Scotland as Lord Balmerino. By contrast, Kinloss became an honorary Englishman. Naturalized by act of parliament in 1604, he held manors in Yorkshire and married his only legitimate daughter Christian into the wealthy Cavendish family in 1608 when she was just twelve years old.[151] Mar, Lennox, and Home (earl of Dunbar after 1605) were also based in England but would travel back to Scotland to supervise and report on the progress of specific royal policies that could not be done 'by pen'. Dunbar was exceptionally useful in this respect, so much so that, in 1606, he had to stand down from his English offices because of time away.[152] His place in the English exchequer was given to an Englishman—Sir Julius Caesar—who was sworn a privy councillor the following year.

Lennox, who had kept his post as lord high admiral of Scotland, likewise went north periodically. As James's kinsman, he had considerable status in Scotland, and presumably for that reason the king dispatched him to the northern kingdom as his 'lieutenant' in the summer of 1607 with the mission of getting the Union through the Scottish parliament.[153] Before 1603, Lennox had done little with the governmental posts he held in Scotland, and he showed a similar lack of interest in governing England.[154] Anyway, his influence over policy—especially foreign policy—was limited because of his pro-French and anti-Spanish sympathies. Nonetheless, he signed conciliar letters and, in 1606, received a warrant for properties in the duchy of Lancaster, worth £1,500 a year, 'in consideracon of the longe and faithefull service' he had given as a councillor.[155] English councillors considered him one of their own, and when, in 1609, another Scot, Viscount Haddington, challenged him to a duel 'about some words exchanged between them at Royston', the councillors rallied round, wanting 'to proceed against Haddington, as it was never heard of that a councillor of the king should receive a challenge to a duel'.[156]

★ ★ ★

It is often assumed that James's privy council was riddled with faction.[157] Inevitably, there were rivalries within the body and especially between Cecil and Northampton. Cecil hinted at such jealousies when, in late 1604, he reprimanded his trusted friend Thomas Parry (then ambassador in France) for telling the king that he always operated through the secretary for it 'cast an envy upon me of sole dealing in such things'.[158] Probably, it was to offset the secretary's influence that Northampton stressed his loyalty to Mary, Queen of Scots whose imprisonment and execution could be laid at the hands of Cecil's father. Unquestionably, Cecil and Northampton competed in their financial dealings for, in 1604, Cecil combined with Dorset to create a syndicate that won the lucrative licence to organize and profit from the collection of custom duties known as 'the great farm of customs' against Northampton's rival group; and, each time the lease was renewed, Northampton unsuccessfully mounted a challenge to acquire the farm.[159] Ill feeling between the two men took another course when they found themselves, in 1605, on opposite sides in a star chamber court case that concerned Northampton's kinsman Robert Dudley. Dudley, the bastard son of the earl of Leicester and Douglas Sheffield (née Howard), was claiming the properties of his late father and paternal uncle which had gone to Robert Sidney, Viscount Lisle. Northampton supported Dudley because of the family connection, whereas Cecil sided with Lisle. To make matters worse, when delivering his opinion, Cecil angered Northampton by speaking disparagingly of Dudley and his mother.[160] Disagreements and competition between the two men did not stop there but spilled over into their building projects. Northampton deliberately built a house on the Strand which was far more grandiose in scale and ornamentation than Salisbury House, Cecil's house further down the Strand. Not to be outdone, Cecil tried to enlarge his house and overcome the limitations of its more confined site.[161]

When it came to matters of policy, there were differences in both the religious outlook and international preferences of Cecil and Northampton. Concerning religion, Cecil was considered 'some what puritan in affection', whereas Northampton protected recusants.[162] On foreign policy, Northampton was rightly seen as being 'much in the Spanish interest' while Cecil was thought pro-Dutch and suspicious of Spain.[163] However, these differences did not lead to any open and intense conflicts on the council before Cecil's death—unlike the period of the late 1590s when Essex and Cecil had been at loggerheads over foreign policy.[164] At times, rumours were heard of an 'unkindnes' between the two councillors and of 'contradictions att the councell board', but Northampton for one minimized their importance. Such differences, he told a friend in 1607, occurred 'in all well-guyded councells' and 'betweene the father and the sonne', and his affection for Cecil was strong.[165] The latter statement was almost certainly a lie as was evident after Cecil's death when Northampton openly revealed a contempt for his erstwhile colleague. Nonetheless, during Cecil's lifetime, Northampton reined in his dislike to please James and in the interests of the state.[166] Consequently, the two men co-operated as privy councillors. They complemented each other well when acting as spokesmen for the king at the 1604 Somerset House Conference.[167] They both pushed hard to get James's Union project accepted in parliament, and Northampton spoke in favour of Cecil's 'great contract' despite his own reservations about it.[168] Nor did the two councillors fall out over religion. They were at one in calling for Catholics to be treated with moderation, and neither man stepped out of line from James's religious policy.

Cecil's relationships with other privy councillors were still more collaborative. Dorset leaned on Cecil heavily for advice and referred to him in his will as 'my most special and deerest frend'.[169] Later on, Ellesmere assisted Cecil with the 'great contract' and was bequeathed 300 ounces of gilt plate in Cecil's will 'as a token of the continuaunce of our frendshippe'.[170] Cecil and Suffolk were close friends as well as business partners in spite of rumours flying around the court that Cecil was the lover of Suffolk's beautiful wife.[171] In his will, Cecil left Suffolk a ring worth £200 and referred to their many conversations in which he would communicate his 'dearest thoughtes with him [Suffolk] when ever I have cause, since my first contract of freindshippe with him'. But Cecil also bequeathed to the countess his 'best diamond ringe', worth about £1,000, which he desired her to wear for his sake.[172]

Cecil worked so well with Suffolk and Northampton that James called their threesome 'a trinitie of knaves'.[173] At times, it was a quartet for James liked to add Worcester to his team of key councillors. James explicitly stated his desire that these four men should discuss his weightiest affairs in confidence while the whole council would carry out 'his general errands'.[174] Nor was there any split between the English and Scottish members of the council. Cecil worked well with Lennox and Dunbar while Dunbar and Dorset were good friends.[175]

★ ★ ★

Jean Bodin's *On Sovereignty* made a clear distinction between counsel and command: 'a council is instituted to advise those who exercise sovereign authority in the commonwealth...the council in any well ordered commonwealth should have no power of action [*commander*]'. If the council could enforce its advice, Bodin believed, 'the councillors would rule'.[176] James believed this implicitly. So, for him, the executive function of the privy council was far more important than its role as an advisory body on matters of state. When problems arose that needed immediate solutions, James was as likely to listen to his 'hunting crew'—mainly his gentlemen of the bedchamber who accompanied him at the hunt—as he was to Cecil or indeed to any other privy councillor. Elizabeth had also listened to people outside her formal council, but leading privy councillors (Burghley, Leicester, Walsingham, and Sir Christopher Hatton) were the experts she most relied upon. The same cannot be said of James.

It was in directing the routine business of government that James valued the privy council. Privy councillors made decisions and issued orders to the localities about many areas of life: food, plague, religion, amenities, law and order. When it came to their implementation, the king and the privy council relied on the voluntary service of the county and urban elites. Their cooperation was usually obtained by shared ideological assumptions, a fear of disorder, and the prospect of rewards. Nevertheless, negotiations were often necessary between local officials and either the privy council as a body or individual privy councillors with local links. In this area of government, little had changed, and the role of the privy council was as fundamental under James as it had been under Elizabeth.[177]

10

Parliament and its Members

Parliament was the institution which James found most alien during his early years as king of England; it was quite different from its supposed equivalent in Scotland and far more difficult to handle. Certainly, the king had total control over when and for how long sessions would meet in both realms, but otherwise, the two institutions had little in common.[1] In England, there were two houses: the upper house composed of lay and spiritual lords; the lower house containing two members from thirty-nine of the forty English shires (the exception being Durham), one member from each of the twelve Welsh counties, and representatives from enfranchised boroughs and (from 1604) the universities of Oxford and Cambridge.[2] By contrast, the Scottish assembly was unicameral, its membership consisting of burgh members, representatives of the nobility, laird commissioners from the shires, and a handful of clerics.

The English parliament was by far the larger body. In 1604, it comprised ninety-four lay peers and twenty-six bishops in the upper house while crown lawyers, usually senior judges, often attended to give legal advice but had no vote.[3] In the lower house, there sat some 478 members (ninety knights of the shire and the remainder burgesses).[4] The exact number in the Scottish chamber varied, but 109 representatives were recorded as sitting in 1612. Contested elections were more common in Scotland than in England. About 80 per cent of English and Welsh members of parliament were selected rather than elected; a local consensus was reached before election day and no-one stood against the approved candidate at the hustings.[5] In Scotland, contested elections for shire commissioners were introduced in 1587 but had long been the norm for burgh members, although admittedly the franchise in towns was increasingly becoming restricted.

Most important, the role of the monarch differed in each institution. In England, he or she opened each new parliament at Westminster but then retired to Whitehall Palace during the debates. By contrast, the Scottish monarch was normally in attendance throughout the whole parliamentary proceedings and consequently could direct and comment on business. James much preferred the Scottish system. A lower house, he declared, had developed in England only because their kings had grown 'greate and lazie' and the number of boroughs had increased; consequently, whereas the commons' speeches had previously been delivered in the presence of the king, 'nowe the kinge may not knowe what is don in the lower house' yet 'nothing can be concluded without him'.[6]

The physical layout of the two parliaments reflected the dissimilar role of the monarch in each. The Scottish chamber was arranged in a horseshoe with the king sitting in the centre, *primus inter pares*, his nobility on his left and commissioners of the burghs and shires on his right. At Westminster, the chamber of the lower house (which met in St Stephen's Chapel) was also laid out in a horseshoe shape, but it was the speaker who presided and sat 'somewhat higher, that he may see and be seene of them all'. Privy councillors and the monarch's chief officers were positioned next to him; the citizens of London and York sat on his right-hand side beneath the councillors; otherwise, the knights and burgesses took places where they liked. In the upper house, a throne was fixed in the centre to be used by the monarch on the rare occasions he or she attended. Below the throne sat the lord chancellor, 'the voyce and orator of the prince', while to the left were benches for the lay peers and to the right for the archbishops and bishops, each sitting in strict order of rank and precedence.[7]

Another significant contrast was that in Scotland parliamentary sessions lasted fewer than two weeks, and sometimes only a few days; in 1584, for example, the parliament passed forty-nine acts in just two days. In England, sessions usually continued for several weeks or even months before being either prorogued or dissolved by the monarch. This difference arose because, in Scotland, the legislative programme was managed by a steering committee of about forty members, known as the 'lords of the articles', who had diligently scrutinized much of the proposed legislation and negotiated with the monarch in advance of the session.[8] No such prior management occurred in England. Instead, there were multiple readings of bills: three readings (and debates) as well as committee meetings for items of legislation in the two houses. What was more, members of the English parliament enjoyed a freedom of speech, allowing them to offer the monarch counsel and present lengthy grievances, whereas in Scotland not everyone was entitled to participate in the parliamentary debate.[9]

Because of these structural differences, Cecil and other privy councillors briefed James in advance about the running of English parliaments. They also gave him advice about how to handle problems that arose. But, partly because the advice was not always sound, parliamentary sessions never proceeded anything like as smoothly as the king wanted. From the opening of his first parliament in March 1604 until its dissolution in February 1611, the king and the house of commons clashed bitterly over a range of issues, including the proposed Union, royal finances, and Puritan grievances. James was often angry at what he saw as an attack on his prerogative, while the commons was defensive at what it experienced as an assault on its privileges. Although important statutes were passed on a variety of matters, the king failed to achieve the legislation most dear to him: in 1606 and 1607, a 'perfect' Union and the English naturalization of all Scots born after his accession (called the *post-nati*); and, in 1610, the 'great contract', a lump sum required to dissolve his debts and a deal devised to provide him with a substantial annual grant. The most vocal members of the commons were equally frustrated that, in all five sessions of this parliament, they were unable to secure the reforms in Church and state for which they clamoured.

Why was the relationship between the king and commons so fraught? For a long time now, historians have rejected an older view that it was because the commons as a body sought to extend its powers at the expense of the crown and was naturally oppositional to the monarch. No longer do historians today view the parliamentary conflict under James as a step down the road to the Civil War of the 1640s. Since at least the 1980s, scholars have recognized that early Stuart MPs were not consistently resisting royal policies nor seeking to extend their place in the constitution. It was rather that their devotion to preserving the privileges of the lower house and to promoting the interests of their locality and the commonwealth as a whole frequently turned many into outspoken critics of royal policies. Some of their grievances—purveyance and the sacking of nonconforming ministers—had roots back into Elizabeth's reign, and members of the commons now expected and demanded their redress, especially as James had posed as a reformer on his progress to London. Some parliamentary concerns, however, were new—notably the projected Union, the financial profligacy of the king, and the extension of impositions.

Also new was disquiet about James's understanding of kingship for some of his assertions in *The Trew Law* were unsettling. Although James had expressed divine right principles that were shared by his predecessors, he had gone beyond them to assume an extreme monarchical position. He had maintained, for example, that kings were 'above the law, as both the author and giver of strength thereto' and had downplayed parliament's role when declaring that 'general lawes, made publikely in parliament, may upon knowen respects to the king by his authoritie bee mitigated, and suspended upon causes onely knowen to him'.[10] Such statements contradicted the long-held opinions of English lawyers and constitutional thinkers and hence conflicted with Jacobean MPs' understanding of monarchical powers.[11] Bilson's divine right sermon at James's coronation the previous year may have increased anxieties, as probably did the Latin legend on the coronation medal that entitled the king as 'Caesar Augustus of Britain, Caesar the heir of the Caesars'.[12] Such imperial imagery looked incompatible with parliamentary rights. Several of James's utterances in the early part of his English reign probably also created alarm. Famously, when, in 1608, Coke reminded him that 'the common law protecteth the king', James shouted in anger that this was 'a traiterous speech: for the king protecteth the lawe and not the lawe the king'.[13] On several other occasions too, James spoke of himself as the source not the subject of law.

Some MPs did suspect that James intended to put his monarchical principles into practice and expand the royal prerogative at parliament's expense. Their suspicions appeared well founded given James's frequent use of royal proclamations—making law without parliament. In contrast to Elizabeth who had issued only five proclamations in her final years of life, James released thirty-two during his first nine months as king of England and 267 altogether throughout his reign.[14] Protests were soon heard. In April 1607, one MP called it 'an unlawful course' to punish men for failing to obey proclamations. In 1610 the lower house as a whole rallied against proclamations that were altering existing laws or introducing measures that had been previously rejected by parliament.[15] In 1611, Coke and three other judges ruled that the king could not create any new offence by his prerogative, but James continued to issue proclamations for that very purpose.[16]

Another reason for the commons' anxiety related to impositions. In 1606, the court of the exchequer judged that John Bate, a merchant of the Levant Company, had to pay new customs duties levied without parliamentary consent [viz. impositions]. Two concerns immediately arose. First, the case laid down the worrying principle that the king could act outside the common law for the general benefit of the people, *salus populi*. Second, levying impositions was effectively taxing without consent and hence contrary to

England's laws and customs; if accepted as legal, thought many MPs, everyone's lands and goods would be vulnerable to seizure and England would become a tyranny.[17] Furthermore, the money raised from impositions could be so great that parliaments need no longer be summoned.

James's ways of managing the commons did not help sessions to run harmoniously. In the first place, his overlong speeches dwelt too often on the principles of divine right kingship, which ruffled rather than smoothed relations. By contrast, Elizabeth had been emollient as well as sharp-tongued in her speeches and had largely avoided discussion of her prerogative. Second, because of his ennoblements, James had no first-rate privy councillors in the commons to present the crown's case, steer debates, and respond quickly to troublesome members. Eight privy councillors had sat in Elizabeth's lower house in 1589 and five in 1601; by contrast, only two (both junior figures) were present there during the first session of parliament in 1604, increasing to only three in the fourth and fifth.[18] Privy councillors would have been helpful in taking the lead in the lower house. Without their presence, it often sounded like a Tower of Babel. Perhaps just as important, the commons felt the lack of privy councillors in their house signified that the king held them in little esteem.[19] Nonetheless, we should not assume that the commons was free from governmental influence. Conferences between the two houses allowed Cecil, Ellesmere, and Northampton to speak to as many as fifty or a hundred MPs at once. Additionally, many privy councillors had kin, friends, and clients sitting in the commons and used them to assist James's control of the house. The crown could also rely upon MPs who held posts in the royal household—about forty in 1604 and sixty-two between 1605 and 1610. Although these men could not always be counted upon to support royal policies, they tried to be helpful whenever they could. According to one recent assessment, just over 60 per cent of speeches by members who also held court positions supported James.[20] A few household men also acted as James's informants and go-betweens. Aston, for instance, was a member who frequently acted as the king's messenger to and from the lower house, sat on committees, and was appointed to the joint conferences of the two houses that dealt with matters of importance. By such means, the king was kept abreast of debates in the house and could intervene if he thought it necessary, which he often did.[21]

Notwithstanding the noise and disputes, most members rarely, if ever, found their voices in the commons; only about three or four dozen made regular contributions and just a dozen or so dominated debates and committees. Among this latter group were Sir Francis Bacon, Nicholas Fuller, Sir Francis Hastings, Sir Edward Hoby, Laurence Hyde, Richard Martin, Sir George More, Sir Edwin Sandys, Sir Robert Wingfield, Sir Robert Wroth, and Sir Henry Yelverton.[22] Bacon—a brilliant orator and ambitious politician—usually employed his skills on behalf of the crown, but most of the others were—in the words of the historian Nicholas Tyacke—'a combination of critics and reformers'.[23]

The bulk of those who took the lead criticizing royal practices and policies had received some legal training, usually at the inns of court, and were consequently knowledgeable about precedents in common law.[24] Tyacke also identified the 'most coherent among them' as 'certain puritans', men who displayed their godly credentials by voting not to sit on the Sabbath but to attend on Ascension Day and who made it their mission to bring godly reforms to England.[25] All of them were old hands in parliament and had been equally assertive, and sometimes troublesome, under Elizabeth. However, they should not be thought of as an oppositional group since they did not always vote together nor were they consistently hostile to government measures. They also had different views about the policies they wanted to be followed.

Outside the debating chambers, the wider public had a keen interest in the goings-on in parliament, not least because individual MPs were expected to forward the interests of their locality and patron. Some kept diaries, which might be communicated to friends or patrons; others sent news of proceedings to select individuals, even passing on copies of speeches or grievances raised in the debating chambers or committees.[26] Yet far less private reportage of James's first parliament has survived than of his later ones.[27] One unofficial peep into parliamentary life from this earlier period was a humorous poem, entitled 'Censure of the Parliament Fart'. Written by a member of the commons and prompted by one of his colleague's farting during the debates on the naturalization of Scots in 1607, each of the verse couplets offered a witty portrait of each member present in the chamber by characterizing his response to the fart. The poem circulated widely in manuscript, its popularity arising not only from its irreverence but also because the fart expressed what many people felt about James's policy.[28]

Such instances aside, parliamentarians were very protective of the 'secrecy' of proceedings in the two chambers. On the rare occasions it was breached, the culprits became subject to parliamentary censure. John Thornborough, bishop of Bristol, was forced to make an abject apology in the house of lords, in May 1604, after the publication of his printed pamphlet revealing discussions on the Union in the commons, his misconduct made worse in members' eyes because he went on to refute each one of their objections in turn.[29] The commons, moreover, could become incensed when its proceedings were publicly disparaged. In June 1604, the anti-Puritan cleric Dr John Howson was named and shamed for some 'speeches of scandal and scorn to this house'; what he actually said is unrecorded but was presumably related to the commons' attempts at ecclesiastical reform.[30] Two years later, some MPs successfully called for the arrest of Dr Roger Parker, a precentor of Lincoln Cathedral, who 'verie indiscretly' inveighed against the 'proceedings in the lower house' in a sermon at Paul's Cross; although the king deemed his words merely 'presumptuous', the commons thought them seditious.[31] Of course no-one could complain when James chose to give his own version of parliamentary business; his speeches were put on sale to explain why the Union project was shelved in 1607 and why the 'great contract' collapsed in 1610.

★ ★ ★

James planned for his first English parliament to sit immediately after his coronation. The plague, however, put paid to this notion, and it was not until February 1604 that the hustings to select MPs took place. In readiness, James issued a proclamation in January charging electors not to choose 'superstitious' persons (meaning Catholics), those noted for 'their turbulent humors' (Puritans), bankrupts, or outlaws.[32] This order was highly unusual and was to cause serious problems during the session. On the advice of his lord chancellor, Baron Ellesmere, James also stipulated that the election returns should be brought to the court of chancery for approval, another order that led to trouble.[33]

In the proclamation, James also stated the parliament's purpose. It was, he declared, to fulfil his 'earnest desire' to redress abuses and so 'answere that expectation, which (by their joyfull maner of receiving us) wee perceived they had conceived of our government'. Taking his 'earnest desire' to heart, the commons expected a wide programme of reforms: all wanted tighter laws against recusancy; the majority desired changes to purveyance and wardship; and many were keen for reforms relating to religion and 'the reformation of manners'.[34] Members were consequently gravely disappointed with James's opening speech to parliament on 19 March. There, he again referred to his subjects' joyful welcome at his accession but now made no mention of the reform of abuses. Indeed, he warned the commons against having too large a legislative programme, as there would be no time for sufficient deliberation, and 'the making of too many lawes in one parliament will bring in confusion'. His own agenda in parliament, said the king, was a formal Anglo-Scottish Union, a policy that commanded little support among his listeners. James continued with comments about religious groups which were equally not to their liking. After dismissing Puritans as a discontented sect, he spoke kindly of lay Catholics, whom he thought 'well minded men and peaceable subjects', misguided rather than reprobate, and in need of instruction not persecution.[35] In neither his proclamation nor opening speech did James request a subsidy—the usual reason for summoning parliament—because the monies granted in Elizabeth's last parliament of 1601 were still being collected and because he anyway expected his parliament to vote him tonnage and poundage [the customs duty on wine and wool] for life, as was customary at the beginning of each reign. This omission at least would have pleased the commons.

Perhaps in reaction to the king's speech, some members of the commons demonstrated from the start a determination to maintain the independence of their chamber. Instead of the unanimous acclamation of the crown's nominee (Sir Edward Phelips) as speaker of the house, as was customary, silence followed his nomination. Then 'other names were muttered'—including Hastings, Bacon, Hoby, Montagu, and Martin—and it had to be put to a vote.[36] The house ultimately rallied around Phelips for want of agreement on an alternative, but there was evidently concern that he might be the mouthpiece of the king or lord chancellor rather than their own. And this apprehension proved not unjustified. In his acceptance speech, Phelips openly spoke of James as 'the ymage and representation of God upon earth', and throughout the session he generally guided debates in the crown's interest.[37] Probably, it was in part to free themselves from his authority that the commons employed the procedural device of 'the committee of the whole house'—which suspended the role of the speaker—during the 1607 and 1610 sessions when contentious matters of state were to be debated.[38]

Four days after Phelips's election, the first battle began. Members leapt to defend their parliamentary privileges when their fellow MP Sir Francis Goodwin was excluded from the house. Goodwin had defeated Sir John Fortescue (the seventy-one-year-old privy councillor who was a veteran of seven previous parliaments) as the senior member elected for

Buckinghamshire, but the clerk of the crown (based in the court of chancery) afterwards discovered that Goodwin was technically an outlaw because he had not repaid some small debts. The clerk therefore held another election in which Fortescue retained his seat. Spokesmen in the commons objected on two counts. First, they maintained that Goodwin's outlawry was no good cause for exclusion despite the king's earlier proclamation. Second, they argued that the commons not chancery should be the judge in a disputed election for otherwise chancery could control the composition of the house. The row dragged on for several weeks, much to the irritation of James who wanted the commons to get on with discussing the Union.

In one sense, the Goodwin–Fortescue case was simply the continuation of a long-running dispute about the respective jurisdictions of the commons and chancery. But Conrad Russell has argued that such strong feelings over the election dispute may have arisen because of parliamentary fears that James was planning to create new constituencies and use his prerogative to allow Scots to be elected to parliament. If so, the commons possibly felt the need to assert its control over parliamentary elections and resist crown interference, while James had an incentive to back chancery as his instrument.[39] It is impossible to know for sure, but—whatever the cause—the Goodwin–Fortescue election dispute escalated into a serious political confrontation between the king and commons.

After reviewing the case, the commons ejected Fortescue from the house. That should have ended the matter, but, on 27 March, the lords made known their dissatisfaction with this proceeding and called for a joint conference at which they could tell the commons the 'reasons for their dislike'. The initiative came from Ellesmere and Cecil: Ellesmere was seeking to protect chancery's jurisdiction while Cecil was horrified at the exclusion from the house of an 'antient' privy councillor. The commons, however, considered the matter beyond the scope of the lords and rejected their suggestion for a meeting. This time, James intervened. He had listened to his councillors (no doubt Ellesmere and Cecil) and 'conceived himself engaged and touched in honour'. He was 'engaged' because he thought (or had been told) that his prerogative was endangered since chancery was the king's court of equity; he was 'touched in honour' because he had previously ordered that outlaws should not be elected.[40] He therefore summoned representatives of the commons—including twelve lawyers—to explain themselves before him at Whitehall. After much debate, the house voted that a different commons' delegation should go to the king 'not to give the reasons of our judgmente in that case but to satysfye him of the erevocabliness [irrevocableness] of our judgments'.[41]

The meeting took place on 28 March. There James dismayed the commons. Although he stated that he had no preference for either Fortescue or Goodwin and 'no purpose to impeach' the commons' privileges, he declared that their rights derived solely from him and 'should not be turned against him'. He pointed out that his judges—led by Chief Justice Popham—had ruled that Goodwin was unable to take his place as an outlaw and that the commons had no right to arbitrate in election disputes. James then demanded that the commons should confer with his judges in the upper house.[42] The reaction of the commons was mixed. Some members rejected any compromise on the basis that, if they submitted on this issue, 'the free election of the country is taken away, and none shall be chosen but such as shall please the king and council'. Other members—including Bacon—thought it wise to hold a conference with the lords to avoid a further altercation with the king. All seemingly concurred with Yelverton that they could not go back on their original decision for 'our judgment first given hath bounde our tonges'. If resolutions of the commons did not hold, said Yelverton, there could be no security or continuity in the state.[43] It was finally agreed to put down in writing the reasons for their standing firm in refusing to debate the matter further.

By then, the king had moved to Royston from where he expected to receive a written confirmation that the commons would speak with his judges. After a few days of silence, he felt 'offended' that the house had not responded positively to his 'more than loving proposition' and 'fatherly conclusion' that 'yf they were in the wrong towards us, they should not be ashamed to acknowledge it'. Moreover, he was perturbed by reports that the commons was persisting in taking upon itself the right 'to judge both of the opinion of the judges and of our royall prerogative'. This was unacceptable to him. On 1 April, James ruled that all other parliamentary matters be put on hold until the Buckinghamshire election dispute was resolved.[44] At this point, he believed his prerogative was at stake.

Two days later, the commons gave their answer to the king in writing. They began with asserting their loyalty and denying any 'thought to offend' him. They next repeated their reasons for disagreeing with his judges. Precedent, they argued, gave chancery the authority to receive election returns but not to judge them; and in matters relating to their privileges, the lower house was—and had always been—a court with 'sufficent power to discerne and determine' without the intervention of the lords. They then added a new argument. Their investigations into the handling of the elections now revealed that Goodwin was not an outlaw at all. This 'humble answer' was then delivered to the lord chancellor in the upper house.[45]

Angered by the commons' continuing resistance, James immediately returned to London to hold a two-hour meeting with the speaker. We do not know what was said, but at its conclusion Phelips was told to impart a message to the commons that attempted to be both conciliatory and authoritarian. James admitted that he had been 'distracted in judgment' and acknowledged the commons' privileges, but he 'commanded as an absolute king' that they should confer with the judges in his and his privy council's presence. Upon receiving this message, 'there grew some amazement, and silence; but at last one [member] stood up, and said, the prince's command is like a thunderbolt; his command upon our allegiance, like the roaring of a lion: to his command there is no contradiction'.[46]

That same afternoon, a delegation from the commons met the king again. James 'was somwhat angry at first but afterwards the matter was pacyfyed' with the two sides reaching a compromise solution: both Fortescue and Goodwin would be displaced, and a new election be held in which neither man would stand for the seat.[47] James had decided to back down for several good reasons. He realized that the commons' case was stronger than he had originally been advised. Additionally, ambassadors were reporting news of the conflict abroad, creating bad publicity for the new regime. Most important of all, the king needed the lower house's goodwill if his Union project was to proceed successfully.[48]

The Easter break that began on 6 April allowed tempers to cool. After the adjournment, the king and commons publicly mended their bridges. On behalf of the commons, the speaker gave effusive thanks to the king, expressing 'what wonder they conceived in his judgment; what joy in his grace; what comfort they had in his justice; what approbation they made of his prudence; and what obedience they yielded to his power and pleasure'. On his side, James gracefully accepted the commons' 'grave, dutiful, and obedient answer', reiterated his respect for their privileges, and gave thanks to them with the words 'that he had rather be a king of such subjects, than to be a king of many kingdoms'. He then exhorted the commons to get on with urgent business, meaning the Union.[49]

However, no sooner was the Buckinghamshire dispute settled than the commons turned its attention to another case of parliamentary privilege.

Four days before the opening of parliament, Sir Thomas Shirley, the member for Steyning in Sussex, had been clapped into the Fleet prison for debt. Believing that freedom from arrest was an essential parliamentary privilege which had been established successfully under Elizabeth, the commons ordered that a writ of habeas corpus be issued to obtain Shirley's freedom and allow him to take his seat.[50]

Shirley's case was less contentious as neither the king nor lords opposed the principle of parliamentary immunity from arrest.[51] But it was tricky to resolve because of legal technicalities. Determined to assert the lower house's power in matters of privilege, members refused to call upon chancery to issue the habeas corpus writ to secure Shirley's release; and without a writ from chancery, the warden of the Fleet refused to free the prisoner for fear of becoming liable for his debt. To break this deadlock, the commons committed the warden to the Tower and sent their own sergeant to the Fleet to release Shirley. There, the officer encountered the warden's wife who, fearful of disobeying her husband (or so she claimed), would not deliver the prisoner. Infuriated by the married couple's intransigence (the warden still would not budge), a majority in the commons voted, on 9 May, 'to free him [Shirley] with force', but they held back when the speaker warned them against breaking the law.

The next day, the commons seemed to find a solution in statute. Members drafted a bill that liberated Shirley, saved the warden from incurring his debt, and made sure the money owed would be paid to the creditor after the parliamentary session ended. The bill passed both houses within two days. However, the lords pointed out that it could not be signed by the king until the end of the session, timing which would prevent Shirley from taking his seat before then. Wanting the matter to be over, an exasperated James sent a message to the house that '*in verbo principis*' he would give his royal assent at the session's end. Accordingly, on 15 May, Shirley entered the house and took his seat; and four days later the warden was released from the Tower and brought kneeling into the lower house where he confessed 'his error and presumption'. Accepting his apology, the house pardoned him.[52]

Even with the satisfactory conclusion of both cases, some members worried that James had not explicitly recognized that the lower house enjoyed 'fundamentall priviledges' which had been held since 'tyme immemoryall'.[53] They became still more concerned at the beginning of the next parliamentary session in 1606, when the king directed the speaker to permit both Goodwin and Fortescue to fill two seats that had been vacated since the previous session with no by-election. As one member explained: 'I am a little jelous [suspicious] what maie follow if wee receave burgesses by his Majestie's comendacions.'[54] Despite such objections, the two men did take up the vacant seats. Nonetheless, thereafter, the speaker issued a writ for by-elections whenever a member died and so the commons won its battle with chancery in gaining control over elections and membership.[55] Ellesmere would probably have fought back, had he had strong backing, but James and other privy councillors were resistant to chancery interfering again in electoral matters. It would waste too much parliamentary time.[56]

★ ★ ★

As was clear from his opening speech, James wanted this parliament to devote itself to the Union. Once the privilege cases were resolved, the issue did indeed occupy more parliamentary time than any other matter. However, the voices raised against it surprised and affronted the king, even though Cecil had warned him in advance that the measure could run into difficulties. Both houses contained members who were strongly opposed to the creation of a new political entity, Great Britain. The lords were less outspoken, relying on the lower house to do the work of rejecting the measure. Consequently, as one of the commons put it, the lords 'clad angel-like were received into Abraham's bosom, while we fried in the furnace of the king's displeasure'.[57]

Initially, it looked as if there would be no problem. No one apparently objected when, ten days into the session, Sir William Maurice (member for Caernarvonshire) recited an old Welsh prophecy, translated by another member as:

A king of British blood in cradle crowne[d]
  With lion mark shall join all British ground
Restore the cross and make the isle renowne[d].[58]

Likewise, the matter was passed over on the last day of March, when Maurice again spoke up for Union, this time during the debate to recognize the king's title to the English crown.[59] The lower house was then preoccupied with the Buckinghamshire election case and left well alone.

However, once the Buckinghamshire dispute was resolved, the question could be postponed no longer. James informed the commons, on 12 April, that his one wish was 'at his death to leave one worship to God; one kingdom, intirely governed; one uniformity in laws'. The next day, Ellesmere conveyed to both houses James's roadmap to achieve his ends: first, that a commission would be appointed to determine the exact form of Union; and second, that James should take the new title of king of Great Britain.[60] It was then agreed that the lords and commons should set up a joint committee to finalize arrangements.

However, before any meeting of a commission was held, the commons began a debate that revealed the divisiveness of James's proposals. Although some speeches endorsed his projected Union and name change, a storm of protests was heard.[61] The brilliant orator Edwin Sandys (the forty-two-year-old member for Stockbridge) took the lead.[62] A 'perfect' Union—where two kingdoms were united in government, laws, and title—he argued, was only possible when one was 'wonne by the sworde and conquered'. Historical and present examples of multiple monarchies demonstrated that unions brought about by marriage or election could never be 'perfect'.[63]

The renaming of England and Scotland 'Great Britain' caused the greatest storm, with members contending that a new title denoted a new kingdom. If England ceased to exist, they maintained, so too would its laws, including the common law upon which all their rights and privileges depended as well as existing international treaties.[64] Furthermore, they feared the change of name would disparage the realm because 'a new erected kingdome must take the latest and lowest place' in precedence among kingdoms. Sandys also questioned whether parliament had the right to introduce such constitutional changes: surely the English parliament had no power to legislate to alter the laws of Scotland nor had it the authority to act on behalf of all Englishmen? Overall, he recommended that the nature of the Union be decided before any change of name be concluded and that the wider country be consulted on so great a matter.[65] While Sandys focused on historical precedents and legal arguments to make his case, other members drifted into anti-Scottish sentiment and language. Fuller, for example, used a xenophobic analogy to incite fear that Union would bring hordes of impoverished Scots into England: if the boundaries of two flocks of sheep at pasture were removed, he declared, 'the flocke in the worse ground will come in to the better and eat that as bare as theyr owne'.[66]

On learning of these objections, James delivered messages to both houses. Given on 20 April, it was delivered to the commons the next day. Unfortunately, we cannot be sure of his exact words because they have not survived in their original form and can only be accessed in different reports. In one account, he expressed his astonishment at the commons' 'curious carpinge'; in another, he complained that their doubts 'were but curiosities of ignorant persons such as sought to finde knots in bulrushes' and that 'he liked not to have his deliberacons questioned'. In both accounts, he briskly dismissed the commons' arguments. A change in name, he admonished, did not mean a loss of status: after all, a baron suffered no such 'diminution' when he became an earl. His intention, he said, was not 'to alter or innovate the fundamentall lawes, priviledges, and good customes of this kingdome' but simply that all the laws and customs of the two halves of his kingdom should be 'welld in one, as they are all one body, under one heade'. It was especially important that the laws of succession were brought into line, he declared, so that 'the crowne of Scotlande should be ever adherent and follow the succession of the bloud of England'. The way forward, he maintained, was for the appointment of English and Scottish commissioners who would discuss and reach an agreement on the exact changes. Once they had made their report, it could be debated in parliament.[67]

At the same time, James asked the judges to give their legal opinion as to whether he could use the name of Britain 'without the direct abrogation of all the lawis'.[68] No doubt he expected their verdict would bolster his case, but he was to be disappointed. On 28 April, the judges ruled that any change in his title would result in 'an utter extinction of all the lawes now in force'.[69] We can imagine how Sandys and his fellow members gloated when told this judgment on 1 May. But any gloating was short-lived. The same day, a letter from the king was read out to the house which demonstrated the commons' battle was far from won. Written in his own hand, it expressed James's frustration and anger at what he saw as wasted weeks spent in nit-picking debates. He made no mention of his judges' verdict but simply demanded an end to all further discussion. He had 'given over wrangling upon wordis', and he craved 'no conclusion to be taken at this tyme' but required the appointment of a commission to draft a form of Union that would later be discussed in the two houses. Any further attempt to thwart the process of Union, James denounced as an act of blasphemy, a spit in the face of God, for they would be 'praeferring warre to peace, trouble to quyetnes, hatred to love, weakenes to greatnes, and division to union; to sowe the seidis of discorde to all oure posterities; to dishonoure youre king'.[70] Faced with James's rage and intransigence, the commons agreed to go ahead with appointing the commission, which was to be composed of Scots and Englishmen. Even then, the two houses tussled over its exact language. The final wording of the statute repeated James's words and revealed the limits of Union, for it laid down that the English commissioners would not introduce to parliament any scheme 'to alter and innovate the fundamental and ancient laws, privileges, and good customs of this kingdom'.[71] James's fury was evident in his closing speech to parliament. There, he berated 'the pertness and boldnes of some members' and warned that they would 'extort nothing by violence' from him in the matter of the Union.[72]

★ ★ ★

While James was pushing for his pet project, some in the commons were seeking a reform of abuses in the state. Although in his January proclamation James had expressed his readiness to hear and act on their grievances, the debates that followed went nowhere and added to the ill-feeling between the king and commons.

Sir Robert Wroth (member for Middlesex) opened the batting on 23 March, the first working day of the session. A veteran of nine Elizabethan parliaments, in most of which he had spoken out against monopolies and purveyance, Wroth put forward a seven-point programme of reform that included tackling these two abuses. Among the other reforms was the abolition of wardship and the confirmation of the new prayer book drawn up by convocation after the Hampton Court Conference. The remainder dealt with the abolition of the export of iron ordnance, dispensations from the penal statutes against recusants, and the removal of the abuses of the exchequer.[73] Wroth's speech was greeted with silence. Members were uncertain how to proceed because most of his proposals touched the royal prerogative. Furthermore, since Wroth was known to be Cecil's client, it was unclear whether he was acting on his own initiative or on behalf of the privy council. Breaking the silence, Sir Edward Montagu (member for Northamptonshire and brother of the dean of the chapel royal) brought up three different grievances: enclosure (a particular problem in the Midlands), the suspension of ministers 'for not observing some ceremonies' (an acute concern in his county), and the 'intollerable burthen' and abuses in the consistory court of Canterbury. The house then agreed to refer all the issues raised by Wroth and Montagu to two large committees.[74]

As to be expected, the religious grievances broached by Montagu were objectionable to many bishops, especially Richard Bancroft, then bishop of London and soon-to-be archbishop of Canterbury.[75] Wroth's demand that parliament confirm the new prayer book was likewise intolerable to Bancroft since it implicitly affirmed parliamentary sovereignty over the

Church, a principle that he and most of the upper clergy denied. Under Elizabeth, the commons had been barred from initiating religious reforms; religion, she had insisted, was to be dealt with by the assembly of the clergy at convocation. James now overturned this principle; on 13 April, he implicitly admitted the commons' right to discuss ecclesiastical reform. Immediately, an alarmed Bancroft lobbied James to prevent this happening, and three days later the king sent the commons a message that 'before they intermeddled' with such reforms they should confer with members of convocation.[76] At once, several of the commons strongly objected because such a move would jeopardize both their desired reforms and parliamentary liberties. They pointed out 'that there was no precedent of any conference with a convocation' and that 'clarks of the convocation weare not theyr peeres'. The next day the commons 'utterly refused' the bishops' request for a meeting in the convocation house at Westminster Abbey. Instead, they offered to confer with them in the painted chamber of the upper house where the bishops would be present as spiritual peers, not senior churchmen. Under pressure from James—and possibly the lay lords—the bishops 'yielded'.[77] As far as James was concerned, the compromise was minor and, besides, he wanted to mollify the commons, again to obtain their support for Union. Nevertheless, the concession still signified that parliament had the power to initiate and carry through religious reforms, a power that Elizabeth had never conceded. But, thanks to the intransigence of the bishops, the reform agenda of the commons got nowhere in the joint conferences. As to be expected, Bancroft would not permit any degree of nonconformity even when ministers otherwise carried out their duties well. More surprisingly, the commons' attempts to extirpate pluralism and provide for a learned clergy stalled. On 4 June, Bancroft read out a statement from convocation 'inhibiting' the bishops from conferring with members of the lower house because 'the laity had not to meddle in these matters'.[78]

Bancroft's statement had the support of James who had been persuaded that the Puritan MPs were little different from Scottish Presbyterians. In May, the king had become so alarmed when a few of them had demanded a revision of the thirty-nine articles that he immediately told Bancroft to reaffirm the official statement of faith in convocation.[79] Soon afterwards, James agreed that the canons produced in convocation did not need to be passed in parliament, a verdict that restored the independent legislative power of the Church as an autonomous body. As a result, the 1604 session ended without the passing of any significant religious reforms. The only statute concerning religion was 'for the due execution' of statutes against Catholics.

★ ★ ★

The 1604 session also failed to pass statutes reforming purveyance and wardship. Before parliament opened, Dorset and Cecil were giving serious thought to the abolition of both these sources of royal revenue, provided that parliament gave the king financial compensation for their loss.[80] Together purveyance and wardship brought in 10 to 15 per cent of the crown's yearly income and would need replacing with a large annual cash payment. Quite possibly, Cecil had actually encouraged his client Wroth to raise the issues of purveyance and wardship so that a debate on their future would begin.[81] Parliamentary support for abolition would certainly help him override the opposition to change from vested interests who benefited from the practices.

Over the next weeks, the lower and upper houses worked closely together to draft an agreed bill.[82] On 31 March, a committee of lawyers brought in a bill against purveyance, but the house soon began to realize that any statute would be unacceptable to the king since it encroached upon his prerogative. Consequently, after a second reading, the bill was replaced by a petition to the king. Moderate in content, it did not call for the abolition of purveyance and simply asked him 'to confirm, and put in execution, the laws already made'.[83] Since there was no obvious attack on his prerogative, James was sympathetic, affirmed his desire to redress the 'great grievances', and allowed representatives of the commons to discuss the issue with the privy council and lords.[84]

Given the language of the petition, James fully expected the commons to be satisfied with a promise and commitment to iron out abuses, enforce existing statutes, and extend compositions. They were not. Many members wanted a complete overhaul or abolition and, for this purpose, began further discussions with the upper house. On 9 May, representatives of both houses arrived at what seemed like a workable solution: the shires would contribute £50,000 a year to buy out purveyance.[85] However, when put before the commons, some members questioned its wisdom. Those who judged purveyance illegal rejected the notion that the king could demand an income in compensation for its loss. Those from localities which were free of purveyance worried that their electors might balk at contributing to a national composition. Speakers also voiced misgivings about the proposed arrangement out of fear that it might create a precedent for permanent direct taxes at a national level. Many—probably the majority—acknowledged that the royal household required some money from the state but quibbled about how much; one member thought £20,000 quite sufficient. When all these points—and more—had been heard over several sittings, the commons decided to defer any decision: members would consult their constituencies and bring their electors' views to the next session of parliament.[86] Unsurprisingly, kicking the can down the road satisfied no-one.[87]

The proposal to offer the king an annual sum in place of purveyance inspired some members to reanimate the issue of wardship that had lain dormant for weeks. On 11 May, Sandys reintroduced the grievance during the debate on purveyance. As seen, he had already made a name for himself in speaking against the Union; he now came to the notice of the house again by proposing that composition for wardship 'might go hand in hand' with that of purveyance. This approach reflected Cecil's preference at that time, and it is likely that Sandys was putting forward the secretary's solution for reform. However, the motion was rejected. Instead, the house agreed that wardship should be treated 'singly' and that a conference be held with the upper house to discuss framing a petition against all the king's historic feudal dues. On 19 May, the lords—led by Cecil—appeared ready to back a form of composition that would replace wardship. Sandys then headed a committee in the lower house which drew up a petition detailing the abuses in wardship, recommending the buying out of feudal tenures, and outlining ways it could be done.[88]

A week later, Cecil unexpectedly came out against Sandys's proposal. His *volte-face* was largely because of the urgency of James's financial needs. Composition would be a complicated and lengthy process, and the crown could not afford to lose receipts from wardship—which brought in about £67,000 a year—while the changes were being enacted. If change 'shold hang long in suspense' because of divisions in parliament and the complexity of proposed composition schemes, thought Cecil, it would be highly prejudicial to the king and cause 'an exceeding decrease of his revenues' just as royal expenses were rising. Additionally, Cecil was facing strong lobbying from officials in the court of wards who would lose status, salaries, and bribes, if wardship were abolished.[89]

Almost certainly, Cecil conveyed his new thinking to Wroth. At any rate, the MP did an astounding U turn when Sandys brought his draft petition before the commons on 26 May. Wroth, who had raised the issue in the first place, now spoke forcefully against the measure, as did members of the lords later that day when Sandys brought the proposed reform before a joint meeting. According to one in the commons' delegation, the lords (no names mentioned) accused the lower house of 'inconsiderateness' in demanding 'more of the king than of any of his predecessors since or before the [Norman] Conquest' and of endeavouring 'to deprive the king of his prerogative'. This sudden and unexpected withdrawal of official support enraged the commons against the upper house, and they furiously denied the accusations against them.[90]

After the Whitsun recess, on 30 May, James called 'the whole house' to attend upon him at Whitehall where they received a lashing of his tongue.[91] We have no record of James's words, but they were evidently wounding enough for members to decide to draft a petition in self-defence. The outcome was the 'Form of Apology and Satisfaction', a document explaining parliamentary rights to a foreign king.[92] Although it was once thought important in the development of the English constitution, its authors were not radicals or members of an opposition party. The motion to write it came from Sir Thomas Ridgeway, who often spoke in favour of the government's programme. His purpose in proposing the document, he explained, was to clear up 'misinformations', which had been the cause 'of all the discontentfull and troublesome proceedings' in parliament and to:

> in all humility informe his Majestie in the truthe and clearenes of the actions and intentions of the house from the beginning, thereby to free yt from the scandall of levity and precipitation, as also of the proceeding in particuler touching the said matter of wardship, with this speciall care that a matter so advisedly and gravely undertaken and proceeded in might not die or bee buried in the hands of those that first bred yt.[93]

Phelips, the speaker, seconded it, and the final document was brought into the commons on 20 June. Its tone was respectful, but its content was implicitly critical of recent royal conduct. First, it asserted that the commons' privileges were of right, not of the king's grace as James claimed. Second, it stipulated that laws concerning religion needed the consent of parliament. Third, it confirmed the commons' recent victories, namely that they were the sole judge of election returns and enjoyed freedom from arrest and free speech. Finally, it expressed the need to reform purveyance and wardship. The petition, however, was lost in committee, possibly because it was thought too radical or provocative. Although never presented to the king, he came to hear of it. That he was angered by its impertinence is evident from his speech of 7 July proroguing parliament, which was delivered, as was traditional, before both houses.

There, James praised the lords in the upper house for their 'discretion, modesty, judgment, care, and fidelity'. But he rebuked those in the lower house who had caused him trouble. Whereas in Scotland, he was treated with great respect, he said, here in England the members found fault with his every proposition. Although he did not suspect them of disloyalty, he censured them as 'idle heads' and rash. Among the troublesome members, he went on, were 'some of a new religion framed to theyr owne appetite', who sought to build a 'new Jerusalem' and had no tolerance of their fellowmen; and he was astonished that they 'had been so great, so proude, or so dominant in the house'. James then reiterated his commitment to the Union, which he declared was natural, godly, and in the interests of both peoples, but he dismissed a reform of purveyance on the grounds that the existing laws just needed proper execution. Referring to the 'Apology', he wished its authors would have spoken 'with more modesty' of their liberties.[94] His feelings made plain, James closed parliament.

In spite of these tensions and ill feeling, the 1604 session passed thirty-nine private acts and thirty-three public statutes. Overall, it was more legislatively productive than any Elizabethan parliament, and some of its statutes were significant.[95] Of the latter, one was an act against witchcraft which stiffened penalties for the offence and extended the crime from 'maleficium' (the harmful use of magic), as laid down in an earlier Elizabethan statute, to demonism, apostasy, and conspiracy. Although this new definition was in accord with Scottish practice and reflected James's own thinking in *Daemonologie*, most historians do not think the king was directly responsible for the bill's introduction or amendments. Nonetheless, its timing does suggest that his accession and the printing of his book on the subject stimulated the commons to introduce the measure. Even so, prosecutions remained relatively low except for a spike in trials from 1645 to 1647 until its repeal in 1736.[96]

Another significant measure was a new Game Law which allowed only those of noble and gentry status with incomes of £40 a year or more to hunt, thereby excluding the lesser gentry. Again, James does not seem to have been responsible for its introduction, but it certainly gained his approval since he believed that overhunting had led to a shortage of game that affected his enjoyment of the sport. The statute was contentious and deeply resented by those lesser gentlemen banned from hunting; the sport, after all, was a sign of gentility and social standing.[97]

★ ★ ★

The second session of this parliament was postponed twice. Originally due to open on 7 February 1605, it was initially prorogued until 23 October for two reasons. First, James wanted to deny Puritans a parliamentary platform in their campaign against the imposition of conformity to the prayer book.[98] Second, James and Cecil expected opposition to the Union project, the main purpose for the session, and required more time to win people round.[99] In need of a subsidy to meet his expenses, James demanded 'loans' from his subjects during the summer to tide him over.[100]

In October, parliament was prorogued again, this time until Tuesday 5 November. Cecil wanted the extra weeks to persuade leading MPs to support a subsidy.[101] But, if rumours were correct, Cecil had his work cut out, and the expectation was that supply would be refused:

> for many members openly declare that as there is no war with Spain, no war in Holland, no army on the Scottish border—which they say cost the late queen upwards of a million a year in gold—they cannot understand why the king, who has the revenues of Scotland, should want money.[102]

In November, the session was again prorogued, but this time because of the Gunpowder Plot. The government explained that it needed time to focus on extracting all the conspirators and bringing them to justice. But before the prorogation, Lord Chancellor Ellesmere placed the commissioners' report on Union—the 'Instrument—with the clerk of the parliament in preparation for future discussion.[103]

When parliament met on 21 January 1606, the commons was so slow to start discussing the Union that, on 11 April, Fuller moved that the subject be postponed for lack of time. The lords agreed, and a bill was passed deferring consideration of the 'Instrument' until the next session.[104] The commons was gleeful, hoping that the proposal would go away permanently, and indeed the Venetian ambassador thought members might be right and nothing more would be heard of it since the issue was 'so full of difficulty'.[105]

With the Union out of the way, this parliamentary session concerned itself with anti-Catholic legislation and the presentation of the commons' grievances. As far as the former was concerned, king and parliament were at one.[106] Both houses and the king worked together to pass 'very sharp' laws against recusants and priests, though admittedly not as sharp as a few members desired.[107] Throughout the session, parliament expressed concern about the king's safety, especially amid rumours of further attempts on his life.[108] In the same spirit of loyalism, the commons—albeit somewhat belatedly—agreed to three subsidies and fifteenths (worth then nearly £400,000), for which there was 'no other precedent in times of peace'.[109]

Nonetheless, not all went well. Purveyance 'was the maine matter, which bred truble on all sides', as almost a repeat of 1604. By now, the commons' spokesmen were intent upon its abolition. This time, however, the king referred the issue to his judges who 'overruled all on the prerogative side' and delivered their verdict that 'the prerogative was not subject to law but that it was a transcendent above the reach of parlement'. Understandably, members were dismayed, even alarmed, at what they considered a dangerous principle. Attempting to pacify them, James said that 'in kindness he would doe much, but upon constraint nothing'; in other words, members could expect some reformation of purveyance from him if his prerogative was not touched.[110] Accordingly, on 23 April, James issued a proclamation to crack down on abuses. When it was read to the lower house, members spent half an hour 'in idle looking one upon an other', powerless to bring about the significant change they had been considering.[111] Church reform equally made no progress. In February, the commons moved that a 'colleccion of all greavances' be drawn up and, before parliament ended in May, it was presented as a petition to the king.[112]

Before the next session reconvened on 18 November 1606, James, in consultation with his councillors and justices, gave what he called 'mature deliberacon' to the commons' petition of grievances.[113] Cecil and others also drew up answers to the objections to Union which MPs had propounded in 1604.[114] All seemed ready for a productive session. It turned out otherwise. James's opening speech did not get it off to a good start. He criticized those he termed the 'tribunes of the people, whose mouths could not be stopped, either from the matters of the Puritanes or of the purveyance'. He also smeared those who opposed the Union as 'men of humourous or malicious minds' and went on to dismiss each of their objections in turn. Speaking for an hour and a half, James aimed 'to perswade the passage of the act and "Instrument" of the Union'.[115] The 'Instrument' had recommended freedom of commerce between the two realms, the abolition of the separate legal status of the borders, mutual naturalization, and the abolition of hostile laws between England and Scotland. These now needed to be discussed and passed into law.

A lack of enthusiasm for these proposals slowed down proceedings. After more than a week spent on determining the correct procedure for discussions, it was agreed that the lords should take responsibility for introducing bills on naturalization and the borders, the topics which were thought most controversial and likely to cause conflict with the king, while the commons would lead on commerce and hostile laws. However, there were several peers in the upper house as opposed to naturalization as there were members in the lower. Consequently, there was little chance of an easy passage in the lords, let alone the commons.[116]

The following two weeks saw debates in the lower house that displayed 'confusion and disorder, and no conclusion'.[117] To make matters worse, anti-Scottish prejudices tainted many speeches.[118] In the upper house, it had been agreed that normal rules would be suspended and every member could 'deliver his mind and meaning upon any point, as occasion may serve, by as often speech as he will', but their debates are frustratingly unrecorded.[119] On 13 December, the two houses held a joint conference on the easier topics of abolishing hostile laws and facilitating commerce, but nothing was achieved by the Christmas break which started on 18 December.

When parliament reconvened on 10 February 1607, it still got nowhere on the Union. Eventually, in the debate about naturalization, the commons rejected the automatic naturalization of *post-nati* (Scots born after James's accession in 1603), as proposed in the 'Instrument', and which the judges had anyway considered to be legal without need of statutory confirmation.[120] Just before the Easter recess, on 31 March, James intervened. Before members of both houses, in the great chamber at Whitehall, he made a gracious and conciliatory appeal. He spoke of his two kingdoms as 'two twinnes', not as two wives or parts of his body as he had in previous speeches to parliament. Borrowing the language of scripture, he repeated the metaphor of Union as a divine institution like the marriage at Cana. He no longer upbraided the commons but admitted his mistake in thinking Union would be easy to achieve: 'The error was my mistaking: I knew mine owne end, but not others' feares.' The commons, he went on 'had reason to advise at leasure upon so great a cause; for great matters doe ever require great deliberation'. Nonetheless, they needed to make some progress: 'Betweene foolish rashnesse, and extreame length, there is a middle way. Search all that is reasonable; but omit that which is idle, curious, and unnecessary;

otherwise, there can never be a resolution or end in any good worke.' James then reiterated his reasons for seeking Union and answered objections presented against it.[121] It was a very good speech but had no noticeable impact. After the houses reassembled on 26 April, the Union project made no further progress. Its opponents, notably Sandys, rejected the 'Instrument' and instead called for a new commission to report on how to achieve a 'perfect union' of parliaments, laws, and institution. Given that the Scots would not accept a fusion of the two realms, Sandys's proposal was generally viewed as a stratagem to muddy the waters and stymie even a limited Union—which indeed it was.[122]

In desperation, after the Easter recess on 2 May, James again summoned members of the commons to Whitehall. This time, he vented his frustration in no uncertain terms. He claimed Sandys had deliberately misunderstood his previous speech and warned the house to 'tempt not the patience of your prince' but, instead, speedily to 'proceed with as much as can be done at this time, and make not all you have done, frustrate'.[123] But he knew when he was beaten and implicitly let drop the proposals for the borders, commerce, and naturalization. Only a bill for the abolition of hostile laws was introduced in the commons, which—after a great deal of resistance—passed both houses at the beginning of July just before the end of the session.[124]

There was no question of calling another parliamentary session to reintroduce further bills to achieve James's once cherished plan for Union.[125] When, in 1610, a lone MP 'hotly revived' the matter again, 'there was no little interruption and whistling of the lower house, which took no great taste *en ce potage rechauffé*'.[126]

★ ★ ★

Whatever the commons wanted, the final two sessions of James's first parliament had to be devoted to the dire problem of royal finances.[127] Before it met on 9 February 1610, Cecil—now lord treasurer—had advised James to make a serious attempt to cut back his expenditure or else the commons would resist both subsidies and structural reforms.[128] It did not work: the crown debt remained enormous, and some members held James responsible. One of them, Thomas Wentworth, said reforms would be to no purpose unless the king diminished 'his charge and expences'. Indeed, Wentworth went further. He proposed petitioning the king to 'diminish his charge and live of his owne without exacting of his poore subjects' especially in peacetime;

and if he refused, a law should force him to do so as it had done under Richard II and Henry IV.[129]

In a speech before a joint conference of both houses on 15 February, arranged by the lords, Cecil had to admit to the parlous state of royal finances and entreat immediate supply and long-term support. Trying to appeal to the commons' loyalty to the crown, he first linked Henry's upcoming investiture and new independence with the immediate need for money. But looking at the bigger picture, Cecil explained that James's ordinary expenses each year greatly exceeded his revenues despite having received £450,000 in subsidies from parliament since his accession. As a result, he said, the debt for his ordinary expenses stood at £300,000, a sum which was in fact lower than it had previously been.[130] As for the nature of James's expenses, Cecil did an excellent job in explaining them away. He itemized the late queen's debt, the cost of her funeral, the need for 'magnificence' at royal entries and during the visit of Christian IV, the births and burials of two princesses, and the grand entertainments of ambassadors, envoys, and commissioners who came to England on state business. All this outlay, said Cecil, was absolutely essential for maintaining the king's honour and reputation. Answering the charge that James should be less generous to courtiers, Cecil declared that 'bounty was a disease that few complained of in Queen Elizabeth's days' and that many of those present—including himself—had benefited from it. He admitted that the queen had been more frugal, but if James 'did not give, I should think his subjects lived in a miserable climate'. The purpose of this parliament, concluded Cecil, was to grant supply 'as may make this state both safe and happy', and in return James would consider granting 'favors which are in his power to do' and which parliament proposed 'for the public good'.[131]

Cecil's two-hour speech—acclaimed as 'an excellent oration'—provided a stark but convincing assessment of the state of royal finances: 'the grounds and strength of his arguments were so energeticall, and his speech so persuasive as it seemeth to have given very good satisfaction both to the minds and judgments of all the howse'.[132] Members immediately began to consider a range of ways to improve the king's yearly income: fining papists; confiscating their land; removing impositions and customs from farmers who profited from the deals; and granting the king 'a greate yearly allowance' in lieu of purveyance. However, on 19 February, Thomas Wentworth called on the king to live out of his own means (which would be customs, crown lands, and feudal revenues). He reckoned without Sir Julius Caesar—chancellor of the exchequer since 1606—who dismissed Wentworth's proposal as absurd. James's expenses, stated Caesar 'in angry manner', amounted to £1,400 a day, excluding the interest on his debts; to discharge what he owed, the king required a lump sum of £600,000; and, to prevent future debt, he needed an annual payment of £200,000.[133] At a joint conference of the commons and lords on the 24th, Cecil confirmed these figures and declared that the king was willing to relinquish ten minor sources of income, including purveyance, in return for the annual sum, but significantly wardship was not part of the deal.[134]

On 28 February, this proposed 'great contract' was debated in the lower house. Despite the name, it was not intended as a 'contract', meaning a reciprocal arrangement, for Cecil was demanding substantial extra revenues with some concessions, 'nothing more than redress of grievances'.[135] The proposal immediately ran into difficulties. Not only were the sums requested huge and unprecedented but, additionally, members were unwilling to grant a fixed annual sum unless James also relinquished wardship.[136] At first, James would not hear of it. Apart from anything else, he was uncomfortable about a grant following on from some form of compensation: 'in order, honor, and matter itself, contribution hath the first place and to retribute before you contribute is nothing else but to deal with me in the way of bargain'.[137] Of more substance, James declared wardship a no-go area. As he told Cecil, it was 'like a precious stone set and inherent in his crowne' and 'he could not in honor now make it away from himself and his successors'. However, desperation for funding and no doubt the advice of Cecil led to a rethink, and he allowed the commons to consider wardship as part of the package.[138] At that moment, there seemed good hope that the difficulties would be ironed out and an agreement reached. But the 'daily discussions' surrounding wardship proceeded 'very slowly', since the commons found 'such a labyrinth of difficulties' that they could make little progress. A key difficulty was that the abolition of wardship required the extinction of the tenures by which the king held them, and that would create all kinds of legal problems.[139]

Another difficulty was a growing suspicion of the king's motives. A furore arose, on 23 February, over passages buried in an academic law dictionary, called *The Interpreter* (1607), which were read out to the house.[140] The offending sections were deemed 'dangerous' since they tended 'greatlie to the derogation' of the common law, the liberties of the subjects, and the power of parliament. According to one MP, the book's author, the civil lawyer Dr John Cowell, vicar-general of Canterbury, had offered a 'presumptuous novelty' in asserting that the two houses could only make law by the king's goodwill and that the king was above the law with the right to alter it.[141] That the commons were so angry about Cowell's book several years after it had first been published reveals the members' concern about James's divine right views and the direction in which they were taking him. A sermon preached at court, on 11 March 1610, on the text 'render unto Caesar' by Samuel Harsnett, bishop of Chichester, intensified their unease for he had argued that the king could tax without parliamentary consent.[142] James—supported by his judges—was already imposing new customs duties by right of his prerogative. Would he go further and rule without parliament if Cecil's 'great contract' went through? To prevent such an occurrence, members reminded the commons of the statutes passed under Edward I 'that a parliament should be called once every year and oftener if need be'.[143] But the anxiety did not go away.

James could not afford to allow these concerns to get in the way of the parliamentary negotiations for supply and support. Money was far more important for him at this time than abstract claims about his prerogative. To pacify parliament, Cowell was held for a while under a form of house arrest and made to answer for his claims before the king and privy council.[144] Then, on 21 March, the king summoned the lords and commons to the banqueting house at Whitehall and delivered what was said to have been 'a most eloquent and excellent speech, to the exceeding joye, admiracon of all that heard him'.[145] It is actually somewhat surprising that his listeners approved of the speech so effusively for James began by comparing kings to God:

> for God maketh and unmaketh so do they; God hath a power of lyffe and death, soe have they; God is accomptible to noe man, noe more are they; God advanceth and pulleth downe and soe doe they; all things are within the power of God and soe are the goods of the subject in the disposing of the king.[146]

One member, though, did wish James had been 'more spareing' in comparing the deity with princes' sovereignty.[147] More pleasing was the main part of his speech in which he distanced himself from both Cowell and Harsnett. Stating that kings in settled kingdoms must obey the laws, he promised to abide by the common law which he averred to hold dear. He stressed his love for his people and announced his intention to issue a proclamation condemning and banning Cowell's book. The speech ended with a reminder of parliament's main purpose, namely to offer supply. His lord treasurer had explained his need—'which is not usuall for kings to doe to their subjects'—now he wanted action. Here again, James tried to be conciliatory, saying: 'The people owe supply and support to their prince but what supply they will gyve is in their power', and he would not ask for more than his people could bear. However, he clearly thought they could bear a lot more than they had hitherto given.[148]

James's speech may have 'satisfied the houses that he did not assume any such extravagant authority as was spoken of in the book', but it did not result in any settlement of the king's financial needs.[149] The commons put discussions about immediate supply on hold while it worked on the tricky terms for the 'great contract'. On 26 March, it offered James a fixed annual grant of £100,000, only half the sum originally requested, in return for the abolition of wardship and feudal tenures. It was unacceptable.[150] The grant might compensate for the crown's loss of income but would not bring in additional revenues. Besides, James had no intention of renouncing his role as a feudal overlord by abolishing knights' service and other tenures. It was 'a matter too prejudiciall and dishonorable both to himself and the gentilitie of England to abolish the noblest tenure of his kingdom and reduce all his subjects, base and noble, to one tenure of lands'.[151]

After the Easter recess, James began negotiations for a new offer. In return for abolishing wardship, he demanded £300,000 as the annual sum (which amounted to £200,000 more than his present income from wardship) and £600,000 for immediate supply. The commons were 'very much distasted and stricken dumbe' with what they thought to be an outrageous demand 'so far exceeding reason and the worth of those things'. They remained silent, waiting for James to make 'some more reasonable proposition unto them or break absolutely the bargain'.[152] As the commons anticipated, Cecil and James came back with new terms. Cecil indicated that the king would go down to the original £200,000 p.a. and the commons could add 'any flower to the deal which would not deface the royal garland or prerogative'. In other words, they could include any other small source of royal income in the package which would not touch the prerogative. Unimpressed, the commons rejected this offer too, and to Cecil's dismay, on 24 April, they began debating impositions, which was outside the scope of the negotiations.[153]

On 8 May, Cecil used the occasion of the assassination of Henry IV of France to urge the commons 'not to delay to give him [James] every satisfaction' now that 'a still heavier burden' was laid upon him including military action in Jülich-Cleves.[154] But members were in no mood to submit to the king's demands. They also ignored the privy council's message of 11 May, commanding them not to call the king's powers or prerogatives into question. Instead, they continued to debate impositions.[155] Furious at their disobedience, James summoned the commons and lords into the great chamber at Whitehall, on 21 May, and repeated the order. Directing his words to the commons, he told them to 'leave to the king that which is his in power' and seek only to redress any 'burden and inconvenience'. Taking away impositions, he said, would dramatically reduce his power and 'make a king a duke of Venice'; how dutiful was it for his subjects to deprive him of a power that all their previous kings and even 'two women before him' had exercised? Nor was the time right. 'Is it a fit matter to dispute of taking away £70,000 a year from me when you are called to consider of supply and support for me?' As well as this severe reprimand, James delivered a warning: it had pleased him to call parliament to hear its advice but 'the more wayward you shall be, I shall be the more unwilling to call you to parliament for such behavior will make me call you the seldomer to council'.[156]

James's speech disconcerted, even alarmed, the commons. In their opinion, his order endangered their right to talk about 'any of the subjects in particular or the commonwealth in generall without restraint or inhibition'.[157] It was true, pointed out Bacon, that Elizabeth had often prohibited debate on matters concerning the crown—her marriage, the succession, and religion—but these 'were things so proper to herself' whereas impositions touched their goods and were 'greevances to the commonwealth'.[158] In protest, the commons sent 'with all humble dutie' a petition to the king in which they declared their 'ancient and fundamentall' right to 'debate freely all matters which do properly concerne the subject'; and these included impositions which were causing 'much sorrow and discomfort'. They had no intention, the petitioners wrote, to challenge the royal prerogative, only 'to know the reasons' why the recent Bate's case had declared impositions legal.[159]

Faced with this remonstration, James caved in. He 'graciously' allowed a group of twenty members of the commons to present their petition to him in the drawing chamber at Greenwich Palace, which was itself a mark of respect. After pouring over the petition's contents, he delivered a speech to the delegation that was equally respectful. Acknowledging misunderstandings on both sides, he protested that he had no intention of eradicating any parliamentary privileges and limiting free speech. His earlier commands, he said, were intended only to get the commons back on track to remedy his great need for money. His concern had been that nothing had thus far been achieved and yet time was short before the heat of the summer began, given 'the holie daies' and the investiture of his son as prince of Wales. Accepting the commons' petition, he allowed them to discuss impositions as a grievance but urged them to concentrate on his financial wants and not 'take away with one hand what they give with the other and so bring to pass that the cause of the parliament be defeated'. To avoid mutual suspicions in the future, he also recommended that ten or twelve members 'might come privately' and 'in plaine and homely manner talke' to him for 'his access was free' to them. When reported back, the commons appeared well satisfied and began again conferring with the lords about the way forward.[160]

However, after Henry's investiture on Monday 4 June, James began having second thoughts about pursuing the 'contract', possibly after listening to 'a variety of opinions from a number about him, especially the Scotts' and possibly too his son Henry, who was totally opposed to the abolition of wardship.[161] Their line of reasoning against the 'contract' was that bargaining was unseemly; that James would have to yield too much of his prerogative; that the gains seemed too small and his needs too great. On 11 June, therefore, James asked the commons, through Cecil, for an immediate £500,000 and suggested suspending further discussion of both the 'contract' and their grievances until a new parliamentary session in the autumn. In the meantime, he promised not to add any new impositions.[162]

Although there was little dispute about postponing the 'contract', the majority opinion was against granting supply without redress of grievances. If they went home 'with nothing for the good of the commonwealth', said one, their constituencies 'would say [we have] bene all this while like children in ketching [catching] butterflies'. So, the next morning, James undertook to hear and respond to their grievances in expectation that they would afterwards vote him a large sum of money.[163] After lengthy discussions, the commons drew up a long list on a wide variety of subjects, including impositions, purveyance, deprived nonconforming ministers, the court of high commission, the royal use of proclamations, and the abolition of the council of Wales. On 7 July, the petition was delivered to the king, who received it ungraciously and commented acerbically that the document was long enough to cover his chamber's wall.[164] His only substantial concession was a promise to levy no *future* impositions except by parliament, an outcome thought 'not wholly satisfactory'.[165] Four days later, the commons voted James one subsidy and one fifteenth (worth only £100,000), which was 'but a drop in a cistern of water' and less than the normal grant.[166]

Somewhat surprisingly, the commons continued to deliberate on the 'contract', during the last few weeks of the parliament. After 'long debate', progress was at last made when, on 13 July, members agreed to an annual grant of £180,000, a sum 'which the lower house thought too great and his Majesty too lytle'. To put the proposal to James, 'fower great counsellors' (Cecil, Suffolk, Northampton, and Worcester) rode to Theobalds, 'where they long debated the weight of this great busyness'. James eventually concluded that he would accept £200,000, but no less.[167] When put to the vote in the commons, it was accepted by a majority of about sixty upon certain conditions that included the dissolution of the court of wards and abolition of purveyance.[168] Many, including James, thought it was a 'a goode and sound resolucon', and Cecil received praise for his role.[169]

However, such optimism was misplaced. Two other important matters had still to be determined: first, how the £200,000 was to be levied. Any new tax, especially a land tax, would be very unpopular; and why should localities which did not benefit from the abolition of purveyance contribute to the annual grant? Second, there was the problem 'with what cords we shall bind Sampson's hands', meaning what security could be given to bind the prerogative permanently.[170] For these reasons, the commons began to have second thoughts over the summer when they discussed the 'contract' with their constituents.[171] At the same time, opposition began to mount on the government's side. It was to be expected that vested interests would be hostile: the purveyors and officers of the court of wards would lose their offices if the contract went through. But, some members of the privy council feared that the renunciation of wardship nibbled away at the royal prerogative for little gain. Wardship, explained Sir Julius Caesar, was 'the fairest flowers for proffit and commaund in all his garland', yet James was surrendering it for about £85,000 and with much dishonour and quite possibly dangerous consequences.[172] To make matters worse, the commons made clear that it was planning to add all kinds of extras—especially the abolition of feudal tenures and impositions—to the 'contract'.[173] All this made James question whether he had given up too much; after all, his debts had risen and the interest on them would eat up most of the yearly grant the commons promised.

When parliament met again on 16 October, it was poorly attended; even the speaker was absent because of illness. Were members voting with their feet against endorsing the contract? Certainly, those present did not focus on the 'contract', and for more than a week 'nothing of moment was done'.[174] On the 25th, Cecil intervened, warning the commons: 'if the parliament relieve him [the king] not, you leave him in great extremity, and the consequence is dangerous both to the king and the people'. If they were to change the contract's original terms, it would fail and the consequences for them would be dire: 'I do not say the king shall send you an Empson and a Dudley, but this I say, the king must not want.' Empson and Dudley were the officials of Henry VII whose financial extortions had led to their execution by Henry VIII. The king 'will not do injustice to his subject; he will not do all he may do. But more than he hath done he must do'.[175] In other words, James would not behave tyrannically but he would use his prerogative to its full extent in order to extract whatever money was needed to meet his wants.

Not for the last time, the commons could not agree about how to proceed and what to do. There seemed to be as many opinions as voices. Then, on 6 November, James weighed in with new demands: a supply of £500,000 to pay off his debts in addition to the £200,000 subsidy already voted, and another unspecified sum to compensate the officers of the court of wards. Only this huge sum would provide for the 'repair of his wants and establishing of his estate', and it had to be agreed before he would 'perfect the contract'.[176]

In answer, the house spent two dayes in deliberation and 'returned that the state was not able to bear it'. When put to a vote, only a handful approved the 'contract'. Hoping to get at least some supply, Cecil offered the house a range of solutions to various grievances, such as reform of the penal laws, the repeal of obsolete laws, and, most significantly, no new impositions to be levied without parliamentary approval.[177] Most in the house could not be persuaded, one member notably complaining that the king's needs were not their responsibility.[178] Without even attempting a vote on supply, James, with much 'displeasur', formally prorogued the house until 9 February 1611.[179]

It is easy to play the blame game for the failure of the 'great contract'. James's demands were huge and unprecedented, so it is understandable that there was resistance to them. His flagrant extravagance and partiality towards the Scots contributed to the commons' dislike of his proposals.[180] But MPs can be criticized for failing to appreciate the need for structural reform to put crown finances on a sounder footing. The majority wanted the removal of the most lucrative sources of royal revenue—impositions, wardship, and purveyance—without either offering adequate compensation or realizing that compensation was simply not enough to cover the king's needs. The xenophobic speeches of some members put James's back up, while James's harping on the royal prerogative put up theirs. Perhaps it is more surprising that the discussions went on for so long and that a compromise was patched up in June than that the contract ultimately fell apart.

★ ★ ★

Bruised by his first encounter with the English parliament, James wanted no more. On 7 December, he ranted against the commons to Cecil, concluding with the words: 'this lower howse, by their behaviour, have perelled and annoyed our health, wounded our reputation, emboldened all ill natured people, encroched upon maney of our priviledges, and plagued our purse with their delayes'.[181] Two months later he dissolved the house. A new parliament would not be called until 1614; in the meantime, he concentrated on securing a large dowry for his sons. Only when that came to nothing did James reluctantly call another. That one went still more badly! After that, James spent seven years without a parliament, relying on impositions, windfalls, and loans to get by. His 1621 parliament proved no more compliant for new issues divided the king from the commons. Nevertheless, James's last parliament in 1624 was arguably the most successful of the reign since seventy-three statutes were then enacted in just over three months.[182] But the price for this legislative success was political failure. James's harmonious relations with parliament—lords and commons—came only after he agreed to their (and his son's) demands for a war against Spain, a reversal of his long-term foreign policy.

PART 3

Religion and Politics

11

Protestants and Puritans

If James expected the Hampton Court Conference to end all heated disagreements among English Protestants, he was badly mistaken. Until at least 1610, religious divergences and divisions were exposed and widely aired in parliament and the press, while parishes suffered from disruptions, sometimes serious, when Puritan ministers were 'presented' for nonconformity before their bishops and threatened with suspension or deprivation. The early years of James's reign did not constitute a peaceful period for the Church. From James's perspective, the fault lay with his Puritan subjects, whom he branded disobedient troublemakers 'ever discontented with the present government'.[1] Puritans, though, blamed the bishops and especially Bancroft, archbishop of Canterbury from December 1604 until November 1610. In my view, the political and religious turbulence arose because of the king's determination, after 1604, to enforce the traditional liturgical ceremonies retained in the 1559 Elizabethan settlement. In so doing, he renewed and intensified the acrimonious debates that had scarred the Church under his predecessor.

Puritan agitation centred on the revised 1604 prayer book and the 141 canons approved by the convocation of Canterbury in September that same year. Both were ratified not by parliament but by the king's letters patent, a written order that reinforced the king's prerogative over religion and the royal supremacy over the Church. The revisions to the prayer book did not come close to meeting the Puritan objections raised at Hampton Court. At James's insistence, the amendments were merely insertions of 'some declaration and enlargement by waie of explanation' to counter incorrect doctrine, and none was 'contrarye to any thinge that is allready conteyned in that booke nor to any of our lawes or statute'.[2] Furthermore, Puritans found unacceptable the few concessions made to their spokesmen at Hampton Court. That absolution [forgiveness of sins] was in future to be called 'the absolution or general remission of sins' still smacked to them of 'papishe absolucon', while the rite of confirmation, they claimed, was actually 'made worse' by the new wording which called for episcopal 'laying of hands upon children baptized'.[3] Although lay baptism was now disallowed, as Puritans had requested, the new prayer book retained prayers for the rite in private houses at 'time of necessity' [when a baby was close to death], a rubric that implied baptism was still necessary for salvation.[4]

The 1604 canons authorized and detailed these and other ceremonies that Puritans found offensive: the sign of the cross in baptism was declared legitimate; stone fonts were to be used instead of basins in all churches; and even worse, canon 69 implied again that baptism was necessary for salvation, since ministers who failed to baptize an infant close to death would be suspended for three months.[5] Surplices were to be worn by ministers at all services, and copes by celebrants of communion in cathedrals.[6] Additionally, the canons demanded not only strict conformity to the prayer book but also clerical subscription to the three articles set down by Whitgift in 1583, one of which affirmed that the prayer book was in accordance with the Word of God.[7] Those who refused to follow the prayer book to the letter and would not subscribe to the articles would not be permitted to preach or hold a benefice. Moreover, subscription had to be given 'willingly and *ex animo*' [from the heart], a demand designed to put a stop to the previous practice of allowing Puritans to use their own form of words in a qualified subscription. This loophole had basically let many Puritans off the hook under Elizabeth and enabled them to retain their livings.[8] It was unsurprising that the new canons would be anti-Puritan since convocation was dominated by cathedral chapters, bishops, and their diocesan officials.

Like Elizabeth before him, James was fully behind—and indeed often led from the front—the bishops' campaign to impose conformity.[9] Both monarchs believed that unity of doctrine and liturgy would 'settle a perpetuall peace in the Church of God', whereas a lack of uniformity would be 'the occasion of scandal' and impede 'the suppression of the Romishe idolatrye and superstition'.[10] Equally important, disobeying the law by failing to follow the prescribed prayer book was judged a dangerous challenge to royal authority. Accordingly, on 5 March 1604, James issued a proclamation upholding the new prayer book and requiring the clergy and secular officers 'to doe their dueties in causing the same to be obeyed and in punishing offendours according to the lawes of the realm'.[11] It was his resolve on this issue that led him to choose Bancroft as the new archbishop of Canterbury after Whitgift's death rather than the other main contender Tobie Matthew, bishop of Durham, who was considered more sympathetic to nonconforming ministers.[12]

Naturally, James wanted to avoid a serious confrontation with the Puritan clergy and their lay supporters. He also recognized the difficulty in finding sufficient qualified and godly ministers to replace deprived incumbents. The upshot was that, shortly after the house of commons approved, in 1604, a petition of dispensation for some ministers, James agreed that the bishops could give 'some tyme of probation' to those nonconforming ministers 'whose gifts of learninge and myld condition may promise hope of good to follow'.[13] A month later, on 16 July, he issued a proclamation, which gave the clergy until 30 November that year to obey the law. Even so, conform they must. As he explained, 'our duetie towards God requireth at our hands that what untractable men doe not performe upon admonition, they must bee compelled unto by authoritie'.[14] Once the November deadline had expired, the king demanded the immediate deprivation of disobedient ministers and their replacement with clergy 'of learning and integrity'.[15] On 10 December 1604, fourteen privy councillors ordered Bancroft, on the king's behalf, to ensure the execution of the royal order for conformity. The same month, James pressed the reluctant Bishop Thomas Dove of Peterborough—whose large diocese contained several Puritan centres—to deprive disobedient ministers.[16]

When it came to subscription, James was prepared to compromise. He remained determined to see subscription imposed upon all the colleges of the Universities of Oxford and Cambridge for he judged it would be possible 'to confute [invalidate] all the Puritans in the kingdom' if they saw 'so great an number of learned men in a universitye to consent so fully in one'.[17] However, he decided to let bishops take a more relaxed approach to imposing subscription on the parish clergy. In December 1604, he laid down that ministers would not have to subscribe to the three articles in the canons, provided that they fully observed the ceremonies in the prayer book.[18] This shift did not mark a softening towards Puritans. Rather, James's reasoning was that ministers who subscribed could after 'the storme is passed never parforme a worde and proteste that thaire subscription was only *ex iusto metu* [out of a proper fear]'; but, if they conformed and yet afterwards refused to subscribe to the prayer-book ceremonies that they had already performed, 'it wolde be a meanes to make thaire vanities appeare, and everie man to pitie thaim the lesse'.[19]

Confident that the king was still committed to 'his purpose to work an uniformity', Bancroft accepted, and possibly had even advised, this tactic. Accordingly, he directed the bishops not to demand immediate subscription from those Puritans who were 'contented to observe' the ceremonies and 'fully to conform themselves'. The hope was that they would subscribe in the near future.[20] Most bishops were relieved. Sympathetic to their 'brothers in Christ', they were 'loath to proceed too rigorously in casting out and depriving so many well reputed of for life and learning'. Moreover, since the number of Puritans standing firm against subscription was far greater than anyone had originally 'suspected', the bishops—for practical reasons—wanted to keep godly preachers in their posts if at all possible.[21] Consequently, they were all too ready to follow the recommendation proffered by Anthony Rudd, bishop of St David's, in the 1604 convocation that ministers of tender consciences who stood out 'stiffly' against subscription should be treated leniently as long as they were not schismatics nor open disturbers of the state; otherwise, their godly ministry would be severely missed and the episcopate would become an object of hatred, thereby encouraging Presbyterianism.[22]

In total, only eighty to ninety ministers (out of some 9,000) were deprived, 85 per cent of them between December 1604 and December 1606.[23] Puritans at the time, however, alleged that the number of deprivations was greater. In 1606, Henry Jacob estimated that 'three hundred, or there-aboutes... [had] in one yeere and a litle more, been turned out of Christ's service'.[24] In 1607, Samuel Hieron, a minister from Modbury (Devon), assessed the number as '275 at the least'.[25] Given these estimates, it is hardly surprising that MPs loudly protested about their silenced brethren in the parliamentary sessions of 1604, 1606, and 1610. Nathanial Bacon, in the 1606 session, called for the restoration of 260 ministers whom he claimed had already been deprived.[26] Maybe the Puritan complainants were exaggerating for effect, but just as likely they were including curates and lecturers who did not have a benefice (therefore technically could not be deprived) and ministers who were brought before their bishop but held onto their posts.[27] In June 1607, the commons referred in their petition to '300 deprived, suspended, or silenced'.[28]

Why were so few—a mere 1 per cent—of the clergy deprived? Undoubtedly, a fair number conformed under the pressure and consequently retained their livings. But we also see episcopal leniency operating to keep nonconforming or partially conforming godly clergy within the ministry. Taking advantage of the shift away from subscription, some bishops chose to interpret Bancroft's phrase 'contented to observe' far more loosely than either he or James had intended. As a result, in certain dioceses, Puritan ministers who merely gave assurances of future obedience were allowed to continue *in situ*. William Chaderton, bishop of Lincoln, for example, accepted no more than a *promise* of conformity from Thomas Wooll, a Puritan who had been reported to him for saying that he would turn his surplice into a 'cushion to sitt on' rather than wear it. Similarly, the bishop accepted without question a churchwarden's word that Thomas Humfrey, the rector of Grainsby, would in future wear the surplice and 'intended' to use the sign of the cross in baptism.[29] Chaderton was not alone. Richard Vaughan, bishop of London until 1607, was reputed to have 'permitted all the godly ministers [of Essex] to live peaceably and to enjoy liberty in their ministry'.[30] Additionally, some bishops returned deprived ministers to their posts or found them a place elsewhere, once they had promised future obedience.[31] Famously, Tobie Matthew, when archbishop of York, restored the semi-separatist Richard Bernard to his living at Worksop in 1607 and later protected him when the minister was charged with minor acts of nonconformity surrounding baptism.[32]

Puritan laypeople, too, protected nonconforming ministers, just as they had under Elizabeth. Thanks to Sir William Strode, Hieron kept his cure at Modbury although suspended five times by Bishop William Cotton of Exeter.[33] The Presbyterian Thomas Brightman likewise held onto the rectory of Haynes in Bedfordshire until his death in 1607 owing to the protection of Sir John Osborne.[34] The troublesome minister Robert Catelin was restored to his living shortly after the mayor, aldermen, and JPs of Northampton wrote to Cecil with the endorsement that he had served his parish 'peacablie and painfullie' for the past fourteen years.[35] These and many other ministers who kept their livings were as committed nonconformists as those who were ejected, but they were rescued because of their connections and the high esteem in which influential laypeople held their preaching abilities and pastoral care.

When patrons could not save nonconforming ministers from deprivation, they tried to help in other ways. So, after suspension, John Dod was settled into the family church of the Drydens, which Sir Erasmus Dryden claimed had been a priory and hence exempt from the jurisdiction of the bishop of Peterborough.[36] Similarly, the 'religious gentleman' Alexander Redich, who had previously supported Arthur Hildersham, brought William

Bradshaw, a nonconforming lecturer under Elizabeth and James, into his household near Burton-on-Trent as a chaplain; shortly afterwards, Redich used his influence with Bishop Overton to acquire for Bradshaw a licence to preach within the diocese of Coventry and Lichfield.[37] Nor was Bradshaw the only Puritan preacher who survived the purge of nonconformists, various others being employed as lecturers by Puritan town corporations, such as Coventry. Not all lay Puritan help, though, was successful. To take one example, Sarah Venables, the wealthy widow of a London merchant, left a substantial bequest for 'poor ministers' ejected from their livings, but after her death the prerogative court of exchequer decided that the money should instead be distributed to 'such preaching conformable ministers' or their widows and children who were in need.[38] Likely, this judicial decision owed something to the influence of the king.

Unsurprisingly, James strongly disapproved of the support given to Puritans. It is true that he responded to complaints in the 1610 parliament about the silenced ministers with the promise that he would personally go through the lists of deprivations, assess which ones offered 'better hope of conformity', and then 'take such order in that behalf, as in our princely wisdom we shall hold most fit and convenient for the good and peace of the Church'.[39] However, there is no evidence that he did examine the lists or personally restore any deprived ministers. On the contrary, he complained a few years later that certain 'ministers which heretofore have bene silenced are suffered for to preache'. John Dod, Robert Cleaver, and Robert Catelin, he picked out by name. James was especially outraged to hear that Catelin, when questioned by a bishop, had answered he would 'weare a surplesse, or knele at the communion or do some such like but once', and a year or two afterwards would not conform at all. James insisted that the minister should be in 'perpetuall conformitye' so that the people of Northampton would 'no longer be borne with all in there refractory disposition'.[40] The early years of James's reign, therefore, saw a war of attrition between the king and anti-Puritan bishops on the one hand and the nonconforming clergy and their supporters on the other.

★ ★ ★

As had occurred under Elizabeth, Puritan ministers and their friends did not take the campaign to impose conformity lying down. Some sought legal remedies and some took to a variety of media to publicise its injustice. The legal remedies were based on the argument that subscription to the prayer book and the deprivation of ministers were both illegal. People 'learned in the lawe' (possibly Nicholas Fuller was one) maintained that subscription to the prayer book was not covered by legislation, for the only statute (an act of 1571) demanding subscription required ministers to swear to the truth of the thirty-nine articles of faith, nothing else.[41] In any event, claimed one minister, John Burges, those appointed to a benefice during the previous reign should not have to subscribe as they had already done so (albeit in a qualified form) under Elizabeth.[42] Regarding deprivations, ministers and their supporters appealed to Magna Carta in their claim that the Church was acting illegally. In a personal plea to the king, the wife of an ousted minister asserted that Magna Carta had laid down: 'none ys to be disseised of his freehold (of which nature his beneficeis) but by the lawe of the land'. She therefore insisted that her husband should 'peaceblie enjoye' his benefice 'till such tyme as he shalbe evicted and ejected by a due course of lawe', meaning by the common law in a secular court.[43] Likewise pleading their rights under Magna Carta, deprived ministers frequently sought writs of prohibition to allow their cases to be transferred from the ecclesiastical courts to the common-law courts. Calls for Magna Carta to be applied in these cases were also presented in the public domain by MPs and polemicists.[44]

These legal challenges were not upheld by the government. In February 1605, justices sitting in star chamber deemed that the ecclesiastical court of high commission had the power of deprivation.[45] They also ruled that 'noe [writ of] prohibition doth lye in that case [concerning deprivations] against the judges ecclesiasticall'.[46] This judgment was hardly unexpected since it was derived from an Elizabethan test case, Cawdrey's case of 1591, which had confirmed the right of high commission and other ecclesiastical courts to deprive ministers who refused to hold services in accordance with the Elizabethan prayer book.[47] A few months later, James's privy council ordered the chief justices not to allow any prohibitions except 'in cases of necessitie'.[48] Yet, despite the new orders, the common-law judges continued to issue prohibitions in cases that started in the ecclesiastical courts, much to the anger of Bancroft and like-minded bishops.

In 1607, a new legal case challenged the competence and powers of high commission. It arose from the actions of the common lawyer and London MP Nicholas Fuller, who had been engaged in Cawdrey's case and consistently disputed the power of high commission and use of the *ex officio* oath (which allowed self-incrimination) under Elizabeth.[49] Horrified by the early Jacobean deprivations, Fuller launched an attack on the ecclesiastical court in both parliament and the common-law courts. In June 1607, he introduced a parliamentary bill designed to revise and restrain high commission's power and jurisdiction.[50] Around the same time, he condemned the ecclesiastical court as 'popish and antichristian' in a fiery speech before the king's bench [a common-law court], while defending two Puritans, jailed for contempt of court by high commission for refusing to take the *ex officio* oath.[51] Arguing for writs of prohibition and *habeas corpus* on his clients' behalf, Fuller maintained—as he had in parliament—that high commission was exceeding its authority and exploiting the capacious and vague powers it had been wrongly granted in the crown's letters patent that established the court. His argument depended on the principle that the monarch could only delegate powers whose limits had been laid out by statute law, in this case the Act of Supremacy.[52] Safe from prosecution when attacking high commission in the commons, Fuller was placed under arrest soon after parliament's prorogation in July. Incarcerated in the Fleet prison, he was indicted by high commission for 'schism', 'erroneous opinions', and 'malicious impeachment' of the king's authority in ecclesiastical causes.[53] In response, Fuller promptly sought and received a writ of prohibition to allow his own case to be heard before common-law judges, who were at that time in recess.

James was deeply perturbed at this course of events. He had long thought Fuller to be a 'villain' and agitator because the MP had not only been a strong advocate for Puritans but also a key opponent of Union. But the matter ran deeper than personal animosity. Fuller's attack on high commission (and Elizabeth's letters patent) threatened the royal prerogative. Partly with this in mind, James told Cecil:

> I prophecie unto you that quensoever [whensoever] the eclesiasticall dignitie together with the king's gouvernemente thairof shall be turnid in contempte and beginne to evanishe in this kingdome, the kinge's heirof shall not long after prosper in thaire gouvernement and the monarchie shall fall to ruine quhiche [which] I praye god I maye never live to see.[54]

Cecil concurred: if allowed, the judges' writ of prohibition, 'soe absurdly granted', and Fuller's 'insolencye' would be a disquieting precedent for further 'mischief'. Ultimately, predicted Cecil, it could 'begett an apparent change of our happy govenement (noe monarchy being able to stand where the Church is in anarchy)'.[55] In total accord, king and minister worked together behind the scenes against Fuller. What Cecil did is not exactly specified, but both Bancroft and James were later thankful for his 'discreete handling of the judgis'.[56]

In September 1607, the writ of prohibition was set aside with the result that (in the words of Dudley Carleton) 'poore Nick is nickt as before'.[57] But, owing to the sensitivity of the case, a conference was summoned in late September to hear Fuller's arguments.[58] The judges who attended were the twelve common-law justices and the barons of the exchequer. Apparently, they were divided among themselves, but James made it clear how their verdict should go. He demanded the 'effectual acomplishment of his royall and just determinacon' and exhorted that 'if the judges denyed it', they and Fuller should be called before the privy council 'to be censured therin in his Majestie's presence'.[59] Predictably, the judges ruled against the prohibition. But the majority might well have reached this decision even had the king not leaned on them. It was perfectly reasonable for them to conclude that Fuller's case should come within the jurisdiction of high commission since he had been accused of schism, unquestionably a spiritual offence. In October, Fuller was found guilty, fined £200, and sentenced to prison during the king's pleasure.[60]

But, if down, Fuller was not out. He endeavoured to overturn the punishment by obtaining a writ of *habeas corpus* for himself on the grounds that the only legal precedents for an ecclesiastical court imprisoning offenders had occurred 'in the time of darknes' before the break with Rome. As before, he claimed that the powers given to the court in Elizabeth's letters patent were invalid since they went beyond those set out in statute law.[61] Because of its political nature, James's attorney-general (Sir Henry Hobart) took up the case against him. By this time, there was considerable public interest in its outcome. Fuller's arguments in defence of his two Puritan clients had already gone into print on a secret press, and it was obvious to many that both the power of high commission and the use of prohibitions in all manner of cases were now at stake.[62] As one gentleman asked another litigant who had secured a writ of prohibitions for himself in an entirely different kind of lawsuit (one concerning a disputed will): 'Do you thinke the Lord Archbyshoppe will suffer suche abuse?' And he went on to ponder if common-law judges would now hold off hearing any case brought to their courts by writ of prohibitions until the verdict in Fuller's case was known.[63] Because of its legal significance, when the case of *habeas corpus* was heard in the king's bench on 24 November, it played to a full house.[64]

Deciding to defend himself, Fuller initially lost the case, but the judges then agreed he could have another hearing, this time with a legal representative. Two days later, a judgment was reached: the authority of the letters patent (and hence authority of high commission) was upheld; and Fuller's imprisonment was deemed legal. However, the judges also reaffirmed the right of the common-law courts to issue prohibitions if high commission were ever to encroach on temporal matters going beyond the powers set down in the letters patent.[65] On hearing the verdict on Fuller, James reportedly said wryly: 'the judges had don well for them selfes as well as for him, for that he [James] was resolved if they had don otherwise, and mainteyned their *habeas corpus*, he wold have committed them'. As for their judgment on prohibitions, James 'spake angerily that by their leaves they should not use their libertie therin but be proscribed'.[66] Following this up, James was noticeably more sensitive to lawyers' attempts to take cases away from his prerogative courts; he attempted to 'stretch his prerogative to the uttermost' and limit the granting of prohibitions.[67] But as far as high commission was concerned, James reassured parliament, in 1610, that complaints against it would be redressed and that the court would only hear 'exorbitant causes'.[68]

Having lost his case, Fuller paid his fine but to secure his freedom he had no other recourse than to throw himself on the king's mercy, which James granted on condition that he made a 'humble submission' in writing. After the prisoner reluctantly agreed, he was released on 5 January 1608.[69] However, within weeks he was rearrested and, for a short time, placed in the Tower. He was now accused of having allowed his arguments against the ecclesiastical court to be printed on a secret press. Pleading ignorance, deploring the publication of the pamphlet, and reneging on some of its arguments, Fuller was freed in mid-April.[70] But he was not silenced for he continued to denounce high commission in the 1610 parliament.[71]

Fuller was not the first Puritan or common lawyer to challenge the jurisdiction and powers of high commission, but his case brought the dispute into the open and captured public attention. It also set the scene for conflict between James—wary about attacks on his prerogative—and Sir Edward Coke, who was chief justice of common pleas from 1606 to 1613, a conflict that resulted in Coke's dismissal, in 1616, as chief justice of king's bench.[72] Furthermore, Fuller's arguments had a long-time significance, for they were reused after his death during the session of the Long Parliament of 1640 to 1642 when high commission together with the other prerogative courts were attacked and abolished.[73] In the short term, though, the outcome did not end prohibitions but on the contrary made it more difficult for Puritans to use the legal instrument.

★ ★ ★

Aside from seeking legal remedies, Puritans resorted to sermons, manuscript libels, petitions, and the press to obtain public support and halt the drive for conformity. Given the bishops' control of the pulpit, not many clerics could preach against the episcopal crackdown, although there are examples of a few brave, or foolhardy, individuals who did. Their sermons have mainly not survived, but those who got into trouble included Robert Brooke of Enstone in 1605, William Pemberton before the king at Newmarket in 1609, and Alexander Cooke, vicar of Louth, who refused to give a copy of his sermon against ceremonies to his bishop.[74] The most notorious incident concerned John Burges, a renowned preacher and nonconforming clergyman, who had long enjoyed the protection of powerful lay patrons and a lenient bishop. His contemporary at the University of Cambridge, the Calvinist James Montagu, dean of the chapel royal, had invited him to preach at Greenwich before the king, on Tuesday 19 June 1604, as an audition for an appointment to be a chaplain for Prince Henry. Deciding to act as the spokesperson for other nonconforming clergy, Burges took the path of honesty over discretion. His text was out of 122 Psalms: 'For my brethren and neighbours' sake I wil now speake peace unto thee.' Using King David as the model, Burges spoke frankly about the various ways James fell short of the biblical exemplar and implicitly threatened him with God's wrath if he failed to take care of religion and bring peace to the Church. Burges concluded with a classical parable: a servant Pollio broke a priceless crystal glass of his master Vedius in the presence of Emperor Augustus and was condemned to be cut up and fed to fishes. Aghast at this barbaric punishment, Augustus not only reversed the sentence but also smashed the remaining glasses in the set so that 'they might not be the occasion of the like vigorous sentence afterwards'. The moral was that James should remove all the ceremonies of the Church to avoid injustice and ensure peace.[75]

Burges's sermon gravely offended the king. Unlike Elizabeth who had frequently faced down or ignored critical sermons, James sent the preacher to the Tower. Burges then penned a long apology, which was barely an apology at all as he reiterated his objections to ceremonies and the imposition of conformity. Before first the privy council and afterwards Bancroft and Montagu, Burges denied any Presbyterian opinions, accepted that the use of the cross in baptism and the wearing of a surplice in services were 'not unlawfull' in themselves, and affirmed subscription to the three articles with a certain 'limitation' which expressed his scruples about the prayer book. He also swore that he had spoken independently and not at the promptings of other people. However, when it came down to it, Burges would not conform, and James would not let him get away with it. Brought before Chaderton of Lincoln in October 1604, Burges refused a new form of subscription which did not include his 'limitation'. He lost his living the following January.[76]

Burges's sermon was quite mild compared to the most outrageous of the manuscript libels attacking the policy of conformity. A piece of doggerel, entitled 'The Lamentation of Dickie for the Death of Jockie', made its first appearance in late March 1604. Pinned to Whitgift's hearse at his funeral, the 'lewde writinge' mocked and excoriated both Whitgift ('Jockie') and his successor at Canterbury, Bancroft ('Dickie'), in a dramatic way. Subverting the convention of honouring the dead by attaching eulogies to a hearse, the verse disparaged Whitgift by mocking his name and characterizing him as:

> Reformer's hinderer, trew pastor's slanderer,
>   The papists' broker, the atheists' cloker
> The ceremonye's procter, the latyn docter
>   The dumb doggs' patron, non resid[e]ns' champion.

The 'persecutor' Bancroft was no better for he now hoped 'to play Jhocky alone'.[77] Whether or not anyone read the piece while it was fixed to the hearse is unknown, but the text certainly went round the Puritan community.[78] The following year, a copy was found in the rooms of Thomas Bywater who was already in trouble with the king. Under questioning, Bywater fingered the author as Lewis Pickering, a Northamptonshire Puritan with influential contacts at court. Pickering admitted to passing on the libel secretly to Bywater but denied pinning it to the hearse.[79] When his case was brought before star chamber in May 1605, he also refuted a charge of seditious libel on the grounds that the subject 'being a deade man, he tooke it no offence'. Nonetheless, he was found guilty and sentenced to one year's imprisonment, a heavy fine, and time in the pillory.[80] The harshness of the punishment was because the judges understood Pickering's libel to be part of a widely organized Puritan campaign. He was evidently an associate of Bywater, who was himself accused at that time of plotting with other accomplices 'in there sermons and praiers' to 'stirre the people to desyre a reformacyon, which is not tolerable in a monarchie but in a democracie'.[81] In the event, however, Pickering was released before the year was up and relieved of the fine.[82]

Bywater's rooms had been searched because he had written a book, said to be 'of very treasonable and seditious contentes' and entitled 'The errors of the king of Great Britain', which he had delivered to the king at Ware in February 1605.[83] Following the strategies of other petitioners, the book's tone was deliberately respectful, offering advice, and not making demands, but it nonetheless criticized all aspects of the king's government including his ecclesiastical policy.[84] Since James had come to the throne, alleged Bywater:

> Popery wonderfully hath increased...and it is worse with the Puritan, better with the papist then ever in the good queen's days. Imprisonment of good ministers is as ordinary, or more, then of papists; all favour is shewed to the dumbe ministery, and much favour unto popery; but disgrace & disfavour to zelous and faithful ministers.

Puritans, Bywater went on, 'desireth nothing but what is in your Majestie's own words and writings'.[85] Like Burges and Pickering, Bywater had important patrons: he was then chaplain to Lord Hunsdon and had been a tutor to Lord Sheffield's children. But neither man could, or would, protect him.[86] So, Bywater was first sent to the Tower and then removed to the Clink, which was not much better.

★ ★ ★

The timing of Bywater's petition identifies him as one of the many Puritans who were petitioning James to end the drive for conformity.[87] During the winter of 1604, a fresh Puritan petitioning campaign had got under way. Numerous appeals were brought directly to the king, especially while he was out hunting. The first, supposedly from two hundred yeomen of Essex from around Royston, was handed to him on Tuesday 20 November—ten days before the official deadline for conformity—and pleaded for the retention of 'faithfull pastors' who were under threat of deprivation.[88] On 30 November—the deadline day—three ministers presented a petition and 'booke of reasons' against subscription to James, who was then hunting at Hinchingbrooke. Both were drawn up by 'thirty-two prominent divines' from the diocese of Lincoln, one of whom was Arthur Hildersham, who had been an organizer of the Millenary Petition the previous year; another minister was John Burges, who was then under threat of deprivation.[89] A third petition—this time from twenty-eight Huntingdonshire laymen—also reached the king sometime in November.[90] A fourth from 'twelve senior Lancashire gentry' greeted James as he rode to Royston, on 7 December, after a brief visit to London.[91] In addition to presenting objections to the prayer book, all these petitions expressed concern that 'good and understanding ministers' would be replaced with 'idle drones' and that the only beneficiaries of the deprivations would be 'the comon adversaries', in other words Catholics.[92] Nor were these the only petitions sent to James around this time. Among others, he received a petition from twenty-two preachers of London and the suburbs, and from twenty-seven Warwickshire ministers.[93] This was evidently a co-ordinated effort, as had been the petitions of 1603.

On the surface, James showed a willingness to engage with the petitioners and ministers under threat of deprivation. He spoke at some length to those from Lincoln diocese and instructed them to write down their objections to the prayer book and canons and direct them to Dean Montagu and their own bishop.[94] However, as far as is known, nothing came of these referrals. Similarly, James instructed those from Essex to send 'ten of the wisest among them' to declare their grievances before the privy council.[95] But, according to the Venetian ambassador: 'The orders he did give to the council were that when the petitioners appeared, they or the principal among them were to be arrested.'[96] Meanwhile, James ordered investigations into the signatories of the various petitions to determine if they were Presbyterians and political agitators.[97]

At the same time, James remained committed to seeing through his policy of punishing all non-observers of prayer-book rituals. In late November, he had assured his council that he was 'farre from yeilding any thing for feare of thaire popularitie'; on the contrary, 'if my eye ether spare or pittie any of the disobedient, then lett me incurre both the shame and the harme in Goddis name'.[98] As already mentioned, in December he pressed Bishop Dove to begin the deprivations in Northamptonshire.

In reaction, on 9 February 1605, a group of forty-five Northamptonshire gentlemen, many of them JPs, presented James with yet another petition. Among the signatories were the two local MPs—Sir Valentine Knightley and Sir Edward Montagu—as well as Sir Frances Hastings, an MP for Somerset. Although Hastings had no power base in Northamptonshire, he had worked with the county's members in the 1604 parliament to remedy

Puritan grievances and had also been a mainstay of the Puritan cause in parliament under Elizabeth. He later claimed responsibility for drawing up this petition.[99] As had earlier petitioners, the Northamptonshire gentry crafted their petition to emphasize their moderation and loyalty. They made no demands that James change his policy but rather prostrated themselves upon their knees at his feet to 'most humblie begge and crave' him 'to moderate the extremitie' of his order; and they concluded with a prayer for the preservation of his person.[100] Denying any subversive intent, the leaders afterwards explained that their intention was merely to offer 'a certaine kinde of testimonial or certificate of the godlines, paynefullnes, and fruitefullness of the reverend pastors and preachers dispersed throughout our countrye' who were now at risk of deprivation.[101]

The king, however, did not see it that way at all. As far as he was concerned, their petition amounted to dissent which was tantamount to treason. He reminded his privy councillors and bishops that the revolt in the Netherlands and troubles in Scotland had begun with a petition about religion.[102] His privy councillors and justices evidently agreed, or at least did not dare to disagree. At a hurriedly called session of star chamber in February, the Northamptonshire petition was judged 'near to treason and felony'. The purported reason for this verdict was that the Puritan organizers had clearly 'tended to the raising of sedition, rebellion, and discontent among the people' because they had intimated that 'many thousands' of the king's subjects would be discontented if James did not grant their request, a threat they intended to fulfil. Privy councillors at the meeting also declared that 'some of the Puritans involved had raised a false rumor of the king' in saying that he intended to grant toleration to Catholics, an offence judged 'heinously fineable by the rules of common law' and statute.[103]

The three MPs, thought to be the ringleaders of the Northamptonshire petition, were hauled before the privy council. Each had to write a letter of submission to the king and promise dutiful obedience in the future. After Montagu and Hastings resisted putting their names to the submission drafted by the privy council, they were stripped of their local offices and ordered to retire to the country.[104] Thanks to his brother's intervention, Montagu made a new submission which James grudgingly accepted. Pardoned, the MP recovered his offices. But Hastings never held public office again, although he continued to sit in parliament.[105] Even so, compared to Sir Erasmus Dryden, he got off quite lightly. The privy council had 'sentenced it to be against the lawes to gather handes in favour of persons refusinge conformity', and Dryden was imprisoned first in the Tower and then the Fleet for nearly a month because he had been instrumental in organizing the signatories to the petition.[106]

* * *

In addition to petitions, which were addressed not only to the king but also to privy councillors and bishops thought sympathetic, Puritans employed print to make their case.[107] Because of government censorship, many works came off a secret press, usually that of William Jones.[108] Jones had first shown himself to be active on behalf of Puritans on the morning of 15 May 1604, when he handed two documents to the speaker of the commons on his way to the lower house. One was a bill of attainder charging Bancroft with treason for conspiring with papists (notably Watson, the priest behind the Bye Plot) to print books that imperilled the realm. The second contained a list of articles that provided evidence for the charge. This accusation had been raised at the Hampton Court Conference and was brought up again because of Puritan consternation at the new prayer book and canons coming out of convocation. The objective was to discredit Bancroft, but it failed dismally. The king refused to allow parliament to discuss the bill and retained his trust in Bancroft.[109]

Jones was not acting alone here but rather in cahoots with Puritan ministers and MPs. Likewise, when printing unlicensed works, Jones was collaborating with other Puritans, not just the authors but also the people who financed the print runs and distributed the copies.[110] Eventually, in 1609, Jones was caught and accused in star chamber of publishing sixteen 'scandalous, factious, and seditious bookes and pamphletts' tending to the 'begettinge of schism, errors, and disorder in the Church'.[111] These works included copies (partial or full) of the London and Lincolnshire petitions of 1605, the arguments of Nicholas Fuller, and another petition of 1606 directed ostensibly to parliament but targeting a wider 'public' readership.[112]

One tactic of the Puritan pamphlets was to defend the nonconforming ministers on grounds of their characters. Those who had lost their livings, wrote one supporter, preached 'knowledge, godlines, loyalty, peace, and love' in contrast to those (obviously Catholics) who were 'ignorant of all duty to God and man, and therefore prophane, irreligious, contentious, and apt to sedition and rebellion'. Despite their pains, continued this anonymous writer, such godly ministers and their families were to be turned out of their homes and livings.[113] It was shameful, added another, that bishops ejected 'preaching ministers, otherwise unreprovable for life and doctrine', yet tolerated 'unpreaching ministers, scandalous in life, and ignorant of doctrine'.[114] A further tactic of the Puritan was to dismiss the validity of prayer-book ceremonies and the necessity of wearing of the surplice, repeating arguments that had first emerged in the 1560s.

As under Elizabeth, the Puritan print campaign under James was designed to appeal to parliament and the wider public in the hope that they would induce the monarch to redirect policy. Additionally, some tracts were dedicated to James himself, urging him to 'take a more exact knowledge' of their cause by reading their works or holding an 'indifferent, honest, and reasonable' conference in which Puritans would choose their own spokesmen against the 'prelates'.[115] Like the petitioners, all the pamphleteers presented themselves as loyalists who were writing in the interests of the commonwealth, not some 'factious' group as their opponents charged. And, indeed, they were loyal in the sense that they accepted monarchical rule and refuted George Buchanan-type theories of resistance. Most of them—including some who were Presbyterian—also accepted the royal supremacy. The Presbyterian civil lawyer William Stoughton, for instance, aimed to show, in a tract of 1604, 'how the discipline by pastors and elders may be planted without any derogation to the king's royal prerogative'.[116] Like Stoughton, William Bradshaw stated unambiguously his adherence to 'the same authoritie and supremacie in all causes and over all persons civill and ecclesiasticall, graunted by statute to Queene Elizabeth'. Even if monarchs apostatized, went on Bradshaw, subjects 'ought to acknowledge and yeald the said supremacie unto them'.[117] These Puritans therefore contested James's belief that all Puritans were a 'secte, ennemies to all kings and to me only because I ame a king' and his dictum at Hampton Court that a presbytery 'as well agreeth with a monarchy as God and the devil'.[118]

Nonetheless, despite their protestations of loyalty and moderation, all nonconforming Puritans were flouting royal orders. They justified their refusal to comply by referring to 'Christian liberty', meaning that they had to follow the scriptures and disobey the bishops in those important matters of religion which touched their consciences for otherwise they would be guilty of 'sinne against God'.[119] As a polemical point, they took pains to distinguish themselves from recusant Catholics who 'pretend the like colour and scruple of conscience' when refusing to attend church. Catholics, they said, obeyed the pope's commands rather than the king's, whereas nonconforming Protestants never doubted that 'obeying princes are thinges so expressly commaunded that none ought to pretend conscience to the contrarye'.[120]

Complementing their loyalist rhetoric, Puritans denied they were separatists. Even Presbyterians who were radical in their ecclesiology claimed they wanted to stay within the national Church, and the majority envisaged a system of pastors and elders who worked locally and nationally in synods.[121] Others were more radical in that they hoped for a Church closer to what today we label 'parish congregationalism': the establishment of pastors, elders, and deacons within autonomous individual congregations without any need for synods. But, until such dreams were realized, all these Presbyterians believed Protestants should stay within the Established Church. As Bradshaw explained, although the prayer book was imperfect and contained 'some devises and inventions of man', it was certainly good enough because 'the true worship of God (not withstanding) is prescribed in it'.[122] Henry Jacob—a London Presbyterian so active in the Sussex petitioning campaign of 1603 that he was briefly imprisoned in the Clink—for a time concurred.[123] Like Bradshaw a semi-Congregationalist, Jacob, in a 1604 tract, described the Church of England as a true Church through which one might obtain salvation and seek a full reformation. In a direct appeal to the king, he referred to him as 'the soveraign power here, to give generall redresse to these our not only temporall but also spirituall grievances in our consciences'.[124] It was only later, after 1609, that Jacob moved into the more radical semi-separatist position for which he is better known and, only in 1616, that he founded an independent, covenanted congregation in Southwark, London.

Nonetheless, several deprived Puritan ministers and their congregations did turn to fully fledged separatism.[125] At a meeting held in 1606 at the Coventry home of Sir William and Lady Isabel Bowes, a small group of Puritans discussed withdrawal from the Established Church on the basis that its worship was 'corrupt'. The majority decided to stay, partly on the grounds that leaving would only benefit Catholics, but several of the participants rejected the Church of England as a 'false Church' and founded their own congregations outside it. The three leaders of this separatist movement were John Robinson (originally from Norwich), Richard Clifton (from Bawtry, Nottinghamshire), and John Smyth (from nearby Gainsborough, in Lincolnshire). Their activities in England came to a halt when Tobie Matthew, newly appointed archbishop of York, began a drive against separatist communities and their leaders.[126] To avoid arrest and imprisonment

Robinson and Clifton, together with a congregation from Scrooby in Nottinghamshire, escaped to Amsterdam in 1608. Soon afterwards, Robinson moved to Leiden where his congregation grew to about three hundred at its height. It was members of this group who sailed on the *Mayflower*, in 1620, to the New World under the leadership of William Brewster. Sometime between 1607 and 1608, Smyth too moved to the Netherlands, taking with him worshippers from Gainsborough. There he became still more radicalized and promoted adult baptism. When he later joined a branch of the Dutch Mennonites, a split occurred in his congregation, and a breakaway group led by Thomas Helwys returned to England in 1611. The following year, Helwys and twelve congregants established the first Baptist church at Spitalfields, London.[127]

★ ★ ★

Such separatist communities were not new to England. During Elizabeth's reign, they had operated underground, usually meeting in private houses and using their own form of worship. They rejected the parish church and 1559 prayer book not just because of its 'popish' remnants but because scripted prayer prevented the spirit from working within believers. However, separatists went into decline after three of their leaders—John Greenwood, John Penry, and Henry Barrow—were hanged in 1593.

Memory of these earlier congregations, together with the formation of new ones, provided ammunition for conformists in their own preaching and printing operation against nonconformity. All nonconforming Puritans were now tarred with the separatist brush. To take just a few examples: Bancroft's chaplain, Thomas Rogers, gave the name 'Schismatic' to one of the speakers defending nonconformity in his tract upholding traditional ceremonies.[128] Oliver Ormerod, rector of Little Wenham, Suffolk, whose stated aim was to bring his readers to 'a full detestation of the Puritan-faction', likened deprived ministers to German Anabaptists, papists, and the Elizabethan separatists executed in 1593.[129] In a printed sermon, originally preached before James in 1607, the royal chaplain Martin Fotherby conflated nonconforming Puritans with Presbyterians and separatists and urged his listeners 'for the safety of the whole, to cut off such festered and infected partes'.[130]

Other conformist polemicists were less vitriolic in tone, but most still linked nonconforming ministers with separatism and argued that their wilfulness risked creating a dangerous schism in the Church. Another of

Bancroft's chaplains, William Covell, denounced the intransigents as 'immodest, disturbers of the unitie and peace both in the Church and the commonwealthe' and censured their resistance to subscription as a 'peevish [peverse] refusal' that served only 'to make a schisme'.[131] The deeply anti-Catholic Gabriel Powel took a similar line. He began his own tract gently enough, calling the nonconforming ministers his 'brethren', loyal to the king, and far less dangerous than Catholics. Quoting an aphorism of the Elizabethan bishop of London, John Aylmer, Powel stated approvingly:

> If I were in the company but of one papist, I might justly feare the losse of my life, but being amongst ten thousand precisians well might I be affrayde of my byshoprike, but never of my throate. The one would cut my coate, and the other my throate.[132]

However, Powel went on to condemn the 'precisians' as harshly as had other conformists, branding them: 'schismaticall ministers' who were being punished 'for giddie innovation and noveltie, for faction, schism, and impugning the magistrate's auctority, or disturbing the peace and quietnesse of the Church'. These ministers had 'withdrawne their hands from the plough, making a manifest schisme and disturbing the peace of the Church' and sowing 'the tares of sedition, schism, and faction'. Parishioners should therefore cease pitying their 'unfaithfull and ungratefull pastours [who] have dealt so unkindly and undutifully with them'.[133]

Those urging conformity generally argued that the matters in dispute were not central to doctrine but rather 'petty and small'.[134] Addressing 'discontented' Puritans directly, Samuel Gardiner argued 'the oddes betweene you and us are not of that importance to devide and sunder you from us', and he urged conformity so that 'we might all proceede in the common cause of religion'.[135] He and like-minded conformists asserted that all the ceremonies in dispute were 'adiaphora', matters indifferent and not central to doctrine, so there was absolutely no reason for Protestants not to perform them when a Christian monarch and his bishops commanded it. In the words of Powel: 'God hath given absolute power and authoritie unto the Church over all indifferent actions, rites, and outward ceremonies to dispose of them, for her owne conservation, utilitie, decencie, order, and discipline.'[136] The king went much further, telling MPs: 'ministeris by disobedience to the king's authoritie and ordinances of a setled Churche in indifferent things do prove thaimselfis to be nothing ellis indeid but seditiouse schismatikes'.[137]

Puritan clergy responded with the obvious question: if these ceremonies were 'of no great moment', why should they be enforced at all?[138] Consequently, conformist polemicists had to justify the prayer-book ceremonies as well as decry Puritan clergy as schismatics. They did so in many sermons and tracts, often at inordinate length and rarely saying anything new.[139] Put briefly, the core of their arguments was relatively simple: none of the ceremonies in dispute were idolatrous as Puritans claimed. The sign of the cross was not an idol, because it was not worshipped; on the contrary, it was an ancient 'gesture' that 'cannot be ill, when our doctrine is good'. Kneeling at communion, likewise, was a long-established 'gesture' and not a sign of adoration that implied Christ's presence in the consecrated elements. As for the surplice, it was used 'without any superstitious opinion' and only for 'comlinesse, order, and decency'. Uniformity on all these matters was necessary to prevent 'papists' taking advantage of the 'multiplicitie and varietie of gestures' to bring in their own superstitious practices.[140] What was more, declared a few, these minor ceremonies were not the true corruptions in the Church; people should look instead to Sabbath-breaking, immoral behaviour, and blasphemy ('the southerne oaths and northerne curses'). Those that did not and focused instead on church ceremonies were hypocrites.[141]

Conformist writings were aimed at different readerships. Some targeted waverers, partial conformists, or ejected clergy in the hope of bringing them back into the fold. Thomas Sparke, who had been a Puritan representative at Hampton Court but afterwards conformed (according to him, thanks to James's public interventions and private conversations), professed to be putting forward his reasons for conforming in print in order 'to perswade others so to doe likewise'.[142] Francis Mason claimed that he was addressing his call for obedience to nonconformists who 'have bene carried away rather of weaknesse then of wilfulnesse', and that his purpose was 'to quiet and settle the unresolved conscience'.[143] However, the abusive tone of many other polemicists suggests that they believed their readership already held a negative view of 'Puritans' and hence would be in sympathy with James's conformist policy. And they were probably correct; as already seen, the seedbed of anti-Puritanism had been sown at the popular level during the 1590s and seems to have grown stronger during the first decade of James's reign.

Judging from court records and libels, anti-Puritan feeling existed widely in the country.[144] Ministers such as Samuel Hieron were thought divisive when they denounced the sins of dead parishioners in funeral sermons or when others, such as Anthony Lapthorne, admonished living members of the congregation from the pulpit for their ungodly lives.[145] Puritan officials often faced hostility and contempt when they attempted to suppress popular local festivities and impose sabbatarianism.[146] In Dorchester (Dorset), where the godly held positions of power, three libels circulated that attacked the Puritan laity as self-righteous hypocrites and nonconforming ministers as seditious given that 'what our king commands, that they do deny'.[147] In Bridport (also in Dorset), a libellous poem reproached the 'Puritans' of the town for moral hypocrisy and self-righteousness, while another accused specific men and women known to be religious reformers of using their holy conventicles for the satisfaction of carnal desires.[148]

Hostility to Puritans was also expressed on the London stage, both reflecting and intensifying anti-Puritan sentiments. Jonson's *The Alchemist* and Shakespeare's *Measure for Measure* are the best-known examples. The plot of Jonson's satire centres around Ananias and Tribulation, two 'brethren from Amsterdam', being duped by two London rogues. For comic effect, Jonson mocks the language of zealous precisionists as when Ananias objects to Latin and Greek as a 'heathen language', corrects the con man Subtle for saying 'Christmas' not 'Christ-tide', damns bells as 'profane', interjects that 'idle starch' in linen is 'indeed an idol', and hates traditions as 'popish all'. Tribulation, meanwhile, uses religious language to mask his greed and argues that sharp practice is justified so long as it is done for godly purposes. The hypocrisy of both men is there for all to see when they prefer the gold which they are seeking to go to themselves and their congregation, not to orphan children.[149]

An altogether more subtle play, Shakespeare's *Measure for Measure* (1604) also critiques Puritan hypocrisy. Despite his professed godliness, the zealous Puritan ruler Angelo lusts after Claudio's sister Isabella and carries out an act of fornication with a woman he wrongly believes to be her. Angelo then breaks his promise to Isabella that he would free her brother if she slept with him. At the same time, the play presents a Puritan dystopia. While everyone in the play agrees that sexual licence requires punishment, they (and the audience) think Angelo's imposition of the death penalty on Claudio for the sin of premarital sex is excessive and disproportionate.[150]

★ ★ ★

Although Protestants in England were divided over the liturgy of the Established Church and the nature of a godly society, they were in total accord on at least three important matters. Most obviously they had a common enemy in Roman Catholicism. The call for the vigorous prosecution of Catholic recusants came from bishops as well as Puritans, and vituperative anti-Catholic language suffused the religious literature produced by Puritans and anti-Puritans alike. They all habitually identified the pope as the Antichrist, the antithesis of true religion, who had to be anathematized and combated.[151] The Gunpowder Plot merely proved for them the perfidy of Roman Catholics, while the controversy over the oath of allegiance (discussed in chapter 12) united Protestants in horror at papal claims.[152] This deep prejudice of the 'other' helped keep a bond of unity within the Protestant Church and community.

Another bond of unity was the predestinarian theology which was embedded (albeit imprecisely) in the thirty-nine articles of faith, widely taught in the universities and preached in the parishes.[153] It is true that some influential theologians and preachers were turning away from a rigid predestination with its emphasis on God's eternal decree which determined who were the elect and who the reprobate, although, before 1612, such 'avant-garde' anti-Calvinist views remained marginal.[154] It is also true that predestinarians diverged in their understanding of the theology. The hardest line stated that merit played no part in salvation and that the elect could not fall from grace (called the 'perseverance of the saints'), whereas others—admittedly a minority view—were ready to allow human merit a place, however modest, in the divine scheme. Nonetheless, during this early Jacobean period, these theological differences were kept in check. It was only later in the reign and under Charles I when Puritans became alarmed at anti-predestinarian preaching that the resulting fissures endangered the inclusiveness of the Protestant Church.[155]

Finally, all Protestants valued preaching and agreed on the need to establish a learned preaching ministry in every parish. Indeed, as already mentioned, an argument used by bishops and Puritans alike against the deprivations was that the places left vacant would be filled with inadequate preachers or non-residents. From the moment that James set foot on English soil, he listened and responded to the numerous petitions demanding sufficient and satisfactory preachers in every parish. Unlike Elizabeth, who was suspicious of preaching and concerned more about the moral worth than the educational level of ministers, James valued sermons as a godly tool for conversion and edification.[156] Yet, despite Elizabeth's attitude, measures to improve the learning of the parish clergy had started during her reign.

In 1584, Whitgift introduced canons which insisted upon a higher standard of learning for ordinands. He also attempted to improve preaching and provide in-service training in the scriptures and reformed texts for ministers already in post who were not graduates. Estimating that, in his first year as archbishop, there had been no more than 2,000 candidates with university degrees for ordination, Whitgift was pleased to report that, in 1603, there were about 4,000 graduates and 4,840 clergymen licensed to preach.[157] Moreover, the laity who relished sermons had access to them in print if not in the pulpit, for during Elizabeth's reign over a thousand were published.[158] Under James, these efforts continued, providing another reason for Puritans to stay within the Church. Many Jacobean bishops imposed strict standards for ordination, and a few continued or introduced vocational training schemes for clerics. The bishops of London and Gloucester retained pre-existing schemes aimed at identifying and improving the quality of poor-performing clerics, while Bishop Watson of Chichester took remedial action after being shamed by the Puritan petitioning campaign which exposed clerical shortcomings in his diocese. Additionally, vocational training for non-preaching clergy was introduced in Salisbury (1613) and Hereford (1614).[159]

More, of course, needed to be done. It was generally recognized that one major obstacle to producing a high-grade preaching clergy was the poverty of many livings, which led to pluralism, non-residence, and the employment of poorly qualified curates or ministers. As James pronounced in the July after his accession: 'no one thing is so greate ympedyment [to a preaching clergy] then want of competent lyving to maintaine learned men' in our kingdom.[160] He was right. Because so many parishes in the large diocese of Coventry and Lichfield were inadequately endowed, fewer than one-quarter of its clergy were graduates in 1603 and fewer than one-fifth of its total clergy was licensed to preach.[161]

James was determined to take immediate action to remedy the problem. One way forward, he thought, was to return impropriated tithes [those tithes which went to the lay owners of a benefice] held by the crown and universities back to the Church so that they might be 'converted againe to the right use for which they were first instituted', namely maintaining preachers.[162] Whitgift, however, immediately put a stop to the universities losing such a valuable source of income which, he claimed, was being used to support poor scholars.[163] Regardless, James pursued his ultimate objective. In October 1603, he ordered the bishops to carry out a survey that would focus on the quality of ministers and investigate what each living was worth in each parish of their diocese. His purpose was to find out if the Puritans' own surveys were accurate as well as to get bishops to take the problem seriously.[164]

From the surveys, it was clear that many livings were too impoverished to maintain a resident preaching minister and the issue was discussed at the Hampton Court Conference. The answer, the bishops believed, was to change or end the system of impropriated tithes.[165] Accordingly, in 1604, they sponsored a measure in the house of lords that would allow a 'portion to be assigned out of every impropriation for the maintenance of a preaching minister'. To Bancroft's disgust, the commons out of self-interest rejected the bill at its first reading. It was sheer hypocrisy, he told James, that laymen considered it legal and legitimate to 'reap the tithes of two benefices' when they condemned pluralism and non-residence.[166] All James could therefore do in that session to improve the financial position of the Church was to revoke the 1559 Act of Exchange, which had been used under Elizabeth to denude dioceses of much of their landed property. The king was influenced by the bishops' arguments that their authority could not be upheld if they continued to lose local estates to the crown. However, despite his initial enthusiasm for improving the revenues of the Church, James was not prepared to restore the impropriated tithes in the hands of the crown. On the contrary, in 1607, he negotiated with two syndicates of London businessmen to sell some in order to provide pensions for courtiers.[167]

Notwithstanding the general unwillingness to return their impropriated tithes to the Church, everyone continued to complain about pluralism, non-residence, and the lack of preaching. To show that he was taking steps to curtail the abuses and answer critics in parliament, James ordered Bancroft, in April 1605, to collect the names of pluralist clergy and assess 'the sufficiency' of curates in every parish where the incumbent was non-resident. James had no intention of removing pluralists from any benefice, but he insisted that they abide by articles 41 and 44 of the 1604 canons and provide 'an able and sufficient curate' who could preach in their place, if necessary by paying out a higher stipend.[168] Again confronted with grievances about pluralism in the 1610 session of parliament, he announced his intention to 'lay a strict charge upon the bishops, under the pain of our displeasure' to ensure that pluralists would provide a preacher for the benefice in which they did not reside. Afterwards, he told Bancroft to carry this through and suspend any pluralist who refused to co-operate.[169] James and the bishops' efforts led to some improvement, but poorer livings continued to be filled with 'very mean ministers' for otherwise the cure would lie vacant. Consequently, bills were presented in all parliaments, between 1614 and 1629, with proposals for augmenting the income of the clergy, but to no great effect.[170]

★ ★ ★

James had far greater success in carrying through another reform requested at the Hampton Court Conference. There, John Reynolds had called for all the different versions of the English bible then in circulation to be replaced with one reformed translation 'to stand as warranted for all'. The various bibles in use were the Great Bible of Henry VIII's reign, the Bishops' Bible (originally produced in 1568) which was customarily read in churches, and the more reader-friendly 1560 Geneva Bible—known as the 'People's Bible'—which was studied privately in homes. As Reynolds pointed out, all the bibles contained mistranslations, but the bishops seemed satisfied with the existing Great and Bishops' Bibles.[171] At any rate, an anonymous account of the Hampton Court Conference, which reflected their viewpoint, maintained that Reynolds's motion was 'little debated and so passed over as a matter of no great moment'.[172] Furthermore, one of the 1604 canons instructed the placement of the 'Bible of the largest volume' in all parish churches, meaning either the folio versions of the Great or Bishops' Bible.[173] Without doubt, most bishops disapproved of the Geneva Bible's provocative marginalia as well as some of its renditions, which were Presbyterian in tone and meaning.

James, however, supported Reynolds in his request for 'one uniforme translation'. In 1602, he had urged 'earnestly' a new translation of the bible for Scotland and now favoured the same for England, especially as—like the bishops—he considered the Geneva Bible was 'the worst of all' translations and disliked its marginal commentaries. It was not only that the notes often 'enforce a sence further then the texte will beare', he said at the Hampton Court Conference, but also that too many of them were 'very partiall, untrue, seditious, and savouring too much of daungerous and trayterous conceites'.[174] Specifically offensive to James was the marginal note on Exodus 1:19 which seemingly legitimated disobedience to monarchs because it called 'lawful' the disobedience of Pharaoh's midwives in rescuing Moses. Another commentary James found loathsome was the note on 2 Chronicles 15:16 that justified, even praised, the deposition and murder of an ungodly ruler. There, Asa was criticized for a lack of zeal in deposing instead of killing his idolatrous mother. For these reasons, James's preference was that the new translation should be based on the Bishops' Bible.[175]

In early summer 1604, James ordered the appointment of fifty-four scholars with specialist language skills to produce a new English bible.[176] The translators were swiftly selected, probably by Lancelot Andrewes, dean of Westminster, and the two Regius professors of Hebrew at Oxford and Cambridge. The team included two key spokesmen on the Puritan side at the Hampton Court Conference: Reynolds (a renowned Greek scholar) until his death on 21 May 1607 and Chaderton (a scholar of Greek, Hebrew, and Latin). Anti-Calvinists—such as John Overall—were also represented. Bancroft was the 'chiefe overseer' of the project. The translators were then divided into 'companies': two based in Cambridge, two in Oxford, and two in Westminster.[177] Each company began work during the summer on drafting a separate portion of the translation, possibly co-operatively or maybe individually on different chapters—the sources do not reveal which.[178] Following this stage of the process, a separate revisory committee, consisting of two members from each of the six companies, was convened in London to review and revise the various parts of the translation produced.

The translators were immediately issued with an official set of fourteen instructions (later a fifteenth was added), which were probably drawn up by the king or, at the very least, devised in consultation with him. The first directed that the Bishops' Bible was 'to be followed and as little altered as the truth of the originall will permitt'. To ensure that the translators worked from 'the right text', they were given an unbound copy of the 1602 edition which they could 'if they wished' annotate. Another instruction (the sixth) commanded that the new translation should contain no marginal notes other than those explaining Hebrew or Greek words which could not be translated succinctly in the text. A further key instruction directed that 'the ould ecclesiasticall words [were] to be kept, viz. the word Churche not to be translated congregation etc', the translation that most Puritans preferred.[179]

Nonetheless, many passages in the new translation derived directly from the Geneva Bible. Additionally, the translators went back to the bibles of Henry VIII's reign in accordance with the last of James's instructions that these sources were to be 'used where they agree better with the text than the Bishops' Bible'. The Bishops' Bible had anyway been heavily indebted to these Henrician bibles, which themselves were influenced by

William Tyndale's translations. More surprisingly, the translators of the New Testament also turned to the scholarly Catholic Rheims translation.[180] Hence, the new bible, published in May 1611, was constructed from an amalgam of sources as well as drawing on the best Hebrew and Greek scholarship of the day.

Overall, the King James Version was far more conservative than the Geneva Bible. Not only did the word 'congregation' disappear but so did the word 'tyrant', which had appeared four hundred times in the Geneva Bible. The lack of marginalia took away the aid and incentive for independent thought and embodied the notion that exegesis belonged properly to the clergy alone. Now, the bible operated—as Lori Anne Ferrell has observed—less as a means 'for individual edification and group study', as godly Protestants required, than as a vehicle for corporate worship.[181]

The lack of marginalia was criticized at the time as a major weakness. As one commentator complained, 'many seeming riddles are read, if the words be but read' without explanation.[182] It was probably for this reason that the Geneva Bible remained popular, reprinted again in 1616; the last early modern reprinting in its entirety took place as late as 1644. Editions of the King James Bible in smaller formats also sold well, being used by families alongside their existing bibles. It took longer for the folio editions to replace the Bishops' Bible in parish churches. The price was high, and no royal or episcopal order demanded its purchase. Only under Charles I was there a drive for all parishes to buy and use the King James Version.[183]

★ ★ ★

According to Richard Edes, the Jacobean succession was 'change...without change. A change of the governor, but not of the religion and government of the land'.[184] Fundamentally, this observation is correct, but the change of governor did inspire some changes in the religious climate at court and in the country. As already mentioned, James's personal enjoyment of sermons and his resolution to plant good preachers in all parishes of England and Ireland contrasted strongly with Elizabeth's preference for prayer over sermons and her disdain for preaching as a godly tool for conversion and edification. At court, James doubled the number of sermons held in the chapel royal each week and made regular attendance compulsory, even when he was away hunting. He increased the pool of chaplains who would 'wait on' the chapel royal, because he added to it preachers who had impressed him when outside the court. Likewise, he encouraged sermons in the parishes.

After the Gunpowder Plot, he pressed Bancroft to introduce a regular Tuesday sermon, and he allowed the restoration of licensed preaching training exercises (called prophesyings) which had been banned by Elizabeth in the archdiocese of Canterbury. Putting pressure on bishops, he added impetus to the process whereby all new ordinands were to be university graduates.

A committed Calvinist, James had a far deeper interest in theology than had Elizabeth. The queen had left doctrinal teachings to theologians, maybe because of her gender or her limited knowledge in such matters. Unlike James, she confessed to her ignorance of God's will in relation to predestination and even reduced the doctrine to adiaphora.[185] Because of his interest in intellectual debates about religion, James appeared more at home in the company of clerics than was Elizabeth. Sure, she was close to her personal chaplains, almoners, and Archbishop Whitgift, but these relationships lacked the ease and intimacy that James enjoyed with his favourite preachers and clergy, whether Patrick Galloway, James Montagu, or Lancelot Andrewes, whom he would sometimes invite to dine with him informally. Unlike Elizabeth, who had kept bishops off the privy council for twenty-five years, James came to increase the episcopal presence and, in 1621, appointed Bishop Williams as lord keeper and head of the judiciary. James also brought the bishop of London into star chamber, though he was neither a privy councillor nor judge. At court James revived the posts of dean of the chapel royal and clerk of the closet in 1603, which Elizabeth had allowed to lapse, their duties handed over to the lord chamberlain.[186]

However, continuities in the Church across both reigns outweighed the contrasts, especially during the early Jacobean years. At court, the chapel royal retained its institutional structure and ceremonial practices in line with the canons.[187] In the country, as already seen, progress continued to be made in improving the quality of the parochial clergy, while the problem of impoverished cures remained unsolved. Turning to bishops, Kenneth Fincham's archival research has revealed that both the late Elizabethan episcopate and the new Jacobean appointments included energetic pastors as well as able administrators. Furthermore, under both supreme governors, the episcopal bench was diverse in its theological stance and contained both conformists and protectors of Puritans.[188] Although early Stuart bishops exercised more secular power than their Elizabethan counterparts, this development did not occur until after 1615. Before that date, the archbishop of Canterbury was the only cleric to sit on the privy council. Similarly, the number of clerics on the commission of the peace expanded significantly only after 1616.[189]

The supreme governors were similar in as many ways as they were different. Despite his own joy in debating theology, James—like Elizabeth—considered the tricky issue of predestination to be a matter suitable only for scholars in the universities to discuss and openly debate. For this reason, he too refused to endorse the 1595 Lambeth articles and have them attached to the thirty-nine articles in the revised prayer book, as Puritans had wanted.[190] Notwithstanding his love of preaching, James took exception to politically driven sermons. His treatment of Burges was harsh, and when his foreign policy came under attack later in the reign, he clamped down on the number and nature of sermons. Preachers, for example, were ordered not to 'meddle with these matters of state', while the church authorities were told to 'be more warie and choice in licensing preachers'.[191] Elizabeth would have approved!

Both monarchs apparently shared the same taste in public services. When it came to the Sunday morning service at court, they usually heard abbreviated services—lasting about thirty minutes—and took communion monthly not weekly.[192] On special occasions, the two of them preferred more elaborate ceremonies despite James's Calvinist upbringing. For example, at the garter service when Prince Charles was invested in May 1611, it was reported that:

> the clergy, robed in rich copes and purple cottas began to chaunt [chant] certain prayers and hymns in English, then the epistle, the gospel, and the creed; then other prayers and psalms to a great music of organs and wind instruments, and a multitude of voices that made a harmony worthy the ears of a mighty monarch.[193]

Like Elizabeth, James enjoyed church music. Indeed, one of James's earliest measures after his accession was to increase the wages of the choristers of the chapel royal that had been frozen because of the wars.[194]

James—like Elizabeth—was a staunch defender of the doctrine and ceremonies contained in the authorized prayer book. The changes he permitted in 1604 were 'small' (by his own admission).[195] Moreover, James rejected further attempts to introduce modifications or innovations. Here, Elizabeth's motto *'semper eadem'* [always the same] applied equally well to him. As shown above, both monarchs resisted nonconformity and vigorously asserted the royal supremacy. Indeed, the enforcement of conformity under James resulted in more deprivations than the one initiated by Whitgift with Elizabeth's support in the 1580s. Indeed, the early Jacobean Church experienced the greatest purge of Protestant clergy from the accession of Elizabeth until the Civil War.[196] What is more, subscription was systematically imposed on new ordinands and candidates for a living, as had been demanded in two of the 1604 canons. As a result, a new generation of conformists entered the ranks of the clergy during James's reign, many of them deeply hostile to Puritans.[197]

Looking ahead beyond the timeframe of this book, I need to mention that the Jacobean Church enjoyed a short period of relative calm after the appointment, in 1611, of George Abbot as archbishop of Canterbury.[198] Again, this is evidence for continuity since there had likewise been a period of relative harmony in the Elizabethan Church after Edmund Grindal's elevation to the archdiocese of Canterbury in 1575. In the eyes of both archbishops, propagating 'true' Protestant doctrine mattered far more than the problem of godly pastors who would not accept unimportant ceremonies. Hence, they both took a relatively moderate stance towards Puritans who were not troublemakers, and the court of high commission under Abbot's presidency focused on negligent, not nonconforming, clergy.[199] During their archiepiscopates, moreover, anti-Puritan discourse died down because of resurgent Protestant fears of a Catholic threat, and, with the lack of overt conflict, the godly retained confidence in the Established Church.[200]

However, the peace did not last long. Both archbishops quickly lost the trust of their monarch, who anyway had a different outlook from their primates. Grindal and Elizabeth famously clashed over prophesyings and the nature of the royal supremacy. Because Abbot was more anti-Catholic and less anti-Puritan than James, the archbishop could not persuade the king to execute missionary priests and found himself sometimes unable to protect high-profile nonconforming ministers whom conformist opponents had brought to James's attention.[201] Furthermore, after 1618, the king's policies dismayed and alienated the godly. In 1618, he issued a Book of Sports which authorized certain recreations after divine service on the Sabbath; and during the 1620s, he pursued a Spanish marriage for Prince Charles and suspended the penal laws against Catholics to make it happen. When Protestant criticisms and protests created an uproar, he responded by clamping down on political sermons and 'scandalous' books and pamphlets to silence his opponents. At the same time, James extended his favour to anti-Calvinist divines since Calvinists were his most vocal critics. By the time James died in 1625, twelve anti-Calvinists sat on the episcopal bench, half the total number, and they were promoting ceremonial reforms in their dioceses which were offensive to the godly.[202] All in all, James left as troubled a legacy for his heir as Elizabeth had bequeathed him. Unfortunately, Charles managed the legacy less well. His inflexibility and determination to drive religion in an anti-Calvinist direction shattered the fragile unity of Church and state in all his realms. But that is another story.

12

Catholics and Recusants

It was not only the Puritans who sought a new church settlement in 1603. Catholics were desperate for James to repeal the Elizabethan recusancy laws or, better still, the 1559 Act of Uniformity; and a fair number were convinced that the new king would be amenable to change. Some of them took heart from promises James had allegedly made while king of Scotland that he would allow English Catholics to practise their religion, if not publicly then in their own homes.[1] Others imagined that James had long been a secret Catholic but not shown his hand for fear of putting in jeopardy his title to the English crown.[2] Equally unrealistically, several maintained that James would 'in tyme suffer himself to be rightlie informed in religion' and would until then agree to 'mitigation or release of our miseries'.[3] For a while, Robert Persons affected to share this degree of optimism. Distancing himself from his 1595 treatise which had favoured the succession of the Infanta Isabella, Persons declared, in May 1603, that he had the previous week found 'many things' to admire in *Basilikon Doron*, which had 'exceedingly comforted' him about James's character.[4] Admittedly, it did not take him long to become disenchanted. When reading *The Trew Law* in July, the Jesuit realized that the king's treatment of absolute monarchy was incompatible with Catholic ecclesiology and that there seemed little chance of a change in James's thinking.[5]

English Catholics wasted no time before entering the political fray. Immediately upon Elizabeth's death, they embarked upon a petitioning campaign framed to show James their loyalty and the injustice of the penal laws against them. Some approached him in Scotland;[6] still more came forward to hand over their written petitions as he progressed to London.[7] Following an agreed strategy, the spokesmen expressed joy at his accession, and the tenor of their petitions was loyalist and moderate. One supplication, for example, presented no specific demands at all but simply reminded the king how Catholics had immediately recognized him as the 'lawfull and rightfull kinge of the realme' and promised future 'zeale and dutye' in his service. Other petitioners did ask for toleration but merely requested 'the free use of religion, yf not in publicke churches at the lest in private howses' and 'if not with approbation, yet with toleration, without molestation'.[8]

This early Catholic petitioning campaign mirrored that of the Puritans in 1603. So, from his very first days as king of England, James was confronted with irreconcilable demands from his new subjects, all of whom purported to be loyal and moderate. He reacted similarly to both religious groups. Although he took badly pleas that he believed were accompanied with threats, he otherwise displayed a readiness to reform proven abuses.[9] In the case of Catholics, he promised not to hound them but to treat them fairly as long as they remained 'quiet and decently hidden'.[10] As a practical measure, he demanded in April an investigation into their complaints that greedy exchequer officials were bleeding recusants dry through fines.[11] Among other hopeful signs for Catholics, James appointed semi-conformists as privy councillors, showed favour to recusants on his progress to London—even dubbing some of them knights—and took action on behalf of individual Catholics who petitioned him about specific injuries.[12] No wonder some Protestants feared that James might make further concessions, especially since it was widely rumoured that he was seeking peace with Spain and that Philip III would demand religious toleration before signing a treaty. These fears no doubt fuelled the anti-Catholic sentiment so evident in the accession literature greeting the new king.[13] Yet Protestants need not have worried for, in late June, James 'compelled' recusants to pay the next biennial instalment of fines.[14] By that time, moreover, some Catholic priests and laypeople had already felt betrayed by James's evident unwillingness to introduce meaningful toleration, and these men devised or joined the Bye Plot described in chapter 3.

Just after Copley's revelation of the conspiracy, James moved to appease disaffected Catholics who up till then were loyal. He summoned to his presence a deputation of Catholics, headed by Sir Thomas Tresham, and pledged that recusancy fines would be suspended provided that Catholics remained loyal to the state; he also stated that those who took the oath of supremacy would be eligible for office.[15] While the latter offered nothing substantially new, abating or ending recusancy fines was an innovative and valuable concession. True to his word, James allowed the remission of fines for those convicted of recusancy in both England and Scotland.[16] He justified the decision on the grounds that 'pecuniarye paynes weare inconvenient meanes to reduce men's mynds from errours [in religion] to trewth'.[17] But in reality, James wanted to keep onside the powerful Catholic nobility and gentry, especially during the months when the Bye Plot was under investigation. Probably, too, he thought to woo the Spanish king to the peace table by intimating that Catholics could expect favourable treatment from him. Political expedients rather than principle lay behind his act of partial toleration in July 1603.

James had no intention of permitting full toleration even if Catholics proved loyal. He retained the Elizabethan ban on priests entering the realm and issued a proclamation, on 22 February 1604, for the expulsion of all Jesuits and seminary priests who were found in the kingdom after 19 March.[18] As he well knew, a deficiency of priests would make it impossible for Catholics to receive the sacraments, the lifeblood of their faith. James gave two reasons for his order. First, the priests' missionary efforts were resulting in an increase in the number of recusants and, second, their loyalty to him could never be absolute since they had to submit to the pope's authority at their ordination.[19] As James later told the 1604 parliament, papal authority limited the royal supremacy and, worse still, popes sanctioned the deposition and assassination of monarchs, 'thinking it no sinne but rather a matter of salvation'.[20]

★ ★ ★

As the date of James's first parliament drew nearer, Catholics stepped up their political agitation. In several towns and shires they began to organize themselves to elect members who would represent their interests.[21] Mirroring again the concurrent Puritan campaign, Catholics, in the autumn of 1603, were 'imployed to goe upp and down to gett oute a petission for tolleration of relgigion'.[22] According to the bishop of Durham, Catholics held 'meetinges and devises' at which 'their solicitours' persuaded men, women, and children 'in a greate longe schedule of parchement to subscribe their names to a supplicacon' for presentation to the king.[23] The objective was to persuade the king to repeal all the anti-Catholic laws on the statute book.

While many petitions were handed to the king directly, some were aimed at a wider public, whether local or national. All of them reiterated the past and present loyalty of the Catholic priesthood and laity. The very short 'Seminaries' Supplication', which was pinned upon Wigan Cross in

Lancashire, in March 1604, remonstrated against the unwarranted continuance of 'ould woonted perssecutions' after Catholics had shown great devotion to James's mother and support for his title after her death; and it ended not with a call for civil disobedience but with a prayer for God to mitigate the 'wrath' against the Catholic community and to give its members a 'christian patiens to induer for our Lord', signing off 'God save the king'.[24] Likewise, the seminary priest John Colleton emphasized Catholic loyalty in his 1604 *Supplication* addressed to the king and parliament. Unlike Protestants and Puritans, wrote Colleton, Catholics censured 'all sortes of rebellion' and 'would presently flocke to the banner of your Majestie and with the effusion of their best bloud guarde and protect your royall person'. If James were to 'licence the practise of our religion in private houses without molestation to priest or lay person', he would obtain the active service of Catholics, who with their great numbers and political connections could make the realm secure 'against all worldly attempts foraine and domesticall'.[25] Similar points were made in *A Petition Apologeticall*, supposedly written by one John Lecey. Not only had the community shown 'zeale and promptitude' in recognizing his title the previous year, declared Lecey, but additionally it had long displayed a commitment to the principle of hereditary monarchy. It was they, not Protestants, he repeated several times, who had upheld the rightful title of Mary, Queen of Scots to the English throne.[26] To allay James's fears about dual loyalties, Lecey proposed that priests and lay Catholics alike could take an oath saying:

> Wee doe, and will acknowledge due unto your Majesty from us, what soever is due for a subject unto his prince and soveraigne, either by the lawe of nature, or by the word of God, or hath beene used by any Catholike subject towardes your Highnes' Catholike progenitors.[27]

Lecey was not the only Catholic to suggest an oath of obedience. In January 1603, thirteen appellants had signed a 'Protestation of Allegiance' requesting toleration in return for a declaration of loyalty. Later in 1603, the Catholic exile and theologian Matthew Kellison offered to swear an oath to obey the law 'in all temporal causes' and defend the royal family 'with the laste droppe of our bloud'.[28] These proposals got nowhere at the time but, as we shall see, Catholic offers of an oath may well have been the genesis of James's later policy.

The arguments in these petitions and pamphlets cut no ice with most Protestants. Only a small minority believed that the danger from Catholics was any less severe under James than it had been under Elizabeth. For most Protestants, the circumstances of 1603—the Bye Plot, the assertiveness of northern Catholics, and the arrival of priests in greater numbers from the Continent—provided sufficient evidence that the Catholic threat was real and the professed loyalism of the petitioners a sham. Catholics, they believed, were 'wolves in sheep's clothing'.[29] The king's suspension of the recusancy fines, consequently, created general alarm, especially in the north; this leniency, Archbishop Matthew Hutton of York warned Cecil, had led to 'papists and recusants' growing 'mightily in number, courage, and insolencye'.[30]

During 1604, therefore, James was subjected in sermons, pamphlets, and parliamentary speeches to demands for tougher measures against all recusants. The anti-Catholic discourse—which included responses to Catholic petitions and polemic—naturally made much of the 'daungerous and damnable propositions' that the pope had the right to excommunicate and depose princes, but often it also espoused a spiritual and scriptural perspective. Pamphleteers exhorted the king to 'tolerate no papists to live and to blaspheme our God with idolatrie and false worship among your Christian subjects'.[31] Likewise, in a sermon preached before James in May 1604, Henry Hooke (incidentally no lover of Puritans either) cautioned the king against introducing any toleration for 'idolaters and heretiques' and indeed urged harsher laws to prevent them disturbing 'the peace of Jerusalem'.[32]

While not proposing to repeal the penal laws against Catholics, James did offer, in 1604, to examine the existing ones carefully 'in case they have bene in times past further or more rigorously extended by judges then the meaning of the law was', thereby harming 'the innocent as of guiltie persons'. The guilty, he believed, were the priests and the newly converted; the innocent, those who were 'quiet and well minded' but had been educated in 'venim in place of wholesome nutriment'.[33] The commons, however, were not interested in easing the penalties on the Catholic community, even though individual MPs, like other Protestants, would often plead for favourable treatment towards their own Catholic kin or close acquaintances.

★ ★ ★

In June 1604, a bill to exile priests and enforce the penalties for recusants passed the commons. Brought before the lords, its wording was judged imperfect, and the bill was modified. However, at its third reading, a storm erupted when the leading Catholic peer Anthony Browne, second Viscount Montague, declared his 'open and earnest disent' to the measure and then 'enveighed against the whole state of religion' established in England. He defended his Church and faith on the grounds that they were in accordance with scripture and the early Church, and he alleged that the truth of the old Church was what drew people away from the new.[34] Predictably, the lords found his speech 'very offensive', and Montague was instantly placed in the Fleet prison where he remained until he made a public apology before the house several days later. That he suffered no worse was because the lords wanted to avoid turning him into a martyr. As for the bill, it passed both houses, and the king allowed it to go into law.[35] James's approval should have come as no surprise. Not only was it in line with his February proclamation but he had also told his privy councillors shortly before the parliament met that his relaxation of recusancy fines was designed only as a one-year concession to reward Catholics for not opposing his accession and that he now intended to fortify all the laws against them 'saving for blood, from which he had a natural aversion'.[36] It is likely that James also countenanced another bill introduced into the commons that was against printing 'popish' pamphlets, but anyway it was dropped 'through weariness and want of time'.[37]

The parliamentary session over, fines again began to be collected and the courts came down hard on recusants.[38] About a thousand recusants from Yorkshire and six hundred from Lancashire with 'fewe' or 'none of the better sort omitted' were indicted in one session of the northern circuit in early 1605.[39] The banishment of priests was put into operation: twenty-one were taken from prisons and shipped abroad in September 1604, and early the next year recusant homes were again searched for priests. Those found were imprisoned and threatened with execution, as happened at Oxford 'when a priest was actually taken up to the gallows to terrify him and the others, and to induce them to leave the country'.[40] Regardless of James's stated opposition to the death penalty, local justices carried out several executions of Catholics: the seminary priest John Sugar and his lay follower Robert Grissold were hanged, drawn, and quartered at Warwick in July 1604; the layman Laurence Baily met his end in Lancaster either in August or September the same year, condemned for helping an apprehended priest.[41]

Understandably, Catholics swiftly became disillusioned. As one anonymous petitioner put it: despite the king denouncing 'war' against them at his accession, he was now carrying out 'all maner of persecution' against them. Catholics had been expecting to enter 'that land of promise wherin they should take breath from the Egiptian impositiones wherwith for so many yeares they weare oppressed', but they were now subjected to heavier financial exactions than those imposed by Elizabeth. He warned that Catholics were not a weak people to be trampled upon but 'more mightie and honorable' than Protestants and Puritans.[42] In a petition to the king, a kinsman of Montague Thomas Pounde protested against the recent executions and supposedly begged James 'to spare the innocent, lest God, who is to judge justices, avenge the blood of his own'. For this audacity, he was brought before star chamber, sentenced to the pillory, and remanded in prison. Had foreign ambassadors not intervened, his punishment would have been more extreme.[43]

Not all Catholics blamed the king personally: recusants in Herefordshire thought he was 'drawne to execute lawes contrarie to his liking' by his privy council.[44] And this may have been partially true. Although James was demanding conformity and ordering the expulsion of priests, he did not want to squeeze recusants dry nor carry through the death penalty in cases other than treason.[45] His desire for a peace with Spain was another consideration for leniency. But James came under considerable pressure from some councillors and all bishops, and it was difficult for him to maintain and justify any laxity towards recusants while simultaneously coming down hard on nonconforming Protestants.

★ ★ ★

The new onslaught against recusants and priests led to unrest. In the spring of 1605, one Yorkshire recusant was sent to the pillory and had an ear cut off for speaking seditious words as well as beating up a minister in church.[46] In Wells that summer, a disturbance occurred when John Lund and armed followers tried to prevent the arrest of his recusant wife.[47] The most serious tumult occurred during Whitsun that same year. It began when forty or fifty men bearing weapons rescued a prisoner who had been arrested for attending, with other armed men, the Catholic burial of an excommunicated woman near Hereford.[48] Following on from this incident, 'a most daungerous riott' broke out nearby when attempts were made to take into custody recusants and priests who were present at an open mass. Spreading throughout Herefordshire and Monmouthshire, the disorder was deemed so severe that, in July, James and the council dispatched the local nobleman and crypto-Catholic earl of Worcester to suppress it by either force or negotiation. Worcester chose negotiation; he rounded up the ringleaders, but even they were treated leniently.[49]

Catholic protests in these areas were not new, but the open defiance and unrest appear to have had a sharper edge in the years immediately following

James's accession. Disappointment resulted in desperation, disaffection, and a reluctance to abide by the pope's instruction that English Catholics should refrain from sedition and a resort to arms.[50] Although his testimony is suspect, the superior of the Jesuits, Henry Garnet, later claimed to have prevented four additional 'tumults', which would otherwise have erupted.[51]

Worse was to come. During 1604, a small group of recusant gentlemen plotted to bring about a terrorist attack and armed rising with the intent of achieving a *coup d'état* and the re-establishment of Catholicism. Their plan was to blow up the house of lords on the day that the king, queen, and heir apparent were attending the opening of parliament. The blast would kill most of the Protestant elite and carry a symbolic force since it was in parliament that the Protestant Church had been established and the punitive laws against Catholics introduced. But that was not all. Exploiting the chaos that would ensue, the conspirators proposed to raise a Catholic army in the Midlands, capture the king's daughter, nine-year-old Elizabeth—then living at Combe Abbey near Coventry—proclaim her queen, and march down to London to crown her and dismantle the Protestant Church.[52] Despite this plot being associated today with Guy Fawkes, its architect was actually Robert Catesby, a Northamptonshire gentleman, who had a charismatic personality and wide circle of connections within the recusant community.[53] Despairing of Spanish aid, especially after Philip III had opened peace negotiations with James, Catesby had resolved around Lent 1604 to take direct action himself. In his view, Spain promised much but delivered nothing.[54] So, unlike the Catholic plotters of Elizabeth's reign who looked to Spain or France for assistance with a foreign army, he decided to go it alone.

Over the following year, Catesby recruited twelve men, all sworn to secrecy. Fawkes, who had fought for Spain in the Netherlands for about twenty years, was enlisted because he was unknown to the English government and skilled in using explosives. The other core conspirators were Catesby's cousin John or Jack Wright (a Yorkshireman from the East Riding), Wright's cousin Thomas Wintour (from Worcestershire), and Sir Thomas Percy, who was Wright's brother-in-law as well as the fourth cousin and estate manager of the earl of Northumberland. Except for Fawkes, these men had joined Essex's abortive rising in 1601; all were second generation recusants; and most had strong familial connections. The other men enlisted were needed for specific tasks, such as digging the tunnel or caretaking the house where the gunpowder was initially stored; two were brought into the conspiracy by December 1604 and three in March 1605. The brothers of Thomas Wintour (Robert) and John Wright (Christopher) were among them.

Catesby had originally planned for Fawkes to mine a tunnel built under the old Palace of Westminster from an adjacent dwelling house which Percy had leased in July 1604 for that purpose.[55] However, about the beginning of March 1605, the ground floor vault beneath the house of lords which had been used for coal storage was vacated by its tenant, and Percy took over the lease. This was a much better location. The conspirators hid the gunpowder there, ready for Fawkes to set alight with a long fuse once parliament eventually sat.[56] Around the same time, Catesby stockpiled armour and weapons in his family home in Northamptonshire, ready for the rising in the Midlands. To avoid suspicion, he let it be known that he was planning to raise a regiment of English Catholics to fight for Spain in the Netherlands.

Because the king's three prorogations of parliament delayed the action, Catesby began to run out of the money which was needed for renting houses and purchasing munitions. For this reason, in the autumn of 1605, he revealed the plot to Ambrose Rookwood (a gentleman from Suffolk), Sir Everard Digby (from Rutland), and Francis Tresham (the eldest son of Sir Thomas, from Rushton, Northamptonshire), all wealthy Catholic landowners. Rookwood agreed to help because he 'loved and respected' Catesby 'as his owne life' despite his scruples about spilling 'so much blood'.[57] Digby was likewise troubled about the loss of life, especially the deaths of the seventeen Catholic peers who would be attending parliament. However, Catesby assured both men that an order would be given 'as that non of them should loose any of theyr friends'.[58] Tresham was less easily won over. Besides his concern about killing Catholic peers, he thought the plot, even if successful, was a terrible idea since it would give Protestants 'just cause to enkindle them against us'. Unsuccessfully trying to talk Catesby out of it, he kept his distance from the conspiracy other than providing some money.[59] At the end of September, Rookwood and his wife moved with his family into Clopton House, and in October Digby sent his household to Coughton Court, both houses in Warwickshire, so that they would be on hand to raise the Midland revolt.[60]

The plans started to unravel about ten days before the opening of parliament. Around 26 October, Catesby and Fawkes—who were staying at a house occupied by the Catholic Anne Vaux in Enfield Chase—received news from London that Henry would not be accompanying his father to parliament. The conspirators had already worked out that Percy (created a gentleman pensioner through the influence of Northumberland) would abduct Prince Charles but they now needed to arrange how to capture Henry, a considerably more difficult task. Far worse for the conspirators, on

Saturday 26 October, William Parker, Baron Monteagle, received an anonymous letter in a disguised hand while he was at dinner in his house at Hoxton. Allegedly, it had been given to his footman 'in the streetes, he knew not by whome'.[61] Possibly penned by his brother-in-law Tresham, the letter warned Monteagle to stay away from parliament on 5 November because those who attended would 'receyve a terrible blowe'.[62] The baron, who had been a committed recusant under Elizabeth and also involved in the Essex rising, had announced, on James's accession, that 'he had done with all former plots' and 'was resolved to stand wholly for the king'.[63] In this frame of mind, he straightaway took the message to Cecil, who was then dining with Northampton, Suffolk, and Worcester at Whitehall.[64] At least two other Catholic barons—Henry Mordaunt, fourth Baron Mordaunt (a friend of Catesby) and Edward Stourton, tenth Baron Stourton (another of Tresham's brothers-in-law and friend of Catesby)—may also have received a warning to absent themselves from parliament, but they kept quiet.

Since the king was safely hunting in Royston, Cecil awaited his return before revealing the letter. During this time, the secretary probably put out feelers to his network of informants to discover what, if anything, they knew of a plot. By the time of James's return on 31 October, the privy councillors in the picture had already agreed that Suffolk (as lord chamberlain) would take special care to search the warren of rooms around the chamber of the upper house but not before the parliamentary session was due to meet. They decided to wait in order not to scare off any conspirators. On 1 November, James agreed with this strategy. According to the information which the privy council gave out on 5 November, James on reading the letter to Monteagle 'toke hold of the last sentence and said he conceived it might be som plott to be performed with powder, remembring his father', Lord Darnley, who had been staying at a house blown up in an assassination attempt.

The conspirators had learned about Monteagle's letter on 27 October—possibly through the servant who had read it out to the baron. But because the government appeared not to be carrying out further enquiries, they decided to stick to their plan.[65] On Monday 4 November, Fawkes went to the vault to check all was well, and there he encountered Suffolk and Monteagle who were searching the palace. Learning that the room's tenant was the gentleman pensioner Percy, they assumed Fawkes was some sort of servant and were not suspicious at the sight of the large pile of brushwood and faggots which concealed the gunpowder. But after remembering that

Percy was a Catholic and asking themselves why he should be renting a vault in Westminster when he had his own house in London, Suffolk and Monteagle agreed a further examination was required. James concurred, reciting one of his maxims: 'either do nothing or else to do that which might make all sure'.[66]

Around 11.00 p.m. that night, the keeper of Whitehall and Westminster palaces, Sir Thomas Knyvett, returned to the room beneath Westminster Hall. There he met Fawkes, booted and spurred, who gave his name as John Johnson. When Fawkes's pockets were emptied, a tinder box, touchwood, and some matches were found. Knyvett immediately arrested him and embarked upon a 'diligent and careful' inspection of the room where he found thirty-six barrels of gunpowder, enough to blow up the entire palace of Westminster and surroundings. Fawkes was taken straight to the Tower to be interrogated, if necessary under torture, for so the king instructed.[67]

Measures were immediately put in place to apprehend Percy who was obviously implicated. A proclamation informing people of the plot and calling for the traitor's capture alive was issued on the 5th. The same day, orders were sent out for the closure of ports to prevent both his escape and the potential arrival of foreign troops.[68] Percy's house in London was also searched.[69] Horrified by the news learned from rumour as well as the proclamation, 'popular feeling' in London was aroused. As reported by the Venetian ambassador: 'Catholics fear heretics, and vice versa; both are armed; foreigners live in terror of their houses being sacked by the mob that is convinced that some, if not all, foreign princes are at the bottom of the plot.'[70] More specifically, William Waad, the lieutenant of the Tower, was worried lest there would be attacks on the Spanish ambassador's lodgings.[71] Nevertheless, all remained calm, and the mood soon turned from anger to relief. In the evening, church bells rang out and bonfires were lit to celebrate the king's deliverance.[72]

The interrogations of Fawkes began immediately, but before torture was applied, he gave out little information, not even his real name.[73] According to one correspondent (who had heard it second or third hand), the prisoner was brought to Whitehall shortly after his arrest to be asked by James 'how he could conspire so hideous a treason against his children and so many innocent souls'. In response, Fawkes allegedly replied: 'that it was true, but a dangerous disease required a desperate remedy'. Then, turning towards the Scottish courtiers, he spat out that 'his intent was to have blown them back into Scotland'.[74] This oft-quoted account, which seems to prove the anti-Scottish dimension of the conspiracy, is somewhat questionable given that Princess Elizabeth's guardian John, Lord Harington of Exton told his cousin the following January: 'His Majesty did sometime desire to see these men, but said he felt himself sorely appall'd at the thought, and so forbare.'[75] Nonetheless, evidence did emerge that the conspirators both hated the Scots and were ready to exploit the general anti-Scottish sentiment in England.[76] The usually well-informed Venetian ambassador heard in December that a paper found among the prisoners' effects listed the houses of the Scots in London; and when questioned, the prisoners admitted: 'it was intended, after the explosion of the mine, to massacre all the Scottish in this country, for they could not submit to the share which their natural enemies now had in the government'.[77] Additionally, according to Fawkes's confession, the proclamation to declare Elizabeth II was 'to have protested agaynst the Union and in noe sort to have meddeled with religion', wording devised to garner broad support for the new regime.[78]

★ ★ ★

The conspirators learned of Fawkes's detention early the same day. The first phase of their plot foiled, they decided to put into operation the second part and raise the Midlands in revolt. Catesby, Percy, and John Wright—closely followed by Rookwood and afterwards Wintour—hastily fled to join Digby, who had arranged to meet local Catholic gentlemen at the Red Lion Inn at Dunchurch, a few miles east of Coventry. The meeting was set up under the guise of a hunting party which might recruit soldiers to fight in a Catholic regiment in the Netherlands. The actual intention, though, was for Digby to persuade the gentlemen and their retainers to march on London, presumably capturing Elizabeth on the way. So, after the hunt on the 5th, Digby told them that a massacre of Catholics was intended in London and they had to forestall the Protestants or perish.[79] Most of the assembled gentlemen, however, were disbelieving. And when Catesby and his friends arrived at the inn shortly after supper with news of the plot's miscarriage and Fawkes's capture, they slipped away.[80] Whether or not they would have joined a Catholic rising had the king been murdered is of course unknown, but almost all refused to join a rebellion with the king alive. Nonetheless, some eighty or so men rode that night to Warwick Castle where they seized ten fresh horses and galloped off to Norbrook, the home of John Grant, another of the original conspirators.

Alerted by the Warwick raid to the whereabouts of the traitors and fearing that 'some great rebellion' was at hand, the earl of Devonshire was appointed 'general' to command a force of 1,200 gentlemen, 'partly English, partly Scottish', to defeat the rebels. However, it soon became apparent that it was not needed. Instead, local authorities—the deputy lord lieutenants, sheriffs, and JPs of the Midland counties—raised troops to maintain order and capture the insurgents.[81] To keep Elizabeth safe, Harington removed her on his own initiative into Coventry, 'a place of farr more safetie', both in respect of its position and 'for the loyall affection' of the citizens.[82]

Over the next two days, the rebels wandered from one Catholic house to another across Warwickshire and Worcestershire, their leaders trying to rouse the shires by declaring themselves for God and the country. When 'one of the country people' said in response that he was for God, the king, and the country, the rebels cried out 'kill him'. No new supporters joined them, many recusants refused assistance, and their force was shrinking through desertions. Servingmen especially were desperate to escape and throw themselves on the king's mercy.[83]

At about 10.00 p.m. on 7 November, the rump of perhaps fourteen men crossed the county border into Staffordshire and reached Holbeach House, the home of the recusant Steven Littleton who had joined the rebels at Dunchurch. By now exhausted, the fugitives were carelessly drying out some damp gunpowder before a fire when it exploded, burning Catesby and Rookwood and blinding Grant. Knowing that they were being followed by government forces, Wright suggested that they throw the rest of the gunpowder on the fire so that 'they might all together be blown up'.[84] But instead they decided to fight. When Wintour—absent at the time of the accident—returned to the house after failing to recruit support, he asked Catesby, Percy, the Wrights, Rookwood, and Grant what they intended to do. 'They answered: "we meane here to dye".'[85] And die most of them did.

The next morning, at about 11.00 a.m., the sheriff of Worcestershire Sir Richard Walsh and his company of trained soldiers attacked Holbeach House. Instead of surrendering, several of the rebels—notably Catesby, Wintour, Percy, and Wright—'did resist' in a last stand.[86] Wintour was shot in the right shoulder as he went into the courtyard and wounded again as he retreated into the house. While the soldiers broke down the door, Wintour stood shoulder to shoulder with Catesby and Percy, brandishing swords in a final gesture of defiance. John Street of Worcester later claimed to have slain Percy, Catesby, and Wright 'at two shootes' and to have hurt Rookwood 'sore beside' with a wound to his right arm, but his account was contradicted by Wintour who maintained in one of his confessions that Wright was killed in the courtyard. The injured Rookwood and Wintour (who was wounded again with a pike struck in his belly) survived and were placed under arrest, but Catesby, Percy, and Wright could not be saved, much to Street's disgust as he had hoped to gain the reward for Percy's capture.[87] Thomas Lawley, who tried to revive the casualties, found that 'their wounds beinge many and grevous, and no surgeon at hande, they became uncurable'. The problem, he explained, was made worse because 'such was the extreame disorder of the baser sorte' that while he 'tooke up one of the languishinge traitors, the rude people stripped the rest naked', not caring for their lives or honour.[88] Although the bodies of the slain were immediately buried, the privy council ordered they should be dug up, disembowelled, and 'their quarters to be sett upp in some principall townes where they most led their life'. The heads of Percy and Catesby were to be sent to London for display.[89]

Over the next days, some twenty-six conspirators were arrested and delivered to London for interrogation and imprisonment.[90] Already incarcerated in the Tower (in addition to Fawkes) were Tresham and Lords Montague, Mordaunt, and Stourton. Another one soon to join them was Northumberland.[91] The commissioners investigating the plot in London suspected him of involvement because of his relationship to Percy. They also conjectured that the plotters had intended to make him lord protector of England during Elizabeth's minority, had their coup been successful. In fact, no direct evidence could be found to implicate the earl, and so he was never brought to trial, merely prosecuted in star chamber on a series of smaller charges.[92]

But was Northumberland the intended lord protector? Of course, a man of high status such as the earl would have been needed to lead a new Catholic government, but the historian Michael Hodgett has identified an intriguing alternative candidate: Catesby's brother-in-law Sir Robert Dudley, the bastard of Robert Dudley, earl of Leicester and Douglas Sheffield. After Dudley had lost his suit in star chamber to claim his family's properties, he was unquestionably disaffected. He was also inclined towards Catholicism.[93] Possibly, therefore, Catesby intended him to assume the leadership of the Midlands rising and become the future protector of the realm. Kenilworth Castle in Warwickshire (which was specifically left to Dudley in his father's will) would have made an excellent base for the rising. But, if that was the plan, it was thwarted, in July 1605, when Dudley abandoned his wife and left the country accompanied by his lover Elizabeth Southwell disguised as his page. His absence, suggests Hodgett, left a huge hole in the conspiracy, which Catesby tried to fill with Digby, whose youth and lack of connections in the Midlands made unsuitable for the role.[94] Whatever the truth, Dudley went on to enjoy freedom and status abroad, whereas Northumberland was condemned to imprisonment during the king's pleasure, remaining in the Tower until June 1621.

★ ★ ★

Over the winter months, the commissioners in London took confessions from the captured conspirators, their wives, servingmen, and lesser folk—innkeepers, carters, barbers—about their interactions with the traitors.[95] Informers passed on the names of people—usually prominent recusants—whom they thought might be involved, and they too were questioned. Many of those interrogated claimed ignorance or else refused to reveal what they knew, but the details of the plot as outlined above can be pieced together from the confessions of the principals. Admittedly, a few admissions might have been extracted under torture, but the confessions are generally consistent with each other. The belief of a few historians that the fullest ones—especially those of Thomas Wintour—were forgeries or at least tampered with has been persuasively rebutted by Mark Nicholls.[96] His 'clinching proof' is the frustration of the interrogators that Wintour and almost all the other key conspirators 'obstinately' refused 'to be accusors' of the priests no matter 'what torture soever they be putt to'. Nicholls also correctly dismisses the allegation that Cecil fabricated the plot through his *agents provocateurs* with the aim of damaging the priests. If this had been the secretary's underhand plan, why did more than a month pass before the government began the hunt for Garnet and other prominent Jesuits?[97]

Most of the lay conspirators denied that the priests 'knew any thing in particular' and refused to implicate them in the plot.[98] Nevertheless, it became obvious to privy councillors that priests were involved. Fawkes admitted that Gerard had given the sacrament to the conspirators to 'performe their vowe' of secrecy, although the priest did not know its purpose.[99] Similarly, other conspirators affirmed that they had received the sacrament as they travelled on the run between safe houses, even though they denied that the priests knew about the treason. Only Thomas Bates (Catesby's yeoman retainer) admitted that he had confessed the 'very daungerous peece of work' to a priest, who was named Greenway (an alias for Fr Oswald Tesimond) and had been given absolution because the slaughter 'was for a good cause'.[100]

By mid-January 1606, the government knew enough for the king to order the arrest of three Jesuits: Garnet, Gerard, and Tesimond.[101] The latter two escaped abroad, but Garnet hid first in Coughton Court and then Hindlip Hall near Worcester, from where he wrote a letter to the privy council denying any involvement in the plot.[102] On 27 January, after an eight-day search of Hindlip, Garnet was found concealed in a cramped and foul-smelling priest's hole together with another Jesuit, Edward Oldcorne. Two lay brothers, Nicholas Owen and Ralph Ashley, were captured in the same house when they tried to escape. On 6 February, the prisoners were brought down to London for interrogation.[103]

On the very same day as Garnet was taken, eight of the surviving conspirators were put on trial at Westminster Hall. Seven of them—Fawkes, the Wintour brothers, Grant, Rookwood, Bates, and Robert Keyes (who had looked after the gunpowder)—pleaded not guilty and were tried together that morning. Digby, who pleaded guilty, was tried separately later the same day. Tresham was not one of their number because he had already died in the Tower, seemingly of natural causes.[104] Both trials were a public spectacle with people paying to sit or stand in the public enclosure. The king and queen watched the proceedings from a private space. Given the considerable public interest, an anonymous writer and the printer John Windet saw an opportunity to make money by producing a narrative of the trial and description of the men's later execution.[105]

The chief prosecutor was Attorney General Coke, who was intent on drawing 'certain comparisons' between the 'Powder Treason' and the Bye and Main Plots in order to demonstrate the evil purposes of all Catholics, whether laymen, Jesuits, or appellants. All these men, pronounced Coke, were 'joined in the end like Sampson's foxes' [a reference to Judges 15:4]. Most of the prisoners said little at the trial, but Digby spoke at some length of his motives in joining the treason: 'the friendship and love' he bore Catesby; 'the cause of religion'; James's broken promises to Catholics; and the fear of 'harder laws from this parliament against recusants'. Not allowing criticisms of James to stand unchallenged, Coke immediately dismissed the prisoner's claim that the king had made any promise of religious toleration. Northampton and Cecil then rallied round the king, also pouring scorn on the 'false and scandalous report of some further hope and comfort yielded to the Catholicks for toleration or connivance, before his [James's] coming to the crown'. No-one, said Northampton, knew better than he that before his accession James had made absolutely patent his intention 'to bind all subjects in one kingdom to one law concerning the religion established'. The king, went on Northampton, had left men in no doubt of his 'constancy' in upholding the religion of his youth. Cecil too spoke out to defend the king's honour and clear James from 'all imputation and scandal of irresolution in religion'. As to be expected, the jury 'stayde not longe' in convicting the accused.[106]

Three days later, on Thursday 30 January, four of the prisoners—Digby, Robert Wintour, Grant, and Bates—were taken from the Tower and drawn on traitors' hurdles through streets lined with guards towards Paul's Churchyard. On the scaffold, the condemned men each said a few words, crossed themselves, and recited some Latin prayers, before they were hanged, drawn, and quartered. The next day, it was the turn of the others. This time the scaffold was erected within the Old Palace Yard at Westminster, not far from the parliament house they intended to destroy. In their very short speeches, all but Keyes apologized for their offence. All of them died as Catholics, Rookwood praying for the conversion of the king. Fawkes was so 'weak with torture and sickness' that he was barely able to climb up to the scaffold. Perhaps taking pity on him, the hangman helped hang him high, allowing the fall to break his neck and sparing him the excruciating pain of disembowelment.[107]

The executions over, the seven privy councillors investigating the plot now turned their attention to the two Jesuits captured on 27 January. Imprisoned in adjacent cells in the Tower, the priests were deliberately allowed to communicate through a hatch, which they mistakenly thought was unnoticed by the gaolers. 'Brought into a foole's paradise', they had 'divers conferences' which were overheard by '2 most skilfull men in all tongues'. By this ruse, the government ascertained that Garnet had received 'intelligence of the Gunpowder treason in confession', a key element in the charge against him.[108] To obtain an explicit admission, he was examined twenty-three times and possibly put to the rack. Eventually, on 8 March, he owned up to his advance knowledge of the plot but explained that he had learned of it under the sacred seal of confession and therefore could not divulge it to the authorities.[109]

On 28 March, Garnet was arraigned in the Guild Hall, charged with conspiring to kill the king and his heir, to stir sedition, and overthrow religion.

The trial, which lasted from 8.00 a.m. until 7.00 p.m., again aroused great public interest. The king attended 'privately'; and noted among the spectators were Lady Arbella, the countess of Suffolk, and other members of the queen's household, though not Anna herself.[110] Representing the crown, Coke sought to prove that Garnet was the author of the plot, involved at every stage in its preparation, and hence more guilty than the actual actors.

Coke's speech was predominantly a diatribe against the pope and the Jesuits. He denounced Garnet as 'a doctor of five Ds', which were 'dissimulation, deposing of princes, disposing of kingdomes, daunting and deterring of subjects, and destruction'. The last four related to papal bulls of excommunication, while dissimulation was thought particular to the Jesuits. Since the 1590s, Protestant propaganda had represented dissimulation or equivocation as a stratagem adopted by Jesuits to advance their evil mission and lie under oath. But, in Garnet's trial, Coke had additional reason to reference equivocation. In Tresham's rooms in the Inner Temple, he had found a 62-page manuscript treatise that gave guidance on how to equivocate. It suggested practices such as using ambiguous words, telling only part of the truth or—more shockingly—applying a mental reservation which might include speaking only part of a sentence out loud and then silently finishing it or adding a qualification in one's head. Jesuits viewed equivocation as essential for survival in a hostile world and no sin in the eyes of God, but Coke labelled it 'simple lying' and 'fearful and damnable blasphemy'.[111]

Garnet pleaded not guilty to the charge of treason and defended himself against all Coke's accusations. He explained that the papal right of deposition did not extend to monarchs born into heresy and was directed only against apostates. In fact, James had been baptized a Catholic, so was technically an apostate, but that was conveniently forgotten. Garnet also upheld the doctrine of equivocation. In relation to the specific charges regarding the plot, he denied his consent to a Spanish invasion, Catholic insurrection, and Catesby's project. However, he admitted foreknowledge. As in the previous trials, Cecil and Northampton had their say. After fifteen minutes' consultation, the jury found the defendant guilty as charged, and the judges sentenced him to death. His execution was delayed until after 3 May, probably because the government still hoped 'to win much out of him'. His fellow Jesuit, Edward Oldcorne, who had been tried in Worcester, was executed there a month earlier alongside three others.

During Garnet's wait, he made several more declarations and statements.[112] He still hoped for a reprieve through the intervention of the Spanish ambassador, but to no avail.[113] He was hanged, drawn, and

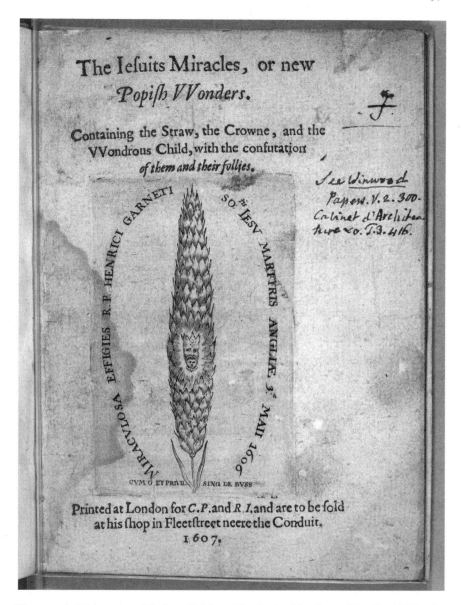

Figure 16. Title page of Robert Pricket, *The Jesuits Miracles, or New Popish Wonders* (1607) © The Huntington Library, San Marino, California.

quartered in Paul's Churchyard, London. In his speech on the scaffold, he denounced the treasonous plot but reiterated his defence that he could not violate the sacred seal of confession. Maybe thanks to the king's order, the hangman lessened Garnet's pain by ensuring he was dead before he was disembowelled.[114] His remains were then dispersed to avoid any gathering of relics, but in vain. Catholics throughout Europe quickly came to venerate an ear of corn on which, it was said, a perfect likeness of the martyr had miraculously appeared from the blood which had spattered on it. For Catholics, it was evidence of the hand of God at work and led to calls for Garnet's beatification; for Protestants, the story was proof of Catholic deceptiveness in creating a forgery to breed superstition.[115] Robert Pricket's book denouncing 'popish' miracles displayed on the title page the miraculous bloodstained ear of wheat with the image of Garnet's face (see Figure 16).[116]

★ ★ ★

Unlike its attempted silence over the Main and Bye Plots, the government sought to publicize and control the narrative of the Gunpowder Treason. From the moment that the plot was detected until the spring of 1606, the king's printer Robert Barker produced texts that provided readers with an official version of the traumatic event. These took various forms: the proclamations ordering the arrest of the traitors; the king's speech before parliament on 9 November; sermons denouncing the plot; and several books detailing the confessions and trials of key conspirators.[117] The ostensible purposes of these publications were to convey gratitude for the plot's discovery and to quell 'divers uncertaine, untrue, and incoherent reports'.[118] But they all went well beyond this remit, for James and his ministers deliberately utilized the event to create mythologizing accounts that enhanced the king's right to the throne and publicized his role as the protector of Protestantism. After the difficulties he had confronted in the 1604 session of parliament, it made good sense to exploit the plot in this way.

One theme emerging in the governmental publications was that the king was a providential, even prophetic, monarch. He was portrayed as the person responsible for perceiving the true nature of the threat which had been hinted at obliquely in the letter to Monteagle. In his speech to parliament, James indulged in self-praise to promote this image:

> wherein a generall obscure advertisement was given of some dangerous blow at this time, I did upon the instant interpret and apprehend some darke phrases

therein, contrary to the ordinary grammer construction of them, (and in another sort then I am sure any divine or lawyer in any universitie would have taken them) to be meant by this horrible forme of blowing us up all by powder, and thereupon ordered that search to be made, whereby the matter was discovered, and the man apprehended.[119]

But it was not just royal wisdom that saved the day. As recorded in *A True and Perfect Relation*, Coke explained how the king had been 'divinely illuminated by Almighty God' to demand the search.[120] The king was therefore characterized here (and indeed elsewhere) as the agent for one of God's 'great deliverances'.

The theme of 'great deliverances' was evident in all governmental writings. James compared the 'great and miraculous delivery' of himself, his parliament, and the 'whole body of this estate' with Noah's preservation from the flood.[121] In a sermon delivered at Paul's Cross on the Sunday following the plot's discovery, Bishop Barlow chose another scriptural analogy. His chosen text came from Psalms 18:50, which allowed him to praise James as a providential king on a par with King David who had received numerous deliverances from God.[122] Neither king nor bishop presented the Gunpowder Treason as the culmination of the Catholic plots attempted under Elizabeth, although Barlow did refer to Catholic regicidal writings during her reign. Instead, James drew a parallel with the Gowrie plot of 1600: 'it pleased God to graunt mee two such notable deliveries upon one day of the weeke, which was Tuesday, and likewise one day of the moneth, which was the fifth; thereby to teach me, that as it was the same devill that still persecuted me'.[123] This correspondence enabled James both to promote the deliverance as personal to himself and to downplay the Catholic nature of the Gunpowder Plot, as the Gowrie conspirators had been Protestants.[124] It was left to Coke and others to bring the Elizabethan Catholic plots into the providential story and tell a deeply anti-Catholic story. Whether in verse or pamphlets, the story was soon told of how God 'saved his anointed'—both Elizabeth and James—'wonderously'.[125]

Like James, many others portrayed the plot as the work of the devil. In his sermon, Barlow branded in vivid terms 'this late horrible treason' as satanic, describing how gunpowder could ignite a fiery hell, and calling Fawkes 'divill of the vault'.[126] The thanksgiving service recited in churches at the time and on the plot's anniversary condemned the 'devilish enterprise' of 5 November.[127] One writer described the pope—the author of the 'treason of all treasons'—as the vicar of the devil, whose triple crown represented murder, treachery, and treason.[128] Letter writers shared this language. When reporting the news to his friend, John Chamberlain labelled the plot a 'develish conspiracie', while the council of Scotland penned thanks for the king's 'happy delyverie frome the abhominable conspiracie so inhumanelie contryved by the devill' and his supporters.[129] The trope of the 'divilish plot' was also taken up in popular verse. Picking up on Barlow's labelling of Fawkes as the 'divell of the vault', IH—possibly John Hynd—entitled his verse by that name and called Catesby and Percy 'hel's blacke fiends'.[130] Meanwhile, a sixteen-year-old scholar from Westminster School imagined Percy and Catesby in hell, deservedly suffering 'the endlesse payne' of punishment for their treason.[131]

While some—possibly most—Protestants believed all Catholics were engaged in the devil's work, since their 'practise is murthering of soules and bodies', James made a distinction between those who accepted the Roman Church's seditious teachings and those who were 'blinded' by erroneous theological doctrines and 'superstitions' yet remained 'good and faithfull subjects'.[132] Cecil followed suit, reiterating the king's pronouncement in parliament that he would not condemn the general for the particular.[133] This attempt to isolate disloyal Catholics had political purposes: to quench Protestant anger against the whole community and so prevent a massacre; and to enable James to keep amity with the Catholic European powers.

For James and others, the most devilish Catholics were the Jesuits. In *A True and Perfect Relation*, Garnet (with a long list of aliases to demonstrate his deceptiveness) was named before the lay conspirators in the indictment, and it was he, Gerard, and Tesimond who were alleged to have persuaded the others that 'all heretiques were accursed' and 'it was lawfull and meritorious' to kill the king and his Protestant subjects.[134] In a speech, reported in *A True and Perfect Relation*, Northampton took Garnet's activities back to 1586 to associate him with other attempts of the pope and their Jesuitical agents to assassinate an English monarch and incite a Spanish invasion.

★ ★ ★

Although conspiracies to murder monarchs were not new to Britain nor the Continent, the Gunpowder Treason was distinct because it intended the 'destruction' of the whole governing class. Nothing like it had ever been attempted before; and it also came within a hair's breadth of success. Rightly called a 'treason without paralell', such as 'the like was never ever heard or read', the plot came to exert a powerful hold on the popular imagination and became the subject of pamphlets, popular ballads, poems, and secular songs.[135] Yet, despite the uniqueness of the event, many of these works echoed Coke in drawing a parallel with the earlier (less serious) Catholic attempts against Elizabeth. Calls were made, too, for 1605 and 1588 to be commemorated as Protestant days of thanksgiving:

> Mongst years let eighty eight bee chroniched
>   Mongst days November fift bee kalendred
> To God let both bee hallowed
>   With hearts and tonges solemnized
> With hymnes and songes eternized.[136]

And, indeed, the commemorations of 1605 usually recalled 1588.[137]

Since the king discouraged plays which featured contemporary monarchs, early Jacobean dramatists alluded to the plot only indirectly. But the allusions would surely have been as obvious to audiences then as they are to literary critics today. As seen in chapter 1, Heywood's *Part 2* looked back at Catholic plots against Elizabeth and the 1588 invasion attempt, while Dekker's *Whore of Babylon* employed an allegorical device to tell its story of Catholic perfidy. Additionally, the plot line of Barnabe Barnes' *The Devil's Charter* (produced at court during the Christmas season of 1606–07)— concerning Pope Alexander VIII's charter with the devil to destroy all powers opposed to his hellish reign—speaks for itself. The language in the play, moreover, conjured up the 1605 Plot by using phrases such as 'arcane plots and intricate designes... to darte downe fire and thunder on their foes' and 'with my lint-stocke gave fire to the traine'.[138]

Shakespeare's *Macbeth* is, in some respects, a Gunpowder play as well. How could spectators at the first performance of *Macbeth* in 1606 not relate the murder of an earlier Scottish king to the recently failed attempt on James's life? Additionally, like Barnes, Shakespeare used words associated with the plot: 'blow', 'combustion', and 'destruction'. At various points in the play, moreover, Garnet's defence of equivocation can be heard; indeed, some scholars have contended that the whole play is about equivocation. Specifically, when opening the castle gate, the Porter declares in Act 2, Scene 2 (lines 8–11): 'Faith, here's an equivocator, that could swear in both the scales against either scale; who committed treason enough for God's sake yet could not equivocate to heaven;' while in Act 4, Scene 2 (lines 44–57), Lady Macduff talks to her son about who should be hanged as a traitor. Nonetheless, unlike Barnes's *The Devil's Charter* and Decker's *Whore of Babylon*, Shakespeare's *Macbeth* is not an anti-Catholic play but rather a meditation on the sources of human evil and the dangers of equivocation; as one literary critic has explained, the play explores the charisma of treason as well as its destructive qualities.[139]

With its emphasis on lying and its depiction of a world of conspiracy in which it is unclear who is telling the truth, Ben Jonson's *Volpone* was probably another indirect response to the Gunpowder Plot. Its puns on the word 'lie' could well have been jokes based on what was known about the 'Treatise of Equivocation'. Like *Macbeth*, it was not anti-Catholic—hardly surprising as Jonson was himself presented for recusancy shortly before the writing and performance of the play in 1606.[140]

Pictures as well as words reminded people of the plot. Free-standing engravings of the conspirators were printed on the Continent, reflecting the international fascination with the plot. The famous group portrait of eight conspirators was produced in two impressions with information provided in Latin or German. The same group portrait was reproduced in a broadside

Figure 17. A broadside on the Gunpowder Plot (1606), British Museum 1848,0911.451 © The Trustees of the British Museum.

containing three more scenes which depicted the traitors drawn on wicker hurdles by horses, their bodies dismembered on the scaffold, and their heads on spikes; the text here was mainly in German but included French and Latin (see Figure 17).

Thomas Percy was given a print of his own, also apparently for the foreign market as the text was in German and Latin.[141] Nor was Henry Garnet forgotten. Entitled *Princeps Proditorum* [Leader of the Traitors], a woodcut represents him holding the pope's pardon; and beneath his figure are two columns of six verses in English accusing him and the pope of the abhorrent doctrine of equivocation.[142]

The first English printed image of the plot still in existence was published in 1612 and is complex in its imagery (see Figure 18). The broadside, 'The Papists' Powder Treason', is in the form of a triumphal arch decorated with tableaux, plaques, and allegorical figures. In the centre above the arch is the plaque inscribed 'Jacob's stone erected in aeternal memorie of the divine bountie in England's preservation from ye hellish pouder plot intended for the blowinge up of ye parliament howse, 1605'. On its left side are the kneeling figures of James, Henry, and Charles; and on the right are Anna and Elizabeth. In the lower margin are ten stanzas of a poem.[143]

Other surviving English prints date from the next decade. Although equally complex in their iconography, they all emphasize the plot's devilish nature and providential outcome in response to the specific political contexts of the time.[144]

Other than prints and church memorials, few material objects serving as commemorations of the plot have survived. One, though, is a medal in silver and bronze that was struck in Holland but circulated in England. The front face depicts a snake among lilies and roses, symbolizing Jesuit intrigue and deception. The inscription reads 'DETECTVS. QVI. LATVIT. S.C.' [He, who concealed himself, is detected. By order of the senate of Holland]. The reverse bears the tetragrammaton [the name of God in Hebrew letters] in a circle of thorns, with an inscription paraphrasing Psalm 121: 'NON DORMITASTI ANTISTES IACOBI' [You (i.e. God), the keeper of James, have not slept].[145] One other surviving material object of interest is an ornamental marble plaque set around 1608 into a wall of the council chamber in the Tower where prisoners were generally interrogated. Along its top are the chiselled and painted coats of arms of Chief Justice Popham and the eight privy councillors who oversaw the interrogations of the plotters, while the arms of Coke and William Waad, lieutenant of the Tower, are situated on

Figure 18. 'The Papists' Powder Treason' © Lambeth Palace Library, London.

the left-hand and right-hand pilasters respectively. A Latin inscription in the central panel testifies to the 'perfidious and serpentine impiety' of the conspirators and their accomplices, whose names are listed in a panel below. On the same wall as the monument is a portrait of James, the two working together to remind later prisoners how monarchs punished traitors.[146]

The long-term memory of the plot was kept alive less by the immediate media responses than by the annual thanksgiving services and celebrations on its anniversary. As ordered by the king and authorized by parliament, the day was treated as a 'red-letter' holiday throughout Britain and marked by a special morning service of thanksgiving with a set form of prayers and sometimes a special sermon which harped on Britain's deliverance and preservation from papal plots. To celebrate the deliverance, many parishes paid for the pealing of church bells, lighting of bonfires (*feux de joie*), public drinking, or solemn processions. This commemoration of 5 November continued for more than two centuries, fuelled by specific moments of anti-Catholicism.[147] It was not until 1859 that the statute establishing the religious service on the anniversary was eventually revoked in parliament and by royal warrant.

★ ★ ★

Despite his later reputation for cowardice, James reacted to the plot with considerable aplomb. Understandably, his immediate reaction was to retreat into his bedchamber but, before the month was out, he decided to leave London with a few trusted companions 'for his usual amusement of the chase', thereby ignoring the advice of his wife and councillors who feared he would be exposed to an assassination attempt outside his palace. He was 'resolved', reported the Venetian ambassador, 'to rely on the divine mercy and to place his pleasure above his peril'.[148] James remained in the country till Christmas and, on his return to Whitehall, participated in the usual revels as if nothing had happened.[149]

Immediately upon the capture of Fawkes, the king demanded that every servant in his and the queen's household should take the oath upholding the royal supremacy over all spiritual and temporal 'things or cawses' and denying papal authority and jurisdiction in England.[150] But it was evident to many that more was needed to safeguard the king and the realm. When parliament resumed on 21 January 1606, the dominant emotion of MPs was fervently anti-Catholic. While some agreed with Sir Francis Bacon that the older generation of 'papists' were 'rather superstitious than seditious', parliament nonetheless enacted two new statutes that struck at the entire community of recusants and semi-conformists.[151] One of them—'to prevent and avoid dangers which grow by popish recusants'—restricted further their right to travel, bear arms, or enter the professions. They were barred from law and medicine, could not take a degree in the universities, nor become officers in the militia or navy. Convicted recusants were also ordered to leave London and its precincts. To prevent a new generation of recusants growing up, their children had to be baptized and attend services in the Church of England or else their parents would face a £100 fine.[152]

The other statute explicitly blurred the distinction between loyal and seditious Catholics for it warned that all those who 'adhere in their hearts to the popish religion' could easily be infected to execute 'treasonable conspiracies and practices'. Seeking to penalize all those who were 'popishly affected', the statute imposed heavy fines on occasional conformists who did not attend church regularly, or for the whole service, or receive communion every year. The penalty for not receiving communion was £20 in the first year, £40 in the second, and £60 in the third year and thereafter. As for hardened recusants, instead of paying a regular fine of £20 a month in lieu of attending services, they were now subjected to the confiscation of two-thirds of their property 'till every such offender shall conform him or herself respectively'. Recusant wives would be imprisoned until their husband paid the fine; if widowed, they would lose their right to two-thirds of their jointure [inheritance] and right to share in their late husband's goods. Masters and mistresses were to be responsible for ensuring that their servants attended services on pain of a fine of £10 a month. Some of these clauses went considerably further than Elizabethan statutes, which had held back from insisting upon Catholics taking communion.[153]

Part and parcel of this statute was another novelty: the imposition of an oath of allegiance on all known recusants and semi-conformists over the age of eighteen.[154] The oath came into operation on 22 June 1606. The penalty for refusing it was imprisonment until it was tendered again; a second refusal would incur a charge of *praemunire* [the offence of asserting or assisting papal jurisdiction in England], which would result in the loss of all property and imprisonment at the king's pleasure. A simple oath of allegiance to the king might have been acceptable to most Catholics; many were also prepared to repudiate the pope's power to depose a sovereign. However, this oath required the taker to 'abhorre, detest, and abjure' the 'damnable doctrine' of the papal deposing power 'as impious and heretical'. This was far more difficult for Catholics to swallow, first, because they believed that it was beyond the competence of secular powers to judge what was heresy and, second, because the words touched upon the spiritual power of the pope and amounted to 'denyenge the aucthoritie and power of the Churche', which was a matter of faith.[155] Furthermore, unlike the 1559 oath of supremacy, the

1606 oath did not allow for any casuistry or ambiguity because the swearer had to 'subscribe his name unto the othe' and confirm that it had been taken 'without any equivocation, or mental evasion, or secret reservation whatsoever'.[156] Loopholes were thereby closed.[157]

The exact purpose of the oath is unclear, and historians have offered variant possibilities. Should we take James at his word when he claimed to be simply separating the disloyal minority of Catholics from moderates who gave him their allegiance while living as recusants?[158] Or did the oath have the greater purpose of seeking to assert the king's sovereignty and increase royal control over his Catholic subjects?[159] Or was the oath actually a subtle policy of divide and rule, intended mainly to drive a wedge between those Catholics prepared to take the oath in return for some toleration and hardliners who would not?[160] Historians are divided on this issue.

Undeniably, the oath reflected James's belief in the divine right of kings—how could a pope depose a sovereign appointed by God?—and James took advantage of the Gunpowder Plot to call himself again God's lieutenant and demand total obedience from his Catholic subjects. Almost certainly, the oath's timing arose because the plot reignited in James's mind concerns about papal claims and doubts about Catholic loyalty. Less convincing, though, are the king's professions of moderation. The statutory measures introduced in 1606 were restrictive and severe on all Catholics, not just those who refused the oath. Besides, taking the oath did not protect nonconforming Catholics from the recusancy laws, especially after 1610 when a higher level of enforcement was implemented as a kneejerk reaction to the assassination of Henry IV of France.[161] In 1610, moreover, James ordered that all recusants—whether or not they took the oath—should be excommunicated and those excommunicated should not have a Christian burial.[162] In practice, the oath was sometimes treated as a supplement to the recusancy laws. Alarmed by the 'multitude of recusants' in his diocese, Robert Bennet, bishop of Hereford, urged Ralph Lord Eure, lord president of the council of Wales, 'to minister unto them the oath of allegiance, hoping thereby, if they be not reduced to conformitie, yet should be restrayned from theire publique assemblies and generall conventicles, and more feared from intertayning of preests'.[163]

Possibly, James imagined that all Catholics bar the extremist few would conform and had no expectation that the oath would be divisive. However, whether intended or not, the oath did indeed split the English Catholic community. All Catholics experienced the oath as a crisis of conscience:

since oaths were sacrosanct, they would endanger their souls if they took it; but, if they refused, they risked a charge of treason. Not all made the same choice, but the majority succumbed. The then head of English Catholics, George Blackwell, took and defended the oath from London's Clink prison; likewise, the Benedictine monk, Thomas Preston, published works defending the oath after initially opposing it.[164] Under huge pressure, many lay Catholics also caved in: the staunch recusant Lady Stonor, for example, swore the oath in 1612 after two previous refusals.[165] In the North Riding of Yorkshire, fifty-six (thirteen of them gentry) took the oath compared to twenty-four (four gentry) who refused.[166] Some recusants swore the oath after JPs in their area allowed it to be taken with some kind of qualification.[167]

A small minority of Catholic priests and laypeople stayed firm in their refusal, ignoring the threat of execution.[168] Eighteen priests were condemned to death under James for refusing the oath, some of whom were Jesuits, some secular priests, and four missionary Benedictines (of whom three were executed, while the other died in prison). Several had refused to take the oath because it contained matters of faith but offered to swear to the section 'which only contains allegiance to my sovereign'.[169] As another Catholic explained, if the oath had concerned only 'temporal allegeaunce,... no true English subjecte, being offred the same but would take it hartelie and willinglie'. But given that the oath contained contested points of doctrine, how could any person 'safely sweare that thinge to be true which is doubtfull and questionable'? Cleverly, the objector also made the point: 'the oath beinge tendred under great penaltie to the refuser, how can anie man truelie sweare that he doeth take yt hartelie and willinglie?'[170] Lay gentry who refused the oath were usually treated more lightly. Gentlemen like William Vavasour lost their freedom and property but not their lives. Some gentry who refused the oath avoided the harshest punishment by paying a substantial fine as a pardon or a bribe; an unknown number went into hiding or travelled from house to house to evade taking the oath.[171]

★ ★ ★

Those who refused the oath were following the directives of Pope Paul V who issued *brevi* in 1606 and 1607 proscribing the oath on grounds of doctrine and admonishing any who swore it.[172] Robert and Cardinal Robert Bellarmine, the leading Jesuit theologian, also unequivocally condemned the oath and criticized Blackwell for his surrender. Deeply offended by their interventions, James began to prepare a reply that justified the oath. Helped by Dean Montagu, he worked on it while they were at Royston in December 1607. The next February, the king's quarto book of 112 pages, entitled *Triplici Nodo, Triplex Cuneus:* ['A triple wedge for a triple knot'] *or An Apologie for the Oath of Allegiance*, went into print. No author of the book was named, but the royal coat of arms was stamped opposite its first page, so few had any doubt about who had written it. Anyway, Latin and French translations were afterwards given to foreign ambassadors, who were told that James 'did not wish his name to appear for reasons which he would subsequently explain'.[173]

Preserving anonymity, the king's argument was presented in the third person. The speaker in the text argued that the oath had been misunderstood by its critics for its purpose was to demand civil obedience not religious conformity. Indeed, the oath—stated the speaker—was conceived as a favour to Catholics who did not want to be regarded as traitors in the aftermath of the Gunpowder Plot. It was the pope not the king who was telling Catholics to choose between their faith and their 'naturall obedience' to their sovereign. Although the king was concerned to obtain his subjects' civil rather than spiritual obedience, the speaker nevertheless defended the king's right to enter the spiritual domain. Injunctions could be found in scripture, he declared, that 'subjects are bound to obey their princes for conscience sake, whether they were good or wicked princes'.[174]

James's intervention ignited a pamphlet war between the king and Continental Catholics which gave rise to over 150 publications on the issue circulating throughout Europe.[175] Questions surrounding the spiritual and political authority of the pope were of pan-European interest, not least because of a dispute that had exploded in late 1605 between Paul V and Venice over ecclesiastical jurisdiction, privileges, and property. To bring the Italian republic into line, the pope, in the spring of 1606, imposed an interdict prohibiting all religious rites and services on Venice. Venice reacted by banning papal bulls, expelling the Jesuits, and ordering the clergy to carry out their religious duties anyway. Rome poured out anti-Venetian propaganda, and Venice responded in kind. While posing as a neutral mediator, Henry IV of France supported the pope, although his ambassador to Venice and Gallicans in the Sorbonne opposed papal pretensions. Philip III also backed the pope and deployed a large army to northern Italy in case military force was needed to obtain Venice's submission. The dispute was, however, soon settled without resort to arms. Nonetheless, issues relating to papal power and authority were still raw. So, while Venetian and Protestant writers leapt to James's defence, Rome saw James's appropriation of spiritual power as a dangerous precedent that had to be resisted. This was why Persons and Bellarmine entered the polemical fray in 1608.[176]

Persons's reply to James in 1608 was directed to English Catholics with the aim of encouraging unity against the oath, whereas Bellarmine, writing in Latin, addressed his response to the international scholarly community.[177] It was Bellarmine's text, written under a pseudonym, which particularly 'disturbed' James, but not so much because of the force of the cardinal's theological arguments as because of the personal attack on his integrity. In the *Responsio* (1608), Bellarmine revealed and quoted from a letter James had sent to Clement VIII, in 1599, in which the king had used the styles of the pope's title and recommended a Scottish-born Catholic bishop to be appointed a cardinal. Furious at the insinuation that he had previously recognized papal authority and understanding that his reputation as 'an honest man' was at stake, the king accused Lord Balmerino, his secretary of state in Scotland, of forging his signature on the letter, an act of treason. James's name was ostensibly cleared, in October 1608, when Balmerino confessed that he had surreptitiously placed the letter 'wherewith your Majestie is falslie taxed' among others for signing in an 'abuse of your Majestie's trust'. Almost certainly, Balmerino was covering for his sovereign, and, perhaps for this reason, the death sentence pronounced at his trial in March 1609 was commuted to one of house arrest for life. True or not, the affair 'was causing much talk' in London and seems to have reinforced James's reputation for duplicity.[178]

Meanwhile, James called on Lancelot Andrewes to answer Bellarmine's *Responsio* in a Latin treatise for the international scholarly community. Concurrently, he made ready to republish the *Triplici Nodo* with a new title and under his own name.[179] At Christmas 1608, he gathered theologians around him as he went through revisions to the text and brought in the classical scholar Sir Henry Savile to help with the Latin version. By the spring, while at Theobalds, James was said to be 'so wholy possest' with his book that till it 'be finished to his liking, he can brooke no other sport nor business'.[180] First issued in April, it had to be recalled because of errors; only after revision by four bishops was it finally printed in May 1609.[181] By then, if not before, James was fully aware of the theological and political implications of the oath in the European context and had decided to make an appeal to both Protestant and Catholic princes to join him against the pope.

For this purpose, he composed a lengthy introduction, called a *Premonition*, which was dedicated to Emperor Rudolph II and told all Christian princes that his cause was also theirs: 'the cause is generall, and concerneth the authoritie and priviledge of kings in generall, and all supereminent temporall powers'. All princes, James warned, should consider 'what a feather he [Bellarmine] pulls out of your wings when he denudeth you of so many subjects and their possessions in the pope's favour'. As for the pope, he was the Antichrist unless he renounced 'medling with princes in any thing belonging to their temporall jurisdiction'. Princes, he suggested, should consider holding a general council to reunite Christendom, one from which both Jesuits and Puritans would be debarred.[182]

James's book was well received in England among Protestants, especially Puritans: 'all sorts that have yt or heare of yt doe embrace yt', reported a Northamptonshire gentleman who believed approval of the royal stand against the pope made it easier for him to collect the subsidy in his county.[183] But foreign rulers were the readers whom James was targeting. He arranged for deluxe copies to be presented as royal gifts to both Catholic and Protestant rulers of Europe. The most elaborate of these quarto volumes were bound in crimson velvet, edged with gold lace, and with 'corner-pieces of solid gold stamped with the rose, the thistle, the lion, and the lilies'. Where there was no resident ambassador on site to hand over the book, James sent out special envoys to deliver a presentation copy: the Scottish poet Robert Ayton, a gentleman of the privy chamber, took it to Protestant German princes; the Catholic John Barclay was the envoy to Emperor Rudolph, the king of Hungary, and the Catholic dukes of Bavaria, Lorraine, Savoy and Tuscany; a third Scot was dispatched to deliver it to the kings of Denmark and Poland; and a fourth to Sweden.[184] It was not unusual for a king to offer a printed polemical work to another ruler, but it was very unusual for the gift to be distributed simultaneously to a large number of European rulers and for it to be authored by the donor king.[185]

The Protestant princes accepted the book enthusiastically. Welcoming James as defender of the Christian faith and protector of the 'true Church', they no doubt hoped that he would now join their newly formed political league, the Protestant Union.[186] The response of the Catholic powers was either ambivalent or downright hostile since the pope had prohibited the reading of the book upon pain of excommunication.[187] The doge of Venice took his copy ceremoniously as a royal gift and 'proof of the continuance of that good-will' which James had always shown the republic. Its government, however, had no intention of disobeying the pope, and so the doge deposited the book unread in the public archives and banned its publication within Venetian territories. This provoked the ire of the English ambassador Sir Henry Wotton, who declared it 'a downright offence' and carried 'a graver injury than the favour implied by accepting it'. James, though, was more sanguine about the matter and was careful not to let it disturb his good relations with the republic.[188] Henry IV also accepted his copy of the book, even though he said James would have done better to have remained silent, but he too had no intention of offending the pope. He consequently told the papal nuncio that he was bound to accept a gift from a friend but had not read the book and simply passed it over to theologians.[189]

Neither the archdukes nor the Spanish king would take their copies. Two hours before the English ambassador Thomas Edmondes was due to see Archduke Albert on his return to Brussels and hand over James's gift, he was notified that his audience would be cancelled if he intended to present the book 'in respect there was so much spoken therein against the pope and the doctrine of their Church'. Edmondes showed his annoyance at the rebuff by cancelling the audience, thereby restoring the honour balance between the archdukes and the king.[190] Likewise, the English ambassador to Spain, Charles Cornwallis, was told in no uncertain terms that Philip III 'would never receive, much less give reading to any book containing matter derogatory' to his religion or the papacy. Cornwallis tried to explain that the book did not deal with matters of faith but only with papal claims which affected all rulers, but he made no headway.[191] Somewhat later, the king's envoy to Savoy could not, 'in spite of reiterated efforts', succeed in making the duke take the book.[192] Even worse, the emperor refused the envoy an audience.[193]

James's book was far from ending the controversy. Because polemicists and their sponsors were determined to leave no attack unanswered, writings for or against the arguments contained in the book persisted in England and on the Continent for several years. By the end of 1610, James's own book had appeared in multiple languages in at least twenty editions.[194] German, Flemish, Spanish, and Dutch theologians also entered the debate. But having ignited it, James decided not to take up his pen again (or at least not until 1616 when he produced the *Remonstrance for the Right of Kings*).[195] Instead, he sponsored and helped finance the foundation of Chelsea College, in 1609, for the very purpose of 'handling controversies in religion' and producing anti-Roman Catholic tracts.[196] With the murder of Henry IV in 1610, attacks on papal powers were given a new lease of life for Jesuit justifications of tyrannicide were believed to have inspired the assassin.[197]

One of the English authors who contributed to the controversy was John Donne, who is more famous today for his poetry. His prose work *Pseudo-Martyr*, printed in January 1610, defended the oath of allegiance and affirmed that those who refused to take it could not be deemed religious martyrs since the oath concerned only temporal, not spiritual, matters.[198] Many literary critics have viewed this endorsement of the oath as part of Donne's obsessive quest for advancement in royal service.[199] And, indeed, there was much in *Pseudo-Martyr* to please the king: Donne dedicated the work to him in words adapted from the queen of Sheba to King Solomon; he lavished praise on the king's writings; and he presented scriptural arguments in support of Catholics taking the oath. Yet, as some scholars have come to appreciate, there was a more serious intellectual intent behind Donne's scholarly defence of James's policy, whether it was to explore matters of conscience or questions related to sovereignty.[200] Unlike many other Protestant polemicists who entered the debate, Donne avoided language that vilified Catholics. A convert to Protestantism, he was sympathetic to the Catholic dilemma.

The tracts relating to the allegiance controversy began to die down after 1614, although several works continued to be published as late as 1620. The long pamphlet war exposed and heightened the religious and political tensions throughout Europe as well as in England. It was not just that Europe was split into rival Churches but also that Catholics in many states were divided among themselves over the extent and nature of papal powers. Some historians have seen James as the voice of moderation amidst the extremists on all sides of these debates but, although his rhetoric was sometimes more inclusive, he was little different from other European rulers who tried to impose confessional conformity on their states and marginalize—even persecute—Catholics and Puritans who would not obey the Established Church.

★ ★ ★

Henry IV's assassination made life still more difficult for English Catholics. The commons, in 1610, petitioned the lords to agree to measures 'for safety of his Majestie's person, preservatioun of the state, and better observation of the lawes now in force'.[201] James, equally concerned about his safety, implemented the parliamentary recommendations in a proclamation of 2 June. Around the same time, a house-to-house search for Jesuits and seminarians was ordered in London and southern towns, principally in recusants' properties; once caught, the priests were to be banished.[202] The following year, James spoke 'very earnestly and sharply' against those lords who harboured priests with intent to kill him and instructed JPs and bishops to administer the oath of allegiance to Catholics again. His promotion of George Abbot—the most junior bishop on the bench—to succeed Bancroft at Canterbury was made in part because, as bishop of Coventry and Lichfield, he had shown himself to be indefatigable in policing Catholic priests and laity.[203] And, indeed, the archbishop soon renewed pressure on recusants: Lord Montagu, Lord Vaux, and his mother Lady Vaux, for example, were imprisoned for refusing the oath of allegiance.[204] Recusancy fines were more rigorously collected: one estimate is that, between 1606 and 1612, the annual sum from fines was no more than £10,000 but that, by 1614, it had increased to £24,000 a year.[205]

James's attitude and policy towards Catholics differed little from that of his predecessor. It is true that far more priests and laypeople were executed under Elizabeth than under James; the Catholic Church recognizes twenty-five martyrs between 1604 and 1618 as against 189 martyrs between 1570 and 1603.[206] But the pope had not excommunicated James and called for his deposition as he had Elizabeth in a bull which Jesuits brought to England. Moreover, in the 1580s and 1590s, England was at war against Catholic Spain, and the priests and their harbourers were believed to be a fifth column for England's enemies. Officially at peace with all the Catholic powers, the king did not want to incite them into a crusade against him by persecuting their co-religionists.

It is also true that the crown's income from recusancy fines nosedived in the first few years of James's reign, never to recover fully. However, historians now realize that this occurred only in part because of the king's leniency. At least as important were two other circumstances: first, some Catholic gentlemen slipped into occasional conformity to avoid paying fines; and second, exchequer officials sometimes preferred to compound with convicted recusants to obtain a steadier, if somewhat smaller, revenue stream.[207]

Both monarchs associated allegiance to the pope with treason, although it was the 1606 oath that first connected the two in law. They both claimed to be tolerant in matters of conscience, not seeking windows into their subjects' souls, and they were indisputably more concerned about the political implications of loyalty to the pope than the spiritual dangers arising from erroneous matters of faith. Like Elizabeth, James protected individual recusants and was criticized in some quarters for insufficient rigour towards them.[208] Both monarchs honoured those recusant and semi-conforming nobles and gentry who were patently not involved in conspiracies by visiting their homes, allowing them at court, or permitting them promotions. Pauline Croft has shown how the Jacobean regime 'consciously' encouraged some leading Catholic gentry families to buy the title of baronet.[209] The monarchs were not alone in such leniency. During both reigns, many Protestants shielded their Catholic kin, clients, and neighbours who were not considered marginal or troublemakers by helping them get round many of the discriminatory laws and, in some cases, allowing them to hold onto local offices and sit as JPs.[210] Social status and connections frequently trumped religious affiliation. Furthermore, there were those who believed in showing charity to their Catholic neighbours, people like Shakespeare's son-in-law, the Puritan physician John Hall, who gave his services to Catholics and Protestants alike in his religiously divided community.[211]

Nonetheless, the overall Catholic experience under James during the first half of his reign was as difficult as it had been under Elizabeth. Fines had to be paid; their homes were periodically searched for priests and arms; and they often faced harassment by JPs. No wonder recusants were disappointed and angry at the lack of change. Only when negotiations for a marriage between Prince Charles and the infanta Maria Anna of Spain became serious, in the early 1620s, did Catholics have a brief respite from fines, but this Spanish match and fears of toleration aroused such fervent anti-Catholicism that it rocked political stability.

13

Union and Empire

Unlike the previous two chapters which reveal continuities, this one argues for change. Although the idea of an Anglo-Scottish Union did not come out of the blue, James's attempt to create a Union after 1603 was so controversial that for a time it replaced the Elizabethan succession issue as a major cause of conflict between monarch and commons. By 1607, the Union project had pretty much failed in parliament, but James's efforts to bring his two realms closer together set in motion tensions that lasted throughout the reign and beyond. In England, there was not only disquiet about an imagined flood of Scots moving south but also a suspicion of the political ideas James articulated during the Union debates. In Scotland, there was political resistance (mainly unsuccessful) when James brought English practices into the Kirk and an armed rising in 1639 when Charles I attempted to introduce a new prayer book into his northern realm. Multiple kingdoms were common in Europe but also very difficult to manage, as the revolt of the Netherlands had already demonstrated in the late sixteenth century and the revolts of Catalonia and Portugal were to do in 1640.[1]

James of course also inherited the kingdom of Ireland in 1603. Although he had no intention of absorbing that realm into his new political union, his rule there differed from that of his predecessor in one crucial respect, largely resulting from the Union project. Whereas Elizabeth had tried to keep the Scots out of Ireland, James encouraged them to settle there in the new plantations established in the north. The ongoing Scottish immigration was to change the cultural and religious landscape of Ulster and ultimately differentiate it from the rest of Ireland.

England's colonization of America effectively began under James. The imperial ambitions of Jacobeans in the New World were no different from those of Elizabethans; what was different was their actualization. Despite a shaky start, a settlement became well established at Jamestown and soon was followed by the foundation of further colonies in Virginia, New England, and the West Indies. Initially left behind in the scramble for colonies, England under the Stuarts came to rival the Dutch and French in their expansion into the Americas.

For all these reasons, James's accession in 1603 should be seen as a key date in both British and imperial history. Under its Scottish king, England retained its political independence, but it acquired a new appellation (Great Britain), a new relationship with Scotland, a new (shared) plantation in Ireland, and new Atlantic colonies. These developments, all of which began during the first decade of his reign, are the subject of this chapter.

★ ★ ★

Even before Elizabeth died, James had hinted at his desire to unite England and Scotland in more than just a union of crowns. The two nations, he wrote in *Basilikon Doron*, were 'both but one Ile of Britaine and alreadie joined in unitie of religion and language', so despite previous Anglo-Scottish wars 'the uniting and welding of them hereafter in one by all sorts of friendship, commerce, and alliance' would 'produce and maintain a naturall and inseparable unitie of love amongst them'.[2] Once James was proclaimed king of England, he immediately repeated this aspiration. In his first proclamation in Scotland after his accession was announced, he declared that his two crowns were 'now unitid and incorporat' and that his two peoples should 'conjoine thameselffis as ane [one] natioun under his Majestie's authoritie'.[3] Then on 3 April, when bidding Scotland farewell, he affirmed that his two realms would now be 'joined in wealth, in religion, in hearts, and affections'.[4]

James immediately took steps to make Union a reality, starting with the appointment of Scots to the English privy council, privy chamber, and household offices.[5] He also inched it forward in three proclamations directed at his English subjects. The first of 8 April established the relative value of Scottish and English coins as a primary stage in bringing the two currencies into line. Scottish coins were to be legal tender in England, with the relative value of £12 Scots to £1 English.[6] A second proclamation of 19 May dismantled the frontier between England and Scotland, renaming the borderlands as the 'middle shires', and gave notice that legislation would soon be introduced into parliament for the Union 'to be perfited'.[7] In the third proclamation of 8 July, James simply declared his 'equall affection' for each of his kingdoms and his determination 'to be an universall and equall sovereign to them both'.[8]

Issuing royal proclamations, however, was hardly likely to persuade his English subjects of the benefit of Union. On the contrary, using prerogative powers seemed a threat to the authority of parliament and looked like arbitrary rule. In some quarters, it was even seen as amounting to an act of conquest, comparable to that of the Normans in 1066, since—according to English legal thought—the only authority which could change law without consent was that of conquest.[9]

James publicized the Union project visually too. His first great seal contained the arms of Scotland and (for the first time) of Ireland, while its legend told of the Union of the three realms under one king and the end of ancient feuds between England and Scotland.[10] His silver accession and coronation medals, which depicted him as a Roman emperor wearing a toga and crowned with laurel, acclaimed him in Latin as 'Emperor of the whole island of Britain and king of France and Ireland' (the former) and as 'Caesar Augustus of Britain, Caesar the heir of the Caesars' (the latter).[11] James also signalled the Union in the hat badge he wore in life and in many of his early portraits. The 'greate and riche jewell' of five main stones was called the 'Mirror of Great Britain', although whether many knew of this is questionable.[12] However, on the new issue of coins (21 May 1603) James was entitled king of England and Scotland separately, and he had to wait a year before the second issue made a change to his title and introduced a legend signifying Union.

★ ★ ★

James's vision of an Anglo-Scottish Union was not new. As early as 1521, John Mair of Haddington, a Scottish professor of philosophy and theology in Paris, made the case for a dynastic union in which neither kingdom would subdue the other and their joint ruler would be called king of Britain.[13] Then in 1547, the Edinburgh merchant James Henrisoun wrote a pamphlet maintaining that the two realms had no natural boundary and shared a common ancestor, the legendary Brute (a descendant of the Trojan Aeneas) who had conquered the whole island of Britain well before the Romans. With a dynastic union between Edward VI and Mary, Queen of Scots on the agenda (a marriage that of course never happened), Henrisoun urged 'these two realms should grow into one' in an equal relationship. A committed Protestant, Henrisoun went beyond Mair's political union to envisage a godly one.[14]

The same message of equality and godly union was conveyed in England by Edward VI's lord protector, the earl of Somerset, during his invasion of Scotland. In his *Epistle or Exhortacion*, he proclaimed: 'We offer love, we offer equalities and amity.'[15] However, the military realities of the time—Somerset laying waste much of Lowland Scotland and placing garrisons along the east coast as far north as Dundee—convinced most Scots that the English were embarking on a policy of conquest and an imperial union, not one of equals. Nonetheless, the prospect of a Britain united in the cause of godly reform remained an ideal among some Scottish and English Protestants.[16]

Under Elizabeth, the unionist dream became more contentious because of its links to the question of the succession. English Protestants who opposed the title of Mary, Queen of Scots downplayed the similarities between the two realms, argued that the Scottish monarch was an alien born outside the allegiance of the English monarch, and emphasized the long history of warfare between the two realms. Those who supported Mary's (and later James VI's) right to the succession denied the Scots were aliens, wrote of Britain as a geopolitical entity, and endorsed the foundation myth of the legendary Brute conquering the whole island of Britain. They added, moreover, the equally mythic account of Brute dividing the island among his three sons and giving his eldest, Locrine, the kingship of England and feudal overlordship over the younger sons who became the kings of Scotland and Wales.[17] The claim of Anglocentric imperialism embodied in this myth, however, was naturally rejected by the Scots who supported James's succession. Consequently, some dismissed the Brute story as a fabrication while others fell back on a counter-mythology, that of an unbroken line of forty-five sovereign Scottish kings dating back to 330 BCE when Fergus I, originally from Ireland, took the throne.[18] Significantly, James did not mention Brute in the original Scottish version of *Basilikon Doron*, but introduced it to the English edition.

Perhaps because the Union project was not a novel idea in either England or Scotland, James initially underestimated opposition to it. He also had reason to think that it would be easy to achieve as the theme of Union was prevalent in the panegyric welcoming him to England. Many of the poems he would not have read, nor was he likely to have come across *A Welch Bayte to Spare Provender* which discussed approvingly 'the aptnesse of the English and the Scotte to incorporate and become one entire a monarchie'.[19] But almost certainly he had heard, and may have read, Samuel Daniel's *Panegyrike*

Congratulatory, delivered at the house of the countess of Bedford in Rutland, in which stanza 2 pronounced:

> Shake hands with Union, O thou mightie state,
>   Now thou art all great Brittaine, and no more,
> No Scot, no English now, nor no debate:
>   No borders but the ocean, or the shore,
> No wall of Adrian serves to seperate
>   Our mutuall love, nor our obedience,
> All subjects all to one imperiall prince.[20]

Additionally, as already described in chapter 6, the iconography on the arches devised for the royal entry of 1604 celebrated Union.

That the proponents of Union so often metaphorically compared it to the marriage of Henry VII and Elizabeth of York—which had brought together the warring families of Lancaster and York—intimates that they were contemplating merely a union of crowns that would bring perpetual peace to the warring nations of England and Scotland. This kind of 'imperfect union' was common in Europe and would allow the two realms to preserve their independence and retain their own privy council, parliament, laws, Church, and other institutions. However, one weakness of this constitutional arrangement was that it could easily be dissolved, as had happened in 1523 when Sweden finally seceded from the 1397 Kalmar Union, a personal union of the three Scandinavian kingdoms of Sweden, Denmark, and Norway.

For this very reason, James wanted more than a dynastic union and favoured a 'perfect union', which would lead to a convergence of laws, customs, and peoples.[21] The king also preferred this kind of union because of his belief—buttressed by reading the French political thinker Jean Bodin—that a divided sovereignty was harmful to a monarchy.[22] Yet there were very few examples of a 'perfect union' in contemporary Europe that had not been formed by conquest. One of them was the union of Poland and Lithuania, which had begun in 1386 with the marriage of Poland's Queen Jadwiga to the grand duke of Lithuania and had through negotiation become, in 1569, a parliamentary union whereby Lithuania (the weaker unit) was 'incorporated and perpetually united' to Poland (the stronger); or at least that was how the constitutional set-up was understood in England, even though the reality was far more complex.[23] Some English supporters of James's programme—possibly James too—thought this sort of commonwealth was an apt model to follow.[24]

Another model of 'perfect union' was Wales's absorption into England seventy years earlier by act of parliament. When James spoke of the 'union of Wales to England' (significantly saying 'to' not 'and') in his speech of 19 March 1604 to parliament, he seemed to imply that a similar 'incorporated' model of union was in his mind.[25] However, the Welsh example was unacceptable to the Scots. After all, Wales had initially been joined to England by conquest not marriage; and such a union would result in Scotland losing its separate identity. If there was to be a 'perfect union', the Scots demanded one that was 'mutuall and reciproque, not the translatioun of the estait of ane kingdome in ane other, not of Scotland as subaltern to England'.[26] Their parliament would agree to nothing less, and legislation enacting Union had to pass through both the English and Scottish parliaments.

The Kirk too objected to the prospect of the incorporation model of union not least because it would require changes to Scotland's religion, or so most ministers believed. Commissioners of the synods queried that since 'the realms could not be united without unioun and conformitie of the Kirk's government and worship', how could that happen 'unlesse the one gave place to the other?'[27] For this reason, Presbyterian ministers held fasts and preached against the Union, and the Scottish parliament passed an act that declared the 'establissit' Church was non-negotiable.[28] Robert Pont, a minister of the Kirk, who ostensibly favoured James's policy, had one of his speakers in an imaginary dialogue about Union warn that England would rule Scotland because 'the stronger ever draweth to itself the weaker'.[29]

Whatever form it would take, James's endgame was a 'perfect union': England and Scotland united in one monarchy—Great Britain—where there would be one law and one society though not total uniformity in the customs of each place.[30] But the king's advisers and other commentators thought this too ambitious a project for the present. In a short address to the king in 1603, Sir Francis Bacon (a keen advocate of Union) cautioned against moving with too much haste. Like the king, he recognized that the best kind of Union required '*compositio* and *mistio*, putting together and mingling'—a mingling which entailed 'union in name, union in language, union in laws, and union in employments'. But to obtain a 'perfect mixture' in nature and science, time was of the essence, and the 'unnatural hasting thereof doth disturb the work and not dispatch it'. The same would be true, he believed, when attempting a political, constitutional, and legal Union.[31] Similarly, the antiquary Sir Henry Spelman (decidedly less keen on Union) considered the two realms needed at least seven years to get used to each other before there was any talk of a formal tighter relationship.[32]

James listened to Bacon's advice, which was almost certainly reinforced by Cecil, and decided to go for a less far-reaching programme than the Union he had originally envisaged. Opposing voices raised in his 1604 session of parliament also convinced him of the need to proceed slowly. Believing that a natural union between the two realms had already been created on his accession, since sovereignty resided in his person, James later told parliament: Union 'is now perfect in my title and descent, though it be not an accomplisht and full union: for that, time must ripen and work'. His requirements in the present parliament, therefore, were only measures to bring his two kingdoms closer together since 'hee that buildeth a ship must first provide the timber'. All that was needed for the immediate future was the removal of existing distinctions between the two realms: the border, bars to commerce, the different names for each territory, and the two separate legal identities of his subjects.[33] Mistakenly, James did not anticipate that even these relatively modest changes would create enormous difficulties.

★ ★ ★

In spite of English MPs' vocal opposition to a statutory Union, parliament agreed, in 1604, to a bilateral commission which would discuss the issue. The Scottish parliament followed suit, but only after its members were 'admonished by the king that their prompt obedience could alone avert his severe displeasure'.[34] From October to December 1604, forty-eight English commissioners and thirty-one Scots met every few days in the painted chamber at Westminster with the goal of drawing up a set of proposals for a Union to be put before the next session of parliament.[35] Ellesmere headed the commission, and among its English members were Cecil, Northampton, and Bacon; among the Scottish members were Lord Chancellor Fyvie and the eminent jurist and historian Sir Thomas Craig of Riccarton.

Impatient for Union, James did not await the commission's report before introducing symbolic measures to advance unity via his royal prerogative. On 20 October 1604, a proclamation enacted the name change that MPs had decried earlier that year. Thinking it 'unreasonable that the thing, which is by the worke of God and nature so much in effect one, should not be one in name', James declared his assumption of 'the name and stile of king of Great Brittaine, France, and Ireland', an ancient name 'which God and time have imposed upon this isle'. However, to avoid legal and constitutional issues, James agreed its usage would not be extended to 'any legal proceeding, instrument, or assurance, until further order be taken on that behalf'.[36] The proclamation was read out with great pomp in London and afterwards in Edinburgh, but it was ill received in both realms. People were appalled and protests heard. The government soon laid its hands on what James called a 'crewallie villanouse pasquil', which railed against the king 'for the neme of Brittaine', and an ex-soldier, Edward Smith, was imprisoned for writing a 'ballade or dyttie' upon the dissolution of the garrison at Berwick, presumably an anti-Union verse.[37]

A few of the English protesters simply disliked the name 'Britain' and might possibly have accepted 'Albion' as an alternative.[38] How could England take on the name of a land, declared one, whose inhabitants had been 'an ydolatrous nation and worshippers of divels' and who, at the beginning of Christianity, were 'thrust owt into the mountanes where they lived long like theefes and robbers and are to this day the most base, presantly perfidious people of the world'?[39] Most objectors, however, were opposed to any name change at all, mainly out of national pride. They were distressed that the historic name of England would sink into oblivion and feared that the new name risked demoting their country in matters of precedence within the international community, since 'Great Britain' could no longer claim antiquity.[40] A number raised constitutional issues too, asking how the island could have one name when there existed two separate laws and governments.[41] Additionally, there was a secondary anxiety. By again relying on proclamation to obtain his goal, James seemed to be treating parliament with contempt and even acting as if he had personally conquered England.[42]

Another important act of symbolism for James was the new coinage of 1604 created for both realms. Enforced in England by a proclamation of 16 November, the coinage was to be of 'one uniforme standard and allay'.[43] On the coins was stamped James's new style, 'king of Great Britain and Ireland', while their Latin legends repeated mottoes in praise of unity. Translated into English, the gold £1 and guinea coins were inscribed with: 'I will make them one nation' (a providential quotation from Ezekiel 37:22 referring to the union of Israel and Judah).[44] On the larger silver sixpence, the inscription read: 'What God has joined together, let no man put asunder' (Matthew 19:6), a quotation that James had previously brought into his March 1604 speech to parliament.[45] On the half-crown was: 'Henry [united] the roses, James the kingdoms', a sentiment James had articulated in the same speech.

Also stamped on some of the coins was the Scottish thistle united with the English rose.[46] As far as we know, the coins were used without complaint.

As a final symbolic act, James commissioned heralds to design a new flag for Great Britain, one that would combine England's vertical red cross of St George on a white field with Scotland's diagonal white St Andrew's cross on a blue field. It was a difficult commission since it was nigh impossible for the Scottish and English crosses to have equal priority. Several designs were produced, and eventually, in August 1606, a prototype was approved and made obligatory by another proclamation. However, because the English cross was superimposed upon and obscured the St Andrew's cross, Scottish sailors refused to fly the new ensign.[47]

These symbols of Union were incompatible with the growing sense of separate national identities fostered in both realms during the previous century. In England, the Reformation and wars against France (under Henry VIII) and Spain (under Elizabeth) had done a great deal to stimulate English patriotism. At the same time, the language of nationhood was being instilled in the reading public, playgoers, and scholars. Holinshed's *Chronicles* of 1577 and 1587 comprised three separate histories of England, Scotland, and Wales; Shakespeare brought to life the triumphs and failures of numerous English kings from John to Richard III. Meanwhile, the Society of Antiquaries (founded in 1586 and disbanded in 1607) generated scholarly investigations into English institutions and a passion for England's past antiquities. Typical among its members were the lawyer Joseph Holland, who delivered papers about old English manuscripts and 'divers antiquities in coin', and Sir Robert Cotton (Northampton's research assistant), who carried out investigations into the etymologies and antiquity of English towns, castles, and offices.[48] Although William Camden (a founding member of the society) published *Britannia*, a topographical study of England, Scotland, and Ireland, he recognized the separateness of the three national identities and was at best sceptical about the Brute legend.[49] A number of antiquarians, moreover, looked to the Germanic origins of England and identified Anglo-Saxons—not Britons—as the originators of their language, culture, and race.[50]

Scots too possessed a strong sense of their own national identity. Around the time of James's accession, various items went into print that publicized Scotland's ancient royal genealogy (108 kings in the space of 1,933 years) and its long history of independence overcoming England's attempts at conquest.[51] Like the English, Scottish antiquaries preserved and collected old literary and historical texts, while several new histories of Scotland had appeared during the sixteenth century in both manuscript and print.[52] The Scots may have been inferior to their southern neighbours in terms of population and resources, but they considered themselves at least their equal in dignity and status.

★ ★ ★

Recognizing the need to win over hearts and minds, James ensured that pro-Union material was made available to the reading public. His 19 March speech to parliament, which elaborated upon the benefits of Union, was immediately put into press. His proclamation of 20 October was similarly printed and pretty much a propaganda piece in answering objections to the name change. James also ordered, or authorized, the publication of pro-Union tracts composed by Scots and Englishmen, and these were supplemented with pamphlets written by men who were either ideologically committed to Union or on the make, seeking royal patronage by advocating James's policy. Overall, eleven pro-Union tracts (five of them by Scots) were printed, while many more circulated in manuscript before 1607, the bulk between May and October 1604.[53] How convincing they were is anyone's guess.[54]

Additionally, in Scotland, the royal printer Robert Waldegrave (a puritan exile from England) produced for sale, in 1603, a book of Scottish prophesies that included several verses predicting James's rule over a united Britain. His purpose was to present Union as a Scottish enterprise and not an English attempt to absorb the northern kingdom. One prophesy, supposedly pronounced by Sibylla, queen of Austria, foretold how 'the Ile of Brittane shal be in al joy and peace' during the reign of a king, interpreted by the editor as James VI of Scotland.[55] Two others—'the prophecie of Bertlington' and Thomas the Rhymer—predicted that:

The Frenche wife shal beare the sonne
Shal weild al Bretane to the sea.
  And from the Bruce's blood shall come.[56]

Scottish readers would have recognized Mary, Queen of Scots, the widow of Francis II, as the 'Frenche wife' whose line descended from Robert the Bruce.

The pro-Union tracts were generally more prosaic. Naturally, they all stated the general benefits of Union: unity meant strength, concord, and prosperity. Like marriage,

> Union is heaven's good, the best of state,
>   Whom good doth joyne, let no man seperate.[57]

In the case of England and Scotland, the specific advantages listed were an end to criminals escaping justice by fleeing over the frontier and the disappearance of the borderlands, then commonly viewed as 'most subject to incursions, spoiles, rapines, and other detestable outrages'.[58] Unionists also downplayed or dismissed objections, called 'inconveniences', which opponents had raised in parliament. John Thornborough, bishop of Bristol, countered the protests about the new name of Britain with the assertion (also made by James) that the name was not new at all.[59] Equally unfounded, Unionists maintained, was the worry that automatic naturalization would result in the Scots descending upon England in droves and taking 'the best offices alone'. James would not especially favour the Scots, asserted writers, because 'he is king of both, he is father of both, and (being equally charged by the King of Kings with both) owing unto both one duty, he will give unto both one affection'.[60] Besides, 'such is his Majestie's royall disposition to chuse the best from the most'.[61]

To legitimize the name change and Union, many tracts appealed to both mythology and divine providence. The story of Brute was frequently retold, and several genealogies drawn to prove that James was lineally descended from the 'first inhabiter of this ile of Brittayne'.[62] Likewise invoked to demonstrate the historic, if mythical, unity of the island were King Arthur and Emperor Constantine, whom the medieval chronicler Geoffrey of Monmouth had deemed kings of the Britons.[63] Taking up the providential theme further, the Anglo-Scot John Gordon, dean of Salisbury, upheld Union as an apocalyptic imperative. Spuriously claiming the word Britannia had its etymology in the Hebrew language, Gordon translated 'Brit' as 'covenant', 'an' as 'there', and 'iah' as 'of God'. When put together, the syllables signified that 'in this iland the covenant of God was to be established', and they foretold James's 'happy and blessed Union in one religion and one kingdome'.[64] According to this worldview, Union was God's plan and anyone who rejected it was guilty of blasphemy.[65]

Most pro-Union tracts also focused on historical and recent unions in order to show what was possible and what desirable. They veered towards similar conclusions. Full ('perfect') unions formed by conquest—especially the annexations of the ancient world—were deemed liable to civil unrest and hence undesirable. Anyway, they were dismissed as irrelevant in the present circumstances since neither England nor Scotland had been conquered by the other. Partial unions formed by a marriage or election were judged likely to be temporary, especially if there were different laws of succession in each kingdom. They might also be unstable, as in the case of Spain where several risings had occurred in the Aragonese kingdom because it had not been 'well incorporated and cemented with the other crownes'.[66] Partial unions formed by succession where each sovereign kingdom retained its separate laws, privileges, and customs—such as that achieved when Portugal was joined to Spain in 1580—were considered more likely to be stable, though again unlikely to last in perpetuity.[67] This kind of imperfect union appealed to those—mainly Scots—who appreciated that England and Scotland were both independent sovereign states and who favoured a sort of federal system in which each of the two kingdoms would retain its own laws and parliaments.

Stability and permanence, Unionists generally concluded, could only be achieved when there was a full union created by marriage and succession. However, such instances were rare. As already seen, the commonwealth of Poland and Lithuania was one example, but the disadvantage of this model was that the full merger had not taken place immediately.[68] Another was the incorporation of Brittany into France through the marriages of its duchess Anne to French kings in 1491 and 1499.[69] This precedent was especially liked by Unionists who favoured the creation of a single unitary state and was also thought applicable to an Anglo-Scottish Union. France and Brittany, wrote John Hayward, had 'commonly received the same civill lawes' and so their 'perfect union' had been 'both more easie and also more sure'; and since 'the fundamental lawes' of England and Scotland 'doe well agree', he went on, 'to reduce the lawes of England and Scotland into one bodie, it seemeth the change will not bee great'.[70] The model also worked well for those English Unionists who asserted that Scotland, like the semi-autonomous province of Brittany, had never been an independent state since it paid homage to its feudal overlord, the king of England.[71] It was consequently rejected by the Scots.

The two most sophisticated of the Unionist authors were Scots: the humanist and poet David Hume of Godscroft, and Sir Thomas Craig of Riccarton. Both wrote their treatises in Latin: Hume for an international scholarly circle, and Craig in manuscript for the king.[72] Hume's vision of Britain was the most radical of all the Unionist writers. He was not just interested in political forms nor looking for previous precedents; he wanted to create a reformed society in which British men (not of course women) would be active citizens 'involved in the business of government'. His long-term aim was to erase the separate identities of Scots and English and bring 'one people into existence' who would be equal citizens in a fully integrated 'British commonwealth'. To achieve this fusion, the two separate kingdoms had to merge in everything, except their laws. They would share the same institutions: a British council of state, one parliament meeting at York, and one Church organized along Presbyterian lines. New cross-country regional councils would be established in Lancaster, York, London, Edinburgh, and possibly Aberdeen; and a fifth of the members of each council would come from the other country.[73] In a second part of his treatise (which was left unpublished), Hume set out still more ambitious proposals; here he recommended that the youth of Scotland should be educated in the Universities at Oxford and Cambridge while English youth should attend a university in Scotland.[74] Out of sync with the prevailing sentiments of the time, Hume's dream remained just that.

Craig's *De Unione Regnorum Britanniae Tractatus* was far more practicable in its espousal of Union. Writing after his time on the Union commission, Craig argued for the amalgamation of the two kingdoms into a single realm with a new name and reformed polity. In this new state there would be concordance (not uniformity) in religion, ecclesiastical discipline, coinage, language, laws, customs, and government. Some compatibilities, he wrote, already existed, but they needed to be extended and inconsistences removed. To take the example of law, because the legal systems of England and Scotland were based on common feudal principles and contained elements of civil law, in Craig's view (like Hayward's) it would not be difficult to fashion one body of law common to both, thereby 'promoting the union of the countries into one body politic'.[75] A pragmatist, Craig recognized that the two kingdoms would not 'submit to identical laws and systems', but over time the introduction of piecemeal and careful harmonization on the basis of common principles would result in a union.[76] The model here was the England historically formed from the variety of Anglo-Saxon kingdoms. Craig's farsightedness appealed to James and was shared by Englishmen, such as Bacon and Ellesmere, who, aside from Union, were keen to see legal reforms.

★ ★ ★

The commissioners who set to work in 1604 did not have as their remit the creation of a 'perfect union', not least because the Scottish parliament had forbidden its representatives to discuss one. Nonetheless their task was not easy, for there were many irreconcilabilities and technicalities to resolve. The Scots demanded the abolition of hostile laws on England's statute books, but exactly which ones were unambiguously hostile? The English wanted the removal of 'priviledges' in the Scots' commercial arrangements with France, but they were part of a Franco-Scottish treaty which would be difficult to rescind even if there were a willingness to do so.[77] By what means could English commissioners agree to the automatic naturalization of Scots while restricting their poorer neighbours' rights to land and offices in England, restrictions that the king anyway refused to set down in writing? Yet, remarkably, all the 'essentiall' points were agreed upon within six weeks and written up in an 'Instrument' which made four recommendations: the repeal of hostile laws, abolition of the borders, freedom of commerce, and mutual naturalization.[78]

James oversaw the writing of the Instrument. He intervened to correct early drafts, for instance passing on to Fyvie 'his jugement and corrections' regarding naturalization.[79] He also demanded changes to the preface of the finished document. The commissioners, he quibbled, said they *desired* (rather than required) a perfect Union and *hoped* (rather than demanded) that parliament would accept it. The preface, he told Cecil, had to go or else a new one containing his amendments had to be written.[80] The changes were made, but the original wording intimates that the commissioners were not wholeheartedly behind the document or else feared that the commons would not approve it. If the French ambassador is to be believed, it was probably the former; he reported that both the Scottish and English commissioners secretly hoped parliament would reject their work. As for James, he was probably more apprehensive about the Instrument's reception in parliament than he cared to admit.[81] Anyway, he ended up shelving it for nearly two years while he tried to drum up support. As already seen, he prorogued parliament several times in 1605; moreover, in January 1606, he did not object to, and may even have encouraged, a bill to defer debate on the Instrument until the next session because discussions held in committee about the repeal of hostile laws had raised much 'adoe' and proved acrimonious.[82]

When the Union question was reopened in the parliamentary session of late 1606, opposition to the Instrument's recommendations had not diminished. None was without controversial elements, but the call for freedom of commerce and mutual naturalization aroused the greatest objections.[83]

MPs spurned free trade for non-ideological reasons. First, they believed that the removal of customs duties between the two realms would result in a serious loss of royal revenues, sums which would then have to be raised by other means. Second, merchants testified before the commons that freedom of commerce would be of no benefit to England owing to Scotland's 'povertie', 'the barrenness of theire comodities', and the continuation of Scotland's privileged commercial relationship with France. Because the two countries produced the same goods and Scotland's were cheaper, being of poorer quality, merchants lobbied for them to be kept out of England by tariffs. Their petitions that 'all might remane as it did withowt further uniting' carried considerable weight in the commons, even though the collection of tariffs on domestic goods had been suspended since the spring of 1604 to no ill effects.[84]

When naturalization came to be discussed, the debates became more rancorous. The Instrument assumed that those Scots who were born after James's accession (the so-called *post-nati*) would be automatically naturalized in England but that the *ante-nati* (those born before 1603) would require a statute of naturalization to become English citizens. However, many MPs rejected automatic naturalization on the basis that Scotland would remain a foreign nation under the present arrangements. While the Scots 'contynue a distinct bodie from us', asserted Sir Edwin Sandys, 'it is no reason to communicate all the benefites of our state with them'. Sir Henry Neville agreed and asked whether it would be safe, honourable, or beneficial for England 'to give naturalization to those that are obliged to an other nation [France] in treaties of common hostilitie against this kingdome'. Automatic naturalization, concluded the leading opponents, would be possible only in a unitary British state in which the Scots were subject to English laws and had representatives in a British parliament. They consequently called for the establishment of a new commission to create a 'perfect union' of laws, parliaments, and judicial institutions. As a tactic, it was masterly for they—and James—knew very well that this form of 'perfect union' involved an incorporation totally unacceptable to the Scots.[85]

After a fruitless attempt to win over the commons, James became furious. He accused their leaders of speaking 'against duty, almost allegiance' and resorted to threats.[86] However, seeing he was beaten, James let Union drop. This was a decision that was greeted with as much relief in Scotland as in England. The Scots were less strident in their opposition, partly out of deference to their king and partly because they preferred to leave the English parliament to impose the veto.

Parliament's outright rejection of Union is often attributed to the xenophobia, even racism, of MPs.[87] Unquestionably, their speeches exposed deep-seated prejudices against the Scots, often related to their poverty. In a debate about removing barriers to commerce in December 1606, Fuller said that 'Scots in other cuntreys were more like pedlars then marchants', while another member 'with a bitter word against owr neighbours' called them 'the beggarly Scots'.[88] In the 1607 debate on naturalization, Christopher Pigott delivered such an 'invective against the Scotts and Scottish nation, using many words of scandal and obloquy' that James sent him to the Tower.[89] Others used more moderate language but were equally obsessed with the imagined outcome of Scots moving to England in search of a better life. To counteract the effects, they insisted upon a range of restrictions that should be legally imposed if naturalization went ahead. These included demands that the Scots should pay the same taxes and be liable to English laws, which sounded reasonable, but also that no Scot could hold a wardship or marry a ward or become an archbishop or bishop or head of a college. Going still further, some members proposed, 'though lamely', that Scots should be debarred from the county offices of JPs, sheriffs, and jurors.[90] James had tried to convince them that no formal restrictions would be necessary, because he had no intention of promoting Scots 'to such and such places' until the 'maturitie' of time had 'pece and pece' removed any 'distinction of nations, as it hath allreaddie don heir betwixt Englande and Wales'.[91] However, given the privileged role of the Scots in the bedchamber, his words seemed hardly credible.

There was, though, far more to opposition than xenophobia. Structural problems and constitutional concerns were as important in wrecking James's Union project in parliament. Despite all the rhetoric of similarities between James's two realms, there were glaring differences between them, as opponents of Union were swift to spotlight. The Scots, wrote Spelman, were more similar in language to the Irish than to the English. And, indeed, the language of the Highlands and Isles was largely Gaelic (known then as 'Irish') while the 'Scotis' or 'Inglis' spoken by Lowlands Scots was distinctive in its accent and idioms, all of which were often difficult for many English to penetrate.[92] Also, glossing over the truth was the assertion in pro-Union tracts that 'the fundamentall lawes (as they are termed) of both kingdomes and crownes doe well agree' and that 'in other lawes of government they hold good conformitie'.[93] Again, Spelman pointed out the difference: Scotland's laws, he wrote, were Continental, closer to the French system than to the English common law which was based on precedent and made by judges not a legislator.[94] Other divergences of importance were that the Kirk was largely Presbyterian while the Church of England was Episcopalian, and Scotland's parliament was unicameral while England's had two chambers. Because England was more heavily populated and by far the wealthier of the two realms, any political equality in a 'perfect union' would be problematic.[95] When it came to their economies, the two kingdoms were in fact too close: producing the same goods, they operated as competitors rather than trading partners.[96] Because of these circumstances, it was hard for English MPs to feel British and accept even a watered-down Union.

Furthermore, James's insistent claim that the two kingdoms were already united in his person had constitutional implications that alarmed MPs.[97] The spokesmen against Union believed England and Scotland to be as far apart in 1603 as they had been before since the two realms were two different bodies politic. For them, a body politic was more than just its head [the king]; it had a body [people], life [the laws], even a soul [the execution of laws]. Sovereignty, therefore, resided in a kingdom's laws not in the person of a ruler, and Scots were 'noe natural subjects to the soveraigntie of Englande'.[98] Simply put, because the king reigned over two different kingdoms with different laws and parliament, he held two sovereignties not one. To admit otherwise, these members averred, was to put England's laws and liberties under threat and walk blindfold down the road towards arbitrary monarchy. Such considerations, together with the king's extended use of his prerogative, aroused deep anxieties. Suspicions of James's kingship as much as hatred of the Scots scuppered the Union project.

★ ★ ★

Despite this defeat, James remained determined to bring about greater cohesion between his two realms. And he had some success. With help from his judges, he got his way over *post-nati* naturalization. A majority decided in 'Calvin's case' that his subjects born in Scotland after his accession had the same legal status in England as his English subjects. The case arose in 1607 when the trustees of a boy born in Edinburgh in 1605 initiated two civil suits in the English law courts over his right as a Scot to hold property in England. The boy Robert Calvin (originally Colville) had inherited tenements in Shoreditch and Bishopsgate, London, but the men who were then in possession of the properties refused to surrender them. Their defence was that Calvin could neither own a freehold in England nor issue a writ against them because he was an alien. The lawyers for Calvin's trustees, however, argued that *post-nati* Scots were not aliens as they owed allegiance to the English king. The suits, therefore, raised the same issues as were then being debated in parliament. For this reason, James decided to use the case 'to give an end to this question'. Presumably through his influence, the suits were transferred to the exchequer chamber to be heard as one case in front of the lord chancellor, the barons of the exchequer, and the common-law justices, fourteen men in all.[99]

Among the five common lawyers for the defendants were Richard Hutton and Lawrence Hyde, who as MPs opposed the naturalization of Scots. Francis Bacon, James's solicitor general, and Henry Hobart, the attorney general, argued for the plaintiffs on behalf of the crown.[100] They won. In 1608, all but two of the justices determined that the *post-nati*—unlike the *ante-nati*—were not to be regarded as aliens in England.[101] The immediate effect of the case was negligible since few *post-nati* were of an age to benefit from the verdict. Nonetheless, it was an immensely important ruling. Basing their judgment on the argument that there was no difference between the person of the king and his body politic, the judges dealt a legal blow to the political theory of the King's Two Bodies, which had held sway for centuries. Moreover, the principle of naturalization derived from Calvin's case—namely that someone's birth in a territory within the king's dominion made that person a natural-born subject in all the king's lands—remained part of English law until 1981.[102]

Ante-nati Scots continued to be naturalized by English statute on a case-by-case basis. To integrate them further into his newly formed Britain, James encouraged them to intermarry into the nobilities and gentry of England. As king of Scotland, he had used marriage as a tool to heal bad blood between different families; now he promoted intermarriage as a step towards forging a British identity.[103] To advance such matches, James would on occasion use the lure of patronage. Learning that a marriage was being treated between Sir William Auchterlony's heir and the daughter of Sir Hugh Bethell in 1606, James wrote to the girl's father: 'We have thought good to let you knowe that your willingnes to the finishing of that match is to us a testimony of yor respect to us.' His 'willingness', James continued, would assure Bethell of royal favour in any 'reasonable matter' because 'we have no greater desire then that this union of these kingdomes on our person be corroborate in the heartes of our subjects of either realme by mutuall affynities and connection of bloud to establish the same to posterity'.[104]

The first Anglo-Scottish wedding occurred as early as 1603 when Sir John Kennedy married Elizabeth Brydges, the daughter of Giles, second Lord Chandos. Unfortunately, Kennedy already had a wife alive in Scotland, and his marriage to Elizabeth ended in scandal.[105] More successful were the marriages of Hay, Haddington, Erskine, Lennox, Argyll, and Aubigny to English brides. Although in most Anglo-Scottish marriages the husband was a Scot, Dunbar's daughter wed Suffolk's eldest son; Christian, the thirteen-year-old daughter of Kinloss, was foisted on the eighteen-year-old Sir William Cavendish, later earl of Devonshire; and Margaret, James's first cousin, married Nottingham. Overall, between 1603 and 1638, some thirty Anglo-Scottish marriages were celebrated. Nevertheless, outside the English court, intermarriage was negligible, and James's attempt to create a British aristocracy can hardly be judged a success.[106]

Although James made no attempt to amalgamate the two realms' key institutions, namely the privy council and parliament, he did seek convergence elsewhere, although not always successfully. In October 1607, for example, he called for informal discussions to be held about creating greater 'concurrence' and 'uniformitie of the lawes' of England and Scotland, but ultimately these talks came to nothing.[107] James also tried, but failed, to bring the two different systems of nobility into alignment. The Scots objected because noble privileges in Scotland were far wider than in England, and they would 'not submit to any diminution of the same'.[108] The English, too, disliked any integration of the two nobilities as shown when they murmured against the earl of Argyll claiming precedence over Pembroke at dinner 'as being now become all Britaines'.[109] James had to be content with installing Scots into the English order of the garter (see Appendix 3).[110]

James had success in introducing English-style JPs and parish constables to Scotland. Since the JPs were given wide responsibilities that went beyond their role as magistrates, the innovation extended royal authority throughout Scotland, which was undoubtedly part of the king's aim.[111] Successful too was James's decision to create one diplomatic corps for the two realms, a feature of most European multiple kingdoms. Everyone appreciated that it would be absurd and expensive to maintain parallel diplomatic representation at foreign courts, so no-one in England objected. Besides, Englishmen held posts in the more prestigious courts of Madrid, Brussels, Paris, and the Hague, whereas Scots conducted diplomacy as agents in Denmark, Sweden, and Poland.[112] On the cultural side, James extended the Scottish Gowrie

Day into England and ensured that Gunpowder Treason Day was celebrated in all his realms.[113]

James initially had no intention of imposing convergence within religious practice in recognition that it would create a furore in Scotland and might restart debates in England about revising the English prayer book, just when he was demanding conformity to its rites. Nonetheless, James continued his pre-1603 moves to assert the royal supremacy, diminish the power of the Presbyterian synods, and extend the number and role of bishops in Scotland, all measures which as a by-product would advance Anglo-Scottish ecclesiastical convergence.[114] Because his man on the spot, Alexander Seton, earl of Dunfermline, was a Catholic and unable to deal with the Kirk effectively, James gave Dunbar the task of carrying out negotiations there and ensuring the relevant legislation passed the Scottish parliament.[115] He was 'mervelously well pleased' with Dunbar, in the summer of 1606, when the episcopal revenues of thirteen sees were restored to their bishops.[116]

James's programme inevitably reignited a confrontation with the Kirk from which he and Dunbar did not shrink. In 1606, Dunbar ensured that oppositional Presbyterian ministers were brought to trial and convicted for having held a banned general assembly at Aberdeen the previous year. Six were imprisoned, and eight more—including Andrew Melville—were summoned to appear before the king in London. Their first formal audience with the king took place at Hampton Court on 20 September, and they had several more interviews with him thereafter. On Sunday the 21st, the ministers had to endure hearing the Sabbath sermon delivered by Bishop Barlow in the chapel royal, the first of many anti-Presbyterian sermons they were made to attend over the next ten days.[117] Unimpressed, the ministers displayed 'violent opposition' and consequently, in November, were placed in the custody of individual English bishops for further instruction to 'reclayme' them from opinions 'contrarie to this Church'.[118] Six were eventually allowed to return to Scotland, but not Melville nor his nephew James. Andrew was charged with treason because he had penned a satirical Latin epigram on an English altar and abused Bancroft in person. After several years in the Tower, he was exiled to France. James was detained in the north of England until his death in 1613.[119]

Their leaders out of the way, the Kirk soon caved in. In July 1608, Dunbar arrived again in Edinburgh 'with a great traine' to underline his status as James's lieutenant before attending the Kirk's general assembly at Linlithgow. There, in the king's name, he agreed to anti-Catholic measures, and in return the bishops 'gott a great vantage'; they could operate as commissioners of the assembly and permanent moderators of the presbyteries where they resided.[120] The next year, Dunbar attended the Scottish parliament that enacted the restoration of bishops to 'their livings, jurisdictioun, and place'.[121] Then, in 1610, a nominated assembly approved royal decrees ordaining episcopal powers and responsibilities.[122] By these means, the thirteen medieval dioceses of Scotland were restored, and the bishops stood at the head of the Presbyterian system as agents of the crown.

Gaining confidence from this success, James later attempted alterations in Scotland's religious worship, one of which demanded that communicants should receive the bread and wine 'meiklie and reverendlie upone their knees'. This order caused a furore in Edinburgh after 1618, as it was thought idolatrous, and serious trouble was only averted when the Protestants in the Scottish privy council refused to impose conformity.[123] However, the disturbances and disobedience revealed a fissure in the union of crowns that cracked wide open when Charles I endeavoured to impose an English prayer book on Scotland in 1637. Opposition then escalated into rebellion and civil war.

These attempts at integration and convergence were initiated by James to effect Union without statutory constitutional change. Simultaneously, he made efforts to eradicate the traditional border between his two realms. On his accession, he immediately abolished the wardenries that had previously been responsible for law and order in the frontier regions of both England and Scotland, now designated the 'middle shires'. In the lord wardens' place, he appointed lord lieutenants who were given the task of making the shires 'as peaceable and ansourable as any other pairt' of Britain.[124] However, since James assigned the earl of Cumberland to serve over the three border counties in England and Lord Home (later Dunbar) over those in Scotland, the division between the realms was effectively retained.[125]

In a further move to erase the frontier, James set up a commission, in February 1605, which was composed of five Scots and five English justices. An Englishman was 'to be commander of the rest for the first three months, and then one of the Scottish side for three months, and so afterwards alternately'. The commissioners were given extensive powers to administer the whole 'middle shires' and rid the area of hardened criminals. To execute this task, they had the assistance of two forces of mounted border guards.[126] Yet again, the two realms remained largely separate as the commissioners and border guards operated mainly within their own countries.[127]

The commission failed to meet James's expectations and was dissolved in September 1607.[128] Not long afterwards, the king appointed Dunbar, whose sizeable estates and connections were on both sides of the border, as a lieutenant with jurisdiction over the whole 'middle shires', but he served in the English counties with Cumberland's heir.[129] Over three years, the earl 'purged the bordours of all the cheiffest malefactouris, rubbars, and brigantis as war wount to regnne' there.[130] Yet, despite this achievement, the experiment of a more integrated Anglo-Scottish approach was not sustained after Dunbar's death in January 1611. Within a short time, the role of lord lieutenant disappeared from Scotland while it continued in the border shires of England. The separate legal systems and commissions functioning on each side of the border operated once again, and the networks of border officials and families rarely crossed into the opposite realm. An invisible border therefore remained intact, and the people living there usually referred to themselves as 'English' or 'Scottish', not British.[131]

★ ★ ★

Nevertheless, the name 'Great Britain' came to be extensively used in the material and print culture of early Jacobean England. As already seen, the new nomenclature was officially sanctioned, appearing on coins and medals. In an unforeseen consequence, which surely pleased James, the name 'Britain's Bourse' was printed on the frontispiece of the many books sold in the London shopping arcade (opened in April 1609) which had been given that name. Hence part of the book trade acquired a British identity.

In these early years, 'Britain' rather than 'England' appeared in many book titles, and not just those that were part of the polemical literature in support of Union. In many cases, the change of name was merely cosmetic. Sir John Clapham's revamped 1602 *Historie of England* was, in 1611, renamed *Historie of Great Britain*, a narrative which began with the origin of the name Britain 'first known to the Romans', but then discounted Scotland, and ended with King Egbert 'the first English monarch'.[132] *A New Almanack Indifferently Serving this Whole Monarchie of Great Britaine*, produced by Thomas Rudston in 1610, sounded 'British' in scope, but entirely ignored Scotland when listing the best routes to London from a variety of towns in England and Wales.[133] Similarly, except for his tract's title—*A Souldier's Wishe to Briton's Welfare*—Barnabe Rich referred only to 'England', never 'Britain', in the 1604 text.

Other writers took more seriously the change in England's name and saw their task as informing readers about their British roots. The Lincolnshire historian Edward Ayscu began his 'history of our famous island of Britaine' with a 'briefe declaration' of its first inhabitants before recounting what he intended to be an impartial account of the 'many leagues and happy mariages between the two kingdoms of this Iland'.[134] However, Ayscu never passed over the opportunity to draw attention to the instances when Scottish monarchs paid homage to their English counterparts, and he clearly saw England as the superior partner in the relationship. The title page of the book showed where his priorities lay for, in a small sketch map of the British Isles, 'Scotia' and 'Hibernia' are disproportionately dwarfed by 'Anglia'.[135]

Like Ayscu, John Speed proffered a description of Ancient Britain in his 1611 *History of Great Britaine*, and his account was not brief. In over 150 two-columned folio pages, Speed assessed the various etymologies of Britain's name, described the 'manners and customes' of its people, and explained the form of its government. Nonetheless, once Speed moved into post-Norman history, he was utterly Anglocentric; concentrating on English monarchs, he had little to say about those of Wales and Scotland except when the English defeated them in battle.[136]

Both Speed and Ayscu dismissed the notion of Brute as the founder of Great Britain. But, since Brute was germane to James's Union project, he found a secure place not just in Union tracts and royal genealogies but in chronologies printed in almanacs and the imaginative writings of several early Jacobean poets.[137] The Londoner Edward Wilkinson, for example, celebrated James's accession with a story in verse of Brute's arrival 'with Trojan youth' in the island where 'built he a new Troy' with 'lawes both good and witty'.[138] On 29 October 1605 (shortly before the Union was supposed to be reopened in parliament), Anthony Munday's pageant celebrating the inauguration of London's lord mayor recreated 'the antiquitie of Brytaine', with the conquering Brute as its lead character who blessed James as a 'second Brute', reuniting 'those sundred lands in one'. Yet, despite this theme, Munday's text was unashamedly or perhaps unconsciously Anglocentric. Given its context, it is hardly surprising that London was 'Troya Nova' and the Thames the 'queene of all Britanniae's streames', but the only other rivers mentioned in the pageant were the Humber and Severn.[139]

Michael Drayton's long chorographical poem *Poly-Olbion* had Brute on the frontispiece (designed by the engraver William Hole), together with Julius Caesar, Hengist the Saxon, and William the Norman, all conquerors of Albion/Great Britain, which was depicted as a woman seated within a triumphal arch. In the text, Drayton lionized 'the Godlike Brute' whose story dominates the first song and whose bloodline runs through the whole poem. In the fifth song comes the prophesy that a king would descend from the marriage which 'conjoined the white-rose and the red':

> By whom three sever'd realms in one shall firmlie stand,
>   As Britain-founding Brute first monarchiz'd the land.[140]

Yet sitting alongside each of Drayton's songs is a prose commentary by the antiquary John Seldon that injects a note of scepticism about the legends in the poem. Seemingly, Drayton did not expect his readers to accept the story of Brute as historical truth but presented him as a character revived through the power of poetry and put to topical use.[141]

Brute and his sons figured in other Jacobean poems and perhaps ten late Elizabethan plays.[142] But these legendary persons are absent from early Jacobean plays. Instead, dramatists conjured up Britain's ancient past through other characters and stories which equally well served the purpose of topicality. The anonymous Elizabethan play *The True Chronicle History of King Leir* (performed in 1594) was printed in 1605 at a time when Union was a current political issue, and Shakespeare's *King Lear* was staged before James and his court during the Christmas season of 1606, when the parliamentary debates about Union were at their height. The latter was printed in 1608 just after parliament's rejection of James's scheme. Since the plot of both plays concerned a British king creating and inhabiting a divided realm, their contemporary flavour was obvious. However, their plots were not identical. In giving his drama a tragic ending, Shakespeare moved away from both *King Leir* and Holinshed's *Chronicles*, the shared source, in which Lear and Cordelia did not die but were restored to the throne.[143] Because their deaths, civil war, and foreign invasion resulted from Shakespeare's Lear dividing up his kingdom, the play has often been interpreted as pro-Union.[144] However, it is better to see it as more elliptical. As one literary critic explains, the tragedy stems not so much from Lear dividing his kingdom as from his seeking to hold onto power after doing so. Furthermore, the play negates the fictive pro-Union prophecy that a king with Brute's blood would again sit on the throne, because the childless deaths of Lear's daughters extinguish the British king's royal dynasty.[145]

Another legendary British king was the inspiration for Shakespeare's *Cymbeline*, which was quite possibly performed at court and in the public theatre to celebrate Henry's investiture of 1610.[146] Although it would be reductive to construe *Cymbeline* as a pro-Union play, it does evoke Jacobean language surrounding the failed project.[147] Throughout, 'Britain' is mentioned twenty-nine times (in contrast to *Lear*'s three), while separation, fragmentation, and disharmony are the play's central themes until the last act when all is resolved with actions and words of revival, restoration, reunion, and peace, the language of pro-Union polemic. The supposedly dead sons of Cymbeline are restored to their father, 'whose issue/Promises Britain peace and plenty'. The Romano-Briton Postumus is reunited with his wife, Cymbeline's daughter Innogen. Cymbeline's final speeches resound with phrases of peace and harmony: 'My peace we will begin'; 'Let/A Roman and British ensign wave/Friendly together', while the final sentence is: 'Ere bloody hands were washed with such a peace.'[148] Of course, this language of peace also references James's irenic foreign policy, but it is within a British context.

The conflict between Ancient Britain and Classical Rome is the subject of *The Tragedie of Bonduca*, written by Francis Beaumont and John Fletcher.[149] Performed several years after Union had been defeated (in 1611 or 1613–14), the play considers the nature of a British identity as well as that of colonialism. Its two main characters—the legendary Boudicca (Bonduca), queen of the Iceni tribe, and her cousin Caractacus (Caratach)—hold opposing views of Rome: the former despising Romans as 'vitrous' and 'tyrants'; the latter admiring Roman courage and honour, despite fighting against the invaders. In Act 4, Bonduca dies by her own hand after military defeat and, in the last scene of Act 5, Caratach is treated honourably by the Romans; 'a brave' foe, he becomes 'a noble friend'. With the deaths of Bonduca, her two daughters, and nephew Hengo, the independent Britain they fought for is extinct, but a Roman Britain is born from the newly forged peace. As Bonduca counsels Rome: 'If you will keep your laws and empire whole,/Place in your Romaine flesh a Britain soul.'[150]

These dramas exposed thousands of playgoers to a mythical Ancient Britain and might too have 'taught the unlearned some knowledge' of the past, as the playwright Thomas Heywood claimed.[151] But the plays do not look back nostalgically on an Ancient Britain in support of James's Union. As with Munday's pageant, Britain in these plays did not comprise the whole island. After all, Lear, Cymbeline, Boudicca, and Caractacus supposedly lived after the division of Brutus's kingdom in a land that was called Britain but corresponded to what was later named England. What the plays did was explore the British component in England's national identity, an identity formed by many conquering peoples.[152] It is doubtful that this theme would have been of much interest to playgoers had not a Scot been sitting on England's throne and attempting a measure of Union.[153]

★ ★ ★

One of James's kingdoms, Ireland, of course remained outside Britain for he held the title 'king of Ireland' separate from the new one of 'king of Great Britain'. The realm of Ireland was ruled through a lord deputy, Irish privy council, and a parliament based in Dublin. Nonetheless, James thought in terms of a triple monarchy and was keen to make Ireland British. His main approach was to encourage Scots to settle alongside the English in parts of the north. From 1604, he allocated lands in Down and the Ards confiscated from Con O'Neill of Clandeboye (who had rebelled in 1601) to James Hamilton, James's agent who had settled in Dublin. Likewise, in 1604, James ignored the vehement objections of Sir Arthur Chichester, soon to be lord deputy, and confirmed an earlier large grant of land in Antrim to Sir Randal Macdonnell.[154] When James began the Ulster plantation in 1609, he awarded about half the land grants to Scottish applicants. Most of the Scottish undertakers were minor lairds, but Lennox and his brother Aubigny were also grantees.[155] Scottish migration into Ireland, James believed, would help create a British Isles, as well as guarantee its security.[156]

Additionally, James gave positions in the Irish Church to Scots. Before 1612, three held six bishoprics in Ireland, and they employed their countrymen as ministers and preachers.[157] Scots were brought into the government too. As early as August 1603, Sir James Fullerton was made muster-master general, responsible for the important task of demobilizing the greater part of the English army and, in 1606, he was sworn onto the Irish privy council, the first Scot ever to serve on that body. Two more Scots were appointed privy councillors before 1612 and a further eight before the end of James's reign in 1625. In truth, the Scottish councillors barely participated in the government policy or administration, and David Edwards has judged James's attempts to 'britannize' the Irish administration by bringing in Scots a failure.[158] But, at the very least, their formal inclusion had a symbolic importance.

James was considerably more successful in emasculating the Gaelic chieftains and lords. At first, it seemed they had retained their independence and status after the Nine Years' War, for the peace left many in power. Mountjoy had offered the defeated rebels a generous settlement in the Treaty of

Mellifont of 30 March 1603, and soon afterwards Tyrone and his ally Rory O'Donnell, lord of Tyrconnell, went to the English court and obtained a royal pardon. On the advice of Cecil and Mountjoy, James restored to Tyrone his lordship and earldom in Ulster and made O'Donnell earl of Tyrconnell. Lesser Irish rebels were pardoned too and given legal title to their lands.

However, many in the army and civilian government were incensed at the leniency of the peace terms. Among the critics were Chichester and the new attorney-general Sir John Davies. These 'servitors' (as those Englishmen engaged in both military and civilian service in Ireland were called) were equally at odds with London's policy of using persuasion rather than coercion to advance Protestantism in Ireland.[159] James's government was looking for stability after the long war, whereas the more ideologically driven servitors wanted all Catholic priests to be expelled and conformity imposed on the Old English Catholics, if necessary by force. Royal officials in Dublin, therefore, tried to push the king and English privy councillors into pursuing a tougher policy towards not just the Irish lords but also the Old English who were the descendants of Ireland's twelfth-century Anglo-Norman settlers and had largely remained loyal to England during the Nine Years' War. While Mountjoy, now earl of Devonshire, retained his influence as lord lieutenant of Ireland, a strong voice for moderation was heard in the English privy council. However, once he lost royal favour and afterwards died, the Irish government and army felt freer to attack the power and authority of the Ulster earls as well as come down hard on recusants living in the Pale, which encompassed much of Dublin, Kildare, Meath, West Meath, and Louth.

On the ground, the army—stationed in garrisons in Ulster or along its borders—treated Tyrone and Tyrconnell with scant respect. Captains and soldiers were able to get away with rape, theft, extortion, and murder, leaving the Irish earls powerless to protect their people or get compensation for their relatives, the essential function of lordship.[160] The earls' position as Irish lords was further damaged when the government converted Gaelic land tenures into freeholds and tenancies, abolished the lords' right to impose private taxes, initiated investigations into Tyrone's proprietorial rights, and planned to introduce shires with sheriffs, JPs, and assizes.[161] The earls' estates were additionally endangered when George Montgomery, the new bishop of Derry, Raphoe, and Clogher, laid claim to the ecclesiastical lands in his dioceses (which covered much of the two lordships). Montgomery's explicit mission to spread 'the Reformation' and the 'civilising of the barbarous manners' of the Irish nation further infuriated Tyrone who self-identified as the champion of Irish Catholicism.[162]

At the same time, Chichester's administration began a drive against recusancy in the areas it controlled. The lord deputy issued mandates in the king's name ordering designated Catholics to attend Protestant services on pain of severe prosecution. Recusants would be subjected to fines of up to £200 for contempt of the council's authority, a much higher sum than stipulated in the Irish Act of Uniformity. This 'mandates policy' was initiated in 1605 in Dublin, where sixteen Old English gentlemen were targeted. When protests arose, Chichester ordered the arrest of the ringleaders, one of whom was Tyrone's brother-in-law Sir Patrick Barnewall.[163]

Confronted with complaints from Ulster lords and Dublin Catholics, James demanded Chichester proceed more moderately. In the wake of the Gunpowder Plot, he and his councillors feared that the present peaceful protests might escalate into an armed Catholic rising. Given the crown's financial difficulties, the last thing it needed was for Ireland to go up again in flames. So, after reading Tyrone's complaints, James and the English privy council ordered Chichester to 'seek to control' the army and 'carefully protect the earl from any unnecessary molestation' for as long as he remained obedient to the state. To retain the earl's trust, James decided to arbitrate personally in the proprietorial disputes involving him so that the judicial review would not be left to men biased against him. He also rejected a proposal to establish an Ulster presidency which would have challenged the earl's power in his lordship.[164]

Additionally, James and the privy council wanted Chichester to pull back from the 'compulsory course' he had begun towards the Old English Catholics. They advised he take 'a temperate course between both extremes, neither yielding any hope of toleration of their superstition, nor startling the multitude by any general or rigorous compulsion'. All but one of the prisoners, they ordered, should be released and the way forward should henceforward be 'admonition, persuasion, and instruction' with the punishment of only a few as examples so that 'the rest may be kept in awe'.[165] Yet, despite this order, Chichester persisted in the 'mandates policy' based on coercion and extended it outside Dublin to Munster. Many Catholics conformed under the pressure, but discontent seethed at the harshness.

These were just the circumstances that might cause a rising, and, in the early summer of 1607, London heard disturbing news that the earls were plotting to lead a pan-Catholic rebellion (uniting the Gaelic Irish and the

Old English Catholics) with Spanish support. Several in England questioned the truth of the rumours as they had been heard before and the main informant this time (Lord Howth) was thought unsound. Historians today, however, are certain that Tyrone was in league with Spain and planning to lead the Old English Catholics in a rebellion to defend Catholicism. Whether the Old English were themselves involved in treason is harder to assess.[166]

Even with uncertain intelligence, the government could not afford to take chances, especially as enclosure riots were then disturbing the Midlands of England while, in Scotland, highlanders had seized three royal castles.[167] The English privy council therefore ordered an immediate end to the 'mandates policy' and instructed Chichester to arrest Tyrone if investigation proved the rumours correct. In the meantime, James commanded Tyrone to come to London for a hearing of a contentious proprietorial dispute and possibly considered detaining the earl there. Certainly, Tyrone received a warning from Archduke Albert that the summons of July 1607 was a ploy to get him to court where he would be put under arrest. Panicked, Tyrone embarked on what has become known as the 'flight of the earls'.[168]

On 3 September, Tyrone met up with Tyrconnell at Rathmullan in Donegal with the intent of leaving for Spain. Together with nearly forty members of their family, they set off the next day and, after twenty days of rough seas, they landed at Quilleboeuf in Normandy. Straightaway, their arrival on the Continent instigated diplomatic tensions. When Henry IV ignored English demands for the earls' extradition and allowed them safe passage to the Spanish Netherlands, Cecil vented his fury on the French ambassador. Cecil then put pressure on the Habsburgs to hand over the fugitives. Philip III and the archdukes were caught between a rock and a hard place: their religious role as protectors of Catholics and their political need to stay on good terms with England. In the end, they took a middle course, pouring honours on the Irish earls but denying them access to Spain and encouraging them to stay in Rome, where they would receive a pension from the pope.[169]

Meanwhile, in Ireland, a series of injustices and personal insults provoked the previously loyal lord of Inishowen, Sir Cahir O'Doherty, into an impromptu rising. On 19 April 1608, he captured the garrison at Derry, took English hostages—including Bishop Montgomery's wife and sister— and raised rebellion across north Donegal as far east as Armagh. Seemingly, he hoped the English would seek to redress his grievances given the unsettled state of the north and the general expectation that the Ulster earls would return with foreign 'succours and support'. However, O'Doherty miscalculated. Chichester was not a man for appeasement. The lord deputy stood firm, and dispatched forces to storm the rebels' main stronghold. After its surrender, O'Doherty was killed in battle on 5 July, and the rising collapsed.[170]

O'Doherty's rebellion—still more than Tyrone's flight—destroyed James's confidence that the lesser Irish lords could be counted loyal subjects. He consequently agreed with Chichester's plan to seize the land of all the Gaelic lords and chieftains in the province, even those who had not supported Tyrone and O'Doherty, and implement a widespread policy of plantation [colonization]. Plantations had begun in other parts of Ireland during the second half of the sixteenth century, but many of the English colonial settlements had not survived the upheavals and massacres that took place during the Nine Years' War. As with the earlier plantations, the goal in 1608 was first to secure the province from foreign invasion and domestic unrest and second to reform 'the religion and manners' of the Irish and 'reduce them to better civilitie'.[171] Hand in hand with the planting of Protestant settlers, the crown worked to clear Ulster of disruptive elements. Thousands of alleged traitors (those who escaped hangings) and 'idle swordsmen' (unemployed highly trained soldiers) were transported from the north to Sweden where many were conscripted to serve in Charles IX's army against Russia. When listing his service to the crown in 1614, Chichester declared with pride: 'besides the cuttinge of manie bad members and disloyall offenders within the lande, I have sent awaie above 6,000 of the same inclination and profession into the warres of Sweden'.[172]

The plantation plans were finalized in May 1610 and included measures designed to overcome the weaknesses of previous ones: for instance, the planners allocated smaller, more manageable estates (ranging from 1,000 to 2,000 acres), insisted that the grantees had to be resident in Ireland for at least the first five years, and required colonists to live in clusters to ensure their security. The grantees (called undertakers) fell into three main groups: English and Scots, servitors, and 'deserving' Gaelic Irish. The parcels of land offered to the English and Scottish undertakers were roughly equal in size: 81,500 acres in total for the English, 81,000 acres for the Scots, just over one-third of the whole. These British undertakers were initially required to settle English and Scottish immigrants onto their lands as either freeholders or tenants, but under Charles I Irish tenants were permitted to take up leases too. Gaelic Irish grantees faced no restrictions on who was to farm their lands but could not demand Irish exactions from tenants. The scheme also set aside land in Counties Coleraine and Tyrone (to be renamed Londonderry) for twelve London livery companies, which in return were expected to develop two towns (Londonderry and Coleraine) into the commercial hubs of the settlements trading directly with London. The Irish Church and Trinity College, Dublin, received land too.[173]

Although it took time, the Ulster plantation flourished. As many as 15,000 adult British men were planted there by Charles I's reign, and 100,000 people had migrated to Ireland by 1641.[174] However, the plan to make the island British was slow to take off. The first generation of English, Scots, and Irish settlers mainly lived separately, prayed separately, and avoided intermarriage.[175] Moreover, the English deeply resented the Scots; they failed to see why the lands in Ulster should be shared with others since they had subdued the province at great cost to their own lives and finances.[176] In the short term, James's plantation policy imposed stability on Ulster; however, in the longer term, the deep grievances of the displaced Irish against the new landowners exploded in the massacres that followed a rebellion which started in 1641.

★ ★ ★

James's kingship of Ireland both reflected and impacted upon his rule over the Highlands and Islands of Scotland. During the 1590s, James had attempted to bring these areas under more effective centralized control and eradicate their Gaelic customs and culture by demilitarizing the clans and establishing colonies of Lowland settlers in the Western Isles. The Scottish king's motives were partly political (to acquire greater royal control over the area), partly financial (to collect taxes there), and partly cultural (to 'plant civilitie' in 'barbarous' regions).[177] As it turned out, colonization proved unworkable before 1603, especially in Lewis where the inhabitants turned on the new settlers in 1601 and forced those who survived to flee.[178] For practical reasons, James had to revert to the Scottish crown's traditional policy of delegating responsibility for enforcing law and order in the Highlands and North Isles to the marquess of Huntly and in the Western Isles to Archibald Campbell, seventh earl of Argyll.[179]

After the flight of the Ulster earls, the Western Isles seemed to pose a security threat to the Irish plantation project. Because Scottish mercenaries from there had sometimes fought for Tyrone during the Nine Years' War, fears were expressed that they might well intervene in Ulster. Taking advantage of the union of crowns, James now decided to vanquish the clans in the Western Isles by applying a military strategy that involved all three realms.[180] His original plan—conveyed to Chichester in January 1608—was for a British expedition under Andrew Stewart, third Lord Ochiltree, to be sent to the Isles: Scotland would raise the main army; England would provide some forces, shipping, and ammunition; and Ireland would send several hundred men.[181] Keen to comply, Chichester earmarked some four hundred men for the venture and offered his services 'towards the planting and settlement therof'.[182] When O'Doherty rebelled in April, this plan had to be abandoned as Chichester could spare no troops. Nevertheless, still taking a British perspective, James dispatched the Ochiltree expedition from Scotland, supported by an English naval force, to protect his Irish province, subdue the Hebridean clans, and expropriate their lands.[183]

The military operation was immediately successful, but instead of implementing colonization, as originally intended, James was persuaded to negotiate and compromise with the clans. Mainly because he could not afford to suppress resistance, he allowed his negotiator, Andrew Knox, to reach a collaborative settlement in 1609 (known as the Iona Statutes) with the chiefs and Hebridean elite. They agreed to set up Presbyterian churches in their midst, abandon many of their Gaelic customs, and send their sons to be educated in the Scottish Lowlands where they would learn to speak and read English.[184] Like the plantation programme in Ireland, the plan for the Western Isles was for the Gaelic peoples to be 'civilized', just as the Ancient Britons had been by the Romans.[185] The same rationalization was used by the colonists who settled in Virginia.

★ ★ ★

The triple monarchy of England, Scotland, and Ireland was often referred to as an empire since 'empire' was then understood as the agglomeration of many kingdoms under one ruler. Speed used empire in this sense when he entitled his 1611 geographical study a *Theatre of the Empire of Great Britain* and praised James as the 'inlarger and uniter of the British Empire' in its preface (see Figure 19).

However, the word 'empire' had two additional meanings, both of which could be applied to the British Isles under James. The first was derived from the Roman conceptions of *imperium* and denoted sovereignty.[186] That 'this realm of England is an empire' was articulated in the 1533 statute of

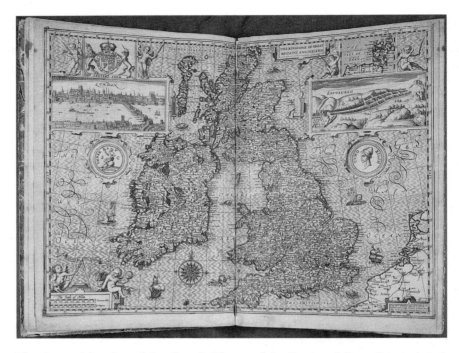

Figure 19. Map from John Speed, *Theatre of the Empire of Great Britain* (1611). The map shows Ireland almost attached to Scotland in order to emphasize that Great Britain was a geographical as well as a dynastic unit. Reproduced with the permission of Special Collections, Leeds University Library, The Whitaker Collection, 9 fol.

Henry VIII, which separated England from the jurisdiction of Rome, and meant that the kingdom was subject to no earthly power other than the monarch. This was the principle that lay behind James's own dispute with the papacy (discussed in chapter 12). The second meaning emerged from the sixteenth-century European overseas expansions and associated empire with colonization.[187] The plantations in Ireland were part of this process, although whether we can call that kingdom a colony is a matter of dispute among historians. But, at the very least, similar justifications for colonization were applied to the plantations in both Ireland and North America.[188]

One of the main proponents of overseas colonization under Elizabeth had been Richard Hakluyt, the writer and compiler of exploration narratives. His 'Discourse of Western Planting' (1584) was a long memorandum, composed at Sir Francis Walsingham's request, to enlist the queen's support for Ralegh's scheme for settling a large tract of land on the eastern coast of

North America. Hakluyt listed numerous reasons for backing the venture: an evangelical obligation; opportunities for prosperity from rich resources, trade, and agriculture; the employment of England's surplus and unproductive population; and a means to curtail Spanish expansionism in the New World. Hakluyt's later encyclopaedic compilation *The Principall Navigations* (first edition 1589, an enlarged second edition 1598–1600) extended these arguments and was constructed to appeal to England's sense of nationhood and spirit of adventure.[189]

Ralegh's project did secure royal support. In 1584, Elizabeth granted him a patent for the settlement of Virginia (named after the Virgin Queen as another intended enticement), but the colony proved a failure. The first group of male settlers on Roanoke Island in 1585 took flight after their relationship with the local Algonquians, on whom they depended for food, broke down. A second attempt in 1587 to settle men, women, and children on Roanoke also failed. The colony's governor, John White, returned home to fetch supplies, but by the time a naval convoy arrived in 1590 to bring relief the colonists had mysteriously disappeared.[190] The only outcome of note from these experiments was the exquisite watercolours made by White, adapted in engravings by Theodor de Bry to illustrate Thomas Harriot's pamphlet *A Brief and True Report of the New Found Land of Virginia*. The text and pictures describe the flora, fauna, and peoples of the area in attractive detail.

After the Roanoke disasters, colonization in North America was not attempted again under Elizabeth. The risks were too great, and shipping in the Atlantic was being used for privateering, offering quick profits, and other maritime strategies in the war against Spain. So, despite the reputation of Elizabeth's sailors as the first founders of the British Empire, England's colonial achievement in the Americas before 1603 was practically nil.[191] Nonetheless, Jacobean promoters of colonization saw themselves as inheritors of this earlier imperial past, and they targeted places which had been already located by Elizabethans for their own settlements.

James's 1604 peace with Spain, which prohibited privateering, redirected attention towards colonization in areas outside existing Iberian settlement. James supported the process by granting a monopoly to two joint stock companies, on 10 April 1606, to colonize an area on the east coast of North America, roughly between today's Canadian border and Cape Fear River in North Carolina. The London company—the Virginia Company—was given responsibility for all colonies established south of the forty-first parallel (cutting through present-day New York and Pennsylvania). The second company—the Plymouth branch—included merchants from Bristol, Exeter, and Plymouth and was to colonize the lands further north. The extent of the physical space granted for exploration and settlement was defined by the wish to avoid Florida (a Spanish area of influence) and the Newfoundland fisheries.[192] Other companies formed for projects across the Atlantic during the timescale of this book were the Newfoundland Company (1610) and Somers Islands/Bermuda Company (1612).

Merchants were not the only investors in the Virginia Company; soldiers, lawyers, nobles, and gentry also came to be backers. MPs were heavily involved: all but three names on the original 1606 Virginia charter sat in the commons.[193] Some of the men already encountered in this book—Richard Martin, Sandys, Bacon, Lennox, and Southampton—were members of the company. Holding shares in other trading companies, most investors were looking for short- to medium-term financial returns, but profit was not their only goal. The dominant theme of the charters of 1606 and 1609, as well as the company's promotional literature, was that the establishment of the colony would serve God in bringing Christianity and 'human civility' to the 'infidels and savages living in those parts'. The company's intention, or so it professed, was to teach the 'savages' of the New World the religion, laws, and customs of the old and create 'a new Brittaine in another world'. Another claim was that the colony would enhance the honour of the king and 'nation'. Expanding James's territories would boost his reputation abroad; and embarking on virile colonial ventures would prevent the nation sinking into 'effeminacy' now that the Spanish war had ended. Also, not forgotten were such practical advantages as removing 'idle persons' and 'papists' into employment overseas.[194] For the most part, the aims and justifications reiterated those made earlier by Hakluyt.

Just before Christmas 1606, the Virginia Company sent out three ships carrying some 104 male passengers across the Atlantic. Sailing from London, the colonists arrived at the mouth of Chesapeake Bay towards the end of April, and the next month they settled some fifty miles upstream on swampy land belonging to the Paspahegh tribe in the territory of Tsenacomoco. The settlement was named Jamestown in honour of the king. But, since the site was poor, the climate unhealthy, and the settlers (many of them gentlemen or craftsmen) inexperienced in farming, the colony struggled to survive during its first decade, its viability not helped by poor governance and feuding among the leaders. During these early years, countless settlers died; the colony was not self-sufficient, requiring provisions from relief ships; and the investors made no profit.[195] Yet, against all odds, the colony did survive, unlike the previous settlements in Roanoke. The achievement could not have happened without the initial protection and aid offered by the Powhatans, the tribe which exercised a form of overlordship in the region and already had long experience of Europeans.[196] Relations with their chieftain Wahunsonacock were co-operative at the start, and he allowed the exchange of corn and pelts for metal goods and textiles. This co-operation was cemented into a quasi-alliance after he adopted John Smith, the *de facto* governor of the colony, as a *werowanve* [local chieftain, or vassal] and took settler boys into the tribal communities to learn the local languages and serve as hostages for the colonists' good behaviour.[197] However, relations deteriorated after Smith launched a series of raids in 1608 against local Indian settlements that included women and children.[198]

Because the colony depended upon relief ships to bring in new colonists as well as supplies, the colony was costly. To save their investment, the Virginia Company requested and received a new charter from James in 1609, which allowed it to sell stock to the public; for £12 10s, each new stockholder was promised land in Virginia. The offer was widely advertised, and enough money was raised to fund nine ships for Virginia. The convoy set out in June 1609, but after seven weeks at sea it ran into a hurricane, and the ships were scattered. While eight of them transporting several hundred passengers made it to Jamestown, the flagship *Sea Venture* was wrecked just off present-day Bermuda. About 150 people on board made a dramatic escape to the largely uninhabited island where they spent the winter and spring in some comfort, eating pigs and seabirds. Among them was the soldier Sir Thomas Gates, who had been appointed deputy governor by the Virginia Company, and two men—William Strachey and Silvester Jourdain—who later wrote accounts of the landing at Bermuda. These circulated in London before being printed and may have influenced Shakespeare's *The Tempest*.[199]

Building two smaller ships from the salvage and local trees, the shipwrecked men escaped Bermuda and landed at Jamestown in May 1610. The colony that greeted them was close to collapse. Injured in a gunpowder explosion, Smith had departed for England the previous October, and, from that time onwards, the local tribes had refused to provide the colonists with food, not least because they were suffering themselves from a severe drought. During that winter—known as the 'starving time'—some 80 per cent of the three hundred or so settlers either died of starvation or were killed when they tried to forage outside their settlement. Those who lived may have resorted to cannibalism for one report stated that a Mr Collines salted his dead wife's corpse to survive.[200]

Aghast at the state of the settlement, Gates decided to take the survivors back to England. But, sailing down the James River, he encountered a fleet sent by the Virginia Company with fresh supplies and colonists led by Thomas West, Baron de la Warr, the newly appointed governor. Cheered by these reinforcements, Gates turned back. The following year another experienced soldier, Sir Thomas Dale, joined the colony as lord marshal. The new arrivals brought discipline to the demoralized settlers by introducing martial law to curb crime and strict regulations to improve sanitation and living conditions.[201]

De la Warr stayed only ten months in Virginia, but the colony continued to thrive under the deputy governors, first Gates and then Dale. However, the deputy governors' drive to extend the colony worsened the settlers' relations with local tribes, resulting in a cycle of violent attacks and vicious reprisals. Although the colonists were winning encounters, they were all too ready to end the warfare. A peace was agreed in 1614, sealed by a marriage between an English settler, John Rolfe, and Pocahontas, the daughter of Wahunsonacock, whom the colonists had kidnapped the previous year. The peace lasted until 1622.[202]

★ ★ ★

Back in England there was huge interest in Virginia, generated by the many sermons preached and publications printed to promote the Jamestown settlement as well as the general prayers offered for its success.[203] Readers devoured the stories of settlers. Londoners wondered at and sometimes intermingled with the small numbers of women, children, and young men from Tsenacomoco who came to England and were lodged in the homes of merchants and ministers in the City.[204]

Learning from earlier Spanish accounts and their own experiences, colonists and Londoners had little doubt about the humanity and powers of reason held by the indigenous peoples. Travel narratives testified to their use of language, desire for sociability, and organization of a civil society.[205] Some early Jacobeans may also have been influenced by Montaigne's essay 'Of the Canniballes' which was translated by Florio in 1603 and argued that 'there is nothing barbarous or savage in this nation by anything that I can gather, excepting, that every one gives the title of barbarism to everything that is not in use in his own country'.[206] Nonetheless, the word 'savage' was applied to the Powhatans. Their semi-nomadic lifestyle and illiteracy made them appear uncultured while their goods—jewellery and animal skins—were judged crude. Only their tobacco was valued although not by everyone. James urged his subjects not to imitate the 'maners of the wilde, godlesse, and slavish Indians' to take up 'this uncivill tricke' of smoking.[207]

For many in England, the 'Indians' resembled the Ancient Britons before the arrival of the Romans. All the natives needed was their own Roman emperor to bring them into civilization. As one ballad rang out in 1612:

> Who knowes not England once was like
>   a wildernesse and savage place,
> Till government and use of men,
>   that wildnesse did deface:
> And so Virginia may in time,
>   be made like England now
> Where long-loud peace and plenty both
>   sits smiling on her brow.[208]

While comparing themselves to the Romans, the English wanted to be distinguished from the Spanish colonizers of the Americas. Preaching to raise funds for the Virginia Company, William Crashaw, in 1609, maintained that, unlike the conquistadores, 'we will take nothing from the savages by power nor pillage, by craft nor violence, neither goods, lands nor libertie, much lesse life'. The purpose of the English enterprise, he maintained, was the conversion of 'our brethren, for the same God made them', and while fair trade with 'a heathen' was legitimate, a Christian could take nothing from him 'against his will'.[209] Nevertheless, other supporters of colonization were more than ready to expropriate the land of the 'natives' on grounds that they had not been exploiting it properly and were failing to realize its potential. Ironically, this latter group—which also began to argue that the natives were irredeemably 'savages'—came to rely on Spanish texts to provide justifications for expanding into Powhatan territory. And over time, they won the argument.[210]

During the early years of the colony at Jamestown, the morality of dispossessing the Powhatans was contested. The issue was imaginatively explored in at least two plays on the London stage. As we have seen, *Bonduca*, set in Britain at the time of the Roman invasion, broached questions about national identity. At the same time, though, it drew upon and raised questions about the colonial experience: Caratach fights to keep the invader off his land; Corporal Judas complains of the hardships and starvation that the Romans (colonizers) are facing; and the Britons have one leader (Caratach) capable of being civilized in Rome and another (Bonduca) who would rather die than do so. In asking whether the Romans or the Britons deserve to win the conflict, the play contemplates the morality of the colonial enterprise.[211]

The relationship between Shakespeare's *The Tempest* and the colonial experience has long been debated. All agree that the playwright was influenced by Montaigne's essay on 'cannibals', but many scholars today refute earlier notions of interpreting the play within a colonial context.[212] Of course, Prospero's isle was not Bermuda nor Virginia, and indeed it was firmly placed in the Old World. Nonetheless, the speeches of Caliban (an anagram of ca[n]nibal), the only character born on the island, might well have prompted discussions about the rights and nature of native peoples in those places. Similarly, questions of sovereignty and possession are aired through the rival claims of Caliban and Prospero to the island, issues relevant to Jacobeans interested in the Virginia enterprise. We do not know how Jacobeans responded to the play, but it is hard today not to hear the pain of dispossession in Caliban's speech of Act 1, Scene 2:

This island's mine, by Sycorax my mother,
   Which thou tak'st from me. When thou cam'st first,
Thou strok'st me and made much of me, wouldst give me
   Water with berries in 't, and teach me how
To name the bigger light, and how the less,
   That burn by day and night. And then I lov'd thee
And showed thee all the qualities o' th' isle,
   The fresh springs, brine-pits, barren place and fertile:
Curs'd be I that did so! All the charms
   Of Sycorax, toads, beetles, bats, light on you!
For I am all the subjects that you have,
   Which first was mine own king. And here you sty me
In this hard rock, whiles you do keep from me
   The rest o' th' island.[213]

★ ★ ★

James was pivotal in the attempt at Union and the drive for empire. The initiative for Union was solely his, even though he had the support of a handful of reformers and loyal individuals. For him, Union was a providential imperative: God had chosen him and his lineage to rule over the peoples of Britain and Ireland, and they had a religious duty to unite in common allegiance to him and his family, just as the members of a Scottish clan owed allegiance to the individual chosen to head it.[214] Hence, when his parliaments rejected Union and did not yield to the providence of God, their decision was 'to spit and blaspheme in his face'.[215] The impetus for plantation in Ireland, though, came from the servitors, but James made sure that it should be part of his British project. As for empire, James declared his subjects' right to settle in territories unoccupied by any Christian prince and granted the Virginia Company its charter as a scheme that might bring the crown financial rewards. He hoped this approach would avoid confrontations with Spain but, as we shall see in the next chapter, in this he was mistaken.

Although James I's accession launched and moulded many of the initiatives described here, his attempts to unify his territories continued a process of state formation and integration that had long predated his inheritance of the English crown and was occurring in other European states.[216] Similarly, western expansion had been attempted (albeit unsuccessfully) under Elizabeth and was likewise a European development. After the establishment of the Spanish and Portuguese empires in the early sixteenth centuries, the Americas had become a magnet attracting not just England but also France and the United Provinces. These processes were not inevitable, nor did they take the same form in all countries; different milieux and contingency determined their nature and outcomes. And one contingent influence in Britain was the accession of James to the English throne.

14

The Habsburgs and the Dutch

It is a bad mistake to think that James came to the English throne with 'an ignorance of diplomacy and the politics of mainland Europe'.[1] Far from it! The Scottish king had long proved adept at international relations. During the 1590s, he productively cultivated his Protestant in-laws in Denmark and Germany and came to be considered a key figure in that powerful dynastic network of rulers. Although he remained neutral in the major conflicts taking place in western Europe, he managed to retain the goodwill of all the warring participants. Grateful to James for allowing Scottish volunteers and mercenaries to fight on their side against Spain, the Dutch States General maintained diplomatic and commercial ties with the king. So did Henry IV of France, who even sought James as a husband for his sister. The Spanish kings and archdukes were certainly suspicious of James but, at least on the surface, they seemed appreciative of his messages of friendship and hints that he might convert to Catholicism. Only with Elizabeth was James's relationship tense and bad-tempered; even so, the Anglo-Scottish defensive alliance of 1586 still held.[2]

As Cynthia Fry has expertly explained, James's successes in foreign policy were based on his ability to make vague promises, use plausible deniability, and exploit power dynamics to improve his own and Scotland's position.[3] Building on this experience, James used similar techniques in his relations with the Dutch and the Habsburgs during his first decade as king of England with a similar degree of success. He again tried to avoid military commitments and to appear to all sides as a friendly neutral, even a mediator, in their disputes and wars. He promoted himself as an important figure whose friendship was vital for all rulers to foster, and he held out prospects for dynastic alliances through the marriages of his children. To keep himself at the centre of the international stage, he invited European monarchs and their special representatives to visit him in England for important negotiations.

★ ★ ★

In 1603, James inherited a war with Spain and a treaty of alliance with the Dutch. Guided by Cecil, one of his first acts was to fulfil England's treaty obligations by dispatching the usual contingent of soldiers to the United Provinces to fight against Spain. In a message to the Dutch, he pledged the continuance of aid until he found 'just cause to take another coorse'.[4] Another course was already in his mind and obvious to most observers: 'Everyone concludes that his Majesty's inclination is for peace with Spain', mused Scaramelli, for it was generally known that, 'in his almost private and studious days in Scotland, he used to say that it was a king's duty to govern his people in peace rather than to enlarge his kingdom by force of arms'.[5]

Unfortunately for James, his accession coincided with a critical moment in the war that made withdrawal tricky. Archduke Albert's siege of Ostend was going badly for the Dutch, who had been defending the fortress town since July 1601 with a large band of English soldiers. Casualties were high, and Spanish troops had recently seized some fortified positions around the town. Most of James's advisers, including Cecil, were convinced that a Habsburg victory would be disastrous for England's security since 'the Spanish could keep in that port their vessels both armed and unarmed, and make an arsenal for building others, which owing to their proximity to England would be a standing menace'.[6] James, initially at least, did not appreciate the threat; when the danger that Ostend would fall was brought to the king's notice, he said: 'What of it? Was not Ostend originally the king of Spain's and therefore, now, the archduke's?'[7]

Nonetheless, the Ostend crisis put James on the spot as he had to decide quickly whether to send reinforcements to defend the Dutch. All sides in the war were courting him, and the Dutch were the quickest off the mark. After congratulating him on his accession, the States General exhorted him to continue Elizabeth's assistance 'against the insatiable ambition of the Spaniards' by allowing them to recruit more soldiers in England for Ostend.[8] Shortly afterwards, they dispatched to England a high-level embassy, headed by Frederick Henry of Nassau (the youngest son of William of Orange) and the leading Dutch statesman Johan van Oldenbarnevelt, with the aim of persuading James to step up assistance and cease contemplating peace with

Spain. Arriving in mid-May, it joined with Noel de Caron, the agent of the States General, who had been based at Elizabeth's court since 1591.[9]

Henry IV sent an embassy to England too. James had already let the king know of his 'firme desire' to preserve good relations with all his neighbours, and principally France.[10] But the French king sought more than that. Despite signing a peace with Spain at Vervins, in 1598, he had been surreptitiously funding the Dutch to prevent a Habsburg reconquest of Ostend and wanted James to increase English aid to the United Provinces and continue the war against Spain.[11] To negotiate with James, Henry dispatched, in May, an embassy led by his close friend Maximilien de Béthune, the marquis of Rosny (later duke of Sully). Once in London, Rosny and the Dutch ambassadors were in 'constant consultation' about the best way to handle the king and achieve their common goal.[12] A major problem for them, though, was how the Frenchman could convince James to extend the war against Spain while his own monarch remained at peace with the Habsburgs.[13]

On the other side of the argument, the archdukes wanted James to come to the peace table. They had made overtures to him shortly before Elizabeth's death, when their special ambassador to Edinburgh undertook to assist, not challenge, James's right to the English throne and expressed their hopes for future friendly relations.[14] Once James was proclaimed king, they made ready to send an official delegation to London.[15] Led by the experienced diplomat Arenberg, and three other Flemish commissioners, its ostensible purpose was to compliment James on his accession, but its real intent was both to sever English aid to Ostend and sound out the court's attitude to ending the war.[16] Simultaneously, the archdukes did their best to persuade Philip III to pursue peace: 'it is necessary not to lose time in cultivating' James, wrote Isabella in April 1603, 'for having joined England and Scotland, and being joined to Denmark through his father-in-law [sic], he is about to become lord of the ocean'.[17] Philip was desirous for peace but cautious.[18] James's uncontested accession and the defeat of Tyrone cut off Spanish opportunities to foment risings in England and Ireland. The victory in Ireland, moreover, freed James to increase military aid for the Dutch, if he were so inclined. Philip therefore made it known that he thought the war was but 'a private quarrel' between his father and Elizabeth, and since they were both dead, there was no reason for it to continue.[19] In late April, he ordered his envoy Juan de Tassis (soon to be named count of Villamediana) to go to Brussels and await further instructions before sailing to England.[20]

Both Philip and the archdukes judged the outlook for peace to be reasonably bright since James had informed Albert of his desire to renew

England's 'traditional state of goodwill and friendship' with the Habsburgs.[21] What might stand in its way, though, was the difficulty of securing the right terms and the likelihood of opposition from James's English councillors. Bearing this in mind, Philip was determined not to show himself too eager for a treaty but to adopt instead a wait-and-see approach: hence his instruction to Tassis to remain in Brussels until ordered otherwise.[22] Arenberg would begin negotiations, and Spanish representatives would only enter them if success looked to be imminent.

To ease negotiations, all European rulers and diplomats believed bribery was essential. The Habsburg, Dutch, and French rulers therefore made provision to proffer pensions and expensive jewels to those who might smooth the path to peace. For this purpose, an English Catholic exile, Dr Robert Taylor, came to England to enquire from his co-religionists and friends how much the Habsburgs needed to spend.[23] Even so, the Habsburgs soon found themselves outbid, Arenberg estimating that the Dutch had paid out £30,000 in bribes, the lion's share going to Cecil. Believing 'money was the only means to succeed in England', the count urged the archdukes to provide him with extra sums to disburse.[24] When the Spanish negotiators eventually arrived, they brought with them gold and jewels to win over the English, and all of James's and Anna's leading councillors and courtiers became recipients of Spanish largesse.[25] These 'gifts' did not, of course, guarantee nor necessarily influence their conduct or opinions. The anti-Spanish countess of Bedford, for example, took money from the constable of Castile, in August 1604, as did the pro-French Erskine. Cecil, too, accepted a substantial Spanish pension while continuing to have close ties to and money from the Dutch. Few were as principled as Home [later Dunbar] who accepted only 4,200 ducats from Spain in 1604 in contrast to the 13,327 ducats given to Northampton. Hume also refused a pension from the French and a diamond jewel from the Dutch with the retort to the latter that he did not accept gifts from excommunicates.[26]

★ ★ ★

In the diplomatic exchanges of early to mid-1603, James's official position was that he had not yet made up his mind whether to negotiate a peace treaty with Spain. Assuming a stance like the one he was to take in January 1604 at the Hampton Court Conference, James told both sides that he would hear what they each had to say before announcing his decision. At the same time, he offered to mediate between the States General and the Habsburgs.[27] Nevertheless, it soon became obvious that James had welcomed the Dutch ambassadors 'quite coldly' and was unsympathetic to their cause.[28] In a conference with Cecil, they were told that the king 'was indeed very willing to assist the states, but that he had no desire to ruin himself for them' nor would he commit himself to continue aid.[29] Worse still, during informal conversations, James was said to have expressed disapproval of the Dutch rebellion against their princes and sympathy for the Habsburg claims of sovereignty over the whole Netherlands. The king also declared bluntly that he was not obliged to follow 'the causes of his predecessor' and criticized Henry for supporting the Dutch rebels.[30] Reports of James's seeming indifference to their plight soon reached the Netherlands, reportedly bringing the inhabitants of the Cautionary Town of Flushing 'within an ace of cutting the English garrison to pieces'.[31]

More substantially, James tried to end English privateering against Spain. He issued a proclamation, on 24 April, warning that it must stop, and another, on 23 June, that any ship seized from the Habsburgs or their allies would have to be returned; henceforth, 'privateers' would be treated as pirates.[32] Scaramelli was but one who recognized that this June order was 'striking proof that the king wishes for peace with Spain'.[33] It was, of course, a decision unwelcome to privy councillors such as Cecil, Nottingham, and Cumberland, not to mention merchants, who benefited from privateering.[34]

James showed far more courtesy and affability towards Rosny, partly because he was the close friend of a king not the representative of a republic. Back in France after the visit, the marquis spoke approvingly of his 'frequent access to the king and graciouse usadge'.[35] At their first public meeting, on Sunday 12 June, four days after his arrival, Rosny was delighted to hear James speak 'with the greatest abhorrence' of Spain's 'endeavours to kindle the flames of war among their neighbours'.[36] A few days later, the two men discussed international affairs privately and at length, during which time James emphasized that peace between England and France was secure. Not only had he no interest in England's ancient claim to the French crown and territory but also the two realms shared a common purpose in wanting to prevent the United Provinces coming under the domination of Spain. At dinner on the 20th, James whispered in confidence to Rosny the possibility of a 'double union' of the two royal houses, meaning Anglo-French dynastic marriages.[37]

Rosny's meetings with James's councillors went less smoothly. As the main conciliar spokesman, Cecil focused on the expense of continuing the war against Spain and aid to the Dutch. 'It was not convenient', pointed out

Cecil, 'for the king of England to go to war merely in order that the king of France might live in peace.' Furthermore, at a later conference (in which Nottingham, Northumberland, Mountjoy, and possibly Mar were present), Cecil demanded repayment of the outstanding sums which Elizabeth had loaned both Henry and the States General in the war against Spain before any extra English military action might be taken on their behalf. 'What piqued me most', wrote Rosny in his memoirs, 'was to find these ministers, who were here only to set forth the intentions of the king, impudently substitute their own.'[38] Rosny instantaneously sought another private audience with the king, and the next day he complained to James about Cecil and the rest. Possibly, he also laid before the king his project for a defensive and offensive league against Spain. James was so interested, remembered Rosny later, that he cancelled his hunting party in order to hear the envoy to the end.[39] After four hours of talks, James agreed to sign a treaty of alliance with Henry. He then summoned Cecil, Mar, Mountjoy, Northumberland, and Southampton before him to relay his intention. According to Rosny, 'he reproached Cecil in very strong terms for having, both in his words and actions, acted contrary to his commands' and left the secretary looking very sheepish.[40] Cecil was no doubt taken aback because he had almost certainly been acting according to James's instructions in taking a tough line. Perhaps James had changed his mind and did not want the French to realize it; or perhaps he was performing what Robert Cross has called 'a fantastic moment of political theater' in which he deliberately paraded before Henry's representative and important Englishmen that he alone was the maker of foreign policy, and questions of war or peace depended upon 'his own supreme will'.[41] Maybe too he hoped the French would offer better terms if they thought Cecil opposed a deal.[42] Whatever the cause, Rosny was of course delighted, mistakenly convinced that he had won over the king and foiled his councillors.

Over the next couple of days, James signed a newly drafted treaty which Rosny took back to France. Concluded at Hampton Court at the end of July, it renewed the 'auld alliance' between France and Scotland and the Anglo-French treaties of Elizabeth. Additional terms included James's agreement to allow the Dutch to levy troops in England, which would be paid for by the French but with a third of the cost deducted from the debts Henry owed the English crown. The two kings also agreed that, if one of them was attacked by Spain, the other would come to his aid with a force of at least 6,000 men and James would also send out a squadron to harass

Spain.[43] The French wanted the treaty to be kept secret because it contravened the Treaty of Vervins, and this suited James since it allowed him to negotiate with the Habsburgs.[44] It would be wrong to think—as Rosny evidently did—that the treaty committed James to war against Spain. Rather, James intended to retain the friendship of the two most powerful rulers in Europe just as he had successfully done as king of Scotland. Since this could best be managed if the United Provinces signed a peace with Spain, James hoped to achieve this outcome by mediating between the two sides.[45]

Negotiations with the Habsburgs had proved impossible during Rosny's visit. No sooner had Arenberg arrived in mid-June than he was bedridden with crippling gout, and Tassis was still in Brussels. The English suspected that the inaccessibility of the Habsburg diplomats was intentional since delaying talks until Ostend was taken would strengthen their hand in the negotiations.[46] Very likely, this suspicion had led to James's readiness to sign the treaty with France. It was not until 10 July, around the same time as Rosny departed, that Arenberg had his first formal audience with James and Anna at Windsor. At a private conversation straight afterwards, James reiterated his desire for peace and 'protested that he would not imitate the French by secretly assisting rebels'.[47]

Just then, however, the Main Plot came to light which seemed to implicate Arenberg in a conspiracy to depose the king. The count's protests of innocence rang true and were believed by James, but they put him at a disadvantage since Cobham's confessions bolstered anti-Spanish sentiment at court.[48] Regardless, James displayed great appreciation of Arenberg's gift of beautiful hunting birds and continued to affirm his desire for peace.[49] Explaining away the five or six companies of Scots under Lord Buccleuch that arrived in the autumn to help the Dutch, James insisted that they came from Scotland, not England, and that the soldiers were volunteers, not levied in his name, a stretch of the truth. The archdukes, he offered blithely, could equally well raise troops among his subjects if they so wished.[50]

In the summer, James announced his decision. On 10 August, he told the Dutch of his resolution 'to settle all things' with the Habsburgs, assured them that he would conclude no treaty 'to their prejudice', and asked the States General if it wished to join in the negotiations for a treaty.[51] Within a short time, the reply was a firm 'no'. Refusing to enter talks before their independence was guaranteed, the Dutch entreated James not to negotiate a treaty with the Habsburgs who were, they said, seeking the 'extirpation of the true Christian religion and a general tyranny over all Christendom'.[52]

Ignoring this negative response, James requested the arrival of an envoy from Spain who would be authorized to negotiate a treaty.[53] With these new circumstances, Philip III allowed Tassis—promoted to be count of Villamediana in October—to leave Dunkirk for England.

Tassis arrived on 31 August 1603, but his meeting with the king was delayed because of the plague. He had to trail the court, which was moving around outside London, and then one of his servants died of the illness. Once the negotiations for peace started, they barely got off the ground before they came to a halt for the Spanish envoy had no actual power to conclude a treaty. The English refused to proceed any further 'tyll sufficient authority came out of Spaine', and while they were waiting, Arenberg returned to Brussels for further instructions.[54] Nonetheless, these early talks were not a waste of time. During them, both sides laid down their red lines, which were to remain unchanged when the talks resumed in December. Spain demanded that England should not assist the United Provinces nor trade in the Indies, and England required that English Protestants would not be brought before the Inquisition in any of Spain's territories. As far as the Dutch were concerned, James himself averred that he would not join Spain against them in the Netherlands, 'but he was resolved always to carry an even hand betwixt them both'. Every other issue was left in abeyance.[55]

★ ★ ★

Peace with Spain was a divisive issue in England. As had occurred under Elizabeth, the privy council was split on the issue, with the majority pressing James to continue sending aid to the Dutch and the remainder pushing for a peace treaty.[56] The lack of consensus among the political classes was reflected in the manuscript tracts circulating in 1603 and 1604, which rekindled the intense debate of the late 1590s and reiterated the same arguments as had been presented by pro-peace Burghley and pro-war Essex.[57]

Both sides had a reasonable case to make. The advocates of peace praised it as a Christian ideal but generally focused on its economic and financial benefits. An end to the war, they maintained, would advance commerce, raise the income from customs, and reduce royal expenditure. As for abandoning the Dutch, they claimed that the existing alliance was between the States General and Elizabeth—not James—so ending it would not be a breach of trust; besides, the Dutch were by now strong and prosperous enough to defend themselves if they chose not to join England in a peace treaty.[58]

Most of the pro-war tracts were addressed to the king or Lord Henry Howard, thought to be another promoter of peace, but they were intended for a wider readership and numerous manuscript copies circulated among the political classes. The arguments in them ranged from emotional appeals to the king's reputation and national honour to shrewd assessments of international relations. Their central contention was that, irrespective of the wealth and 'industriousness' of the Dutch, the United Provinces would be unable to continue their struggle alone. They would either have to turn to the French for help or be forced to submit to Spain, and both outcomes would bring 'aequall danger' to England. If the former, England would have 'to suffer Fraunce to be the master of the Netherlands', a highly dangerous consequence. If the latter, the Habsburgs might well invade England and, as masters of the sea, they would be able to land within four hours at whichever part of England they chose, just like previous invaders, the Danes, Saxons, and Normans. Echoing the same arguments that had brought England into the war, these pamphleteers insisted that Spain would not hesitate to attack England once the Dutch were defeated for, like his father, Philip III's aim was to 'make himself a [universal] monarche in Europe', and 'to mayntaine Romish religion' everywhere. The Spanish king, the pro-war lobby insisted, did not want a permanent peace, merely a truce to give himself time to rebuild his resources. According to this view, only a continuation of the war would bring Spain to heel. What was more, a few dreamt, somewhat unrealistically, that England fighting in co-operation with the Dutch would do great things: their combined shipping could command all the trade in the world and even take the Indies from Spain. Anyway, argued the opponents of peace, its benefits were illusory: English merchants would be disadvantaged by the 30 per cent duty recently imposed on all imports to the Iberian Peninsula; the Inquisition would make life hard for Protestants operating in Spanish territories; and the Iberian monopoly on the Americas and East would hold back English attempts to extend into world markets.[59]

The same case for continuing the war was heard in parliament. At a conference between the two houses, on 8 May 1604, Thomas, Lord Scrope, reportedly declared that 'we should be better gainers by war then by peace', not least because of the 30 per cent duty. Four days later, Scrope's brother-in-law and Cecil's first cousin Sir Edward Hoby spoke out at some length against the peace. While echoing the arguments in the tracts, Hoby's speech was still more anti-Spanish. Yet, despite its tone, his opposition to the royal will, and the fact that foreign policy was outside the competence of parliament unless initiated by the king, Hoby was not reprimanded.

Certainly, James did not want to cause a ruckus in the commons while the Union was being debated. Perhaps too, the speech served a useful function by indicating to Spain that a strong war party existed in England and that any treaty had therefore to contain articles in England's interests and not appear an act of surrender.[60]

The loudest voices in England favoured war, yet many people—maybe the majority—were not averse to peace. There was a general war weariness, unsurprising given that the eighteen years of fighting had been burdensome, taxes to pay for it cutting deep into incomes. As a result, apart from one incident of local hostility to the Spaniards in December 1603, Villamediana found the English population welcoming and believed there was a positive anticipation of peace.[61] Some merchants and gentlemen were certainly keen to take advantage of the thaw in Anglo-Iberian relations and obtain licences to trade with Spain if peace were on the horizon.[62]

But no-one wanted peace at any price. Merchants trading overseas were concerned that Spain would offer insufficient concessions and that their interests and those of the country might be sacrificed if the terms were not right. Those operating in the East Indies urged the English negotiators to ensure that 'nothing be concluded to the hinderaunce' of their trade, 'out of which there maye growe so greate a benyfitt and strength to his Majestie's domyniens and the common wealth of this kingedome'.[63] Thomas Alabaster, an Anglo-Iberian merchant and investor in West Indies privateering, warned Cecil that the benefits of peace would be nil unless Spain allowed English merchants freedom from the Inquisition and permission to trade with the East and West Indies. Furthermore, like many others, he wanted a peace that would not endanger the Dutch and was disquieted by the intelligence coming his way that Spain would not make peace unless England handed over the Cautionary Towns of Flushing, Brill, and Rammekins which English troops had garrisoned since 1585. Alabaster's fear was that Spain would play hardball at the peace conference: 'Yt is gennerally voiced abroad in other countries that what honor the king of Spayne lost by the warres hee will now assay to recover by capitulating peace as yf our strength wear most in the armes.'[64] For Alabaster and people like him, England's tough bargaining at the peace conference was vital for otherwise there would be no advantage to a treaty, only danger.[65] But tough bargaining might lead Spain to walk away, so James and the English commissioners had a difficult tightrope to walk.

★ ★ ★

On 21 September 1603, Philip appointed Fernández de Velasco, duke of Frias and constable of Castile, as his extraordinary ambassador to conclude the peace with England. The constable arrived in Brussels shortly before Christmas, and discussions soon began about the location for a peace conference. Spain demanded it take place in the archdukes' territory, not London, for otherwise it would harm their king's reputation and weaken his bargaining position. But James would not hear of it. Although still resolute about the need to end the war, he insisted that the negotiations be held on his home turf.[66] While the dispute was in progress, James and Anna signalled their commitment to a treaty by giving Villamediana precedence over the French representative at the customary Christmas banquets for ambassadors, honouring him during the Twelfth Night revels of 1604, and sponsoring Daniel's masque that had as its theme the benefits of peace. Recognizing the message contained in the masque, Villamediana sent its text to Philip III.[67]

The Spaniards eventually consented to the conference being sited in London. Even if this concession revealed 'an excessive desire for agreement', advised the constable, it delivered 'greater hopes of getting what we want with the talks being close to those rulers, who are most inclined to peace'.[68] James had evidently persuaded the Habsburgs that, if on hand, he could ensure that his negotiators, who were far less keen on a treaty (or so he said), would follow his instructions. However, still unconvinced that the negotiations would be successful, the constable pleaded ill health and remained in Flanders to avoid humiliation were the talks to end in failure. In his place, Allesandro Rovida (senator of Milan) headed the negotiating team in London and worked with Villamediana alongside the archdukes' three commissioners: Arenberg, Jean Richardot (president of the archdukes' privy council), and Louis Verreyken (the archdukes' principal secretary and the audiencier of Brussels).[69] The constable's absence from the talks seemed a discouraging sign, leading many in Spain, and possibly in England, to 'beleve ther wilbe noe peace'.[70] Naturally the Dutch hoped so, but to obtain a military advantage should a treaty be signed, they launched an invasion into Flanders during the spring of 1604.[71]

The conference opened, on Sunday 20 May 1604, in the queen's council chamber at Somerset House where the envoys were staying. The problem of precedence that had sabotaged the late Elizabethan peace talks in Boulogne disappeared with the English acting as hosts. The five men in the Habsburg delegation were directed to sit on the right side of the table 'in respect of the greater honor donne to his Majestie by the sending of the sayd

Figure 20. The Somerset House Conference, 1604. On the right, from back to front, are the earls of Dorset, Nottingham, Devonshire, Northampton, and Cecil, then Viscount Cranborne. On the left, from back to front, are the constable of Castile (who did not attend the conference), Villamediana, Rovida, Arenberg, Richardot, and Verreyken © National Portrait Gallery, London.

commissioners to treate here within this reallme'.[72] Opposite them sat the king's five commissioners Cecil, Northampton, Devonshire, Nottingham, and Dorset (see Figure 20).

None of the English negotiators were pushovers seeking peace at any cost. Cecil repeatedly spoke up for the Dutch, refused to call them rebels, and justified English aid in their 'very just and good cause'. Northampton fought hard during the conference for the right of English merchants to trade with the Indies. Nottingham was thought by some in Spain to be 'wholly French and for his proffitt inclyned to warr' since he had invested heavily in privateering ventures under Elizabeth. Devonshire too was regarded as pro-French. Only Lord Treasurer Dorset was recognized as fully committed to peace with Spain, worried as he was about the state of the public coffers, yet he too was concerned about the vulnerability of the Dutch.[73]

James's selection of commissioners who were thought likely to fight for English interests and not abandon the Dutch did much to prevent political unrest over the talks. However, he did not give them a free hand. Although they were authorized to 'treat and conclude' articles for peace, he gave them instructions that he was 'to be the director and deceder [decider] of all essential circumstances which may occur in the treaty and therein to use the advice of the rest of our privie councell'. This meant, he spelled out, that his commissioners should forbear from agreeing 'in binding manner' to any major point until they had 'first related the same to us and received our approbation or direction'.[74] The commissioners took this to heart and went straight back to the king during the succeeding months whenever they were asked to clarify a point or adjust their position. Although absent, James was therefore a vital participant in the conference.[75] Philip III, by contrast, allowed Villamediana extraordinary freedom in the negotiations, but then he had to because of the slowness of the post.[76]

The preliminary matter for discussion was whether the Habsburgs had satisfactory powers to negotiate a treaty. This was settled when James declared that he preferred 'substance before circumstances and therefore was not willing to insist upon other formallities'.[77] Next, the commissioners sounded out each side's 'dispositions' on areas of disagreement, of which there were four. None of them came as a surprise since they had been discussed both formally and informally in the run-up to the conference. All the same, there was no easy resolution to them.

First, the Habsburgs called for an offensive and defensive league. This was unacceptable to the English commissioners because it would require them to end commerce with the Dutch and prevent volunteers from England fighting in their armies. Consequently, Cecil and the others pushed for 'friendship and amity only, with mutual trade to each other's dominions'. James intervened at this point through his commissioners with the proposal that a league should not be on the agenda at this time, although it might well be in the future. The Spanish delegation reluctantly agreed but then insisted that England should cease aiding the Dutch rebels, a requirement that nearly brought the conference to a close. When Cecil stated that Elizabeth had helped the Dutch but 'as allies and confederates', not rebels, 'the Spanish took offence, and rose to their feet to withdraw'.[78] Only after the English made placatory noises, did they agree to meet again. At this next session (on 31 May), Rovida tried to be conciliatory by styling the Dutch 'enemies', not rebels. However, he repeated his demand that commerce with the Dutch should cease. The English refused. According to the Venetian ambassador, they said that they had hoped for some benefit from the negotiations, but 'instead they were to reap injury; for the prohibition of trade with Holland meant the ruin of all the merchants trading there. They could not be expected to make peace with one prince merely to declare war on another.'[79] Likewise, the English would not agree to prohibit English volunteers from serving in the Dutch army, notwithstanding Habsburg insistence and appeals to the king.

Second, the Habsburgs pressed for the surrender of the Cautionary Towns, but the English commissioners refused to relinquish them because they amounted to a pledge for the outstanding Dutch loan owed to the crown. Third, the English made a bid for free trade with all the Spanish dominions, implicitly the East and West Indies, 'wherein', wrote Cecil, 'we find them as stiff to yield it unto us, no more then we will yield unto them the Cautionary Towns'. Cecil pushed hard for access on grounds that 'it was no way fitt for us to be restreyned in our trade', but Villamediana demanded the insertion of an article in the treaty that explicitly prohibited English merchants from sailing to the East and West Indies.[80] Fourth, the English demanded that their nation be not subjected to the Inquisition. Interestingly, the Habsburgs decided to make no formal requests for the toleration of Catholics in England, probably because they knew it was non-negotiable. In accordance with Arenberg's counsel the previous year, both the archdukes and Philip decided that it should not be demanded as a condition for peace but could be addressed after peace was achieved 'by way of intercession'.[81]

All these issues, bar religious toleration for English Catholics, were debated and fought over in eighteen formal sessions of the conference and in many meetings behind the scenes. At times the negotiations looked to be on the brink of collapse, but the equal determination of James and the Habsburgs to sign a peace resulted in an agreement being reached on most issues, usually by employing a compromise that often looked like a fudge.[82] Regarding the Cautionary Towns, James consented to the suggested Habsburg compromise that the Dutch would be given a deadline for repaying their outstanding debt and, if they failed to meet it, he could assign the towns to whomsoever he chose.[83] However, Cecil soon let the Dutch know that, by this condition, James 'meanethe not to deliver the sayd cautionaryes to any other but to the States United... it beinge always in his Majestie's hands to allow or disallow' their rendition.[84] And indeed, in 1616, James did return the Cautionary Towns to the Dutch and for a third of the price first demanded.[85] When it came to James's subjects fighting for the United Provinces, it was agreed that the garrisons in the Cautionary Towns would not aid them or commit 'any hostile acte' against Spain or the archdukes. However, it was also agreed that volunteer soldiers might serve wherever they wished, whether in the armies of the Dutch or archdukes. As a result, for the first time, Englishmen could fight for Spain without being treated as traitors. Concerning commerce, James said he would 'never restrayne his subjects from trading' in the archdukes' ports, nor would he use his shipping to clear the seas of Dutch privateers for that purpose. However, he did agree to the Habsburgs' demands that English ships should not carry goods between the United Provinces and Spain and that the 30 per cent duty would be paid on goods transported in English ships from Spain into France.[86] As for the Inquisition, after animated debates, Rovida eventually accepted that the institution would not interfere with the private prayers or observances made discreetly by English merchants within their own ships or lodgings.[87] The English also won a small but significant victory on the Indies trade. Villamediana renounced his demand that English traders and seamen would be explicitly banned from the East and West Indies, after James—realizing there was no possibility of obtaining access—consented 'to passe over that point in silence and to leave it undetermined', as it had been in the Treaty of Vervins between France and Spain. The subsequent treaty simply allowed free trade between all the dominions of the two kingdoms 'where commerce existed before the war'.[88] By this means, both sides implicitly accepted that James would forbid his subjects to trade in places already possessed by Spain but left open what might happen elsewhere in the New World.

With the articles formally settled on 14 July, the constable came to England for the formal swearing of the peace. Because he seemed in no hurry to arrive in London, even once he had landed at Dover on 5 August, James became irritated at what seemed a lack of respect and reciprocated by showing no hurry to grant the constable an audience.[89] James continued his summer progress, and the constable had to wait, until late in the week of 16 August, before being given an audience with the king. In the meantime, he was royally entertained at the crown's expense and met with the queen and important courtiers so that the slight did not blow up into an offence.[90] When the king eventually met the constable, the Spaniard was expected to sign secret protocols which had already been prepared: the first granted British ships the right to bring German goods to Spain free of the usual 30 per cent duty; the second specified the degree of religious tolerance for British subjects in Spain and its dominions.[91] Told that the English parliament would never relax the recusancy laws, the constable decided not to press for the insertion of religious toleration for Catholics.[92] He therefore signed, albeit reluctantly.[93]

All this settled, the formal ceremony in which the king swore to uphold the treaty took place on Sunday 19 August. To be acceptable to Spain, the English had arranged that it would be held in the chapel royal at Whitehall Palace (not a church) and contain nothing which 'seemed ecclesiastical'; moreover, the bible to be used was a translation from St Jerome (the Vulgate) that the Plantin Press had printed in Antwerp.[94] By this means, the English had found a ceremonial strategy to bridge the religious divide in the first international treaty between a Protestant and Catholic power.

On the Sunday morning, James escorted the constable and Villamediana into the chapel along with the other commissioners (except for Arenberg, ill again with the gout) and their large retinues to the sound of music and hymns chanted in praise of peace. Cecil handed a parchment copy of the treaty to the constable and read aloud the oath by which both the king and Prince Henry were to bind themselves to the observation of its terms. With their hands on the Gospels, James swore the oath and confirmed the peace. Everyone then cried out 'peace, peace, peace' and 'long live the king', also thrice. Afterwards, those attending withdrew into the great hall, where a grand banquet was held. Amidst the many toasts and exchanges of magnificent gifts, James hinted to the constable that a marriage might be in the offing between the Spanish prince and his daughter: 'he hoped from her name that she might be the means of preserving the kingdoms of Spain and England in friendship and union, unlike that other hostile Elizabeth'. The meal over, the entertainments began. The royal family and courtiers danced together and afterwards viewed from the gallery windows a display of bearbaiting, bullbaiting, and acrobatics in the courtyard. Meanwhile, the same afternoon in London, peace was proclaimed 'at every fifty paces', probably with little joy but certainly without protests or uproar.[95]

With the treaty signed, James made it absolutely clear to Cecil that he had no intention of seeing the constable again, 'the substance of his errand being performed'. Indeed, James intended to recommence his summer progress on the following Tuesday.[96] However, the Spaniard was taken ill the night after the ceremony, and James felt compelled to visit him before setting off on progress. On his recovery, the constable met with the queen and prince—but not the king—before leaving London on the 25th. The elaborate exchange of extravagant gifts which then took place did so without the king's presence.[97] Seemingly, no offence was taken.

★ ★ ★

James had ensured that the treaty's terms were immediately made known to both the Dutch and French in order to reassure them that no secret clauses existed which might cause them harm. In fact, Cecil had kept the agent of the United Provinces 'particularly acquainted' with the progress of the talks, so the articles came as no great surprise.[98] Although not best pleased, the Dutch could at least take comfort from their capture, on 9 August, of Sluis, a Spanish held port near the mouth of the River Scheldt, which had been under siege since May. However, in September, Ostend fell to Spain, and Cecil immediately felt the need to massage those articles which operated 'most darkly or sharply' towards the Dutch.[99]

As far as the French were concerned, their king officially commended James and Cecil for concluding 'this great and weighty action'.[100] Initially, Henry had not been too alarmed by the opening of the Anglo-Spanish negotiations and had simply worked to fortify his special relationship with James by sending him hunting gifts and a special envoy to join him in the chase. To keep Henry onside, James held discussions with the constable about removing the Spanish tariff of 30 per cent from French goods, negotiations which ultimately proved successful. James also gave Henry his word that he would value his friendship above all others and never abandon the Dutch.[101] However, towards the end of 1604, the French king began to doubt James's intentions and trustworthiness; perhaps for the first time, he fully realized that the Anglo-Spanish alliance nullified the treaty negotiated by Rosny.[102] To mollify Henry, James somewhat belatedly sent his cousin Lennox to the French court to 'reciprocate the compliment' of Rosny's embassy, assure Henry of 'the syceritie and constancie' of his love towards him, and pledge that the Anglo-Scottish Union would not change Franco-Scottish amity.[103] Lennox was also instructed to seek a renewal of the 'auld alliance'.[104]

Despite the exchange of mutual protestations of friendship, Lennox's embassy was not a great success.[105] Rosny objected to a clause in the Anglo-Spanish treaty that he said was unfavourable to his king; 'Lennox admitted this but defended the clause.' Henry complained about his ambassador's exclusion from Anna's masque in London as well as about Sir Henry Wotton, James's new ambassador in Venice, who had apparently spoken ill of the

French king. The French were also slow to settle English demands about releasing some merchants whose goods (especially cloth) were thought substandard and had been seized at Rouen. It was only in his last audience with the king that Lennox received 'an assured promise that they should be righted'. Finally, Henry made clear his intention of augmenting his subsidies to the United Provinces and keeping alive their war against Spain.[106]

While Lennox was in France, the terms of the Anglo-Spanish treaty were printed in England. With some justification, it was said that the government had delayed publishing them 'as if they had ben half ashamed or afraid to shew themselves, before they saw how they could be digested'.[107] Once disseminated, there was neither public rejoicing nor open protests. Quite possibly, few people thought the treaty would introduce a permanent state of peace and accepted it cautiously as a welcome breathing space before the next outbreak of hostilities.[108] However, it did not take long before complaints were made that the peace terms could have been more to England's advantage.[109] Even Spaniards were saying, reported Sir Charles Cornwallis (England's resident ambassador in Spain), that the English had sold themselves short in the treaty and that 'England never lost such an opportunity of wynning honor and welth unto it as by relinquishing the war with Spaine'.[110]

★ ★ ★

After the Lennox mission, next on the English diplomatic agenda was the ratification of the treaty abroad, which was scheduled for the spring of 1605. The 66-year-old earl of Hertford and 68-year-old Nottingham, men 'of great birth and qualitie', were dispatched to head embassies to Brussels and Valladolid respectively and witness the oath-taking of the archdukes and Philip III.[111] In his usual spirit of inclusiveness, James ensured that opponents of the peace were included in their retinues.[112]

The importance in which the archdukes held the treaty could be seen in the ceremonial and festivities surrounding its ratification. In late April, Hertford was received at Brussels 'with such a magnifficent trupe of dukes, princes, and other nobility as might well manifeste how highly they did esteeme an ambassage from soe mightie a prince'.[113] The archdukes put aside a whole week to entertain Hertford, which again displayed great 'respect and honor' to the king and reflected 'the joy on the dukes' partes...for the conclusion of this peace'. The entertainments and formal ceremonies mirrored and matched those that had taken place in London the previous year, fulfilling what historians call the 'protocol of reciprocity'. Taking account of English concerns that the oathtaking ceremony might be timed to coincide with a mass 'to the scandall of our religion', the archdukes' arrangements avoided any cause of offence. Paralleling the event in England, the oath-taking was staged in the court chapel 'without the use of any ceremony contrary to the course of our religion'.[114] Afterwards, the envoys were treated to a banquet, dancing, and 'revells' and taken to watch 'very delightfull and costly shewes' of equestrian sports. The succeeding few days were spent at feasts and watching other games.[115]

On the business side, Hertford introduced Sir Thomas Edmondes, the new English ambassador in Brussels, to the archdukes, who had already sent their own resident ambassador to London. Edmondes was to handle any specific issues that arose during the embassy, but Hertford had also received instructions about how to proceed if Albert wanted James to go beyond the wording of the treaty in relation to England's dealings with the Dutch. Both men were told to assure the archdukes of James's 'desier to give sattisfaction in all reasonable matters' but to do or say nothing that was 'to the visible prejudice or apparent breach of newtralitie' with the United Provinces. Edmondes was also to tell the archdukes that James was working to persuade the Dutch 'to come to some termes of pacification', although he found them 'as yet not inclined'.[116] In fact, the difficulties James anticipated passed over easily enough because the Habsburgs were keen for all to run smoothly.[117]

Nottingham's embassy was the more splendid but went less well. His entourage, which included his sons, other kinsmen, nobles, gentlemen, soldiers, and mariners, amounted to at least 650 people and required six ships to transport them and their belongings to Spain. Setting sail, on 5 April, the convoy arrived at Corunna ten days later, but there was a mix-up in the arrangements. To Nottingham's annoyance, he was left stranded in the town for more than a fortnight until an official delegation arrived to escort them to Valladolid, which was then the Spanish capital. The journey—a 248-mile trek—took a fortnight to cover, another irritation for Nottingham.[118] Then, when the embassy made its formal entry on horseback into the town on Thursday 16 May, a sudden torrential shower drenched onlookers and participants alike. Here, Nottingham made a good impression. Refusing to take shelter in a coach, he skilfully manoeuvred his horse into the city even though he was soaked to the skin.[119]

The next three weeks passed in a whirl of meetings and festivities. Like the archdukes, the Spaniards paid close attention to the 'protocol of reciprocity'.[120] In this spirit, Nottingham was treated to a range of entertainments including a bullfight, equestrian games, banquets, and a masque.[121] Reciprocity was likewise shown in the gift-exchanges that took place. Shortly after his arrival, Nottingham officially presented James's and Anna's gifts for the king and queen—including five horses, 'very richly imbroidered' clothes, several beagles, two crossbows, and four 'fowling-pieces'—which were 'very gratiously and royally' accepted. At his departure, on 7 June, Nottingham's baggage was filled with gifts from the king, queen, and other nobles, all perfectly calibrated to match the gifts from the English to the Spaniards. Nottingham personally received jewels estimated at £2,000 as a present from Philip together with jewels, gloves, and perfume 'in great quantity' for his wife.[122] The mutual exchange of resident ambassadors was another vital element in the peace-making process. Sir Charles Cornwallis was introduced to Philip III early in the visit; Pedro de Zúñiga accompanied Nottingham to James's court.

On a couple of occasions, when reciprocity was not maintained, it was experienced as an affront or insult. Nottingham complained bitterly when he was not allowed to dine at the king's table in contrast to the dining arrangements in London where the constable had sat with James. He was placated only when assured that it was the royal custom for the king to eat alone and no disrespect was intended to himself and his master. Even so, this lack of reciprocity was 'somewhat ill taken' and thought 'extraordinary' even after Nottingham's return.[123] Just as contentious, the Spaniards refused to allow the oath-taking ceremony to be performed in a church or royal chapel, as had occurred in London and Brussels. Non-Catholics, they insisted, were not permitted to enter sacred places and, besides, the oath related to a purely secular matter. After some dispute, Nottingham retreated, and the oath-taking, on 30 May, was held in the grand banqueting hall of the royal palace which had probably been built for that very purpose.[124] Despite the location, the ceremony inevitably retained a religious flavour, just as it had in London. Assisted by the cardinal archbishop of Toledo, Philip swore on a crucifix as well as the Vulgate to uphold the original treaty. However, Philip would not swear under oath to uphold the secret articles agreed upon in London (an earlier cause of dispute), and he nearly omitted to sign them under his own hand and seal during the ceremony, which had been the compromise reached. Just before the ceremony was over, Nottingham had to remind the king to sign and hand over the copy.[125]

Another difficulty for the embassy was that Nottingham sometimes found himself wrong-footed when dealing with the sensitive issue of religion. By design, Philip had timed the English visit to coincide with two major Catholic feast days (Whitsunday and Corpus Christi) as well as the baptism of his son and the queen's churching, all of which were celebrated in magnificent Counter-Reformation style. By chance, a new pope was elected during Nottingham's stay, an event also joyously celebrated.[126] Before leaving England, Nottingham had been warned not to do anything that might 'give cause of scandal to the Inquisition' while ensuring that his retinue would 'not be robd of that Christian comfort which cometh by the exercise of God's woord'.[127] So, during all these religious festivities, he had to tread a difficult path: how to avoid offending the Catholic monarchy while remaining true to England's religion. He proved more adept at the former than the latter.

The baptism of Philip III's son on Whitsunday and churching of Queen Margaret passed off easily enough. Not permitted to attend, Nottingham was conveyed to viewing points from where he could admire the grand religious processions and overlook the services.[128] On Corpus Christi Day, however, Nottingham could not prevent some English gentlemen actually joining the procession 'as curious observers with great respect', and on another occasion (according to Cornwallis) the earl 'went down on his knees himself' when encountering the host [a consecrated wafer believed by Catholics to contain the body of Christ] in a religious procession and 'ordered all his suite to do the same'.[129] Furthermore, Nottingham visited a Jesuit seminary where he listened to orations that praised not only the peace but also the Catholic faith while his son went openly to Madrid to see his kinswoman, the elderly duchess of Feria.[130] When Nottingham returned home, Cornwallis used these missteps to take revenge on the lord admiral with whom he had quarrelled over a matter of precedence. In letters, he accused Nottingham of showing too great reverence towards the Catholic religion, denying his Protestant chaplains the opportunity to preach, and making promises to the Spanish ministers that went 'beyond the limits of his commission'. Incurring James's anger, Nottingham retired to the country in disgrace until his friends interceded on his behalf.[131]

★ ★ ★

The treaty ratified, James had to steer his way through the incompatibilities of his position: how to retain the friendship of France and the United Provinces, yet not rupture the newly formed peace. Tensions were inevitable, yet James managed to avoid any diplomatic breach, assisted by international realities: the Dutch and French could not risk him moving fully into the Habsburg camp while the Habsburgs could not afford to see England renewing material aid to the Dutch. Nonetheless, until a truce was signed between the Dutch and Habsburgs in 1609, James actively and successfully used diplomacy to maintain his neutrality and preserve British interests.

After the Treaty of London, there arose two main areas of friction with the United Provinces. One concerned James's refusal to allow the Dutch permission to levy soldiers publicly by the 'stryking of drummes and displaying of ensignes', their usual practice under Elizabeth. Indeed, a recruiting party in Hampshire found itself arrested, in 1605, after it openly and noisily attempted to raise soldiers by this means. Yet the Dutch had no legitimate cause of complaint as the stream of British soldiers in the pay of the United Provinces did not dry up but, on the contrary, reached an all-time high in 1607–08.[132] James allowed his subjects to volunteer for Dutch service, partly because he did not want to see Philip win an outright victory but equally because he feared that the States General might refuse to repay the sums they owed him in reprisal.

The second cause of friction was that the Dutch now treated England's merchant shipping as legitimate prey for attack. Once Anglo-Spanish trade was resumed, Dutch warships in the Channel assailed and looted British vessels bound for ports in the Spanish Netherlands, especially those directed towards Antwerp which was under a Dutch blockade. While James could not ignore his subjects' 'great losses', he was determined to avoid a diplomatic rupture or armed confrontation with the United Provinces over the issue. As his councillors explained, he was caught between two extremities: on the one hand, he recognized that the supply of war materials to the archdukes' ports was 'most prejudiciall' to the United Provinces 'as tending to their utter overthrow'; on the other, he could not suspend such commerce without 'the scandal of doble-dealing' in breaking his treaty with Spain. As a remedy, James urged a general naval disarmament in the Channel or else a meeting in which rules of engagement could be laid down.[133] Neither recommendation got anywhere, and Anglo-Dutch relations remained strained on this particular matter until the truce was signed in 1609.[134] Luckily, James had a very good relationship with Noel de Caron, the States

General's agent in England, which helped smooth over moments of crisis.[135] Similarly, James's representative in The Hague, Sir Ralph Winwood, was a known sympathizer of the Dutch who worked hard to preserve good relations.[136]

Meanwhile, tensions with the Habsburgs arose because they were convinced that James was favouring the Dutch and ignoring his obligations in the peace treaty. Zúñiga remonstrated, for example, when James seemed ready to allow Caron to be upgraded from an agent to an ambassador because this promotion would 'acknowledge their state [the United Provinces] to be legitimate and sovereraigne without respect unto superior', namely Spain.[137] James tried to mollify Zúñiga by promising that Caron would receive no better treatment than before, but the Habsburgs still grumbled. In fact, Caron was not officially advanced to the rank of ambassador until the truce was concluded; then, it became 'the first actuall declaration of their [the United Provinces'] new obtayned souveraigntie'.[138]

Another sign of partiality, complained Zúñiga, was that James made it excessively difficult for the archdukes to recruit British volunteers for their own service. The king had apparently let it be known that:

> although as a friendly neutral he could not refuse the same permission to Spain and the archduke as he had granted to the Dutch, still he will never love nor reckon as a faithful subject anyone who serves a sovereign whose religion is different from his own.

These 'often repeated' words, protested the Habsburgs, deterred British volunteers from fighting in their armies.[139] In fact, though, a steady stream of men enrolled in the archdukes' armies, including some 1,200 to 1,500 British mercenaries and recusants, in 1605, under the Catholic Thomas, Lord Arundel of Wardour.[140] Unquestionably, James and his councillors disapproved of these enlistments, not so much because the recruits would significantly increase Habsburg manpower to the detriment of the Dutch but rather because those 'ill affected in religion' would gain military experience abroad and 'might one day convert their swords to the prejudice of this established government'. The Gunpowder Plot provided some evidence for this dire prediction since Thomas Wintour and Guy Fawkes had at one time fought for Spain. The government therefore decided to staunch the flow and introduced legislation, in 1606, that required all those voluntarily serving a 'forraine prince, state or potentate' to take the oath of allegiance and deposit a substantial 'surety' of about £20 before leaving.[141] Seeking to avoid Habsburg recriminations, England's resident ambassadors in Brussels and Valladolid were instructed to explain that parliament had pushed James into signing this statute, an excuse that the Habsburgs affected to believe but which did not stop their sense of grievance.[142]

Zúñiga also complained about English seamen's attacks on Iberian shipping.[143] With the end of legitimate privateering, thousands of English seamen were employed by foreign cities and states to carry out privateering reprisals against their enemies in the Mediterranean and northern waters. Additionally, some mariners operated independently as pirates, specifically targeting Spanish and Portuguese shipping. Thomas Salkeld and his men established a haven on the Isle of Lundy in the Bristol Channel while other mariners moved their centre of operations from the west of England to Munster in Ireland. On this matter, James was more sympathetic to Spanish protests and did his utmost to stop all forms of piracy. However, piracy in the Atlantic—much anti-Spanish—boomed: Sir Henry Mainwaring claimed that there were ten times as many pirates there in the early seventeenth century as there had been under Elizabeth. Piracy also thrived around the British Isles thanks to the collusion of officials and protection of local landowners.[144] Only after the signing of the 1609 truce did it begin to decline. With war receding in western Europe, many pirate leaders offered to exchange their ships, weapons, and plunder for a pardon and a small pension. Around the same time, insecure bases, poor organization, and waning recruitment started the decline of English piratical activities in the Mediterranean. After 1612, English mariners became the prey rather than the perpetrators of piracy.

Spain's main grievance against James was England's new imperial drive and the establishment of the Jamestown colony. Counting all the Americas to be territories granted to Spain by the pope, Philip viewed the settlement as a serious violation of the 1604 treaty and was minded to take steps 'to prevent the English from settling colonies in North America'.[145] Hearing Spain's complaints via Zúñiga, James stated categorically that the treaty had 'not stipulated that his subjects should not go there' since Virginia was not 'actually possessed' by Spain. He only conceded that Jamestown would not be used as a pirate base to disrupt Spanish shipping, another concern raised by Zúñiga.[146] However, because a Protestant presence in Virginia was thought damaging to Spain's *reputación* and the Catholic Church, Philip got ready, in late 1607, to order his fleet to uproot the colony before its numbers expanded. He only desisted after listening to the advice of the constable of

Castile, Spain's main expert on English affairs. The constable rightly cautioned that military action might endanger the peace as well as worsen Spain's chronic financial difficulties, but he mistakenly opined that the colony was unlikely to survive.[147]

Spanish anger resurfaced as the colony grew. Consequently, in 1609, members of the council of state pronounced that the English had 'as good a right to that countrie [Virginia] as to that of Peru' and recommended military action to oust them. Yet, for fear of breaking the peace, Philip again decided to use only diplomatic means to 'divert' James from 'anie further proceedings of settling in that countrie'.[148] The same happened in 1611 and 1612, for once more Philip and his councillors reached the conclusion that Virginia was not important enough to endanger the peace.[149] Meanwhile, James and Cecil encouraged the construction of intelligence networks to report and assess the danger of Spanish intervention against Jamestown.[150] James's refusal to back down over Virginia yet non-confrontational stance towards Spain helped save the colony and the Treaty of London.

As far as England was concerned, the 1604 treaty was not working well on two counts. The first concerned trade. English merchants and mariners repeatedly protested about their treatment at the hands of Spain's civil authorities and occasionally the Inquisition.[151] Some traders and seamen were thrown into jail or condemned to the galleys while their goods and ships were seized, allegedly because they were involved in smuggling merchandise from the United Provinces or trading outside the limits of the treaty. Furthermore, English merchants complained that Spain consistently tried to disrupt their trade in the Levant, relying on 'papal laws' that prohibited trade with non-Christians.[152] In the summer of 1606, the 'discontentments' grew so 'sore' that one of Edmonde's secretaries in Brussels thought that 'the course proposed for redress', namely reprisals, might 'bring soon both our peace and amity to the wracke'.[153] In the 1607 parliament, 'the question of reprisals was again discussed', Fuller taking the lead while Sandys was sent to ask the lords to support a petition to James, which listed their complaints and called for retaliation.[154] Merchant protests did not die down, and, in August 1607, Cecil—as spokesman for the privy council—told both Habsburg ambassadors that if the 'occasion of complaint' continued it would 'shake very dangerously the foundacon of that amity'.[155] Little changed over the next few months, and Cornwallis was instructed in November to warn the Spaniards that, if nothing substantial was done, the friendship between the two kings would be at risk.[156] To save the treaty, Philip made some recompense to individual merchants and mariners whose sufferings were made known to him, as a gesture of goodwill. But he would not do more, instead repeating grievances about English acts of piracy.[157] The problem remained a troublesome sore in Anglo-Spanish relations.

The second grievance against Spain was political. James and his council were angry that the Habsburgs were not keeping to the pledge that neither side would harbour or aid the other's enemies. Much to James's and Cecil's annoyance, over several years the archdukes refused to extradite two men (Colonel Hugh Owen and the Jesuit William Baldwin) found guilty of complicity in the Gunpowder Plot.[158] Similarly, instead of handing over the Irish earls of Tyrone and Tyrconnell in late 1607, the archdukes—accused Cecil—'were receiving those fugitives into their protection', a charge that the Habsburgs fervently denied.[159] Even worse, just when James was trying to mediate a peace between the Habsburgs and Dutch, he and Cecil heard rumours of Spanish invasion plans on behalf of the Irish earls, which led them to consider whether it might be better for Spain to be bogged down in the Netherlands rather than be free to intervene in Ireland.[160] Yet their suspicions were largely misplaced; the Habsburgs were politically embarrassed by the presence of the Irish fugitives in their territories and did their best to send them on their way to a quiet life in Rome.

★ ★ ★

After the 1604 treaty was ratified, Spain unsuccessfully approached James to act as a mediator to negotiate a peace between the Dutch and the Habsburgs. James was wary to intervene on the stated grounds that the differences between the two sides were irreconcilable and that he would lose influence with them both by interceding.[161] Perhaps too, as the Venetian ambassador cynically suspected, James was content to see no end to the fighting 'because the continuance of war protected him from the Spanish'.[162] Consequently, it came as an unwelcome shock when the archdukes and States General agreed an eight-month ceasefire, in early April 1607, without any forewarning or communication with him. Furious at being 'so apparently neglected', James demanded that the United Provinces immediately send a delegation to England to explain their independent action, which was—he claimed—an infringement of their accord with England.[163] While awaiting their arrival, he turned his attention to what seemed to him the more urgent matter of the Union and let events in the Netherlands take their course. Henry IV filled the vacuum. The French king at once dispatched a delegation to

The Hague led by Pierre Jeannin, who told the States General that the French king would welcome a peace that guaranteed their independence but would give them military support if that were not possible. In fact, Henry preferred the fighting to go on but did not want any longer to cover its costs or risk war with Spain.[164]

James and Cecil continued to believe that a long-term peace in the Netherlands would likely be unattainable on terms that could satisfy and safeguard the United Provinces. Zúñiga had warned them that Philip would never recognize their independence, even though this was an indispensable condition for the Dutch and one already conceded by the archdukes.[165] Apart from the harm to Spanish *reputación*, Philip—supported by the war party in Castile—was convinced that granting such a concession would inevitably result in further rebellions in his empire and the loss of the entire Netherlands. When Philip did capitulate on the 'point of independence' in his ratification of the ceasefire, James and Cecil correctly understood that it was not in perpetuity but only to give the States General 'the right to treat'.[166] Given Spain's intransigence about accepting the loss of its one-time dominion, James and Cecil suspected—also correctly—that Philip had only agreed to start talks because of some 'great necessity' (which was both a shortage of resources and the papal dispute with Venice which threatened war in Italy). Their doubt about the sincerity of Habsburg overtures for peace significantly affected James's and Cecil's interactions with the Dutch throughout 1607 and partly explains their lack of a clear direction in policy over the next few years.

In their meetings with James that summer, the Dutch legation 'let it be quite clearly understood that unless they received certain, prompt, and suitable support in the war they would be obliged to accept the advantageous peace which was now proposed to them'.[167] In a quandary, James sat on the fence. He told the envoys of his unwillingness to see a continuance of the war largely because it was 'repugnant to his owne amitie' with the Habsburgs. Equally bad, to continue their struggle, he recognized that the Dutch would require him to provide subsidies which he could ill afford or else they would turn to the French for additional help.[168] On the other hand, James held back from counselling a peace. Since he and his advisers still believed a permanent one was elusive, he held it safer 'to reserve himselfe from perswading it', for otherwise he would be viewed as 'the author' of an unsuccessful initiative.[169] Were the two sides to agree on a short-term truce, instead of a permanent peace, that too James could not advise, for surely

Spain and the archdukes would resume hostilities once their financial situation had improved and the problems in Italy been resolved.

With all these considerations in mind, James dispatched Sir Richard Spencer to join Winwood in The Hague in August 1607. Their task was to discuss with the French and Dutch what course would best accord with the 'safety' of the United Provinces and 'the present condition' of his own affairs. His 'condition' concerned money; not only could James not provide subsidies if the war continued but he also needed to know how and when the Dutch and French intended to repay their loans to him if peace were secured. Again, he would not press for peace or war, but now he instructed his envoys to convey his conditions for whichever option was followed. If the Dutch chose peace, he and Henry IV had both to be comprehended in the treaty and the terms had to include freedom of conscience in the archdukes' territories and the withdrawal of all Spanish and Italian troops from there. If, however, the States General preferred to continue the war, the Dutch had to be told that he would not supply troops against Spain nor could he assist them financially, unless perhaps he was offered some 'inducement'.[170] Although James kept his options open, contemporaries generally believed that he favoured a peace because he did not want to see French aid to, and influence over, the Dutch that would inevitably occur with the continuation of war.[171] As the Venetian ambassador Zorzi Giustinian astutely noted, the 'real object' of the English government was: 'to protect themselves by the erection of a free state in that country [the United Provinces] which will not, therefore, ever fall into the hands of either Spain or France'.[172] If that objective could be achieved in a peace treaty, James would be satisfied.

Over the next few months, the two envoys in The Hague waited for the Spanish king to change the wording of his supposed recognition of Dutch independence (called the '*agreation*'), the original of which had failed to satisfy the States General. Without it, negotiations for peace could not proceed. When it arrived in mid-October 1607, its wording was still thought 'defective in the forme', yet Winwood and Spencer urged the States General to accept it and 'the sooner the better'. The English envoys knew that their king would provide no material assistance in any new bout of fighting and thought it very unlikely that the French king would fill the gap.[173] Initially, though, James was annoyed at his ambassadors' acceptance of the '*agreation*'. His suspicions of the Habsburgs were then intense, because of their reception of Tyrone, and he wanted to delay a peace. But since he had no intention of aiding the Dutch, James had to retreat and accept the ratification as satisfactory.

It took until December before the United Provinces would consent to the '*agreation*'. Maurice of Nassau (the leader of the war party) had wanted to reject it and only yielded when he eventually despaired of obtaining any substantial aid from either France or England. Once the '*agreation*' was sorted, the commissioners from the archdukes and Spain arrived in The Hague to parley. During these negotiations, England often seemed on the back foot, a position which was quite deliberate for the privy council had advised the English diplomats 'not to be leaders but followers'.[174] Even then, James would not follow blindly. Fearing to be drawn into war, he refused to enter a proposed tripartite defensive league with the French and the Dutch.[175] Only when Henry went it alone and concluded a bilateral treaty with the United Provinces in January 1608, did James agree to negotiate his own bilateral league with the Dutch; presumably he was heeding the warning that his failure to offer them help had given 'the French too much advantage to creep into these men's hearts'.[176]

The Anglo-Dutch treaty, which was signed in June 1608, was pretty much in England's interests since it committed James to very little: he would help the Dutch obtain 'une bonne et asseuree paix'; a defensive league would only operate if that peace was violated; and, in the event of a peace, the Dutch would repay in stages their debt to him.[177] Disappointing to Protestant militants at home and abroad, the treaty nonetheless annoyed the Habsburgs, although Cecil tried to soothe them by maintaining that the alliance 'aymed at nothing else then to a furthering of this peace' since it would force the Dutch to reach terms.[178] Pacifying Spain seemed urgent as rumours were then circulating that Philip was about to negotiate a marriage treaty with Henry, and fears were emerging that the two kings would form a Catholic league against James, whose book against Bellarmine had riled Rome.[179] In fact, neither Philip nor Henry had any intention of breaking with James, and a Habsburg–Bourbon marriage alliance was not arranged until after the assassination of the French king in 1610.[180]

By the summer of 1608, it became evident that James had been right all the time and the two sides were too far apart for a peace treaty to be agreed. The attempts to resolve key issues in dispute—the right of the Dutch to navigate and trade in the Indies and freedom of worship throughout the Netherlands—had left the English mediators 'so harassed that they have scarce time to breathe'.[181] Ultimately, Spain pulled out over the question of religion, its commissioners—supported by Henry and the archdukes—insisting upon the official exercise of Catholicism in the United Provinces, which was unacceptable to the Dutch and opposed by the English.

After this, Winwood and Jeannin tried to urge a truce on both Maurice and Philip.[182] By January 1609, a longish truce looked possible but not on terms favoured by the English: 'the treaty goes forward in the Low Countries and that so fast that, wheras we have spurred them on hitherto, we wold now faine hold them backe with the bridle'.[183] One concern of the English negotiators was that the Dutch were demanding freedom to sail and trade in the East Indies and, if granted, the danger would arise that 'the growing power and commerce of the Dutch by sea will eventually seriously damage the trade of England'.[184] As it was, some English merchants had been fearful that they would lose much of the carrying trade between the southern Netherlands and Spain because the Dutch would 'lett forth their shippes to fraight 1/3 pennie better cheape then we maie'.[185]

Overcoming all obstacles, a twelve-year truce was concluded at Antwerp, on 29 March 1609, and ratified by Philip at the end of June.[186] It was far more than a ceasefire since it comprised thirty-eight articles designed to restore political and commercial relations between the Dutch and the Habsburgs. Its conclusion was a remarkable achievement that owed a great deal to French and English mediation. However, it was built on an ambiguity over whether the United Provinces was being acknowledged as an independent state: Spain thought its recognition was only temporary during the lifetime of the truce; but the Dutch believed their independence had been recognized forever.

In celebration of the truce, the Flemish engraver and printer Hendrick Hondius published a print of the eighteen negotiators, including Spencer and Winwood, which appeared in Dutch, French, and Latin. Additionally, the Antwerp artist and printer Abraham Verhoeven depicted Spencer in a woodcut drawing for a news pamphlet as one of the eight negotiators of the truce.[187] However, in truth, the Habsburgs found the agreement a bitter pill to swallow. In Spain, it was derided as a blow to its *reputación*. In Brussels, the archdukes were troubled that the vagueness of some of its terms favoured the Dutch and called for a new set of negotiations that would settle matters such as the demarcation of the border and the re-opening of the Scheldt.[188] Like Spain, the United Provinces did not view the truce as permanent, and it is surely significant that an official medal struck in Holland in 1609 commemorated not the truce but the States General's alliance with England and France and bore the legend *Contra Vim Tirannorum* [against the power of tyrants].[189] In England, the treaty was treated as a success for James. Its articles were printed, and, on the title page of the publication, James's ambassadors were given credit for their 'mediation and advice'.[190] It seemed an appropriate time for Edward Grimeston to produce his 'description of the eight united provinces now made free', translated from John Petit.[191] Nonetheless, the signing and ratification of the peace passed without any thanksgiving ceremony in London. Perhaps that was far-sighted for the war erupted again when the truce expired, only ending, in January 1648, with the Treaty of Münster which finally recognized the independence of the Dutch republic.

★ ★ ★

Even before the 1609 truce was signed, a new international crisis was brewing in Europe. That spring, a dispute arose over the succession to the duchies of Jülich-Cleves and Berg after the death of its childless Catholic ruler John William on 15 March. The duchies were situated in a vital geopolitical location with Cleves bordering on the United Provinces and Jülich controlling the routes of the rivers Rhine and Meuse. Consequently, the Habsburgs needed the duchies to be in friendly hands; equally, the Dutch and French could not afford to let them slip into the clutches of the Habsburgs.

Although several princes had a claim to succeed, the two with the strongest title were Protestant: John Sigismund, elector of Brandenburg, and Wolfgang William, the son of the palatine count of Neuburg. On hearing of John William's death, both these princes independently sent their forces into the duchies. However, determined to prevent a Protestant succeeding, the Catholic Habsburg emperor, Rudolph II, referred the succession to an imperial court, as was his legal right as the feudal overlord. In response, Brandenburg and Neuburg decided to work together and signed a treaty, on 1 June 1609, whereby they would keep possession of the duchies until impartial princes arbitrated between their rival claims. While Rudolph did nothing, his cousin Archduke Leopold, bishop of Passau and Strasbourg, grabbed the fortress of Jülich, which had until then been held by a Catholic garrison loyal to the Habsburgs.[192]

No-one wanted the dispute to descend into an international armed conflict, and certainly not the archdukes and Philip III. Nevertheless, the danger of just this loomed when German princes began to take sides according to their religious confessions and Henry IV started to contemplate military intervention on behalf of Brandenburg and Neuburg. Henry, it was said, 'desired to make a great noyse in it [rather] then really to prosequute it for the present'.[193] His support would play well with the German princes who, in 1608, had formed themselves into a Protestant Union and might deter the archdukes and Spain from intervening in the dispute. Nonetheless, when Henry moved French troops to its border with the Spanish Netherlands, international tensions were exacerbated.

In January 1610, Henry IV offered Brandenburg and Neuburg full military backing despite the pope thinking the war 'one of religion and not politics'.[194] The king was reacting in part to the hard line taken by the emperor, who had threatened in December to impose an imperial ban on the Protestant claimants and their allies if they did not withdraw from the duchies and accept his arbitration. Having repeatedly spoken of his support for Brandenburg and Neuburg, Henry could hardly abandon them without damaging his international reputation not to mention his strategic security. Rumours flying around, in early 1610, that the archdukes were raising troops to assist Leopold kept Henry on course. In March, he entered an alliance with the Protestant Union of German princes against Leopold and, in April, he concluded an offensive pact with the duke of Savoy for the purpose of invading Spanish-held Milan. Henry was either planning a wider war against the Habsburgs or else aiming to distract Spain from assisting the archdukes and emperor. Spain, incidentally, was remarkably quiet at that time.[195]

Where did James stand in all this? Like Cecil and other interested ministers, he was kept well informed about the various claimants, the nature of their titles, and the dangers arising from the succession dispute.[196] He preferred the title of Brandenburg, a kinsman of his wife, but his first instinct was to encourage the conflict to be resolved by diplomacy no matter who would be proved victorious. If warfare erupted, he would be under pressure to intervene but had no revenues for a fight and no wish to jeopardize his alliance with the Habsburgs. Accordingly, in July 1609, he gave Winwood instructions to put his weight behind the arbitration proposed by the Protestant claimants.[197]

Nevertheless, James well understood that Dutch defences would be badly compromised if Jülich remained in Habsburg hands. Furthermore, for reputational reasons, he did not want the French to be seen as the sole protectors of the Dutch and Protestant Union.[198] For these reasons, James agreed to provide military assistance for Brandenburg and Neuburg in response to urgings from the French and Germans in early 1610. He then commissioned two regiments of British soldiers who were already stationed in the United Provinces to fight in the duchies alongside soldiers raised by France and the Protestant Union. His justification for mobilizing only 4,000 men was that it was in line with 'former precedents' set by Queen Elizabeth who had sent 'not above 4,000 men' for the support of France after 1589.[199] The cost of the army, James fully expected, would be defrayed by the Dutch who could deduct it from their total debt to England. James probably still hoped war could be avoided since 'military opinion' thought Leopold 'weak in money and necessaries' and likely to withdraw from Jülich.[200]

To encourage the emperor and archdukes not to back Leopold, James made it known that his aims were strictly limited. His intention, he declared, was not 'to wrong any authority of the emperor' nor to favour 'any one pretender more than the other' but simply to protect the two German princes then in possession from the 'violence' of the 'intruders' who had no title nor right to the duchies. James wanted the Habsburgs to understand that he was not embarking on a Protestant crusade nor participating in any 'exorbitant purposes' of the French king.[201]

But the Protestant Union and the States General wanted more from the British king. In late March and early April, their ambassadors were assigned to invite him to enter, even lead, the Union and join their league with France. They were to be disappointed. On their arrival, James chose to depart London, leaving the privy council to discuss matters with them, allegedly because he was vexed that their princes and the States General had treated the French king with greater respect, including sending him the more prestigious envoys.[202] The timing of the ambassadors' visit was anyway annoying as a distraction from important parliamentary business related to the 'great contract'. At the same time, keeping his distance had the advantage of keeping him aloof from greater commitments.

Simultaneously, Henry dispatched his own envoy to London to press on James an alliance with France. The proposal was for a defensive treaty modelled largely on Elizabeth's treaty signed with Charles IX of France in 1572. James was ready to negotiate. Hard bargaining took place during April over some extra clauses, especially one related to James's demand that Henry would repay his debt to the English crown.[203] As far as James was concerned, if the French king had the sums available to pay for a military campaign, he could make good the existing debt to him.

While all this was going on, the news arrived that Henry had been stabbed to death on 4 May. The English court was 'stunned' and 'grieved beyond all belief'. James, at the hunt in Royston with the duke of Württemberg, was visibly moved on receipt of the news. The court wore black throughout Whitsuntide, but the formal mourning had to come to an end in June with the investiture of Prince Henry.[204] Although the French king's death put the talk of a league on hold, James did not pull back from his commitment to send troops to Jülich. On the contrary, he reassured his allies that he would meet his obligations and instructed Edmondes, the new ambassador to France, to persuade the French government to honour theirs. An experienced diplomat, Edmondes proved successful, and the minority government under the regency of the dowager queen, Marie de' Medici, reluctantly agreed to scaled-down military operations. As a result, English troops under Edward Cecil marched alongside two French regiments and Dutch forces towards Jülich in July 1610. There, they met the army of the Protestant Union and assaulted the fortress. Thirty-five days afterwards, Leopold surrendered. Subsequently, Brandenburg gained Cleves and Mark, while Neuburg acquired Jülich and Berg.[205]

As a result of the diplomacy surrounding the Jülich–Cleves crisis, James drew close to the Protestant Union. He came further into their orbit after Henry IV's widow negotiated a dynastic double marriage with Spain in 1611. To avoid isolation in the face of this Franco-Spanish rapprochement, James decided upon a marriage alliance with the Elector-Palatine Frederick V. Additionally, James hoped that the marriage would give him leverage among the German Protestants and restrain his son-in-law, who was a militant Calvinist, from embarking on a confessional war against Spain.

★ ★ ★

During his first decade on the English throne, James built up a reputation for himself as a peacemaker and a mediator in international conflicts, so much so that, in August 1612, Swedish ambassadors requested that he 'should intervene to arrange certain differences of great importance between Denmark and Sweden'.[206] James liked to see himself in that light and be represented as a peacemaker at home and abroad. He had written on the virtues of peace in the widely read *Basilikon Doron*, and his personal motto *Beati Pacifici* ('Blessed are the peacemakers' from the sermon on the mount, Matthew 5:9) was emblazoned on his new royal coat of arms.[207] As he settled into his reign in England, James ceased to be depicted wearing a breastplate or armour and was shown in prints, paintings, and medals in fashionable civilian dress.[208]

James, however, was no idealist, no matter the impression he liked to give. On the contrary, he was essentially a realist and pragmatist in his foreign policy.[209] His policies towards Spain and the Dutch, moreover, did not differ greatly from those of Elizabeth before she was dragged into war in the mid-1580s. They both preferred to stay out of foreign conflicts, not least because of England's limited financial and military resources, and to use diplomacy rather than arms to protect their realms against potential foes. Like Elizabeth, James wanted a negotiated settlement in the Netherlands to avoid England being drawn into the war against Spain. Like her too, he sought friendship with Spain to prevent the formation of a Catholic league against England and Spanish intervention in Ireland. Nonetheless, both monarchs were prepared to resort to warfare if necessary. Neither would leave the Dutch to fight alone if they looked to be struggling for survival: not only would a Spanish conquest threaten England's security and be a major blow to European Protestantism but it would be deeply unpopular with their subjects.

James's policy towards France, however, was different from Elizabeth's because of a new set of circumstances. He did not have to worry about France's 'auld alliance' with Scotland nor face the danger that arose from the formation of a Catholic league headed by a powerful and hostile French faction that was related to a potential heir. Religious peace in France—albeit fragile—and the dynastic union with Scotland freed James to develop a working relationship with the French king.

James's pragmatism was to England's advantage. His shrewd assessment of international affairs, his diplomatic experience, and slippery character enabled him to maintain a working relationship with both the Dutch and Habsburgs, to retain England's prestige as an important ally, yet avoid entangling commitments and alliances. In spite of the unpopularity of the peace in some quarters of England, James served his new subjects well in his early foreign policy.

Conclusion

Regime change is a modern concept, first coined by an American newspaperman in the 1920s and becoming popular this century in international relations.¹ Nonetheless, it is a term that can be applied fairly to earlier periods of history when a new dynasty took the throne and introduced new personnel and policies, as James I did in 1603. Although Cecil and other Elizabethan privy councillors remained in post, fresh blood on the council and in the court altered the power base from the previous reign (see Appendix 1). Likewise, the peace with Spain, the Union project, and the crown's acute financial difficulties turned the nation's attention towards a new set of circumstances and problems.

For many years, historians of England treated 1603 as a watershed moment, their books on this period either ending in the year of Elizabeth's death or beginning with James's accession. In part, this division was a legacy of nineteenth-century accounts that projected the causes of the English Civil War back into James's reign. He was held responsible for transforming divine right theories into absolutist principles and practices, while the Jacobean house of commons was thought to have 'seized the initiative' and begun to claim some form of parliamentary sovereignty.²

Historians have long moved away from this interpretation. But their recognition that personal monarchy in the early modern period shaped political life has led them to separate the two reigns as well, this time by focusing on the contrasting personal traits of the two monarchs. They are easy to find. Most notably, Elizabeth was frugal, James profligate; Elizabeth's speeches were terse, James's orations longwinded. In their devotional lives, Elizabeth favoured private prayer, and James public sermons. James thoroughly enjoyed theological disputes and intellectual arguments; Elizabeth preferred to avoid them. Elizabeth was praised for her interactions with her subjects, unlike James who was perceived as inaccessible. Elizabeth wooed her house of commons, whereas James often adopted a confrontational stance; and of course, Elizabeth was a single woman operating within a patriarchal society, whereas James conformed to ideals of masculinity, or at least he did until after 1612 when his relationships with first Robert Carr and then George Villiers aroused hostile comments about his sexuality. All these personal distinctions meant that the style of James's rule was markedly different from that of his predecessor.

There were profounder contrasts too. James's almost obsessional love of hunting and consequent absences from his capital helped shape royal government in a different mould. Although, during his hunting sprees, the king kept control over state business, government by pen often slowed down decision-making and executive orders, while his separation from English courtiers and councillors affected his working relationships. Elizabeth's communications with her principal secretaries had been largely face to face, but James interacted with Cecil for long periods of the year only by letter, sometimes written by himself but more often by Thomas Lake or George Home, earl of Dunbar. Furthermore, James's lengthy periods in the countryside placed a greater responsibility on his wife who came to fill some of the ceremonial void in London; Anna was assigned to entertain special ambassadors during James's absences, and the privy council met in her apartments. In consequence, the ceremonial aspect of royal government became more polycentric.

Another significant contrast was that James, unlike Elizabeth, was a published author. All the queen's proclamations and selected speeches had naturally been printed, as were some of her prayers. But the king put to press a far wider range and number of works: poems, scriptural exegeses, translations, and treatises on political and social issues. Whereas Elizabeth preferred to keep her thoughts to herself and a few select ministers, James broadcasted them to the wider public at home and abroad. *The Trew Lawe* and *Basilikon Doron*, published for English readers in 1603, revealed his theories of kingship; in his *Daemonologie*—also 'Englished' in 1603—James disclosed his interest and belief in witchcraft; and in *A Counterblaste to Tobacco* (1604) he publicized his dislike of the 'common herbe' for smoking. Then in 1608 and 1609, James's *Apologie* provided readers with his manifesto against papal powers. Finally, in what Jane Rickard has called 'his boldest act of authorial self-construction', James gathered his prose works into a large folio volume published in 1616.[3] The king's writings were designed to show off his rhetorical skills of persuasion, display himself as the wise King Solomon, and assert what Kevin Sharpe has called his 'interpretative power over rival voices' as an act of royal authority.[4] Instead of standing apart from political and theological controversies, as Elizabeth had often done, James entered their midst.

While James was admired as an intellectual, this kind of publicity had two potentially perilous political outcomes. First, it eroded some of the mystique surrounding monarchy, which probably explains why no other European early modern monarch had been or was to become a published author. Second, the general message taken from his writings created disquiet among some of his English subjects. James's *The Trew Law* and *Basilikon Doron* had originally been written to serve specific purposes in Scotland when his authority was being challenged by the Kirk and nobility. They were also reactions to previous publications, notably the contract theories of both the Presbyterian George Buchanan and Jesuit Robert Persons. But, in the context of post-1603 England, James's arguments—especially his claim that the king was above the law—seemed sinister, even alarming. To make matters worse, James's re-articulation of his elevated view of kingship in various speeches to parliament led to debates in the lower house about the nature and extent of the royal prerogative, which Elizabeth would never have allowed. Although when under pressure James was prepared to withdraw from some of his more extreme statements, his retreat did not allay the distrust of some parliamentarians. It even grew in intensity when James's actions matched his words, such as when he sidestepped parliament and used a proclamation to create his new title of king of Great Britain and relied on judges to obtain the naturalization of the *post-nati*. Elizabeth's flare-ups with the commons had usually occurred when members badgered her to accept their counsel on what she considered prerogative issues, notably her marriage, the succession, and religious reform. James's conflicts, in his first parliament, frequently arose when the commons refused to implement his will and he afterwards tried to use his prerogative to get his own way.[5] Given this, it is no wonder that, in 1610, members of the commons made such a fuss about John Cowell's *The Interpreter* and Samuel Harsnett's sermon. Nor is it surprising that the commons suspected that, if it were to grant the king a sufficient regular income in the 'great contract', he would cease to summon it.[6]

Furthermore, perhaps because of his lofty approach to his prerogative and because he was a foreigner, James did not properly understand that the scrutiny and criticism of government bills and policies were part of the function of the English parliament. Although he respected free speech in the commons, his own orations made clear that he thought members' reviews and critiques of governmental legislation were fractious, even blasphemous.

Outside parliament, James did not appear to take on board the free speech, known as *parrhesia*, whereby leading subjects conventionally spoke frankly to monarchs in offering advice. While James did not deny the importance of counsel, he was evidently loath to take it and especially whenever his cherished projects were at stake.[7] Certainly, there is no evidence that policies were thrashed out in council as they had been under Elizabeth. It could be that the lack of privy council records during his first decade accounts for this impression, but it is hard to believe that James did allow his privy council to debate the advisability or otherwise of the Union scheme. If he did, then he ignored the views of Cecil and others. It is noticeable too that James did not appreciate or listen to the frank counsel provided by his clergy, especially when it verged on outright criticism. He dismissed Archbishop Matthew Hutton of York's written suggestion that he spend less time hunting as 'a senceles proposition' and 'the foolysht letter that ever hee red'.[8] More significantly, he took a tougher line than Elizabeth had when faced with censures in sermons dressed up as counsel; witness the imprisonment and silencing of John Burges. As evidenced by his conduct at the Hampton Court Conference, we can see that James enjoyed the cut and thrust of theological debate, but he did not want to be told what to do or think, and definitely not that he was wrong.[9]

Historians have disagreed over whether the political ideas expressed in James's writings and speeches amounted to a theory of absolutism.[10] Absolutist theories, which were derived from Continental thinkers such as Jean Bodin, vested sovereign power in the ruler alone and forbade disobedience or resistance to his commands. These thinkers also maintained that kings were accountable only to God, because their power came solely and directly from Him, and hence they entirely rejected the contract theory that James had learned from George Buchanan.[11] The issues here are complex, but James's statements often appear to reflect absolutist theories, as when he asserted that kings made the laws of their realms and were not necessarily bound by them, and that subjects owed obedience to their kings in all circumstances. His belief that he was not accountable to his parliaments or his lawyers or indeed anyone else also smacked of absolutist thinking. Such views had been elaborated in *The Trew Law* before he came to the throne and were given further expression during the oath of allegiance dispute with the papacy. Of course, like Bodin, James maintained that a king should obey divine and natural laws and promote the public good (even though this obedience was not a legal obligation), for otherwise he would be a tyrant. Kings should also abide by the laws of their kingdoms, or at least do so until they believed there were legitimate reasons not to.[12] Nevertheless, the pressure James sometimes put on his judges to support his royal prerogative (see Fuller's case) or policies (over the Union, for example) was another assertion of royal sovereignty and threatened to undermine judicial independence.

James was not alone in having absorbed and generally agreed with Bodin's thinking about sovereignty.[13] Some of his subjects had also read the French jurist's political treatise in French or Latin before its translation into English in 1606, and those who held an exalted view of the royal prerogative came to adopt Bodin's ideas and language in political debates.[14] In judging Bate's case, for example, Chief Baron Fleming pronounced the king's power is 'absolute' for the common good and 'not guided by the rules which direct only at the common law'.[15] Arguably during the 1590s, the outlook of some English jurists and ministers was already moving from the 'mixed monarchy model'; the 'new conformists' among the clergy, for instance, were aiming at 'tilting real political power towards Elizabeth at the expense of the mixed polity'.[16] Nonetheless, others within England—especially some vocal members of the commons—held fast to the Elizabethan political outlook that spoke of England as a 'mixed' commonwealth or government and saw sovereignty as residing in the laws, not the ruler, of a kingdom.[17]

The Union and impositions debates raised these kinds of constitutional issues in James's early parliaments. The commons' hostility towards the monarch's prerogative right to raise new tariffs was not entirely new but became more pronounced under James after the judicial decision in Bate's case declared them legal. The issue of the Union was of course novel, and it too reinforced fears concerning James's ideas about monarchy. Under Henry VIII, England had become part of a composite monarchy with the incorporation of Wales in the mid-1530s and the declaration of Ireland as a separate kingdom in 1542. Now, after 1603, the constitutional status of Scotland was uncertain and problematic. James's new title 'king of Great Britain' put in jeopardy England's common law, while the possible union of laws in a 'perfect union' appeared an even greater danger to its existence. The resulting defence of common law, which became associated in some minds with England's birthright, had the potential for conflict with James's belief that kings made the law and hence were above it.[18] These deliberations on the royal prerogative were not confined to the law courts or houses of parliament, for accounts of the debates on impositions and *post-nati* circulated in commercial copies, as manuscript separates permeated the political culture of the day.[19] While I am far from contending here that a constitutional crisis began in Jacobean England over issues of law, sovereignty, and divine right, I am suggesting that constitutional questions about the extent and nature of the royal prerogative were becoming more evident in political thinking and rhetoric under James.

England's relationship with Scotland was transformed as a result of James's accession. From the English point of view, on the positive side, the back door into England no longer existed and the northern kingdom ceased to be a security threat. But, on the negative, the Union debates and arrival of courtier Scots into London triggered the expression of nasty anti-Scottish prejudices in parliamentary speeches, polemical tracts, popular print, and drama. From the Scots' viewpoint, on the positive side, some of them had access to the bounty of the English crown and the new plantations in Ireland; but on the negative, their king and his court were now centred in London, and attempts were being made to anglicize some of their institutions (including the Kirk) and bring about a degree of congruity in religion. As for Ireland, the end of the Nine Years' War preceded James's accession, and the events that followed probably had little to do with the change in England's dynasty. However, the inclusion of the Scottish Presbyterians in the Ulster plantation was a direct result of James's vision of Union and had a major long-term influence on Anglo-Irish history.

With James's coronation, the Tudor preoccupation with the succession was laid to rest.[20] Problems surrounding the succession had caused dynastic insecurity and political instability throughout the sixteenth century, while the possibility of a contested succession and civil war on Elizabeth's death had cast a shadow over her reign which inspired political activity and influenced popular culture. Although public discussion of the succession had been banned by statute in 1571, polemical pamphlets on the subject circulated privately in manuscript or were printed abroad. Plays for the domestic market alluded to the Elizabethan situation in stories of either past or imagined successions, whether Shakespeare's Wars of the Roses cycle, which explored the effects of rival claims to the English throne, or his *Titus Andronicus* (written in collaboration with George Peele), which used a pseudo-Roman setting to delve into the principles of monarchical succession.[21]

CONCLUSION

During the first decade of James's reign, the immediate succession was no longer a topical matter in England. However, the king's accession was hardly a victory for the hereditary principle, for the panegyric greeting James in 1603 reflected uncertainty about whether the new king had taken the throne as Elizabeth's natural successor or been elected by the privy council or nominated by the queen. Perhaps for this reason, as well as because of the Union question, early Jacobeans were exposed to intellectual inquiries into the nature of successions and monarchies—hereditary and elective—and which kind existed in Britain, and which were to be preferred. As Malcolm Smuts has explained, Shakespeare tackled such matters in *Macbeth* (c. 1606), a play that offered ambivalence not solutions to these questions. After Duncan's death, Macbeth is elected king, yet he is called an 'untitled tyrant' who keeps 'the due of birth' from Malcolm who takes the throne at the end of the play but is himself a flawed character.[22] The witches, moreover, predict a hereditary line from Banquo; and in Act 4 Macbeth has a vision of eight future kings of Scotland, all of them Banquo's descendants, the last of whom is James himself holding triple sceptres.[23] It is hard to imagine this play being written and performed under Elizabeth.

★ ★ ★

Yet, inevitably, not all changed with the new regime. Other than establishing the bedchamber, James did not introduce any radical overhaul of the administration or governance of the realm. The monarchy remained intact in 1603, and its court displayed a similar magnificence to that shown under Elizabeth; indeed, the royal family offered opportunities denied to Elizabeth for royal celebrations, such as the installation of Charles as duke of York, the investiture of Henry as prince of Wales, and the wedding of Princess Elizabeth. Both James and Anna understood the importance of ceremony, spectacles, and a public image, just as had the previous Tudor dynasty. Accusations that James was careless in his dress and had little interest in his appearance are unjustified for he and Anna paid attention to, and considerable sums on, their clothes, jewels, and courtly magnificence. As had his Tudor predecessors—and as did many of his contemporaries on the Continent—James exploited visual media—coins, medals, prints, and portraits—to transmit his authority and policies. Like them, James also appealed directly to his subjects in print (notably after the Gunpowder Plot) and drew on providentialism in his propaganda.[24] Moreover, he continued and indeed extended Elizabeth's practice of encouraging national holidays to celebrate royal anniversaries, just the dates were different. The bellringing which had been customary in some churches on Elizabeth's birthday and accession day were heard again on the anniversaries of James's accession and coronation, on Gowrie Day and 5 November.[25]

Visitors to James's court would have found many similarities in its culture to the previous reign. Elaborate masques were new, but the tilts, tournaments, and garter celebrations continued, showing that neo-chivalry was far from dead under the Scottish king. The 'Barriers' of Prince Henry matched in spectacle the elaborate public relations exercises sponsored by the first earl of Essex during his heyday. The annual court progress to regional communities and residences of prominent individuals continued to take place every summer. Like Elizabeth, James did not add to the stock of royal palaces; but his wife and son created newly refurbished palaces that rivalled those of Henry VIII. They also enhanced royal splendour through their sponsorship of Italianate styles of art, architecture, and garden design, all of which, incidentally, were not entirely new to England but had been encouraged by only a small coterie of Elizabethan courtiers.

In religious life, James's accession brought little change. For the first time since the accession of Edward VI, no new Church settlement was introduced at the outset of a new reign. England remained firmly in the Protestant camp, just as it had been under Elizabeth. Although James was more Calvinist in his theological beliefs, he, no more than she, would allow predestinarian doctrines to become fully part of the Church's official teachings and refused the Puritan request at the Hampton Court Conference to affix the Lambeth articles to the thirty-nine articles or allow explanations upholding predestination to be inserted into the 1604 prayer book. Like Elizabeth, James preferred 'not to stuffe the [prayer] booke with all conclusions theologicall'.[26] And, when later in his reign the doctrine of predestination became hotly contested, James directed that preachers should not 'from henceforth presume to preach in any populous auditorie the deepe points of predestination', because these were 'fitter for the schooles and universities, then for simple auditories'.[27] Elizabeth would have approved. At the same time, James's accession did not usher in a new harmonious post-Reformation interlude after the conflicts of the later Elizabethan period. Puritan pressure for reform and the outcry about suspended and deprived nonconforming clergy continued unabated, while the Gunpowder Plot revealed the lengths to which some disaffected Catholics would go.

Consequently, both monarchs had to wrestle with the contentious question that confronted almost all early modern European rulers: how far had they the right and power to control religious beliefs and behaviour? And in their responses, there was a paper-thin difference between them. Both monarchs understood the royal supremacy to mean that they had the right and duty to impose uniformity of religious practice on their subjects. James upheld the legal position, reached under Elizabeth in Cawdrey's case of 1591, that the monarch had the legal right to deprive nonconforming ministers of their church living, 'because the kinge hath the supreame ecclesisticall power, which he hath delegated to the commissioners whereby they had the power of deprivation by the canon law of the realme'.[28] The hopes of Puritans and Catholics that James would allow greater latitude in worship were illusory. James was no more inclusive of Puritans and Presbyterians than Elizabeth had been (despite short periods of relaxed tensions during both their reigns). Both monarchs equally demanded conformity to adiaphora. It has been said that James was a moderate in his religious views but if 'moderation' is 'tentatively defined as a willingness to take a non-confrontational approach to religious disagreement', James was no moderate.[29]

As for Catholics, Elizabeth and James were happy enough to shelter in their court crypto-Catholic nobles and royal servants whose loyalty they could trust, yet both also agreed to the passage of harsh statutes against recusants. They shared a hatred for Jesuits whom they saw as agents of the pope and supporters of regicide. Undeniably, fewer priests were executed under James, but then the danger from them seemed far less great after the ratification of the 1604 peace with the Habsburgs. Besides, James preferred their banishment to death to avoid disrupting his relationships with the Catholic powers. Nevertheless, James did not entirely abjure the death penalty *per se* for religious dissidents. Not only did priests face executions for refusing to swear the oath of allegiance but he was said to have insisted upon the burning in 1612 of two Protestants who refuted the Trinity. Thankfully, these two men turned out to be the last persons burned for heresy in England, but it was not until 1681 that the last execution of a Catholic took place on English soil.

Notwithstanding the hard line taken towards those who rejected the Protestant Book of Common Prayer, both Elizabeth and James denied that they were making windows into their subjects' souls, claiming instead that they allowed freedom of conscience. And it is true that they were moderates here in comparison to many of their contemporary and later European rulers. They did not drive into exile all the men and women who did not share the beliefs of their Church (as did the Habsburgs during the 1620s) nor encourage local massacres (as had the French crown in 1572 at the Massacre of St Bartholomew). Leaving aside any personal considerations, both Elizabeth and James appreciated that such actions would destabilize the realm far more than would the presence of religious recusants and nonconformists who were not obviously seditious. Nevertheless, both monarchs, backed by their divines, would use oaths when it suited them to penetrate their subjects' consciences and beliefs as part of their campaigns to ensure conformity and loyalty.

In their foreign policy, James and Elizabeth also shared a common approach. Both preferred peace to war and tried to limit their military commitments on the Continent. Neither was attracted to the policy of Protestant militarism favoured by some of their subjects. Financial and military considerations governed their thinking for England could not match the resources of France and Spain. Amity with these Catholic powers was a central plank in both their programmes for much of their reigns, and matrimonial diplomacy played a role at one time or another in their negotiations with the Bourbon and Habsburg monarchs.

Governance in the localities remained the same after 1603. Few additions or removals were made to the commissions of the peace, and the work of JPs continued to grow. Because of alterations in the personnel of the privy council, new networks and relationships had sometimes to be forged between the local elites and the centre, but the structure of politics did not change. Political life in the localities, moreover, was as lively under James as it had been during the Elizabethan years, if not livelier. County gentry and urban citizens continued to discuss the main issues of the day together at quarter sessions and assizes, and sometimes with the members they sent to the commons. Political issues reached the regions through the medium of print. As seen, pamphlets were produced arguing against the royal policy of peace with Spain under both Elizabeth and James, while Puritans and Catholics resorted to print in both reigns to get across their grievances and justify their demands. Other media operated too: verse libels attacking individuals and policies circulated in manuscript, while popular theatre could be an opportunity for laughter at the government's expense and a forum commenting on the issues of the day. What is more, local petitioning to the centre about economic, political, and religious concerns seems to have been on the increase. Despite the authoritarian nature of early modern regimes and their attempts to close down discussions and interventions about 'the 'mysteries of state' (*arcana imperii*), oppositional, even subversive, literature flourished during the late sixteenth and early seventeenth centuries.

For those who had little or no political voice, the accession of James brought little that was new, and their lives went on much as before. Certainly, there were better harvests: good ones experienced from 1603 until 1606 (which were a continuation from Elizabeth's last two years), but only average yields followed before three good harvests from 1618 until 1620.[30] When occasional scarcity came, as in 1608, the privy council resorted to old remedies and reissued the Elizabethan book of orders that demanded prices be controlled and corn distributed during the emergency.[31] The Elizabethan poor laws were left intact. Plague continued to beset urban communities: that of 1603 was especially virulent, deaths running from five to six times their normal level, and plague returned in 1606, 1609, and 1625. In rural areas, despite the enclosure commission that followed the 1607 Midlands Rising, there was no end to wealthier farmers engrossing land and encroaching upon the commons. However, increasingly, the process was becoming more consensual and fewer riots resulted. The drop in wool prices during the early seventeenth century may also have discouraged the increase in flocks of sheep that had so encouraged enclosure. Consequently, enclosure riots became less prevalent as a form of popular protest.

Regime change in 1603, therefore, did not result in a radical break with the past. As we have seen, James shared much of Elizabeth's outlook on religion and politics. Moreover, he saw the value in presenting his reign as a continuation—or a better version—of hers. He well understood that an attempt to change England's institutions would unite much of the political and social elite against him and confirm suspicions that he was acting as a conqueror. Conquerors, it was commonly believed, consolidated their conquests by imposing their own customs and practices on their conquered subjects. Nonetheless, because James could not keep silent whether in his early writings or in his addresses to the English parliament, his views on kingship appeared to many as different and dangerous. Additionally, James's conviction that he had a direct line to God and a duty to bring about God's purpose made him deeply impatient with those who frustrated him and drove him to pursue policies that he believed to be God's will, without the consent of parliament. This goes a long way to explain the new political tensions of James's early years on the English throne. It also helped set the tone of much early Jacobean political culture. Nonetheless, owing to his political shrewdness and flexibility, James avoided being seen as a tyrant while, thanks to his conflict with the papacy, James's Protestant credentials were not in doubt. It was the bishops, especially Bancroft, not the king, who were mainly blamed for the enforcement of conformity. During the latter part of his reign, however, James was far less sure-footed, but that is the subject of another book.

Appendix 1: James's English Privy Council 1603–12

Elizabeth's appointment ★

APPOINTMENTS 1603

Charles Blount, eighth Lord Mountjoy, created earl of Devonshire (July 1603). Appointed master-general of the ordnance (1603). Died 1606.

Edward Bruce, Lord Kinloss. Appointed master of the rolls in chancery (1603). Died 1611.

★Henry Carey, Lord Hunsdon. Died 1603.

★Sir Robert Cecil created Baron Cecil of Essendon (May 1603), Viscount Cranborne (Aug. 1604), earl of Salisbury (May 1605). Retained as principal secretary and master of the court of wards. Appointed lord treasurer (1608). Died 1612.

Thomas Cecil, Lord Burghley, created earl of Exeter (May 1605). Died 1623.

George Clifford, third earl of Cumberland. Appointed governor of the borders (June 1603). Died 1605.

★Sir Thomas Egerton created Baron Ellesmere (July 1603) and Viscount Brackley (1616). Appointed lord chancellor (July 1603). Died 1617.

James Elphinstone created Lord Balmerino (Feb. 1604). Died 1612.

John Erskine, eighteenth or second earl of Mar. Died 1634.

★Sir John Fortescue retained as chancellor of the duchy of Lancaster. Died 1607.

★Sir John Herbert retained as 'second secretary of state'. Died 1617.

Sir George Home created Lord Home of Berwick (July 1604), earl of Dunbar (July 1605). Appointed chancellor of the exchequer (1603–6), keeper of the great wardrobe (1603–6). Died 1611.

★Charles Howard, earl of Nottingham, retained as lord high admiral. Died 1624.

Lord Henry Howard created earl of Northampton (March 1604). Appointed warden of the Cinque Ports (Jan. 1604), lord privy seal (1608). Died 1614.

Thomas Howard, Lord Howard of Walden, created earl of Suffolk (July 1603). Appointed lord chamberlain (Apr. 1603). Died 1626.

★Sir William Knollys created Baron Knollys of Greys (May 1603), Viscount Wallingford (1616). Retained as comptroller [treasurer] of the household. Appointed cofferer to Prince Henry (1606). Died 1632.

Henry Percy, ninth earl of Northumberland, appointed captain of the gentlemen pensioners (May 1603). Deprived (Nov. 1605). Died 1632.

*Sir John Popham retained as lord chief justice. Died 1607.
*Thomas Sackville, Lord Buckhurst, created earl of Dorset (March 1604). Retained as lord treasurer. Died 1608.
*Edward Somerset, fourth earl of Worcester, retained as master of the horse (surrendered 1616). Acted as earl marshal for court ceremonials (1604). Died 1628.
*Sir John Stanhope created Baron Stanhope of Harrington (May 1605). Retained as vice chamberlain of the household. Died 1621.
Ludovick Stuart, second duke of Lennox, created earl of Richmond (1613), duke of Richmond and earl of Newcastle (1623). Appointed lord steward (1616). Died 1624.
*Gilbert Talbot, seventh earl of Shrewsbury. Died 1616.
*Thomas West, third Lord de la Warr. Died 1618.
*John Whitgift, archbishop of Canterbury. Died 1604.
*Sir Edward Wotton created first Baron Wotton (May 1603). Retained as comptroller of the household. Died 1628.
Edward la Zouche, eleventh Lord Zouche. Retained as president of the council of Wales and the marches (1602). Died 1625.

ADDITIONS BEFORE END OF 1612

Archbishop Richard Bancroft of Canterbury (1605).
Sir Thomas Parry (Dec. 1607), chancellor of duchy of Lancaster.
Sir Julius Caesar (July 1607), chancellor of the exchequer (1606).
Sir Thomas Erskine (1610).
Sir Alexander Seton, earl of Dunfermline (1610).
Archbishop George Abbot of Canterbury (1611).
William Herbert, third earl of Pembroke (1611).
Robert Carr, earl of Rochester (1612).

Appendix 2: Lord Lieutenants 1603–12

Bedfordshire: earl of Kent (1586–1615).
Cambridgeshire: earl of Suffolk (1602–26).
Cheshire: earl of Derby (1607–42).
Cornwall: earl of Pembroke replaced Sir Walter Ralegh 1603.
Cumberland and Westmorland: third earl of Cumberland (1603–05); fourth earl of Cumberland (1607–39) jointly with earl of Dunbar (1607–11).
Derbyshire: earl of Shrewsbury (1590/91–1616).
Devon: earl of Bath (1586–1623).
Dorset: Viscount Howard of Bindon (1601–11); Robert Cecil (1611–12) jointly with earl of Suffolk (1611–26).
Durham: vacant until 1615.
Essex: earl of Sussex (1603–29).
Gloucestershire: Baron Berkeley (1603–13).
Hampshire: earl of Southampton (1604–24).
Herefordshire: the lord president of Wales.
Hertfordshire: Robert Cecil (1605–12).
Kent: Lord Cobham (1597–1603); Baron Wotton (1604–20).
Lancashire: earl of Derby (1607–42).
Leicestershire: fourth earl of Huntingdon (1596–1604); fifth earl of Huntingdon (1607–42).
Lincolnshire: earl of Rutland (1603–12).
Monmouthshire: earl of Worcester (1602–28).
Norfolk: earl of Northampton (1605–14).
Northamptonshire: earl of Exeter (1603–23).
Northumberland: see Cumberland.
Oxfordshire: William Baron Knollys (1596–1632).
Rutland: earl of Huntingdon (1596–1604); 1st Baron Harington of Exton (1607–13).
Shropshire: the lord president of Wales.
Somerset: earl of Hertford (1601–21).
Suffolk: earl of Suffolk (1605–26).
Surrey: earl of Nottingham (1585–1624).
Sussex: earl of Nottingham (1585–1608) jointly with earls of Dorset and Northumberland.
Warwickshire: Baron Compton (1603–30).
Wiltshire: see Somerset.
Worcestershire: the lord president of Wales.
Yorkshire: the lord president of the North (Baron Sheffield).

Appendix 3: Installations of Knights of the Garter 1603–12

Henry, duke of Cornwall and earl of Chester. 1603.
Ludovick Stuart, duke of Lennox. 1603.
Henry Wriothesley, third earl of Southampton. 1603.
John Erskine, eighteenth earl of Mar. 1603.
William Herbert, third earl of Pembroke. 1603.
Frederick, duke of Wittenberg, installed 1604 but elected in the year 1597.
Ulric, duke of Holstein. 1605.
Henry Howard, earl of Northampton. 1605.
Robert Cecil, earl of Salisbury. 1606.
Thomas Howard, third Viscount Howard of Bindon. 1606.
Christian IV, king of Denmark and Norway. Awarded 1603, in proxy 1605, in person 1606.
George Home, earl of Dunbar. 1608.
Philip Herbert, earl of Montgomery. 1608.
Charles, duke of York. 1611.
Thomas Howard, twenty-first earl of Arundel. 1611.
Robert Carr, Viscount Rochester. 1611.
Maurice de Nassau. 1612.
Thomas Erskine, Viscount Fenton. 1615.
Sir William Knollys, Baron Knollys of Greys of Greys. 1615.

Abbreviations in Notes

APC	*Acts of the Privy Council*
BL	British Library, London
Bodl.	Bodleian Library, Oxford
CP	Cecil Papers, Hatfield House
CSPDom	*Calendar State Papers, Domestic*
CSPIrel	*Calendar State Papers, Ireland*
CSPVen	*Calendar State Papers, Venice*
CUL	Cambridge University Library
HL	Huntington Library, San Marino, California
HMC	Historical Manuscripts Commission
NLS	National Library of Scotland, Edinburgh
ODNB	*Oxford Dictionary of National Biography, Online*
SP	State Paper in the National Archives, Kew, London, Online

Notes

INTRODUCTION

1. Doran and Kewes, 'Historiographical Perspective' (2014), 4.
2. For a lively narrative of James's accession, De L'Isle, *After Elizabeth* (2005).
3. Wall, 'Religion' (2018), 223–42.
4. Hammer, 'Elizabeth's Unsettling Succession'. For monopolies, ch. 3 of this book.

CHAPTER 1

1. 13 Feb. [NS], *CSPVen*, 9, no. 1132.
2. Wilbraham, *Journal* (1902), pp. 57–8; Nichols, *Elizabeth*, 4, p. 315. Wright, *Clymactericall Yeeres* (1604).
3. Harington, *Nugae Antiquae* (1804), 1, pp. 320–4; Duncan-Jones, '"Smiling"' (2007), 31–47.
4. BL, Lansdowne MS, 512, fol. 42^r; Nichols, *Elizabeth*, 4, p. 211. BL, Sloane MS, 1786, fol. 3^v.
5. Nichols, *Elizabeth*, 4, p. 212; CP183/148; SP12/28, fol.78^v.
6. CP92/18 (2).
7. BL, Additional MS, 22925, fol. 44.
8. Folger, X.c.43; SP14/1, fol. 25.
9. SP12/28, fols 74, 78^v; Bruce, *Correspondence* (1861), p. 72; Loomis, *Death* (2010), pp. 9–10.
10. BL, Lansdowne MS, 512, fol. 42^v. Elizabeth's last extant letters were dated 1 Mar., SP84/62, fols 305, 306.
11. CP102/18; NLS, 33.1.7 (21) no. 44.
12. *CSPVen*, 9, no. 1167.
13. John Guy, however, linked this 'particular episode' to periodontal problems, *Elizabeth* (2016), p. 378.
14. BL, Lansdowne MS, 512, fol. 42^v; Nichols, *Elizabeth*, 4, pp. 212, 214.
15. Loomis, 'Southwell's Manuscript' (1996), 485.
16. Nichols, *Elizabeth*, 4, p. 215; Bruce, *Correspondence*, p. 72; BL, Stowe MS, 150, fol. 180^v; BL, King's MS, 123, fol. 16^r.
17. CP92/57, 37, 39; HMC, *Rutland*, 1 p. 388; Parsons, *Slingsby Diary* (1836), pp. 257–8.
18. BL, Additional MS, 38138, fol. 27^r; Wilbraham, *Journal*, pp. 53–4. According to Northumberland, he and Lords Cobham and Howard of Walden were the only noblemen at court before then, Bruce, *Correspondence*, pp. 1, 73.

19. Wilbraham, *Journal*, pp. 53–4; Bruce, *Correspondence*, p. 73; Dasent, *APC*, 32, pp. 493–4.
20. BL, Additional MS, 11402, fol. 87^r.
21. The draft is probably NLS, 33.1.7 (21) no. 52.
22. Doran, 'Cousins' (2005), 203–34.
23. BL, Lansdowne MS, 153, fols 42^v–3^r; BL, Cotton MS, Titus C.VII, fol. 57$^{r\&v}$; BL, Sloane MS, 1786, fol. 4$^{r\&v}$; Nichols, *Elizabeth*, 4, p. 219; Manningham, *Diary* (1976), p. 207. For a bowdlerized version of the story, BL, King's MS, 123, fol. 59$^{r\&v}$. Wording in the Sloane and Cotton manuscripts implies that Elizabeth was picking up on an earlier conversation with Nottingham before going to Richmond.
24. Manningham, *Diary*, p. 245; *CSPVen*, 10, no. 32; BL, King's MS, 123, fol. 16^v.
25. BL, Lansdowne MS, 512, fol. 43$^{r\&v}$; Nichols, *Elizabeth*, 4, p. 220.
26. Ibid., p. 215; Mares, *Carey Memoirs* (1972), pp. 59–60.
27. For example, Mulcaster, *Verses* (1603), sig. A2^r.
28. BL, Additional MS, 38138, fol. 27^r.
29. Baildon, *Camera Stellata* (1894), p. 164.
30. Clapham was uncertain, *Elizabeth* (1951), pp. 98–9; Scaramelli stated that Elizabeth named James as her successor, *CSPVen*, 10, no. 16; but the French ambassador maintained she named no successor, ibid., no. 32.
31. Nichols, *Elizabeth*, 4, pp. 213, 215; Mares, *Carey Memoirs*, p. 60; SP14/1, fol. 16^r. However, one correspondent wrote that Whitgift was with the queen 'untill the last gaspe', BL, Stowe MS, 150, fol. 180.
32. According to Manningham, Dr Parry was the chaplain with her, *Diary*, p. 207.
33. Nichols, *Elizabeth*, 4, pp. 214–15; Mares, *Carey Memoirs*, p. 60. Parry provided a similar description, Manningham, *Diary*, p. 207. Whitgift wrote that 'shee died most Christianlie', Foster, *Church* (1926), p. xlviii.
34. Hayward, *God's Universal Right* (1603), sig. D4. This message was also conveyed in letters, see BL, Stowe MS, 150, fol. 180^r.
35. Nichols, *Elizabeth*, 4, pp. 224–6.
36. Stow, *Annales* (1615), p. 812.
37. Guy claims the body was not embalmed, *Elizabeth*, p. 388; Whitelock thinks that it was, *Elizabeth's Bedfellows* (2013), pp. 345–6.
38. Manningham, *Diary*, p. 223; Loomis, 'Elizabeth Southwell', 494. Clapham wrote the body was embalmed, *Elizabeth*, p. 112.
39. Nichols, *Elizabeth*, 4, pp. 226–7.
40. NA, LC 2/4/4, fol. 2^r.
41. Folger, V.b.142, fol. 67.
42. See ch. 4.
43. Foster, *Church*, pp. xlviii–xlix.
44. Hayward, *God's Universal Right*; Jackson, *Pastorall Poeme* (1603); Sharpe, *Sermon* (1603); Hooke, *Sermon* (1603).
45. Manningham, *Diary*, p. 209; CP99/80; SP14/1, fol. 16.
46. Clapham, *Elizabeth*, p. 113.

47. Sharpe (1603), *Sermon*, p. 12.
48. BL, Stowe MS, 150, fol. 180^r.
49. CP92/57; Clapham, *Elizabeth*, p. 100.
50. Godskall, *King's Medicine* (1604), sig. G4^v.
51. Dekker, *Wonderfull Yeare* (1603), sig. B2^r.
52. Goodman, *Court* (1839), 2, pp. 56–7; Clapham, *Elizabeth*, p. 99.
53. Donne, *Sermons* (1953), p. 217.
54. Bodl., Tanner MS, 75, fol. 60 [printed in Goodman, *Court*, 2, p. 58]; SP14/1, fol. 28.
55. Hall, *King's Prophecie* (1603), verses 8 and 13.
56. Chettle, *England's Mourning* (1603), sig. G1^r.
57. *CSPVen*, 10, no. 6; Clapham, *Elizabeth*, pp. 110–11.
58. SP14/1, fol. 16; Nichols, *Elizabeth*, 4, p. 227.
59. Whitelock, 'Two Bodies' (2014), 224.
60. Woodward, *Death* (1997), p. 10.
61. Bodl., Ashmole MS, 1729, fol. 62^v [printed in Nichols, *James* (1828), 1, pp. 121–3].
62. Ibid., fols 68^v–9; Nichols, *James*, 1, pp. 121–3; Akrigg, *Letters* (1984), p. 213; CP187/27.
63. *CSPVen*, 10, no. 22.
64. Bodl., Ashmole MS, 1729, fol. 66. Hunsdon died on 9 Sep.
65. SP14/1, fol. 43; *CSPVen*, 10, no. 22.
66. BL, Additional MS, 22925, fols 52^v–3 [Clapham, *Elizabeth*, p. 114].
67. SP14/1, fol. 55.
68. CP99/133; Nichols, *Elizabeth*, 4, pp. 245–6. According to Sir John Fortescue's accounts, it cost £17,301 5s 6d, Folger, X.d.541, fol. 1^r and cited in Shirley, 'Funeral' (1864), 434. For breakdown of costs, Archer, 'City and Court' (2008), 162–3.
69. Dekker, *Wonderfull Yeare*, sig. B2^r; Archer, 'City and Court', 170.
70. *CSPVen*, 10, no. 36; BL, Additional MS, 35324, fols 36, 39.
71. Paule, *Whitgift* (1699), p. 116.
72. The number of mourners varies in the documents. My number is based on the drawing in BL, Additional MS, 35324, fol. 27.
73. Robinson, 'Effigies' (1907), 542.
74. Nichols, *Elizabeth*, 4, p. 233.
75. BL, Additional MS, 35324, fol. 37^v.
76. SP14/1, fols 99–106; HMC, *Various*, 4, pp. 164–5; *CSPVen*, 10, no. 36; Chettle, *England's Mourning*, sigs F2^r–F3^v. For illustrations, BL, Additional MS, 5408 and 35324, fols 27–38^v. For other descriptions, [Niccols], *Expicedium* (1603); Petowe, *Elizabetha Quasi Vivens*. For a modern account, Woodward, *Death*, pp. 87–8.
77. HMC, *Various*, 4, p. 165; Stow, *Annales*, p. 815.
78. Ibid.
79. Dekker, *Wonderfull Yeare*, sig. B2$^{r\&v}$.
80. Stow, *Annales*, p. 815.
81. Dekker, *Wonderfull Yeare*, sig. B2^v.

82. For the production of these printed texts, see Jackson, 'Funeral Procession' (1945), 262–71.
83. *CSPVen*, 10, no. 36.
84. Baildon, *Camera Stellata*, p. 179. Despite its title, [Niccols], *Expicedium. A Funeral Oration* was not the sermon delivered by the bishop at the funeral.
85. Wilbraham, *Journal*, p. 169; Manningham, *Diary*, p. 244.
86. The 'Sermon preached at Q. El funeral' has been recently acquired by the British Library and catalogued in BL, Additional MS 89698. I must thank Dr Andrea Clarke for alerting me to it. See also HMC, *Various*, 4, p. 165; BL, Additional MS, 22925, fol. 53 [Clapham, pp. 114–15].
87. *CSPVen*, 10, no. 36.
88. Ibid., no. 40.
89. For a list of publications, see the Stuart Successions Project Website.
90. Anon, *A Mournefull Dittie* (1603).
91. Shakespeare, *Sonnets* (2010), pp. 20–1; Rickard, *Writing the Monarch* (2015), pp. 11–13.
92. Fenton, *Welcome* (1603), sig. A3^v.
93. Drayton, *Battaile of Agincourt* (1631), p. 268.
94. Nichols, *James*, 1, p. 122.
95. Hall, *King's Prophecie*, verse 21.
96. Nichols, *Elizabeth*, 4, pp. 250–312; Hackett, *Virgin Mother* (1995), pp. 213–34; Loomis, '"Withered Plants"' (2011), 133–50.
97. Anon, *The Poores' Lamentation* (1603), sig. B$^{r\&v}$.
98. Walsham's '"A Very Deborah?"' (2003), 143–68.
99. Hanson, *Time* (1604), p. 5. See also Anon, *Northerne Poems* (1604), sigs B^v, B3^r; Anon, *A Mournefull Dittie*; Mavericke, *Mourning Weede* (1603), fol. 7^v; Anon, *Queene El'zabeth's Losse* (1603), sig. B^r; Rowland, *Ave Caesar* (1603), sig. Aiii^v.
100. Nichols, *Elizabeth*, 4, pp. 278, 345, 744.
101. Ibid., p. 336. See also p. 52.
102. Ibid., pp. 336, 340.
103. Ibid., p. 654.
104. Ibid., p. 668.
105. Leighton, *Vertue* (1603), sig. A2^r; Churchyard, *Verses* (1604); Mavericke, *Seconde Treatise* (1603), fol. 13$^{r\&v}$; Lane, *Elegie* (1603), sig. B3^v; Petowe, *Elizabetha Quasi Vivens*, sig. B3^v; Anon, *Northerne Poems*, sig. B3^v. See also Young, 'Phoenix Reborn', 68–81.
106. Anon, *An Excellent New Ballad* (1603); Daniel, *Panegyrike* (1603), sigs A2^r, A3^r.
107. Pigman, *Grief* (1985), pp. 27–39.
108. For instance, Pricket, *A Souldier's Wish* (1603), sig. C^v.
109. King, 'James I and King David' (2002), 421–53.
110. See ch. 12.
111. For an overview, Levin, 'Elizabeth's Ghost' (2014), 1–16.
112. See *Shorter Title Catalogue* 7592 and 7593.
113. Two examples are Rudd, *Sermon* (1603) and Barlow, *Eagle* (1609).

114. Dekker, *Wonderful Year*, sig. B4ᵛ; HL, HM 116, fol. 37ʳ; BL, Egerton MS, 2877, fol. 16ᵛ; BL, Additional MS, 15227, fol. 2ᵛ; Camden, *Remaines* (1605), p. 378. Chronicles include Speed, *Theatre* (1612) and Camden's *Annales* (1615).
115. It was printed eight times between 1603 and 1639.
116. For deviations from Foxe, Campbell, 'Of Blessed Memory' (2022).
117. Possibly there were originally two plays—one on Gresham and the city traders, the other on Elizabeth—which the printer amalgamated to cash in on the success of Part 1. See Sullivan, *Rhetoric* (2002), p. 176 (note 1).
118. Heywood, *Second Part* (1606), sigs K–K2.
119. Lidster, 'Heywood's I and 2' (2021), 205.
120. For examples, Woolf, 'Two Elizabeths?' (1985), 167–91; Perry, *Jacobean Culture* (1997), pp. 179–82; Bezio, *Staging Power* (2015), pp. 162–9.
121. Howard, 'Thomas Heywood' (2012), 120.
122. First performed before the plot, it was printed in 1606.
123. James VI and I, *Basilikon Doron* (1603), p. 60.
124. Womersley, *Divinity* (2010), p. 189.
125. Dekker, *Whore* (1607), sig. A2ʳ.
126. I disagree with Krantz, 'Whore of Babylon' (1995), 271–91, finding more convincing Schofield, 'Staging Tudor Royalty' (2010), 54–81.
127. Dekker, *Whore*, sig. F2ᵛ.
128. King, *Sermon* (1607), pp. 22–3. See also Pricket, *Jesuits Miracles* (1607), sigs E2ᵛ–3ʳ.
129. Mears, 'Memorials' (2021), 10–11.
130. For monuments, Walker, 'Bones', 273 (note 10). Merritt downplays the influence of the plot on the erection of monuments in London churches, 'Puritans, Laudians' (1998), 953.
131. Bacon, *Felicity* (1651), p. 24.
132. Folger, X.d.541, fol 1ʳ; SP14/13, fols 21ʳ–2.
133. Camden, *Remaines* (1614), pp. 378–9.
134. Sherlock, 'Monuments' (2007), 263–89.
135. Nichols, *James*, 1, p. 252.
136. Hutton, *Merry England* (1994), p. 153.
137. For the song, Rhodes, *A Briefe* (1606), sigs. C2ʳ–3ʳ.
138. Hutton, *Merry England*, pp. 153–4.
139. See ch. 3.
140. Doran, 'Late Raigne' (2021), 156–68.

CHAPTER 2

1. The literature on Mary is vast. For differing views, Wormald, *Mary* (1988) and Guy, *My Heart* (2004). See also Goodare, 'Ainslie Bond' (2014), 301–20.
2. Blakeway, *Regency* (2015); Reid, *Early Life* (2023), pp. 21–86.
3. Anon, 'True Picture' (1634), p. 4; Juhala, 'Household' (2000), 23, 24; Akrigg, *Letters*, p. 41. My thanks to Steven Reid for telling me of the earlier role of Erskine of Gogar.

4. Ibid.
5. Juhala, 'Household'.
6. Pollnitz, *Princely Education* (2015), pp. 264–313.
7. For Young, Sargent, '"Happy"' (2013), 38–58.
8. SP52/26/1, fol. 64^r.
9. Weldon, *James* (1650), p. 55.
10. De Fonteney to Mary, Queen of Scots, HMC, *Salisbury*, 3, pp. 45–59.
11. D'Aubigny was the first cousin of James's father.
12. NLS, 28.3.12, fol. 28^r; Blakeway, 'Morton' (2017), 12–31.
13. Lee, *Solomon* (1990), p. 45.
14. Young, *Homosexuality* (2000), pp. 10, 150; Bergeron, *Homoerotic Desire* (1999), *passim*.
15. *Calendar Border Papers*, 1 (1894), p. 82.
16. SP52/30, fol. 151^r.
17. Melville, *Memoirs* (1827), pp. 275–6.
18. Reid, 'Bairns' (2017), 32–56; Questier, *Dynastic Politics* (2019), p. 143.
19. Ibid., pp. 152–4; Macdonald, 'Subscription Crisis' (1994), 222–5.
20. Grant, 'Brig O'Dee' (1999), 93–109 and 'Friendship' (2017), 57–80.
21. Wormald, 'Gowrie' (2017), 194–206.
22. Groundwater, 'Chasm' (2006), 109–13 and 'Scott-Ker Feud' (2017), 108–10; Grant, 'Friendship', 72–4.
23. For Huntly, Robertson, *Lordship* (2011), pp. 33–5.
24. MacDonald, *Kirk* (1998) and 'General Assembly' (2000), 170–85; Goodare, 'Attempted Coup' (2008), 311–36 and '1596' (2010), 21–48.
25. Mullan, *Episcopacy* (1986), p. 109.
26. For James's adroitness, Wormald, 'Two Kings' (1983), 196–8.
27. Brown, *Kingdom or Province?* (1992), pp. 85–6.
28. Fry, 'Diplomacy' (2014); Sàenz-Cambra, 'Intrigues' (2005), 86–107; Doran, 'Cousins' (2005), 203–34 and 'Polemic' (2014), 215–35.
29. Stevenson, *Wedding* (1997), p. 11.
30. Melville, *Memoirs*, p. 337.
31. *CSPScot*, 10, p. 104.
32. Reid and McOmish, *Corona* (2020), p. 173 (note e).
33. Stevenson, *Wedding*, pp. 79–86; Reid, *Corona*, pp. 183–91.
34. SP52/44, fol. 78^r.
35. Ibid., fol. 83; Riis, *Auld Acquaintance* (1988), 1, p. 263.
36. *CSPScot*, 10, pp. 170, 173.
37. Craig, *Marriage* (1828), pp. 3–11.
38. This is the view of most Scottish historians, although Questier describes the period as 'seemingly total anarchy', *Dynastic Politics* (2019), pp. 188–9.
39. *CSPScot*, 10, pp. 171, 182.
40. Craig, *Marriage*, pp. 12–16.
41. SP52/44, fol. 87 [printed in Craig, *Marriage*, pp. 12–16].
42. Dunnigan, *Eros* (2002), pp. 79–89.
43. McManus, 'Romance' (2000), 180–1 and *Women* (2002), pp. 64–5.

44. *CSPScot*, 10, pp. 211–12.
45. Expressed in his declaration to his subjects, Craig, *Marriage*, p. 13.
46. Ibid.
47. However, Moysie claimed that James arrived 'with buites and all', implying that he wore his travelling gear, *Memoirs* (1830), p. 80.
48. SP52/45, fol. 34; Stevenson, *Wedding*, pp. 49–55, 99.
49. Sauer, *British Poetry* (2008), p. 420.
50. *CSPScot*, 10, pp. 290, 314, 833, 864–5; BL, Cotton MS, Caligula, D.II, fol. 1; NLS, Advocates MS, 33.1.11 (28), no. 45.
51. Ibid., 35.5.3 vol. 3, fol. 269^r.
52. Craig, *Marriage*, Appendix, 1, p. 3.
53. BL, Additional MS, 22958.
54. BL, Cotton MS, Caligula D.I, fol. 357^v; *CSPScot*, 10, pp. 150, 154; HMC, *Salisbury*, 3, p. 430.
55. Craig, *Marriage*, pp. 29–31.
56. SP52/45, fols 34^v, 35^v; *CSPScot*, 10, pp. 298–9, 306.
57. Moysie, *Memoirs*, p. 83; NLS, Advocates MS, 35.4.2, vol. 2, fol. 597^r.
58. Craig, *Marriage*, pp. 37–8; *CSPScot*, 10, p. 863.
59. Ibid., p. 295.
60. Dean, 'State Ceremony' (2013), 305–16.
61. Craig, *Marriage*, Appendix 2, pp. 13–18; NLS, Advocates MS, 35.5.3 vol. 3, fols 239^r–42^r.
62. Ibid.; Stevenson, *Wedding*, pp. 105–6.
63. Calderwood, *Kirk* (1843), pp. 196–8; Reid, *Corona*, pp. 218–35.
64. Gray, 'Royal Entry', 10–37, and Dean, 'Enter the Alien', 267–95.
65. NLS, Advocates MSS, 35.5.3, vol. 3, fol. 293; ibid., 28.3.1, fol. 29^r; ibid., 35.4.2, vol. 2, fols 597^r–8^r; Anon, *Joyfull Receiving* (1590); Stevenson, *Wedding*, pp. ix–x, 60; Moysie, *Memoirs*, pp. 171–2. The best secondary account is Meikle, 'Coronation' (2008), 277–94. See also Lynch, 'Court Ceremony' (2000), 84–7.
66. Reid-Baxter, 'Poetry' (2000), 230–3.
67. Blakeway, '"Newes"' (2016), 546.
68. Doran, 'Cousins' (2005) 203–34; Gausden, 'A Court' (2020), 49–56.
69. National Record Office Scotland, GD205/1/21, 22; GD1/212/55.
70. *CSPScot*, 11, p. 280; Melville, *Memoirs*, 204; BL, Cotton MS, Caligula C.II, fol. 176^v.
71. Bowers, 'True Reportarie' (2005), 3–22.
72. Fowler, *True Reportarie*, sig. C2^v.
73. Reid, *Corona*, pp. 238–43.
74. SP52/54, fol. 34^r.
75. Masson, *Register*, 5 (1882), p. 132.
76. Campbell and Mackechnie, '"Great Temple"' (2011), 91–118.
77. Fowler, *True Reportarie*, sig. B^v; Calderwood, *Kirk*, 5, p. 346; Cameron and Rait, *Warrender Papers*, 2 (1932), pp. 258–62.

78. According to the Dutch ambassadors, 'Henry' was chosen for Henry VIII, Ferguson, *Papers* (1899), 1, pp. 163–4.
79. SP52/54, fol. 25.
80. Ibid., fol. 24^r; BL, Cotton MS, Caligula D.II, fol. 176^r; Mason, '1603' (2020), pp. 7–8.
81. Fowler, *True Reportarie*, sig, B^r.
82. For the racial implications, Fryer, *Staying Power* (1984), p. 4; McManus, *Women* (2002), pp. 82–5.
83. Fowler, *True Reportarie*, sigs D^r–D2^v.
84. Lynch, 'Reassertion' (2003), 1, pp. 224–5.
85. Fowler, *True Reportarie*, ns.
86. Ibid.; Calderwood, *Kirk*, 5, pp. 342–6; NLS, 35.4.2, vol. 2, fols 621^r–2^v.
87. Lynch, 'Court Ceremony' (2000), 89–90.
88. Bowers, '*True Reportarie*', 15.
89. For the children's birth days, Folger, V.b.232, fol. 126^r. For costs of baptisms, Juhala, 'Household', 216–20.
90. BL, Cotton MS, Caligula D.II, fol. 207^r.
91. Meikle, 'Scottish Reactions' (2013), p. 133.
92. SP52/64, fols 59^v, 64^r.
93. Nichols, *Progresses of Elizabeth* (1823), 3, pp. 526–7.
94. SP52/68, fol. 35^v; CP92/130; CP184/15.
95. SP52/68, fol. 63^r.
96. NLS, Advocates MS, 28.3.12, fol. 29^v; ibid., 35.5.3, vol. 3, fols 247^v, 278$^{r\&v}$.
97. Herman, *Royal Poetrie* (2010); Rickard, *Authorship* (2007).
98. Jack 'Music' (2006), 40–1; Clewett, 'Literary Circle', (1973), 447, 450.
99. McCabe, 'Poetics' (2014), 200.
100. *Essayes*, sigs M2^v–3^r; Verweij, *Literary Culture* (2016), pp. 33–5.
101. *Essayes*, sig. Iiiii^v; Kewes, 'Julius Caesar' (2002), 164, 175–8.
102. Sargent, '"Happy"' (2013), 80–5; *Essayes*, sig. Diii^r.
103. Ibid., sig. Niii^r.
104. Ibid., sigs Gii–Iii^v. For commentaries, Wortham, '"Pairte"' (2002), 195–9; Bergeron, 'James's Sexuality' (2002), 361; and Dunnigan, *Eros*, pp. 97–103.
105. Bell, 'Kingcraft' (2002), 161–6.
106. Verweij, '"Booke"' (2014), 115–16, 120–1.
107. Herman, '"Best of Poets"' (2002), 73–7.
108. Neville, *Lachrymae* (1587), sig. K^r.
109. Sidney, *Apologie* (1595), sig. G^r.
110. Herman, *Royal Poetrie*, pp. 165–6.
111. *Vacant Houres* (1591), G4–H^r.
112. For Constable, Lyall, '"Thrie Truear Hairts"' (2003), 186–215.
113. Sharpe, 'King's Writ' (1994), p. 129 and 'Reading' (2002), 21. For James and ecumenism, Patterson, *Reunion* (1997).
114. Stilma, *King Translated* (2012), pp. 92–6.
115. Herman, *Royal Poetrie*, pp. 167–76 and '"Best of Poets"', 78–80; McCabe, 'Poetics', 204–5. See also Fischlin, '"Mercenary Poet"' (2005), 540–59.

116. Lyall, *Montgomerie* (2005), p. 100 (note 97); Richards, 'Gabriel Harvey' (2008), 306, 307, 310.
117. Allot, *England's Parnassus* (1600), pp. 231, 232, 233, 238.
118. Meres, *Palladis* (1598), fol. 284ᵛ. Meres was quoting Richard Barnfield.
119. Vaughan, *Golden-grove* (1600), ns but in the third book.
120. Greene, *Poet's Vision* (1603), sig. Cʳ. The triple crown was of course associated with the pope.
121. Dekker, *Magnificent Entertainment* (1604), sig. C4ᵛ. See ch. 6.
122. May, 'Circulation' (2008), 213–14. Copies are in BL, Additional MS, 22621 and HL, HM198, fols 28ᵛ–9ʳ.
123. Lyall, *Montgomerie* (2005), p. 342 (note 26).
124. Willson, *James VI & I* (1956), p. 25; Goldberg, *Politics* (1989), p. 20.
125. Sig. Aii in both volumes.
126. *Ane Fruitfull Meditatioun*, sigs B3–4ʳ.
127. *Ane Meditation*, sig. Biiiᵛ. For both meditations, see Stilma, 'Religious Writer' (2009), 127–41 and *King Translated*, pp. 183–211.
128. Rickard, 'Word of God' (2006), 136, 138–46.
129. Lyall, 'Marketing' (2002), 211–12.
130. *CSPScot*, 11, p. 337; Stilma, 'Religious Writer' (2009), 138 and *King Translated* (2012), p. 206.
131. Rickard, 'Word of God', 142.
132. SP52/53, fol. 61ᵛ.
133. Normand and Roberts, *Witchcraft* (2000), pp. 78–85; Wormald, 'Witches' (2000), 171. See also Maxwell-Stuart, '1604' (2008), 31–46.
134. [Carmichael], *Newes* (1592), sig. Aivʳ.
135. Ibid., sig. Aivᵛ.
136. Ibid.
137. Bodl., Bodley MS, 165.
138. Goodare, 'Witchcraft Panic' (2002), 51–72 counters Wormald's argument in 'Witches', 178–80, that James was by then becoming increasingly sceptical about diabolic witchcraft. Holmes, 'Witchcraft' (2008) finds Wormald's view 'has much to recommend it'. In my view, while recognizing that fraud sometimes occurred, James accepted the reality of diabolical possession.
139. James VI, *Daemonologie* (1597), p. 51.
140. For an excellent commentary, Rickard, *Authorship*, pp. 98–108. See also Clark, 'Daemonologie' (1977), 156–81.
141. Buchanan, *De Iure Regni Apud Scotos* (printed in 1579 and dedicated to James) and *Rerum Scoticarum Historia* (published 1582).
142. Lake, 'The King' (2004), 243–60.
143. Sommerville, *Writings* (1994), p. 73.
144. Craigie, 'Basilicon Doron' (1948), 22, 24.
145. Sommerville, *Writings*, pp. 5–6, 26–7.
146. Rickard, *Authorship*, pp. 113–16.
147. Lyall, 'Marketing' (2002), 206.

148. *CSPVen*, 11, no. 577; Craigie, 'Basilicon Doron', 25–32; Lyall, 'Marketing' (2002), 207–9, 212–13, 215.
149. Stilma, *King Translated* (2012), pp. 128, 139, 159, 247; Lyall, 'Marketing' (2002), 209; Doelman, 'English Reception' (1994), 1–9.
150. Thomas, 'Renaissance' (2012), 185–203.
151. Pittock, 'Scottish Court Writing' (2000), 16–17; Jack, 'Music', 47–8; Shire, *Song* (1969), pp. 77–9.
152. Pearce, 'Anna' (2019), 149.
153. See chs 7 and 8.
154. Bawcutt, 'Castalian Band', 32, 49. Steven Reid's research 'has found it very hard to recover concrete links between the poets at court in the very early 1580s' (private communication).
155. Clewett, 'Literary Circle', 441, 451, 454; Lyall, *Montgomerie* (2005), pp. 5–8, 63–117.
156. Ibid., pp. 66–7.
157. Verweij, *Literary Culture*, pp. 45–6.
158. Heddle, *Roland Furious*, pp. 7–8, 13.
159. Verweij, *Literary Culture*, pp. 47–8.
160. NLS, MS 2063, 2064.
161. Hudson, *Judith*, sig. Aii^v.
162. SP 52/57, fol. 78^v; *CSPScot*, 12, pp. 80–2; SP 52/66, fol. 111; Wilks, 'Circle' (1987), 81.
163. Thomson, *Painting* (1975), pp. 25–6.
164. Historical Portraits, Image Library, Philip Mould, last accessed March 2022. A larger version is in the Scottish National Gallery, Edinburgh.
165. The Reformation's impact on portraiture should not be exaggerated, see Thomas, 'Renaissance', 198.
166. *CSPVen*, 10, no. 102.
167. Granger, *Biographical History*, 4 (1774), fols 1–26. Examples of the couple's portraits in a series, Johnston, *Inscriptiones* (1602), sig. K3$^{r\&v}$ and *Trewe Description* (1602), ns.
168. Daniel, *Panegyrike* (1603), stanza 43.
169. Bruce, *Letters* (1849), pp. 71, 75–8; SP 52/48, fol. 38; SP 52/56, fol. 87.

CHAPTER 3

1. Baildon, *Camera Stellata*, p. 178.
2. Andrews, 'Caribbean' (1974), 2–3.
3. MacCaffrey, *Elizabeth* (1992).
4. Gajda, 'Debating' (2009), 851–78. See also ch. 14.
5. Morgan, *Tyrone's Rebellion* (1993).
6. O'Neill, 'Kingdom' (2016), 26–47; Carey, 'Campaign' (2004), 205–16.
7. McGurk, *Conquest* (1997).
8. Dietz, *Finance* (1964), pp. 431–2, 440–1.

9. CP22/22.
10. Woodworth, 'Purveyance' (1946), 38.
11. Ibid., 39–52; Croft, 'Parliament' (1985), 9–11; Lindquist, 'Purveyance' (1988), 549–54.
12. Palliser, *Elizabeth* (1983), pp. 292–8.
13. Hoskins, 'Harvest' (1968), 32, 37–8, 42.
14. Ibid.; Archer, *Stability* (1991), pp. 9–16; Sharpe, 'Social Strain' (1995), 192–211.
15. Cummins et al., 'Living Standards' (2016), 12–13; Healey, 'Land' (2011), 152 (note 8).
16. Bohstedt, *Provisions* (2010), pp. 42–5; Walter, *Crowds* (2006), p. 68.
17. Clark, 'Gentry' (2011), 624–5; Healey, 'Commons' (2012), 284; Manning, *Revolts* (1988), pp. 220–9.
18. Ibid., pp. 200–10.
19. Walter, 'Rising' (1985), 90–143.
20. Ibid.; Slack, 'Dearth' (1992), 8–10.
21. Hartley, *Proceedings* (1995), 3, pp. 374–6.
22. SP46/26, fol. 148.
23. Harrison, *Description* (1577), p. 200.
24. SP14/1, fol. 128^r.
25. Bruce, *Correspondence* (1861), p. 59; Trevelyan and Edwards, *Trevelyan Papers* (1872), p. 54.
26. CP 213/119.
27. Bruce, *Correspondence*, p. 59.
28. Sommerville, *Writings*, pp. 37, 48; Bellany, 'The Court' (2011), 118–19.
29. Elizabeth, *Proclamation* (1602).
30. Walsham, *Church Papists* (1993) and *Catholic Reformation* (2014); McClain, *Damned* (2004); Questier, 'Conformity' (2000), 237–61.
31. Lake and Questier, *Archpriest* (2019).
32. Tutino, *Law* (2007), pp. 65–73.
33. Translations of the articles from Latin are in Tyacke, *Anti-Calvinists* (1987), pp. 30–1. For the Barrett case and articles, Tyacke, 'Lambeth Articles' (2022), 1083–9, 1093–8.
34. Strype, *Whitgift* (1822), 2, Book 4, pp. 284, 286.
35. Tyacke, *Anti-Calvinists* (1987), pp. 29–36; Sheils, 'John Whitgift' and Knighton, 'Peter Baro', *ODNB*; Milton, ' "Anglicanism" ' (2006), 159–76.
36. Lake, 'Avant-Garde Conformity' (1990), 113–33; Tyacke, 'Lancelot Andrewes' (2000), p. 12; McCullough, 'Avant-Garde Conformity' (2017), 385.
37. For a historiographical perspective, Lake, *Boxmaker's Revenge* (2001), pp. 11–16.
38. Ferrell, 'Kneeling' (1996), 73. See also, Lake, 'Anti-Puritanism' (2006), especially 85–97.
39. BL, Additional MS, 38492, fols 7–8, 27^r.
40. Shagan, 'Inquisition' (2004), 541–65; Prior, *Confusion* (2012), pp. 26–7.
41. Lake, *Boxmaker's Revenge* (2001), p. 36.
42. For one example, Cust and Lake, *Gentry Culture* (2020), p. 140.

43. Collinson, *Puritan Movement* (1990), p. 388.
44. Black, 'Rhetoric' (1997), 707–25; Hornback, 'Staging Puritanism' (2000), 31–67; Collinson, 'Antipuritanism' (2008), 19–33.
45. Harington, *Nugae Antiquae*, 1, p. 339; CP102/171; CP102/165. For list of petitions, Hoyle, Tankard and Neal, *Petitions* (2006).
46. Wilbraham, *Journal*, p. 57.
47. SP14/1, fol. 243[r].
48. BL, Additional MS, 39829, fol. 93[r].
49. 'A Booke', probably written by Sir Francis Hastings, SP14/11, fol. 216.
50. Martin, *Speache* (1603), sig. B2[r]; Cust, 'Reading' (2016), 197–8.
51. Larkin, *Proclamations*, 1, p. 13.
52. Ibid., pp. 61–3.
53. Braunmuller, *Letter-Book* (1983), pp. 326–9; Mackie, 'Advertisment' (1925), 1–4, of which there are at least seventeen manuscript copies.
54. Hake, *Gold's Kingdome* (1604), sig. B[r].
55. Thorne, *Esoptron* (1603), sig. A3[r].
56. BL, Additional MS, 22601, fols 10–11; SP14/1, fols 64 and 65; HMC, *Various*, 4, p. 166. For its author and circulation, Heaton, '"Petition"' (2006), 105–20. For other complaints about monopolies, Martin, *Speach*; SP14/1, fol. 127[r].
57. SP14/1, fol. 128[r].
58. Ibid.; Bruce, *Correspondence*, p. 59.
59. SP14/1, fols 64, 127–8[v].
60. Ibid., fols 64, 128[v]; Mackie, 'Advertisment', 2; Hake, *Gold's Kingdome*, sig. B[r&v]; Hoyle, 'Masters of Requests' (2011), 564, Table 1.
61. Muldrew, *Economy* (1998), p. 236.
62. Jones, 'Due Process' (1962), 123–50.
63. SP14/1, fol. 64; Martin, *Speach*; Willet, *Ecclesia Triumphans* (1603), no sig. preface. For individual petitions to the king, BL, Lansdowne MS, 266, fol. 5[v].
64. Millington, *True Narration* (1603), sig. E3[r&v].
65. BL, Lansdowne MS, 266, fols 4[v], 5[r], 10[r].
66. CP102/165; SP14/1, fol. 58; Pam, *Enfield Chase* (1984), pp. 31–50; Manning, *Revolts*, pp. 68–9.
67. Hoyle, 'Master of Requests', 564, Table 1.
68. Although surviving manuscript petitions do not mention enclosure, the issue was raised in printed complaint literature: Willet, *Ecclesia Triumphans*, p. 111; Trigge, *Humble Petition* (1604).
69. Ibid., sigs A3[r]–5[r].
70. SP14/1, fol. 64.
71. Willet, *Ecclesia Triumphans* (1603), no sig.
72. Fletcher, *Epistle* (1603), sig. B3[r&v].
73. BL, Sloane MS, 271, fol. 20; BL, Additional MS, 28571, fol. 199 [both printed in Usher, *Reconstruction* (1910), 2, pp. 458–60].
74. BL, Sloane MS, 271, fol. 20. See also BL, Additional MS, 38492, fol. 71; CP103/64.
75. BL, Additional MS, 8978, fols 107[r]–8[v] [printed in Bray, *Canons* (1998), pp. 817–19].

NOTES 495

76. HL, Ellesmere MS, 466.
77. BL, Additional MS, 28571, fols 177, 179; CP103/64; HMC, *3rd Report*, p. 52. See also Collinson, *Puritan Movement*, pp. 453–4.
78. CP101/160–1.
79. SP14/1, fol. 119^r.
80. Akrigg, *Letters*, pp. 206–7. See ch. 5.
81. For Markham, see ch. 5; for Tresham, Kaushik, 'Resistance' (1996), 62 and McKeogh, 'Sir Thomas Tresham', D.Phil. University of Oxford (2017), 158–60.
82. *CSPVen*, 10, no. 40.
83. SP14/1, fols 119–20, 132^v.
84. For details, ch. 13.
85. CP118/36; CP102/16.
86. SP14/4, fol. 204$^{r\&v}$.
87. Powel, *Supplication* (1603), p. 11.
88. Willet, *Ecclesia Triumphans* (1603), Preface to the Reader, no sig.
89. See chs 4 and 6.
90. James's first speech to parliament, Sommerville, *Writings*, p. 144.

CHAPTER 4

1. Firth, *Tracts* (1964), pp. 6–8; Mares, *Memoirs*, pp. 62–4; SP14/1, fol. 15.
2. Firth, *Tracts*, pp. 8, 16; Mares, *Memoirs*, p. 63 (note 1611).
3. CP92/18 (2), 42; CP184/22. The proclamation reached him on 23 Mar.
4. Bruce, *Correspondence*, pp. 7–8.
5. For a full account, Courtney, 'Accession' (2004) and 'Secret Correspondence' (2014).
6. Ibid., p. 47.
7. Akrigg, *Letters*, pp. 206–7.
8. Seventeen nobles signed the proclamation sent to Scotland, Masson, *Register*, 6 (1884), p. 552 and the manuscript copy, SP14/1, fol. 2^r. Three more (Oxford, and Lords Scrope and Norreys) were added to the printed proclamations of 24 Mar., SP14/73, fol. 11; SP14/187, fol. 6; and Larkin, *Proclamations*, 1, pp. 1–4.
9. Ibid.
10. Ibid., p. 2.
11. HMC, *Rutland*, 1, pp. 389–90; Nichols, *James*, 1, pp. 30–1.
12. BL, Additional MS, 18591, fol. 150^v; BL, Stowe MS, 150, fol. 182.
13. For these debates, Doran and Kewes, 'Earlier Succession' (2014), 20–30.
14. Doran, 'James VI and Succession' (2006), 25–42 and 'Polemic', 215–35.
15. Bradley, *Arbella* (1889), 2, p. 136.
16. SP14/3, fol. 134^r; SP14/4, fol. 28^v.
17. Doleman, *Conference*, 2, p. 32.
18. Schneider, 'Kingdom' (2015), 119–41; Loomie, 'Philip III' (1965), 492–514; McCoog, 'View' (2014), 257–70; Borreguero Beltrán, 'Isabel' (2012), 260–3; Pollen, 'Accession' (1903), 572–85.
19. Manningham, *Diary*, pp. 216–24; SP14/22, fol. 26.

20. Manningham, *Diary*, pp. 216–24; SP14/1, fol. 16ᵛ.
21. CP187/19; Manningham, *Diary*, p. 208.
22. Fletcher, *Epistle*, sig. A2ʳ.
23. Sharpe, *Sermon*, pp. 14, 37. For a different interpretation, Kewes, '"Idol"' (2019), 154–6.
24. Hayward, *God's Universal Right*, no sig.; Anon, *England's Wedding Garment* (1603), sig. A3ᵛ; Mavericke, *Second Treatise* (1603), fol. 13ᵛ; Fenton, *Welcome*, sig. Bᵛ; Drayton, *Gratulatorie Poem* (1603), sigs Bʳ–B2ʳ.
25. Buck, *Daphnis* (1605), sigs A3–Bʳ. For genealogies, Trevisan, *Genealogy* (2020).
26. Anon, *Excellent New Ballad* (1603); Buck, *Daphnis*, sigs A–B; Fletcher, *Epistle*, sig. B3ᵛ.
27. Ivic, *Subject* (2020), p. 21.
28. Mosse, *Scotland's Welcome* (1603), pp. 20, 62–6. My thanks to Paulina Kewes for drawing my attention to its significance.
29. Jackson, *Pastorall Poeme*, sig. ¶, 3ᵛ, p. 204.
30. Playfere, *Hearts Delight* (1603), dedicatory epistle to James; Kirby et al., *Sermons at Paul's Cross* (2017), pp. 412–13.
31. Daniel, *Panegyrike*, stanza 12 (sig. B1ʳ), see also stanzas 16, 50, 67.
32. Willet, *Antilogie* (1603), sig.★2ʳ.
33. Rogers, *Anglorum Lacrimae* (1603), sig. B2ᵛ. See also Leighton, *Vertue Triumphant*, sigs A2ᵛ–3ᵛ.
34. Nixon, *Elizae's Memoriall* (1603), sigs C2ᵛ–C3.
35. Anon, *A New Song* (1603); Fletcher, *Epistle*, sig. Bᵛ.
36. CP100/7; Granger, *Biographical History*, 4, fol. 2.
37. *CSPVen*, 10, no. 32.
38. SP14/1, fol. 16ᵛ.
39. Nichols, *James*, 1, pp. 27–9 (note); for Tresham's similar experience at Northampton, HMC, *Various*, 3, p. 122.
40. For proclamations' role in conveying news, Kyle, 'Proclamations' (2015), 774–7.
41. Nichols, *James*, 1, pp. 27, 29, 30, 31, 32 (notes); HMC, *Appendix 7th Report*, p. 452; HMC, *Rutland*, 1–3, p. 390; HMC, *Various*, 8, p. 88; BL, Cotton MS, Vespasian F. VI, fol. 145.
42. CP99/83; BL, Additional MS, 18591, MS, fol. 152.
43. CP99/67.
44. HMC, *Tenth Report*, p. 87.
45. SP63/215, fols 32ʳ, 94ʳ; *Cal. Carew MSS*, 5 (1873), pp. 8–9.
46. SP63/215, fol. 75ʳ.
47. *Cal. Carew MSS*, 5, p. 11; SP63/215, fols 109ᵛ–110ʳ.
48. Ibid., fol. 94ʳ. See also Hutchinson, 'Catholic "Conscience"', 38–57.
49. Ó Buachalla, 'Ideology' (1993), pp. 10–11. My thanks go to Brendan Kane for sending me both the article and the two poems.
50. Ibid.
51. Ibid.; Walter, '"Recusancy Revolt"' (2021), 1–26.
52. *Cal. Carew MSS*, 5, p. 9.

53. SP63/215, fols 75^r, 86$^{r\&v}$; SP63/215, fol. 94^r.
54. Sheehan, 'Revolt' (1983), 3–13.
55. *Cal. Carew MSS*, 5, pp. 9–10.
56. Cited in Sheehan, 'Revolt', 11.
57. Calderwood, *Kirk*, 6, pp. 207–9; Jones, 'Journal' (1953), 243; BL, Stowe MS, 150, fol. 180^v.
58. Bodl., Carte MS, 80, fol. 618^r; BL, King's MS, 123, fols 17^v–18^r.
59. CP134/28; Nichols, *James*, I, pp. 33, 56–7.
60. Bodl., Ashmole MS, 1729, fol. 49.
61. SP14/1, fol. 16^v.
62. NROScot, RH14/3; Manningham, *Diary*, p. 223.
63. Bodl., Ashmole MS, 1729, fols 43$^{r\&v}$, 45^v; Larkin, *Proclamations*, 1, pp. 4–6.
64. *CSPVen*, 10, no. 12.
65. BL, Additional MSS, 18591, fols 154^v–5; ibid., 33051, fol. 53; Bodl., Ashmole MS, 1729, fol. 55^r; SP14/1, fol. 36.
66. Gajda, ' "Popish Plot" ', 115–33.
67. *CSPVen*, 10, no. 40; SP14/1, fol. 43^r.
68. SP14/1, fol. 16^v; Calderwood, *Kirk*, 6, p. 209; Bodl., Ashmole MS, 1729, fol. 43^r.
69. Juhala, 'Household', 170; Woodward, *Death*, p. 19.
70. Meikle, *People* (2013), p. 24.
71. Spottiswoode, *History*, p. 476; Taylor, 'Scottish Privy Council' (1950), 2–3.
72. Calderwood, *Kirk*, 6, pp. 215–16. In *Basilikon Doron* (p. 55) James had advised his son to visit his kingdoms once in three years.
73. Seton, 'Early Years' (1916), 368.
74. Akkerman, *Elizabeth Stuart* (2021), 21–5.
75. CP99/92 and 99/97; Folger, X.d.30, fol. 420 and X.d.426 (116), fol. 178; HMC, *Laing*, I, p. 93.
76. Bodl., Ashmole MS, 1729, fol. 62 [Nichols, *James*, 1, p. 121]; CP187/27.
77. CP99/92 and 97.
78. Nichols, *James*, 1, p. 60; Dugdale, *Time* (1604), sig. A2^v.
79. NLS, Advocates MS, 28.3.12, fol 36^v.
80. BL, Additional MS, 22925, fol. 50.
81. For Elizabethan Berwick, Kesselring, 'Berwick' (2007), 92–112.
82. Nichols, *James*, 1, p. 32.
83. Folger, Z.e.28, fol. 101^v.
84. Millington, *True Narration*, sig. C^r.
85. Ibid., sigs C–C2^r.
86. Ibid., sig. C2^r.
87. Ibid., sig. D^v; SP14/1, fol. 43^r.
88. BL, Egerton MS, 2877, fol. 179^v.
89. Millington, *True Narration*, sig. D^v.
90. Oates, 'Tobie Matthew' (2003), 306.
91. Millington, *True Narration*, sigs C2^v–C3^r.
92. Ibid., sig. C3^v.

93. Ibid., sigs C3^v–4^r.
94. Ibid., sig. D2^r.
95. SP14/1, fol. 43^r.
96. Ibid.; Millington, *True Narration*, sig. D2^r.
97. Akrigg, *Letters*, pp. 212–13.
98. SP14/1, fol. 30.
99. CP99/135; Aubrey, *Brief Lives* (1962), p. 319.
100. BL, Additional MS, 11402, fol. 88^v; Dasent, *APC*, 32 (1907), p. 498; Collier, *Egerton Papers* (1840), pp. 377–80.
101. CP99/110; Collier, *Egerton Papers*, p. 361.
102. SP14/1, fol. 57; CP99/125; Jones, 'Journal', 243.
103. Bodl., Ashmole MS, 1729, fols 56, 76$^{r\,\&v}$.
104. Ibid., fol. 43^r.
105. Ibid., fols 68–89, 78–9; *CSPVen*, 10, nos 12, 36.
106. CP99/135.
107. CP188/13; Doran, 'Jagged Succession' (2020), 452.
108. *CSPVen*, 10, no. 36
109. CP99/125.
110. Millington, *True Narration*, sig. E4^r; HL, Ellesmere MS, 131 [printed in Collier, *Egerton Papers*, p. 369]. For costs at Belvoir, HMC, *Rutland*, 4, pp. 440, 442.
111. Lee, *Solomon* (1990), p. 107.
112. Quarmby, '*Measure for Measure*' (2011), 300–16.
113. Millington, *True Narration*, sig. D3^r.
114. Savile, *Entertainment* (1603), sig. Bi^r.
115. Mackie, 'Advertisment', 2.
116. CP100/155.
117. Bickley, *Gawdy*, p. 130.
118. Mackie, 'Advertisment', 4; Bickley, *Gawdy*, pp. 130, 134, 135, 136.
119. Chapman, *Eastward Ho* (4.1.197–200). The brogue is indicated by his word 'ken' for 'know'.
120. *CSPVen*, 10, no. 40.
121. Millington, *True Narration*, sigs E1^v–2^r.
122. For the practice in Scotland, Chambers, *James* (1830), 2, p. 27.
123. Harington, *Nugae Antiquae*, 1, p. 180.
124. Blague, *Sermon* (1603), sig. B4^v.
125. Rudd, *Sermon* (1603), (ns).
126. Millington, *True Narration*, sig. E4^r.
127. BL, Cotton MS, Caligula E.X, fol. 218^v.
128. CP105/28.
129. SP13/10A, fol. 168.
130. Dasent, *APC*, 32, p. 496; BL, Additional MS, 11402, fol. 88^r.
131. Larkin, *Proclamations*, 1, pp. 13–14.
132. Savile, *Entertainment*, sig. Bii^r.
133. Ibid., sig. Bii^v.

134. BL, Egerton MS, 2877, fos 78–9; NLS, 5831, fols 106ʳ–15ᵛ; HL, Ellesmere MS, 1224; Bodl., Tanner MS, 168, fol. 189ᵛ. See also SP14/1, fols 144–5; HMC, *5th Report*, p. 407.
135. Martin, *Speach*.
136. Savile, *Entertainment*, sigs Biiᵛ–iiiʳ.
137. Millington, *True Narration*, sig. E4ᵛ.
138. Blague, *Sermon*, sig. B4ᵛ.
139. Lancashire, 'Dekker's Accession Pageant' (2009), 39–50.
140. Wilbraham, *Journal*, p. 56.
141. For example, BL, Cotton MS, Caligula E.XII, fol. 343; ibid., Galba E.I, fols 11, 353.
142. Larkin, *Proclamations*, 1, pp. 18–19. See ch. 13.
143. See ch. 14.
144. Collier, *Egerton Papers*, p. 373.
145. CP100/30.
146. Dawson, 'Privy Council' (1950), 627–56.
147. BL, Harley MS, 7007, fol. 16.
148. Mar's mother had just recently died. Fraser, *Memorials*, 2 (1889), pp. 209–13. For a somewhat different story, Calderwood, *Kirk*, 6, pp. 231–2; Spottiswoode, *History*, p. 477.
149. Ibid.; *CSPVen*, 10, no. 69. Akkerman thinks the miscarriage may have been self-induced, *Elizabeth Stuart* (2021), pp. 26–7.
150. NLS, Advocates MS, 31.1.1 (i), no. 10 [printed in Maidment, *Letters* (1838), pp. 53–5].
151. Ibid., p. 50.
152. HMC, *Mar* (1904), pp. 50–2; CP141/277.
153. Masson, *Register*, 6, p. 571.
154. Robert Birrell misdated their arrival from Stirling, NLS, Advocates MS, 28.3.12, fol. 37ʳ.
155. For its organization, Brayshay, 'Journey' (2004), 1–21.
156. Calderwood, *Kirk*, 6, pp. 231–2; NLS, Advocates MS, 28.3.12, fol. 37ʳ.
157. Payne, 'Lucy Russell, Countess of Bedford', *ODNB*; Akkerman, 'Goddess' (2014), 287–93.
158. *CSPDom, 1603–10*, p. 15.
159. Nichols, *James*, 1, pp. 168–75.
160. BL, Cotton MS, Caligula E.X, fol. 342 [burned].
161. SP14/2, fol. 93ᵛ.
162. Ibid., fol. 13.
163. Berry, 'Jonson at Althorp' (2015), 224–7.
164. Jonson, *Cambridge Edition*, 'Particular Entertainment…at Althorp'. See also, Butler, '"Servant"' (1995), 70–2.
165. Samuel Daniel had likewise observed in his *Panegyrike* that flattery would never work on James.
166. Jonson, *Cambridge Edition*, 'Particular Entertainment…at Althorp', especially lines 271–4; Wiggins and Richardson, *British Drama* (2015), pp. 47–8.

167. BL, Stowe MS, 150, fol. 188^v; BL, Cotton MS, Caligula E.X, fol. 278; SP14/2, fols 93^r–4^v; McKeogh, 'Sir Thomas Tresham' (2017), 158–60.
168. Lodge, *Illustrations* (1791), p. 166.
169. Nichols, *James*, 1, p. 194.
170. SP14/2, fols 93^v–4^r.
171. Ibid., fol. 94^r.
172. Béthune and Lennox, *Memoirs*, 3 (1810), p. 68.
173. Pigman, *Grief*, p. 39.
174. SP15/35 fol. 5^v.
175. Anon, *Excellent New Ballad* (1603), verse 23.
176. See McCabe, 'Panegyric' (2019), 19–36.
177. HMC, *Various*, 3, pp. 119–21.
178. SP14/2, fols 238^r–40^r.
179. Cressy, *Dangerous Talk* (2010), pp. 91–3.

CHAPTER 5

1. Kempe, *Loseley* (1836), p. 276.
2. For the Bye Plot, Nicholls, 'Reward' (1995), 821–42.
3. Nicholls, 'William Watson', *ODNB*.
4. Martin and Finnis, 'Appellant Controversy' (2006), 199, 216 (n. 93), 222, 224, 230 (n. 146); Collinson, *Bancroft* (2013), pp. 183–4.
5. Howell, *State Trials* (1816), 2, col. 192.
6. SP14/2, fol. 129^r [Tierney, *Dodd's History* (1841), 4, Appendix, p. i].
7. SP14/3, fols 92, 97.
8. SP14/2, fol. 226^r. For further favour to Rutland, CP99/159.
9. BL, Additional MS, 34218, fol. 224^r.
10. Lake and Questier call the plot 'a frankly ludicrous scheme', *Archpriest*, p. 267.
11. For evil counsel discourse, Lake, *Bad Queen Bess?* (2016).
12. SP14/2, fol. 137^v. For similar argument in Ireland, see ch. 4.
13. CP101/108.
14. Bodl., Carte MS, 205, fols 116–25^v; and BL, Additional MS, 34218, fol. 224$^{r\&v}$.
15. SP14/2, fols 140^v, 143^v [Tierney, *Dodd's History*, 4, Appendix, pp. xxxiii, li]; BL, Egerton MS, 2877 [p. 24], fol. 175^r.
16. Houliston, *Catholic Resistance* (2007), p. 138. Some appellants had reached a concord with Blackwell, see McCoog, *Society*, p. 425.
17. SP14/2, fols 116, 117, 137^r; SP46/60, fol. 73; CP101/44. At their trial, the Bye conspirators were said to have 'voluntarily confessed without rack or torture', BL, Stowe, MS, 396, fol. 69^r.
18. SP14/2, fols 117, 129–35^v, 137–42, especially 138^v [Tierney, *Dodd's History*, 4, Appendix, pp. i–xvi].
19. SP14/2, fol. 117.
20. For proclamation in Edinburgh, Masson, *Register*, 6, pp. 579–81.
21. CP101/58.

22. CP101/34–5 and 44; Dasent, *Acts*, 32, p. 500; SP14/2, fols 122, 169; CP101/112.
23. SP14/2, fol. 122; CP101/57; CP278/3 [printed in Jones, 'Journal', 244].
24. For Grey's friends, Bodl., Carte MS, 80, fol. 608. For Brooke's aunt, NA, PROB 11/89/149. All three men have biographies in the *ODNB*. For their role, Nicholls, 'Trials' (1995), 26–48.
25. SP14/1, fols 43, 155; CP99/135, 162a; CP102/154.
26. SP14/3, fol. 44.
27. BL, King's MS, 123, fol. 97^r.
28. SP14/2, fol. 93; BL, Cotton MS, Caligula E.X, fol. 278; Bodl., Carte MS, 205, fol. 118^v; SP14/3, fol. 44^r.
29. CP101/99.
30. Ibid., 57; SP14/2, fol. 153^r.
31. Ibid., fol. 148.
32. Ibid., fols 153–4, 155 (fair copy).
33. Ibid.; Bodl., Carte MS, 205, fol. 124$^{r\&v}$.
34. Ibid., fols 116–26; ibid., 77, fol. 77^v.
35. SP14/2, fol. 149. Nicholls suggests that Cobham refused to subscribe to his statements 'through a scruple that he had charged Sir Walter unfairly', but Cobham's refusal predated his accusation against Ralegh on 20 Jul., Nicholls, 'Trials' (1995), p. 33.
36. SP14/2, fol. 161^r.
37. SP14/1, fol. 114^r; CP99/111; CP100/33.
38. SP14/2, fols 161^r, 157.
39. Ibid., fol. 163.
40. Ibid., fol. 155^r.
41. Ibid., fol. 157.
42. Nicholls and Williams, *Raleigh* (2011), p. 196.
43. SP14/2, fol. 149.
44. Bodl., Carte MS, 205, fol. 131^v; BL, Egerton MS, 2877 [p. 19], fol. 177; Edwards, *Raleigh*, 2 (1868), p. 388.
45. Bodl., Carte MS, 205, fols 129^v, 131^v, 132^r; BL, Egerton MS, 2877 [p. 19], fol. 177; BL, Additional MS, 34218, fol. 224^v.
46. CP101/87.
47. Munck dates it 19 Jul., but more likely Ralegh's imprisonment occurred after Cobham's outburst, Jones, 'Journal', 244.
48. CP101/82.
49. Larkin, *Proclamations*, 1, pp. 41, 38.
50. Wiggins, *Drama*, 5, p. 86.
51. Petowe, *Caesar* (1603), sig. D3^r.
52. *CSPVen*, 10, no. 105.
53. Devon, *Exchequer* (1836), pp. 6–7; SP15/35, fol. 56.
54. Nichols, *James*, 1, pp. 203–4.
55. Rye, 'Coronation' (1890), 19.
56. Nichols, *James*, 1, pp. 204–5.

57. Shaw and Burtchaell, *Knights* (1906), 1, p. xliii; Nichols, *James*, 1, pp. 206–20; Stow, *Annales* (1631), p. 826.
58. Shaw, *Knights*, 1, pp. 153–6.
59. Stow, *Annales* (1631), p. 827; Nichols, *James*, 1, pp. 206–20.
60. Dugdale, *Time Triumphant*, p. 73. For the cost of the barges, SP14/19, fol. 70^v.
61. Wilbraham, *Journal*, p. 61.
62. *CSPVen*, 10, no. 105; Nichols, *James*, 1, pp. 229–30; Legg, *Order* (1902), pp. lxix–lxxi.
63. The *Liber Regalis* specified a queen consort should wear a jewelled circlet, and the jewels that were to be set in Anna's crown are detailed in HMC, *Laing*, 1, p. 95. The Venetians, however, described the queen's crown as 'plain gold'.
64. SP14/19, fols 55–81; BL, Lansdowne MS, 156, fol. 129^r.
65. The German ambassador wrote that James was accompanied by the archbishops of York and Canterbury, Rye, 'Coronation' (1890), 20.
66. Although the word 'altar' was used in the order of service, Scaramelli scathingly observed it was 'nothing but a common movable table', *CSPVen*, 10, no. 105.
67. For *Liber Regalis*, Strong, *Coronation* (2005), pp. 84–5.
68. For the importance of ritual in legitimation, Sturdy, 'English Coronations' (1990), 239–40.
69. There is no full record of the service used in 1603. My account rests on: SP14/2, fols 208–11^r; BL, Additional MS, 4712, fols 59^r–68^v; HL, Ellesmere, 1222 (35/B/32); Bodl., Rawlinson MS, B.40; Legg, *Order*, pp. lxvii–lxxx, 1–43; Milles, *Catalogue* (1610), pp. 59–60; Anon, *The Ceremonies* (1685); *CSPVen*, 10, no. 105; Rye, 'Coronation' (1890), 18–23.
70. Hunt, 'Bright Star' (2016), 23, 27–9.
71. Peck, 'Kingship' (1993), 81–2.
72. Three formulae were suggested, Legg, *Order* (1902), p. 11.
73. Legg, *Records* (1901), pp. liv–lv; Taylor, *Chapters* (1838), p. 99.
74. James I, *Meditation* (1620), pp. 117–19.
75. Legg, *Order* (1902), p. lxxviii.
76. Bilson, *True Difference* (1585), Dedicatorie (no sig.).
77. Bilson, *Sermon* (1603).
78. Jack, '"A Pattern"' (2004), 74.
79. Brogan, *Royal Touch* (2015), pp. 68–73.
80. Six places (the two shoulders) were listed in HL, Ellesmere, 1222 (35/B/32).
81. *CSPVen*, 10, no. 105.
82. Three sources report the ring was to be placed on the fourth finger of her left hand, SP14/2, fol. 210^r; BL, Additional MS, 4712, fol. 66^v; and HL, Ellesmere, 1222. Another says it was on the forefinger of her right hand, Legg, *Order* (1902), p. 48.
83. Bickley, *Gawdy*, p. 137; HMC, *Sackville* MSS, 2, p. 136; BL, Cotton MS, Caligula E.X, fol. 211^v.
84. CP101/100; SP14/2, fol. 225; Edwards, *Ralegh*, 1, pp. 373–5, 377.

85. BL, Cotton MS, Caligula E.X, fol. 211[r&v]; Bodl., Carte MS, 205, fols 119[v], 120[r], 125.
86. BL, Cotton MS, Caligula E.X, fol. 226.
87. CP101/123.
88. For details, Lake, *Archpriest*, pp. 261–4.
89. SP14/3, fol. 27[r]; CP101/123; Bodl., Carte MS, 205, fol. 136[r&v]; Edwards, *Ralegh*, 2, p. 455.
90. SP14/3, fols 27–30; Bodl., Carte MS, 205, fol. 136[v]; Tierney, *Dodd's History*, pp. xvii–xxix, xxxiv–vii.
91. The indictment, Bodl., Carte MS, 205, fol. 127[r]; Watson's testimony, SP14/3, fol. 65[r].
92. Ibid., fols 44–5[v]; Bodl., Carte MS, 205, fol. 128[v].
93. Bodl., Willis MS, 58, fols 258[v]–9[r].
94. *CSPVen*, 10, no. 164. Gristwood thinks that Arbella may have been complicit in the conspiracy, *Arbella* (2003), pp. 218–20.
95. Devon, *Exchequer*, p. 6; Steen, *Letters* (1994), pp. 176–9, 185.
96. Bodl., Willis MS, 58, fols 258[v]–9[r].
97. Lonchay and Cuvelier, *Correspondance* (1923), 1, p. 173. See ch. 14 for Habsburg bribes.
98. *CSPVen*, 10, no. 71; SP14/4, fol. 202[v]; SP78/49, fol. 225[r&v]; SP84/64, fol. 79[v]; Duerloo, *Dynasty* (2016), p. 171.
99. Edwards, *Raleigh*, 1, pp. 383–4.
100. SP14/4, fol. 160 [Edwards, *Raleigh*, 2, pp. 462–5].
101. BL, Cotton MS, Caligula E.X, fol. 157[v].
102. Nichols, *James*, 1, p. 290.
103. SP14/4, fol. 153.
104. CUL, GBR/0012/MS Add., fol. 50[r].
105. Nichols, *James*, 1, pp. 393–4; Bodl., Willis MS, 58, fol. 251[r].
106. Scudamore was indicted but not arraigned.
107. Nicholls, 'Reward' (1995), 821–42.
108. Bodl., Carte MS, 80, fol. 623[r]; BL, Egerton MS, 2877 [p. 22], fol. 176[r]; Kempe, *Loseley*, pp. 375–7. The previous acquittal was Sir Nicholas Throckmorton in 1554.
109. Kempe, *Loseley*, p. 375; BL, Egerton MS, 2877 [p. 23], fol. 175[v].
110. SP14/3, fol. 119; Nicholls, 'Reward' (1995), 835–7.
111. BL, Egerton MS, 2877 [p. 24], fol. 175[r].
112. Howell, *State Trials*, 2, col. 64; Kempe, *Loseley*, p. 375; BL, Egerton MS, 2877 [p. 23], fol. 175[v]; Stow, *Annales* (1831), p. 830; SP14/3 fol. 98.
113. Stow, *Annales* (1831), p. 830; Bodl., Ashmole MS, 830, fol. 51[v]; BL, Egerton MS, 2877 [p. 23], fol. 174[r].
114. For transcriptions of the trial, I have used: SP14/4, fols 168–89[v]; SP46/61, fols 29–40[v]; Bodl., Willis MS, 58, fols 253[v]–62[v]; BL, Harley MS, 39, fols 275[r]–98[v] (*passim*), 306[r&v], 318[v]–22; BL, Additional MS, 34218, fols 224[r]–6[r] and NLS, MS 5444. The best printed version is Jardine, *Trials* (1832), 1, pp. 400–52.

115. SP46/61, fols 29–31ʳ.
116. HL, HM, 102, printed in Lefranc, 'Ralegh' (1966), 344–5; Edward, *Ralegh*, 1, p. 381.
117. BL, Egerton MS, 2877 [pp. 19–21], fols 176ᵛ–7ᵛ; BL, Additional MS, 34218, fols 224ᵛ–6ʳ; BL, Harley MS, 39, fols 276ᵛ–9; BL, Stowe MS, 396, fols 70ᵛ–82ᵛ; Bodl., Willis MS, 58, fols 253ᵛ–62ᵛ; CUL, Add, 335, fol. 51ʳ–2ᵛ; Bodl., Carte MS, 80, fol. 623ʳ; Lodge *Illustrations* (1791) 3, pp. 214–21; SP14/6, fols 81–3; Jardine, *Trials*, 1, pp. 461–4.
118. For an exception (*c*.1624), BL, Additional, 34218, fols 224ᵛ–6ʳ.
119. For the two-witness rule, Boyer, 'Ralegh Trial' (2005), 883–4, 889.
120. SP46/61, fol. 39ʳ.
121. BL, Egerton MS, 2877, fol. 177ᵛ [p. 19]; Jardine, *Trials*, 1, p. 463.
122. BL, Harley MS, 39, fol. 306ᵛ.
123. Ibid., fol. 290ᵛ. For Arenberg's offers, see ch. 14.
124. SP14/4, fol. 157.
125. In BL, Harley MS, 39, fol. 320ᵛ, the service for Spain was specified as 'intelligence'.
126. SP14/4, fol. 92.
127. NLS, MS 5444, p. 28.
128. Ibid.
129. Bodl., Carte MS, 80, fol. 623ʳ; Jardine, *Trials*, 1, pp. 461–4; SP84/64, fol. 79ʳ.
130. BL, Egerton MS, 2877 [p. 19], fol. 177ᵛ.
131. Doran, 'Ralegh' (2011), pp. 157–74.
132. SP14/4, fol. 156; Lodge, *Illustrations* (1791), 3, p. 217.
133. Bellany, *Libels*, B4–6.
134. Bodl., Carte MS, 80, fol. 623ʳ.
135. Rudick, *Poems* (1999), p. 129, but not everyone includes 'Pilgrimage' in the Ralegh canon.
136. Boyer, 'Ralegh Trial', 900; Nicholls, 'Trials' (1995), 34 and 'Prosecution' (1995).
137. CP101/165; CP102/1; CP187/122; SP14/4, fols 73, 75–8, 80.
138. Ibid., fols 84, 86.
139. Ibid., fol. 202ʳ&ᵛ; Jardine, *Trials*, 1, pp. 459, 460, 467; Bodl., Carte MS, 77, fols 77–8; ibid., 80, fol. 622ʳ&ᵛ; Lodge, *Illustrations* (1791), 3, pp. 218–19; BL, Cotton MS, Caligula E.X, fol. 160ᵛ; BL, Stowe MS, 396, fols 83–6.
140. SP14/4, fols 162–5; Stow, *Annales* (1831), p. 831; Jardine, *Trials*, 1, p. 460; Lodge, *Illustrations*, 3 (1791), p. 219.
141. Bodl., Carte MS, 77, fols 77ᵛ–8ᵛ.
142. Ibid., 80, fol. 622ʳ&ᵛ.
143. Nichols, *James*, 1, p. 269; SP84/64, fol. 78ᵛ.
144. BL, Cotton MS, Caligula E.X, fol. 218ʳ; SP78/49, fol. 75ᵛ; BL, Additional MS, 38138, fol. 27ʳ.
145. SP78/50, fol. 15ʳ; BL, Cotton MS, Caligula C.X, fol. 157ʳ.
146. SP14/3, fols 15, 16; Dasent, *Acts*, 32, p. 502.
147. SP14/3, fol. 134; SP14/4, fols 27, 28; CP193/10; CP102/16.
148. SP14/2, fols 238–40; SP14/3, fols 21, 23; SP14/6, fol. 98.
149. SP14/4, fols 2, 3.

CHAPTER 6

1. Sommerville, *Writings*, p. 49.
2. Both cited in Cox, '"Prince"' (2011), 135.
3. Mackie, 'Advertisment', 3.
4. For James's neglect of his public image, Wilson, *History* (1653), pp. 12–13; Durston, *James* (1993), p. 12.
5. Nichols, *James*, 1, pp. 278, 281.
6. Anon, *Copie* (1603), p. 2.
7. Sommerville, *Writings*, pp. 22–3.
8. Lodge, *Illustrations* (1838), 3, p. 78; BL, Egerton MS, 2877 [p. 23], fol. 174^r.
9. SP14/6, fol. 83; Goodman, *Court*, pp. 87–8, 91–2.
10. Bodl., Carte MS, 80, fol. 626^r.
11. CP102/26 and 41.
12. CP102/49 [printed in Edwards, *Raleigh*, 2, pp. 466–7]. Yet the spy William Sterrell stated it was 'certainly' reported that Brooke repeated the accusations against his brother to the bishop, SP14/6, fol. 83^v.
13. CP102/55.
14. Bodl., Carte MS, 80, fol. 626^r.
15. Ibid.; SP84/64, fol. 84^r. Again, according to Sterrell, Brooke did not retract his words, SP14/6, fol. 83^v.
16. CP102/46, 56, 59, 60.
17. Bodl., Carte MS, 80, fol. 626^v.
18. Ibid.
19. CP102/51 (1) and 47.
20. Ibid., (1).
21. Ibid., 45.
22. CP187/135.
23. HL, Ellesmere MS, 6223.
24. SP84/64 fol. 84^v.
25. Bodl., Carte MS, 80, fols 626–8. The next four paragraphs are based on this source.
26. SP84/64, fols 84^v–5^v.
27. Speed, *Historie* (1623), p. 1244.
28. Ibid.; Anon, *Copie*; SP14/5, fol. 20.
29. Henry IV thought it a mistake, Berger de Xivrey, *Recueil*, pp. 185–6.
30. Anon, *Copie*.
31. CP113/94.
32. Nicholls, *Raleigh* (2011), pp. 226–30, 285–340.
33. SP14/2, fol. 105; BL, Harley MS, 677, fol. 106; BL, Sloane MS, 271, fol. 24; Barton, *'Registrum'*, 1 (1963), pp. 20–1; SP14/2, fol. 108; Oxford University, *Answere* (1603); Covell, *Examination* (1604). For impropriated tithes, see ch. 11.
34. BL, Sloane MS, 271, fol. 20^v; Usher, *Reconstruction*, 1, p. 290. For differing views of James's motives, Fincham and Lake, 'Ecclesiastical Policy' (1985), 171–4, 185; Morgan, 'Popularity' (2018), 202.

35. See ch. 3.
36. Larkin, *Proclamations*, 1, pp. 61–3; Shriver, 'Hampton Court' (1982), 48, 53–5.
37. BL, Sloane MS, 271, fols 23–4.
38. Usher, *Reconstruction*, 2, pp. 331–54; SP14/6, fols 54^v, 84^v–5^r; Winwood, *Memorials*, 2, pp. 13–15; Calderwood, *Kirk*, 6, pp. 162, 241–7; Cardwell, *Conferences* (1849), pp. 161–6. Drafts of Tobie Matthew's letter, Additional MS, 4274, fol. 233 and Egerton MS, 2877, fol. 173.
39. Barlow, *Summe* (1604). A French edition appeared in 1604.
40. Curtis, 'Hampton Court' (1961), 1–16.
41. Hunt, 'Chaderton' (1998), 223.
42. Ibid., p. 211.
43. Barlow, *Summe*, sigs B2^r–3^v.
44. BL, Additional MS, 4274, fol. 233^r.
45. Barlow, *Summe*, sig. P$^{r\&v}$.
46. Winwood, *Memorials*, 2, p. 14.
47. Calderwood, *Kirk*, 6, p. 163; SP14/6, fol. 54^v.
48. BL, Additional MS, 4274, fol. 233^r [printed in Cardwell, *Conferences*, p. 163]; Winwood, *Memorials*, 2, p. 13; Barlow, *Summe*, sig. D2^v.
49. Hunt, 'Chaderton', p. 212.
50. Barlow, *Summe*, sig. E1^v.
51. Usher, *Reconstruction*, 2, p. 343.
52. Barlow, *Summe*, sig. L4^v.
53. Harington, *Nugae Antiquae*, 1, pp. 181–2.
54. Barlow, *Summe*, sigs G1^v–G2^r.
55. On predestination, Tyacke, *Anti-Calvinists* (1987), pp. 9–28.
56. Barlow, *Summe*, sigs L4^r, F2^v.
57. Ibid., sig. L2^v.
58. Ibid., sig. L^r.
59. Ibid., sig. M^v.
60. Ibid., sig. B2^v.
61. Ibid., sig. L3^r.
62. Ibid., sig M2^v.
63. Sommerville, *Writings*, p. 52.
64. Barlow, *Summe*, sig. M4^r.
65. See ch. 3.
66. Barlow, *Summe*, sig. N3^r.
67. Ibid, sig. O4^r. For Chaderton, Shagan, 'Battle' (2005), pp. 127–9.
68. Strype, *Whitgift*, 3, p. 408.
69. Calderwood, *Kirk*, pp. 241–7.
70. For Royston, Thurley, *Palaces* (2021), p. 39.
71. SP 78/51, fols 59^v–60.
72. For individuality of texts, Easterling, 'Entry' (2017), 43–76.
73. For Harrison, Finlayson, '*Arches*' (2020), 176–99.
74. For a modernized composite account, Smuts, 'Entertainment' (2007).

75. For the print history, ibid., pp. 498–9; Easterling, 'Entry', 54–6.
76. Nichols, *James*, 1, p. 325.
77. Manley, *London* (1995), ch. 5; Mardock, *London* (2008), pp. 24–30.
78. Dugdale, *Time*, sig. B^v. The arch viewed was the one created by the Dutch.
79. *CSPVen*, 10, no. 201.
80. Hubbock, *Oration* (1604).
81. Dugdale, *Time*, sig. B2^v; *CSPVen*, 10, no. 201.
82. Ibid.; Hutchings and Cano-Echevarría, 'Account' (2017), 266.
83. *CSPVen*, 10, no. 201; BL, Additional MS, 34218, fols 31^v–2^r. For the costs, Nelson, 'Accounts'; Bergeron, 'Civic Pageant' (2002), 216. Some Londoners refused to donate money for the entry, Nichols, *James*, 1, p. 375.
84. *CSPVen*, 10, no. 201; Stow, *Annales* (1618), p. 448.
85. Mulcaster, *Passage* (1604).
86. Goldberg, *Politics*, pp. 32–3.
87. Harrison, *Archs*; Jonson, *His Part* (1604), sigs A2^r–B4^r.
88. Ibid., sig. B4^v.
89. For the role of music, Butler, 'Musical Transformations' (2020), 202–18.
90. Dekker, *Entertainment* (1604), sigs C2^v–D^r; Parry, *Golden Age* (1981), p. 9.
91. Hood, 'Arch' (1991), 67–82; Archer, 'Royal Ceremonial' (2008), 160.
92. Harrison, *Archs*, sig. E1^v; Dekker, *Entertainment* (1604), sigs D^v–E2^r.
93. Ibid., sig. E2^v.
94. Ibid., sigs E3^r–F2^r.
95. Ibid., sig. F3$^{r\&v}$.
96. Harrison, *Archs*, sig. G^r.
97. Dekker, *Entertainment* (1604), sig. H^r.
98. Ibid., sigs H3^r–I^r; Harrison, *Archs*, sig. H^r. Zeale's speech was Middleton's contribution.
99. Parry, *Golden Age*, p. 18.
100. Taylor and Lavagnino, *Middleton* (2007), pp. 265–6, lines 2268–71, 2287–92.
101. Jonson, *His Part* (1604), sigs C^r–D3^r.
102. Ibid., sigs D3^v–E^v.
103. Dugdale, *Time*, sig. B2^v.
104. *CSPVen*, 10, no. 204; Dunn, '1603/4' (1987), 47.
105. Trevelyan, *Trevelyan Papers*, p. 64.
106. BL, Lansdowne, MS, 512, fol. 80^r; HMC, *Montagu*, p. 41; Dunn, '1603/4', 78–9.
107. It was also reprinted in Stow, *Annales* (1615), pp. 837–44 and the 1616 collection of James's writings.
108. Bergeron, 'Civic Pageant', 213–31.
109. Somerville, *Writings*, pp. 132–46; James I, *Speech* (1604).
110. Jonson, *Cambridge Edition*, A. Panegyre.
111. The first recorded performance of the play was during the Christmas revels of 1604–05 at Whitehall. For its topicality, Bernthal, 'Staging Justice' (1992), 247–69 (though he makes factual errors); Shuger, *Political Theologies* (2001), *passim*.

CHAPTER 7

1. *CSPVen*, 11, no. 856; Akkerman, *Elizabeth Stuart* (2021), pp. 49–50.
2. Chettle, *England's Mourning*, sig. B4r.
3. Hill, *Christ's Prayer* (1606), no sig. nor page; Howell, *State Trials*, 2, col. 236.
4. Lloyd, *Jewels* (1607), sig. A2v.
5. NLS, 2063, no. 98.
6. Rye, *England* (1865), p. 166.
7. Peacham, *Minerva* (1612), p. 13.
8. SP14/26, fol. 82r.
9. Nichols, *James*, 1, pp. 509–12; Bickley, *Gawdy*, pp. 144–5; Rimbault, *Cheque-Book* (1872), pp. 167–9.
10. Mears et al., *National Prayers*, 1 (2013), pp. 259–60.
11. *CSPDom, 1603–10*, p. 217. For James's disappointment, *CSPVen*, 10, no. 363.
12. Rimbault, *Cheque-Book*, p. 170; Stow, *Annales* (1632), p. 883.
13. Lodge, *Illustrations* (1791), 3, pp. 319–20; HMC, *Laing*, 1, p. 109.
14. Lodge, *Illustrations* (1791), 3, pp. 324–5. For both princesses, Green, *Princesses*, 5, pp. 90–9.
15. CP122/71; Lodge, *Illustrations* (1791), 3, p. 323.
16. CP123/151; Lodge, *Illustrations* (1791), 3, p. 325.
17. Nichols, *James*, 2, p. 154; HMC, *De L'Isle*, 3, p. 410; Leech, *Sermon* (1607).
18. CUL, Ee.2.32, fols 1–11.
19. Akkerman, *Correspondence*, 1 (2015), nos 1–3, 7–11; Macdonald, *Letters* (1835), pp. xxxviii–xxxix; CUL, Ee.2.32, fol. 5r.
20. Lindsay and Williamson, 'Myth' (1975), 206.
21. Westerman, *Faithfull Subject* (1608), p. 26; BL, Royal MS, 17 B. XXII, fol. 403r. Westerman viewed the proverb as seditious.
22. Strong, 'Stuart King' (1986), 16–23; Corbin, 'Death' (1966), 131–56, 360–72.
23. *CSPVen*, 12, no. 727.
24. Bickley, *Gawdy*, p. 149.
25. Mares, *Memoirs*, pp. 68–9. Carleton believes the boy was in better shape than I am suggesting, *Charles* (1995), pp. 4–5.
26. *CSPVen*, 11, no. 174.
27. For secretly marrying Seymour in 1610, Arbella was imprisoned in the Tower. He remained on the Continent until 1616.
28. SP14/77, fol. 16; Jansson *Proceedings*, p. 77.
29. Sommerville, *Writings*, p. 42.
30. Meikle, 'Princess' (2008), 130–41.
31. *CJ*, pp. 157–8; NLS, MS 5831, fol. 89r.
32. Nichols, *James*, 1, pp. 545, 546.
33. Meikle, 'Princess' (2008), pp. 135–6.
34. See ch. 4.
35. NLS, 33.1.5 (19), no. 2; *CSPVen*, 10, no. 69.
36. Macdonald, *Letters*, p. xxxii; HMC, *Mar*, p. 50.

37. *CSPVen*, 10, no. 11.
38. For differing views about the timing, Warner, 'Rome' (1905), 124–7; Loomie, 'Catholic Consort' (1971), 305; Meikle and Payne, 'Faith' (2013), 45–69; Davidson and McCoog, 'Convert' (2000), 16–17; Field, 'Anne' (2015), 6–11.
39. Lodge, *Illustrations* (1791), 3, p. 291; Nichols, *James*, 1, p. 114; Rimbault, *Cheque-Book*, pp. 169–70, 171, 172.
40. McCullough, *Sermons* (1998), pp. 170–7; HMC, *De L'Isle*, 3, p. 188.
41. Payne, 'Inventory' (2001), 23–44.
42. Hubbock, *Resurrection* (1606), sig. B1^v.
43. Loomie, 'Catholic Consort' (1971), 305.
44. SP78/51, fol. 15^r.
45. Loomie, 'Toleration' (1963), 24.
46. Bliss, 'Religious Belief' (1889), 110.
47. Bergeron, *Royal Lovers* (1991), pp. 90–1, 139; Lewalski, 'Enacting Opposition' (1993), 15–43, especially p. 25; McManus, *Women*, pp. 98–111, 136–42, 166–82. Payne and Field disagree with these scholars.
48. HMC, *Salisbury*, 18, p. 306.
49. Colvin, *King's Works* (1982), 4 (II), pp. 253–4.
50. CP128/144; SP14/65, fol. 122^r; SP14/70, fol. 30^r; Nichols, *James*, 2, pp. 725, 747; ibid., 3, pp. 88, 97, 98, 135, 186, 220, 231, 238, 480, 495, 498; *CSPVen*, 11, no. 198.
51. Birch, *Court*, 1, p. 71; BL, Harley, MS, 6986, fol. 132; Macdonald, *Letters*, p. xliv.
52. *CSPVen*, 10, no. 739.
53. Marini, 'Diplomacy' (2021), 400; Duerloo, *Dynasty*, p. 174.
54. See ch. 8.
55. SP14/28, fol. 30^r.
56. For example, Jonson, *Cambridge Edition*, Masque of Beauty, 12–14.
57. Sowerby, 'Diplomatic Gifts' (2021), p. 732.
58. Ibid.
59. SP78/51, fols 231^v–2^r.
60. SP78/52, fol. 209.
61. SP14/72, fol. 39^r; Ellis, *Letters*, 4 (1846), p. 172; Murdoch, *Denmark-Norway* (2000), p. 45 (note 4).
62. Payne, 'Women' (2001), 28.
63. Lodge, *Illustrations*, 3 (1791), p. 164; Nichols, *James*, 1, pp. 161–2; *CSPDom, 1603–10*, p. 113; CP219/4.
64. CP191/149; CP194/11; Birch, *Court*, 1, p. 137.
65. CP134/152; CP122/1; CP195/118. However, in 1605 Cecil complained that William Fowler went behind his back to promote certain suits. SP14/13, fol. 34^r.
66. SP14/71, fol. 44^r.
67. Barroll, *Anna* (2001), p. 133.
68. SP14/74, fol. 100^v.
69. SP14/75, fol. 70.
70. SP14/12, fol. 17^r.
71. *CSPVen*, 10, no. 40.

72. Ibid., 12, no. 775.
73. Constable, *Heriot* (1822), Appendix VII, pp. 224–6; SP14/68, fol. 18^r.
74. Vincent, *Dressing* (2003), pp. 13–46; Reynolds, *Style* (2013), pp. 42–3; Field, *Anna* (2020), p. 128.
75. CUL, Dd.1.26.
76. Hearn, *Dynasties* (1995), p. 192.
77. For Spillman, SP14/50, fol. 88; SP14/14, fols 131–2; Constable, *Heriot*, pp. 199–228.
78. Ibid.; Scarisbrick, 'Anne's Jewellery' (1986), 228–36, 'Inventory' (1991), 193–238, and *Jewellery* (1995), p. 69; Field, 'Anne' (2015), 155–79.
79. Constable, *Heriot*, p. 213; Scarisbrick, *Jewellery* (1995), pp. 48, 67, 53–4; Knowles, 'Anna' (2003), 24. For Christian's gift of the C4 jewel, Sowerby, 'Diplomatic Gifts'.
80. Constable, *Heriot*, pp. 201, 203, 204, 205, 206, 207, 212, 215.
81. Devon, *Exchequer, passim*.
82. *CSPDom, 1603–10*, p. 148; Constable, *Heriot*, pp. 222–3; Ungerer, 'Circulation', 152–3.
83. Devon, *Exchequer*, pp. 16, 29, 59; *CSPVen*, 10, no. 739; ibid., 12, no. 253.
84. Ungerer, 'Circulation', 150; Rye, *England* (1865), p. 121.
85. Ibid., pp. 162–4; Sowerby, 'Diplomatic Gifts'.
86. Doc ID 1524, Medici Archive Project, 4184, fol. 11; Hicks, 'Standen', 163–94.
87. *CSPVen*, 10, no. 118.
88. Sowerby, 'Dangerous Gift' (forthcoming). My thanks go to her for sending me the article before publication.
89. Shakespeare, *Henry VIII*, Act 1, Scene 2, ll. 9–81, 125–63; Frye, 'Anne' (2016), 161–93.
90. Nichols, *James*, 2, p. 664.
91. SP14/81, fols 48, 50.
92. CP147/157. The gentleman was Edward Rye. For his case TNA STAC 2/248/2.
93. HMC, *3rd Report*, p. 264; CP111/102.
94. CP134/147; *CSPVen*, 11, no. 466. Balmerino requested her intercession, Fraser, *Elphinstone*, 2, pp. 159–61.
95. CP125/47; Fraser, *Elphinstone*, 2, p. 161.
96. Whitelock states that Anna 'had a decisive influence' in saving his life in 'Political Role' (2016), p. 241. For an alternative explanation, see ch. 12.
97. *CSPVen*, 11, no. 466.
98. Steen, *Letters*, p. 292; Edwards, *Ralegh*, 1, p. 686.
99. CP100/72.
100. CP196/142. The prince invested in a colonial venture, *CSPVen*, 11, no. 449.
101. CP147/157; CP130/174.
102. Riis, *Auld Acquaintance*, 1, p. 272, Table 11.1; Lodge, *Illustrations*, 3 (1791), pp. 206–7.
103. SP14/8, fol. 91.
104. SP14/2, fol. 93^r.
105. SP14/9A, fol. 171; *CSPVen*, 10, no. 118; SP14/67, fol. 212; Payne, 'Women' (2001), pp. 20–44.

106. CP104/64.
107. HMC, *Mar*, p. 59.
108. *CSPVen*, 10, nos 111, 118.
109. Barroll, *Anna* (2001), pp. 90, 111; Orgel, *Illusion* (1991), pp. 37–58.
110. Cano-Echevarria and Hutchings. 'Between Courts' (2012), 97–8. For France, Gough, *Dancing Queen* (2019).
111. *CSPVen*, 11, no. 763; ibid., 12, no. 159. See ch. 8.
112. Field, *Anna* (2020), pp. 56–60.
113. Eiche, 'Richmond' (1998), 10–14.
114. HMC, *Buccleuch*, 3, p. 117.
115. Field, *Anna* (2020), pp. 56–60.
116. Cunningham, *Accounts* (1842), p. xvi.
117. Cole, 'Theobalds' (2017), 71–116; Thurley, *Hampton Court* (2004), pp. 109, 115–16; Folger, X.d.587; CP211/1; Thurley, *Palaces*, pp. 39–46.
118. Stow, *Chronicle* (1832), p. 891; SP14/28, fol. 87^r.
119. Payne, 'Inventory', 36, 38; Campbell, *Flemish Pictures* (1985), pp. xxiv–xxxv; Peacock, 'Portraiture' (1994), p. 212; Hitchmough, 'Portraits' (2020), 248–64.
120. Hill, 'Patronage' (2011), 32–7.
121. *CSPVen*, 12, no. 159.
122. Campbell, *Flemish Pictures*, p. xxxv.
123. Edmond, 'John de Critz', *ODNB*.
124. Devon, *Exchequer*, p. 46; HMC, *Downshire*, 2, 486–7.
125. McLeod, *Lost Prince* (2013), pp. 35–6, 70–1.
126. Ibid., pp. 36–7, 94–5; Hearn, 'Robert Peake', *ODNB*.
127. Reynolds, 'Portraits' (1952), 15; Goldring, *Hilliard* (2019), pp. 259–64.
128. Edmond, 'Isaac Oliver', *ODNB*.
129. Payne, 'Inventory', *passim*.
130. Cunningham, *Accounts*, p. xiv; Wilks, ' "Gallery" ' (2014), 149–72.
131. Medals are in the Greenwich Maritime Museum, British Museum, Museum of London, and Hunterian Collection, Glasgow.
132. Robinson, *Musicke* (1603), sig. Aii^r.
133. Walters, 'Music', 95.
134. Hulse, 'Cecil' (1991), 26, 27, 30.
135. Hauge, 'Seven Tears' (2001), 10–12.
136. Hulse, 'Aristocracy' (1992), 53 and 'Cecil' (1991), 32 (note 33).
137. Hulse, 'Aristocracy', p. 225 (note 153).
138. Hume, *Poeticall Musicke* (1607).
139. Crouch, 'Harmonic Institution' (1980), 16.
140. Cunningham, *Accounts*, p. xiii.
141. Hulse, 'Aristocracy' (1992), p. 219; Walters, 'Music' (2006), 103–4.
142. For the latter, see Munro, *Children* (2005).
143. Gazzard, 'Philotas' (2000), 423–50; Dutton, *Revels* (2022), pp. 175–83. For a more topical reading linked to the Union of Crowns, Cadman, '*Philotas*', 366–7, 373, 377–84.

144. Jonson, *Conversations* (1842), p. 20. The third playwright John Marston was left alone.
145. Braunmuller, *Letter-Book*, pp. 370–89; Dutton, *Revels* (1991), pp. 171–7.
146. Day, *Ile* (1606), sigs A2^v, C^v, E2v; Dutton, *Revels* (2022), pp. 198–200.
147. Birch, *Court*, 1, pp. 60–1; Monro, *Children*, pp. 23–4; Dutton, *Revels* (2022), pp. 152–3.
148. Marcus, 'Literature' (2002), 494–7. The French ambassador reported that the queen attended plays 'in order to enjoy the laugh against her husband', Chambers, *Elizabethan Stage*, 1 (1923), p. 325.
149. Dutton, *Revels* (2022), p. 164.
150. Ibid., pp. 151, 152, 164; Akkerman, 'Bedford' (2014), 294–5. Gausden suggests that Fowler may have aided Daniel's entry into the queen's household, 'A Court', 200.
151. Akkerman, 'Bedford' (2014), 289 (note 9).
152. (1611). ★2^v–4^r; Hamlin, *Essays* (2013), p. 11.
153. Ayton, 'Ayton' (2004), 281–9; Gausden, 'A Court', 169–71; Shire, *Song*, pp. 214–54.
154. For Chaloner, Thrush, *Commons*, 3 (2010), pp. 485–8.
155. Cross, 'British-Spanish Match' (2018), 71–5.
156. SP75/4, fol. 192$^{r\&v}$.
157. Scott, *Somers Tracts*, 2 (1809), pp. 494–6.
158. *CSPVen*, 12, especially nos 334, 371, 499; HMC, *Downshire*, 3, p. 278; Pennini, 'Marriage' (2017), 27–40; Strong, *Monarchy*, 3 (1998), pp. 79–99.
159. *CSPVen*, 12, nos 175, 499.
160. Wilks, 'Forbear' (2001), 59–60; Pennini, 'Marriage', 52.
161. Ibid., 50.
162. Ellis, *Letters*, 3 (1827), pp. 226–8.
163. Folger, V.a.605; Bodl., MS Rawlinson, C. 929, fols 40^r–2^v printed in Gutch, *Collectanea* (1781), 1, pp. 156–60.
164. *CSPVen*, 12, nos 501, 516.
165. Thrush, 'Personal Rule' (2002), 86 and 'French Marriage' (2002), 25–35.
166. Ellis, *Letters*, 3, pp. 226–8; Birch, *Henry* (1760), pp. 309–10.
167. At least five copies of this manuscript circulated in 1612, mpese.ac.uk, accessed 19 June 2020.
168. Seddon, *Holles* (1975), p. 28; Devon, *Exchequer*, pp. 104–5.
169. Payne, 'Inventory', 27–42.
170. *CSPVen*, 11, no. 803. For the Cleves dispute, see ch. 14.
171. Davies, *Chester's Triumph* (1610).
172. Basse, *Helpe* (1619), p. 190; Hannay, *Two Elegies* (1619).
173. *CSPVen*, 11, no. 548; Orrell, 'London Stage' (1978), 167.
174. Dietz, *Finance*, pp. 111–12.
175. SP15/36, fol. 194; CP109/89; SP14/12, fol. 28^r.
176. BL, Additional MS, 58833, fols 12, 18–19^v.
177. Colvin, *King's Works*, 4 (II), pp. 255–61; Field, *Anna* (2020), p. 59.

CHAPTER 8

1. Horrox, 'Caterpillars' (1995), 2.
2. For different meanings of 'court', Cuddy, 'Reinventing' (2000), 59–63.
3. Astington, 'Court Theatre' (2009), 311–12.
4. Adamson, 'Courts', 24–5, 30; Archer, 'Popular Politics' (2000), 28–9.
5. Dillon, *Theatre* (2000), *passim*.
6. Thurley, *Palaces*, pp. 28, 46–52, *Hampton Court*, pp. 109, 115–16, and 'Greenwich Palace' (2006), 126–30.
7. The exception was Robert, earl of Leicester, lord steward 1587–88.
8. Loades, *Tudor Court* (1992).
9. Anderson, *Diplomatic Representatives* (2007), p. 162.
10. Dutton, *Revels* (1991), p. 143.
11. Wright, 'Female Household' (1987), 147–72; Doran, *Circle* (2015), pp. 2–3, 193–5.
12. In 1607, Anna received her own separate establishment below stairs, Seddon, 'Patronage' (1967), 40.
13. Devon, *Exchequer*, *passim*.
14. Cuddy, 'Entourage' (1987), 175–95.
15. Wilbraham, *Journal*, p. 55.
16. In 1610, the number was cut to thirty-two, with a Scot and Englishman added as ushers.
17. Bickley, *Gawdy*, pp. 131, 150–1.
18. Cuddy, 'Entourage' (1987), pp. 173–225.
19. SP14/2, fols 99–100; BL, Harley MS, 589, fol. 197^v.
20. CP103/46.
21. CP213/107.
22. Cuddy, 'Entourage' (1987), pp. 174–84; Juhala, 'Household', *passim*, but especially pp. 146, 140, 150 and 'James VI's Chamber' (2017), 157–8.
23. Sommerville, *Writings*, p. 38.
24. BL, Additional MS, 12497, fols 155^r–6^v, 158^r–9^v, 160^r; SP14/31, fols 227^v.
25. HL, Ellesmere MS, 2737. Lincoln was imprisoned because he was accused of burning down the house of a local enemy, HL, Ellesmere MS, 2733, 2734.
26. Seddon, 'Patronage', pp. 43–4, 16.
27. Masson, *Register*, 14, p. 407.
28. For the relationship between access and favour, Raeymaekers, *One Foot* (2013).
29. Cuddy, 'Entourage' (1987), pp. 218–19.
30. *CSPVen*, 11, no. 443.
31. Thurley, *Palaces*, p. 111.
32. Markham, *Cavelarice* (1607), sig. Xx2^r.
33. Nichols, *James*, 2, p. 438; Winwood, *Memorials*, 2, pp. 54, 205; BL, Cotton MS, Julius C. III, fol. 301^v; *CSPVen*, 11, no. 744.
34. Birch, *Court*, 1, p. 92; Nichols, *James*, 2, p. 287.
35. BL, Cotton MS, Julius C.III, fol. 301^v; Jonson, *Hymenaei* (1606), sig. F^r.
36. SP14/22, fol. 130^v; Ford, *Honor* (1606).

37. SP14/22, fol. 1. For 1610, Birch, *Henry*, p. 184.
38. Stevenson, *Poems* (1910), pp. 249, 270, 308–11.
39. Bergeron, 'Stuart Brothers' (2016), 2–7 and 'Lennox' (2020), 158–60.
40. *CSPVen*, 12, no. 817. See also Winwood, *Memorials*, 3, p. 453.
41. Macpherson, 'Ludovick Stuart', *ODNB*.
42. For his daughter Elizabeth, Masson, *Register*, 7, pp. 440, 696.
43. Dutton, *Shakespeare* (2016), p. 64.
44. For their role as privy councillors, see ch. 9.
45. CP99/145.
46. SP14/6, fol. 3.
47. *CSPVen*, 10, no. 739.
48. Ibid., 12, no. 175.
49. Cuddy, 'Great Contract' (2002), 249–70. See ch. 10.
50. *CSPVen*, 12, no. 175.
51. Thrush, *Commons*, 3 (2010), pp. 68–71.
52. Juhala, 'Chamber', 163.
53. Ibid., 112–13, 304; SP14/1, fol. 43^v.
54. See ch. 10.
55. SP14/60, fols 5^r, 31^r; *CSPDom, 1603–10*, pp. 68, 80, 90, 152, 174, 178, 357, 385.
56. *CSPDom, 1611–18*, p. 5.
57. SP14/43, fols 94, 104, 105; CP116/83; CP122/149; CP120/12.
58. CP106/60.
59. McCoog, *Society*, p. 422.
60. *CSPDom, 1603–10*, pp. 343, 376; ibid., *1611–18*, p. 6.
61. Schreiber, 'James Hay', *ODNB*; Mares, *Memoirs*, p. 66.
62. SP78/51, fols 96$^{r\&v}$, 136^r.
63. Schreiber, 'Hay' (1984), 1–19; Nichols, *James*, 1, p. 247.
64. Osborne, *Memoires* (1658), pp. 124–5.
65. Nichols, *James*, 1, pp. 104–5 (note 3), 247; SP14/17, fol. 30; *CSPDom, 1603–10*, p. 355; HL, Ellesmere MS, 1503; CP188/148.
66. Lindley, 'Masque' (1979), 145.
67. SP15/38, fol. 107; SP46/64, fol. 203; *CSPDom, 1611–18*, p. 5.
68. Brown, 'Scottish Aristocracy' (1993), 558.
69. Winwood, *Memorials*, 3, pp. 181, 403.
70. CP119/68; Nichols, *James*, 2, p. 50.
71. *CSPDom, 1603–10*, pp. 15, 41, 75, 113, 164, 197, 200, 219, 310, 317, 364, 462; SP15/36, fol. 30; CP112/107.
72. SP14/31, fol. 97^v.
73. Folger, X.d.587.
74. CP106/60; SP15/38, fol. 95.
75. Mares, *Memoirs*, p. 66.
76. CP104/57; CP188/81.
77. CP190/111.
78. Bergeron, *Lovers* (1991), pp. 129–30; Wilson, *History* (1653), p. 54.

79. Bellany and McRae, *Libels, passim*.
80. BL, Additional MS, 15476, fol. 92ᵛ. Bellany stated that he became a groom of the king's bedchamber in 1604, *Scandal* (2002), p. 28.
81. SP14/28, fol. 216ʳ.
82. Willson, *James* (1956), p. 337.
83. Harington, *Nugae Antiquae*, 1, pp. 396–7.
84. *CSPDom, 1603–10*, p. 417.
85. Peck, 'Monopolizing Favour' (1999), 57–8.
86. CP134/149. For Sherborne, SP14/43, fol. 17ᵛ; Bellany, *Scandal* (2002), p. 33.
87. CP129/115.
88. SP14/62, fol. 157ʳ; *CSPVen*, 12, no. 217.
89. HMC, *Downshire*, 3, pp. 83, 85, 139.
90. Ibid.
91. Birch, *Court*, p. 191.
92. Winwood, *Memorials*, 3, p. 422; SP14/70, fols 63, 65, 99, 106.
93. For faction after Cecil's death, Bellany, 'Howards' (2011), 537–52 and *Scandal* (2002), *passim*.
94. *CSPVen*, 10, no. 55.
95. BL, King's MS, 123, fol. 142ʳ.
96. Osborn, *Works* (1682), pp. 434, 452.
97. BL, Additional MS, 23723, fols 17ᵛ–18ʳ; Bellany, *Libels*. E.
98. Day, *Ile* (1606), sigs A2ᵛ, Cᵛ, E2ᵛ; Dutton, *Revels* (2022), pp. 198–9.
99. Act 2, Scene 3.
100. Orrell, 'London Stage', 154.
101. For general anti-Scottish sentiment, Wormald, 'Gunpowder' (1985), 141–68.
102. See chs 10 and 13.
103. Rhodes, Richards, and Marshall, *James* (2003), p. 312.
104. HMC, *Laing*, 1, p. 106.
105. HMC, *Portland*, 9, p. 113.
106. Smuts, 'Cultural Diversity', p. 104. Smuts was also referring to the households of aristocratic courtiers.
107. Peck, *Patronage* (1990), pp. 53–6.
108. Payne, 'Women' (2001), 38–44. Cecil bequeathed Lady Walsingham an annuity of £100, NA, PROB 11/119/598 p. 7.
109. For all these people, see *ODNB*.
110. Mishra, *Business* (2018), pp. 65, 70.
111. Payne, 'Women' (2001), 84–9; Field, *Anna* (2020), p. 135.
112. Lonchay, *Correspondance*, 1, p. 156; Payne, 'Women' (2001), 199, 209 *passim*; Fry, 'Perception' (2013), 268–9, 282–3; Loomie, 'Secret Diplomacy' (1994), 231–2, 233.
113. Payne, 'Family Networks' (2016), 164–80; O'Connor, 'Godly Patronage' (2011), 71–83; Hearn, 'Question' (2003), 221–39.
114. HMC, *De Lisle*, 4, pp. 40, 68, 162, 212, 234–5, 278–9, 283, 286–7.
115. Hannay, Brennan, and Lamb, *Sidneys*, 1 (2015), pp. 93–9.

116. Thrush, *Commons, A–C* (2010), pp. 423–4.
117. CP196/92; SP15/35, fol. 66.
118. See Thrush, *Lords*, 3 (2021), pp. 916–21. For an alternative view, Cuddy, 'Southampton' (1993), pp. 121–50.
119. Collier, *Egerton Papers*, pp. 359–61, 363–4; HL, Ellesmere MS, 129.
120. BL, Lansdowne MS, 90, fols 59, 61; Croft, 'Installation' (1992), 181.
121. Wilks, 'Culture' (1987), 1–35, 275–7 and 'Poets' (2016), 159–78.
122. *CSPVen*, 11, no. 393.
123. Croft, 'Installation' (1992), 180–8.
124. Wilks, 'Culture' (1987); Armitage, *Soldier* (2009), pp. 74, 105–21.
125. Ellis, *Letters*, 4 (1846), pp. 166–7; *CSPVen*, 12, nos 356, 373.
126. Wilks, 'Poets' (2016), 166–7.
127. Boran, 'Patrick Young [Junius]' and Marsden, 'Abraham van der Doort', *ODNB*.
128. BL, Additional MS, 39853, fols 16^r, 17^v; Anon, *True Picture* (1634), pp. 2–3; Birch, *Henry*, pp. 85–6.
129. McCullough, *Sermons* (1998), pp. 183–209.
130. Doelman, *Religious Culture* (2000), pp. 37–8.
131. Strong, *Henry* (1986), pp. 14–15 and *Monarchy* (1998), 3, p. 76; Badenhausen, 'Infant Warrior' (1995), 20–37; Parry, *Golden Age*, pp. 64–86.
132. Wilks, 'Poets' (2016), 159–78; White, 'Militant Protestants' (2009), 168–70; Murray, 'Letters Patent' (2012), 1–16.
133. Sommerville, *Writings*, pp. 32–3. See ch. 14.
134. Hawkins, *Silver Coins* (1841), p. 156; Kenyon, *Gold Coins* (1884), pp. 138–9, 145, 146; Cook, ' "Stampt" ' (2019), 307–9.
135. [Cotton], *Answer* (1655), p. 5.
136. *CSPVen*, 11, no. 801.
137. Ibid., nos 457, 463; HMC, *Downshire*, 2, p. 276; Gausden, 'A Court', 107.
138. *CSPVen*, 10, no. 360.
139. See ch. 12.
140. Nichols, *James*, 2, pp. 287, 441, 609, 759; *CSPVen*, 10, nos 204, 360, 716; ibid., 11, nos 216, 838, 856; Orrell, 'London Stage', 161; Gausden, 'A Court', 100-8.
141. *CSPVen*, 12, nos 34, 302, 309; ibid., 11, nos 580, 588.
142. SP14/9, fol. 15^v.
143. *CSPVen*, 10, nos 216, 517; ibid., 11, nos 228, 245, 261, 497, 894.
144. Strong, *Cult* (1999), p. 168.
145. *CSPVen*, 12, no. 236; Jefferson, 'Garter Installation' (2001), 141–50. For James and garter ceremonies, Gausden, 'A Court', 81–92.
146. Nichols, *James*, 1, pp. 593–7; SP14/61, fols 70–1; Heal, *Gifts* (2014), pp. 129–32.
147. Nichols, *James*, 1, pp. 593 (note 1), 594–6.
148. HMC, *De Lisle*, 4, p. 155; Payne, 'Women' (2001), 137.
149. *CSPDom, 1603–10*, p. 655.
150. Devon, *Exchequer*, pp. 49, 54, 58; *CSPDom, 1603–10*, p. 419.
151. Birch, *Henry*, pp. 99, 138.
152. *CSPVen*, 15, no. 456; HMC, *Downshire*, 2, p. 259; ibid., 3, p. 276.
153. SP78/51, fol. 57^r.

154. CP195/70.
155. *CSPVen*, 11, nos 109, 112; Orrell, 'London Stage', 160.
156. Dutton, *Shakespeare*, p. 82.
157. SP14/31, fol. 56[r&v].
158. Astington, 'Court Theatre', 314.
159. Wiggins, *Drama* (2012), pp. 51–2.
160. Clifford, *Diaries*, p. 27.
161. Wiggins, *Drama* (2012), p. 52; Jones, 'Journal', 259–60.
162. Wilbraham, *Journal*, p. 66.
163. Steen, *Letters*, p. 197; Pitcher, 'Daniel's Masque' (2013).
164. Cano-Echevarria and Hutchings, 'New Document' (2012), 245–7.
165. Ibid., 245–7; Daniel, *Vision* (1604), sig. A4[v].
166. Ibid., *passim*.
167. SP14/6, fol. 53[v]; Botonaki, 'Elizabeth's Presence' (2011), 140–57 and 'Queenship' (2013), 137–9.
168. SP14/6, fol. 53[v].
169. Wade, 'Queen's Courts' (2003), 61.
170. Packer, 'Jewels' (2012), 201–22.
171. *CSPVen*, 10, no. 332; SP14/12/6, fols 8[v]–9, 28[r&v]; Winwood, *Memorials*, 2, p. 44. The official accounts state that the *two* masques played that Christmas came to £4,000, SP14/14, fol. 132.
172. Ibid.; SP14/37, fol. 193[r].
173. See ch. 13.
174. Jonson, *Cambridge Edition*, Masque of Blackness.
175. Hall, *Darkness* (1995), pp. 128–37; Andrea, 'Black Skin' (1999), 246–81. For the 'negation of African racial difference' and 'a race-making innovation', Hutson, *Insular Imagining* (2023), 220–44.
176. Lewalski, 'Enacting Opposition', 15–43, especially 31–3; Fiorato, 'Performance' (2016), 256–66; McManus, 'Jacobean Fantasies' (2008), 437–74.
177. SP14/12, fol. 28.
178. HL, HM 55674, fols 6[v]–7[r].
179. *CSPVen*, 11, no. 127.
180. Ungerer, 'Circulation', 156–7.
181. Jonson, *Cambridge Edition*, Masque of Beauty, 8, 12, 13, 19.
182. See chs 13 and 14.
183. Jonson, *Cambridge Edition*, Masque of Beauty, 15, 17.
184. Burtin, *Ambassades*, 3 (1750), pp. 121–7.
185. Jonson, *Cambridge Edition*, Masque of Queens, 11, 13, 15, 22, 23, 27.
186. For the anti-masque, Paleit, *War* (2013), p. 164; Ravelhofer, *Masque* (2006), pp. 187–99; Daye, 'Balet Comique' (2014), 185–207.
187. Ravelhofer, *Masque*, pp. 19, 20.
188. Anon, *True Picture* (1634); Cornwallis, *Henry* (1641), pp. 13–15; Jonson, *Cambridge Edition*, Barriers, 12. For a non-chivalric interpretation, Council, 'Chivalry' (1980), 271–2.
189. HMC, *Downshire*, 2, p. 216.

190. Bergeron, 'Creating Entertainments' (2008), 433–49.
191. Anon, *The Order* (1610), especially sigs E4^v, F3^r.
192. Parry, 'Jacobean Masque' (1993), pp. 96–8.
193. Birch, *Court*, p. 152.
194. Jonson, *Hymenaei* (1606); Curran, *Marriage*, (2009), pp. 43, 47–56.
195. BL, Cotton MS, Julius C.III, fol. 301$^{r\&v}$.
196. Curran, *Marriage*, pp. 61–75. But Lindley suggests that the masque expressed reservations about the Union project, 'Masque', 145.
197. MacCray, *Beaumont Papers* (1894), pp. 16–17.
198. Literary scholars have long debated whether masques were panegyrics or subversive; Orgel, *Illusion* (1975); Butler, *Political Culture* (2008).
199. SP14/76, fol. 99^r.
200. *CSPVen*, 10, no. 623; ibid., 11, nos 117, 700.
201. *CSPDom*, 1603–10, pp. 312, 413; ibid., 1611–18, pp. 23, 58; CP129/89; *CSPVen*, 11, nos 216, 858.
202. SP14/44, fol. 166^v.
203. *CSPVen*, 12, no. 612; Cole, 'State Apartment' (2010), 24, 37.
204. Nichols, *James*, 2, pp. 538, 550, 553. For other plays at Oxford, Sandis, 'Drama' (2017), 60–1, 63–9.
205. *CSPVen*, 12, no. 612.
206. Ibid., 11, no. 285.
207. Wiggins, *British Drama* (2015), pp. 97–9.
208. Nichols, *James*, 2, pp. 132, 136, 138.
209. *CSPVen*, 11, nos 248, 255.
210. BL, Additional MS, 11402, fol. 113^r.
211. Ibid., fol. 114^r; *CSPVen*, 10, no. 716.
212. Davies, 'Limitations' (1992), 315–20.
213. Anon, *Welcome* (1606); Roberts, *Entertainement* (1606), pp. 8, 11–15.
214. CP119/162.
215. *CSPVen*, 10, no. 556; Anon, *Welcome* (1606), pp. 12–16; Davies, 'Limitations', pp. 324–5.
216. *CSPVen*, 10, no. 560.
217. Anon, *Welcome* (1606), pp. 17–25.
218. Burtin, *Ambassades*, 1, pp. 249, 261; Roberts, *Farewell* (1606), sigs B2^v–B3^r.
219. Ibid., sigs B3^v–C^r.
220. SP14/23, fol. 14^r.
221. Srigley, 'Hamlet' (2002), 168–92.
222. Christian had been installed *in absentia* in 1605, Folger, X.d.291.
223. SP14/23, fol. 14^r; Stow, *Chronicle* (1632), pp. 885–9.
224. HL, Ellesmere MS, 251, 252; SP14/23, fols 15^r–16^v.
225. CP117/97.
226. For an alternative view, Meikle, 'Once a Dane' (2019), 177.
227. Burtin, *Ambassades*, 1, p. 296. Birch, *Court*, p. 67; Heal, *Gifts*, p. 153.
228. SP14/23, fol. 14^r.

229. *CSPVen*, 10, no. 573; Burtin, *Ambassades*, 1, pp. 310–11.
230. SP14/23, fol. 13ᵛ.
231. Burtin, *Ambassades*, 1, p. 259; SP15/38, fol. 95; SP14/22, fol. 150ʳ&ᵛ (wrongly calendared under 1603).
232. Davies, 'Limitations', p. 316.
233. Burtin, *Ambassades*, 1, p. 311.
234. *CSPVen*, 10, no. 564.
235. HMC, *De L'Isle*, 3, p. 276.
236. SP14/22, fol. 150; Burtin, *Ambassades*, 1, pp. 244–5.
237. Ibid., p. 260.
238. SP14/23, fol. 13ᵛ; Harington, *Nugæ Antiquæ*, 2, pp. 126–8. De la Boderie made no such observation when reporting the visit, Burtin, *Ambassades*, 1, pp. 260–1.
239. Anon, *Welcome* (1606), p. 8.
240. SP14/12, fols 8ᵛ–9ʳ.
241. *CSPVen*, 10, nos 72, 169, 179; ibid., 11, no. 801; Walters, 'Music', p. 83.
242. *CSPVen*, 11, no. 792.
243. Ibid., 12, no. 516.
244. See ch. 14.
245. Brown, 'Scottish Aristocracy', 545, 546.
246. Dietz, *Finance*, p. 108.
247. CUL, Ll.4.8, fols 85ʳ–90ʳ.
248. Dietz, *Finance*, p. 108.
249. Ashton, 'Finance' (1957), p. 27.
250. HMC, *Rutland*, 1–3, p. 396.
251. CUL, Add, 335, fols 70ᵛ, 72–7ʳ.
252. Wakeman, *Salomon's Exaltation* (1605), especially pp. 53, 58–9, 61, 65; *CSPVen*, 10, no. 739.
253. Marcus, 'Literature', p. 487; Smuts, 'Progresses' (2002), 289; Kiséry, *Hamlet's Moment* (2016), p. 5.
254. Smuts, *Culture* (1987), pp. 73–84; McRae, *Literature* (2004), pp. 26–32, 36.

CHAPTER 9

1. *CSPVen*, 10, no. 739.
2. Crankshaw, 'Privy Council'.
3. Kesselring and Mears, 'Star Chamber' (2021), 9–10, 12–13.
4. Blakeway, 'Privy Council' (2016), 23–44; Goodare, *Government* (2004), pp. 128–31.
5. SP15/35, fols 29ʳ–32ʳ; CP100/30–2.
6. Cole, *Portable Queen* (1999), pp. 35–6.
7. Lodge, *Illustrations* (1791), 3, p. 268.
8. BL, Additional MS, 11402, fol. 98ʳ.
9. CP134/52.
10. SP14/12, fols 17ʳ, 165.
11. Akrigg, *Letters*, p. 234. See also CP134/48; Nichols, *James*, 2, p. 203.

12. CP111/151.
13. Lodge, *Illustrations* (1791), 3, p. 245; *CSPVen*, 10, no. 313.
14. Birch, *Court*, p. 133.
15. *CSPDom, 1603–10*, nos 104, 118, 120.
16. *CSPVen*, 10, no. 295.
17. CP134/33; CP104/74.
18. SP14/8, fol. 112.
19. CP107/148. See also CP188/79; CP126/77.
20. SP14/14, fol. 115.
21. CP117/88.
22. CP188/40.
23. CP115/64; CP123/93; CP192/69; CP193/133.
24. SP14/13, fol. 29.
25. CP103/114; CP192/72.
26. *CSPDom James, 1623–25*, p. 535.
27. *CSPVen*, 10, no. 301.
28. Ibid., no. 526.
29. Bellany, *Libels*, D3–D4, D9.
30. Davies, *Microcosmos* (1603), p. 121; Leighton, *Vertue* (1603), sigs E^v–E2^r.
31. MacDonald, 'Consultation' (2016), 194–204.
32. As one example, CP189/100.
33. Mears, *Queenship* (2005), *passim*.
34. BL, Additional MS, 11402.
35. HL, Ellesmere MS, 1763, fol. 1^v.
36. BL, Sloane MS, 1435, fols 144–55; CUL, Ll.4.8, fols 47–70^r, 77–97^v, 80–101^r. For Cecil's position papers, also see Croft, 'A Collection'.
37. Cited in Wormald, 'Two Kings' (1983), 202.
38. See ch. 10.
39. *CSPVen*, 10, no. 713.
40. CP Petitions 2072, 2020.
41. Patterson, *Urban Patronage*, pp. 35–6, 42, 156, 245–54.
42. SP14/1, fol. 127^v.
43. BL, Additional MS, 11402, fol. 101^r.
44. Ibid., fols 101^v–2^r.
45. Forster, 'Local Community' (1977), p. 197.
46. Lists of JPs appointed under the great seal are missing from 1603 until 1615.
47. Hankins, 'Local Government' (2003), 110–11.
48. Youngs, 'Petty Sessions' (1982), 201–2; Cust, *Gentry Culture*, pp. 126–7.
49. Saunders and Day, *Nathaniel Bacon* (1915), pp. xx–xxi, 24–6.
50. HL, Hastings MS, Box 1, no. 17; *CJ*, 1, p. 450.
51. BL, Additional MS, 11402, fol. 127^r; HMC, *Rutland*, 1–3, pp. 405, 406.
52. Larkin, *Proclamations*, 1, pp. 152–4.
53. Walter, *Crowds*, p. 20.
54. Lodge, *Illustrations* (1791), 3, p. 321.

55. Ibid.; Bridges, *Northamptonshire*, 2 (1791), p. 206.
56. BL, Additional MS, 11402, fol. 127^r.
57. *CSPVen*, 11, no. 11; Larkin *Proclamations*, 1, pp. 154–8.
58. Ibid., pp. 161–2.
59. Bridges, *Northamptonshire*, p. 206; Hindle, 'Insurrection' (2008), 21–61.
60. CP193/141; CP122/30 and 53; Gay, 'Midland Revolt' (1904), 219–37.
61. BL, Additional MS, 11402, fol. 128$^{r\&v}$; SP14/28, fol. 61^v.
62. SP14/1, fol. 147^r; BL, Additional MS, 11402, fol. 88^v; Dasent, *Acts*, 32, p. 498.
63. SP14/1, fol. 147^r. In 1618, there were twenty-seven, and thirty-five in 1623, Turner, *Privy Council*, 1, (1927), p. 73.
64. For example, CP188/78.
65. See ch. 10 and Appendix 1.
66. Arenberg reported that James had initially named his Scottish secretary as 'secretary of state', Lonchay, *Correspondance*, 1, p. 150.
67. Coakley, 'Cecil' (1970), p. 77.
68. Wilbraham, *Diary*, p. 106.
69. McCavitt, *Chichester* (1998), pp. 28, 164.
70. CP134/49, 59.
71. CP123/66; SP14/1, fol. 40^r.
72. Smith, 'Secretariats' (1968), 493–7, 501.
73. Evans, *Secretary* (1923), pp. 62–4.
74. Thrush, *Lords* (2021), 2, pp. 517–57, *passim*.
75. Thomas, 'Developments' (1982), pp. 105–8.
76. Ibid.; Dietz, *Finance*, p. 134.
77. See ch. 10.
78. Croft, 'Baronets' (2000), 265–7.
79. Davison, 'Bounty' (1973), 26–53. The book was printed in 1611.
80. See ch. 14.
81. Lodge, *Illustrations* (1791), 3, p. 365.
82. Thrush, *Lords*, 2 (2021), pp. 535–6.
83. Ibid., p. 554.
84. Lindquist, 'Last Years' (1986), 23–41.
85. SP14/15, fol. 169^r; Lodge, *Illustrations* (1791), 3, p. 380.
86. Hill, 'Journal', 317, 320, 321, 322, 323; Cuddy, 'King's Chambers' (1987), p. 62.
87. *CSPVen*, 12, nos 446, 452, 462, 503, 524; Nichols, *James*, 2, pp. 438, 444.
88. CP134/87; SP14/27, fol. 26^v.
89. *CSPVen*, 11, no. 826; Thrush, *Lords*, 2 (2021), p. 519; Stone, 'Fruits' (1961), 95.
90. HL, Ellesmere MS, 1203 [printed in Gutch, *Collectanea*, 1, pp. 122–5, 128].
91. Croft, 'Reputation' (1991), 43–69.
92. HMC, *Portland*, 9, p. 100; Wilbraham, *Journal*, p. 106; for Dorset's assessment, TNA, PROB 11/113/77. 2, p. 4.
93. Lodge, *Portraits* (1747), p. 6.
94. Healy, 'Revenue' (2015), 209, 87–8, 264.
95. BL, Additional MS, 11402, fols 103^r–5^r.

96. Heaton, '"Petition"', 115–17; Gutch, *Collectanea*, p. 122; Bellany, *Libels*, B15–16.
97. Zim, 'Poet' (2006), 199–223; Town, 'House' (2010), 75–82.
98. BL, Additional MS, 11402, fol. 138^v; TNA, PROB 11/113/77. 2.
99. For Egerton's conflicts with his wife HL, Ellesmere MS, 213 and 214.
100. Ibid., 162, 163, 164, 166, 167.
101. CP116/151; CP112/22.
102. CP106/91.
103. HL, Ellesmere MS, 1211, fol. 7, 1762, 1763; Folger, Z.e.1, fols 4^r–5^v.
104. HL, Ellesmere MS, 456, fol. 2^r; 438; 439.
105. Ibid., 1521, fol. 2^r.
106. Ibid., 263, 451, 456, 1211, fol. 8, 2007, 2011, 2613; Knafla, *Law* (1977).
107. Kenny, *Admiral* (1970), pp. 250–4.
108. Nottingham was ready to sell the office of lord admiral to Suffolk, but his price was too high. Thrush, *Lords*, 3 (2021), pp. 120–1.
109. *CSPVen*, 10, no. 141; Kenny, *Admiral*, pp. 264–72.
110. Macdonald, *Letters*, pp. xliv–xlvi; Dasent, *Acts*, 32, p. 498; Kenny, *Admiral*, pp. 275–6.
111. See ch. 14.
112. Peck, 'Problems' (1976), 835; Thrush, *Lords,* 3 (2021), pp. 120–1.
113. After the coronation, James appointed a commission of six men to carry out the role of earl marshal, Worcester being but one of them.
114. Lodge, *Illustrations* (1791), 3, pp. 268–9, 273–4, 282–3, 378–80, 381; Nichols, *James*, p. 467; CP188/70.
115. Thrush, *Lords*, 3 (2021), pp. 635–9.
116. Lloyd, *States-men* (1665), p. 393.
117. For Sterrell, Martin and Finnis, 'Anthony Rivers' (2002), 39–74.
118. Loomie, 'Toleration' (1963), p. 17.
119. Goodman, *Court*, 2, p. 106.
120. Spence, 'Pacification' (1977), 96, 99–105; ch. 13.
121. SP14/20, fols 82^v–3^r; for the affair, Rickman, *Love* (2008), pp. 111–39.
122. *CSPVen*, 10, no. 34.
123. For the plot, ch. 12.
124. For biographies of Howard, see Peck, *Northampton* (1982); Thrush, *Lords*, 3 (2021), pp. 138–73; Croft, 'Henry Howard', *ODNB*.
125. *CSPVen*, 11, no. 245; BL, Additional MS, 11402, fol. 138^v.
126. SP14/60, fol. 9.
127. CP134/72; CP 104/74; Bellany, *Libels*, B2, KI iv. Items listed in the inventory upon his death also point to Howard's Catholicism, Shirley, 'Inventory' (1869), pp. 350, 355, 357, 371, 373.
128. Howell, *State Trials*, 2, p. 80. See ch. 12.
129. Peck, *Northampton*, pp. 55–7.
130. CUL, Gg.5.18, fol. 5^r; Bellany, *Libels*, B2; Burtin, *Ambassades*, 2, p. 200. For a near contemporary critique, Wilson, *History*, sig. B2^r.
131. Jonson, *Conversations*, p. 22.

132. Guerci, 'Northumberland House' (2010), 2.
133. Peck, *Northampton*, p. 101.
134. SP14/15, fol. 158.
135. McGowan, *Commissions* (1971), pp. xiv–xvi, 4–5; *CSPVen*, 11, no. 539; SP14/41; Peck, 'Problems', 835–40.
136. SP14/15, fols 146, 158.
137. Sherlock, 'Monuments', 276–7.
138. Bacon, *Essays* (1894), p. 184. See also ch. 12.
139. Akrigg, *Letters*, pp. 250, 252, 254, 288; Lodge, *Illustrations* (1791), 3, p. 325.
140. SP14/23, fol. 13^r.
141. SP14/68, fol.18; CP134/66; CP134/71; Akrigg, *Letters*, pp. 257, 263.
142. Shirley, 'Inventory', p. 375; BL, Additional MS, 15649.
143. Another possibility is that his uncle used his influence with James, Thrush, *Lords*, 3 (2021), p. 187.
144. SP14/60, fol. 9.
145. CP134/66; CP134/71.
146. Croft, 'Thomas Howard', *ODNB*.
147. See ch. 3.
148. Mackie, 'Advertisement', p. 2.
149. *CSPVen*, 10, no. 55.
150. BL, Additional MS, 11402, fol. 89^r; Dasent, *Acts*, 32, p. 498.
151. Lodge, *Illustrations* (1791), 3, pp. 351–2; Zulager, 'Edward Bruce, Lord Kinloss', *ODNB*.
152. For Dunbar in Scotland, Fraser, *Elphinstone*, 2 (1897), pp. 150, 152–3; ch. 13.
153. *CSPVen*, 11, nos 37, 52.
154. McLaughlin, 'Lennox' (2017), 136–54.
155. Folger, L.d.915.
156. *CSPVen*, 11, no. 444.
157. Smith, 'Politics' (2003), p. 244.
158. SP78/50, fols 82^v–3^r.
159. Peck, *Patronage* (1990), p. 35.
160. Baildon, *Star Chamber*, pp. 219, 220–1; Thrush, *Lords*, 3 (2021), p. 151; Leader, *Dudley* (1895), pp. 45, 48, 175. In his will, Northampton paid Dudley's debts, Shirley, 'Inventory', p. 376.
161. Thrush, *Lords*, 3 (2021), p. 151; Guerci, 'Northumberland House', pp. 345–8, 354–86.
162. CP123/66; Croft, 'Cecil's Religion' (1991), 781, 784.
163. *CSPVen*, 10, no. 714.
164. Peck, *Northampton*, pp. 29–30, 79; Croft, 'Cecil's Religion', 781.
165. BL, Additional MS, 39853, fol. 83^r.
166. Croft, 'Reputation' (1991), 63.
167. See ch. 14.
168. Foster, *Proceedings*, 1 (1966), pp. 35–6.
169. TNA, PROB 11/113/77.2, pp. 3–4.

170. Ibid., 11/119/598, p. 5; HL, Ellesmere MS, 1203, fols 1–6.
171. The king even made a joke to Cecil to that effect, Akrigg, *Letters*, p. 234.
172. TNA, PROB 11/119/598, p. 5.
173. CP134/66.
174. HMC, *Salisbury*, 16, p. 254.
175. For Dorset and Dunbar, TNA, PROB 11/113/77.2, p. 5.
176. Cited in Paul, *Counsel* (2020), p. 176.
177. For a case study, Cust, *Gentry Culture*, pp. 119–57.

CHAPTER 10

1. For English parliaments: Thrush and Ferris, *Commons*, 6 vols (2010) and *Lords*, 3 vols (2021). For Scottish parliaments: Brown, 'Political Participation' (2016), 1–33; MacDonald, 'Legislative Process' (2011), 601–17; Brown and MacDonald, *Parliament in Context* (2010), pp. 18–20, 123, 125; Macdonald, *Burghs* (2007); Goodare, 'Scottish Parliament' (2004), 147–72.
2. Thrush, *Commons*, 1 (2010), p. 48.
3. The number of lay peers grew with James's creations, Thrush, *Lords* (2021), 1, p. 99.
4. Thrush, *Commons*, 1 (2010), p. 372. Overall, 562 people were returned to parliament between 1604 and 1610, Kilroy, 'Demographic Study' (2021), 5.
5. Gruenfelder, *Elections* (1981), pp. 3–9.
6. HL, Ellesmere MS, 1763, fol. 2^r. See also Thrush, *Commons*, 1 (2010), pp. 372–3.
7. Smith, *De Republica* (1583), pp. 36–7, 39; Hooker, *Parliament* (1577), p. 164. My thanks to Andrew Thrush for the latter reference.
8. Nonetheless, some Scottish acts were redrafted and amended before their final registration, MacDonald, 'Legislative Process', 610.
9. Thrush, *Commons*, 1 (2010), p. 373.
10. Sommerville, *Writings*, p. 75.
11. Baker, *Magna Carta* (2017), pp. 339–40.
12. For Bilson's sermon, ch. 5; for the medal, BM, G3, EM.316.
13. Chan Smith, *Coke* (2014), p. 176; Baker, *Magna Carta*, pp. 367–8.
14. Heinze, 'Proclamations' (1982), p. 240; Brooks, *Law* (2008), p. 408.
15. Thrush, *Commons*, 1 (2010), pp. 5–7.
16. Poole, *Reason of State* (2015), pp. 23–4.
17. Ibid., p. 27.
18. Willson, *Privy Councillors* (1940), p. 99; Thrush, *Commons*, 1 (2010), pp. 371, 378–9.
19. Ibid., p. 379.
20. Ibid., 1, pp. 159–61; Kilroy, 'Demographic Study', 19–20.
21. For example, *CJ*, 1, pp. 169, 189–90.
22. Munden, 'Commons' (1985), Appendix A, p. 326.
23. Tyacke, 'Biography' (2013), 536.
24. Kilroy, 'Demographic Study', 13–16.
25. Tyacke, 'Biography' (2013), 538; Russell, *Parliaments* (2011), p. 147.

26. Winwood, *Memorials*, 3, p. 129; Bickley, *Gawdy*, p. 143.
27. Millstone, *Manuscript* (2016), pp. 99–101.
28. There are variant versions, some of only 40 lines others at over 225, Callaghan, 'Performing Politics' (2006), 121–38.
29. *CJ*, 1, p. 226; Thornborough, *Discourse* (1604).
30. *CJ*, 1, p. 235.
31. Ibid., pp. 312–13; CP111/14.
32. Larkin, *Proclamations*, 1, pp. 66–70. For draft in Ellesmere's hand, HL, Ellesmere MS, 2590.
33. Thrush, *Commons*, 1 (2010), pp. 68–9.
34. SP14/6 fol. 181^r.
35. Sommerville, *Writings*, pp. 132–46. See also ch. 6.
36. BL, Lansdowne MS, 512, fols 80^v–1^r; SP14/6, fol. 198^r; *CJ*, 1, pp. 141; Dunn, '1603/4', 49, 52; Thrush, *Commons*, 1 (2010), pp. 219–20.
37. HL, Ellesmere MS, 2608, fol. 2$^{r\&v}$.
38. Thrush, *Commons*, 1 (2010), pp. 398–9. The procedure also allowed members to speak more than once in a day, Kyle, *Theater* (2012), p. 5.
39. Russell, 'Parliaments 1593–1606' (1990), p. 211.
40. *CJ*, 1, pp. 154–6; SP14/7, fols 57–8^v; Winwood, *Memorials*, 2, pp. 18–19; BL, Cotton MS, Titus F.IV, fol. 7^v; Thrush, '1604' (2007), 305–6; Russell, *Parliaments* (2011), pp. 28–30.
41. BL, Cotton MS, Titus F.IV, fol. 7^v.
42. *CJ*, 1, pp. 157–9; BL, Additional MS, 48044, fols 302–4^v.
43. BL, Cotton MS, Titus F.IV, fols 8^r–10^v; *CJ*, 1, 157–8, 939; Healy, 'Debates' (2001), 35–6; BL, Additional MS, 48116, fol. 214^r.
44. SP14/7 fol. 1; CP104/117.
45. Among the manuscript copies in a seventeenth-century hand, SP14/7, fols 5–7; BL, Additional MS, 48044, fols 302–4^v; BL, Sloane MS, 1856, fols 39^v–62; Stowe, MS, 180, fols 11–12^v. See also *CJ*, 1, pp. 161–2, 162–5, 165–6.
46. *CJ*, 1, pp. 166–7. In Proverbs, the wrath of a king is compared to the roaring of a lion.
47. Bickley, *Gawdy*, pp. 143–4.
48. Winwood, *Memorials*, 2, pp. 18–19.
49. *CJ*, 1, pp. 169–71.
50. BL, Lansdowne MS, 512, fols 86^v–7^r; Dunn, '1603/4', 75–6; Stapylton, 'Freedom' (2016), 75–111; Prothero, 'Shirley's Case, 1604' (1893), 733–40.
51. *CJ*, 1, p. 204.
52. Ibid., pp. 204, 205, 214–15.
53. SP14/8, fols 134–5^r [fols 134–9^v]; a copy, BL, Lansdowne MS, 312, fols 120–32^v.
54. Willson, *Bowyer's Diary* (1977), p. 15.
55. SP14/52, fol. 143 [32].
56. Hirst, 'Elections' (1975), 851–62; Knafla, *Law*, p. 256.
57. HMC, *Portland*, 9, pp. 12–13.
58. HMC, *Buccleuch*, 3, p. 84.

59. *CJ*, 1, pp. 160–1.
60. Healy, 'Debates' (2001), 66–7; *CJ*, 1, pp. 169–71.
61. SP14/7, fol. 99$^{r\&v}$.
62. Thrush, *Commons*, 6 (2010), pp. 165–7; Rabb, 'Sandys' (1964), 646–70. Most historians treat Sandys as Cecil's client, but Cuddy argued he was a client of Southampton, Cuddy, 'Southampton' (1993), 127–8.
63. SP14/7, fols 161^r, 232^v. For the Union, see ch. 13.
64. BL, Additional MS, 4149, fol. 123^r; SP14/7, fols 79, 151^v; HL, Ellesmere MS, 1226.
65. *CJ*, 1, pp. 178, 950–1; SP14/7, fols 161$^{r\&v}$, 234^v; 151–2^r, 166–78^v; HL, Ellesmere MS, 1226; BL, Cotton MS, Julius F.VI, no. 39.
66. SP14/7, fol. 234^v. See also ch. 13.
67. SP14/7, fols 130–4, 231$^{r-2^r}$, 234^v, 237^{v-9}; *CJ*, 1, pp. 180–1.
68. SP14/7, fols 79, 232^r.
69. Ibid., fol. 284^r.
70. *CJ*, 1, p. 193; SP14/8, fol. 2$^{r\&v}$.
71. Statute I Jac.I cap. II.
72. SP14/8, fols 187$^{v-8^v}$.
73. Thrush, *Commons*, 6 (2010), pp. 863–7.
74. Dunn, '1603/4', 143–4; Healy, 'Debates' (2001), 43–4; *CJ*, 1, pp. 150–2; BL, Lansdowne MS, 512, fol. 92$^{r\&v}$; BL, Cotton MS, Titus F.IV, fol. 4^v.
75. Whitgift died in Feb. 1604 and Bancroft was translated to Canterbury on 10 Dec.
76. BL, Lansdowne MS, 512, fol. 156; Healy, 'Debates' (2001), 68–70; Thrush, *Lords*, 2 (2021), pp. 69–70, *Commons*, 1 (2010), pp. 21–2.
77. Strateman, '"Policies"' (1951), 55; *CJ*, 1, pp. 172–3, 175–6, 177–8; *LJ*, 2, pp. 280–1, 281–3; BL, Lansdowne MS, 512, fol. 156^r.
78. *CJ*, 1, 234–5; Russell, *Parliaments* (2011), pp. 41–2; Thrush, *Lords*, 1 (2021), pp. 70–1.
79. Usher, *Reconstruction*, 1, p. 345.
80. *LJ* 2, pp. 265–6; Wilbraham, *Journal*, pp. 62–3; Thrush, *Lords*, 2 (2021), pp. 522, 545.
81. Tyacke, 'Wroth' (1977), 120–5; Croft, 'Purveyance' (1985), 13.
82. *LJ*, 2, pp. 265–6; *CJ*, 1, pp. 199–200.
83. Ibid., pp. 160–1, 162–5, 171–2, 176–7, 185–7, 190–3, 204.
84. Ibid., p. 204.
85. *LJ*, 2, pp. 294–5.
86. *CJ*, 1, pp. 212–13, 222–3; BL, Egerton MS, 2651, fols 20$^{v-2^r}$.
87. HMC, *Portland*, 9, p. 13.
88. Ibid., pp. 134, 136–8; *CJ*, 1, pp. 206–7, 211–12.
89. SP14/52, fols 192–4 (wrongly calendared in 1610). See also Croft, 'Wardship' (1983), 43–4. Russell argues that James was behind the rebuff, *Parliaments* (2011), pp. 23–4.
90. HMC, *Portland*, p. 92; *CJ*, 1, pp. 983–4; *LJ*, 2, p. 309; HMC, *Salisbury*, 23, pp. 137–8.
91. *CJ*, 1, pp. 229–30; Healy, 'Debates', p. 83.
92. Dunn, '1603/4', 1111–36. Among the many manuscript copies, SP14/8, fols 134–9. Notes from it are in CP105/81.

93. CP367/1 p. 19. For Ridgeway, Thrush, *Commons*, 6 (2010), pp. 58–9. Russell suggests Nicholas Fuller was the author, see 'Royal Supremacy' (2000), 28.
94. SP14/8, fols 187–8ᵛ.
95. Dunn, '1603/4', xvi, xvii.
96. Maxwell-Stuart, '1604', pp. 31–46.
97. Rose, 'Hunting' (2020), 16–31.
98. *CSPVen*, 10, no. 313.
99. Ibid., no. 415; Thrush, *Lords*, 2 (2021), pp. 526–7.
100. BL, Additional MS, 11402, fol. 105ʳ.
101. Thrush, *Lords*, 2 (2021), pp. 527–8.
102. *CSPVen*, 10, no. 440.
103. HL, Ellesmere MS, 475.
104. Willson, *Bowyer's Diary*, p. 124; *CJ*, 1, p. 297.
105. Ibid.; *CSPVen*, 10, nos 499, 510.
106. Folger, X.d.428 (59).
107. Winwood, *Memorials*, 2, p. 216; see also ch. 12.
108. Willson, *Bowyer's Diary*, p. 88; *CSPVen* 10, no. 503.
109. SP14/19, fol. 119ʳ.
110. SP14/20, fol. 82ʳ&ᵛ; Cramsie, *Kingship* (2002), pp. 102–3; Russell, *Parliaments* (2011), pp. 48–50, 53–4.
111. Willson, *Bowyer's Diary*, p. 136.
112. Ibid., pp. 33, 149, 158.
113. SP14/23, fols 133, 135–6, 137, 142–4.
114. Ibid., fols 121–2, 126–8.
115. *CJ*, 1, pp. 314–15; Willson, *Bowyer's Diary*, p. 185.
116. *LJ*, 2, pp. 453–4. Hostile peers included Southampton, Burghley, Mounteagle, Arundel, and Pembroke, see Burtin, *Ambassades*, 2, pp. 199–200.
117. *CJ*, 1, p. 329.
118. See ch. 13.
119. *LJ*, 1, pp. 456–7.
120. *CJ*, 1, pp. 332–5.
121. Sommerville, *Writings*, pp. 159–78; *CJ*, 1, pp. 357–63.
122. CUL, Add, 9276; Willson, *Bowyer's Diary*, pp. 267–9, 273. For more details, ch. 13.
123. *CJ*, 1, pp. 366–8; SP14/27, fols 37–8ᵛ; Willson, *Bowyer's Diary*, pp. 287–8.
124. *Statutes*, 4 (b), pp. 1134–7.
125. When the next parliament was called, MPs were surprised that there was 'not one word spoken of the Union', from the government, HMC, *Downshire*, 2, p. 86.
126. Winwood, *Memorials*, 3, p. 119; HMC, *Downshire*, 2, p. 240; Foster, *Proceedings*, 2, pp. 4–5.
127. Ibid., 2, pp. 7–8.
128. CUL, Ll.4.8. MS, fols 3ʳ–4ᵛ, 70–6ʳ.
129. Gardiner, *Debates*, p. 11.

130. Smith, 'Great Contract' (1979), p. 113.
131. Gardiner, *Debates*, pp. 1–9; Foster, *Proceedings*, 2, pp. 9–27; SP14/52, fols 152–5.
132. Winwood, *Memorials*, 3, p. 123.
133. Gardiner, *Debates*, pp. 11–12; Foster, *Proceedings*, 2, pp. 34–6, 358–9.
134. Gardiner, *Debates*, pp. 12–16.
135. Lindquist, 'Failure' (1985), 626.
136. HL, Ellesmere MS, 1211, fols 1–3.
137. Foster, *Proceedings*, 1, p. 20.
138. Ibid., 2, p. 54.
139. Winwood, *Memorials*, 3, pp. 129, 144–5; *CSPVen*, 11, no. 721. For the relationship between wardship and feudal tenures, see Russell, *Parliaments* (2011), pp. 78–9.
140. HMC, *Downshire*, 2, p. 262.
141. Clegg, *Censorship* (2001), pp. 137–43.
142. Foster, *Proceedings*, 1, p. 46.
143. Croft, 'Annual Parliaments' (1996), p. 169.
144. HMC, *Downshire*, 2, p. 262.
145. SP46/166, fol. 218$^{r\&v}$; Winwood, *Memorials*, 3, p. 136.
146. Ibid., p. 141.
147. Ibid.
148. SP14/53, fols 43–4; Foster, *Proceedings*, 1, pp. 45–52.
149. HMC, *Downshire*, 2, p. 267.
150. Ibid., p. 269; Gardiner, *Debates*, p. 30.
151. Winwood, *Memorials*, 3, p. 153.
152. Ibid.
153. Gardiner, *Debates*, 30, pp. 147–52; Foster, *Proceedings*, 2, pp. 73–6; *CJ*, 1, p. 421.
154. *CSPVen*, 11, no. 906; Winwood, *Memorials*, 3, pp. 159–60. See ch. 14.
155. Gardiner, *Debates*, p. 36; Foster, *Proceedings*, 2, pp. 107–8.
156. Foster, *Proceedings*, 1, p. 8; ibid., 2, pp. 100–7; SP14/54, fols 91–3.
157. SP14/193, fol. 156^r.
158. Gardiner, *Debates*, pp. 38–9; Foster, *Proceedings*, 2, pp. 111–12.
159. SP14/193, fols 145, 156–7, 158.
160. Ibid., fol. 104; Foster, *Proceedings*, 2, pp. 114–16.
161. Winwood, *Memorials*, 3, p. 182; *CSPVen*, 11, nos 837, 880.
162. Foster, *Proceedings*, 2, pp. 138–41; Gardiner, *Debates*, p. 57.
163. Ibid., pp. 52–4.
164. Foster, *Proceedings*, 1, pp. 130–3; ibid., 2, pp. 252, 267, 273; Gardiner, *Debates*, p. 123.
165. Wilbraham, *Diary*, p. 105; SP14/56, fol. 40; *LJ*, 2, pp. 656–62.
166. Foster, *Proceedings*, 1, p. 149.
167. SP14/56, fol. 138^r.
168. Winwood, *Memorials*, 3, pp. 193–4; *CJ*, 1, p. 449.
169. SP14/56, fol. 138^v.
170. Winwood, *Memorials*, 3, pp. 193–4.
171. HMC, *Rutland*, 1–3, pp. 424–5; Lindquist, 'Failure', pp. 648–9.
172. HMC, *Rutland*, 1–3, p. 424; Lindquist, 'Failure', pp. 648–9; Gardiner, *Debates*, pp. 164–79.

NOTES 529

173. *LJ*, 1, pp. 656–62.
174. Foster, *Proceedings*, 2, pp. 295–7.
175. Ibid., pp. 299–302.
176. Ibid., pp. 313–16.
177. Ibid., pp. 317–30; Gardiner, *Debates*, p. 133; Russell, *Parliaments* (2011), p. 90.
178. Foster, *Proceedings*, 2, p. 403.
179. HMC, *Rutland*, 1–3, p. 425.
180. Smith largely blamed James, 'Great Contract', pp. 114, 125–6.
181. CP147/162.
182. Harris, *Rebellion* (2014), 219–23.

CHAPTER 11

1. Rhodes, *King James*, p. 299.
2. SP14/6, fol. 64^r.
3. Cardwell, *Conferences*, p. 141; BL, Additional MS, 38492, fol. 12.
4. Buchanan, *Conference* (2009), p. 49.
5. Bray, *Canons*, pp. 303, 305, 307 359, 375.
6. Ibid., pp. 295, 297, 347, 349, 359.
7. See ch. 3.
8. Bray, *Canons*, p. 321. The other two articles affirmed the validity of the royal supremacy and thirty-nine articles of faith.
9. Winwood, *Memorials*, 2, p. 46.
10. CP110/117.
11. Larkin, *Proclamations*, 1, p. 76.
12. Oates, *Moderate Radical* (2018), p. 195; Collinson, *Bancroft* (2013) and 'Succession' (2014), 92–111. Anna was said to be the only one who favoured Matthew, Trevelyan, *Trevelyan Papers*, p. 67.
13. *CJ*, 1, pp. 240–1; SP14/6, fols 169–70.
14. Larkin, *Proclamations*, 1, pp. 88–90.
15. SP14/10A, fol. 162; BL, Additional MS, 11402, fol. 97^r; Cardwell, *Annals* (1839), 2, pp. 89–92, 94.
16. CP10/116. See also Quintrell, 'Royal Hunt' (1980), 41–58.
17. CP134/51; CP103/130; CP107/148; Fincham, 'Oxford' (1997), 183–6; Bondos-Greene, 'Cambridge Puritanism' (1982), 201–8. As chancellor, Cecil enforced royal policy in the University of Cambridge.
18. Cardwell, *Annals*, 2, pp. 69–76; Wilkins, *Concilia* (1737), 4, pp. 408–9.
19. CP134/52.
20. Wilkins, *Concilia*, 4, pp. 409–11.
21. Winwood, *Memorials*, 2, p. 46.
22. BL, Harley MS, 677, fols 42^r–3^v; Babbage, *Puritanism* (1962), pp. 82–4.
23. Ibid., pp. 146–9, 217, 222, 232. Fincham puts the figures between 73 and 83, *Prelate* (1990), pp. 213, 215, 216, Appendix VI, and 'Clerical Conformity' (2000), 139.
24. Jacob, *Offer* (1606), sig. ★3^r.
25. [Hieron], *Dialogue* (1605), sig. A3^v.

26. *CJ*, 1, p. 285.
27. Usher numbered 273 ministers who believed they were under threat of losing their livings, 'Deprivation' (1909), 234–5.
28. *CJ*, 1, pp. 377–9.
29. Foster, *Church*, pp. cxv–cxvi, cviii.
30. Brooks, *Lives*, 2 (1813), p. 232.
31. Usher, 'Deprivation', pp. 239–40; Cahill, 'Coventry and Lichfield', 29.
32. Tan, 'Richard Bernard' (2015), 37, 44, 46–7.
33. Larminie, 'Samuel Hieron', *ODNB*.
34. Foster, *Church*, p. 364; Bozeman, 'Thomas Brightman', *ODNB*.
35. CP103/124.
36. Cliffe, *Puritan Gentry* (1984), pp. 180–1. Dod was ejected in 1611.
37. Clarke, *Lives* (1660), pp. 54, 57–9; Cahill, 'Coventry and Lichfield', 92.
38. Tyacke, *Aspects* (2001), pp. 113–14.
39. *LJ*, 2, pp. 656–62.
40. SP14/77, fol. 163.
41. BL, Additional MS, 38492, fol. 10^r. For Fuller, Thrush, *Commons*, 4 (2010), p. 324.
42. CP108/22.
43. CP Petitions 444. She was referring here to article 29 of Magna Carta.
44. Winwood, *Memorials*, 2, p. 49; SP14/12, fol. 192^v; Thompson, *Magna Carta* (1948), pp. 257–8; Brooks, *Law* (2008), pp. 112–16.
45. SP14/12, fol. 168^r.
46. Ibid. and fol. 192^v.
47. Chan Smith, *Coke*, pp. 190–2; Shagan, 'Inquisition', 541–65.
48. BL, Additional MS, 11402, fol. 100^v.
49. Wright, 'Fuller' (2006), 177–81, 204.
50. The bill was to revise the 1559 Act of Supremacy that had empowered the monarch to establish ecclesiastical commissions by letters patent.
51. The clients were Thomas Ladd of Yarmouth and Richard Mansell of Gloucester.
52. Wright, 'Fuller', p. 196; Chan Smith, *Coke*, pp. 194–5.
53. Usher, *Reconstruction*, 2, pp. 141–2, 145.
54. CP134/126.
55. CP124/135.
56. CP134/128.
57. SP14/28 fol. 87^r.
58. CP124/59.
59. CP122/121.
60. CP124/59.
61. Wright, 'Fuller', 195–6.
62. Anon, *The Argument* (1607); Clegg, *Censorship* (2001), pp. 131–6.
63. SP14/28, fol. 160.
64. CP124/139.
65. CP123/59.

66. CP123/55.
67. SP14/37, fol. 105^v; HL, Ellesmere MS, 2008.
68. Milton, *Second Reformation* (2021), p. 32.
69. SP14/28, fol. 216.
70. Anon, *The Argument* (1607); CP124/59 and 81; Wright, 'Fuller', pp. 198–9.
71. SP14/31, fol. 59^r; Foster, *Proceedings*, 2, p. 396.
72. Chan Smith argues that Coke's actions rose from 'a principled opposition' to the expansion of the court's competence not to the royal prerogative, *Coke*, pp. 181, 196, 278–84.
73. Wright, 'Fuller', 205.
74. CP128/20; Foster, *Church*, pp. lxxii, cvi.
75. CUL, Add., 336, fols 72–7^r. Other copies are in the British, Bodleian, and Folger libraries. The sermon was printed in 1642. For further discussion, McCullough, *Sermons*, pp. 143–5; Lake, 'Goal Posts?' (2000), 179–205.
76. SP14/8, fols 172, 173; BL, Harley, 3791, fols 176–7^r; Babbage, *Puritanism*, pp. 167–73, 381–6. For the significance of the 'limitation', Lake, 'Goal Posts?' (2000), 179–205.
77. Bellany, 'Poem' (1995), 137–64 and 'Libels' (2001), 104–6.
78. CP103/142, fol. 1^v; CP194/49.
79. CP192/18; SP14/13, fol. 73.
80. Baildon, *Camera Stellata*, pp. 223, 226–30.
81. Ibid., p. 224.
82. CP192/7.
83. *CSPVen*, 10, no. 355; CP104/39.
84. CP104/61, fol. 2^r; Baildon, *Camera Stellata*, p. 223.
85. Bodl., MS Rawlinson, B.151, fol. 95^v; Colcough, *Freedom* (2005), pp. 225–8.
86. CP110/45.
87. Babbage, *Puritanism*, pp. 124–46; Sheils, *Peterborough* (1979), pp. 73–7.
88. BL, Harley MS, 677, fol. 44; BL, Additional MS, 38492, fol. 6^r.
89. SP14/10, fol. 192^r; BL, Additional MS, 8978, fol. 116$^{r\&v}$; Anon, *An Abridgement* (1617). Some authorities date the petition as 1 Dec., Elizabeth Allen, 'John Burges', *ODNB*.
90. Winwood, *Memorials*, 2, p. 36.
91. SP14/10, fol. 192^r; BL, Additional MS, 8978, fols 117^r–18^r. Among the signatories was Alexander Redich, the Puritan patron of Arthur Hildersham and William Bradshaw.
92. Cardwell, *Annals*, 2, p. 92; BL, Additional MS, 8978, fol. 117^v.
93. BL, Egerton MS, 2877, pp. 47–8; BL, Harley MS, 3791, fol. 157; BL, Sloane MS, 271, fol. 35; SP14/12, fol. 159; Anon, *Humble Petition* (1605); Sharpe, *Petition* (1605).
94. SP14/10, fol. 192^r; BL, Additional MS, 8978, fol. 16$^{r\&v}$.
95. Winwood, *Memorials*, 2, p. 36.
96. *CSPVen*, 10, no. 313.
97. Ibid.; CP189/42; CP104/24.
98. CP134/52.

99. Cross, *Letters* (1969), p. 90; Newton, 'Hastings' (1998), 917–34. Newton argues the petition was a reaction to James's decision to prorogue parliament, but I think Dove's deprivations were the spur.
100. SP14/12, fol. 162. For a printed version, Cross, *Letters*, pp. 88–9.
101. CP Petitions 57; SP14/12, fol. 213; Cross, *Letters*, pp. 90–2.
102. Barton, *Registrum Vagum*, pp. 155–6.
103. SP14/12, fol. 168^v.
104. Ibid., fol. 169^v; Winwood, *Memorials*, 2, p. 48.
105. For Montagu, HMC, *Buccleugh*, pp. 237–8; Cope, *Life* (1982). Hastings had been a JP, lord lieutenant, and colonel of the militia, see Newton, 'Hastings', 933.
106. CP Petitions 57; SP14/12, fol. 213.
107. For a petition to the bishops, BL, Additional MS, 38492, fol. 3; from the gentlemen of Leicestershire to Cecil, Sir George Home, the earls of Devonshire and Mar, and various gentlemen, BL, Additional MS, 8978, fols 109^r–10^r.
108. Curtis, 'William Jones' (1964), 38–66.
109. Plomer 'Bancroft' (1907), 164–76.
110. Curtis, 'William Jones', 59–60.
111. Ibid., 38, 47–50. According to Clegg, 'Star Chamber' (2005), 66, the action for seditious printing brought against Jones was the only one of its kind during James's reign and also unsuccessful.
112. Anon, *Certaine Arguments* (1606).
113. Ibid., pp. 1–2. See also [Hieron], *Dialogue*, pp. 1–6 and *Defence* (1607).
114. Anon, *Certaine Considerations* (1605), sig. A4^r.
115. Jacob, *Offer*, sigs ★–★4, pp. 3–67.
116. Stoughton, *Assertion* (1604), title page, p. 358.
117. Bradshaw, *Protestation* (1605), pp. 1–3.
118. CP134/53; Barlow, *Summe*, p. 79.
119. For example, Anon, *The Remoovall* (1606), pp. 1–6, 10, 12, 21; BL, Additional MS, 38492, fol. 10^r.
120. Ibid., fol. 46^r.
121. Ha, *Presbyterianism* (2011), p. 77. Ha's findings challenge those of Sprunger, *Trumpets* (1994) and others who have argued that Jacobean Puritans rejected Presbyterianism in favour of a non-separating Congregationalism.
122. Bradshaw, *Unreasonablenesse* (1614), sig. P2^r.
123. Lake, *Moderate Puritans* (1982), pp. 262–78; Morgan, 'Henry Jacob' (2017), 695–727; Burrage, *Dissenters* (1912), pp. 147–65.
124. Jacob, *Reasons* (1604), sig. A2^r–3^v. See also undated letter, Burrage, *Dissenters*, p. 150, where Jacob wrote of the king's 'just and full supremacie' and 'our absolut prophet and sole teacher in all matters of the Church'.
125. For a different type of separatism, 'a species of separatism run amok', Atherton, and Como, 'Edward Wightman' (2005), 1215–50 [quotation p. 1236].
126. Oates, *Moderate Radical*, p. 204.
127. Sprunger, *Dutch Puritanism* (1982), pp. 66–7, 80–2; George, *Robinson* (1982), pp. 57–81; Oates, *Moderate Radical*, p. 204.

NOTES 533

128. Rogers, *Two Dialogues* (1608), *passim*.
129. Ormerod, *Puritane* (1605), *passim* but especially sigs B^v, O^v–O2^v.
130. Fotherby, *Foure Sermons* (1608), the fourth sermon pp. 101–4.
131. Covell, *Examination*, pp. 55–68, 75–93.
132. Powel, *Ministers' Arguments* (1606), p. 11. For Powel's anti-Catholic writing, see ch. 12.
133. Ibid., sigs D2^r, E3^r, G2^v.
134. Ibid., p. 81 [misprint for 18].
135. Gardiner, *Dialogue* (1605), sig. B^v.
136. Powel, *De Adiaphoris* (1607), p. 9. Corinthians 1:14 was his scriptural authority for this point. See also Westerman, *Faithful Subject*, pp. 44–7; Mason, *Authoritie* (1607), sig. E3^r.
137. BL, Cotton MS, Titus F.IV, fol. 169.
138. BL, Additional MS, 38492, fols 24^r, 44–5.
139. For the Elizabethan debates, Lake, *Anglicans?* (1988).
140. Sparke, *Perswasion* (1607), pp. 16–17, 20–1, 24–6; Rogers, *Two Dialogues*, sig. O4^v; Dove, *Defence* (1606), pp. 55–60; Powel, *De Adiaphoris*, p. 82; sermon of Dean Gordon before the king, SP14/13, fol. 160^r.
141. Westerman, *Faithful Subject*, pp. 19–20.
142. Sparke, *Perswasion*, sigs A3^r–C^r.
143. Mason, *Authoritie*, sigs A2^v, C3^v.
144. Haigh, 'Antipuritan' (2004), 682, 685; Maltby, *Prayer Book* (1998), pp. 76–81; Fielding, 'Arminianism' (1993), 118–19.
145. Lake, *Boxmaker's Revenge* (2001), pp. 65, 311–14; Fincham, 'Anthony Lapthorne', *ODNB*. My thanks to Ken Fincham for referring me to Lapthorne.
146. Hutton, *Merry England* (1994), p. 159; Craig, 'Bodies' (2013), 193–5.
147. Collinson, 'Antipuritanism' (2008), pp. 26–7 and 'Ecclesiastical Vitriol' (1995), 150–70. For a sophisticated thought piece, Lake, 'Anti-Puritanism' (2006), 80–97.
148. McGee, 'Puritans' (2003), 52.
149. Jonson, *The Alchemist*. For further commentary, Lake, *Antichrist's Lewd Hat* (2002), pp. 584–6, 600, 605–7.
150. Shakespeare, *Measure for Measure*. For commentaries, Lake, *Antichrist's Lewd Hat*, pp. 628, 699–700; Walsh, *Unsettled Toleration* (2016), pp. 113–25.
151. Milton, *Catholic* (1995), pp. 31–7.
152. See ch. 12.
153. Dixon, *Practical Predestinarians* (2014); Tyacke, *Anti-Calvinists* (1987), pp. 29–86. For an 'enlargement' of the articles, Milton, *Second Reformation* (2021), p. 29.
154. See ch. 3.
155. Tyacke, *Anti-Calvinists* (1987); Fincham, 'Ecclesiastical Policies' (1993), p. 31.
156. Cardwell, *Annals*, 2, pp. 28–92.
157. Cardwell, *Synodalia* (1842), 2, pp. 562–4; BL Harley MS, 280 and 595. See also O'Day, 'Ministry' (1976), pp. 55–76; Ingram, *Church Courts* (1990), p. 87.
158. Green, *Print* (2000), p. 195.
159. Fincham, *Prelate* (1990), pp. 198–206 and 'George Abbot', *ODNB*.

160. SP 14/2, fol. 105^r.
161. 110 were graduates and 82 licensed preachers, Cahill, 'Coventry and Lichfield', 24, 41, 44.
162. SP 14/2, fols 105^r, 107.
163. Ibid., fol. 108.
164. BL, Sloane MS, 271, fol. 24^v.
165. Usher, *Reconstruction*, 2, p. 331. Lucy Kaufman, however, has challenged the view that impropriated tithes greatly affected the quality of the ministry, 'Ecclesiastical Improvements' (2015), 1–23.
166. *CJ*, 1, pp. 244–7; Dalrymple (ed.), *Memorials* (1762), 19–20.
167. Hill, *Economic Problems* (1971), pp. 32–4.
168. Wilkins, *Concilia*, 4, pp. 413–14.
169. Fincham, *Visitation Articles*, 1 (1994), p. 94 and 'Ramifications' (1985), 208–27; *LJ*, 2, 656–62.
170. Milton, *Second Reformation* (2021), p. 31.
171. Norton, *Textual History* (2004), p. 6 states the Geneva Bible was Reynolds's preferred text but Feingold 'Masterpiece' (2018), pp. 2–3, suggests that Reynolds wanted 'a new scholarly enterprise aimed at improving on all existing translations by returning *ad fontes*'.
172. Usher, *Reconstruction*, p. 336.
173. No. 80. The canon's Latin title refers only to holy books (*Libri sacri*), but Bray translates it as 'the great Bible', Bray, *Canons*, pp. 374–5.
174. Spottiswoode, *History*, p. 465; Barlow, *Summe*, pp. 45–6.
175. Ibid., pp. 46–7.
176. Cardwell, *Annals*, 2, pp. 84–6; Usher, *Reconstruction*, 2, p. 357; Norton, *Short History* (2011), pp. 85–6.
177. For the selections, see Feingold, 'Masterpiece', pp. 3–7. For Bancroft's role, Fincham, 'Bible' (2020), 83–4.
178. Miller, 'Geneva Bible' (2017), 530.
179. Usher, *Reconstruction*, 2, p. 357; Norton, *Short History* (2011), pp. 87–90, 94.
180. Miller, 'Geneva Bible', 517–43; Norton, *Short History* (2011), pp. 33–53; Hammond, 'Translations' (2010), 421.
181. Ferrell, *Bible* (2008), p. 92; Nicolson, *Power* (2003), pp. 75, 58; Tadmor, 'Bible' (2016), 387–9.
182. Fuller, *Church History* (1837), p. 247.
183. Norton, *Bible* (2000), p. 87; Fincham, 'Bible' (2020), 78–95.
184. Edes, *Six Sermons* (1604), sig. B2^v.
185. Doran, 'Elizabeth I's Religion' (2000), 707.
186. Foster, 'Clerical Estate' (1993), 161 and 'Bishops' (2017), 84–103; Fincham, *Prelate* (1990), pp. 42–3.
187. Jago, 'Religious Space' (2012), 65, 73–4.
188. Eight new appointments were made between March 1603 and 1612.
189. Fincham, *Prelate* (1990), p. 35; Foster, 'Clerical Estate' (1993), p. 148.
190. Barlow, *Summe*, pp. 39, 40.
191. Abbott, *Kings Majestie's Letter* (1622).

192. McCullough, *Sermons*, p. 71.
193. *CSPVen*, 12, no. 236.
194. McCullough, 'Music' (2013), 122.
195. Larkin, *Proclamations*, 1, p. 76; SP/14/6, fol. 64ʳ.
196. Fincham, 'Clerical Conformity' (2000), 139.
197. Wilkins, *Concilia*, 4, pp. 409–10; Fincham, *Prelate* (1990), pp. 216–20.
198. Fincham, 'George Abbot', *ODNB*.
199. Tyacke, *Aspects* (2001), p. 138; Fincham, 'Abbot', *ODNB*; Fincham, 'Prelacy' (1988), 37, 38; Holland, 'Abbot' (1994), 23–43.
200. Tyacke, *Aspects* (2001), p. 137. Nonetheless, prohibitions were still causing jurisdictional troubles, see Brooks, *Law* (2008), p. 144.
201. Fincham, 'Prelacy' (1988), 45; Holland, 'Abbot', 27–30.
202. Anti-Calvinists held seven English bishoprics by 1617. For a good summary of the 1620s, Harris, *Rebellion*, pp. 190–200, 208–14.

CHAPTER 12

1. Gerard, *Condition* (1871), pp. 23–4; Brogden, 'Herefordshire' (2018), 35.
2. SP14/1, fols 18, 159ᵛ, 261ᵛ; CP100/7; *CSPVen*, 10, no. 16.
3. SP14/1, fol. 155; Loomie, *Spain*, 1 (1973), pp. 42–3.
4. SP14/1, fol. 159ʳ. For Bellarmine's criticisms of the book, Tutino, *Empire* (2010), pp. 23, 122–7.
5. Clancy, 'English Catholics' (1962), 210–11.
6. McCoog, *Society*, p. 415; Lake, *Archpriest* (2019), pp. 253–4; Questier, *Treason* (2022), p. 334.
7. SP14/1, fol. 110; SP14/2, fols 75, 76–8; Bodl., Tanner MS, 82, fol. 160; BL, Additional MS, 29546, fol. 75; ibid., 22848, fol. 121ᵛ; ibid., 39829, fol. 104; HMC, *Various*, 3, pp. 128–32; *CSPVen*, 10, no. 63; Powel, *Supplication* (1603); Bickley, *Gawdy*, pp. 136–7; McCoog, *Society*, pp. 410–11.
8. BL, Additional MS, 39829, fol. 104; SP14/1, fol. 110ᵛ; Powel, *Supplication*, p. 16.
9. James apparently ordered to the Tower four Irish petitioners who arrived with a retinue of eighty men, *Gawdy*, pp. 136–7; *CSPVen*, 10, no. 113.
10. *CSPVen*, 10, nos 36, 38.
11. Bodl., Ashmole MS, 1729, no. 37, fol. 68ʳ&ᵛ.
12. For example, James decided in favour of Thomas Vachel whose property had been seized under Elizabeth, SP15/35, fols 25–7.
13. See ch. 4.
14. *CSPVen*, 10, no. 91.
15. [Lecey], *Petition* (1604), pp. 8–9; *CSPVen*, 10, no. 101.
16. Loomie, *Toleration* (1963), p. 15; HMC, *Various*, 3, p. 138; MacDonald, *Kirk*, (1998), pp. 101–2.
17. CP101/74–7.
18. Larkin, *Proclamations*, 1, pp. 70–3.
19. CP101/74–7; CP135/80.
20. Sommerville, *Writings*, p. 140.

21. Grosvenor, 'Worcestershire Election' (1977), 151–5; Greenslade, *Catholic Staffordshire* (2006), p. 77. Additionally, the recusant Henry Lord Mordaunt tried to have Sir Anthony Mildmay elected for the Northamptonshire seat, Gruenfelder, 'Two Midland' (1976), 241–2.
22. As reported by Lord Sheffield, lord president of the council of the north, CP118/36.
23. SP14/4, fol. 204$^{r\&v}$.
24. SP14/6, fol. 176.
25. Colleton, *Supplication* (1604), sigs A2^r–4^r, G^v.
26. Lecey, *Petition*, pp. 7–9, 30.
27. Ibid., p. 35.
28. Kellison, *Survey* (1603), ns.
29. Sutcliffe, *Supplication* (1604), sigs B^r, C2^v; Powel, *Supplication*, p. 16.
30. For copies, University of Edinburgh, Laing MS, pp. 99–100; CP99/124; CP199/113; BL, Cotton MS, Galba E.I, fol. 115.
31. Powel, *Supplication*, pp. 11, 16; Sutcliffe, *Supplication*, sigs B^r, C2^v, C4^r–D2^v.
32. Hooke, *Sermon* (1604), sigs Ai^v, B^r, Cii^v–Ciii, Civ^{r-v}, D^r.
33. Sommerville, *Writings*, pp. 139–40.
34. Bodl., MS Eng Th. b2, fols 845^r–7^r; BL, Lansdowne MS, 512, fol. 131^v; *LJ*, 2, pp. 327–30; Questier, *Catholicism* (2006), 271–9.
35. BL, Lansdowne MS, 512, fols 139^r–42^v; *LJ*, 2, pp. 334–7; *Statutes*, 4, pp. 1020–2.
36. Winwood, *Memorials*, 2, p. 49.
37. *LJ*, 2, pp. 321–2; *CJ*, 1, pp. 252–3.
38. Dietz, *Finance*, 2, pp. 97 (note 4), 114. But, the sequestered lands for non-payment of fines were leased back to their owners, *CSPVen*, 10, no. 353.
39. CP110/90.
40. *CSPVen*, 10, no. 355.
41. Challoner, *Memoirs* (1741), 2, pp. 6–12.
42. HL, Ellesmere MS, 1221. Gerard made a similar point, *Condition*, p. 25, but did not claim the burdens were worse than those imposed under Elizabeth.
43. [Copinger], *Theatre* (1620), sig. Nn.4^r; Foley, *Records*, 3 (1878), pp. 603–6; Tutino, 'Thomas Pounde' (2004), 31–50, Questier, *Treason* (2022), pp. 340–2.
44. CP190/93.
45. CP188/98; *CSPVen*, 10, no. 373.
46. CP110/92.
47. CP191/31.
48. CP144/219; Brogden, 'Herefordshire', 25–47.
49. CP190/93; CP191/8 and 25; CP111/109; *CSPVen*, 10, nos 384, 390, 397, 408; Brogden, 'Herefordshire', 45–6.
50. CP101/142; *CSPVen*, 10, no. 432.
51. *CSPDom, 1603–10*, p. 228.
52. SP14/216/1, fol. 83^r.
53. For the conspirators, Travers, *Gunpowder Plot* (2005).
54. CP112/91, fol. 1^r; SP14/216/2 fols 6^v–7; Loomie, *Spain*, 1 (1973), pp. 13, 37–8 and *Fawkes in Spain* (1971), pp. 10–12, 22–30.

55. SP14/216/1, fols 8, 9.
56. SP14/216/2, fols 15ᵛ–16ʳ, 47.
57. SP14/16, fol. 119ʳ&ᵛ; SP14/216/2, fol. 50ʳ; SP14/17, fol. 14.
58. SP14/216/2, fol. 48ᵛ.
59. SP14/16, fol. 170.
60. SP14/216/2, fol. 9ʳ.
61. HMC, *Rutland*, 1–3, p. 398.
62. SP14/216/1, fol. 11A; SP14/216/1, fol. 150ʳ. Tresham never confessed to penning the letter.
63. CP112/91, fol. 1ᵛ. In his confession, Garnet indicated that Monteagle had known something about the plot before receiving the letter, Caraman, *Garnet* (1964), pp. 378–81.
64. SP14/216/2, fol. 34ʳ&ᵛ.
65. Ibid., fol. 10ʳ.
66. Ibid., fols 37ᵛ–9ᵛ.
67. Ibid., fols 39ᵛ–40; SP14/216/1, fol. 34; *CSPVen*, 10, no. 442.
68. SP14/16, fol. 18; *CSPVen*, 10, no. 443.
69. Larkin, *Proclamations*, 1, p. 123; SP14/216/1, fol. 28.
70. *CSPVen*, 10, no. 445.
71. SP14/216/1, fol. 26.
72. SP14/16, fol. 41ᵛ.
73. Ibid., fol. 41ʳ.
74. Birch, *Historical View* (1749), p. 239.
75. Harington, *Nugae Antiquae*, 1, p. 373.
76. Wormald, 'Gunpowder' (1985), 161–2.
77. *CSPVen*, 10 no. 456.
78. This part of Fawkes's confession was crossed out, SP14/216, fol. 83ʳ.
79. SP14/216/1, fols 56, 57ʳ, 185; SP14/216/2, fol. 194ʳ&ᵛ; HMC, *Rutland*, 1–3, p. 400.
80. SP14/17, fol. 47ʳ.
81. *CSPVen*, 10, no. 445; SP14/216/1, fols 45, 50, 59. The lord-lieutenants were in London for the parliament.
82. SP14/216/1, fol. 46.
83. Ibid., fols 104, 195ʳ&ᵛ; SP14/216/2, fol. 50ᵛ.
84. Ibid., fol.65ᵛ; Howell, *State Trials*, 2, pp. 182–3.
85. SP14/216/2, fol. 10ᵛ.
86. SP14/216/1, fol. 97; SP14/216/2, fols 10ᵛ–11.
87. CP Petitions 1491.
88. CP113/4; CP191/80.
89. BL, Additional MS, 11402, fol. 108ʳ.
90. HL, Hastings MS, Box 1, no. 11; CP115/36.
91. *CSPVen*, 10, nos 443, 445, 454; SP14/216/181, 182; Montague was not put on trial and was released in Aug. 1606 after paying a fine, SP14/23, fol. 15ᵛ. The other three were brought before star chamber, Baildon, *Camera Stellata*, pp. 287–91, and the barons were released in Aug. 1607, BL, Additional MS, 11402, fol. 115ʳ. See also, Batho, 'Payment', (1958), 42–5.

92. Nicholls, '"Wizard Earl"' (1987), 173–89.
93. For Dudley's suit, see ch. 9.
94. Hodgetts, 'Plot' (2006), 27–30 and 'Coughton' (2009), pp. 93–121. Anthony Milton thinks it most unlikely that Dudley was intended for such a high-status role.
95. BL, Additional MS, 11402, fol. 108$^{r\&v}$.
96. Scarisbrick, 'Whose Plot?' (2006), 2–15; Nicholls, *Gunpowder Plot* (1991), pp. 213–21.
97. CP113/77.
98. Ibid.
99. SP14/216/1, fol. 90^r.
100. Ibid., fol. 65$^{r\&v}$.
101. Larkin, *Proclamations*, 1, pp. 131–3.
102. Barlow, *Sermon* (1606), sig. C4^r; Caraman, *Garnet*, pp. 331–3.
103. CP109/108; Gilbert, 'Habington's Account' (2001), 418; Caraman, *Garnet*, pp. 335, 337–44.
104. Tresham was decapitated after death. BL, Additional MS, 11402, fol. 109^r.
105. Anon, *A True Report* (1606). His short description of the arraignment differed significantly from the official account; for example, Digby pleaded not guilty here and was tried with the others.
106. Willson, *Bowyer's Diary*, p. 10; Bailden, *Camera Stellata*, pp. 251–7; Howell, *State Trials*, cols. 183–4, 187–94.
107. Ibid., cols 197, 215–18.
108. Gilbert, 'Habington's Account', 418; CP115/13; SP14/20, fol. 8^v; Howell, *State Trials*, col. 241.
109. Anon, *Perfect Relation* (1606), sigs Y2^v, Y3^r denied the use of torture, but on 22 Feb., there was an order to put 'the inferior prisoners' to the rack, BL, Additional MS, 11402, fol. 110^r.
110. SP14/20, fol. 8^r.
111. Howell, *State Trials*, col. 234. For equivocation, Tutino, 'Nicodemism' (2006), 534–53; Hadfield, *Lying* (2017), pp. 79–84.
112. SP14/20, fols 3$^{r\&v}$, 5, 32^r; CP115/13; SP14/216/2, fol. 164^r.
113. SP14/20, fol. 9^r; SP14/21, fol. 2^r.
114. Fuller, *Church History* (1837), 3, p. 222.
115. BL, Additional MS, 21203, fols 22^r–3^v; Fuller, *Church History*, pp. 222–4.
116. Pricket, *Jesuits Miracles* (1607).
117. *His Majestie's Speech* (1605) is sometimes known as the *King's Book*. The books were *A True and Perfect Relation* (1606), and an *An Answere* (1606) written by Cecil. See Nicholls, 'King's Book'; Dolan, *True Relations* (2013), pp. 29–46.
118. Anon, *Perfect Relation*, sig. A2^v.
119. *His Majestie's Speech*, sig. B4^r.
120. *Perfect Relation*, sig. K1^v.
121. *His Majestie's Speech*, sigs C4^v–B^v.
122. Barlow, *Sermon*. For a commentary, James, 'Preaching' (2014), esp. pp. 353–60.
123. *His Majestie's Speech*, sig. D4^v.

124. Williamson and Mears, 'Gunpowder Treason Day' (2021), 195.
125. Rhodes, *A Briefe Summe* (1606), sig. B2[r].
126. Barlow, *Sermon*, sig. C3[r&v].
127. Anon, *Prayers* (1606), sigs D2[v]–D3[r].
128. HL, Ellesmere MS, 457, fol. 2[r].
129. SP14/16, fol. 41[r]; CP113/5.
130. [Hynd], *Divell* (1606), sig. D[r].
131. Hawes, *Prosopopeia* (1606), sigs A4[r], B3[r], B3[v]–B4[r], C2[r&v], C3[v], C4[v]. See also CUL, Add, 22, fol. 61[r].
132. *Prayers* (1606), sigs D2[v]–3[r]; *His Majestie's Speech*, sigs C2[r]–3[v].
133. Cecil, *An Answere*, sig. D[v]. For a different interpretation of Cecil's pamphlet, Tutino, *Law* (2007), pp. 124–5.
134. *Perfect Relation*, sigs A4[r]–B2[r].
135. For the quotations, Barlow, *Sermon*, sig. C4[r]; *His Majestie's Speech*, sig. B2[r]. Among popular works, Anon, *Shamefull Downefall* (1606); Allson, *Musicke* (1606), cantos 22, 23. For verses in foreign languages, HL, Ellesmere MS, 1140; Hardin, 'Early Poetry' (1992), 62–79. See also James, *Poets* (2016), *passim*. For Scottish courtier poets, Gausden, 'A Court', 211–13.
136. CUL, Add, 22, fol. 61[r]. See also [Hynd], *Devil* (1606); sig. B3[r].
137. Cressy, *Bonfires* (1989), p. 124.
138. Barnes, *Divil's Charter* (1607), Act 1, Scene 4; Act 3, Scene 2.
139. Herman, 'Gunpowder Plot' (2014), 114–31; Shapiro, *1606* (2015), pp. 209–32; Wills, *Witches* (1995); Lemon, *Treason* (2006), ch. 4.
140. Dutton, *Jonson* (2008); Hadfield, *Lying*, pp. 97–9.
141. Hind, *Engraving* (1955), pp. 390–2.
142. British Printed Images to 1700, bpi8254, bpi7783, bpi8404, bpi7797, bpi693.
143. Hind, *Engraving*, 2, pp. 394–5.
144. Walsham, *Providence* (1999), pp. 253–61.
145. BM, M.7013, 7014, 1885,0406.1; Hunterian, University of Glasgow, GLAHM:38076.
146. Gregory, 'Gunpowder Plot Monument' (2017), 305–20.
147. Cressy, 'Festivities' (2005), pp. 56–7.
148. *CSPVen*, 10, nos 455, 453.
149. Ibid., no. 463.
150. SP14/16, fols 126[v]–7.
151. *CJ*, 1, 265.
152. 2 James I, c. 5, *Statutes*. Much of this law was never enforced.
153. SP14/21, fol. 76[r]; 3 James I, c. 4, *Statutes*. For these reasons, I dispute the argument that the government's response was moderate in the sense of mild, as proposed in Okines, 'Government Reaction' (2004), 278–92.
154. In 1606, nobles were exempt from the oath but could be made to swear it if asked by six privy councillors. In 1609, it was extended to everyone 'of what degree or quality soever', and, in 1610, a statute required all major office holders to take the oath.
155. 3 James I, c. 5, *Statutes*; Clancy, 'English Catholics', 211.

156. 3 James I, c. 5, *Statutes*; SP14/21, fol. 76ᵛ.
157. However, equivocation 'gave reason to believe oaths might be meaningless, so the symbolic act of swearing gave questionable assurance to Protestants', Condren, *Argument* (2006), p. 270.
158. Tending to do so are Milton, *Catholic* (1995), p. 56 and Okines, 'Government Reaction', 278–92.
159. See Sommerville, 'Papalist Political Thought' (2005), 132–5.
160. Taking this view, Questier, 'Loyalty' (1997), 311–29 and 'Loyalism' (2008), 1132–65.
161. HMC, *Rutland*, 1–3, p. 404.
162. Fincham, *Visitation Articles*, 1 (1994), p. 95. Despite this order, excommunicated offenders were generally given a churchyard burial even if denied a formal religious service, Cressy, *Ritual* (1997), p. 465.
163. SP14/49, fol. 44ʳ. As the council had no power over matters of religion, Eure was unable to comply, Questier (1997), 326.
164. Lemon, *Treason*, p. 117; Lazo, 'Catholic Loyalty' (2015); Tutino, 'Thomas Preston' (2010), 91–109.
165. Gifford, 'Oath' (1971), p. 72.
166. Aveling, *Northern Catholics* (1966), pp. 214–15.
167. Brogden, 'Herefordshire', 89–90.
168. Gifford, 'Oath', p. 72; Questier, 'Loyalism' (2008), 1148–9.
169. Pollen, *English Martyrs* (1891), pp. 145–7, 177–80; Lunn, 'English Benedictines' (1969), 149; Gifford, 'Oath', p. 76 (note 1).
170. HL, Ellesmere MS, 2189.
171. Questier, 'Loyalism' (2008); La Rocca, 'Catholic Subjects' (1987), 252–5.
172. HL, Ellesmere MS, 2179, 2180.
173. *CSPVen*, 11, nos 168, 177; Burtin, *Ambassades*, 3, pp. 103–4.
174. *Triplici Nodo*, p. 22; North, 'Debate' (2002), 215–32.
175. Milward, *Religious Controversies* (1978), pp. 89–131.
176. Tutino, *Empire* (2010), pp. 130–1.
177. Persons, *Judgment* (1608).
178. *CSPVen*, 11, nos 340, 354; CP126/67; CP134/98, 23; HL, Ellesmere MS, 1210; Zulager, 'James Elphinstone, First Lord Balmerino', *ODNB*.
179. *CSPVen*, 11, no. 463.
180. SP14/44, fols 189, 190ʳ; *CSPVen*, 11, nos 354, 430.
181. Ibid., nos 497, 503, 511, 580.
182. James, *Apologie*, pp. 1, 21, 107–8, 129.
183. SP14/44, fol. 154ᵛ.
184. *CSPVen*, 11, nos 484, 513, 527, 536, 539, 556; *CSPDom, 1603–10*, p. 514; SP75/4, fol. 141; SP14/51, fol. 12ʳ; Aytoun, *Poems* (1844), p. xxvi.
185. Sowerby, 'Royal Gifts'. My thanks to her for sending it to me before publication.
186. SP81/9, fols 220ʳ, 210ʳ–11ʳ, 217ʳ&ᵛ, 219ʳ, 222.

187. SP99/5, fols 279ʳ–80ʳ; CP227/333. For more on the papal offensive against the book, Patterson, *Reunion* (1997), pp. 97–8.
188. *CSPVen*, 11, nos 561, 562, 572, 592, 614, 617, 625, 635; HMC, *Downshire*, 2, p. 237. Wotton resigned to be replaced by Dudley Carleton.
189. CP127/120; *CSPVen*, 11, no. 554; Gardiner, *Fortescue Papers* (1871), pp. 3–6. French theologians evaluated the book favourably, Burtin, *Ambassades*, 4, pp. 378–9.
190. CP227/305, 308; SP77/9, part 2, fols 52ʳ–3ʳ. Sowerby explains that the cancellation was a rejection of Edmonde's ceremonial obligation to attend upon the archduke after a period of absence, 'Royal Gifts', forthcoming.
191. Winwood, *Memorials*, 3, pp. 66–8.
192. *CSPVen*, 11, nos 579, 585, 590.
193. Ibid., no. 714.
194. Lyall, 'Marketing' (2002), 216.
195. SP14/50, fol. 65.
196. Winwood, *Memorials*, 3, pp. 160–1; Milton, *Catholic* (1995), p. 33.
197. Constantinidou, *Responses* (2017), pp. 216, 226–7; Asch, *Sacral Kingship* (2014), p. 53; Salmon, 'Catholic Resistance' (1991), 252–3.
198. In his breve of September 1606, Paul V urged English Catholics to martyrdom in their fight against the oath, Lemon, *Treason*, p. 116.
199. For the debate on Donne's motives, Adlington, 'Desperate Ambition?' (2011), 718–32; Roebuck, 'Controversial Treatise' (2011), pp. 258–63. For a useful summary of *Pseudo-Martyr*, ibid., pp. 249–63.
200. Leman *Treason*, pp. 123–35; Houlistan, 'An Apology' (2006), 474–86; Read, 'Matter of Sovereignty' (2020), 411–34.
201. HL, Ellesmere MS, 2182.
202. BL, Additional MS, 11402, fols 153ᵛ–4ᵛ.
203. Other reasons for Abbot's elevation were his support for episcopacy in Scotland and the patronage of Dunbar and Cecil. For more on Abbot, ch. 11.
204. Fincham, 'Prelacy and Politics' (1988), 40–5.
205. Dures, *English Catholicism 1558–1642* (Harlow, 1983), p. 51; La Rocca, 'Catholic Subjects', 251–62.
206. Nuttall, 'English Martyrs' (1971), 192.
207. Cogswell, 'Destroyed' (2006), pp. 184, 186–7, 192.
208. For a couple of examples of Elizabeth's leniency to favoured recusants, CP61/44; CP189/24. For James, CP118/159; CP191/53; Lodge, *Illustrations*, 3 (1838), 251–2.
209. Croft, 'Baronets' (2000), 262–81.
210. Milton, 'Qualified Intolerance' (1999), 85–115; Sheils, ' "Getting On" ' (2009), pp. 67–83; Cogan, *Catholic Social Networks* (2021), pp. 158, 164–5, 167–74; Walsham, 'Sociability' (2016); Marshall, 'Confessionalisation' (2016), pp. 40–1, 44–7, 50–1, 62.
211. Walsham, *Charitable Hatred* (2006), p. 91.

CHAPTER 13

1. Historians give different names for multiple kingdoms, Morrill, 'British History' (2006), pp. 44–5; Backerra, 'Personal Union' (2019), pp. 89–111.
2. Somerville, *Writings*, p. 59.
3. Masson, *Register*, 6, p. 553.
4. Calderwood, *Kirk*, 6, p. 216.
5. See chs 8 and 9; Cuddy, 'Union' (1989), 109–10.
6. Larkin, *Proclamations*, 1, p. 7.
7. *Ibid.*, pp. 18–19. The borderlands were present-day Cumberland, Northumberland, Westmorland, and parts of Durham in England and Roxburgh, Selkirk, Peebles, and Dumfries in Scotland.
8. Ibid., 1, p. 39.
9. Kanemura, 'Union Debate' (2014), 162, 165.
10. TNA, SC13/N4.
11. BM, M.6918 and G3,EM.316.
12. Strong, 'Royal Jewels' (1966), 351.
13. Mason, 'Anglo-Scottish Union' (1990), 182–222.
14. Merriman, 'James Henrisoun' (1987), 85–112; Robinson-Self, *Relationship* (2018), pp. 123–30.
15. Murray, *Complaynt* (2002).
16. Williamson, *Consciousness* (1979), pp. 89–96.
17. This narrative originated in Geoffrey of Monmouth's *Historia Regum Britanniae* (*c*.1135).
18. Mason, 'Scotching' (1987), 60–84; Doran, 'Polemic' (2014), 215–35.
19. Powell, *Welch Bayte* (1603), which was printed without licence.
20. *Panegyrike*, sig. A3^r. Daniel presented James with an autograph manuscript copy with slightly different wording, BL, Royal MS, 18A, LXXII.
21. Russell, 'Union' (1994), pp. 238–40, 246–7.
22. Evrigenis, 'Sovereignty' (2019), 1073–88.
23. Mirecka, 'Poland-Lithuania' (2014), 163–6.
24. SP14/7, fols 192–3; Sobecki, 'A Relation' (2014), 1079–97.
25. Sommerville, *Writings*, p. 135.
26. Galloway and Levack, *Six Tracts* (1985), p. 84.
27. Calderwood, *Kirk*, 6, pp. 257, 258.
28. Maidment, *Letters*, p. 60.
29. Galloway, *Six Tracts*, p. 27.
30. Sommerville, *Writings*, pp. 161–2.
31. Bacon, *Letters*, Electronic Edition, 3, pp. 90–9.
32. Galloway, *Six Tracts*, pp. 180–2.
33. Sommerville, *Writings*, pp. 161–78; *CJ*, 1, pp. 366–8; SP14/27, fols 37–8^v.
34. Scott, *Somers' Tracts*, 2, p. 132.
35. Galloway, *Union* (1986), pp. 62–7.
36. Larkin, *Proclamations*, 1, pp. 94–7.

37. SP216/1, fol. 34^v; CP Petitions 1313.
38. Trevisan, *Genealogy*, p. 230.
39. SP14/24, fol. 45^r.
40. HL, Ellesmere MS, 1226; SP14/7, fols 151–2^r.
41. Fraser, *Elphinstone*, 2 (1897), p. 170.
42. SP14/9A, fol. 215; HL, Ellesmere MS, 1226; Russell, 'English View' (2003), 159–60.
43. Larkin, *Proclamations*, 1, pp. 99–102; Galloway, *Union*, pp. 59–60. The minting and proclamation were delayed in Scotland until March 1605.
44. Cook, '"Stampt"', 309–10.
45. Ibid.
46. Grueber, *Coins* (1899), pp. xxxix, 101–3, 104.
47. Larkin, *Proclamations*, 1, pp. 135–6; Masson, *Register*, 7, pp. 498–9; Galloway, *Union*, pp. 82–4.
48. Hearne, *Collection*, 1 (1771), pp. 7, 8, 100, 105; ibid., 2, pp. 65, 97; De Coursey, 'Society of Antiquaries', *ODNB*. Cotton nonetheless wrote a manuscript in support of Union and the name Great Britain, SP14/1, fols 7–9^v.
49. Printed in Latin in 1586, *Britannia* was translated into English in 1610.
50. Parker, 'Recasting England', 393–417.
51. *CSPVen*, 10, no. 132; Monipennie, *Certein Matters* (1603); Mason, '1603' (2020), 413–15.
52. Boece, *Scotorum Historia* (1527), reprinted 1574 and 1575; Buchanan, *Rerum Scoticarum Historia* (1582); Knox, *History of the Reformation in Scotland* (published 1587). Robert Lindsay of Pitscottie's history is extant in sixteen manuscripts.
53. Galloway, *Union*, pp. 48, 56–7; BL, Additional MS, 11600, fols 65^r–72^v (not in Galloway).
54. For the rhetorical strategies employed, Peltonen, *Rhetoric* (2013), pp. 149–63.
55. Laing, *Collection* (1833), pp. 48, 59, 14.
56. Ibid., pp. 16, 25.
57. Harbert, *England's Sorrowe* (1606), sig. C3^r.
58. Galloway, *Six Tracts*, p. 144.
59. Thornborough, *Reuniting* (1605?), p. 10 and *Discourse* (1604), sig. B3^r.
60. Cornwallis, *Union* (1604), sig. B3^v (p. 10); SP14/10A, fols 137–56^r. According to one report, when Cornwallis defended the Union proposal in parliament, he did so 'lamely and, although it seem scarce possible so much worse than his book', Kyle, *Theater*, p. 26.
61. [Skinner], *Rapta Tatio*, sigs C4^v–D^r.
62. Harry, *Genealogy* (1604); Colman, 'Arbor Regalis', MS Latin misc a.1; Hunt et al., 'Lyte' (2016), 169–205; Trevisan, *Genealogy*, passim.
63. For example, Gordon, *Happinesse* (1604), pp. 6, 8, 15, 23.
64. Gordon, *Enotikon* (1604), pp. 22–3, 26.
65. Thornborough, *Reuniting*, p. 10.
66. Bacon, *Discourse* (1603), sig. B4$^{r\&v}$; SP14/7, fol. 172^v; Galloway, *Six Tracts*, pp. 39–41, 56–7. Few Unionists treated the union of Aragon and Castile as a full union.

67. BL, Additional MS, 11600, fols 70ʳ–1ᵛ. Portugal was, in fact, conquered by Spain in 1580.
68. SP14/7, fols 194–6ᵛ.
69. BL, Additional MS, 11600, fols 69ᵛ, 72ʳ.
70. Hayward, *Treatise* (1604), pp. 10, 14.
71. Galloway, *Six Tracts*, pp. 165, 186.
72. Hume, *British Union* (2002); Craig, *De Unione* (1909).
73. Hume, *British Union*, pp. 35–7; Williamson, 'Radical Britain' (2006), pp. 55–68 and 'Hume' (2016), pp. 323–46; Ivic, *Britain*, ch. 3; Wijffels, '*Ius Commune?*' (2002), p. 326.
74. Lindley, 'Hume' (1978), 145–7.
75. Perhaps because Craig argued that English and Scottish laws rested on the same feudal principles, James resisted abolishing feudal tenures in the 'great contract' (see ch. 10), Russell, 'British History' (2002), 63.
76. Mason, '1603' (2020), 415–20; Levack, 'Law' (1994), 213–23; Burgess, *Political Thought*, (2009), pp. 153–61; Russell, 'Topsy' (2007), pp. 71–3.
77. SP14/9A, fols 79–80ʳ.
78. SP15/36, fol. 145. One commissioner—Sir Edward Hoby—did not sign the Instrument—because he was not wholeheartedly behind it, Willson, *Bowyer's Diary*, p. 194. See ch. 10.
79. CP189/44.
80. CP134/101; for the new preface, SP14/10B, fol. 1ʳ&ᵛ.
81. Winwood, *Memorials*, 2, p. 46; Burtin, *Ambassades*, 1, pp. 441–2; Healy, 'Precedent' (2018), 156.
82. SP14/21, fols 27ʳ, 34ʳ&ᵛ.
83. See ch. 10.
84. SP14/24, fols 4ʳ, 12–13, 45ᵛ; Willson, *Bowyer's Diary*, pp. 200, 202 note 1; Galloway, *Union*, pp. 98–103.
85. SP14/26, fol. 152–4ʳ; see also HMC, 29, *Portland*, 9, pp. 121–3.
86. *CJ*, 1, pp. 366-8. See ch. 10.
87. Wormald, 'Gunpowder' (1985), 141–68 and 'Brave New World?' (2005), 22–6.
88. SP14/24, fol. 45ᵛ.
89. *CJ*, 1, pp. 333–4; HMC, *Buccleugh*, 3, pp. 101–11.
90. SP14/26, fols 149ʳ–50ʳ; HMC, *Portland*, 9, pp. 122–3.
91. CP134/53; SP14/10A, fol. 95.
92. Galloway, *Six Tracts*, p. 180; Highley, 'Macbeth' (2004), 54.
93. Hayward, *Treatise*, p. 14.
94. Galloway, *Six Tracts*, p. 180. For the sources of Scottish law, Levack, 'Law' (1994), 216–17.
95. BL, Additional MS, 4149, fol. 125ʳ&ᵛ.
96. Galloway, *Union*, p. 99.
97. SP14/21, fols 25ʳ, 27ʳ, 34ʳ&ᵛ; Russell, 'English View' (2003), 151–63.
98. HL, Ellesmere MS, 1215, fols 1ʳ, 2ʳ.
99. Ibid., 1869; CP122/150, 157; *CSPVen*, 11, no. 78.

100. For Bacon's arguments, HL, Ellesmere MS, 1870; Hobart's speech is no longer extant.
101. SP14/34, fols 12–26ᵛ. For the speech of Sir Christopher Yelverton of the king's bench, HL. Ellesmere MS, 1869.
102. Price, 'Natural Law' (1997), 82–3, 85–6, 116, 121, 136; Kanemura, 'Kingship' (2013), 337–9. As London guilds judged nationality by descent not birth, the children of foreigners were deemed aliens until at least the beginning of the next century, Selwood, ' "English-Born" ' (2005), 728–53.
103. My thanks to Malcolm Smuts for referring me to James's policy in Scotland.
104. SP14/19, fol. 1.
105. SP14/6, fol. 130; CP127/156; SP14/48, fol. 107ᵛ; SP14/66, fol. 106ᵛ.
106. Brown, 'Scottish Aristocracy' (1993), 569–72 and 'British Aristocracy' (1995), 223, 224, 227. For a different view, Morrill, 'Dynasties' (2017), pp. 24–6.
107. CP134/116; CP184/84; CP194/29; CP123/100.
108. *CSPVen*, 11, no. 71; Brown, 'Honour' (2012), 44, 66.
109. Winwood, *Memorials*, 3, p. 117.
110. See Appendix 3.
111. Goodare, *Government* (2004), pp. 203–4.
112. Murdoch, *Denmark-Norway*, pp. 36–40.
113. See ch. 12.
114. Morrill prefers 'congruity' to 'conformity' 'British Patriarchy?' (1994), 215–16.
115. Fraser, *Elphinstone*, 2 (1897), p. 150.
116. SP14/23, fol. 15ʳ; Brown, *Kingdom?* (1992), pp. 88–9.
117. Calderwood, *Kirk*, 6, pp. 567–8; Macdonald, *Kirk* (1998), pp. 113–67; Ferrell, *Polemic* (1998), pp. 125–32.
118. Calderwood, *Kirk*, 6, p. 596; BL, Additional MS, 11402, fol. 124ᵛ.
119. Calderwood, *Kirk*, 6, p. 597; *CSPVen*, 10, nos 592, 632; Reid, *Corona* (2020), p. 214.
120. Calderwood, *Kirk*, 6, pp. 681, 735, 778–9.
121. Ibid., 7, pp. 7, 27–9, 38, 42–5.
122. Mullan, *Episcopacy*, p. 110.
123. Stewart, 'Five Articles' (2007), 1013–36.
124. CP147/158.
125. Groundwater, *Middle March* (2010), p. 90.
126. Ibid., pp. 90–1; HMC, *10th Report*, pp. 229–30.
127. Their correspondence makes this obvious, ibid., pp. 230–6; Groundwater, 'Middle Shires' (2014), 23–40.
128. BL, Additional MS, 11402, fol. 129ʳ; Groundwater, *Middle March* (2010), p. 91.
129. CP192/67; Groundwater, 'Patronage Networks' (2007), 882; Schultz, *National* (2019), pp. 63–5, 67.
130. Maidment, *Letters*, p. 172.
131. Masson, *Register*, 8, pp. 37–8; Groundwater, 'Middle Shires' (2014), p. 120; Schultz, *National Identity*, pp. 2, 65.
132. Clapham, *Historie* (1606), pp. 2, 293; Frénéé-Hutchins, *Boudica's Odyssey* (2016), p. 85.

133. Rudston, *Almanacke* (1610), sigs C^r–C4.
134. Ayscu, *Historie* (1607), sig. A3$^{r\&v}$.
135. Ibid., sig. A3^v; Waucheron, 'Imagined Polities' (2013), 593.
136. Speed, *History* (1611); Woolf, *History* (1998), pp. 65–72.
137. For almanacs, Gilchrist, 'Brutan Histories' (2020), 44.
138. Wilkinson, *Isahak's Inheritance* (1603).
139. Munday, *Triumphes* (1605), sigs Bii^v–Biii^v. For other examples of Munday's Anglocentricity, Hill, 'The Triumphes' (2006), 15–33.
140. Drayton, *Poly-Olbion* (1612), pp. 8, 77.
141. Prescott, 'Marginal Discourse' (1991), 307–28. Other 'Brutan' poems include: Heywood, *Troia Nova* (1609); Harbert, *England's Sorrow*; Ross, *Britannica* (1607).
142. Gilchrist, 'Brutan Histories', 58.
143. Forse, 'King Lear' (2014), 53–72. Significant differences between the quarto and folio versions are discussed in Taylor and Warren, *Division* (1987).
144. Kernan, *King's Playwright* (1995), p. 96.
145. Schwyzer, *Literature* (2004), pp. 158–69. For further discussion of the relationship between Union and *King Lear*, Hutson, *Insular Imagining*, pp. 246–8, 249–52, 269–71.
146. *Cymbeline*, pp. 43–9.
147. For the most extended treatment of *Cymbeline*'s close association with Union, Marcus, *Puzzling Shakespeare* (1988), pp. 121–48.
148. *Cymbeline*, Act 5, ll. 454–7, 459, 477–9, 484–8.
149. For its misogyny, Levin, 'Heroic Queens' (2020), 64–7.
150. Beaumont and Fletcher, *Comedies* (1647), Act 4, ll. 22–3, 203, Act 5, ll. 255–6.
151. Heywood, *Apology* (1612), sig. F3^r.
152. Morrow, 'Speaking England' (2006), iii, 38–112.
153. For two other contemporary plays set in Ancient Britain, Marshall, *Theatre* (2000), pp. 59–60, 64–7.
154. Percival-Maxwell, *Scottish Migration* (1999), pp. 50–60; Gillespie, *Ulster* (1985), pp. 87–9; Connolly, *Contested Island* (2008), pp. 289–90.
155. Edwards, 'Political Change' (2018), p. 48; Margey, 'Plantations' (2018), 574.
156. Edwards argues that James's policy was mainly based on security issues, 'Introduction' (2016), p. 5, but I believe that James's 'British' policy was the more important consideration.
157. Edwards, 'Scottish Officials' (2016), 32.
158. Ibid., pp. 30–9, 41.
159. McCavitt, *Chichester* (1998); Canny, *Plantation* (2001), pp. 168–75.
160. Edwards, 'Plight' (2010), pp. 57–8.
161. Canny, *Plantation* (2001), pp. 179–83; McCavitt, *Chichester* (2001), pp. 130–2; Edwards, 'Political Change' (2018), pp. 56–7.
162. HL, Ellesmere MS, 175.
163. McCavitt, '"Mandates Policy"' (1991), 320–35.
164. *CSPIrel, 1603–1606*, pp. 220–1, 548; McCavitt, *Chichester* (2001), pp. 134–5; Edwards, 'Political Change' (2018), pp. 71–2.

165. *CSPIrel, 1603–1606*, pp. 389–90. See also BL, Additional MS, 11402, fols 121ʳ, 125ᵛ–37ʳ.
166. McCavitt, *Flight* (2002), pp. 2, 60–2 and 'Flight' (1994), 159–60, 165.
167. *CSPVen*, 11, no. 11.
168. See all three works by McCavitt.
169. *CSPVen*, 11, nos 93, 127; BL, Additional MS, 11402, fol. 131ʳ; *CSPIrel, 1606–1608*, pp. 540, 654; McCavitt, *Flight*, pp. 96–110; Lennon, 'Diplomacy' (2010), 77–87.
170. *CSPIrel, 1606–1608*, pp. 659, 524–7, 608; McCavitt, *Flight*, pp. 138–46.
171. SP63/232, fol. 155ʳ&ᵛ.
172. Ibid., fol. 155ᵛ; Dunning and Hudson, 'Transportation' (2013), 422–53.
173. Margey, 'Plantations', 573–5.
174. Ohlmeyer, ' "Civilizinge" ' (1998), 140.
175. Ohlmeyer, *Making Ireland English* (2012), pp. 65–6, 184–5.
176. Edwards, 'Introduction' (2016), 6–7.
177. Lynch, ' "Highland Problem" ' (2000), 208–27. For political and financial motives, Lee, 'Government' (1976), 49–50; for cultural, Sommerville, *Writings*, p. 24.
178. MacGregor, 'Civilizing' (2012), 45–7.
179. For Lewis, Robertson, *Lordship*, pp. 37–40.
180. Masson, *Register*, 8, p. 113.
181. Ibid.; *CSPIrel, 1606–1608*, p. 514.
182. SP63/223, fol. 154ʳ.
183. Cathcart, 'Iona' (2010), 4–27.
184. Ibid.; Macgregor, 'Iona' (2006), 111–81.
185. For the failure of this policy, Ohlmeyer, ' "Civilizinge" ' (1998), 144–5.
186. Armitage, *Ideological Origins* (2000), pp. 30–5.
187. Armitage, 'Elizabethan Idea' (2004), 269–77.
188. Gibney, 'Colony?' (2008), 172–82; Canny, 'Ideology' (1998), 179–202.
189. The bibliography on Hakluyt is immense. Important to read are: Mancall, *Hakluyt's Promise* (2007); Sacks, 'Discourses' (2007), 410–53; the essays in Carey and Jowitt, *Travel Writing* (2012); Young, 'Hakluyt's Voyages' (2018), 1057–80.
190. For the lost colonists, Horning, *Virginian Sea* (2013), pp. 125–7.
191. Andrews, *Trade* (1984); MacMillan, 'Exploration' (2011), 646–62.
192. Games, *Web* (2008), pp. 117–18.
193. Fitzmaurice, *Humanism* (2003), p. 61.
194. Johnson, *Nova Britannia* (1609); Crakanthorpe, *Sermon* (1609), sig. D2ʳ&ᵛ; Quitslund, 'Virginia Company' (2004), 43–114.
195. Kupperman, *Jamestown* (2007), pp. 210–328.
196. For the Powhatans, Horning, *Virginian Sea*, pp. 101–75, *passim*.
197. Games, *Web*, pp. 130, 134–5.
198. Lenman, *Colonial Wars* (2001), pp. 227–8.
199. Kupperman, *Jamestown*, pp. 247–9.
200. Games, *Web*, p. 127.
201. Kupperman, *Jamestown*, pp. 255, 257–8.

202. Lenman, *Colonial Wars*, pp. 228–9.
203. For prayers in early 1610, HMC, *Downshire*, 2, p. 259.
204. Ibid., pp. 48–9; Thrush, *Indigenous London* (2016), pp. 42–4. The Powhatans' first official envoy arrived in 1608; others arrived unofficially.
205. Rome, 'Being Human' (2015), 701–19; Fitzmaurice, 'Moral Uncertainty' (2007), 392–3.
206. Montaigne, *Essays*; Shakespeare quoted from it in *The Tempest*, Act 2, Scene 1, ll. 143–52.
207. *Counterblaste* (1604), sigs B^v, D$^{r\&v}$.
208. Anon, *Lotterie* (London, 1612).
209. Crashaw, *Sermon* (1610), sigs C2^r, C3^r, D3$^{r\&v}$.
210. Fitzmaurice, 'Moral Uncertainty', pp. 396–8, 403–9.
211. Jowitt, 'Colonialism' (2003), 485.
212. Marshall, 'The Tempest', 375–400.
213. Lines, 334–46.
214. I owe the point related to Scotland to Malcolm Smuts.
215. Akrigg, *Letters*, p. 226.
216. Braddick, *State Formation* (2000). For a European perspective, Gustafsson, 'Conglomerate State' (1998), 189–213.

CHAPTER 14

1. Manning, 'Jacobean Peace' (2018), 155.
2. Fry, 'Diplomacy', *passim*.
3. Ibid., p. 137.
4. Bodl, Ashmole MS, 1729, fol. 68^v.
5. *CSPVen*, 10, no. 36. It is a hard to sustain the argument that the policy of ending the war 'originated with Sir Robert Cecil rather than James VI and I', as claimed by Manning, 'Jacobean Peace', 154.
6. *CSPVen*, 10, no. 34.
7. Ibid., nos 36, 39.
8. SP84/64, fol. 1^r; CP134/37.
9. SP78/59, fol. 131$^{r\&v}$; *CSPVen*, 10, no. 36.
10. BL, Cotton MS, Caligula E.X, fols 192, 241.
11. SP78/49, fol. 50^r; Berger de Xivrey, *Lettres*, 6, p. 82.
12. Ibid., p. 84; *CSPVen*, 10, no. 81.
13. Ibid., no. 90.
14. Lonchay, *Correspondance*, 1, pp. 139, 141, 142.
15. Ibid., pp. 140, 144.
16. Ibid. For members of the retinue, Marini, 'Diplomacy', pp. 395–7.
17. Quoted in Hussey, 'America' (1956), 40–1.
18. Lonchay, *Correspondance*, 1, p. 145.
19. *CSPVen*, 10, no. 73.
20. CP100/7; Cross, 'Counterbalance' (2012), 61–2.

21. Lonchay, *Correspondance*, 1, p. 139; Borreguero Beltrán, 'Isabel', pp. 262–3.
22. Lonchay, *Correspondance*, 1, pp. 144, 145.
23. Loomie, 'Toleration' (1963), 18–19, 22; Lonchay, *Correspondance*, 1, pp. 154–5, 156–7, 164.
24. Ibid., pp. 150, 152, 154.
25. *CSPVen*, 10, nos 73, 139; Ruiz Fernández, *England and Spain* (2020), pp. 97–8.
26. Ibid., pp. 98, 108–9; Lonchay, *Correspondance*, 1, pp. 152, 153. These were not just one-off payments; the Spanish court kept numerous English pensioners on their books, Carter, 'Gondomar' (1964), 194–7.
27. *CSPVen*, 10, no. 87.
28. Berger de Xivrey, *Lettres*, 6, p. 112.
29. Béthune, *Memoirs*, 3, p. 110.
30. BL, King's MS, 123, fols 123^r, 144^r, 160^r; *CSPVen*, 10, nos 55, 66.
31. *CSPVen*, 10, no. 73.
32. Larkin, *Proclamations*, 1, pp. 30–1.
33. *CSPVen*, 10, no. 96.
34. Andrews, 'Caribbean' (1974), 5–9.
35. SP78/49, fol. 182$^{r\&v}$.
36. Béthune, *Memoirs*, 3, pp. 74–5, 77. See also, BL, King's, MS, 123, fols 212^v–23^v.
37. Béthune, *Memoirs*, 3, pp. 91–6, 105–6.
38. Ibid., pp. 100–3, 112–14; *CSPVen*, 10, nos 87, 90.
39. Schroder doubts the existence of such a project in 1603, *Trust* (2017), pp. 63–9.
40. Béthune, *Memoirs*, 3, pp. 117–30.
41. Cross, 'Counterbalance' (2012), 142; *CSPVen*, 10, no. 87.
42. Smuts, *Political Culture* (2023), p. 550.
43. Leonard, *Recueil* (1693), pp. 1–3; *CSPVen*, 10, no. 124.
44. Béthune, *Memoirs*, 3, pp. 135–8. The terms were soon leaked, *CSPVen*, 10, nos 141, 147, 161, 162; Duerloo, *Dynasty*, p. 170.
45. *CSPVen*, 10, nos 104, 113, 169. For a different view, Smuts, *Culture*, p. 553.
46. Lonchay, *Correspondance*, 1, pp. 152, 158, 162.
47. Jones, 'Journal', p. 244; HMC, *Salisbury*, 15, pp. 47, 86, 121; BL, Cotton MS, Caligula E.X, fol. 205^v; *CSPVen*, 10, no. 90; Lonchay, *Correspondance*, 1, p. 163.
48. See ch. 5.
49. Duerloo, *Dynasty*, p. 168.
50. Ferguson, *Papers* (1899), p. 187; Lonchay, *Correspondance*, 1, pp. 162, 163; Winwood, *Memorials*, 2, pp. 3, 6–7; Bodl., Ashmole MS, 1729, no. 37.
51. Winwood, *Memorials*, 2, pp. 1–2, 3, 6.
52. CP101/131, translated directly from the French.
53. Winwood, *Memorials*, 2, p. 3.
54. CP187/111, 101/156; *CSPVen*, 10, no. 142; Winwood, *Memorials*, 2, pp. 7–8; Jones, 'Journal', 246.
55. *CSPVen*, 10, no. 142; Winwood, *Memorials*, 2, p. 7.
56. Lonchay, *Correspondance*, 1, p. 160.
57. For the Elizabethan debate, Gajda, 'Debating' (2009), 851–78.

58. 'Considerations Touchinge the Peace', of which there are many copies including BL, Stowe MS, 164, fols 86^r–9^r and Harley MS, 6798, fols 76^r–9^r, 197^r.
59. Anti-peace pamphlets include: John Atkinson, 'A Discourse', Folger, G.a.1, fols 17^r–19^v, 20^r–59^r; ibid., G.b.8, fols 43^r–8^v BL, Additional MS, 34219, fols 1^r–10^v; SP14/2, fols 64^r–72^r; Robert Cotton, 'Discourse', addressed to Lord Henry Howard, BL, Cotton MS, Vespasian C.XIII, fols 158^r–9^r, 160^r–2^r; 'A Discours written by John Askham', BL, Harley MS, 168, nos 115, 117; Walter Ralegh, BL, Cotton MS, Vespasian C.XIII, fols 307^r–11^v; Mackie, 'Advertisment', 1–2.
60. *CSPVen*, 10, no. 230; Thrush, 'Hoby' (2004), 303.
61. Cross, 'Counterbalance' (2012), 202–16; SP94/9, fol. 168^r.
62. SP14/3, fol. 139.
63. CP190/12.
64. SP14/4, fol. 146$^{r\&v}$. For Alabaster's interests, Andrews, 'Caribbean' (1974), 6.
65. SP94/9, fol. 50.
66. *CSPVen*, 10, no. 191.
67. See ch. 8; Cano-Echevarria, 'Between Courts' (2012), 94–5.
68. Quoted in Allen, 'Strategy' (1995), 272 and *Pax Hispanica* (2000), p. 129.
69. Winwood, *Memorials*, 2, pp. 18, 20; SP94/10, fols 11–12^r; Cross, 'Counterbalance' (2012), 173–4, 182–7.
70. SP94/10, fols 13^r, 16^r.
71. Allen, 'Strategy' (1995), 276–8 and *Pax Hispanica* (2000), pp. 131–4.
72. CUL, Dd.9.3. fol. 1^r.
73. Ibid., fol. 17^v; SP94/10, fol. 67^r; Andrews, 'Caribbean' (1974), 6–8, 11.
74. SP94/10, fol. 17$^{r\&v}$; BL, Cotton MS, Vespasian C.XIII, fol. 81.
75. Like Robert Cross, I disagree with Croft who maintained that James 'had surprisingly little to do with the final negotiations for peace with Spain' and was 'conspicuous by his absence', in '"Rex Pacificus"' (2006), pp. 140, 149.
76. Allen, *Pax*, pp. 280–1.
77. CUL, Dd.9.3., fols 13^v–14^r. Cross deals fully with this issue, 'Counterbalance' (2012), 265–9. Croft gives Cecil credit for the breakthrough, '"Rex Pacificus"' (2006), pp. 150–1.
78. *CSPVen*, 10, no. 229.
79. Ibid., no. 233.
80. Winwood, *Memorials*, 2, p. 22; SP94/10, fol. 61; CUL, Dd.9.3., fols 14^v–25^v.
81. Lonchay, *Correspondance*, 1, pp. 174, 175.
82. The terms of the agreement, BL, Cotton MS, Vespasian C.XIII, fols 33–42^v.
83. The debt was estimated as £812,000 in 1604.
84. SP84/64, fol. 161$^{r\&v}$.
85. Anderson, *Diplomatic Representatives* (2007), pp. 150–1.
86. SP84/64, fol. 162^r; SP94/10, fols 54$^{r\&v}$, 55^r.
87. CUL, Dd.9.3., fol. 39$^{r\&v}$.
88. Ibid., fols 21^v, 27^r–8^v; Andrews, 'Caribbean' (1974), 12–13.
89. Jones, 'Journal', 253, 254.
90. SP94/10, fols 93, 95; Velasco, *Relación* (1604), pp. 24–35.

91. Winwood, *Memorials*, 2, p. 29; Whatley, *General Collection* (1732), 2, pp. 131–46. This article was not in the main body of the treaty but attached to it afterwards.
92. Loomie, 'Toleration' (1963), p. 36.
93. For the articles, dated 18 Aug., BL, Cotton MS, Vespasian C.XIII, fols 2–4^r and Anon, *Articles* (1605), sig. F3$^{r\&v}$.
94. Velasco, *La Jornada*, p. 36.
95. Ibid., pp. 36–47; for an English translation, Rye, *England* (1865), pp. 117–24; *CSPVen*, 10, no. 266.
96. CP106/77; *CSPVen*, 10, no. 266.
97. Velasco, *La Jornada*, pp. 47–8; *CSPVen*, 10, no. 267.
98. Winwood, *Memorials*, 2, p. 23.
99. Ibid., 2, pp. 30, 32.
100. SP78/51, fol. 231^v; CP110/137; Berger de Xivrey, *Lettres*, 6, pp. 143, 180–2.
101. SP78/51, fol. 246; SP94/10, fol. 107; Berger de Xivrey, *Lettres*, 6, pp. 281–2.
102. Laffleur de Kermaingant, *Mission de Harlay* (1895), 2, p. 283.
103. *CSPVen*, 10, no. 288; SP78/52 fol. 3^r.
104. CP29/83.
105. SP78/52, fols 1^v, 3^r.
106. *CSPVen*, 10, nos 343, 345, 359; SP78/52, fols 20^r–1^v, 24^v–5; 54$^{r\&v}$; Berger de Xivrey, *Lettres*, 6, pp. 357–60; CP Petitions 1343.
107. Winwood, *Memorials*, 3, pp. 48–9.
108. Bacon was one example, Zeitlin, 'Bacon' (2020), 498.
109. Ibid., 497–8.
110. Winwood, *Memorials*, 2, p. 75.
111. SP77/7, fol. 149; SP77/8/1, fol. 207^r; BL, Additional MS, 11402, fol. 97^r.
112. Sir John Holles and Sir Edward Hoby attended upon Hertford, SP77/7, fol. 130.
113. Ibid., fol. 126^r.
114. SP79/8/1, fol. 207^r; SP79/7, fol. 103^v.
115. SP77/7, fols 153, 163^r; CP227/1, 6. See also, HMC, *Portland*, 9, pp. 94–8, for an account very critical of Hertford but also impressed with the 'most magnificent triumphs, masques, and balls'.
116. SP77/8/1, fols 207–9; SP77/7, fols 102–5.
117. Duerloo, *Dynasty*, pp. 176–7.
118. Cross, 'Counterbalance' (2012), 354–60.
119. Ibid., 367–70. SP94/11, fols 79^r, 106^r, 132^v.
120. Cano-Echevarría, 'Between Courts' (2012), 96–7.
121. SP94/11, fols 124, 128, 134^v.
122. Ibid., fol. 139; Anon, *Royal Entertainement*, pp. 18–19; HMC, *Downshire*, 2, pp. 423–4; Ruiz Fernández, *England and Spain*, p. 106.
123. SP94/11, fols 106^v–8^r; *CSPVen*, 10, no. 396; Bickley, *Gawdy Letters*, p. 157.
124. Cano-Echevarría, 'Between Courts' (2012), 98–100.
125. Winwood, *Memorials*, pp. 69–71, 72; *CSPVen*, 10, no. 383; BL, Cotton MS, Vespasian C.IX, fols 17^v–18. SP94/11, fols 108^v–9^r, 98–100^r, 121; HMC, *Salisbury*, 17, p. 229 (Spanish Version).

126. Anon, *Royal Entertainement*, p. 11.
127. CP110/69.
128. SP 94/11, fols 133ᵛ, 134; Treswell, *A Relation*, pp. 37–8.
129. Cross, 'Counterbalance' (2012), 396–7; *CSPVen*, 10, no. 411.
130. Loomie, 'Toleration' (1963), 43–4; Anon, *Royal Entertainment*, p. 11.
131. *CSPVen*, 10, nos 411, 426; Winwood, *Memorials*, 2, p. 92.
132. Trim, ' "Jacob's Warres" ', 238, 244.
133. SP84/64, fols 197–9; Winwood, *Memorials*, 2, pp. 33, 34; Grayson, 'Anglo-Dutch Relations' (1978), p. 83.
134. Ibid., p. 301.
135. Anderson, *Diplomatic Representatives* (2007), pp. 189–94.
136. McAllister, 'Winwood' (1983), 41–2, 44, 53–4.
137. CP103/91; SP84/64, fol. 230.
138. Winwood, *Memorials*, 3, p. 3; Anderson, *Diplomatic Representatives*, pp. 92, 102.
139. *CSPVen*, 10, nos 374, 404, 436.
140. Ibid., 436; HMC, *Downshire*, 2, p. 429.
141. Article 12, 3 Jas I *c*.4, *Statutes*, 4 prt 2, p. 1074; CP227 p. 180; Croft, 'Serving the Archduke' (1991), 298–304.
142. Winwood, *Memorials*, 2, p. 286.
143. For this and the next paragraph, Senior, *Pirates* (1976), pp. 7–11, 13–14, 43; Appleby, 'Problem' (2006), pp. 41–55 and 'Jacobean Piracy' (2012), pp. 277–300; Hebb, *Piracy* (1994), pp. 7–20.
144. *CSPVen*, 10, nos 146, 181, 208.
145. Brown, *Genesis*, 1 (1890), pp. 91, 121.
146. Ibid., pp. 120–2.
147. CP120/63, 90 (2); CP125/154; Brown, *Genesis*, 1 (1890), pp. 100, 102, 126–7, 144; Goldman, 'Spain' (2011), 427–50.
148. SP94/16, fol. 161ᵛ.
149. Goldman, 'Spain', 448; HMC, *Portland*, 9, p. 107.
150. Flynn, 'Atlantic Politics' (2018), 109–23.
151. Croft, 'Inquisition', (1972), 263.
152. CP206/29; CP120/63; HL, Ellesmere MS, 1626; BL, Additional MS, 11402, fols 120ʳ, 123ʳ; a 1607 petition, SP14/26, fol. 127.
153. HMC, *Downshire*, 2, p. 12; BL, Additional MS, 11402, fol. 119ʳ.
154. *CSPVen*, 10, no. 718; 26 Mar., *CJ*, 1, pp. 354–5; Willson, *Bowyer's Diary*, p. 293. For details, Peck, 'Merchant Grievances' (1981), 537–41.
155. CP227/267, p. 276; Peck, 'Merchant Grievances', 538.
156. BL, Additional MS, 11402, fols 131ʳ–2ᵛ.
157. CP120/63; HMC, *Salisbury*, 19, p. 168.
158. CP227, p. 221; Duerloo, *Dynasty*, pp. 180–3.
159. CP227, pp. 292, 341; *CSPVen*, 11, no. 168. See ch. 13.
160. SP63/222, fol. 266; CP227, pp. 319–21.
161. Burtin, *Ambassades*, 1, pp. 84–8.
162. *CSPVen*, 10, no. 721.

163. Ibid., no. 716; Winwood, *Memorials*, 2, p. 305.
164. HMC, *Downshire*, 2, p. 26; Lee, *James and Henri* (1970), pp. 71–141.
165. *CSPVen*, 11, no. 31.
166. Ibid., 10, no. 727; Duerloo, 'Hawks' (2017), 165.
167. *CSPVen*, 11, no. 34.
168. CP128/86; *CSPVen*, 11, no. 36; Burtin, *Ambassades*, 1, pp. 175–6. Privy councillors felt the same way, BL, Lansdowne MS, 160, fols 112–15^v.
169. CP227, p. 294; Burtin, *Ambassades*, 1, p. 258.
170. Winwood, *Memorials*, 2, pp. 329–35.
171. *CSPVen*, 11, no. 36; HMC, *De Lisle*, 3, p. 396.
172. *CSPVen*, 11, no. 43.
173. Winwood, *Memorials*, 2, p. 358.
174. Birch, *Historical View* (1749), pp. 274–5.
175. Winwood, *Memorials*, 2, pp. 309–10.
176. HMC, *De L'Isle*, 4, pp. 5–6.
177. Rymer and Sanderson, *Foedera*, 16 (1727), pp. 672–3; Winwood, *Memorials*, 2, p. 409. I disagree with Simon Adams who wrote that the treaty was '*correctly* [my italics] interpreted as a sign of weakness', 'Protestant Cause' (1973), p. 163.
178. Winwood, *Memorials*, 2, p. 406, 411–12; HMC, *Salisbury*, 20, p. 212.
179. Winwood, *Memorials*, 2, pp. 406, 410. For James's book, ch. 12.
180. For the marriage alliance, Gough, 'Dynastic Marriage' (2018), pp. 291–8.
181. HMC, *Downshire*, 2, p. 23, Winwood, *Memorials*, 3, p. 59.
182. Jeannon and Winwood did not always work together co-operatively on this joint endeavour, Birch, *Negotiations*, pp. 285–6.
183. SP14/43, fol. 17^v.
184. *CSPVen*, 11, no. 204.
185. CP94/4.
186. The usually given date of 9 Apr. is new style, according to the Gregorian Calendar then in use in the Spanish Netherlands.
187. BM, 1864,0813.3; Helmers, 'Public Diplomacy' (2016), 405.
188. The Dutch assented, and two more conferences took place over the next couple of years, but it was the archdukes who lost out, Vermeir and Roggeman, 'Implementing the Truce' (2010), 817–33.
189. BM, G3, FD.169; Grueber, *English Medals*, p. 10.
190. *Articles* (London, 1609).
191. Grimeston, *Low-Country Common Wealth* (1609).
192. Anderson, *Verge of War* (1999), pp. 18–19, 21–47.
193. SP78/55, fol. 153^r; Winwood, *Memorials*, 3, p. 59.
194. SP78/56, fols 1^r, 7^r–8^r; HMC, *Downshire*, 3, p. 253.
195. Anderson, *Verge of War*, pp. 51–8, 74–8, 81–2, 95–8. For a different view of Henry's motives, Adams, 'The Protestant Cause', p. 167.
196. Winwood, *Memorials*, 3, pp. 19–30, 33, 42, 43–4.
197. Ibid., 3, pp. 53–4, 59.
198. Ibid., p. 57; *CSPVen*, 11, no. 778.

199. HMC, *Downshire*, 2, p. 236. James insisted that two-thirds of the soldiers be English and one-third be Scots.
200. *CSPVen*, 11, nos 821, 856.
201. Winwood, *Memorials*, 3, pp. 112–15, 126–8, 140.
202. Ibid., pp. 153–4; *CSPVen*, 11, nos 894, 897.
203. HMC, *Downshire*, 2, pp. 270, 280, 286; *CSPVen*, 11, nos 838, 857; Lee, *James and Henri* (1970), pp. 161–7. The debt was not paid until 1613.
204. *CSPVen*, 11, nos 906, 936.
205. Anderson, *Verge of War*.
206. *CSPVen*, 12, no. 34; HL, Ellesmere MS, 1646.
207. See for example St Peter's church, Kimberley, Norfolk.
208. BM, 1844,0425.24.
209. This view is shared with and influenced by Smuts, 'Theological Polemics' (2020), 515–50.

CONCLUSION

1. I am grateful to Professor Norman Jones who informed me about the origin of the phrase 'regime change'.
2. For a brief account of the historiography, Smith, 'Politics' (2003), pp. 233–4, 236.
3. Rickard, 'Writings' (2012), 654–64. James's plan to do the same with his devotional works and poetry was never realized.
4. Sharpe, 'King's Writ' (1994), 118.
5. I want to thank Paulina Kewes for discussing this with me.
6. I differ here from Glenn Burgess who argues that in James's reign (unlike Charles's) disagreements arising from self-interest and faction probably 'formed the vast bulk of political disputes', see *Ancient Constitution* (1992), pp. 168–9.
7. Alan R. Macdonald points to the 'consultative decision making' processes in Scotland before 1603 and to the 'sudden reduction in formal consultation' there, after that date. See 'Consultation, Counsel' (2016), pp. 195–204.
8. CP134/48; CP104/48.
9. On James wanting to win any argument, see Lake, '"Free Speech"' (2021), pp. 77–8.
10. Burgess, *Ancient Constitution*; Cromartie, *Constitutionalist Revolution*, chs 6 and 7; and all the works of Johann Sommerville listed in the bibliography. For an especially nuanced approach, Condren, *Argument*, pp. 276–81.
11. Bourdin, *Theological-Political Origins*, pp. 82–90; Sommerville, 'Political Ideas' (1996), 168–72, 188–9.
12. For the relationship between James and Bodin, Evrigenis, 'Sovereignty' (2019), 1073–88.
13. Cromartie, *Constitutionalist Revolution*, pp. 151–4.
14. Evrigenis, 'Sovereignty', 1073–4.
15. Brooks, *Law* (2008), pp. 139–41.
16. Hampson, 'Richard Cosin' (1997), 237.

17. Brooks, *Law* (2008), p. 142.
18. Ibid., pp. 132–5 and *Lawyers* (1998), pp. 224–6.
19. Brooks, *Law* (2008), p. 153.
20. Nenner, *Succession* (1995), *passim*. Paulina Kewes explores the controversies over the Tudor succession question in her forthcoming book *Contesting the Royal Succession*.
21. Kewes, 'Titus Andronicus' (2016), 554.
22. *Macbeth,* Act 4, Scene 3, l. 104; Act 3, Scene 6, l. 25.
23. Smuts, 'Banquo's Progeny' (2008), pp. 226–8; Bezio, *Staging Power*, pp. 171–9.
24. Sharpe, *Image Wars* (2010), pp. 58–117.
25. See for example Freshfield, *Account Books* (1895), pp. 6, 14, 20, 27, 29, 34. Payment for bell ringing was not recorded every year.
26. Barlow, *Summe*, pp. 39, 40.
27. Abbott, *Letter* (1622), sig. A2^v.
28. Shagan, 'English Inquisition' (2004), 541–65.
29. This definition is proposed in Racaut and Ryrie, 'Introduction' (2005), p. 5. For James's moderation, see Questier, *Dynastic Politics* (2009), ch. 5 *passim*.
30. Hoskins, 'Harvest Fluctuations', 32, 46.
31. Sharp, *Famine* (2016), p. 215.

Select Bibliography of Works Cited in Notes

MANUSCRIPTS

Bodleian Library
Ashmole MSS: 830, 1729
MS Bodley: 165
Carte MSS: 74, 77, 80, 205
MS Latin misc a.1
Rawlinson MSS: B.40, B.151, C.929
Tanner MSS: 73, 75, 168, 286, 309, 338
Willis MS: 58

British Library
Additional MSS: 4149, 4274, 4712, 8978, 11402, 11600, 12497, 15227, 15476, 15649, 18591, 21203, 22601, 22621, 22848, 22925, 22958, 23723, 28571, 29546, 33051, 34218, 35324, 38138, 38492, 39829, 39853, 48044, 48116, 58833, 89698
Cotton MSS: Caligula, B.X, C.X, D.I, D.II, E.X, E.XII; Cleopatra F.II; Galba E.I; Julius C.III, F.VI; Titus B.VIII, C.VI, C.VII, F.IV; Vespasian C.XIII, C.IX, F.III
Egerton MSS: 2651, 2877
Harley MSS: 39, 157, 168, 280, 589, 595, 677, 3791, 6798, 6986, 7007
King's MS: 123
Lansdowne MSS: 88, 90, 156, 160, 168, 266, 512, 1172
Royal MSS: 17B, 18A
Sloane MSS: 271, 272, 1435, 1786, 1856
Stowe MSS: 150, 164, 180, 396

Cambridge University Library
Add, 22, 27, 335, 336, 739.2, 4499, 9276, 9277
Dd.1.26, Dd.2.25, Dd.9.3; Ee.2.32, Gg.5.18, Ll.4.8, Mm.4.24
GBR/0012/MS Add

Folger Library, Washington
G.a.1, G.b.8, L.d.915, V.a.605, V.b.232, V.b.142, X.c.43, X.d.291, X.d.426, X.d.428, X.d.541, X.d.587, Z.e.1, 28

Hatfield House
CP (The Cecil Papers online)

558 SELECT BIBLIOGRAPHY OF WORKS CITED IN NOTES

Huntington Library, San Marino, California
Ellesmere MSS (Egerton Family)
Hastings MSS, HAP (Personal and Family)
Hastings MSS, HM

Medici Archive Project
4184, bia.medici.org

National Archives, Kew
State Papers Online: SP12 (Domestic, Elizabeth); SP14 (Domestic, James); SP15 (Domestic Addenda); SP46 (Domestic Supplementary); SP52 (Scotland, Elizabeth); SP63 (Ireland); SP75 (Denmark); SP77 (Flanders); SP78 (France); SP81; SP84 (Holland); SP94 (Spain); SP99 (Venice)
E30/1705 (Exchequer)
LC 2/4/4 (Lord Chamberlain's Department)
PROB 11/89/148; 11/113/77; 11/119/598 (Wills and Probate)
SC13/N4 (Seals)
STAC 2/248/2 (Star Chamber)

National Library of Scotland
Advocates MSS: 28.3.12; 33.1.1 vols 1 & 2; 33.1.5 (19) Missing but in calendar. 33.1.7 (21); 33.1.7 (21, 22); 33.1.9. (26); 33.1.10 (27); 33.1.11 (28); 33.1.13 (30); 33.1.14 (31); 33.1.15 (32); 33.7.19; 35.4.2 vol. 2; 35.5.3 (3); 80.1.1; 81.1.4.
MS 2063; 2064; 2517; 5444; 5831

National Record Office Scotland
GD1/212, 124/10, GD205/1
RH14/3

Material Objects
British Museum: Coins, Medals
The Hunterian Coin Collection, University of Glasgow: GLAHM—medals

PRINTED PRIMARY SOURCES

Abbott, George. *The King's Majestie's Letter to the Lords Grace of Canterbury, Touching Preaching, and Preachers* (London, 1622).
Agar, Ben. *King James, his Apopthegmes, or Table Talk* (London, 1643).
Akkerman, Nadine (ed.). *The Correspondence of Elizabeth Stuart: Queen of Bohemia, Volume 1, 1603–1631* (Oxford, 2015).
Akrigg, G. P. V., *Letters of King James VI & I* (Berkeley, CA, 1984).
Allot, Robert, *England's Parnassus or, The Choysest Flowers of our Moderne Poets* . . . (London, 1600).
Allson, Richard. *An Howre's Recreation in Musicke* (London, 1606).

Anon. *The Joyfull Receiving of James the Sixt of That Name King of Scotland, and Queene Anne his Wife, into the Townes of Lyeth and Edenborough the First Daie of May Last Past. 1590* (London, 1590).

Anon. *Newes from Scotland, Declaring the Damnable Life and Death of Doctor Fian* (London, 1591).

Anon. *A Mournefull Dittie, Entituled Elizabeth's Losse Together with a Welcome for King James. To a Pleasant New Tune* (London, 1603?).

Anon. *A New Song to the Great Comfort and Rejoycing of All True English Harts at Our Most Gracious King James, His Proclamation Upon the 24 of March Last Past in the Cittie of London to the Tune of England's Pride is Gone* (London, 1603).

Anon. *An Excellent New Ballad, Shewing the Petigree of Our Royall King James the First of That Name in England* (London, 1603).

Anon. *England's Wedding Garment. Or A Preparation to King James His Royall Coronation* (London, 1603).

Anon. *Queene El'zabeths Losse, and King James his Welcome* (London, 1603).

Anon. *The Copie of a Letter Written from Master C.S. Neere Salisbury, to Master H.A. at London, Concerning the Proceeding at Winchester...* (London, 1603).

Anon. *The Poores' Lamentation for the Death of Our Late Dread Soveraigne the High and Mightie Princesse Elizabeth... With their Prayers to God for the High and Mightie Prince James* (London, 1603).

Anon. *Weepe with Joy a Lamentation for the Losse of Our Late Soveraigne Lady Queene Elizabeth, with Joy and Exultation for Our High and Mightie Prince, King James, her Lineall and Lawful Successor* (London, 1603).

Anon. *Northerne Poems Congratulating the Kings Majestie's Entrance to the Crowne* (London, 1604).

Anon. *Articles of Peace, Entercourse and Commerce Concluded... In a Treatie at London the 18. Day of August After the Old Stile in the Yeere of our Lord God 1604* (London, 1605).

Anon. *Certaine Considerations Drawne from the Canons of the Last Sinod, and Other the King's Ecclesiasticall and Statue Law... For Not Subscription, For the Not Exact Use of the Order and Forme of the Booke of Common Prayer...* (Middleburg, 1605).

Anon. *His Majesties' Speech in This Last Session of Parliament as Neere His Very Words as Could Be Gathered at the Instant. Together with a Discourse of the Maner of the Discovery of This Late Intended Treason, Joyned with the Examination of Some of the Prisoners* (London, 1605).

Anon. *The Royal Entertainement of the Right Honourable the Earl of Nottingham Sent Ambassador from his Majestie to the King of Spaine* (London, 1605).

Anon. *To the Kinge's Most Excellent Majestie the Humble Petition of Two and Twentie Preachers in London and the Suburbs Thereof* (London, 1605).

Anon. *A True and Perfect Relation of the Whole Proceedings Against the Late Most Barbarous Traitors, Garnet a Jesuite, and His Confederats Contayning Sundry Speeches Delivered by the Lords Commissioners at Their Arraignments...* (London, 1606).

Anon. *A True Report of the Arraignement and Execution of the Late Traytors* (London, 1606).

Anon. *Certaine Arguments to Perswade and Provoke the Most Honorable and High Court of Parliament Now Assembled... to Promote and Advance the Sincere Ministery of the*

Gospel; as Also Zealously to Speake For the Ministers Therof Now Degraded, Deprived, Silenced, or Admonished, or Afterward Like to be Called Into Question, For Subscription, Ceremonyes, Strict Observation of the Booke of Common Prayer, or For Other Conformitie (William Jones's secret press, 1606).

Anon. *Prayers and Thanksgiving to be Used by All the Kings Majestie's Loving Subjects, For the Happy Deliverance of his Majestie, the Queene, Prince, and States of Parliament, From the Most Traiterous and Bloody Intended Massacre by Gunpowder, the 5 of November 1605* (London, 1606).

Anon. *The King of Denmarke's Welcome Containing his Arivall, Abode, and Entertainement, both in the Citie and Other Places* (London, 1606).

Anon. *The Remoovall of Certaine Imputations Laid Upon the Ministers of Devon: and Cornwall* ([Middleburg], 1606).

Anon. *The Shamefull Downefall of the Pope's Kingdome Contayning the Life and Death of Steeven [sic] Garnet, the Popes Chiefe Priest in England: Being Executed in Paules Church-yard in London the 3. of May Last. 1606* (London, 1606).

Anon. *The Argument of Master Nicholas Fuller, in the Case of Thomas Lad, and Richard Maunsell, his Clients Wherein it is Plainely Proved, that the Ecclesiasticall Commissioners Have No Power, by Vertue of their Commission, to Imprison, To Put to the Oath Ex Officio* (London, 1607).

Anon. *The Order and Solemnitie of the Creation of the High and Mightie Prince Henrie* (London, 1610).

Anon. *London's Lotterie with an Incouragement to the Furtherance Thereof for the Good of Virginia, and the Benefite of this Our Native Countrie, Wishing Good Fortune to All That Venture in the Same[.] To the Tune of Lusty Gallant* (London, 1612).

Anon. *An Abridgement of that Booke which the Ministers of Lincoln Diocese Delivered to his Majestie Upon the First of December 1605* (Leiden, 1617).

Anon [W.H.]. *The True Picture and Relation of Prince Henry his Noble and Vertuous Disposition...* (Leyden, 1634).

Anon. *An Abstract or Brief Declaration of the Present State of His Majestie's Revenew, with the Assignations and Defalcations upon the Same* (London, 1651).

Anon. *The Ceremonies, Form of Prayer and Services used in Westminster Abbey at the Coronation of King James I* (London, 1685).

Aubrey, John. *Aubrey's Brief Lives*, edited by Oliver Lawson Dick (reprint, London, 1987).

Ayscu, Edward. *A Historie Contayning the Warres, Treaties, Marriages, and Other Occurrents Betweene England and Scotland, From King William the Conqueror* (London, 1607).

Aytoun, Sir Robert. *The Poems of Sir Robert Aytoun*, edited by Charles Roger (Edinburgh, 1844).

Bacon, Francis. *A Briefe Discourse* (London, 1603).

Bacon, Francis. *The Letters and Life of Francis Bacon*. Electronic Edition, vol. 3 (Charlottesville, VA, 1998).

Baildon, William Paley (ed.). *Les Reportes des Cases in Camera Stellata: From the Original MS of John Hawarde* (London, 1894).

SELECT BIBLIOGRAPHY OF WORKS CITED IN NOTES 561

Barlow, William. *The Summe and Substance of the Conference Which, It Pleased his Excellent Majestie to Have . . . at Hampton Court. January 14. 1603* (London, 1604).
Barlow, William. *The Sermon Preached at Paule's Crosse, the Tenth Day of Nouember Being the Next Sunday After the Discoverie of This Late Horrible Treason* (London, 1606).
Barlow, William. *The Eagle and the Body Described in One Sermon Preached before Queene Elizabeth of Precious Memorie, in Lent. Anno 1601* (London, 1609).
Barnes, Barnabe. *The Divil's Charter* (London, 1607).
Barton, Thomas F. *The 'Registrum Vagum' of Anthony Harrison. Part I*, Norfolk Record Society Publications, 32 (1963).
Barton, Thomas F. *The 'Registrum Vagum' of Anthony Harrison. Part 2*, Norfolk Record Society Publications, 33 (1964).
Basse, William. *A Helpe to Discourse* (London, 1619).
Beaumont, Francis and John Fletcher. *Comedies and Tragedies* (London, 1647).
Bellany, Alistair and Andrew McRae (eds). *Early Stuart Libels: An Edition of Poetry from Manuscript Sources*, http://www.earlystuartlibels.net/ [accessed 20 September 2022].
Berger de Xivrey, Jules. *Recueil de Lettres Missives de Henri IV*, tome 6 (Paris, 1853).
Béthune, Maximilien de and Charlotte Lennox (eds). *The Memoirs of the Duke of Sully, Prime-Minister to Henry the Great*, vol. 3 (London, 1810).
Bickley, Frances B. and Isaac Herbert Jeayes (eds). *Letters of Philip Gawdy of West Harling, Norfolk, and of London to Various Members of his Family, 1579–1616*. Roxburghe Club (London, 1906).
Bilson, Thomas. *The True Difference Between Christian Subjection and Unchristian Rebellion* (London, 1585).
Bilson, Thomas. *A Sermon Preached at Westminster Before the King and Queene's Majesties, at Their Coronations on Saint James his Day, Being 28* [sic] *July* (London, 1603).
Birch, Thomas. *An Historical View of the Negotiations Between the Courts of England, France, and Brussels from the year 1592–1617: Extracted Chiefly from the MS. State Papers of Sir Thomas Edmondes . . . and of Anthony Bacon . . .* (London, 1749).
Birch, Thomas. *The Life of Henry, Prince of Wales, Eldest Son of King James I* (Dublin, 1760).
Birch, Thomas (ed.). *The Court and Times of James the First*, 2 vols (London, 1848).
Blague, Thomas. *A Sermon Preached at the Charterhouse Before the King's Majestie, on Tuesday, the Tenth of May* (London, 1603).
Bradley, E. T. (ed.). *Life of the Lady Arbella Stuart*, Part 2 (London, 1889).
Bradshaw, William. *A Consideration of Certaine Positions Archiepiscopall* (William Jones's secret press, 1605).
Bradshaw, William. *A Protestation of the King's Supremacie Made in the Name of the Afflicted Ministers, and Opposed to the Shamefull Calumniations of the Prelates* (William Jones's secret press, 1605).
Bradshaw, William. *The Unreasonablenesse of the Separation* (Dort, 1614).
Braunmuller, A. R. *A Seventeenth-Century Letter-Book: A Facsimile of Folger MS V.a.321* (Newark, London, and Toronto, 1983).
Bray, Gerard (ed.). *Anglican Canons, 1529–1947* (Woodbridge, 1998).

Bridges, John (ed.). *The History and Antiquities of Northamptonshire*, vol. 2 (Oxford, 1791).
British Printed Images to 1700, https:bpi1700.org.uk
Brown, Alexander. *The Genesis of the United States*, vol. 1 (Boston, MA, 1890).
Bruce, John. *Letters of Queen Elizabeth and King James VI. of Scotland*, Camden Society, 46 (London, 1849).
Bruce, John. *Correspondence of King James VI of Scotland with Sir Robert Cecil and Others in England, During the Reign of Queen Elizabeth: With an Appendix Containing Papers Illustrative of Transactions Between King James and Robert Earl of Essex...*, Camden Society, 78 (London, 1861).
Buchanan, Colin (ed.). *The Hampton Court Conference and the 1604 Book of Common Prayer* (np, 2009).
Burrage, Champlin. *Early English Dissenters in the Light of Recent Research 1550–1641: Vol. 2, Illustrative Documents* (Cambridge, 1912).
Burtin, Paul Denis (ed.). *Ambassades de Monsieur de la Boderie, en Angleterre Sous La Règne d'Henri IV et La Minorité de Louis XIII (1605–11)*, vols 1–4 (Paris, 1750).
Calderwood, David. *History of the Kirk of Scotland*, vols 4–6 (Edinburgh, 1843–45).
Calendar of Border Papers, Volume 1: 1560–95, edited by Joseph Bain (London, 1894), British History Online, http://www.british-history.ac.uk/cal-border-papers/vol1 [accessed 15 June 2021].
Calendar of the Carew Manuscripts: Preserved in the Archiepiscopal Library at Lambeth, edited by J. S. Brewer, William Bullen, vol. 5 (London, 1873).
Calendar of State Papers Domestic: James I, 1603–1610, 1611–18, 1623–25, edited by Mary Anne Everett Green (London, 1857), British History Online, http://www.british-history.ac.uk/cal-state-papers/domestic/jas1/1603-10 [accessed 16 September 2022].
Calendar of State Papers, Ireland, 1603–1606 and 1606–1608, edited by C. W. Russell and John P. Prendergast (London, 1872, 1874), British History Online, http://www.british-history.ac.uk/cal-state-papers/ireland [accessed 16 September 2022].
Calendar of State Papers, Scotland, Volume 10: 1589–1593, edited by William K. Boyd and Henry W. Meikle (Edinburgh, 1936), British History Online, http://www.british-history.ac.uk/cal-state-papers/scotland/vol10 [accessed 16 September 2022].
Calendar of State Papers Relating To English Affairs in the Archives of Venice, Volume 10: 1603–1607, Volume 11: 1607–1610, Volume 12: 1610–1613, edited by Horatio F. Brown (London, 1900, 1904), British History Online, http://www.british-history.ac.uk/cal-state-papers/venice/vol10/vol11/vol12 [accessed 16 September 2022].
Camden, William. *Remaines of a Greater Worke, Concerning Britaine* (London, 1605 & 1614).
Cameron, Annie I. and Robert S. Rait (eds). *The Warrender Papers*, vol. 2 (Edinburgh, 1932).
Cano-Echevarria, Berta and Mark Hutchings. 'The Spanish Ambassador and Samuel Daniel's Vision of the Twelve Goddesses: A New Document', *English Literary Renaissance*, 24 (2012), 223–57.
Cano-Echevarria, Berta and Mark Hutchings. 'Between Courts: Female Masquers and Anglo-Spanish Diplomacy, 1603–5', *Early Theatre*, 15 (2012), 91–108.

Cardwell, Edward. *Documentary Annals of the Reformed Church of England*, vol. 2 (Oxford, 1839).
Cardwell, Edward. *Synodalia: A Collection of Articles of Religion, Canons, and Proceedings of Convocations in the Province of Canterbury, from the Year 1547 to the Year 1717*, 2 vols (Oxford, 1842).
Cardwell, Edward. *A History of Conferences and Other Proceedings Connected with the Revision of the Book of Common Prayer from the Year 1558 to the Year 1690* (Oxford, 3rd edition, 1849).
[Carmichael, James.] *Newes from Scotland, Declaring the Damnable Life and Death of Doctor Flan* (London, 1592).
Cecil, Robert. *An Answere to Certaine Scandalous Papers, Scattered Abroad Under Colour of a Catholicke Admonition* (London, 1606).
Challoner, Richard. *Memoirs of Missionary Priests as well Secular as Regular: and Other Catholics of Both Sexes, that have Suffered Death in England on Religious Accounts From the Year of Our Lord 1577 to 1684* (London, 1741).
Chettle, Henry. *England's Mourning Garment: Worne Heere by Plaine Shepheards, in Memorie of their Sacred Mistresse, Elizabeth* (London, 1603).
Churchyard, Thomas. *Sorrowfull Verses made on [...] Death of Our Most Soveraigne Lady Queene Elizabeth, My Gracious Mistresse* (London, 1604).
Clapham, Sir John. *The Historie of Great Britannie Declaring the Successe of Times and Affaires in that Iland* (London, 1606).
Clapham, John. *Elizabeth of England: Certain Observations Concerning the Life and Reign of Queen Elizabeth*, edited by Evelyn Plumer Read and Conyers Read (Philadelphia, 1951).
Clarke, Samuel. *The Lives of Two and Twenty English Divines Eminent in their Generations for Learning, Piety, and Painfulnesse in the Work of the Ministry, and for their Sufferings in the Cause of Christ* (London, 1660).
Clifford, D. J. H. (ed.). *The Diaries of Lady Anne Clifford* (Stroud, 1990).
Colleton, John. *A Supplication to the Kings Most Excellent Majestie Wherein, Severall Reasons of State and Religion are Briefly Touched...* ([London,] 1604).
Collier, John Payne (ed.). *The Egerton Papers*, Camden Society, 12 (London 1840).
Constable, Archibald (ed.). *Memoirs of George Heriot, Jeweller to King James*, Appendix VII, Extracts from Accounts and Vouchers. 1605–1615 (Edinburgh, 1822).
[Copinger, John]. *The Theatre of Catholique and Protestant Religion Divided into Twelve Bookes* (St Omer, 1620).
Cornwallis, Sir Charles. *The Life and Death of Our Late Most Incomparable and Heroique Prince, Henry Prince of Wales* (London, 1641).
Cornwallis, Sir William. *The Miraculous and Happie Union of England and Scotland by How Admirable Meanes it is Effected; How Profitable to Both Nations, and How Free of Inconvenience Either Past, Present, or to be Discerned* (London, 1604).
[Cotton, Robert.] *An Answer Made by Command of Prince Henry to Certain Propositions of Warre and Peace* (London, 1655).
Covell, William. *A Modest and Reasonable Examination, of Some Things in Use in the Church of England, Sundrie Times Heretofore Misliked* (London, 1604).

Craig, James Thomson Gibson. *Papers Relative to the Marriage of King James the Sixth of Scotland, with the Princess Anna of Denmark: A.D. MDLXXXIX, and the Form and Manner of Her Majesty's Coronation at Holyroodhouse, A.D. MDXC* (Edinburgh, 1828).

Craig, Sir Thomas. *De Unione Regnorum Britanniae Tractatus*, edited and translated by C. Sanford Terry, Scottish History Society (Edinburgh, 1909).

Crakanthorpe, Richard. *A Sermon at the Solemnizing of the Happie Inauguration of Our Most Gracious and Religious Soveraigne King James* (London, 1609).

Crashaw, William. *A Sermon Preached in London Before the Right Honourable Lord LaWarre* (London, 1610).

Croft, Pauline (ed.). 'A Collection of Several Speeches and Treatises of the Late Lord Treasurer Cecil, and of Observations of the Lords of the Council Given to King James Concerning His Estate and Revenue in the Years 1608, 1609 and 1610', *Camden Miscellany*, 29, Camden 4th series, 34 (London, 1987).

Cross, Claire (ed.). *The Letters of Sir Francis Hastings 1574–1609*, Somerset Record Society, 69 (Frome, 1969).

Cunningham, Peter. *Extracts from the Accounts of the Revels at Court* (London, 1942).

Dalrymple, David (ed.). *Memorials and Letters Relating to the History of Britain in the Reign of James the First* (Glasgow, 1762).

Daniel, Samuel. *A Panegyricke Congratulatorie Delivered to the King's Most Excellent Majestie* (London, 1603).

Daniel, Samuel. *The Vision of the 12. Goddesses Presented in a Maske the 8. of January, at Hampton Court: by the Queene's Most Excellent Majestie, and Her Ladies* (London, 1604).

Dasent, John Roche. *Acts of the Privy Council of England, Volume 32: 1601–1604* (London, 1907), British History Online, http://www.british-history.ac.uk/acts-privy-council/vol32 [accessed 12 October 2018].

Davies, John. *Microcosmos: The Discovery of the Little World, Thereof* (London 1603).

Davies, Richard. *Chester's Triumph in Honor of her Prince As it Was Performed Upon S. Georges Day 1610. in the Foresaid Citie* (London, 1610).

Day, John. *Ile of Guls* (London, 1606).

Dekker, Thomas. *1603. The Wonderfull Yeare. Wherein is Shewed the Picture of London Lying Sicke of the Plague* (London, 1603).

Dekker, Thomas. *The Whole Magnificent Entertainment Given to King James, Queen Anne His Wife and Henry Frederick the Prince...* (London, 1604).

Dekker, Thomas. *The Whore of Babylon* (London, 1607).

Devon, Frederick (ed.). *Issues of the Exchequer: Being Payments Made Out of His Majesty's Revenue During the Reign of James I* (London, 1836).

Doleman, R. *A Conference About the Next Succession to the Crown of Ingland*, pt I (Antwerp, 1595).

Donne, John. *The Sermons of John Donne*, edited by George R. Potter and Evelyn M. Simpson, vol. 1 (Berkeley and Los Angeles, 1953).

Dove, John. *A Defence of Church Government Dedicated to the High Court of Parliament...* (London, 1606).

Drayton, Michael. *To the Majestie of King James. A Gratulatorie Poem* (London, 1603).

Drayton, Michael. *Poly-Olbion* (London, 1612).
Drayton, Michael. *The Battaile of Agincourt* (London, 1631).
Dugdale, Gilbert. *The Time Triumphant Declaring in Briefe, the Arival of our Soveraigne Liedge Lord, King James into England, his Coronation at Westminster: Together with his Late Royal Progresse, from the Towre of London Through the Cittie, to his Highnes Manor of White Hall...* (London, 1604).
Dunn, Brian Russell. 'Commons Debates 1603/4', Ph.D., Bryn Mawr College (1987).
Edes, Richard. *Six Learned and Godly Sermons: Preached Some of Them Before the King's Majestie, Some Before Queen Elizabeth* (London, 1604).
Edwards, Edward. *The Life of Sir Walter Ralegh, Based on Contemporary Documents Preserved in the Rolls House, the Privy Council Office, Hatfield House, the British Museum and Other Manuscript Repositories, British and Foreign, Together with his Letters*, 2 vols (London, 1868).
Ellis, Sir Henry (ed.). *Original Letters Illustrative of English History*, 2nd series, vol. 3 & 3rd series, vol. 4 (London, 1827 and 1846).
Fenton, John. *King James His Welcome to London with Elizae's Tombe and Epitaph, and Our King's Triumph and Epitimie. Lamenting the One's Decease, and Rejoycing at the Other's Accesse* (London, 1603).
Ferguson, James. *Papers Illustrating the History of the Scots Brigade in the Service of the United Netherlands, 1572–1782*, vol. 1 (Edinburgh, 1899).
Fincham, Kenneth (ed.). *Visitation Articles and Injunctions of the Early Stuart Church*, vol. 1: 1603–25. Church of England Record Society (Woodbridge, 1994).
Firth, C. H. (ed.). *Stuart Tracts 1603–1693* (New York, 1964).
Fletcher, Robert. *A Briefe and Familiar Epistle Shewing His Majestie's Most Lawfull, Honourable and Just Title to All His Kingdomes with an Epitaph or Briefe Lamentation for the Late Majestie Royall of Most Famous, Godly, and Honourable Memory...* (London, 1603).
Florio, John. *Queen Anna's New World of Word or Dictionarie of the Italian and English Tongues* (London, 1611).
Foley SJ, Henry. *Records of the English Province of the Society of Jesus*, vol. 3 (London, 1878).
Ford, John. *Honor Triumphant. Or The Peeres' Challenge, by Armes Defensible, at Tilt, Turney, and Barriers in Honor of All Faire Ladies...* (London, 1606).
Foster, C. (ed.). *The State of the Church in the Reigns of Elizabeth and James I*, vol. 1, Lincoln Record Society, 23 (Horncastle, 1926).
Foster, Elizabeth Read. *Proceedings in Parliament 1610*, 2 vols (New Haven, CT, 1966).
Fotherby, Martin. *Foure Sermons Lately Preached... The Second at Canterbury, at the Lord Archbishops Visitation. Septemb. 14. anno 1607. The Third at Paules Crosse, Upon the Day of our Deliverance from the Gun-powder Treason. Novemb. 5. anno 1607. The Fourth at the Court, Before the King's Majestie. Novemb. 15. Anno 1607...* (London, 1608).
Fraser, Sir William. *Memorials of the Earls of Haddington*, 2 vols (Edinburgh, 1889).
Fraser, Sir William. *The Elphinstone Family Book of the Lords Elphinstone, Balmerino and Coupar*, vol. 2 (Edinburgh, 1897).

Freshfield, Edwin (ed.). *The Account Books of the Parish of St. Bartholomew Exchange in the City of London, 1596–1698* (London, 1895).
Fuller, Thomas. *The Church History of Britain*, vol. 3 (London, 1837).
Galloway, Bruce R. and Brian P. Levack (eds). *The Jacobean Union: Six Tracts of 1604* (Edinburgh, 1985).
Gardiner, Samuel. *A Dialogue or Conference Betweene Irenaeus and Antimachus, About the Rites and Ceremonies of the Church of England* (London, 1605).
Gardiner, Samuel Rawson (ed.). *Parliamentary Debates in 1610. Edited From the Notes of a Member of the House of Commons*, Camden Society (London, 1862).
Gardiner, Samuel Rawson (ed.). *The Fortescue Papers*, Camden Society (London, 1871).
Gerard, John. *The Condition of Catholics Under James I: Father Gerard's Narrative of the Gunpowder Plot*, edited by John Morris (London, 1872).
Gilbert, C. Don (ed.). 'Thomas Habington's Account of the 1606 Search at Hindlip', *Recusant History*, 25 (2001), 415–22.
Godskall, James. *The King's Medicine for This Present Yeere 1604* (London, 1604).
Goodman, Godfrey. *The Court of King James the First*, edited by John. S. Brewer, 2 vols (London, 1839).
Gordon, John. *England and Scotland's Happinesse in Being Reduced to Unitie of Religion, Under Our Invincible Monarke King James* (London, 1604).
Gordon, John. *Enotikon or A Sermon of the Union of Great Brittannie, in Antiquitie of Language, Name, Religion, and Kingdome ... Preached in Presence of the King's Majestie at Whitehall* (London, 1604).
Granger, James. *A Biographical History of England from Egbert The Great to The Revolution*, 2nd edition, vol. 4 (London, 1774).
Greene, Thomas. *A Poet's Vision, and a Prince's Glorie* (London, 1603).
Grimeston, Edward. *The Low-Country Common Wealth Contayninge an Exact Description of the Eight United Provinces. Now Made Free* (London, 1609).
Gutch, John. *Collectanea Curiosa; or Miscellaneous Tracts, Relating to the History and Antiquities of England and Ireland, ... and a Variety of Other Subjects ...*, vol. 1 (Oxford, 1781).
Hake, Edward. *Of Gold's Kingdome, and this Unhelping Age Described in Sundry Poems Intermixedly Placed After Certaine Other Poems of More Speciall Respect: and Before the Same is an Oration or Speech Intended to Have Bene Delivered by the Author Hereof unto the King's Majesty* (London, 1604).
Hall, Joseph. *The King's Prophecie: Or Weeping Joy* (London, 1603).
Hannay, Patrick. *Two Elegies, on the Late Death of Our Soveraigne Queene Anne with Epitaphes* (London, 1619).
Harbert, William. *England's Sorrowe or, A Farewell to Essex with a Commemoration of the Famous Lives, and Untimely Deaths of Many Woorthie Personages which have Lived in England* (London, 1606).
Harington, Sir John. *Nugae Antiquae: Being a Miscellaneous Collection of Original Papers, in Prose and Verse; Written During the Reigns of Henry VIII: Edward VI, Queen Mary, Elizabeth and King James* selected by Henry Harington, arranged by Thomas Park, 2 vols (London, 1804).

Harrison, Stephen. *The Archs of Triumph Erected in Honor of the High and Mighty Prince. James the First of That Name. King, of England. and the Sixt of Scotland* (London, 1604).
Harrison, William. *The Description of England: The Classic Contemporary Acccount of Tudor Social Life*, edited by Georges Edelen (Washington DC and New York, 1994).
Harry, George Owen. *The Genealogy of the High and Mighty Monarch, James, by the Grace of God, King of Great Brittayne &c. With his Lineall Descent from Noah, by Divers Direct Lynes to Brutus, First Inhabiter of this Ile of Brittayne and From him to Caldwaluder, the Last King of the Brittish Bloud...* (London 1604).
Hartley, T. E. *Proceedings in the Parliaments of Elizabeth I*, vol. 3 (Leicester, 1995).
Hawes, Edward. *Trayterous Percyes & Catesbyes Prosopopeia* (London, 1606).
Hayward, John. *God's Universal Right Proclaimed: A Sermon Preached at Paule's Crosse, the 27. of March 1603...* (London, 1603).
Hayward, John. *A Treatise of Union of the Two Realmes of England and Scotland* (London, 1604).
Healy, Simon (ed.). 'Debates in the House of Commons 1604–1607', in Chris R. Kyle (ed.), *Parliament, Politics and Elections 1604–1648*, Camden Society, 5th series, 17 (Cambridge, 2001), pp. 13–147.
Hearne, Thomas. *A Collection of Curious Discourses Written by Eminent Antiquaries Upon Several Heads in Our English Antiquities*, vols 1–2 (London, 1771).
Heywood, Thomas. *If You Know Not Me, You Know No Bodie. (Part One)* (London, 1605).
Heywood, Thomas. *The Second Part of Queene Elizabeth's Troubles* (London, 1606).
Heywood, Thomas. *Troia Nova* (London, 1609).
Heywood, Thomas. *An Apology for Actors* (London, 1612).
Heywood, Thomas. *If You Know Not Mee, You Know No Body* (London, 1639).
[Hieron, Samuel]. *A Short Dialogue Proving that the Ceremonyes, and Some Other Corruptions Now in Question, Are Defended, by None Other Arguments Then Such as the Papists Have Heretofore Used; And Our Protestant Writers Have Long Since Answered* (London, 1605).
[Hieron, Samuel]. *A Defence of the Ministers' Reasons for Refusall of Subscription to the Book of Common Prayer and of Conformitie* (London, 1607).
Hill, L. M. (ed.). 'Sir Julius Caesar's Journal of Salisbury's First Two Months and Twenty Days as Lord Treasurer: 1608', *Bulletin of the Institute of Historical Research*, 45 (1972), 311–27.
Hill, Robert. *Christ's Prayer Expounded, a Christian Directed, and a Communicant Prepared* (London, 1606).
Hind, Arthur M. *Engraving in England in the Sixteenth and Seventeenth Century*, vol. 2 (Cambridge, 1955).
Historical MSS Commission, *Third Report* (London, 1872).
Historical MSS Commission, *Fifth Report* (London, 1878).
Historical MSS Commission, *Seventh Report, Appendix* (London, 1879).
Historical MSS Commission, 9, *Calendar of the Manuscripts of the Most Hon. The Marquis of Salisbury K.G. Preserved at Hatfield House*, vols 3, 15, 17, 19, 20 (London, 1883–1940).

Historical MSS Commission, *10th Report*, Appendix part IV, The Manuscripts of Lord Muncaster (London, 1885).
Historical MSS Commission, 12, *The Manuscripts of His Grace the Duke of Rutland, G.C.B., Preserved at Belvoir Castle*, 4 vols (London, 1888–1905).
Historical MSS Commission, 29, *Report on the Manuscripts of the Duke of Portland Preserved at Welbeck Abbey*, vol. 9 (London, 1923).
Historical MSS Commission, 45, *Report on the Manuscripts of the Duke of Buccleugh and Queensbury, Preserved at Montagu House, Whitehall*, vol. 3 (London, 1926).
Historical MSS Commission, 55, *Report on the Manuscripts in Various Collections*, vols 4, 6, 8 (London, 1901–14).
Historical MSS Commission, 60, *Report on the Manuscripts of the Earl of Mar and Kellie at Alloa House* (London, 1904).
Historical MSS Commission, 72, *Report on the Laing Manuscripts in the University of Edinburgh*, vol. 1 (London, 1914).
Historical MSS Commission, 75, *Report on the Manuscripts of the Marquis of Downshire, Preserved at Easthampstead Park, Berks*, vols 2 and 3 (London, 1924–40).
Historical MSS Commission, 77, *Report on the Manuscripts of Lord De Lisle and Dudley Preserved at Penshurst Place, Kent*, vols 3–5 (London, 1925–42).
Historical MSS Commission, 80, *Calendar of the Manuscripts of The Right Honourable Lord Sackville of Knole, Sevenoaks, Kent*, vol. 2 (London, 1966).
Hooke, Henry. *A Sermon Preached Before the King at White-hall, the Eight of May 1604* (London, 1604).
Hooker, John. *Parliament in Elizabethan England: John Hooker's 'Order and Usage'*, edited by V. F. Snow (New Haven, CT and London, 1977).
Howell, Thomas Bayley. *A Complete Collection of State Trials and Proceedings for High Treason and Other Crimes and Misdemeanors from the Earliest Period to the Year 1783*, vol. 2 (London, 1816).
Hubbock, William. *An Oration Gratulatory to the High and Mighty James of England, Scotland, France, and Ireland, King, Defendor of the Faith, &c. On the Twelft Day of February Last Presented, When his Majesty Entered the Tower of London...* (Oxford, 1604).
Hubbock, William. *Great Brittaine's Resurrection: or the Parliament's Passing Bell* (London, 1606).
Hudson, Thomas. *The Historie of Judith in Forme of a Poeme* (Edinburgh, 1584).
Hume, David. *The British Union: A Critical Edition of David Hume of Godscroft's De Unione Insulae Britannicae*, edited by Paul J. McGinnis et al. (Aldershot, 2002).
Hume, John Robert. *History of the Hume Family* (St Louis, MO, 1903).
Hume, Tobias. *Captaine Hume's Poeticall Musicke Principally Made for Two Basse-viols* (London, 1607).
Hutchings, Mark and Berta Cano-Echevarría. 'The Spanish Ambassador's Account of James I's Entry into London, 1604 [with Text]', *The Seventeenth Century*, 33 (2017), 255–77.
Hutton, Leonard. *An Answere to a Certaine Treatise of the Crosse in Baptisme* (Oxford, 1605).

[Hynd, John] I.E. *The Divell of the Vault* (London, 1606).
Jackson, Thomas. *David's Pastorall Poeme: or Sheepeheard's Song, Seven Sermons, on the 23. Psalme of David, Whereof the Last Was Preached at Ashford in Kent, the Day Whereon our Gracious King Was There Proclaimed* (London, 1603).
Jacob, Henry. *Reasons Taken Out of God's Word and the Best Humane Testimonies Proving a Necessitie of Reforming Our Churches in England* (Middleburg, 1604).
Jacob, Henry. *A Christian and Modest Offer of a Most Indifferent Conference, or Disputation, About the Maine and Principall Controversies Betwixt the Prelats, and the Late Silenced and Deprived Ministers in England* (London, 1606).
James VI of Scotland. *The Essayes of a Prentise, in the Divine Art of Poesie* (Edinburgh, 1584).
James VI of Scotland. *Ane Fruitfull Meditatioun Contening ane Plane and Facill Expositioun of ye 7.8.9 and 10 versis of the 20 chap. of the Reuelatioun in Forme of ane Sermone* (Edinburgh, 1588).
James VI of Scotland. *Ane Meditatioun upon the xxv, xxvi, xxvii, xxviii, and xxix Verses of the XV Chapt. of the First Buke of the Chronicles of the Kingis* (Edinburgh, 1589).
James VI of Scotland. *His Majestie's Poeticall Exercises at Vacant Houres* (Edinburgh, 1591).
James VI of Scotland. *Daemonologie in Forme of a Dialogue, Divided into Three Bookes* (Edinburgh, 1597).
James VI and I. *Basilikon Doron, Or His Majestie's Instructions to His Dearest Sonne, Henry the Prince* (London, 1603).
James I of England. *A Counterblaste to Tobacco* (London, 1604).
James I of England. *The King's Majestie's Speech, as it was Delivered by Him in the Upper House of the Parliament* (London, 1604).
[James I of England]. *Triplici Nodo, Triplex Cuneus. Sive Apologia Pro Iuramento Fidelitatis: Adversus Duo Brevia P. Pauli Quinti, & Epistolam Cardinalis Bellarmini, ad G. Blackwellum Archipresbyterum Nuper Scriptam. Authoritate Regiâ* (London, 1607).
James I of England. *An Apologie for the Oath of Allegiance First Set Foorth Without a Name, and Now Acknowledged By The Authour, the Right High and Mightie Prince, James... Together with a Premonition of His Majestie's, to Most Mightie Monarches, Kings, Free Princes and States of Christendome* (London, 1609).
James I of England. *A Meditation Upon the 27. 28. 29. Verses of the xxvii Chapter of Saint Matthew. Or a Paterne for a King's Inauguration* (London, 1620).
Jansson, Maija (ed.). *Proceedings in Parliament 1614* (Philadelphia, 1988).
Jardine, David. *Criminal Trials*, vol. 1 (London, 1832).
Johnson, Robert. *Nova Britannia* (London, 1609).
Johnson, Robert. *Nova Britannia Offering Most Excellent Fruites by Planting in Virginia...* (London, 1609).
Johnston, John. *Inscriptiones Historicae Regum Scotorum* (Amsterdam, 1602).
Johnston, John. *A Trewe Description, of the Nobill Race of the Stewards Succedinge Lineallie to the Croun of Scotland unto this Day...* (Amsterdam, 1602).
Jones, Howard Vallance. 'The Journal of Levinus Munck', *The English Historical Review*, 68 (1953), 234–58.

Jonson, Ben. *His Part of King James His Royall and Magnificent Entertainement Through His Honorable Cittie of London, Thurseday the 15. of March. 1603* ... (London, 1604).

Jonson, Ben. *Hymenaei: or The Solemnities of Masque, and Barriers Magnificently Performed on the Eleventh, and Twelfth Nights, from Christmas; at Court: to the Auspicious Celebrating of the Marriage-Union, Betweene Robert, Earle of Essex, and the Lady Frances* (London, 1606).

Jonson, Ben. *The Alchemist*, www.gutenberg.org/files/4081/4081-h/4081-h.htm [accessed 10 September 2023].

Jonson, Ben. *Notes of Ben Jonson's Conversations with William Drummond of Hawthornden January, M.DC.XIX* (London, 1842).

Jonson, Ben. *The Cambridge Edition of the Works of Ben Jonson Online*.

Journal of the House of Commons, Volume 1: 1547–1629 (London, 1802), British History Online, http://www.british-history.ac.uk/commons-jrnl/vol1 [accessed 23 June 2018].

Journal of the House of Lords, Volume 2: 1578–1614 (London, 1767–1830), British History Online, http://www.british-history.ac.uk/lords-jrnl/vol2 [accessed 23 June 2018].

Kellison, Matthew. *A Survey of the New Religion, Detecting Manie Grosse Absurdities Which it Implieth* (Douai, 1603).

Kempe, A. J. (ed.). *The Loseley Manuscripts* (London, 1836).

King, John. *A Sermon Preached in Oxon: The 5. of November 1607* (Oxford, 1607).

Kirby, W. J. Torrance, P. G. Stanwood, Mary Morrissey, and John N. King. *Sermons at Paul's Cross, 1521–1642* (Oxford, 2017).

Laffleur de Kermaingant, Pierre Paul. *L'Ambassade de France en Angleterre Sous Henri IV. Mission de Christophe de Harlay, Comte de Beaumont (1602–1605)*, tome 2 (Paris, 1895).

Laing, D. (ed.). *Collection of Ancient Scottish Prophecies in Alliterative verse, Reprinted from Waldegrave's Edition 1603* (Edinburgh, 1833).

Lane, John. *An Elegie Upon the Death of the High and Renowned Princesse, Our Late Soveraigne Elizabeth* (London, 1603).

Larkin, James F. and Paul L. Hughes (eds). *Stuart Royal Proclamations, Vol. 1: Royal Proclamations of King James I 1603–1625*. Oxford Scholarly Editions Online (Oxford, 2013).

Latham, Agnes and Joyce Youings (eds). *Letters of Sir Walter Ralegh* (Exeter, 1999).

Lecey, John. *A Petition Apologeticall, Presented to the Kinge's Most Excellent Majesty, by the Lay Catholikes of England in July Last* (Douai [i.e. England by secret press], 1604).

Leech, Jeremy. *A Sermon, Preached Before the Lords of the Councel, in K. Henry the Seaventh's Chappell. Sept. 23. 1607 At the Funerall of the Most Excellent & Hopefull Princess, The Lady Marie's Grace* (London, 1607).

Legg, J. Wickham (ed.). *The Coronation Order of King James I* (London, 1902).

Legg, Leopold G. Wickham. *English Coronation Records* (London, 1901).

Leighton, William. *Vertue Triumphant, or A Lively Description of the Foure Vertues Cardinall Dedicated to the Kings Majestie* (London, 1603).

Leonard, Frederic. *Recueil de Traitez de Paix*, vol. 5 (Paris, 1693).

Lloyd, David. *The States-men and Favourites of England* (London, 1665).

Lloyd, Lodowick. *The Choyce of Jewels* (London, 1607).

Lodge, Edmund. *Portraits of Illustrious Personages* (London, 1747).
Lodge, Edmund (ed.). *Illustrations of British History, Biography, and Manners, in the Reigns of Henry VIII, Edward VI, Mary, Elizabeth, and James I, Exhibited in a Series of Original Papers*, vol. 3 (London, 1791).
Lodge, Edmund (ed.). *Illustrations of British History, Biography and Manners in the Reigns of Henry VIII... [to] James I, in Papers from the MSS. of the Families of Howard, Talbot and Cecil*, 2nd edition, vol. 3 (London, 1838).
Lonchay, Henri and Joseph Cuvelier (eds). *Correspondance de la Cour d'Espagne sur les Affaires des Pays-Bas au XVII Siècle*, vol. 1 (Brussels, 1923).
Loomie, Albert J. *Spain and the Jacobean Catholics, vol. 1 1603–1612*, Catholic Record Society, 64 (1973).
Loomis, Catherine (ed.). 'Elizabeth Southwell's Manuscript Account of the Death of Queen Elizabeth [with text]', *English Literary Renaissance*, 26 (1996), 482–509.
Macdonald, Alexander (ed.). *Letters to King James the Sixth from the Queen [and Others]. From the Originals in the Library of the Faculty of Advocates* (Edinburgh, 1835).
Mackie, J. Duncan (ed.). '"A Loyall Subiecte's Advertisment" as to the Unpopularity of James I's Government in England, 1603–4', *The Scottish Historical Review*, 23 (1925), 1–17.
Maidment, James (ed.). *Letters and State Papers During the Reign of King James the Sixth, Chiefly from the Manuscript Collections of Sir James Balfour of Denmyln* (Edinburgh, 1838).
Manningham, John. *The Diary of John Manningham of the Middle Temple 1602–3*, edited by Robert Parker Sorlien (Hanover, NH, 1976).
Mares, F. H. (ed.). *The Memoirs of Robert Carey* (Oxford, 1972).
Markham, Gervase. *Cavelarice, or The English Horseman Contayning All the Arte of Horse-manship* (London, 1607).
Marston, John. *The Dutch Courtesan*, edited by David Crane (London, 2014).
Martin, Richard. *A Speach Delivered, to the King's Most Excellent Majestie in the Name of the Sheriffes of London and Middlesex* (London, 1603).
Mason, Francis. *The Authoritie of the Church in Making Canons and Constitutions Concerning Things Indifferent and the Obedience Thereto Required... Delivered in a Sermon Preached in the Greene yard at Norwich the Third Sunday after Trinitie, 1605.* (London, 1607).
Masson, David. *Register of the Privy Council of Scotland*, vols 5–8 (Edinburgh, 1882–87).
Mavericke, Radford. *Three Treatises Religiously Handled and Named According to the Severall Subiect of Each Treatise: The Mourning Weede. The Morning's Joy. The King's Rejoycing* (London 1603).
McGowan, A.P. (ed.). *The Jacobean Commissions of Enquiry 1608 and 1618* (London, 1971).
Mears, Natalie, Alasdair Raffe, Stephen Taylor and Philip Williamson (with Lucy Bates) (eds). *National Prayers: Special Worship Since the Reformation, Volume I: Special Prayers, Fasts and Thanksgivings in the British Isles 1533–1688* (Woodbridge, 2013).
Melville of Halhill, James. *Memoirs of His Own Life* (Edinburgh, 1827).
Meres, Francis. *Palladis Tamia Wits' Treasury Being the Second Part of Wits' Common Wealth* (London, 1598).

Middleton, Thomas. *Thomas Middleton: The Collected Works*, edited by Gary Taylor and John Lavagnono et al. (Oxford, 2007).

Milles, Thomas. *The Catalogue of Honor or Tresury of True Nobility, Peculiar and Proper to the Isle of Great Britaine* . . . (London, 1610).

Millington, Thomas. *The True Narration of the Entertainment of his Royall Majestie, From the Time of his Departure from Edenbrough; Till his Receiuing at London with All or the Most Speciall Occurrences* (London, 1603).

Monipennie, John. *Certein Matters Concerning the Realme of Scotland* (London, 1603).

Montagne, Michel de. *Essays* translated by Charles Cotton, www.gutenberg.org files [accessed 18 August 2020].

Mosse, Miles. *Scotland's Welcome: a Sermon Preached at Needham in the Countie of Suff. on Tuesday, April 5, 1603* . . . (London, 1603).

Moysie, David. *Memoirs of the Affairs of Scotland, 1577–1603*, edited by J. Dennistoun, Maitland Club (Edinburgh 1830).

Mulcaster, Richard. *The Passage of Our Most Drad Soveraigne Lady Quene Elyzabeth I* (London, 1559, reprinted 1604).

Mulcaster, Richard. *The Translation of Certaine Latine Verses written Uppon her Majestie's Death, Called A Comforting Complaint This Onely Way I Could Declare My Thankefull Mind* (London, 1603).

Munday, Anthony. *The Triumphes of Re-united Britania* (London, 1605).

Murray, James A. H. (ed.). *The Complaynt of Scotlande, A.D. 1549* (Woodbridge, 2002).

Nelson, Alan. 'Lord Chamberlain Accounts', http://socrates.berkeley.edu/~ahnelson/SHAX/lc1604.html [accessed 8 February 2017].

Neville, Alexander. *Academiae Cantabrigiensis Lachrymae Tumulo Noblilissimi Equitis, D. Philippi Sidneii Sacratae* (London, 1587).

[Niccols, Richard]. *Expicedium, A Funeral Oration, Upon the Late Deceased Princesse Elizabeth Queen of England By Infelice Academico Ignoto. Wherunto Is Added, the True Order of Her Highnes Funerall* (London, 1603).

Nichols, John. *The Progresses, Processions, and Magnificent Festivities of King James the First*, vols 1–3 (London, 1828).

Nichols, John. *The Progresses and Public Processions of Queen Elizabeth I: A New Edition of the Early Modern Sources*, vol. 3, edited by Elizabeth Goldring, Faith Eales, Elizabeth Clarke and Jayne Elisabeth Archer (Oxford, 2014).

Nixon, Anthony. *Elizae's Memoriall. King James his Arrivall. And Rome's Downefall* (London, 1603).

Ormerod, Oliver. *The Picture of a Puritane* (London, 1605).

Orrell, John (ed.). 'The London Stage in the Florentine Correspondence, 1604–1618', *International Theatre Research*, new series, 3 (1978), 157–76.

Osborne, Francis. *Historical Memoires on the Reigns of Queen Elizabeth and King James* (London, 1658).

Oxford University. *The Answere of the Vicechancelour, the Doctors, both the Proctors, and other the Heads of Houses in the Universitie of Oxford* (Oxford, 1603).

Parsons, Daniel (ed.). *The Diary of Sir Henry Slingsby, of Scriven* (London, 1836).

Peacham, Henry. *Minerva Britanna Or A Garden of Heroical Deuises, Furnished, and Adorned with Emblemes and Impresa's of Sundry Natures* (London, 1612).

Persons, Robert. *The Judgment of a Catholicke English-man Living in Banishment for His Religion* (Saint Omer, 1608).

Petowe, Henry. *Elizabetha Quasi Vivens: Eliza's Funerall: A Few Aprill Drops Showred on the Hearse of Dead Eliza* (London, 1603).

Playfere, Thomas. *Heart's Delight. A Sermon Preached at Paul's Crosse in London in Easter Terme. 1593* (London, 1603).

Pollen, John Hungerford. *Acts of English Martyrs Hitherto Unpublished* (London, 1891).

Potter, George R. and Evelyn M. Simpson (eds). *The Sermons of John Donne*, 10 vols (Berkeley, CA, 1953).

Powel, Gabriel. *The Catholikes' Supplication unto the Kings Majestie; for Toleration of Catholike Religion in England; with Short Notes or Animadversions in the Margine: Whereunto is Annexed Parallel-wise, a Supplicatorie Counterpoyse of the Protestants, unto the Same Most Excellent Majestie...* (London, 1603).

Powel, Gabriel. *A Consideration of the Deprived and Silenced Ministers' Arguments, for Their Restitution to the Use and Libertie of their Ministerie Exhibited in Their Late Supplication, Unto the Honorable States Assembled in this Present Parliament* (London, 1606).

Powel, Gabriel. *De Adiaphoris Theological and Scholastical Positions, Concerning the Nature and Use of Things Indifferent...* (London, 1607).

Powell, Thomas. *A Welch Bayte to Spare Provender. Or, A Looking Backe Upon the Times Past* (London, 1603).

Pricket, Robert. *A Souldier's Wish* (London, 1603).

Pricket, Robert. *The Jesuits Miracles, or New Popish Wonders* (London, 1607).

Reid, Steven J. and David McOmish (eds). *Corona Borealis: Scottish Neo-Latin Poets on King James VI and His Reign, 1566–1603* (Glasgow, 2020).

Rhodes, John. *A Briefe Summe of the Treason Intended Against the King & State, When They Should Have Been Assembled in Parliament. November. 5. 1605...* (London, 1606).

Rhodes, Neil, Jennifer Richards, and Joseph Marshall (eds). *King James VI and I: Selected Writings* (Aldershot, 2003).

Rich, Barnabe. *A Souldier's Wishe to Briton's Welfare* (London, 1604).

Rimbault, Edward F. (ed.). *The Old Cheque-Book, or Book of Remembrance, of the Chapel Royal, from 1561–1744*, Camden Society, new series, 3 (London, 1872).

Roberts, Henry. *The Most Royall and Honourable Entertainement, of the Famous and Renowmed King, Christiern the Fourth, King of Denmarke...* (London, 1606).

Roberts, Henry. *England's Farewell to Christian the Fourth, Famous King of Denmarke...* (London, 1606).

Robinson, Thomas. *The Schoole of Musicke* (London, 1603).

Rogers, Thomas. *Anglorum Lacrimae in a Sad Passion Complayning the Death of our Late Soveraigne Lady Queene Elizabeth: Yet Comforted Againe by the Vertuous Hopes of our Most Royall and Renowned King James: Whose Majestie God Long Continue* (London, 1603).

Rogers, Thomas. *Two Dialogues, or Conferences (About an Old Question Lately Renued, and by the Schismaticall Company, Both by Printed Pamphlets, and Otherwise to the Disturbance of the Churches Quiet, and of Peaceable Minds, Very Hotly Pursued.)*... (London, 1608).

Ross, John. *Britannica* (1607), trans. Dana F. Sutton. University of Birmingham (2010). https://philological.cal.bham.ac.uk/ross/apologiatrans.html#1 [accessed July 2020].

Rowland, Samuel. *Aue Caesar. = God Save the King The Joyfull Ecchoes of Loyall English Hartes, Entertayning his Majestie's Late Arivall in England. With an Epitaph Upon the Death of her Majestie Our Late Queene* (London, 1603).

Rudd, Anthony. *A Sermon Preached at Richmond before Queene Elizabeth of Famous Memorie, Upon the 28. of March, 1596* (London, 1603).

Rudd, Anthony. *A Sermon Preached at Greenwich before the King's Majestie Upon Tuesday in Whitson Weeke being the 14. of June. 1603* (London, 1603).

Rudick, Michael (ed.). *The Poems of Sir Walter Ralegh: A Historical Edition* (Tempe, Arizona, 1999).

Rudston, Thomas. *Rudston 1610: A New Almanacke and Prognostication... But Like Indifferently Serving This Whole Monarchie of Great Brittaine* (London, 1610).

Rye, William Brenchley. *England As Seen by Foreigners in the Days of Elizabeth and James the First* (London, 1865).

Rye, William Brenchley. 'The Coronation of King James I, 1603', *The Antiquary*, 22 (1890), 18–23.

Rymer, Thomas and Robert Sanderson (eds). *Foedera, Conventiones, Literae Foedera, Conventiones, Literae, Et Cujuscunque Generis Acta Publica, Inter Reges Angliae, Et Alios Quosuis Imperatores, Reges, Pontifices, Principes*, 2nd edition, vol. 16 (London, 1727).

Saunders, H. W. and Anstel Day (eds). *The Official Papers of Sir Nathaniel Bacon of Stiffkey, Norfolk, as Justice of the Peace, 1580–1620*, Camden Society, 3rd series, 26 (London, 1915).

Savile, John. *King James His Entertainment at Theobalds with His Welcome to London, Together with a Salutatorie Poeme* (London, 1603).

Scarisbrick, Diana. 'Anne of Denmark's Jewellery Inventory', *Archaeologia*, 109 (1991), 193–238.

Scott, Walter (ed.). *A Collection of Scarce and Valuable Tracts... Selected From an Infinite Number in Print and Manuscript, in the Royal, Cotton, Sion, and Other Public, as well as Private, Libraries; Particularly That of the Late Lord Somers*, vol. 2, 2nd edition (London, 1809).

Seddon, P. R. (ed.). *Letters of John Holles 1587–1637*, Thoroton Society, 38 (Nottingham, 1975).

Shakespeare, William. *The Tempest*, edited by Frank Kermode (London, 1954).

Shakespeare, William. *Measure for Measure*, edited by J. W. Lever (London, 1965).

Shakespearre, William. *Henry VIII*, edited by Barbara A. Mowat and Paul Werstine (New York, 2007).

Shakespeare, William. *Shakespeare's Sonnets*, edited by Katherine Duncan-Jones (London, 2010).

Shakespeare, William. *Cymbeline*, edited by Valerie Wayne (London, 2017).

Sharpe, Leonell. *A Sermon Preached at Cambridge before the University, the Knights, and Chiefe Gentlemen of the Shiere, the Mayor and Townesmen, the 28. of March* (Cambridge, 1603).

[Sharpe, Leonell]. *To the Kinges Most Excellent Majestie the Humble Petition of Two and Twentie Preachers in London and the Suburbs Thereof* (London, 1605?).

Shirley, Evelyn Philip (ed.). 'Inventory and Will of Henry Howard, Earl of Northampton', *Archaeologia*, 42 (1869), 347–78.

[Skinner, Sir John]. *Rapta Tatio: The Mirrour of His Majestie's Present Government, Tending to the Union of His Whole Iland of Brittonie* (London, 1604).

Smith, Thomas. *De Republica Anglorum* (London, 1583).

Sommerville, Johann P. (ed.). *King James VI and I: Political Writings* (Cambridge, 1994).

Sparke, Thomas. *A Brotherly Perswasion to Unitie, and Uniformitie in Judgment and Practise Touching the Received, and Present Ecclesiasticall Government, and the Authorised Rites and Ceremonies of the Church of England* (London, 1607).

Speed, John. *Theatre of the Empire of Great Britaine* (London, 1612).

Speed, John. *The History of Great Britaine Under the Conquests of Ye Romans, Saxons, Danes and Normans* (London, 1611, 1614).

Speed, John. *The Historie of Great Britaine Under the Conquests of the Romans, Saxons, Danes and Normans* (London, 1623).

Spottiswoode, John. *The History of the Church of Scotland...*, 3rd edition (London, 1668).

Statutes of the Realm, vol. 4. Part 2, edited by John Raithby (London, 1819).

Steen, Sara Jayne (ed.). *The Letters of Lady Arbella Stuart* (Oxford, 1994).

Stevenson, David. *Scotland's Last Royal Wedding: The Marriage of James VI and Anne of Denmark* (Edinburgh, 1997).

Stevenson, George (ed.). *Poems of Alexander Montgomerie, and Other Pieces from Laing MS. no. 447* (Edinburgh, 1910).

Stoughton, William. *An Assertion for True and Christian Church Policie* ([Middelburg], 1604).

Stow, John. *The Annales, or a Generall Chronicle of England, Begun First by Maister John Stow, and After him Continued and Augmented with Matters Forreyne, and Domestique, Aunciet and Moderne, Unto the Ende of This Present Yeere 1614 by Edmond Howes* (London, 1615, 1618, 1631, 1632).

Strateman Sims, Catherine. '"Policies in Parliaments": An Early Seventeenth-Century Tractate on House of Commons Procedure', *Huntington Library Quarterly*, 15 (1951), 45–58.

Strype, John. *The Life and Acts of John Whitgift D.D.*, 5 vols (Oxford, 1822).

Sutcliffe, Matthew. *The Supplication of Certaine Masse-priests Falsely Called Catholikes* (London, 1604).

Taylor, Gary and John Lavagnino (eds). *Thomas Middleton, Vol. 2: Thomas Middleton and Early Modern Textual Culture* (Oxford, 2007).

Thornborough, John. *A Discourse Plainely Proving the Evident Utilitie and Urgent Necessitie of the Desired Happie Union of the Two Famous Kingdomes of England and Scotland by Way of Answer to Certaine Objections Against the Same* (London, 1604).

Thornborough, John. *The Joiefull and Blessed Reuniting the Two Mighty and Famous Kingdomes, England and Scotland into Their Ancient Name of Great Brittaine* (Oxford, 1605?).

Thorne, William. *Esoptron Basilikon. Or A Kenning-Glasse for a Christian King* (London, 1603).

Tierney, M. A. (ed.). *Dodd's Church History of England... from the Commencement of the Sixteenth Century to the Revolution in 1688*, 5 vols (London, 1839–43).

Treswell, Robert. *A Relation of Such Things as Were Obserued to Happen in the Journey of the Right Honourable Charles Earle of Nottingham L. High Admirall of England, His Highnesse Ambassadour to the King of Spaine...* (London, 1605).

Trevelyan, Sir Walter Calverley and Sir Charles Edward (eds). *Trevelyan Papers*, Camden Society, 151 (1872), Part III.

Trigge, Francis. *To the King's Most Excellent Majestie. The Humble Petition of Two Sisters the Church and Common-wealth: For the Restoring of their Ancient Commons and Liberties, which late Inclosure with Depopulation, Uncharitably Hath Taken Away...* (London, 1604).

Usher, Roland G. *The Reconstruction of the English Church*, 2 vols (New York and London, 1910).

Vaughan, William. *The Golden-grove Moralized in Three Bookes* (London, 1600).

Velasco, Juan Fernández de. *Relación de la Jornada del Excelentissimo Condestable de Castilla, a las pazes entre España y Inglaterra, que se concluyeron y juraron en Londres por el mes de Agosto, Año 1604* (Valencia, 1604).

Wakeman, Robert. *Salomon's Exaltation, a Sermon Preached Before the King's Majestie at None-such, April. 30. 1605* (Oxford, 1605).

Weldon, Anthony. *The Court and Character of King James* (London, 1650).

Westerman, William. *The Faithfull Subject: or Mephiboseth and Salomons Porch: or A Caveat For Them That Enter Gods House: in Two Sermons Preached at Paules Crosse* (London, 1608).

Wilbraham, Roger. *The Journal of Sir Roger Wilbraham, Solicitor-General in Ireland and Master of Requests for the Years 1593–1616*, edited by Harold Spencer Scott, Camden Miscellany, 10 (London, 1902).

Wilkins, David. *Concilia Magnae Britanniae et Hiberniae*, vol. 4 (London, 1737).

Wilkinson, Edward. *Isahak's Inheritance: Dew to our High and Mightie Prince, James the Sixt of Scotland, of England, France and Ireland the First* (London, 1603).

Willet, Andrew. *Ecclesia Triumphans: That is, the Joy of the English Church for the Happie Coronation of the Most Vertuous and Pious James...* (London, 1603).

Willet, Andrew. *An Antilogie or Counterplea to An Apologicall (He Should Have Said) Apologeticall Epistle Published by a Favorite of the Romane Separation, and (as is Supposed) One of the Ignatian Faction* (London, 1603).

Willson, David Harris (ed.). *The Parliamentary Diary of Robert Bowyer 1606–1607* (Minneapolis, 1977).

Wilson, Arthur. *The History of Great Britain Being the Life and Reign of King James First* (London, 1653).

Winwood, Ralph. *Memorials of Affairs of State in the Reigns of Q. Elizabeth and K. James I, Collected (Chiefly) From the Original Papers of... Sir Ralph Winwood*, edited by E. Sawyer, 3 vols (London, 1725).

Wright, Thomas. *A Succinct Philosophicall Declaration of the Mature of Clymactericall Yeeres, Occasioned by the Death of Queene Elizabeth* (London, 1604).

SECONDARY SOURCES

Adams, Simon. 'The Protestant Cause: Religious Alliance with the European Calvinist Communities as a Political Issue in England 1585–1630', D.Phil., University of Oxford (1973).

Adamson, John. 'The Tudor and Stuart Courts', in *idem* (ed.), *The Princely Courts of Europe: Ritial, Politics and Culture Under the Ancien Régime 1500–1750* (London, 1999), pp. 95–117.

Adlington, Hugh. 'Do Donne's Writings Express His Desperate Ambition?', in Jeanne Shami, Dennis Flynn, and M. Thomas Hester (eds), *The Oxford Handbook of John Donne* (Oxford, 2011), pp. 718–32.

Akkerman, Nadine. 'The Goddess of the Household: The Masquing Politics of Lucy Harington-Russell, 1601–1604', in Nadine Akkerman and Birgit Houben (eds), *The Politics of Female Households* (Leiden, 2014).

Akkerman, Nadine. *Elizabeth Stuart: Queen of Hearts* (Oxford, 2021).

Allen, Paul C. 'The Strategy of Peace: Spanish Foreign Policy and the *Pax Hispanica*', Ph.D., Yale University (1995).

Allen, Paul C. *Philip III and the Pax Hispanica 1598–1621: The Failure of Grand Strategy* (New Haven and London, 2000).

Anderson, Alison D. *On the Verge of War: International Relations and the Jülich-Kleve Succession Crises (1609–1614)* (Boston, MA, 1999).

Anderson, Roberta. *Foreign Diplomatic Representatives to the Stuart Court during the Seventeenth Century. Part 1: 1603–1625* (AHDS, 2007).

Andrea, 'Bernadette. 'Black Skin, the Queen's Masques: Africanist Ambivalence and Feminine Author(ity) in the Masques of Blacknesse and Beauty', *English Literary Renaissance*, 29 (1999), 246–81.

Andrews, K. R. 'Caribbean Rivalry and the Anglo-Spanish Peace of 1604', *History*, 59 (1974), 1–17.

Andrews, Kenneth R. *Trade, Plunder and Settlement* (Cambridge, 1984).

Appleby, John C. 'The Problem of Piracy in Ireland 1570–1630', in Claire Jowitt (ed.), *Pirates? The Politics of Plunder, 1550–1650* (Basingstoke, 2006), pp. 41–55.

Appleby, John C. 'Jacobean Piracy: English Maritime Depredation in Transition, 1603–1625', in Cheryl A. Fury (ed.), *The Social History of English Seamen, 1485–1649* (Woodbridge, 2012), pp. 277–300.

Archer, Ian W. *The Pursuit of Stability: Social Relations in Elizabethan London* (Cambridge, 1991).

Archer, Ian W. 'Popular Politics in the Sixteenth and Early Seventeenth Centuries', in Paul Griffiths and Mark S. R. Jenner (eds), *Londinopolis: Essays in the Cultural and Social History of Early Modern London* (Manchester, 2000), pp. 26–46.

Archer, Ian W. 'City and Court Connected: The Material Dimensions of Royal Ceremonial, ca. 1480–1625', *Huntington Library Quarterly*, 71 (2008), 157–79.

Armitage, David. *The Ideological Origins of the British Empire* (Cambridge, 2000).

Armitage David. 'The Elizabethan Idea of Empire', *Transactions of the Royal Historical Society*, 14 (2004), 269–77.

Armitage, David R. *The Complete Soldier: Military Books and Military Culture in Early Stuart England 1603–1645* (Leiden, Boston, 2009).

Asch, Ronald G. *Sacral Kingship Between Disenchantment and Re-enchantment: The French and English Monarchies 1587–1688* (New York, 2014).

Ashton, Robert. 'Deficit Finance in the Reign of James I', *Economic History Review*, 10 (1957), 15–29.

Astington, John H. 'Court Theatre' in Richard Dutton (ed.), *The Oxford Handbook of Early Modern Theatre* (Oxford, 2009), pp. 307–22.

Atherton, Ian and David Como. 'The Burning of Edward Wightman: Puritanism, Prelacy and the Politics of Heresy in Early Modern England', *The English Historical Review*, 120 (2005), 1215–50.

Aveling, Hugh. *Northern Catholics: The Catholic Recusants of the North Riding of Yorkshire 1558–1790* (London, 1966).

Ayton, James. 'Sir Robert Ayton—The Last Castalian: Time for a Reappraisal', *Studies in Scottish Literature*, 33 (2004), 281–9.

Babbage, Stuart Barton. *Puritanism and Richard Bancroft* (London, 1962).

Backerra, Charlotte. 'Personal Union, Composite Monarchy and "Multiple Rule"', in Elena Woodacre, Lucinda H. S. Dean et al. (eds), *The Routledge History of Monarchy* (Abingdon, 2019), pp. 89–111.

Badenhausen, Richard. 'Disarming the Infant Warrior: Prince Henry, King James, and the Chivalric Revival', *Papers on Language and Literature*, 31 (1995), 20–37.

Baker, John. *The Reinvention of Magna Carta 1216–1616* (Cambridge, 2017).

Barroll, Leeds. *Anna of Denmark, Queen of England: A Cultural Biography* (Philadephia, 2001).

Batho, G. R. 'The Payment and Mitigation of a Star Chamber Fine', *The Historical Journal*, 1 (1958), 40–51.

Bawcutt, Priscilla. 'James VI's Castalian Band: A Modern Myth', *The Scottish Historical Review*, 80 (2001), 251–9.

Bell, Sandra J. 'Kingcraft and Poetry: James VI's Cultural Policy', in Peter C. Herman (ed.), *Reading Monarch's Writing: The Poetry of Henry VIII, Mary Stuart, Elizabeth I, and James VI/I* (Tempe, Arizona, 2002), pp. 155–77.

Bellany, Alastair. 'A Poem on the Archbishop's Hearse: Puritanism, Libel and Sedition After the Hampton Court Conference', *Journal of British Studies*, 34 (1995), 137–64.

Bellany, Alastair. 'Libels in Action: Ritual, Subversion and the English Literary Underground, 1603–42', in Tim Harris (ed.), *The Politics of the Excluded, c.1500–1850* (Basingstoke, 2001), pp. 99–124.

Bellany, Alastair. *The Politics of Court Scandal in Early Modern England* (Cambridge, 2002).

Bellany, Alastair. 'The Court', in Suzanne Gossett (ed.), *Thomas Middleton in Context* (Cambridge, 2011), pp. 117–25.

Bellany, Alastair. 'The Rise of the Howards at Court', in Dennis Flynn, M. Thomas Hester, and Jeanne Shami (eds), *The Oxford Handbook of John Donne* (Oxford, 2011), pp. 537–52.

Bergeron, David. *Royal Family, Royal Lovers: King James of England and Scotland* (Columbia, MO, 1991).

Bergeron, David. *King James and Letters of Homoerotic Desire* (Iowa, 1999).

Bergeron, David M. 'King James's Civic Pageant and Parliamentary Speech in March 1604', *Albion*, 34 (2002), 213–31.

Bergeron, David M. 'Creating Entertainments for Prince Henry's Creation (1610)', *Comparative Drama*, 42 (2008), 433–49.

Bergeron, David M. 'The Stuart Brothers and English Theatre', *Renaissance Papers 2015*, 20 (2016), 1–12.

Bergeron, David M. 'The Duke of Lennox and Civic Entertainments', in J. Caitlin Finlayson and Amrita Sen (eds), *Civic Performance: Pageantry and Entertainments in Early Modern London* (Abingdon, 2020), pp. 157–75.

Bernthal, Craig A. 'Staging Justice: James I and the Trial Scenes of Measure for Measure', *Studies in English Literature, 1500–1900*, 32 (1992), 247–69.

Berry, Ralph. 'Ben Jonson at Althorp: Stage Direction as Memoir', *Notes and Queries*, 62 (2015), 224–7.

Bezio, Kristin M. S. *Staging Power in Tudor and Stuart English History Plays: History, Political Thought, and the Redefinition of Sovereignty* (Farnham, 2015).

Black, Joseph. 'The Rhetoric of Reaction: The Martin Marprelate Tracts (1588–9), Anti-Martinism, and the Uses of Print in Early-Modern England', *The Sixteenth Century Journal*, 28 (1997), 707–25.

Blakeway, Amy. *Regency in Sixteenth-Century Scotland* (Martlesham, 2015).

Blakeway, Amy. ' "Newes from Scotland" in England, 1559–1602', *Huntington Library Quarterly*, 79 (2016), 533–59.

Blakeway, Amy. 'The Privy Council of James V of Scotland 1528–1542', *The Historical Journal*, 59 (2016), 23–44.

Blakeway, Amy. 'James VI and James Douglas, Regent Morton', in Miles Kerr-Peterson and Steven J. Reid (eds), *James VI and Noble Power in Scotland 1578–1603* (Abingdon, 2017), pp. 12–31.

Bliss, William. 'The Religious Belief of Anne of Denmark', *The English Historical Review*, 4 (1889), 110.

Bohstedt, John. *The Politics of Provisions: Food Riots, Moral Economy, and Market Transition in England, c. 1550–1850* (Farnham, 2010).

Bondos-Greene, Stephen A. 'The End of an Era: Cambridge Puritanism and the Christ's College Election of 1609', *The Historical Journal*, 25 (1982), 197–208.

Borreguero Beltrán, Cristina. 'Isabel Clara Eugenia: Daughter of the Spanish Empire', in Tonio Andrade and William Reger (eds), *The Limits of Empire: European Imperial Formations in Early Modern World History, Essays in Honour of Geoffrey Parker* (Farnham, 2012), pp. 257–80.

Botonaki, Effie. 'Elizabeth's Presence in the Jacobean Masque', in Alessandra Petrina and Laura Tosi (eds), *Representations of Elizabeth I in Early Modern Culture* (Basingstoke, 2011), 140–57.

Botonaki, Effie. 'Anne of Denmark and the Court Masque: Displaying and Authoring Queenship', in Debra Barrett-Graves (ed.), *The Emblematic Queen: Extra-Literary Representations of Early Modern Queenship* (Basingstoke, 2013), 133–54.

Bourdin Bernard. *The Theological-Political Origins of the Modern State: The Controversy between James I of England and Cardinal Bellarmine*, trans. Susan Pickford (Washington DC, 2011).

Bowers, Rick. 'James VI, Prince Henry, and *A True Reportarie* of Baptism at Stirling 1594', *Renaissance and Reformation*, 29 (2005), 3–22.

Boyer, Allen D. 'The Trial of Sir Walter Ralegh: The Law of Treason, the Trial of Treason and the Origins of the Confrontation Clause', *Mississippi Law Journal*, 74 (2005), 869–901.

Braddick, Michael J. *State Formation in Early Modern England c. 1550–1700* (Cambridge, 2000).

Brayshay, Mark. 'Long-Distance Royal Journeys: Anne of Denmark's Journey from Stirling to Windsor in 1603', *The Journal of Transport History*, 25 (2004), 1–21.

Brogan, Stephen. *The Royal Touch in Early Modern England: Politics, Medicine and Sin* (London, 2015).

Brogden, Wendy Elizabeth. 'Catholicism, Community and Identity in Late Tudor and Early Stuart Herefordshire', Ph.D., University of Birmingham (2018).

Brooks, Benjamin. *The Lives of the Puritans, Containing a Biographical Account of Those Divines who Distinguished Themselves in the Cause of Religious Liberty, from the Reformation Under Queen Elizabeth, to the Act of Uniformity in 1662*, 3 vols (London, 1813).

Brooks, Christopher W. *Lawyers, Litigation and English Society Since 1450* (London, 1998).

Brooks, Christopher W. *Law, Politics and Society in Early Modern England* (Cambridge, 2008).

Brown, Keith M. *Kingdom or Province? Scotland and the Regal Union, 1603–1715* (Basingstoke, 1992).

Brown, Keith M. 'The Scottish Aristocracy, Anglicization and the Court, 1603–38', *The Historical Journal*, 36 (1993), 543–76.

Brown, Keith M. 'The Origins of a British Aristocracy: Integration and its Limitations Before the Treaty of Union', in Steven G. Ellis and Sarah Barber (eds), *Conquest and Union: Fashioning a British State* (London, 1995), pp. 222–49.

Brown, Keith M. 'Honour, Honours and Nobility in Scotland between the Reformation and the National Covenant', *The Scottish Historical Review*, 91 (2012), 42–75.

Brown, Keith M. 'Toward Political Participation and Capacity: Elections, Voting, and Representation in Early Modern Scotland', *Journal of Modern History*, 88 (2016), 1–33.
Brown, Keith M. and Alan R. MacDonald (eds). *Parliament in Context, 1235–1707* (Edinburgh, 2010).
Burgess, Glenn. *The Politics of the Ancient Constitution: An Introduction to English Political Thought, 1603–1642* (Basingstoke, 1992).
Burgess, Glenn. *British Political Thought* (Basingstoke, 2009).
Butler, Katherine. 'Musical Transformations of the City Soundscape: King James I's Entry into London in 1604', in J. Caitlin Finlayson and Amrita Sen (eds), *Civic Performance Pageantry and Entertainments in Early Modern London* (Abingdon, 2020), pp. 200–18.
Butler, Martin. '"Servant, but not a Slave": Ben Jonson at the Jacobean Court', *Proceedings of the British Academy*, 90 (1995), 65–93.
Butler, Martin. *The Stuart Court Masque and Political Culture* (Cambridge, 2008).
Cadman, Daniel. 'Th'Accession of these Mighty States': Daniel's *Philotas* and the Union of Crowns', *Renaissance Studies*, 26 (2012), 365–84.
Cahill, Michael. 'The Diocese of Coventry and Lichfield', Ph.D., University of Warwick (2001).
Campbell, Heidi Olson. '"Of Blessed Memory": The Recasting of Elizabeth I as England's Protestant Patron Saint, 1603–1645', *Anglican and Episcopal History*, 91 (2022), 429–54.
Campbell, Ian and Aonghus Mackechnie. 'The "Great Temple of Solomon" at Stirling Castle', *Architectural History*, 54 (2011), 91–118.
Campbell, Lorne. *The Early Flemish Pictures in the Collection of Her Majesty the Queen* (Cambridge, 1985).
Canny, Nicholas P. 'The Ideology of English Colonization: From Ireland to America', in David Armitage (ed.), *Theories of Empire* (Aldershot, 1998), pp. 179–202.
Canny, Nicholas. *Plantation in Ireland 1603–1622* (Oxford, 2001).
Caraman, Philip. *Henry Garnet 1555–1606, and the Gunpowder Plot* (London, 1964).
Carey, Daniel and Claire Jowitt (eds). *Richard Hakluyt and Travel Writing in Early Modern Europe* (Farnham, 2012).
Carey, Vincent. '"What Pen Can Paint or Tears Atone?": Mountjoy's Scorched Earth Campaign', in Hiram Morgan (ed.), *The Battle of Kinsale* (Wicklow, 2004), pp. 205–16.
Carleton, Charles. *Charles I: The Personal Monarch*, 2nd edition (London, 1995).
Carter, Charles H. 'Gondomar: Ambassador to James I', *The Historical Journal*, 7 (1964), 189–208.
Cathcart, Alison. 'The Statutes of Iona: The Archipelagic Context', *Journal of British Studies*, 49 (2010), 4–27.
Chambers, E. K. *The Elizabethan Stage*, vol. 1 (Oxford, 1923).
Chambers, Robert. *The Life of King James the First*, 2 vols (Edinburgh, 1830).
Chan Smith, David. *Sir Edward Coke and the Reformation of the Laws: Religion, Politics and Jurisprudence, 1578–1616* (Cambridge, 2014).

Clancy SJ, Thomas. 'English Catholics and the Papal Deposing Power, 1570–1640', *Recusant History*, 6 (1962), 205–27.
Clark, Matthew. 'The Gentry, the Commons, and the Politics of Common Right in Enfield, c.1558–c.1603', *The Historical Journal*, 54 (2011), 609–29.
Clark, Stuart. 'King James's Daemonologie: Witchcraft and Kingship', in Sydney Anglo (ed.), *The Damned Art: Essays in the Literature of Witchcraft* (London, 1977), pp. 156–81.
Clegg, Cyndia Susan. *Press Censorship in Jacobean England* (Cambridge, 2001).
Clegg, Cyndia Susan. 'Censorship and the Courts of Star Chamber and High Commission in England to 1640', *Journal of Modern European History*, 3 (2005), 50–80.
Clewett Jr, Richard M. 'James VI of Scotland and his Literary Circle', *Aevum*, 47 (1973), 441–54.
Cliffe, J. T. *The Puritan Gentry: The Great Puritan Families of Early Stuart England* (London, 1984).
Coakley, Thomas M. 'Robert Cecil in Power: Elizabethan Politics in Two Reigns', in Howard S. Reinmuth Jr (ed.), *Early Stuart Studies: Essays in Honour of David Harris Willson* (Minneapolis, 1970), pp. 64–94.
Cogan, Susan. *Catholic Social Networks in Early Modern England: Kinship, Gender, and Coexistence* (Amsterdam, 2021).
Cogswell, Thomas. 'Destroyed for Doing my Duty: Thomas Felton and the Penal Laws Under Elizabeth and James', in Kenneth Fincham and Peter Lake (eds), *Religious Politics in Post-Reformation England: Essays in Honour of Nicholas Tyacke* (Woodbridge, 2006), pp. 177–92.
Colclough, David. *Freedom of Speech in Early Stuart England* (Cambridge, 2005).
Colclough, David. *The Oxford History of Popular Print Culture, Volume 1: Cheap Print in Britain and Ireland to 1660* (Oxford, 2011).
Cole, Emily V. 'The State Apartment in the Jacobean Country House, 1603–1625', Ph.D., University of Sussex (2010).
Cole, Emily. 'Theobalds, Hertfordshire: The Plan and Interiors of an Elizabethan Country House', *Architectural History*, 60 (2017), 71–116.
Cole, Mary Hill. *A Portable Queen* (Amherst, MA, 1999).
Collinson, Patrick. *The Elizabethan Puritan Movement* (Oxford, 1990).
Collinson, Patrick. 'Ecclesiastical Vitriol: Religious Satire in the 1590s and the Invention of Puritanism', in John Guy (ed.), *The Reign of Elizabeth I: Court and Culture in the Last Decade* (Cambridge, 1995), pp. 150–70.
Collinson, Patrick. 'Antipuritanism', in John Coffey and Paul C. H. Lim (eds), *The Cambridge History of Puritanism* (Cambridge, 2008), pp. 19–33.
Collinson, Patrick. *Richard Bancroft and Elizabethan Anti-Puritanism* (Cambridge, 2013).
Collinson, Patrick. 'Bishop Richard Bancroft and the Succession', in Susan Doran and Paulina Kewes (eds), *Doubtful and Dangerous: The Question of Succession in Late Elizabethan England* (Manchester, 2014), pp. 92–111.
Colvin, H. M. (ed.). *The History of the King's Works*, vol. 4 (London, 1982).

Condren, Conal. *Argument and Authority in Early Modern England: The Presupposition of Oaths and Offices* (Cambridge, 2006).
Connolly, S. J. *Contested Island: Ireland 1460–1630* (Oxford, 2008).
Constantinidou, Natasha. *Responses to Religious Division c. 1580–1620: Public and Private, Divine and Temporal* (Leiden, 2017).
Cook, B. J. '"Stampt With Your Own Image": The Numismatic Dimension of Two Stuart Successions', in Paulina Kewes and Andrew McRae (eds), *Stuart Succession Literature: Moments and Transformations* (Oxford, 2019), pp. 303–18.
Cope, Esther S. *The Life of a Public Man, Edward, First Baron Montagu of Boughton* (Philadelphia, 1981).
Corbin, Peter Francis. 'A Death and a Marriage', Ph.D., University of Birmingham (1966).
Council, Norman. 'Ben Jonson, Inigo Jones, and the Transformation of Tudor Chivalry', *English Literary History*, 47 (1980), 259–75.
Courtney, Alexander. 'The Accession of James VI to the English Throne, 1601–1603', M.Phil., University of Cambridge (2004).
Courtney, Alexander. 'The Scottish King and the English Court: The Secret Correspondence of James VI, 1601–3', in Susan Doran and Paulina Kewes (eds), *Doubtful and Dangerous: The Question of Succession in Late Elizabethan England* (Manchester, 2014), pp. 134–51.
Craig, John. 'Bodies and Prayer in Early Modern England', in Natalie Mears and Alec Ryrie (eds), *Worship and the Parish Church in Early Modern Britain* (Farnham, 2013).
Craigie, James. 'The Basilicon Doron of King James I', *The Library*, s5-III (1948), 22–32.
Cramsie, John. *Kingship and Crown Finance Under James VI and I, 1603–1625* (Woodbridge, 2002).
Crankshaw, David. 'The Tudor Privy Council, c.1540–1603', gale.cengage.co.uk/images/Crankshaw-Privy-Council.pdf [accessed 5 October 2017].
Cressy, David. *Bonfires and Bells* (London, 1989).
Cressy, David. *Birth, Marriage and Death: Ritual, Religion, and the Life-cycle in Tudor and Stuart England* (Oxford, 1997).
Cressy, David. 'Four Hundred Years of Festivities', in Brenda Buchanan et al. (eds), *Gunpowder Plots* (London, 2005), pp. 49–79.
Cressy, David. *Dangerous Talk: Scandalous, Seditious, and Treasonable Speech in Pre-Modern England* (Oxford, 2010).
Croft, Pauline. 'Englishmen and the Spanish Inquisition, 1558–1625', *The English Historical Review*, 87 (1972), 249–68.
Croft, Pauline. 'Wardship in the Parliament of 1604', *Parliamentary History*, 2 (1983), 39–48.
Croft, Pauline. 'Parliament, Purveyance and the City of London, 1589–1608', *Parliamentary History*, 4 (1985), 9–34.
Croft, Pauline. 'The Religion of Robert Cecil', *The Historical Journal*, 34 (1991), 773–98.

Croft, Pauline. 'The Reputation of Robert Cecil: Libels, Political Opinion and Popular Awareness in the Early Seventeenth Century', *Transactions of the Royal Historical Society*, 1 (1991), 43–69.

Croft, Pauline. 'Serving the Archduke: Robert Cecil's Management of the Parliamentary Session of 1606', *Historical Research*, 64 (1991), 289–304.

Croft, Pauline. 'The Parliamentary Installation of Henry, Prince of Wales', *Historical Research*, 65 (1992), 177–93.

Croft, Pauline. 'The Debate on Annual Parliaments in the Early Seventeenth Century', *Parliaments, Estates & Representation*, 16 (1996), 163–74.

Croft, Pauline. 'The Catholic Gentry, the Earl of Salisbury and the Baronets of 1611', in Peter Lake and Michael Questier (eds), *Conformity and Orthodoxy in the English Church c1560–1660* (Woodbridge, 2000), pp. 262–81.

Croft, Pauline. '*Rex Pacificus*, Robert Cecil, and the 1604 Peace with Spain', in Glenn Burgess, Roland Wymer, and Jason Lawrence (eds), *The Accession of James I: Historical and Cultural Consequences* (Basingstoke, 2006), pp. 140–54.

Cromartie, Alan. *The Constitutionalist Revolution: An Essay on the History of England, 1450–1642* (Cambridge, 2006).

Cross, Robert Stuart Davis. 'To Counterbalance the World: England, Spain, and Peace in the Early 17th Century', Ph.D., Princeton University (2012).

Cross, Robert. '"The Onely Soveraigne Medecine": Religious Politics and Political Culture in the British-Spanish Match, 1596–1625', in Valentina Caldari and Sara J. Wolfson (eds), *Stuart Marriage Diplomacy* (Woodbridge, 2018), pp. 67–94.

Crouch, Linda. 'Salomon de Caus's Harmonic Institution: An Annotated Translation and Introduction', MA, University of Ohio (1980).

Cuddy, Neil. 'The King's Chambers: The Bedchamber of James I in Administration and Politics, 1603–1625', D.Phil., University of Oxford (1987).

Cuddy, Neil. 'The Revival of the Entourage: The Bedchamber of James I, 1603–25', in David Starkey et al. (eds), *The English Court from the Wars of the Roses to the Civil War* (Harlow, 1987), pp. 175–95.

Cuddy, Neil. 'Anglo-Scottish Union and the Court of James I, 1603–1625', *Transactions of the Royal Historical Society*, 39 (1989), 107–24.

Cuddy, Neil. 'The Conflicting Loyalties of a "Vulgar Counselor": The Third Earl of Southampton, 1597–1624', in J. Morrill, P. Slack, and D. Woolf (eds), *Public Duty and Private Conscience in Seventeenth-Century England: Essays Presented to G.E. Aylmer* (Oxford, 1993), pp. 121–50.

Cuddy, Neil. 'Reinventing a Monarchy: The Changing Structure and Political Function of the Stuart Court', in Eveline Cruickshanks (ed.), *The Stuart Courts* (Stroud, 2000), pp. 59–85.

Cuddy, Neil. 'The Real, Attempted "Tudor Revolution in Government": Salisbury's 1610 Great Contract', in G. W. Bernard and S. J. Gunn (eds), *Authority and Consent in Tudor England* (Aldershot, 2002), pp. 249–70.

Cummins, Neil, Morgan Kelly, and Cormac Ó Gráda. 'Living Standards and Plague in London, 1560–1665', *Economic History Review*, 69 (2016), 3–34.

Curran, Kevin. *Marriage, Performance, and Politics at the Jacobean Court* (Farnham, 2009).

Curtis, Mark H. 'Hampton Court Conference and its Aftermath', *History*, 46 (1961), 1–16.
Curtis, Mark. 'William Jones: Puritan Printer and Propagandist', *The Library*, 5th series, 19 (1964), 38–66.
Cust, Richard and Peter Lake. *Gentry Culture and the Politics of Religion: Cheshire on the Eve of Civil War* (Manchester, 2020).
Davidson, Peter and Thomas McCoog SJ. 'Father Robert's Convert—the Private Catholicism of Anne of Denmark', *Times Literary Supplement*, 25 November (2000), 16–17.
Davies, H. Neville. 'The Limitations of Festival: Christian IV's State Visit to England in 1606', in J. R. Mulryne and Margaret Shewring (eds), *Italian Renaissance Festivals and their European Influence* (Lampeter, 1992), pp. 311–35.
Davison, Peter. 'King James's Book of Bounty: From Manuscript to Print', *The Library*, 5th series, 28 (1973), 26–53.
Dawson, John P. 'The Privy Council and Private Law in the Tudor and Stuart Period: ii', *Michigan Law Review*, 48 (1950), 627–56.
Daye, Anne. 'The Role of Le Balet Comique in Forging the Stuart Masque: Part 1 The Jacobean Initiative', *Dance Research* 32 (2014), 185–207.
De Lisle, Leanda. *After Elizabeth: The Death of Elizabeth and the Coming of King James* (London, 2005).
Dean, Lucinda H. S. 'Crowns, Wedding Rings, and Processions: Continuity and Change in Representations of Scottish Royal Authority in State Ceremony, c.1214–c.1603', Ph.D., University of Stirling (2013).
Dean, Lucinda H. S. 'Enter the Alien: Foreign Consorts and their Royal Entries into Scottish Cities, c. 1449–1594', in R. Mulryne and A.M. Testaverde with I. Aliverti (eds), *The Iconography of Power: Ceremonial Entries in Early Modern Europe* (Farnham, 2015).
Dietz, Frederick C. *English Public Finance 1558–1641*, 2nd edition (London 1964).
Dillon, Janette. *Theatre, Court and City 1595–1610: Drama and Social Space in London* (Cambridge, 2000).
Dixon, Leif. *Practical Predestinarians in England, c. 1590–1640* (Farnham, 2014).
Doelman, James. '"A King of Thine Own Heart": The English Reception of King James VI and I's *Basilikon Doron*', *The Seventeenth Century*, 9 (1994), 1–9.
Doelman, J. 'The Accession of King James I and English Religious Poetry', *Studies in English Literature 1500–1900*, 34 (1994), 19–40.
Doelman, James. *King James I and the Religious Culture of England* (Cambridge, 2000).
Dolan, Francis E. *True Relations: Reading, Literature, and Evidence in Seventeenth-Century England* (Philadelphia, 2013).
Doran, Susan. 'Elizabeth I's Religion: The Evidence of her Letters', *The Journal of Ecclesiastical History*, 51 (2000), 699–720.
Doran, Susan. 'Loving and Affectionate Cousins? The Relationship between Elizabeth I and James VI of Scotland 1586–1603', in Susan Doran and Glenn Richardson (eds), *Tudor England and its Neighbours* (Basingstoke, 2005), pp. 203–34.

Doran, Susan. 'James VI and the Succession', in Ralph Houlbrooke (ed.), *James VI and I: Ideas, Authority and Government* (Farnham, 2006), pp. 25–42.

Doran, Susan. 'Elizabeth I and her Favourites: The Case of Sir Walter Ralegh', in Donald Stump, Linda Shenk, and Carole Levin (eds), *Elizabeth I and the Sovereign Arts* (Tempe, AZ, 2011), pp. 157–74.

Doran, Susan. 'Polemic and Prejudice: A Scottish King for an English Throne', in Susan Doran and Paulina Kewes (eds), *Doubtful and Dangerous: The Question of Succession in Late Elizabethan England* (Manchester, 2014), pp. 215–35.

Doran, Susan. *Elizabeth I and her Circle* (Oxford, 2015).

Doran, Susan. '1603: A Jagged Successsion', *Historical Research*, 93 (2020), 443–65.

Doran, Susan. 'The Late Raigne of Blessed Queene Elizabeth: Memory and Commemoration of Elizabeth I in Early-Jacobean England', *Groniek Historisch Tijdschrift*, 227 (2021), 156–68.

Doran, Susan and Paulina Kewes. 'Introduction: A Historiographical Perspective', in Susan Doran and Paulina Kewes (eds), *Doubtful and Dangerous: The Question of Succession in Late Elizabethan England* (Manchester, 2014), pp. 3–19.

Doran, Susan and Paulina Kewes. 'The Earlier Elizabethan Succession Question Revisited', in Susan Doran and Paulina Kewes (eds), *Doubtful and Dangerous: The Question of Succession in Late Elizabethan England* (Manchester, 2014), 20–44.

Duerloo, Luc. *Dynasty and Piety: Archduke Albert (1598–1621) and Habsburg Political Culture in an Age of Religious War* (London, 2016).

Duerloo, Luc. 'Hawks, Doves, and Magpies: The Business of Faction at the Court of the Archdukes', in Ruben Gonzalez Cuerva and Alexander Koller (eds), *Europe of Courts, A Europe of Factions* (Leiden, 2017), pp. 156–75.

Duncan-Jones, Katherine. '"Almost Always Smiling": Elizabeth's Last Two Years', in Elizabeth H. Hageman and Katherine Conway (eds), *Resurrecting Elizabeth I in Seventeenth-Century England* (Madison NJ, 2007), pp. 31–47.

Dunn, Brian Russell. 'Commons Debates 1603/4', Ph.D., Bryn Mawr College (1987).

Dunnigan, Sarah M. *Eros and Poetry at the Courts of Mary Queen of Scots and James VI* (Basingstoke, 2002).

Dunning, Chester S. L. and David R. C. Hudson. 'The Transportation of Irish Swordsmen to Sweden and Russia and Plantation in Ulster (1609–1613)', *Archivium Hibernicum*, 66 (2013), 422–53.

Durston, Christopher. *James I* (London, 1993).

Dutton, Richard. *Ben Jonson, Volpone, and the Gunpowder Plot* (Cambridge, 2008).

Dutton, Richard. *Mastering the Revels: The Regulation and Censorship of English Renaissance Drama* (Basingstoke, 1991 and 2022).

Dutton, Richard. *William Shakespeare: Court Dramatist* (Oxford, 2016).

Easterling, Heather C. 'Reading the Royal Entry (1604) in/as Print', *Early Theatre*, 20 (2017), 43–76.

Edwards, David. 'The Plight of the Earls: Tyrone and Tyrconnell's "Grievances" and Crown Coercion in Ulster, 1603–7', in Mary Ann Lyons and Thomas O'Connor (eds), *The Ulster Earls and Baroque Europe: Refashioning Irish Identities 1600–1800* (Dublin, 2010), pp. 53–76.

Edwards, David. 'Introduction: Union and Separation', in Simon Egan and David Edwards (eds), *The Scots in Early Stuart Ireland: Union and Separation in Two Kingdoms* (Manchester, 2016), pp. 1–28.

Edwards, David. 'Scottish Officials and Secular Government in Early Stuart Ireland', in Simon Egan and David Edwards (eds), *The Scots in Early Stuart Ireland: Union and Separation in Two Kingdoms* (Manchester, 2016), pp. 29–61.

Edwards, David. 'Political Change and Social Transformations, 1603–1641', in Jane Ohlmeyer (ed.), *The Cambridge History of Ireland, Volume 2: 1550–1730* (Cambridge, 2018), pp. 48–71.

Eiche, Sabine. 'Prince Henry's Richmond, the Project by Constantino de' Servi', *Apollo*, 148 (November 1998), 10–14.

Evans, Florence M. Greir. *The Principal Secretary of State* (Manchester, 1923).

Evrigenis, Joannis D. 'Sovereignty, Mercy, and Natural Law: King James VI/I and Jean Bodin', *History of European Ideas*, 45 (2019), 1073–88.

Feingold, Mordechai. 'Birth and Early Reception of a Masterpiece: Some Loose Ends and Common Misconceptions', in Mordechai Feingold (ed.), *Labourers in the Vineyard of the Lord: Scholarship and the Making of the King James Version of the Bible* (Leiden, 2018), pp. 1–29.

Field, Jemma Aeronny Jane. 'Anne of Denmark and the Arts in Jacobean England', Ph.D., University of Auckland (2015).

Field, Jemma. 'Dressing a Queen: The Wardrobe of Anna of Denmark at the Scottish Court of King James VI, 1590–1603', *The Court Historian*, 24 (2019), 152–67.

Field, Jemma. *Anna of Denmark: The Material and Visual Culture of the Stuart Courts* (Manchester, 2020).

Ferrell, Lori Anne. 'Kneeling and the Body Politic', in Donna B. Hamilton and Richard Strier (eds), *Religion, Literature and Politics in Post-Reformation England, 1540–1688* (Cambridge, 1996), pp. 70–88.

Ferrell, Lori Anne. *Government by Polemic: James I, the King's Preachers, and the Rhetorics of Conformity, 1603–1625* (Stanford, CA, 1998).

Ferrell, Lori Anne. *Bible and the People* (New Haven, CT, 2008).

Fielding, John. 'Arminianism in the Localities: Peterborough Diocese, 1603–1642', in Kenneth Fincham (ed.), *The Early Stuart Church, 1603–1642* (Basingstoke, 1993), pp. 93–113.

Fincham, Kenneth. 'Ramifications of the Hampton Court Conference in the Dioceses, 1603–9', *The Journal of Ecclesiastical History*, 36 (1985), 208–27.

Fincham, Kenneth. 'Prelacy and Politics: Archbishop Abbot's Defence of Protestant Orthodoxy', *Historical Research*, 61 (1988), 36–64.

Fincham, Kenneth. *Prelate as Pastor: The Episcopate of James I* (Oxford, 1990).

Fincham, Kenneth. 'Oxford and the Early Stuart Polity', in Nicholas Tyacke (ed.), *The History of the University of Oxford, Volume IV: Seventeenth-Century Oxford* (Oxford, 1997), pp. 179–210.

Fincham, Kenneth. 'Clerical Conformity from Whitgift to Laud', in Peter Lake and Michael Questier (eds), *Conformity and Orthodoxy in the English Church c. 1560–1660* (Woodbridge, 2000), pp. 125–58.

Fincham, Kenneth. 'The King James Bible: Crown, Church and People', *The Journal of Ecclesiastical History*, 71 (2020), 77–97.
Fincham, Kenneth and Peter Lake. 'The Ecclesiastical Policies of James I', in *Journal of British Studies*, 24 (1985), 169–207.
Fincham, Kenneth and Peter Lake. 'The Ecclesiastical Policies of James I and Charles I', in Kenneth Fincham (eds), *The Early Stuart Church 1603–1642* (Basingstoke, 1993), pp. 23–49.
Finlayson, J. Caitlin. 'Stephen Harrison's *The Arches of Triumph* (1604) and James I's Royal Entry in the London Literary Marketplace', in J. Caitlin Finlayson and Amrita Sen (eds), *Civic Performance* (Abingdon, 2020), pp. 176–99.
Fiorato, Sidia. 'Anna of Denmark and the Performance of the Queen Consort's Sovreignty', in Sidia Fiorato and John Drakakis (eds), *Performing the Renaissance Body: Essays on Drama, Law, and Representation* (Berlin, 2016), pp. 247–72.
Fischlin, Daniel. ' "Like a Mercenary Poet": The Politics and Poetics of James VI's *Lepanto*', in Sally Mapstone (ed.), *Older Scots Literature* (Edinburgh, 2005), pp. 540–59.
Fitzmaurice, Andrew. *Humanism and America* (Cambridge, 2003).
Fitzmaurice, Andrew. 'Moral Uncertainty in the Dispossession of Native Americans', in Peter C. Mancall (ed.), *The Atlantic World and Virginia, 1550–1624* (Chapel Hill, NC, 2007), pp. 383–409.
Flynn, Kelsey. 'The Atlantic Politics of Stuart Diplomacy', in Valentina Caldari and Sara J. Wolfson (eds), *Stuart Marriage Diplomacy* (Woodbridge, 2018), pp. 109–23.
Forse, James H. 'To Die or Not to Die, That is the Question: Borrowing and Adapting the King Lear Legend in the Anonymous *The True Chronicle History of King Leir* and Shakespeare's *King Lear*', *Ben Jonson Journal*, 21 (2014), 53–72.
Forster, G. C. F. 'The English Local Community and Local Government 1603–1625', in Alan G. R. Smith (ed.), *The Reign of James VI and I* (London and Basingstoke, 1977), pp. 195–213.
Foster, Andrew. 'The Clerical Estate Revitalised', in K. Fincham (ed.), *The Early Stuart Church, 1603–1642* (Basingstoke, 1993), pp. 139–60.
Foster, Andrew. 'Bishops, Church and State, c.1530–1646', in Anthony Milton (ed.), *The Oxford History of Anglicanism*, I (Oxford, 2017), pp. 84–103.
Frénéé-Hutchins, Samantha. *Boudica's Odyssey in Early Modern England* (Abingdon, 2016).
Fry, Cynthia. 'Perception of Influence: The Catholic Diplomacy of Queen Anna and Her Ladies, 1601–1604', in Nadine Akkerman and Birgit Houben (eds), *The Politics of Female Households: Ladies-in-Waiting Across Early Modern Europe* (Leiden, 2013), pp. 265–85.
Fry, Cynthia Ann. 'Diplomacy & Deception: King James VI of Scotland's Foreign Relations with Europe (c. 1584–1603)', Ph.D., University of St Andrews (2014).
Frye, Susan. 'Anne of Denmark and the Historical Contextualisation of Shakespeare and Fletcher's Henry VIII', in James Daybell (ed.), *Women and Politics in Early Modern England, 1450–1700* (Abingdon, 2016), pp. 181–93.
Fryer, Peter. *Staying Power: The History of Black People in Britain* (London, 1984).

Fuller, Thomas. *The Church History of Britain from the Birth of Jesus Christ until the Year MDCXKVIII...*, edited by James Nichols, 3 (London, 1837).
Gajda, Alexandra. 'Debating War and Peace in Late Elizabethan England', *The Historical Journal*, 52 (2009), 851–78.
Gajda, Alexandra. 'Essex and the "Popish Plot"', in Susan Doran and Paulina Kewes (eds), *Doubtful and Dangerous: The Question of Succession in Late Elizabethan England* (Manchester, 2014), pp. 115–33.
Galloway, Bruce. *The Union of England and Scotland 1603–1608* (Edinburgh, 1986).
Games, Alison. *The Web of Empire: English Cosmopolitans in an Age of Expansion, 1560–1660* (Oxford, 2008).
Gausden, Christopher Paul. 'The Literary Culture of the English Court, c. 1590–1612', D.Phil., University of Oxford (2020).
Gay, Edwin F. 'The Midland Revolt and the Inquisitions of Depopulation of 1607', *Transactions of the Royal Historical Society*, 18 (1904), 195–244.
Gazzard, Hugh. '"Those Graue Presentments of Antiquitie" Samuel Daniel's Philotas and the Earl of Essex', *The Review of English Studies*, 51 (2000), 423–50.
George, Timothy. *John Robinson and the English Separatist Tradition* (Macon, GA, 1982).
Gibney, John. 'Early Modern Ireland: A British Atlantic Colony?', *History Compass*, 6 (2008), 172–82.
Gifford, J. W. 'The Controversy of the Oath of Allegiance', D.Phil., University of Oxford (1971).
Gilchrist, Kim. '"The Wonder is, He Hath Endured So Long": King Lear and the Erosion of the Brutan Histories', *Shakespeare*, 16 (2020), 40–59.
Gillespie, Raymond. *Colonial Ulster: The Settlement of East Ulster, 1600–1641* (Cork, 1985).
Goldberg, Jonathan. *James I and the Politics of Literature: Jonson, Shakespeare, Donne and Their Contemporaries* (Stanford, CA, 1989).
Goldman, William S. 'Spain and the Founding of Jamestown', *The William and Mary Quarterly*, 68 (2011), 427–50.
Goldring, Elizabeth. *Nicholas Hilliard: Life of an Artist* (New Haven, CT and New York, 2019).
Goodare, Julian. 'The Scottish Witchcraft Panic of 1597', in Julian Goodare (ed.), *The Scottish Witch-Hunt in Context* (Manchester, 2002), pp. 51–72.
Goodare, Julian. *The Government of Scotland 1560–1625* (Oxford, 2004).
Goodare, Julian. 'The Scottish Parliament and its Early Modern "Rivals"', in *Parliaments Estates and Representation*, 24 (2004), pp. 147–72.
Goodare, Julian. 'The Attempted Scottish Coup of 1596', in Julian Goodare and Alasdair Macdonald (eds), *Sixteenth-Century Scotland: Essays in Honour of Michael Lynch* (Leiden, 2008), pp. 311–36.
Goodare, Julian. 'The Scottish Presbyterian Movement in 1596', *Canadian Journal of History*, 45 (2010), 21–48.
Goodare, Julian. 'The Ainslie Bond', in Steve Boardman (ed.), *Kings, Lords and Men in Scotland and Britain: Essays in Honour of Jenny Wormald* (Edinburgh, 2014), 301–20.

Gough, Melinda J. *Dancing Queen: Marie de Medicis Ballets at the Court of Henri IV* (Toronto, 2018).
Gough, Melinda J. 'Dynastic Marriage, Diplomatic Ceremonial, and the Treaties of London (1604–05) and Antwerp (1609)', in Valentina Caldari and Sara J. Wolfson (eds), *Stuart Marriage Diplomacy* (Woodbridge, 2018), pp. 288–301.
Grant, Ruth. 'The Brig O'Dee Affair, the Sixth Earl of Huntly and the Politics of the Counter-Reformation', in Julian Goodare and Michael Lynch (eds), *The Reign of James VI* (Edinburgh 2000), pp. 93–109.
Grant, Ruth. 'Friendship, Politics and Religion: George Gordon, Sixth Earl of Huntley and King James VI, 1581–1595', in Miles Kerr-Peterson and Steven J. Reid (eds), *James VI and Noble Power in Scotland 1578–1603* (Abingdon, 2017), pp. 57–80.
Gray, Douglas. 'The Royal Entry in Sixteenth-Century Scotland', in Sally Mapstone and Juliette Wood (eds), *The Rose and the Thistle: Essays on the Culture of Late Medieval and Renaissance Scotland* (East Linton, 1998), pp. 10–37.
Grayson, John Christopher. 'From Protectorate to Partnership: Anglo-Dutch Relations 1598–1625', Ph.D., University of London (1978).
Green, Ian. *Print and Protestantism in Early Modern England* (Oxford, 2000).
Green, Mary Anne Everett. *Lives of the Princesses of England from the Norman Conquest*, vol. 5 (London, 1857).
Greenslade, Michael. *Catholic Staffordshire 1500–1850* (Leominster, 2006).
Gregory, Alden. 'An Early Seventeenth-Century Gunpowder Plot Monument and a Portrait Relief of James I in the Queen's House at the Tower of London', *The Sculpture Journal*, 26 (2017), 305–20.
Gristwood, Sarah. *Arbella: England's Lost Queen* (London, 2003).
Grosvenor, Ian D. 'Catholics and Politics: The Worcestershire Election of 1604', *Recusant History*, 14 (1977), 149–62.
Groundwater, Anna. 'The Chasm Between James VI and I's Vision of the Orderly "Middle Shires" and the "Wickit" Scottish Borderers Between 1587 and 1625', *Renaissance and Reformation*, 30 (2006), 105–32.
Groundwater, Anna. 'From Whitehall to Jedburgh, the Role of Patronage Networks in the Government of the Scottish Borders, 1603 to 1625', *The Historical Journal*, 53 (2010), 871–93.
Groundwater, Anna. *The Scottish Middle March, 1573–1625: Power, Kinship, Allegiance* (Woodbridge, 2010).
Groundwater, Anna. 'The Middle Shires Divided: Tensions at the Heart of Anglo-Scottish Union', in Sharon Adams and Julian Goodare (eds), *Scotland in the Age of Two Revolutions* (Woodbridge, 2014), pp. 23–40.
Groundwater, Anna. 'He "Made Them Friends in His Cabinet": James VI's Suppression of the Scott-Ker Feud', in Miles Kerr-Peterson and Steven J. Reid (eds), *James VI and Noble Power in Scotland 1578–1603* (Abingdon, 2017), pp. 98–116.
Grueber, Herbert A. *A Guide to the Exhibition of English Medals* (London, 1891).
Grueber, Herbert A. *Handbook of the Coins of Great Britain and Ireland in the British Museum* (London, 1899).
Gruenfelder, J. K. 'Two Midland Parliamentary Elections of 1604', *Midland History*, 3 (1976), 241–55.

Gruenfelder, John K. *Influence in Early Stuart Elections, 1604–1640* (Columbus, OH, 1981).
Guerci, Manolo. 'The Construction of Northumberland House and the Patronage of its Original Builder, Lord Henry Howards, 1603–14', *The Antiquaries Journal*, 90 (2010), 1–60.
Gustafsson, Harald. 'The Conglomerate State: A Perspective on State Formation in Early Modern Europe', *Scandinavian Journal of History*, 23 (1998), 189–213.
Guy, John. *My Heart Is My Own: The Life of Mary Queen of Scots* (London, 2004).
Guy, John. *Elizabeth: The Forgotten Years* (London, 2016).
Ha, Polly. *English Presbyterianism, 1590–1640* (Stanford, CA, 2011).
Hackett, Helen. *Virgin Mother, Maiden Queen: Elizabeth I and the Cult of the Virgin Mary* (New York, 1995).
Hadfield, Andrew. *Lying in Early Modern English Culture: From the Oath of Supremacy to the Oath of Allegiance* (Oxford, 2017).
Haigh, Christopher. 'The Character of an Antipuritan', *The Sixteenth Century Journal*, 35, (2004), 671–88.
Hall, Kim F. *Things of Darkness: Economies of Race and Gender in Early Modern England* (Ithaca, NY and London, 1995).
Hamlin, William M. *Montaigne's English Journey: Reading the Essays in Shakespeare's Day* (Oxford, 2013).
Hammer, Paul E. J. 'Elizabeth's Unsettling Succession', *Huntington Library Quarterly*, 78, (2015), 553–61.
Hammond, Gerald. 'Translations of the Bible', in Michael Hattaway (ed.), *A New Companion to English Renaissance Literature and Culture* (Oxford, 2010), pp. 419–29.
Hampson, James E. 'Richard Cosin and the Rehabilitation of the Clerical Estate in Late Elizabethan England', Ph.D., University of St Andrews (1997).
Hankins, Jeffrey R. 'Local Government and Society in Early Modern England: Hertfordshire and Essex c.1590–1630', Ph.D., Louisiana State University (2003).
Hannay, Margaret P. *Mary Sidney, Lady Wroth* (Farnham, 2010).
Hannay, Margaret P., Michael G. Brennan, and Mary Ellen Lamb (eds). *The Ashgate Research Companion to The Sidneys, 1500–1700, Volume 1: Lives* (Farnham, 2015).
Hardin, Richard F. 'The Early Poetry of the Gunpowder Plot: Myth in the Making', *English Literary Renaissance*, 22 (1992), 62–79.
Harris, Tim. *Rebellion: Britain's First Stuart Kings* (Oxford, 2014).
Hauge, Peter. 'Dowland's Seven Tears, or the Art of Concealing the Art', *Dansk årbog for Musikforskning*, 29 (2001), 9–36.
Hawkins, Edward. *The Silver Coins of England* (London, 1841).
Heal, Felicity. *The Power of Gifts: Gift Exchange in Early Modern England* (Oxford, 2014).
Healey, Jonathan. 'Land, Population and Famine in the English Uplands: A Westmorland Case Study, c.1370–1650', *Agricultural History Review*, 59 (2011), 151–75.
Healey, Jonathan. 'The Political Culture of the English Commons, c.1550–1650', *Agricultural History Review*, 60 (2012), 266–87.
Healy, Simon. 'Crown Revenue and the Political Culture of Early Stuart England', Ph.D., Birkbeck, University of London (2015).

Hearn, Karen (ed.). *Dynasties: Painting in Tudor and Jacobean England 1530–1630* (London, 1995).

Hearn, Karen. 'A Question of Judgement: Lucy Harington, Countess of Bedford, as Art Patron and Collector', in Edward Chaney (ed.), *The Evolution of English Collecting* (New Haven and London, 2003), pp. 221–39.

Heaton, Gabriel. '"The Poor Man's Petition": Anthony Atkinson and the Politics of Libel', *Huntington Library Quarterly*, 69 (2006), 105–20.

Hebb, David Delison. *Piracy and the English Government 1616–1642* (Aldershot, 1994).

Heddle, Donna. *John Stewart of Baldynneis Roland Furius: A Scots Poem in its European Context* (Leiden, 2008).

Heinze, R. W. 'Proclamations and Parliamentary Protest, 1539–1610', in D. J. Guth and J. W. McKenna (eds), *Tudor Rule and Revolution: Essays for G.R. Elton from his American Friends* (Cambridge, 1982), pp. 237–59.

Helmers, Helmer. 'Public Diplomacy in Early Modern Europe', *Media History*, 22 (2016), 401–20.

Herman, Peter C. '"Best of Poets, Best of Kings": King James and the Scene of Monarchic Verse', in Mark Fischlin and Daniel Fortier (eds), *Royal Subjects: Essays on the Writings of James VI and I* (Detroit, 2002), 61–103.

Herman, Peter C. *Royal Poetrie: Monarchic Verse and the Political Imaginary of Early Modern England* (Cornell, 2010).

Herman, Peter C. '"A Deed Without a Name", the Gunpowder Plot and Terrorism', *Journal for Cultural Research*, 18 (2014), 114–31.

Hicks, Leo. 'The Embassy of Sir Anthony Standen in 1603', Part III: *Recusant History*, 6 (1962), 163–94.

Highley, Christopher. 'The Place of Scots in the Scottish Play: Macbeth and the Politics of Language', in Will Maley and Andrew Murphy (eds), *Shakespeare and Scotland* (Manchester, 2004), 53–66.

Hitchmough, Wendy. 'Setting' the Stuart Court: Placing Portraits in the "Performance" of Anglo-Spanish Negotiations', *Journal of the History of Collections*, 32 (2020), 245–64.

Hill, Christopher. *Economic Problems of the Church* (London, 1971).

Hill, Robert. 'Art and Patronage: Sir Henry Wotton and the Venetian Embassy 1604–1624', in Marika Keblusek and Badeloch Vera Noldusp (eds), *Double Agents: Cultural and Political Brokerage in Early Modern Europe* (Leiden, 2011), pp. 27–58.

Hill, Tracey. '"Representing the Awefull Authoritie of Soveraigne Majestie": Monarchs and Mayors in Anthony Munday's The Triumphes of Re-uinited Britania', in G. Burgess, R. Wymer, and J. Lawrence (eds), *The Accession of James I: Historical and Cultural Consequences* (Basingstoke, 2006), 15–33.

Hindle, Steve. 'Imagining Insurrection in Seventeenth-Century England: Representations of the Midland Rising of 1607', *History Workshop Journal*, 66 (2008), 21–61.

Hirst, Derek. 'Elections and the Privileges of the House of Commons in the Early Seventeenth Century: Confrontation or Compromise?', *The Historical Journal*, 18 (1975), 851–62.

Hodgetts, Michael. 'The Plot in Warwickshire and Worcestershire', *Midland Catholic History*, 12 (2006), 16–34.

Hodgetts, Michael. 'Coughton and the Gunpowder Plot', in Peter Marshall and Geoffrey Abbot Scott (eds), *Catholic Gentry in English Society: The Throckmortons of Coughton from Reformation to Emancipation* (Farnham, 2009), pp. 93–121.
Holland, Susan. 'Archbishop Abbot and the Problem of "Puritanism"', *The Historical Journal*, 37 (1994), 23–43.
Holmes, Clive. 'Witchcraft and Possession at the Accession of James I: The Publication of Samuel Harsnett's *A Declaration of Egregious Popish Impostures*', in John Newton (ed.), *Witchcraft and the Act of 1604* (Leiden and Boston, MA, 2008), pp. 69–90.
Hood, Gervase. 'A Netherlandic Triumphal Arch for James I', in Susan Roach (ed.), *Across the Narrow Seas: Studies in the History and Bibliography of Britain and the Low Countries. Presented to Anna E. C. Simoni* (London, 1991), pp. 67–82.
Hornback, Robert. 'Staging Puritanism in the Early 1590s: The Carnivalesque, Rebellious Clowns Anti-Puritan Stereotype', *Renaissance and Reformation*, 24 (2000), 31–67.
Horning, Audrey. *Ireland in the Virginian Sea* (Chapel Hill, NC, 2013).
Horrox, Rosemary. 'Caterpillars of the Commonwealth? Courtiers in Late Medieval England', in Rowena E. Archer and Simon Walker (eds), *Rulers and Ruled in Late Medieval England* (London, 1995), pp. 1–16.
Hoskins, W. G. 'Harvest Fluctuations and English Economic History, 1480–1619', *The Agricultural History Review*, 12 (1968), 28–46.
Houliston, Victor. 'An Apology for Donne's Pseudo-Martyr', *The Review of English Studies*, new series, 57 (2006), 474–86.
Houliston, Victor. *Catholic Resistance in Elizabethan England: Robert Persons's Jesuit Polemic, 1580–1610* (Aldershot, 2007).
Howard, Jean E. 'Thomas Heywood', in Ton Hoenselaars (ed.), *The Cambridge Companion to Shakespeare and Contemporary Dramatists* (Cambridge, 2012), pp. 120–33.
Hoyle, Richard W., Danae Tankard, and Simon R. Neal. *Heard before the King: Registers of Petitions to James I, 1603–16 England and Wales. Court of Requests.* List & Index Society (Kew, 2006).
Hoyle, R. W. 'The Masters of Requests and the Small Change of Jacobean Patronage', *The English Historical Review*, 126 (2011), 544–81.
Hulse, Lynn. 'The Musical Patronage of Robert Cecil, First Earl of Salisbury (1563–1612)', *Journal of the Royal Musical Association*, 116 (1991), 24–40.
Hulse, Lynn Mary. 'The Musical Patronage of the English Aristocracy, c. 1590–1640', Ph.D., University of London (1992).
Hunt, Alice. 'The Bright Star of the North: James I and his English Coronation', *Medieval English Theatre*, 38 (2016), 22–37.
Hunt, Arnold. 'Laurence Chaderton and the Hampton Court Conference', in Susan Wabuda and Caroline Litzenberger (eds), *Belief and Practice in Reformation England: A Tribute to Patrick Collinson from his Students* (Aldershot, 1998), 207–28.
Hunt, Arnold, Dora Thornton, and George Dalgliesh. 'A Jacobean Antiquary Reassessed: Thomas Lyte, the Lyte Genealogy and the Lyte Jewel', *The Antiquaries Journal*, 96 (2016), 169–205.

Hussey, Roland Dennis. 'America in European Diplomacy, 1597–1604', *Revista de Historia de América*, 41 (1956), 1–30.
Hutson, Lorna. *England's Insular Imagining: The Elizabethan Erasure of Scotland* (Cambridge, 2023).
Hutton, Ronald. *The Rise and Fall of Merry England* (Oxford, 1994).
Ingram, Martin. *Church Courts, Sex and Marriage 1570–1640* (Cambridge, 1990).
Ivic, Christopher. *The Subject of Britain, 1603–25* (Manchester, 2020).
Jack, R. D. S. 'Music, Poetry and Performance at the Court of James VI', *John Donne Journal*, 25 (2006), 37–63.
Jack, Sybil M. '"A Pattern for a King's Inauguration": The Coronation of James I in England', *Parergon*, 21 (2004), 67–91.
Jackson, W. A. 'The Funeral Procession of Queen Elizabeth', *The Library*, 4th series, 26 (1945), 262–71.
Jago, James Sherrinton. 'The Dissemination and Reassessment of Private Religious Space in Early Modern England', Ph.D., University of York (2012).
James, Anne. 'Preaching the Good News: William Barlow Narrates the Fall of Essex and the Gunpowder Plot', in Torrance Kirby and P. G. Stanwood (eds), *Paul's Cross and the Culture of Persuasion in England, 1520–1640* (Leiden, 2014), pp. 345–60.
James, Anne. *Poets, Players and Preachers: Remembering the Gunpowder Plot in Seventeenth-century England* (Toronto, 2016).
Jones, W. J. 'Due Process and Slow Process in the Elizabethan Chancery', *American Journal of Legal History*, 6 (1962), 123–50.
Jefferson, Lisa. 'A Garter Installation Ceremony in 1606', *The Court Historian*, 6 (2001), 141–50.
Jowitt, Claire. 'Colonialism, Politics and Romanization in John Fletcher's "Bonduca"', *Studies in English Literature, 1500–1900*, 43 (2003), 475–94.
Juhala, Amy L. 'The Household and Court of King James VI', Ph.D., University of Edinburgh (2000).
Juhala, Amy L. '"For the King Favours Them Very Strangely": The Rise of James VI's Chamber, 1580–1603', in Miles Kerr-Peterson and Steven J. Reid (eds), *James VI and Noble Power, 1578–83* (Abingdon, 2017), 155–76.
Kanemura, Rei. 'Kingship by Descent or Kingship by Election? The Contested Tide of James VI and I', *Journal of British Studies*, 52 (2013), 317–42.
Kanemura, Rei. 'Historical Perspectives on the Anglo-Scottish Union Debate: Re-reading the Norman Conquest in the 1610s', *History of European Ideas*, 40 (2014), 155–76.
Kaufman, Lucy. 'Ecclesiastical Improvements, Lay Impropriations, and the Building of a Post-Reformation Church in England, 1560–1600', *The Historical Journal*, 58 (2015), 1–23.
Kenny, Robert W. *Elizabeth's Admiral: The Political Career of Charles Howard Earl of Nottingham 1536–1624* (Baltimore and London, 1970).
Kernan, Alvin. *The King's Playwright* (New Haven and London, 1995).
Kewes, Paulina. 'Julius Caesar in Jacobean England', *The Seventeenth Century*, 17 (2002), 155–86.

Kewes, Paulina. '"I Ask Your Voices and Your Suffrages": The Bogus Rome of Peele and Shakespeare's Titus Andronicus', *The Review of Politics*, 78 (2016), 551–70.

Kewes, Paulina. '"The Idol of State Innovators and Republicans": Robert Persons's Conference about the Next Succession (1594/5) in Stuart Britain', in Paulina Kewes and Andrew McCrae (eds), *Stuart Succession Literature: Moments and Transformations* (Oxford, 2019), pp. 149–204.

Kenyon, R. L. *The Gold Coins of England* (London, 1884).

Kesselring, K. J. '"Berwick is our England": Local and National Identities in an Elizabethan Border Town', in Norman L. Jones and Daniel Woolf (eds), *Local Identities in Late Medieval and Early Modern England* (Basingstoke, 2007), pp. 92–112.

Kesselring, K. J. and Natalie Mears. 'Introduction: Star Chamber Matters', in *idem*, *Star Chamber Matters: An Early Modern Court and its Records* (London, 2021), pp. 1–18.

Kilroy, Deborah. 'All the King's Men? A Demographic Study of Opinion in the First English Parliament of James I, 1604–10', *Parliaments, Estates and Representation*, 41 (2021), 1–23.

Kiséry, András. *Hamlet's Moment: Drama and Political Knowledge in Early Modern England* (Oxford, 2016).

Knafla, Louis. A. *Law and Politics in Jacobean England: The Tracts of Lord Chancellor Ellesmere* (Cambridge, 1977).

Knowles, James. '"To Enlight the Darksome Night, Pale Cinthia Doth Arise": Anna of Denmark, Elizabeth I and the Images of Royalty', in Clare McManus (ed.), *Women and Culture at the Courts of the Stuart Queens* (New York, 2003), pp. 21–48.

Krantz, Susan E. 'Thomas Dekker's Political Commentary in The Whore of Babylon', *Studies in English Literature, 1500–1900*, 35 (1995), 271–91.

Kupperman, Karen Ordahl. *The Jamestown Project* (Cambridge, MA, 2007).

Kurland, Stuart M. '*Hamlet* and the Stuart Succession?', *Studies in English Literature, 1500–1900*, 34 (1994), 279–300.

Kyle, Chris R. *Theatre of State: Parliament and Political Culture in Early Stuart England* (Stanford, CA, 2012).

Lake, Peter. *Moderate Puritans and the Elizabethan Church* (Cambridge, 1982).

Lake, Peter. *Anglicans and Puritans? Presbyterianism and English Conformist Thought from Whitgift to Hooker* (London, 1988).

Lake, Peter. 'Lancelot Andrewes, John Buckeridge, and Avant-Garde Conformity at the Court of James I', in Linda Levy Peck (ed.), *The Mental World of the Jacobean Court* (Cambridge, 1990), pp. 113–33.

Lake, Peter. 'Moving the Goal Posts? Modified Subscription and the Conformity in the Early Stuart Church', in Peter Lake and Michael Questier (eds), *Conformity and Orthodoxy in the English Church, c.1560–1660* (Woodbridge 2000), 179–205.

Lake, Peter. 'Ministers, Magistrates and the Production of "Order" in Measure for Measure', *Shakespeare Survey*, 54 (2001), 165–81.

Lake, Peter. *The Boxmaker's Revenge: 'Orthodoxy', 'Heterodoxy' and the Politics of the Parish in Early Stuart London* (Manchester, 2001).

Lake, Peter with Michael Questier. *The Antichrist's Lewd Hat: Protestants, and Players in Post-Reformation England* (New Haven, 2002).

Lake, Peter. 'The King (the Queen) and the Jesuit: James Stuart's True Law of Free Monarchies in Context/s', *Transactions of the Royal Historical Society*, 6th series, 14 (2004), 243–60.

Lake, Peter. 'Anti-Puritanism: The Structure of a Prejudice', in Kenneth Fincham and Peter Lake (eds), *Religious Politics in Post-Reformation England: Essays in Honour of Nicholas Tyacke* (Woodbridge, 2006), pp. 80–97.

Lake, Peter. *Bad Queen Bess?* (Oxford, 2016).

Lake, Peter. ' "Free Speech" in Elizabethan and Early Stuart England', in Robert Ingram, Jason Peacey, and Alex W. Barber (eds), *Freedom of Speech, 1500–1850* (Manchester, 2021), pp. 63–97.

Lake, Peter and Michael Questier. *All Hail to the Archpriest: Confessional Conflict, Toleration, and the Politics of Publicity in Post-Reformation England* (Oxford, 2019).

Lancashire, Anne. 'Dekker's Accession Pageant for James I', *Early Theatre: A Journal Associated with the Records of Early English Drama*, 12 (2009), 39–50.

La Rocca, John J. SJ. 'James I and his Catholic Subjects, 1606–1612: Some Financial Implications', *Recusant History*, 18 (1987), 251–62.

Lazo, Katherine Shreve. 'Catholic Loyalty in Jacobean England: Thomas Preston's Appeal to the English Catholic Laity over the 1606 Oath of Allegiance', MA, Vanderbilt University (2015).

Leader, John Temple. *Life of Sir Robert Dudley, Earl of Warwick and Duke of Northumberland* (Florence, 1895).

Lee Jr, Maurice. *James I and Henri IV* (Urbana, IL, 1970).

Lee Jr, Maurice. 'James VI's "Government of Scotland after 1603" ', *The Scottish Historical Review*, 55 (1976), 41–53.

Lee Jr, Maurice. *Great Britain's Solomon: James VI and I in His Three Kingdoms* (Urbana and Chicago, IL, 1990).

Lefranc, Pierre. 'Ralegh in 1596 and 1603: Three Unprinted Letters in the Huntington Library', *Huntington Library Quarterly*, 29 (1966), 344–5.

Lemon, Rebecca. *Treason by Words: Literature, Law, and Rebellion in Shakespeare's England* (Ithaca, NY, 2006).

Lenman, Bruce. *England's Colonial Wars* (Harlow, 2001).

Lennon, Colm. 'The Flight of the Earls in British-Spanish Diplomacy', in Mary Ann Lyons and Thomas O'Connor (eds), *The Ulster Earls and Baroque Europe: Refashioning Irish Identities, 1600–1800* (Dublin, 2010), pp. 77–87.

Levack, Brian P. 'Law, Sovereignty and the Union', in Roger A. Mason (ed.), *Scots and Britons: Scottish Political Thought and the Union of 1603* (Cambridge, 1994), pp. 213–37.

Levin, Carole. 'Elizabeth's Ghost: The Afterlife of the Queen in Stuart England', *Royal Studies Journal*, 1 (2014), 1–16.

Levin, Carole. 'Heroic Queens in the Age of the Stuart Kings: Elizabeth and Boudicca', *Parergon*, 37 (2020), 51–76.

Lewalski, Barbara Kiefer. 'Enacting Opposition: Anne of Denmark and the Subversions of Masquing', in her *Writing Women in Jacobean England* (Cambridge, MA, 1993), pp. 15–43.

Lidster, Amy. '"With Much Labour Out of Scattered Papers": The Caroline Reprints of Thomas Heywood's 1 and 2 *If You Know Not Me You Know Nobody*', *Renaissance Drama*, 49 (2021), 205–28.
Lindley, David. 'David Hume, *De Unione Tractatus Secundus*', *The British Library Journal*, 4 (1978), 145–7.
Lindley, David. 'Who Paid for Campion's Lord Hay's Masque', *Notes and Queries*, 26 (1979), 144–5.
Lindquist, Eric N. 'The Failure of the Great Contract', *The Journal of Modern History*, 57 (1985), 617–51.
Lindquist, Eric N. 'The Last Years of the First Earl of Salisbury, 1610–1612', *Albion*, 18 (1986), 23–41.
Lindquist, Eric N. 'The King, the People and the House of Commons: The Problem of Early Jacobean Purveyance', *The Historical Journal*, 31 (1988), 549–70.
Lindquist, Eric N. 'The Case of Sir Francis Goodwin', *The English Historical Review*, 114 (1989), 670–7.
Lindsay, Barbara N. and J. W. Williamson. 'Myth of the Conqueror: Prince Henry Stuart and Protestant Militancy', *The Journal of Medieval and Renaissance Studies*, 5 (1975), 203–22.
Loades, David. *The Tudor Court* (Bangor, 1992).
Loomie, Albert J. 'Toleration and Diplomacy: The Religious Issue in Anglo-Spanish Relations, 1603–1605', *Transactions of the American Philosophical Society*, 53 (1963), 1–60.
Loomie, A. J. 'Philip III and the Stuart Succession in England, 1600–1603', *Revue Belge de Philologie et d'Histoire*, 43 (1965), 492–514.
Loomie, A. J. 'King James I's Catholic Consort', *Huntington Library Quarterly*, 34 (1971), 303–16.
Loomie, Albert J. SJ. *Guy Fawkes in Spain: The 'Spanish Treason' in Spanish Documents* (London, 1971).
Loomie, Albert J. 'Spanish Secret Diplomacy at the Court of James', in Malcolm R. Thorp and Arthur Joseph Slavin (eds), *Politics, Religion & Diplomacy in Early Modern Europe: Essays in Honour of De Lamar Jensen* (Kirksville, MO, 1994), pp. 231–44.
Loomis, Catherine. *The Death of Elizabeth I: Remembering and Reconstructing the Virgin Queen* (New York, 2010).
Loomis, Catherine. '"Withered Plants Do Bud and Blossom Yeelds": Naturalizing James I's Succession', in Robert S. Sturges (ed.), *Law and Sovereignty in the Middle Ages and the Renaissance* (Turnhout, 2011), pp. 133–50.
Lunn OSB, Maurus. 'English Benedictines and the Oath of Allegiance 1606–1647', *Recusant History*, 10 (1969), 146–64.
Lyall, Roderick J. 'The Marketing of James VI/I: Scotland, England and the Continental Book Trade', *Quaerendo*, 32 (2002), 204–17.
Lyall, Roderick J. '"Thrie Truear Hairts": Alexander Montgomerie, Henry Constable, Henry Keir and Cultural Politics in Renaissance Britain', *The Innes Review*, 54 (2003), 186–215.

Lyall, Roderick J. *Alexander Montgomerie: Poetry, Politics and Cultural Change in Jacobean Scotland* (Tempe, AZ, 2005).

Lynch, Michael. 'Court Ceremony and Ritual during the Personal Reign of James VI', in Julian Goodare and Michael Lynch (eds), *The Reign of James VI* (Edinburgh, 2000), pp. 71–92.

Lynch, Michael. 'James VI and the "Highland Problem"', in Julian Goodare and Michael Lynch (eds), *The Reign of James VI* (Edinburgh, 2000), pp. 208–27.

Lynch, Michael. 'The Reassertion of Princely Power in Scotland: The Reigns of Mary Queen of Scots and King James VI', in Martin Gosman, A. A. MacDonald, and Arie Johan Vanderjagt (eds), *Princes and Princely Culture, 1450–1650*, 2 vols (Leiden, 2003), I, pp. 199–238.

MacCaffrey, Wallace T. *Elizabeth I: War and Politics, 1588–1603* (Princeton, 1992).

MacColl, Alan. 'The Meaning of "Britain" in Medieval and Early Modern England', *Journal of British Studies*, 45 (2006), 248–69.

MacDonald, Alan R. 'The Subscription Crisis and Church–State Relations 1584–1586', *Scottish Church History Society*, 35 (1994), 222–55.

MacDonald, Alan R. *The Jacobean Kirk, 1567–1625: Sovereignty, Polity, and Liturgy* (Aldershot, 1998).

MacDonald, Alan R. 'James VI and the General Assembly', in Julian Goodare and Michael Lynch (eds), *The Reign of James VI* (Edinburgh, 2000), pp. 170–85.

MacDonald, Alan R. *The Burghs and Parliament in Scotland c. 1550–1651* (Aldershot, 2007).

MacDonald, Alan R. 'Consultation and Consent Under James VI', *The Historical Journal*, 54 (2011), 287–306.

MacDonald, Alan R. 'Consulation, Counsel, and the "Early Stuart" Period in Scotland', in Jacqueline Rose (ed.), *The Politics of Counsel in England and Scotland, 1286–1707* (Oxford, 2016), pp. 193–210.

MacGregor, Martin. 'The Statutes of Iona: Text and Context', *The Innes Review*, 57 (2006), 111–81.

MacGregor, Martin. 'Civilizing Gaelic Scotland: The Scottish Isles and the Stewart Empire', in É. Ó Ciardha and M. Ó Siochrú (eds), *The Plantation of Ulster: Ideology and Practice* (Manchester, 2012), pp. 33–54.

MacMillan, Ken. 'Exploration, Trade and Empire', in Susan Doran and Norman Jones (eds), *The Elizabethan World* (Abingdon, 2011), 646–62.

Maltby, Judith. *Prayer Book and People in Elizabethan and Early Stuart England* (Cambridge, 1998).

Mancall, Peter C. *Hakluyt's Promise* (New Haven, 2007).

Manley, Lawrence. *The Literature and Culture in Early Modern London* (Cambridge, 1995).

Manning, Roger B. *Village Revolts: Social Protest and Popular Disturbances in England, 1509–1640* (Oxford, 1988).

Manning, Roger B. 'The Jacobean Peace, The Irenic Policy of James VI and I and its Legacy', *Quidditas*, 39 (2018), 148–81.

Manuscript Pamphleteering in Early Stuart England, mpese.ac.uk [accessed 11 December 2022].

Marcus, Leah S. *Puzzling Shakespeare* (Berkeley, CA, 1988).

Marcus, Leah S. 'Literature and the Court', in David Loewenstein and Janel M. Mueller (eds), *The Cambridge History of Early Modern English Literature* (Cambridge, 2002), pp. 487–511.

Mardock, James D. *Our Scene is London: Ben Jonson's City and the Space of the Author* (New York and London, 2008).

Margey, Annaleigh. 'Plantations, 1550–1641', in Jane Ohlmeyer (ed.), *The Cambridge History of Ireland, Volume 2: 1550–1730* (Cambridge, 2018), pp. 555–83.

Marini, Mirella. 'The Dynastic Diplomacy of the Princely Count of Arenberg at the Stuart Court in 1603', *The Seventeenth Century*, 36 (2021), 389–411.

Marshall, Peter. 'Confessionalisation and Community in the Burial of English Catholics, c.1570–1700', in Nadine Lewycky and Adam Morton (eds), *Getting Along? Religious Identities and Confessional Relations in Early Modern England: Essays in Honour of Professor W.J. Sheils* (Abingdon, 2016), pp. 57–75.

Marshall, Tristan. 'The Tempest and the British Imperium in 1611', *The Historical Journal*, 41 (1998), 375–400.

Marshall, Tristan. *Theatre and Empire: Great Britain on the London Stages Under James VI and I* (Manchester, 2000).

Martin, Patrick and John Finnis. 'The Identity of Anthony Rivers', *Recusant History*, 26 (2002), 39–74.

Martin, Patrick and John Finnis. 'The Secret Sharers: "Anthony Rivers" and the Appellant Controversy, 1601–2', *Huntington Library Quarterly*, 69 (2006).

Mason, Roger A. 'Scotching the Brut: Politics, History and National Myth in Sixteenth-Century Britain', in *idem*, *Scotland and England* (Edinburgh, 1987), pp. 60–84.

Mason, Roger A. 'Kingship, Nobility and Anglo-Scottish Union: John Mair's *History of Greater Britian* (1521)', *The Innes Review*, 41 (1990), 182–222.

Mason, Roger A. '1603: Multiple Monarchy and Scottish Identity', *History*, 105 (2020), 402–21.

Maxwell-Stuart, P. G. 'King James's Experience of Witches and the 1604 English Witchcraft Act', in John Newton and Jo Bath (eds), *Witchcraft and the Act of 1604* (Leiden, 2008), pp. 31–46.

May, Steven W. 'The Circulation in Manuscript of Poems by King James VI and I', in James M. Dutcher and Anne Lake Prescott (eds), *Renaissance Historicisms: Essays in Honor of Arthur F. Kinney* (Newark, DE, 2008), pp. 206–24.

McAllister, Charles Maffitt. '"The Boisterous Secretarie": The Political Career of Sir Ralph Winwood', Ph.D., University of Virginia (1983).

McCabe, Richard. 'The Poetics of Succession 1587–1605: The Stuart Claim', in Susan Doran and Paulina Kewes (eds), *Doubtful and Dangerous: The Question of Succession in Late Elizabethan England* (Manchester, 2014), pp. 192–211.

McCabe, Richard A. 'Panegyric and its Discontents: The First Stuart Accession', in Paulina Kewes and Andrew McCrae (eds), *Stuart Succession Literature: Moments and Transformations* (Oxford, 2019), pp. 19–36.

McCavitt, John. 'Lord Deputy Chichester and the English Government's "Mandates Policy" in Ireland, 1605–1607', *Recusant History*, 20 (1991), 320–35.

McCavitt, John. 'The Flight of the Earls', *Irish Historical Studies*, 29 (1994), 159–73.
McCavitt, John. *Sir Arthur Chichester: Lord Deputy of Ireland* (Belfast, 1998).
McCavitt, John. *The Flight of the Earls* (Dublin, 2002).
McClain, Lisa. *Lest We Be Damned: Practical Innovation and Lived Experience Among Catholics in Protestant England, 1559–1642* (New York and London, 2004).
McCoog SJ, Thomas M. 'A View from Abroad: Continental Powers and the Succession', in Susan Doran and Paulina Kewes (eds), *Doubtful and Dangerous: The Question of Succession in Late Elizabethan England* (Manchester, 2014), pp. 257–70.
McCoog SJ, Thomas M. *The Society of Jesus in Ireland, Scotland, and England, 1598–1606: "Lest Our Lamp be Entirely Extinguished"* (Leiden, 2017).
McCullough, Peter. *Sermons at Court: Politics and Religion in Elizabethan and Jacobean Preaching* (Cambridge, 1998).
McCullough, Peter. 'Music Reconciled to Preaching: A Jacobean Moment', in Natalie Mears and Alec Ryrie (eds), *Worship and the Parish Church in Early Modern Britain* (Aldershot, 2013), pp. 109–29.
McCullough, Peter. 'Avant-Garde Conformity in the 1590s', in Anthony Milton (ed.), *The Oxford History of Anglicanism, Volume 1: Reformation and Identity c.1520–1662* (Oxford, 2017), pp. 380–93.
McGee, C. E. 'Puritans and Performers in Early Modern Dorset', *Early Theatre*, 6 (2003), 51–66.
McKeogh, Katie. 'Sir Thomas Tresham (1543–1605) and Early Modern Catholic Culture and Identity 1580–1610', D.Phil., University of Oxford (2017).
McLaughlin, Adrienne. 'Rise of a Courtier: The Second Duke of Lennox and Strategies of Noble Power Under James VI', in Miles Kerr-Peterson and Steven J. Reid (eds), *James VI and Noble Power in Scotland 1578–1603* (Abingdon, 2017), pp. 136–54.
McLeod, Catherine (ed.). *The Lost Prince: The Life and Death of Henry Stuart* (London, 2013).
McManus, Clare. 'Marriage and the Performance of the Romance Quest: Anne of Denmark and the Stirling Baptismal Celebrations for Prince Henry', in L. A. J. R. Houwen, A. A. MacDonald, and S. L. Mapstone (eds), *A Palace in the Wild: Essays on Vernacular Culture and Humanism in Late-Medieval and Renaissance Scotland* (Leuven, 2000), pp. 175–98.
McManus, Clare. *Women on the Renaissance Stage: Anna of Denmark and Female Masquing in the Stuart Court (1590–1619)* (Manchester, 2002).
McManus, Clare. 'When is a Woman not a Woman? Or, Jacobean Fantasies of Female Performance (1606–11)', *Modern Philology*, 105 (2008), 437–74.
McRae, Andrew. *Literature, Satire and the Early Stuart State* (Cambridge, 2004).
Mears, Natalie. *Queenship and Political Discourse in the Elizabethan Realms* (Cambridge, 2005).
Mears, Natalie. 'Memorials of Queen Elizabeth I in Early Stuart London', *The Seventeenth Century*, 37 (2021), 1–22.

Meikle, Maureen M. 'Anna of Denmark's Coronation and Entry into Edinburgh, 1590: Cultural, Religious and Diplomatic Perspectives', in Julian Goodare and Alasdair A. Macdonald (eds), *Sixteenth-Century Scotland: Essays in Honour of Michael Lynch* (Leiden, 2008), pp. 277–94.

Meikle, Maureen M. 'A Meddlesome Princess: Anna of Denmark and Scottish Court Politics, 1589–1603', in Julian Goodare and Michael Lynch (eds), *The Reign of James VI* (Edinburgh, 2008), pp. 126–41.

Meikle, Maureen M. *The Scottish People* (Raleigh, NC, 2013).

Meikle, Maureen M. 'Scottish Reactions to the Marriage of the Lady Elizabeth, "First Dochter of Scotland"', in Sara Smart and Mara Wade (eds), *The Palatine Wedding of 1613* (Wolfenbuttel, 2013), pp. 131–43.

Meikle, Maureen. 'Once a Dane, Always a Dane? Queen Anna of Denmark's Foreign Relations and Intercessions as a Queen Consort of Scotland and England, 1588–1619', *The Court Historian*, 24 (2019), 168–80.

Meikle, Maureen M. and Helen Payne. 'From Lutheranism to Catholicism: The Faith of Anna of Denmark (1574–1619)', *The Journal of Ecclesiastical History*, 64 (2013), 45–69.

Merriman, Marcus. 'James Henrisoun and "Great Britain": British Union and the Scottish Commonweal', in Roger Mason (ed.), *Scotland and England 1286–1815* (Edinburgh, 1987), pp. 85–112.

Merritt, J. F. 'Puritans, Laudians, and the Phenomenon of Church-Building in Jacobean London', *The Historical Journal*, 41 (1998), 935–60.

Miller, Jeffrey Alan. '"Better as in the Geneva": The Role of the Geneva Bible in Drafting the King James Version', *Journal of Medieval and Early Modern Studies*, 47 (2017), 517–43.

Millstone, Noah. *Manuscript Circulation and the Invention of Politics in Early Stuart England* (Cambridge, 2016).

Milton, Anthony. *Catholic and Reformed: The Roman and Protestant Churches in English Protestant Thought* (Cambridge, 1995).

Milton, Anthony. 'A Qualified Intolerance', in A. Marotti (ed.), *Catholicism and Anti-Catholicism in Early Modern English Texts* (Basingstoke, 1998), pp. 85–115.

Milton, Anthony. '"Anglicanism" by Stealth: The Career and Influence of John Overall', in Kenneth Fincham and Peter Lake (eds), *Religious Politics in Post-Reformation England: Essays in Honour of Nicholas Tyacke* (Woodbridge, 2006), pp. 159–76.

Milton, Anthony. *England's Second Reformation: The Battle for the Church of England 1625–1662* (Cambridge, 2021).

Milward, Peter SJ. *Religious Controversies of the Jacobean Age* (London 1978).

Mirecka, Martyna. '"Monarchy as it Should Be"? British Perceptions of Poland-Lithuania in the Long Seventeenth Century', Ph.D., University of St Andrews (2014).

Mishra, Rupali. *A Business of State: Commerce, Politics, and the Birth of the East India Company* (Cambridge, MA, 2018).

Morgan, Hiram. *Tyrone's Rebellion: The Outbreak of the Nine Years War in Tudor Ireland* (London, 1993).
Morgan, John. 'Henry Jacob, James I, and Religious Reform, 1603–1609: From Hampton Court to Reason-of-State', *Church History*, 86 (2017), 695–727.
Morgan, John. 'Popularity and Monarchy: The Hampton Court Conference and the Early Jacobean Church', *Canadian Journal of History*, 53 (2018), 197–232.
Morrill, John. 'A British Patriarchy? Ecclesiastical Imperialism Under the Early Stuarts', in Anthony Fletcher and Peter Roberts (eds), *Religion, Culture and Society in Early Modern Britain: Essays in Honour of Patrick Collinson* (Cambridge, 1994), pp. 209–37.
Morrill, John. 'Thinking About the New British History', in David Armitage (ed.), *British Political Thought in History, Literature and Theory* (Cambridge, 2006), pp. 23–46.
Morrill, John S. 'Dynasties, Realms, Peoples and State Formation, 1500–1700', in Robert von Friedeburg and John S. Morrill (eds), *Monarchy Transformed: Princes and their Elites in Early Modern Europe* (Cambridge, 2017), pp. 17–43.
Morrow, Christopher L. 'Speaking England: Nationalism(s) in Early Modern Literature and Culture', Ph.D., University of Texas A&M (2006).
Muldrew, Craig. *The Economy of Obligation* (Basingstoke, 1998).
Mullan, David George. *Episcopacy in Scotland: The History of an Idea 1560–1638* (Edinburgh, 1986).
Munden, R. C. 'The Defeat of Sir John Fortescue: Court Versus Country at the Hustings?', *The English Historical Review*, 93 (1978), 811–16.
Munden, R. C. 'Government and Opposition: Initiative, Reform and Politics in the House of Commons 1597–1610', Ph.D., University of East Anglia (1985).
Munro, Lucy. *Children of the Queen's Revels: A Jacobean Theatre Repertory* (Cambridge, 2005).
Murdoch, Steve. *Britain, Denmark-Norway and the House of Stuart, 1603–1660* (East Linton, 2000).
Murray, Catriona. 'The Pacific King and the Militant Prince? Representation and Collaboration in the Letters Patent of James I, creating his son, Henry, Prince of Wales', *Electronic British Library Journal*, 8 (2012), 1–16.
Murray, Catriona. *Imaging Stuart Family Politics: Dynastic Crisis and Continuity* (London, 2017).
Nenner, Howard. *The Right to be King: The Succession to the Crown of England, 1603–1714* (Chapel Hill, NC, 1995).
Newton, Diana. 'Sir Francis Hastings and the Religious Education of James VI and I', *The Historical Journal*, 41 (1998), 917–34.
Nicholls, Mark. 'The "Wizard Earl" in Star Chamber: The Trial of the Earl of Northumberland, June 1606', *The Historical Journal*, 30 (1987), 173–89.
Nicholls, Mark. *Investigating Gunpowder Plot* (Manchester, 1991).
Nicholls, Mark. 'Treason's Reward: The Punishment of Conspirators in the Bye Plot of 1603', *The Historical Journal*, 38 (1995), 821–42.

Nicholls, Mark. 'Sir Walter Ralegh's Treason: A Prosecution Document', *The English Historical Review*, 110 (1995), 902–24.

Nicholls, Mark. 'Two Winchester Trials: The Prosecution of Henry, Lord Cobham, and Thomas, Lord Grey of Wilton, 1603', *Historical Research*, 68 (1995), 26–48.

Nicholls, Mark. 'Discovering Gunpowder Plot: The King's Book and the Dissemination of News', *Recusant History*, 28 (2007), 397–415.

Nicholls, Mark. 'Strategy and Motivation in the Gunpowder Plot', *The Historical Journal*, 50 (2007), 787–807.

Nicholls, Mark and Penry Williams. *Sir Walter Raleigh: In Life and Legend* (London, 2011).

Nicolson, Adam. *Power and Glory: Jacobean England and the Making of the King James Bible* (London, 2003).

Normand, Lawrence and Gareth Roberts. *Witchcraft in Early Modern Scotland* (Exeter, 2000).

North, Marcy L. 'Anonymity's Subject: James I and the Debate over the Oath of Allegiance', *New Literary History*, 33 (2002), 215–32.

Norton, David. *A History of the English Bible as Literature* (Cambridge 2000).

Norton, David. *A Textual History of the King James Bible* (Cambridge, 2004).

Norton, David. *The King James Bible: A Short History from Tyndale to Today* (Cambridge, 2011).

Nuttall, Geoffrey F. 'The English Martyrs 1535–1680: A Statistical Review', *The Journal of Ecclesiastical History*, 22 (1971), 191–7.

Ó Buachalla, Brendhán. 'James our True King: The Ideology of Irish Royalism in the Seventeenth Century', in D. George Boyce, Robert Eccleshall, and Vincent Geoghegan (eds), *Political Thought in Ireland Since the Seventeenth Century* (London, 1993), pp. 7–35.

Oates, Rosamund Brigid Mary. 'Tobie Matthew and the Establishment of the Godly Commonwealth in England: 1560–1606', Ph.D., University of York (2003).

Oates, Rosamund. *Moderate Radical: Tobie Matthew and the English Reformation* (Oxford, 2018).

O'Callaghan, Michelle. 'Performing Politics: The Circulation of the "Parliament Fart"', *Huntington Library Quarterly*, 69 (2006), 121–38.

O'Connor, Marion. 'Godly Patronage: Lucy Harington Russell, Countess of Bedford', in Johanna I. Harris and Elizabeth Scott-Baumann (eds), *The Intellectual Culture of Puritan Women, 1558–1680* (Basingstoke, 2011), pp. 71–83.

O'Day, Rosemary. 'The Reformation of the Ministry 1558–1642', in Rosemary O'Day and Felicity Heal (eds), *Continuity and Change: Personnel and Administration of the Church in England* (Leicester, 1976), pp. 55–76.

O'Neill, James. 'A Kindom Near Lost: English Military Recovery in Ireland 1600-03', *British Journal for Military History*, 3 (2016), 26–47.

Ohlmeyer, Jane H. '"Civilizinge of those Rude Partes": Colonization within Britain and Ireland, 1580s–1640s', in Nicholas Canny (ed.), *The Oxford History of the British Empire, Volume I: The Origins of Empire: British Overseas Enterprise to the Close of the Seventeenth Century* (Oxford, 1998), pp. 124–47.

Ohlmeyer, Jane. *Making Ireland English: The Irish Aristocracy in the Seventeenth Century* (New Haven, CT, 2012).

Okines, A. W. R. E. 'Why Was There So Little Government Reaction to Gunpowder Plot?', *The Journal of Ecclesiastical History*, 55 (2004), 275–92.

Orgel, Stephen. *The Illusion of Power: Political Theater in the English Renaissance* (Berkeley, CA, 1991).

Packer, Daniel. 'Jewels of "Blacknesse" at the Jacobean Court', *Journal of the Warburg and Courtauld Institutes*, 75 (2012), 201–22.

Paleit, Edward. *War, Liberty, and Caesar: Responses to Lucan's Bellum Ciuile, ca. 1580–1650* (Oxford, 2013).

Palliser, D. M. *The Age of Elizabeth, England Under the Later Tudors 1547–1603* (Harlow, 1983).

Pam, David. *The Story of Enfield Chase* (Enfield, 1984).

Parker, Brett. 'Recasting England: The Varieties of Antiquarian Responses to the Proposed Union of Crowns, 1603–1607', *Journal of Medieval and Early Modern Studies*, 43 (2013), 393–417.

Parry, Graham. *The Golden Age Restor'd: The Culture of the Stuart Court, 1603–42* (Cambridge, 1981).

Parry, Graham. 'The Politics of the Jacobean Masque', in J. R. Mulryne and Margaret Shewring (eds), *Theatre and Government Under the Early Stuarts* (Cambridge, 1993), pp. 87–117.

Patterson, Catherine. *Urban Patronage in Early Modern England: Corporate Boroughs, the Landed Elite, and the Crown, 1580–1640* (Stanford, CA, 1999).

Patterson, W. D. *King James VI and I and the Reunion of Christendom* (Cambridge, 1997).

Paul, Joanne. *Counsel and Command in Early Modern English Thought* (Cambridge, 2020).

Payne, Helen. 'Aristocratic Women and the Jacobean Court, 1603–1625', Ph.D., University of London (2001).

Payne, Helen. 'Aristocratic Women, Power, Patronage and Family Networks at the Jacobean Court, 1603–1625', in James Daybell (ed.), *Women and Politics in Early Modern England, 1450–1700* (Abingdon, 2016), pp. 164–80.

Payne, M. T. W. 'An Inventory of Queen Anne of Denmark's "Ornaments, Furniture, Householde Stuff and Other Parcells" at Denmark House', *Journal of the History of Collections*, 13 (2001), 23–44.

Peacock, John. 'The Politics of Portraiture', in Kevin Sharpe and Peter Lake (eds), *Culture and Politics in Early Stuart England* (Basingstoke, 1994), pp. 199–228.

Pearce, Michael. 'Anna of Denmark: Fashioning a Danish Court in Scotland', *The Court Historian*, 24 (2019), 138–51.

Peck, Linda Levy. 'Problems in Jacobean Administration: Was Henry Howard, Earl of Northampton, a Reformer?' *The Historical Journal*, 19 (1976), 831–58.

Peck, Linda Levy. 'The Earl of Northampton, Merchant Grievances and the Addled Parliamant of 1614', *The Historical Journal*, 24 (1981), 533–52.

Peck, Linda Levy. *Northampton: Patronage and Policy at the Court of James I* (London, 1982).

Peck, Linda Levy. *Court Patronage and Corruption in Early Stuart England* (London, 1990).

Peck, Linda Levy. 'Monopolizing Favor: Structures of Power in the Early Seventeenth Century English Court', in J. H. Elliott and L. W. B. Brockliss (eds), *The World of the Favorite* (New Haven and London, 1999), pp. 54–70.
Peltonen, Markku. *Rhetoric, Politics and Popularity in Pre-revolutionary England* (Cambridge, 2013).
Pennini, Andrea. 'Marriage Proposal: Seventeenth-Century Stuart-Savoy Matrimonial Prospects and Politics', in Paola Bianchi (ed.), *Turin and the British in the Age of the Grand Tour* (Cambridge, 2017), pp. 27–40.
Percival-Maxwell, M. *The Scottish Migration to Ulster* (Belfast, 1999).
Perry, Curtis. *The Making of Jacobean Culture: James I and the Renegotiation of Elizabethan Literary Practice* (Cambridge, 1997).
Pigman III, G. W. *Grief and the Renaissance Elegy* (Cambridge, 1985).
Pitcher, John. 'Samuel Daniel's Masque *The Vision of the Twelve Goddesses*: Texts and Payments', *Medieval and Renaissance Drama in England*, 26 (2013), 17–42.
Pittock, Murray. 'From Edinburgh to London: Scottish Court Writing and 1603', in Eveline Cruickshanks (ed.), *The Stuart Courts* (Thrupp, Stroud, 2000), pp. 13–28.
Plomer, H. R. 'Bishop Bancroft and a Catholic Press', *The Library*, new series, 8 (1907), 164–76.
Pollen, J. H. 'The Accession of King James I', *The Month*, 103 (1903), 572–85.
Pollnitz, Aysha. *Princely Education in Early Modern Britain* (Cambridge, 2015).
Poole, Thomas. *Reason of State: Law, Prerogative and Empire* (Cambridge, 2015).
Prescott, Anne Lake. 'Marginal Discourse: Drayton's Muse and Selden's "Story"', *Studies in Philology*, 88 (1991), 307–28.
Price, Polly. 'Natural Law and Birthright Citizenship in Calvin's Case (1608)', *Yale Journal of Law and the Humanities*, 73 (1997), 73–145.
Prothero, G. W. 'The Parliamentary Privilege of Freedom from Arrest, and Sir Thomas Shirley's Case, 1604', *The English Historical Review*, 8 (1893), 733–40.
Quarmby, Kevin A. 'Narrative of Negativity: Whig Historiography and the Spectre of King James VI and I in *Measure for Measure*', *Shakespeare Survey*, 64 (2011), 300–16.
Questier, Michael C. 'Sir Henry Spiller, Recusancy and the Efficiency of the Jacobean Exchequer', *Historical Research*, 66 (1993), 256–66.
Questier, Michael C. 'Loyalty, Religion and State Power in Early Modern England: English Romanism and the Jacobean Oath of Allegiance', *The Historical Journal*, 40, (1997), 311–29.
Questier, Michael C. 'The Politics of Religious Conformity and the Accession of James I', *Historical Research*, 71 (1998), 14–30.
Questier, Michael. 'Conformity, Catholicism and the Law', in Peter Lake and Michael Questier (eds), *Conformity and Orthodoxy in the English Church, c. 1560–1660* (Woodbridge 2000), pp. 237–61.
Questier, Michael C. *Catholicism and Community in Early Modern England: Politics, Aristocratic Patronage and Religion c. 1550–1640* (Cambridge, 2006).
Questier, Michael C. 'Catholic Loyalism in Early Stuart England'. *The English Historical Review*, 123 (2008), 1132–65.
Questier, Michael. *Dynastic Politics and the British Reformations, 1558–1630* (Oxford, 2019).

Questier, Michael. *Catholics and Treason: Martyrology, Memory, and Politics in the Post-Reformation* (Oxford, 2022).

Quintrell, B. W. 'The Royal Hunt and the Puritans, 1604–5', *The Journal of Ecclesiastical History*, 31 (1980), 41–58.

Quitslund, Beth. 'The Virginia Company, 1606–1624: Anglicanism's Millennial Adventure', in Richard Connors and Andrew Colin Gow (eds), *Anglo-American Millenialism, from Milton to the Millerites* (Leiden, 2004), pp. 43–114.

Rabb, Theodore K. 'Sir Edwin Sandys and the Parliament of 1604', *The American Historical Review*, 69 (1964), 646–70.

Racaut, Luc and Alec Ryrie. 'Introduction: Between Coercion and Persuasion', in idem, *Moderate Voices in the European Reformation* (Aldershot, 2005), pp. 1–12.

Raeymaekers, Dries. *One Foot in the Palace: The Habsburg Court of Brussels and the Politics of Access in the Reign of Albert and Isabella 1598–1621* (Leuven, 2013).

Ravelhofer, Barbara. *The Early Stuart Masque: Dance, Costume, and Music* (Oxford, 2006).

Read, David. 'More Than Half His Mind: John Donne's *Pseudo-Martyr* and the Matter of Sovereignty', *The Seventeenth Century*, 35 (2020), 411–34.

Reid, Steven. 'Of Bairns and Bearded Men: James VI and the Ruthven Raid', in Miles Kerr-Peterson and Steven J. Reid (eds), *James VI and Noble Power in Scotland 1578–1603* (Abingdon, 2017), pp. 32–56.

Reid, Steven J. *The Early Life of James VI: A Long Apprenticeship 1566–1585* (Edinburgh, 2023).

Reid-Baxter, Jamie. 'Politics, Passion and Poetry in the Circle of James VI: John Burel and His Surviving Works', in L. A. J. R. Houwen, A. A. MacDonald, and S. L. Mapstone (eds), *A Palace in the Wild: Essays on Vernacular Culture and Humanism in Late-Medieval and Renaissance Scotland* (Leuven, 2000), pp. 199–248.

Reynolds, Anna. *In Fine Style: The Art of Tudor and Stuart Fashion* (London, 2013).

Reynolds, Graham. 'Portraits by Nicholas Hilliard and his Assistants of King James I and his Family', *Walpole Society*, 34 (1952), 14–26.

Richards, Jennifer. 'Gabriel Harvey, James VI, and the Politics of Reading Early Modern Poetry', *Huntington Library Quarterly*, 71 (2008), 303–21.

Rickard, Jane. 'The Word of God and the Word of the King: The Scriptural Exegesis of James VI and I and the King James Bible', in Ralph Houlbrooke (ed.), *James VI and I: Ideas, Authority and Government* (Aldershot, 2006), pp. 135–49.

Rickard, Jane. *Authorship and Authority: The Writings of James VI and I* (Manchester and New York, 2007).

Rickard, Jane. 'The Writings of James VI and I and Early Modern Literary Culture', *Literature Compass*, 9 (2012), 654–64.

Rickman, Johanna. *Love, Lust, and License in Early Modern England: Illicit Sex and the Nobility* (Aldershot, 2008).

Riis, Thomas. *Should Auld Acquaintance Be Forgot: Scottish-Danish Relations c. 1450–1707*, vol. 1 (Odense, 1988).

Robertson, Barry. *Lordship and Power in the North of Scotland: The Noble House of Huntly, 1603–1690* (Edinburgh, 2011).

Robinson, Joseph Armitage. 'On the Funeral Effigies of the Kings and Queens of England', *Archaeologia*, 60 (1907), 517–70.
Robinson-Self, Phil. *Early Modern Britain's Relationship to its Past: The Historiographical Fortunes of the Legends of Brute, Albina and Scota* (Kalamazoo, 2018).
Roebuck, Graham. 'The Controversial Treatise', in Jeanne Shami, Dennis Flynn, and M. Thomas Hester (eds), *The Oxford Handbook of John Donne* (Oxford, 2011), pp. 249–64.
Rome, Alan S. 'Being Human in Early Virginia', *Renaissance Studies*, 29 (2015), 701–19.
Rose, Thomas. 'Hunting in Early Stuart England: Status, Sociability, and Politics', Ph.D., University of Nottingham (2020).
Ruiz Fernández, Óscar Alfredo. *England and Spain in the Early Modern Era: Royal Love, Diplomacy, Trade and Naval Relations, 1604–25* (London, 2020).
Russell, Conrad. 'English Parliaments 1593–1606: One Epoch or Two?', in David M. Dean and Norman. L. Jones (eds), *The Parliaments of Elizabethan England* (Oxford, 1990), pp. 191–213.
Russell, Conrad. 'The Anglo-Scottish Union 1603–1643: A Success?', in Anthony Fletcher and Peter Roberts (eds), *Religion, Culture and Society in Early Modern Britain: Essays in Honour of Patrick Collinson* (Cambridge, 1994), pp. 238–56.
Russell, Conrad. 'Parliament, the Royal Supremacy and the Church', *Parliamentary History*, 19 (2000), 2–37.
Russell, Conrad. 'Is British History International History?', in Allan Macinnes and Jane Ohlmeyer (eds), *The Stuart Kingdoms in the Seventeenth Century* (Dublin, 2002), 62–9.
Russell, Conrad. 'James VI and I and Rule Over Two Kingdoms: An English View', *Historical Research*, 76 (2003), 151–63.
Russell, Conrad. 'Topsy and the King: The English Common Law, King James VI and I, and the Union of Crowns', in Buchanan Sharp and Mark Charles Fissel (eds), *Law and Authority in Early Modern England: Essays Presented to Thomas Garden Barnes* (Newark, DE, 2007), pp. 64–76.
Russell, Conrad, Richard Cust, and Andrew Thrush. *King James VI and I and his English Parliaments* (Oxford, 2011).
Sacks, David Harris. 'Discourses of Western Planting: Richard Hakluyt and the Making of the Atlantic World', in Peter C. Mancall (ed.), *The Atlantic World and Virginia, 1550–1624* (Chapel Hill, NC, 2007), pp. 410–53.
Sàenz-Cambra, Concepción. 'James VI's *Ius Suum Conservare*: His Intrigues with Spain, 1580–1603', *International Review of Scottish Studies*, 30 (2005), 86–107.
Salmon, J. H. M. 'Catholic Resistance Theory, Ultramontanism and the Royalist Response', in J. H. Burns and Mark Goldie (eds), *The Cambridge History of Political Thought* (Cambridge, 1991), pp. 219–53.
Sandis, Elizabeth. 'A Coming of Age: Drama at St John's College, Oxford in the Early Modern Period', D.Phil., University of Oxford (2017).
Sargent, Gillian. ' "Happy Are They That Read and Understand": Reading for Moral and Spiritual Acuity in a Selection of Writings by King James VI and I', Ph.D., University of Glasgow (2013).

Scarisbrick, Diana. 'Anne of Denmark's Jewellery: The Old and the New', *Apollo*, 123 (1986), 228–36.
Scarisbrick, Diana. *Tudor and Jacobean Jewellery* (London, 1995).
Scarisbrick, J. J. 'Whose Plot was it?', *Midland Catholic History*, 12 (2006), 2–15.
Schneider, Christian. 'A Kingdom for a Catholic? Pope Clement VIII, King James VI/I, and the English Succession in International Diplomacy (1592–1605)', *The International History Review*, 37 (2015), 119–41.
Schofield, Scott James. 'Staging Tudor Royalty: Religious Politics in Stuart Historical Drama (1603–1607)', Ph.D., University of Toronto (2010).
Schreiber, Roy E. 'The First Carlisle: Sir James Hay, First Earl of Carlisle as Courtier, Diplomat and Entrepreneur, 1580–1636', *Transactions of the American Philosophical Society*, 74 (1984), 1–202.
Schroder, Paul. *Trust in Early Modern International Political Thought, 1598–1713* (Cambridge, 2017).
Schultz, Jenna M. *National Identity and the Anglo-Scottish Borderlands, 1552–1652* (Woodbridge, 2019).
Schwyzer, Philip. *Literature, Nationalism, and Memory in Early Modern England and Wales* (Cambridge, 2004).
Seddon, P. R. 'Patronage and Officers in the Reign of James I', Ph.D., University of Manchester (1967).
Selwood, Jacob. '"English-Born Reputed Strangers": Birth and Descent in Seventeenth-Century London', *Journal of British Studies*, 44 (2005), 728–53.
Senior, C. M. *A Nation of Pirates: English Piracy in its Heyday* (Newton Abbot, 1976).
Seton, Walter W. 'The Early Years of Henry Frederick, Prince of Wales, and Charles, Duke of Albany [Charles I] 1593–1605', *The Scottish Historical Review*, 13 (1916), 366–79.
Shagan, Ethan H. 'The English Inquisition: Constitutional Conflict and Ecclesiastical Law in the 1590s', *The Historical Journal*, 47 (2004), 541–65.
Shagan, Ethan. 'The Battle for Indifference in Elizabethan England', in Luc Racaut and Alec Ryrie (eds), *Moderate Voices in the European Reformation* (Aldershot, 2005), pp. 122–44.
Shapiro, James. *1606: William Shakespeare and the Year of Lear* (London, 2015).
Sharp, Buchanan. *Famine and Scarcity in Late Medieval and Early Modern England: The Regulation of Grain Marketing, 1256–1631* (Cambridge, 2016).
Sharpe, Jim. 'Social Strain and Social Dislocation, 1585–1603', in John Guy (ed.), *The Reign of Elizabeth I* (Cambridge, 1995), pp. 192–211.
Sharpe, Kevin. 'The King's Writ: Royal Authors and Royal Authority in Early Modern England', in Kevin Sharpe and Peter Lake (eds), *Culture and Politics in Early Stuart England* (Basingstoke, 1994), pp. 117–38.
Sharpe, Kevin. 'Reading James Writing: The Subjects of Royal Writings in Jacobean England', in Daniel Fischlin and Mark Fortier (eds), *Royal Subjects: Essays on the Writings of James VI and I* (Detroit, MI, 2002), pp. 15–36.
Sharpe, Kevin. *Image Wars: Promoting Kings and Commonwealths in England, 1603–1660* (New Haven, CT and London, 2010).

Shaw, W. M. A. and G. D. Burtchaell. *The Knights of England*, vol. 1 (London 1906).
Sheehan, Anthony J. 'The Recusancy Revolt of 1603: A Reinterpretation', *Archivium Hibernicum*, 38 (1983), 3–13.
Sheils, W. J. *The Puritans in the Diocese of Peterborough 1558–1610* (Northampton 1979).
Sheils, W. J. '"Getting On" and "Getting Along" in Parish and Town', in Benjamin J. Kaplan, Bob Moore, Henk F. Van Nierop, and Judith Pollman (eds), *Catholic Communities in Protestant States: Britain and the Netherlands c. 1570–1720* (Manchester, 2009), pp. 67–83.
Sherlock, Peter. 'The Monuments of Elizabeth Tudor and Mary Stuart: King James and the Manipulation of Memory', *Journal of British Studies*, 46 (2007), 263–89.
Shire, Helena Mennie. *Song, Dance and Poetry of the Court of Scotland Under King James VI* (Cambridge, 1969).
Shirley, E. P. 'Funeral and Tomb of Queen Elizabeth', *Notes and Queries*, 3rd series, 5 (28 May 1864), 434.
Shriver, Frederick. 'Hampton Court Re-visited: James I and the Puritans', *Journal of Ecclesiatical History*, 33 (1982), 48–71.
Shuger, Debora K. *Political Theologies in Shakespeare's England: The Sacred and the State in Measure for Measure* (Basingstoke, 2001).
Slack, Paul. 'Dearth and Social Policy in Early Modern England', *Social History of Medicine*, 5 (1992), 1–17.
Smith, Alan G. R. 'The Secretariats of the Cecils, circa 1580–1612', *The English Historical Review*, 83 (1968), 481–504.
Smith, Alan G. R. 'Crown, Parliament and Finance: The Great Contract of 1610', in Peter Clark, Alan Smith, and Nicholas Tyacke (eds), *The English Commonwealth, 1547–1640* (Leicester, 1979), pp. 111–27.
Smith, David L. 'Politics in Early Stuart Britain 1603–1640', in Barry Coward (ed.), *A Companion to Stuart Britain* (Oxford, 2003), pp. 233–52.
Smuts, R. Malcolm. *Court Culture and the Origins of a Royalist Tradition in Early Stuart Tradition* (Philadelphia, 1987).
Smuts, Malcolm. 'Cultural Diversity and Cultural Change at the Court of James I', in Linda Levy Peck (ed.), *The Mental World of the Jacobean Court* (Cambridge, 1991), pp. 99–112.
Smuts, R. Malcolm. 'Material Culture, Metropolitan Influences and Moral Authority in Early Modern England', in Curtis Perry (ed.) *Material Culture and Cultural Materialism* (Brussels, 2001), pp. 203–24.
Smuts, R. Malcolm. 'Progresses and Court Entertainments', in Arthur F. Kinney (ed.), *A Companion to Renaissance Drama* (Oxford, 2002), pp. 281–93.
Smuts, R. Malcolm. 'The Whole Royal and Magnificent Entertainment', in Gary Taylor and John Lavagnino (eds), *Thomas Middleton, Volume 2: Thomas Middleton and Early Modern Textual Culture* (Oxford, 2007), pp. 498–501.
Smuts, Robert Malcolm. 'Banquo's Progeny: Hereditary Monarchy, the Stuart Lineage and *Macbeth*', in James M. Dutcher and Anne Lake Prescott (eds), *Renaissance Historicisms: Essays in Honour of Arthur F. Kinney* (Newark, DE, 2008), pp. 225–40.

Smuts, R. Malcolm. 'Theological Polemics and James I's Diplomacy', *Journal of Medieval and Early Modern Studies*, 50 (2020), 515–50.

Smuts, R. Malcolm. *Political Culture, the State, and the Problem of Religious War in Britain and Ireland, 1578–1625* (Oxford, 2023).

Sobecki, Sebastian. 'John Peyton's A Relation of the State of Polonia and the Accession of King James I, 1598–1603', *The English Historical Review*, 129 (2014), 1079–97.

Sommerville, Johann P. 'The Royal Supremacy and the Episcopacy: "jure divino"', *The Journal of Ecclesiastical History*, 34 (1983), 548–58.

Sommerville, Johann P. 'English and European Political Ideas in the Early Seventeenth Century: Revisionism and the Case of Absolutism', *Journal of British Studies*, 35 (1996), 168–94.

Sommerville, Johann P. 'The Ancient Constitution Reassessed: The Common Law, the Court and the Languages of Politics in Early Modern', in R. Malcolm Smuts (ed.), *The Stuart Court and Europe: Essays in Politics and Political Culture* (Cambridge, 1996), pp. 39–64.

Sommerville, Johann P. *Royalists and Patriots: Politics and Ideology in England 1603–1640*, 2nd edition (London, 1999).

Sommerville, Johann P. 'Papalist Political Thought and the Controversy over the Jacobean Oath of Allegiance', in Ethan H. Shagan (ed.), *Catholics and the 'Protestant Nation': Religious Politics and Identity in Early Modern England* (Manchester, 2005), pp. 162–84.

Sowerby, Tracey. 'Early Modern Queens Consort and Dowager and Diplomatic Gifts', *Women's History Review*, 30 (2021), 723–37.

Sowerby, Tracey A. 'The Dangerous Gift as Diplomatic Tool? Relics and Cross-confessional Gift-giving at the Turn of the Seventeenth Century', in T. A. Sowerby et al. (eds), *The Dangers of Gifts from Antiquity to the Digital Age* (Abingdon, 2021).

Sowerby, Tracey. 'Royal Gifts, Religious Polemics, and Diplomatic Ceremonial: The Reception of James VI/I's *Apologie*' (forthcoming).

Spence, R. T. 'The Pacification of the Cumberland Borders, 1593–1628', *Northern History*, 13 (1977), 59–160.

Sprunger, Keith. *Dutch Puritanism: A History of English and Scottish Churches of the Netherlands in the Sixteenth and Seventeenth Centuries* (Eugene, OR, 1982).

Sprunger, Keith. *Trumpets from the Tower: English Puritan Printing in the Netherlands, 1600–1640* (Leiden, 1994).

Srigley, Michael. '"Heavy-headed Revel East and West": Hamlet and Christian IV of Denmark', in Gunnar Sorelius (ed.) *Shakespeare and Scandinavia: A Collection of Nordic Studies* (Newark and London, 2002), pp. 168–92.

Stapylton, Keith A. T. 'The Parliamentary Privilege of Freedom from Arrest, 1603–1629', Ph.D., University College London (2016).

Stevenson, David. *Scotland's Last Royal Wedding: The Marriage of James VI and Anne of Denmark* (Edinburgh, 1997).

Stewart, Laura A. M. 'The Political Repercussions of the Five Articles of Perth: A Reassessment of James VI and I's Religious Policies in Scotland', *The Sixteenth Century Journal*, 38 (2007), 1013–36.

Stilma, Astrid. 'King James VI and I as a Religious Writer', in Crawford Gribben and David George Mullan (eds), *Literature and the Scottish Reformation* (Abingdon and New York, 2009), pp. 127–41.

Stilma, Astrid. *A King Translated: The Writings of King James VI & I and their Interpretation in the Low Countries 1593–1603* (Farnham, 2012).

Stone, Lawrence. 'The Fruits of Office: The Case of Robert Cecil, First Earl of Salisbury, 1596–1612', in F. J. Fisher (ed.), *Essays in the Economic and Social History of Tudor and Stuart England in Honour of R. H. Tawney* (Cambridge, 1961), pp. 89–11.

Strong, Roy. 'Three Royal Jewels: The Three Brothers, the Mirror of Great Britain and the Feather', *The Burlington Magazine*, 108 (1966), 350–3.

Strong, Roy. 'Henry, Prince of Wales: England's Lost Stuart King', *History Today*, 36 (1986), 16–23.

Strong, Roy. *Henry, Prince of Wales and England's Lost Renaissance* (London, 1986).

Strong, Roy. *The Tudor and Stuart Monarchy: Pageantry, Painting, Iconography*, vol. 3, *Jacobean and Caroline* (Woodbridge, 1998).

Strong, Roy. *The Cult of Elizabeth* (London, 1999).

Strong, Roy. *Coronation: A History of Kingship and the British Monarchy* (London, 2005).

Sturdy, David J. 'Continuity Versus Change: Historians and English Coronations of the Medieval and Early Modern Periods', in János M. Bak (ed.), *Coronations* (Oxford, 1990), pp. 228–45.

Sullivan, Ceri. *The Rhetoric of Credit: Merchants in Early Modern Writing* (Cranbury, NJ, 2002).

Tadmor, Naomi. 'The Bible in English Culture: The Age of Shakespeare', in R. Malcolm Smuts (ed.), *The Oxford Handbook of the Age of Shakespeare* (Oxford, 2016), pp. 384–97.

Tan, Amy Grant. 'Richard Bernard and his Publics: A Puritan Minister as Author', Ph.D., Vanderbilt University (2015).

Taylor, Gary and Michael Warren (eds). *The Division of the Kingdoms: Shakespeare's Two Versions of King Lear* (Oxford, 1987).

Taylor, William. 'The Scottish Privy Council, 1603–1625, its Composition and its Work', Ph.D., University of Edinburgh (1950).

Taylor, William Cooke. *Chapters on Coronations* (London, 1838).

Terry, C. S. *Scottish Parliaments, its Constitution and Procedures* (Glasgow, 1905).

Thomas, Andrea. 'The Renaissance', in T. M. Devine and Jenny Wormald (eds), *The Oxford Handbook of Modern Scottish History* (Oxford, 2012), pp. 185–203.

Thomas, David. 'Financial and Administrative Developments', in Howard Tomlinson (ed.), *Before the English Civil War* (Basingstoke, 1983), pp. 103–22.

Thompson, Faith. *Magna Carta, its Role in the Making of the English Constitution 1300–1629* (Minneapolis, MN, 1948).

Thomson, Duncan. *Painting in Scotland 1570–1650* (Edinburgh, 1975).

Thrush, Andrew. 'The Personal Rule of James I, 1611–1620', in Thomas Cogswell, Richard Cust, and Peter Lake (eds), *Politics, Religion and Popularity in Early Stuart Britain: Essays in Honour of Conrad Russell* (Cambridge, 2002), pp. 84–102.

Thrush, Andrew. 'The French Marriage and the Origins of the 1614 Parliament', in Stephen Clucas and Rosalind Davies (eds), *The Crisis of 1614 and the Addled Parliament* (Burlington, VT, 2002), 25–35.

Thrush, Andrew. 'Commons v. Chancery: The 1604 Buckinghamshire Election Dispute Revisited', *Parliamentary History*, 26 (2007), 301–9.

Thrush, Andrew. *The History of Parliament: The House of Lords 1604–1629*, 3 vols (Cambridge, 2021).

Thrush, Andrew and John P. Ferris (eds). *The History of Parliament: The House of Commons 1604–1629*, 6 vols (Cambridge, 2010).

Thrush, Coll. *Indigenous London: Native Travelers at the Heart of Empire* (New Haven, 2016).

Thurley, Simon. *Hampton Court* (London and New Haven, 2004).

Thurley, Simon. 'Architecture and Diplomacy: Greenwich Palace Under the Stuarts', *The Court Historian*, 11 (2006), 125–33.

Thurley, Simon. *Palaces of Revolution: Life, Death & Art at the Stuart Court* (London, 2021).

Town, Edward. 'A House "Re-edified"—Thomas Sackville and the Transformation of Knole 1605–1608', Ph.D., University of Sussex (2010).

Travers, James. *Gunpowder: The Players Behind the Plot* (Kew, 2005).

Trevisan, Sara. *Royal Genealogy in the Age of Shakespeare* (Cambridge, 2020).

Trim, David. 'Fighting "Jacob's Warres": English and Welsh Mercenaries in the European Wars of Religion: France and the Netherlands', Ph.D., University of London (2003).

Turner, Edward Raymond. *The Privy Council of England in the Seventeenth and Eighteenth Centuries*, vol. 1 (Baltimore, 1927).

Tutino, Stefania. '"Makynge Recusancy Deathe Outrighte"? Thomas Pounde, Andrew Willet and the Catholic Question in Early Jacobean England', *Recusant History*, 27 (2004), 31–50.

Tutino, Stefania. 'Between Nicodemism and "Honest" Dissimulation: The Society of Jesus in England', *Historical Research*, 79 (2006), 534–53.

Tutino, Stefania. *Law and Conscience: Catholicism in Early Modern England, 1570–1625* (Burlington, 2007).

Tutino, Stefania. *Empire of Souls: Robert Bellarmine and the Christian Commonwealth* (Oxford, 2010).

Tutino, Stefania. 'Thomas Preston and English Catholic Loyalism: Elements of an International Affair', *The Sixteenth Century Journal*, 41 (2010), 91–109.

Tyacke, Nicholas. 'Wroth, Cecil and the Parliamentary Session of 1604', *Bulletin of the Institute of Historical Research*, 50 (1977), 120–5.

Tyacke, Nicholas. *Anti-Calvinists: The Rise of English Arminianism c.1590–1640* (Oxford, 1987).

Tyacke, Nicholas. 'Sir Edwin Sandys and the Cecils: A Client–Patron Relationship', *Historical Research*, 64 (1991), 87–91.

Tyacke, Nicholas. 'Religious Controversy', in idem (ed.), *The History of the University of Oxford, Volume IV: Seventeenth-Century Oxford* (Oxford, 1997), 569–619.

Tyacke, Nicholas. 'Lancelot Andrewes and the Myth of Anglicanism', in Peter Lake and Michael Questier (eds), *Conformity and Orthodoxy in the English Church, c.1560–1660* (Woodbridge, 2000), pp. 5–33.

Tyacke, Nicholas. *Aspects of English Protestantism c.1530–1700* (Manchester, 2001).
Tyacke, Nicholas. 'Puritan Politicians and King James VI and I, 1587–1604', in T. Cogswell, R. Cust, and P. Lake (eds), *Politics, Religion and Popularity in Early Stuart Britain* (Cambridge, 2002), pp. 21–44.
Tyacke, Nicholas. 'The Puritan Paradigm of English Politics, 1558–1642', *The Historical Journal*, 53 (2010), 527–50.
Tyacke, Nicholas. 'Collective Biography and the Interpretative Change of Early-Stuart Parliamentary History', *Parliamentary History*, 32 (2013), 531–54.
Tyacke, Nicholas. 'The Lambeth Articles (1595) and the Doctrinal Stance of the Church of England', *The English Historical Review*, 137 (2022), 1082–117.
Ungerer, Gustav. 'Juan Pantoja de la Cruz and the Circulation of Gifts Between the English and Spanish Courts in 1604/5', *Shakespeare Studies*, 26 (1998), 145–86.
Usher, Roland G. 'Nicholas Fuller: A Forgotten Exponent of English Liberty, *American Historical Review*, 12 (1907), 743–60.
Usher, Roland G. 'The Deprivation of Puritan Ministers in 1605', *The English Historical Review*, 24 (1909), 232–46.
Vermeir, René and Tomas Roggeman. 'Implementing the Truce: Negotiations Between the Republic and the Archducal Netherlands, 1609–10', *European Revue of History*, 17 (2010), 817–33.
Verweij, Sebastian. '"Booke, go thy Wayes": The Publication, Reading, and Reception of James VI/I's Early Poetic Works', *Huntington Library Quarterly*, 77 (2014), 111–31.
Verweij, Sebastian. *The Literary Culture of Early Modern Scotland: Manuscript Production and Transmission* (Oxford, 2016).
Vincent, Susan. *Dressing the Elite: Clothes in Early Modern England* (Oxford, 2003).
Wade, Mara R. 'The Queen's Courts: Anna of Denmark and Her Royal Sisters: Cultural Agency at Four Northern European Courts in the Sixteenth and Seventeenth Centuries', in Clare McManus (ed.) *Women and Culture at the Courts of the Stuart Queens* (Basingstoke, 2003), pp. 49–80.
Walker, Julia. 'Bones of Contention: Posthumous Images of Elizabeth and Stuart Politics', in her *Dissing Elizabeth: Negative Representations of Gloriana* (London, 1998), pp. 252–76.
Wall, Alison. 'Religion and the Composition of the Commissions of the Peace, 1547–1640', *History*, 103 (2018), 223–42.
Walsh, Brian. *Unsettled Toleration: Religious Difference on the Shakespearean Stage* (Oxford, 2016).
Walsham, Alexandra. *Church Papists: Catholicism, Conformity and Confessional Polemic in Early Modern England* (London, 1993).
Walsham, Alexandra. *Providence in Early-Modern England* (Oxford, 1999).
Walsham, Alexandra. '"A Very Deborah?" The Myth of Elizabeth I as a Providential Monarch', in Susan Doran and Thomas S. Freeman (eds), *The Myth of Elizabeth* (New York, 2003), pp. 143–68.
Walsham, Alexandra. *Charitable Hatred: Tolerance and Intolerance in England, 1500–1700* (Manchester, 2006).

Walsham, Alexandra. *Catholic Reformation in Protestant Britain* (Farnham, 2014).

Walsham, Alexandra. 'Supping with Satan's Disciples: Spiritual and Secular Sociability in Post-Reformation England', in Nadine Lewycky and Adam Morton (eds), *Getting Along? Religious Identities and Confessional Relations in Early Modern England: Essays in Honour of Professor W. J. Sheils* (Abingdon, 2016), pp. 29–55.

Walter, John. 'A Rising of the People'? The Oxfordshire Rising of 1596', *Past and Present*, 70 (1985), 90–143.

Walter, John. *Crowds and Popular Politics in Early Modern England* (Manchester, 2006).

Walter, John. 'The "Recusancy Revolt" of 1603 Revisited, Popular Politics, and Civic Catholicism in Early Modern Ireland', *The Historical Journal*, 65 (2021), 1–26.

Walters, Myfanwy. 'The Court Culture of James I: The Music and Ceremony in Early Seventeenth-Century London', Ph.D., University of London (2006).

Waucheron, Sarah. 'Imagined Polities, Failed Dreams, and the Beginnings of an Unacknowledged Britain: English Responses to James VI and I's Vision of Perfect Union', *Journal of British Studies*, 52 (2013), 575–96.

White, Jason. 'Militant Protestants: British Identity in the Jacobean Period, 1603–1625', *History*, 94 (2009), 154–75.

Whitelock, Anna. *Elizabeth's Bedfellows: An Intimate History of the Queen's Court* (London, 2013).

Whitelock, Anna. 'The Queen's Two Bodies: The Image and Reality of the Body of Elizabeth I', in Sean McGlynn and Elena Woodacre (eds), *The Image and Perception of Monarchy in Medieval and Early Modern Europe* (Cambridge, 2014), pp. 207–25.

Whitelock, Anna. 'Reconsidering the Political Role of Anna of Denmark', in Joanne Paul and H. R. Matheson-Pollock (eds), *Queenship and Counsel in the Early Modern World* (Basingstoke, 2016), pp. 237–58.

Wiggins, Martin. *Drama and the Transfer of Power in Renaissance England* (Oxford, 2012).

Wiggins, Martin and Catherine Richardson (eds). *British Drama 1533–1642: A Catalogue, Volume 5: 1603–1608* (Oxford, 2015).

Wijffels, Alain. 'A British *Ius Commune*? A Debate on the Union of the Laws of Scotland and England During the First Years of James', *Edinburgh Law Review*, 6 (2002), 315–55.

Wilks, Timothy. 'The Court Culture of Prince Henry and his Circle, 1603–1613', D.Phil., University of Oxford (1987).

Wilks, Timothy. '"Forbear the Heat and Haste of Building": Designers at Prince Henry's Court', *The Court Historian*, 6 (2001), 49–65.

Wilks, Timothy. '"Paying Special Attention to the Adorning of a Most Beautiful Gallery": The Pictures in St James's Palace, 1609–49', *The Court Historian*, 10 (2014), 149–72.

Wilks, Timothy. 'Poets, Patronage, and the Prince's Court', in R. Malcolm Smuts (ed.), *The Oxford Handbook of the Age of Shakespeare* (Oxford, 2016), pp. 159–78.

Williamson, Arthur. *Scottish National Consciousness in the Age of James VI: The Apocalypse, the Union and the Shaping of Scotland's Public Culture* (Edinburgh, 1979).

Williamson, Arthur. 'Radical Britain: David Hume of Godscroft and the Challenge to the Jacobean British Vision', in Glenn Burgess et al. (eds), *The Accession of James I: Historical and Cultural Consequences* (Basingstoke, 2006), pp. 48–68.

Williamson, Arthur H. 'David Hume, Richard Verstegan, and the Battle for Britain', in Malcolm Smuts (ed.), *Age of Shakespeare* (Oxford, 2016), pp. 323–46.
Williamson, Philip and Natalie Mears. 'James I and Gunpowder Treason Day', *The Historical Journal*, 64 (2021), 185–210.
Wills, Gary. *Witches and Jesuits: Shakespeare's Macbeth* (Oxford, 1995).
Willson, D. H. *Privy Councillors in House of Commons* (Minneapolis, 1940).
Willson, D. H. *King James VI & I* (London, 1956).
Womersley, David. *Divinity and State* (Oxford, 2010).
Woodward, Jennifer. *The Theatre of Death: The Ritual Management of Royal Funerals in Renaissance England 1570–1625* (Woodbridge, 1997).
Woodworth, Allegra. 'Purveyance for the Royal Household in the Reign of Queen Elizabeth', in *Transactions of the American Philosophical Society*, new series, 35 (1946), 3–86.
Woolf, Daniel. *The Idea of History in Early Stuart England: Erudition, Ideology, and 'The Light of Truth' from the Accession of James I to the Civil War* (Toronto, 1998).
Woolf, D. R. 'Two Elizabeths? James I and the Late Queen's Famous Memory', *Canadian Journal of History*, 20 (1985), 167–91.
Wormald, Jenny. 'James VI and I: Two Kings or One', *History*, 68 (1983), 187–209.
Wormald, Jenny. 'Gunpowder, Treason, and Scots', *Journal of British Studies*, 24 (1985), 141–68.
Wormald, Jenny. *Mary Queen of Scots: A Study in Failure* (London, 1988).
Wormald, Jenny. 'The Union of 1603', in Roger A. Mason (ed.), *Scots and Britons: Scottish Political Thought and the Union 1603* (Cambridge, 1994), pp. 17–40.
Wormald, Jenny. 'The Witches, the Devil and the King', in Terry Brotherstone and David Ditchburn (eds), *Freedom and Authority: Scotland c.1050–c.1650. Historical and Historiographical Essays Presented to Grant G. Simpson* (East Lothian, 2000), pp. 165–80.
Wormald, Jenny. 'O Brave New World? The Union of England and Scotland in 1603', in T. C. Smout (ed.), *Anglo-Scottish Relations from 1603–1900* (Oxford, 2005), pp. 13–35.
Wormald, Jenny. 'The Gowrie Conspiracy: Do We Need to Wait Until the Day of Judgment?', in Miles Kerr-Peterson and Steven J. Reid (eds), *James VI and Noble Power in Scotland 1578–1603* (Abingdon, 2016), pp. 194–206.
Wortham, Simon. '"Pairte of My Taill Is Yet Untolde": James VI and I, the *Phoenix*, and the Royal Gift', in Daniel Fischlin and Mark Fortier (eds), *Royal Subjects: Essays on the Writings of James VI and I* (Detroit, MI, 2002), pp. 182–204.
Wright, Pam. 'A Change in Direction: The Ramifications of a Female Household, 1558–1603', in David Starkey et al. (eds), *The English Court from the Wars of the Roses to the Civil War* (Harlow, 1987), pp. 147–72.
Wright, Stephen. 'Nicholas Fuller and the Liberties of the Subject', *Parliamentary History*, 25 (2006), 176–213.
Young, Alan R. 'The Phoenix Reborn: The Jacobean Appropriation of an Elizabethan Symbol', in Elizabeth H. Hageman and Katherine Conway (eds), *Resurrecting Elizabeth I in Seventeenth-Century England* (Madison, NJ, 2007), pp. 68–81.
Young, Michael B. *King James and the History of Homosexuality* (Houndmills, 1999).
Young, Sandra. 'Richard Hakluyt's Voyages: Early Modern Print Culture and the Global Reach of Englishness', *The Sixteenth Century Journal*, 49 (2018), 1057–80.

Youngs Jr, Frederic A. 'Towards Petty Sessions: Tudor JPs and Divisions of Counties', in DeLloyd J. Guth and John W. McKenna (eds), *Tudor Rule and Revolution* (Cambridge, 1982), pp. 201–16.

Zeitlin, Samuel Garrett. 'Francis Bacon and the 1604 Treaty of London', *History of Political Thought*, 41 (2020), 487–504.

Zim, Rivkah. 'A Poet in Politics: Thomas Sackville, Lord Buckhurst and First Earl of Dorset (1536–1608)', *Historical Research*, 79 (2006), 199–223.

Index

For the benefit of digital users, indexed terms that span two pages (e.g., 52–53) may, on occasion, appear on only one of those pages.

Abbot, George, archbishop of
  Canterbury 212, 351–2, 387–8,
  541 n.203
Accession Day
  Elizabeth's 33–4
  James's 33–4, 221, 226, 234
Adams, Simon 553 n.177
ambassadors and envoys to England 196,
  199–200, 211–13, 230, 234, 243,
  246–7, 294, 358–9, 382–3, 431–2,
  440, 512 n.148, 548 n.204
  see also Arenberg, Caron
  French 13, 19, 103, 221–2, 228, 235–7,
    241–3, 250–1, 403, 432, 440, 446–7,
    519 n.238
  see also Rosny
  Spanish 211, 241–2, 363, 370–2,
    449, 452–4
  see also constable of Castile and Tassis
  Venetian 9, 18, 21–2, 107–8, 115–16,
    136, 141, 189, 204–5, 212, 223, 228,
    239, 251, 254, 257–9, 305, 334,
    363–4, 379, 431, 434, 442–3, 455–7
America 6, 390–1, 423, 453–4
  colonial expansion 201, 390–1, 422–4,
    426, 429, 454
  English attitudes towards indigenous
    peoples 424–8
  Jamestown 390–1, 424–6, 453–4
  Virginia project 423–6, 428–9
Andrewes, Lancelot 84, 140–1, 234, 347,
  349, 384–5
Anna of Denmark, queen consort 4, 34,
  46, 53–4, 213, 217, 224–5, 272,
  529 n.12
  character 5, 247, 444–5, 475

  coronation in England 136–8, 141–2,
    168, 502 nn.63,82
  coronation in Scotland and royal
    entry 46–9
  custody of Prince Henry 119–20, 191
  deaths of children 54–5, 186–8, 248
  diplomatic role 193–4, 197, 199–200,
    211, 237–8, 241–2, 440–1,
    444–6, 466
  family 43, 45–8, 50, 52, 54–5, 70,
    185–6, 189, 191, 196–200, 204–5,
    213–14, 240–1, 251, 280, 461
  see also Christian IV
  fertility 53, 70, 185–7, 189
  houses 192–3, 472
  see also Greenwich, Oatlands,
    Somerset House
  household 119–20, 191–2, 194–5, 202,
    207–11, 218, 229–31, 273, 369–70,
    379–80, 513 n.12
  intercessor 172, 200–1
  jewels 48–9, 196–200, 230, 238–9, 241
  jointure 202
  marriage 42–3, 45
  marriages of children 193–4, 196,
    211–13, 241
  miscarriages 50, 119, 186, 499 n.149
  and music 175, 207–9
  patronage of the arts 69, 122,
    202–11, 472
  politics while in England 193–5, 227
  portraits of 69, 194, 197–8, 205, 207, 233
  progress to Bristol 1613 200
  progress to London 1603 19, 120–2,
    201, 233
  progresses with James 246–7, 472

618 INDEX

Anna of Denmark, queen consort (*cont.*)
   relationship with James 5, 67, 190–6,
      209–10, 379, 512 n.148
   religion 92–3, 141–2, 191–2, 211
   royal entry 1604 168–70, 172,
      175, 177–8
   theatre companies 209–10
   wardrobe 196–7
   see also masques
Anne Boleyn 1, 185, 201
archdukes of the Spanish Netherlands 1,
   41–2, 74, 98–9, 132–3, 386, 418, 432,
   440, 443–4, 447–8, 451–3, 455–62,
   553 n.188
   Albert, archduke of Austria 74, 98,
      386, 418, 431–3, 448
   Isabella Clara Eugenia, infanta-
      archduchess of Austria 82–3, 98–9,
      104–5, 193–4, 432
Arenberg, Charles de Ligne, prince
   count of 521 n.66
   Main Plot 132–4, 144–5, 148–51, 436
   peace negotiations 193–4, 199, 432–3,
      436–7, 440–1, 445
Aston, Roger 223–5, 256, 288
Ayton, Sir Robert 210–11, 385

Bacon, Sir Francis 31, 114–15, 267, 288–9,
   293, 379–80, 395–6, 402, 407, 424
ballads 23–4, 49, 100–1, 123–4, 374–5,
   396–7
Bancroft, Richard
   as bishop of London 86, 126, 128–30,
      163–4, 166–7, 299–301, 349,
      526 n.75
   as archbishop of Canterbury 321–4,
      327–9, 331–3, 336, 339–40, 345–9,
      387–8, 409, 475–6
Barlow, William, dean of Chester, bishop
   of Rochester, bishop of Lincoln
   and Hampton Court Conference 162,
      164–5, 167
   sermons 373, 409
Basilikon Doron 29–30, 63, 66, 81, 87–8,
   90–1, 139, 154–5, 165–6, 170, 172–4,
   180, 190, 196, 219–20, 233, 259–60,
   353, 391, 393, 463, 466–7, 497 n.72
bedchamber of King James 4, 38,
   218–26, 228–30, 252–3, 260, 266,
   282–3, 379, 405, 471–2
   grooms of 158–9, 278

Bellarmine, Cardinal Robert
   382–5, 458
Berwick upon Tweed 19, 38–9, 107,
   110–11, 113–14, 120–1, 396–7
bible 29, 36–7, 47–8, 51, 61–3, 65, 81,
   105–6, 346, 445, 525 n.46
   Geneva Bible 86, 346–8, 534 n.171
   Hebrew Bible 36, 174, 200
   King James Version 348
   translation of 29, 346–8
Bilson, Thomas, bishop of Winchester
   138–9, 157–8, 161–4
bishops
   in England 11, 13–15, 19–20, 83–6,
      90–2, 94, 96–7, 137, 140–1, 154–5,
      161–7, 169–70, 188, 235, 284–5,
      299–300, 321–7, 335–8, 340, 342–50,
      359, 384–5, 387–8, 409, 475–6,
      534 n.188, 535 n.202
   in Scotland 40–1, 53–4, 409–10
   see also individual bishops
Blackwell, George 82, 128, 381–3
Blague, Thomas, dean of
   Rochester 115–18
Blount, Charles, Lord Mountjoy 75,
   105–6, 112–13, 135–6, 415–16,
   434–5
   as earl of Devonshire 209–10, 265–6,
      274–5, 365, 441, 477
Bodin, Jean 394, 468–9
borders 41, 43–4, 109–10, 274, 306–8,
   391–2, 394, 396, 400, 402–3,
   410–11, 535 n.7
Bradshaw, William 325–6, 337–8,
   531 n.91
Britain 2–3, 172, 175, 239–41, 243–4,
   296–9, 379, 391–3, 395–402, 407,
   410–15, 421, 424, 427–9
   British 6, 50–2, 55, 61–2, 110, 170,
      251–2, 407, 411–12, 414–15, 420
Brutus/Brute 172, 176–7, 392–3, 398,
   400, 412–15
Brooke, Frances, countess of Kildare 120,
   148–50, 194
Brooke, George 129–33, 142–6, 150–1,
   156–7, 160, 505 n.12
Brooke, Henry, Lord Cobham 3–4,
   107–8, 129–34, 136, 142–5, 147–51,
   156–8, 276, 436, 483 n.18, 501 n.35
Browne, Anthony Viscount
   Montague 357–9, 366, 537 n.91

Bruce, Edward, Lord Kinloss 116, 152–3, 271, 279–80, 408
Buchanan, George 36–7, 64–6, 337
Burges, John 252–3, 326–7, 331–4, 350, 468
Burgess, Glenn 554 n.6
Bywater, Thomas 332–3

Caesar, Sir Julius 269, 280, 309–10, 315
Camden, William 10–11, 398
Carey, Lady Elizabeth 189, 194
Carey, Henry, Lord Hunsdon 18, 57–60, 333
Carey, Sir Robert 13–14, 95–6, 103–4, 106–7, 110–11, 189
Carleton, Dudley 158–9, 175–6, 249–51, 329, 541 n.188
Caron, Noel de 431–2, 451–2
Carr, Robert, later Viscount Rochester 5, 195, 220–1, 226–7, 230–1, 235, 465–6, 515 n.80
Catelin, Robert 124–5, 325–6
Catholics
　anti-Catholic 17, 24, 26–31, 46–7, 50–1, 84–5, 93, 111, 123, 138, 140, 164–7, 199–200, 232–4, 305–6, 333, 337–43, 351–2, 354, 356–7, 368–70, 374, 379–82, 386, 389, 409–10
　appellants 82–3, 126, 356
　disillusionment with James 126, 353–4, 358–60, 368–9, 389, 470
　executions of 358–9, 382, 388
　Jesuits 39–40, 58–9, 61, 64, 81–3, 92–3, 98, 124–6, 128, 143, 156, 233–4, 273–4, 355, 359–60, 367–8, 370, 374, 377–8, 382–8, 450
　occasional conformists 82, 354, 359, 379–81, 388
　pamphlets 355–6
　penal laws against 127–9, 179, 299, 316, 351–8, 379–81, 388, 444–5
　petitions 92–4, 353–6, 358–9, 535 n.9
　priests 81–3, 92–3, 105–6, 126, 128, 154–5, 200, 351–2, 354–8, 367–8, 381–2, 387–8, 416
　recusants 11–12, 112, 276–7, 337–8, 354, 356–60, 365, 368–9, 379–82, 387–9, 452–3, 536 n.38, 540 n.162
　see also Ireland, nobility, oath of allegiance, pope, plots
Cautionary Towns 433–4, 439, 443–4

Cecil, Robert 3–5, 107, 116, 124, 130, 152, 212, 224, 231, 279, 282, 296, 299, 325, 418, 433–4, 465, 477, 529 n.17
　and Anna 187, 194–5, 200, 202, 229–30, 241, 268–9
　and Elizabeth I's funeral and tomb 18, 31–2, 187
　and Carr 226–7
　and Fuller's case 328–9
　'great contract' 223, 226–7, 267–8, 281–2, 286, 310, 312–17, 462, 467, 544 n.75
　and Gunpowder Plot 333, 361–2, 367–70, 374
　illnesses and death 5, 195, 266, 268–9, 278
　and James I 265–9, 278, 524 n.171
　and James I's accession 13, 15, 87, 95–6, 276, 412
　James I's minister and councillor 87, 159, 218–19, 222–3, 228, 231, 256–60, 265–8, 288, 396, 415–16, 431, 434–5, 445–6, 454–6, 458, 466, 521 n.66
　local influence 261
　and Main and Bye Plotters 144–7, 150, 152
　and other councillors 281–2
　rewards for service 186, 267–9
　and royal finances 246–7, 266–7, 269–70, 301–3, 308–12, 315–16
　and Somerset House Conference 440–4, 548 n.5
　under Elizabeth I 9–11, 13, 62–3, 80–1, 89, 265–6, 272
　unpopularity of 152–3, 209–10, 228, 230–1, 258–9, 269
Cecil, Thomas
　as second Baron Burghley 3–4, 109, 116, 527 n.116
　as earl of Exeter 186, 263–4, 274
Cecil, William, Baron Burghley 10–13, 57–8, 76
Chaderton, Laurence 166–7, 347
Chaderton, William. bishop of Lincoln 324–5, 332
Chaloner, Sir Thomas 194, 211–12, 229–31
Chamberlain, John 17, 103, 107, 236, 373–4
Chapman, George 23, 209–10, 221–2

Charles, prince 36–8, 54–5, 108–9, 185, 189–90, 194, 207, 235, 240–4, 350–2, 361–2, 389, 508 n.25
  Charles I 343, 348, 351–2, 390, 410, 419–20, 471–2
Charterhouse 9, 115–18
Chettle, Henry 17
Chichester, Sir Arthur 415–21
Christian IV, king of Denmark 45, 199, 207–9, 221, 238–9, 261
  visit to England 247–51, 309
chronicles 26–7
  Holinshed's *Chronicles* 398, 413
  Speed's *Historie* 160, 412
  Stow's *Annales* 21
Clarke, William 129–30, 143, 145–6, 156
clergy 109, 140, 323
  preaching ministry 161, 343–6, 534 n.161
  see also Puritans
Clifford, George, third earl of Cumberland 51, 89–90, 121, 123, 274, 410, 434
coins 26–7, 34, 207, 233, 391–2, 397–8, 411, 471–2
Coke, Sir Edward 531 n.72
  and common law 267–8, 286–7, 330–1
  treason trials 89–90, 145, 148–9, 368–70
  A True and Perfect Relation 373–4
Colt, Maximilian 31, 186–7
commerce 38–9, 76–7, 251–2, 427, 439, 443–4, 451–2, 459
  Anglo-Dutch 442–3
  Anglo-Scottish 306–8, 403–6
  Anglo-Spanish 76–7, 439, 451–2, 454–5
  Levant Company 76–7, 258, 287–8, 454–5
  with Indies 250, 437, 443–4, 459
Constable, Henry 59–60
constable of Castile, Fernández de Velasco, the fifth duke of Frías 199, 224, 433, 440–1, 444–6, 449–50, 453–4
Copley, Sir Anthony 128–9, 133, 145, 147, 155–6, 160, 354–5
Cornwallis, Sir Charles 212, 386, 447, 449–50, 454–5

Cornwallis, Sir William 247, 543 n.60
corruption 3, 80–1, 94, 114–15, 180, 253, 259, 270–3, 277–9, 433
  in Church 162–3, 167
court calendar 234–7, 245–6
Cotton, Sir Robert 267, 277–8, 398, 536 n.46
Craig, Sir Thomas of Riccarton 396, 401–2, 544 n.75
Croft, Pauline 388–9, 550 nn.75,77
Cross, Robert 434–5, 550 n.75
Cuddy, Neil 219–20, 526 n.62

Daemonologie 63–4, 66, 242, 304, 466–7
Daniel, Samuel 6, 23, 72, 101, 209–11
  Panegyrike Congratulatory 16–17, 23, 393–4, 499 n.165, 535 n.20
  The Vision of Twelve Goddesses 237–8, 440
  Tethys' Festival 243–4
David, Old Testament king 22–4, 26, 61–2, 90, 93, 101, 168–9, 174, 331, 373
De Critz, John 31, 205–6
Dekker, Thomas 16, 19, 21, 26–7, 29–30, 118, 167–8, 175, 375
Denmark 41–3, 46, 49–51, 63, 203, 207–9, 230, 247, 255, 394, 408–9, 430, 432, 463
  see also Anna, Christian IV
Denmark House *see* Somerset House
Devereux, Robert, second earl of Essex 10, 15–16, 68, 73–5, 80–1, 107–8, 127, 130, 149, 160, 209–10, 230–1, 261, 273–4, 276, 281–2, 361–2, 437, 472
Devereux, Robert, third earl of Essex 15–16, 221, 231, 244–5, 279
divine providence 23–4, 29–30, 33–4, 101, 174, 372–3, 377, 379, 397–8, 400, 429
Dod, John 325–6
Donne, John 6, 16, 387
Douglas, James, fourth earl of Morton 35, 38
Dove, Thomas, bishop of Peterborough 323, 325–6, 334
Drayton, Michael 23, 412–13
Drummond, Jane, Lady Roxburgh 230
Dryden, Sir Erasmus 325–6, 335–6

Du Bartas, Guillaume de Salluste, sieur 42–3, 56, 58, 68
Dudley, Robert 281, 366–7, 523 n.160, 538 n.94
Dunfermline 54–5, 194

Edinburgh 4, 38, 40–3, 48, 54–5, 59–60, 63, 68, 95, 103–4, 107–8, 110, 113–15, 119–20, 126–7, 201, 255, 392, 396–7, 401–2, 406–7, 409–10, 432
Edmondes, Thomas 386, 448–50, 454–5, 462–3, 541 n.190
Edwards, David 415, 546 n.156
Egerton, Sir Thomas, Baron Ellesmere, and Viscount Brackley 13, 89, 151–2, 165–6, 231, 260, 271–2, 296–7, 396, 401–2, 477
 as lord chancellor 150, 271, 290–1, 293–4, 305, 406–7
 and parliament 288, 290–6
Elizabeth, princess, daughter of James and Anna 54, 108–9, 119–22, 189–90, 194, 205–6, 218, 229–30, 242–4, 246–7, 360, 363–5
 marriage 185, 189–90, 194, 211–12, 445
 wedding 196, 214–15, 245, 471–2
Elizabeth of York 1, 22, 96, 100, 394
Elizabeth I, queen of England 1–2, 35–6, 55, 57–8, 65, 138, 154, 170, 175–6, 178, 196–8, 204–5, 207–9, 214, 217–18, 235, 242, 268–9, 278–9, 322–3, 326–7, 333, 349, 461–2
 coffin 15, 17, 20–2, 123–4
 criticisms of 73, 80–1, 121–2, 289, 331–2
 cultural memory of 26–31
 deathbed 13–15, 484 n.23
 death 14–16, 25–6, 87, 95–6, 103–6, 123, 130, 172, 176–7, 465
 embalming 15, 17, 484 nn.37, 38
 eulogies to 22–6, 30–1, 117, 189
 finances 75–6, 196–7, 214–15
 funeral 18–22, 123–4, 485 n.68
 health 9–11, 16, 95–6
 household 3, 18–20, 76, 217–18, 220, 229–30
 image 73, 238
 mourning for 15–17, 19–20, 22–3, 123–4
 policies 38, 73–4, 83–5, 116–17, 351–2, 388–9, 463–4, 474
 progresses 246, 472
 relationship with James VI 12–13, 40, 44, 50–1, 54, 72, 97, 101, 191–3, 273
 religion 92–3, 343–4, 350–1, 472–4
 tomb 31–2
 see also succession, Spain
Elphinstone, James, Lord Balmerino 46, 116, 201, 280, 384, 510 n.94
empire 51–2, 172–4, 177, 421–3, 429
enclosure 78–9, 89–90, 200, 263–4, 299, 418, 475, 494 n.68
engravings 26–7, 69, 71, 102–3, 376–8, 459–60
Erskine, Annabella, countess of Mar 36, 47–8
Erskine, John, first earl of Mar 35–6
Erskine, John, second earl of Mar 35–6, 39, 116, 119–20, 123, 190–1, 195, 224, 280, 434–5
Erskine, Sir Thomas, later Lord Fenton 224, 408, 433

faction 5, 40, 72, 107–8, 119–20, 227, 229–31, 274, 281–2
Fawkes, Guy 29, 360–4, 366–9, 373–4, 379–80, 452–3, 537 n.78
 see also Gunpowder Plot
Feingold, Mordechai 534 n.171
Fergus, king of Scotland 65, 105, 393
Ferrell, Lori Anne 348
Fincham, Kenneth 349–50, 529 n.23
Fletcher, Robert 90, 99–100
Florio, John 210–11, 426–7
Fortescue, Sir John 3–4, 106–7, 222–3
 Fortescue versus Goodwin 291–6
Fowler, William 50, 53–4, 68, 186, 209–10, 509 n.65, 512 n.150
Foxe, John 23–4, 26–7, 29, 201
France 2, 11–12, 31–2, 38, 44, 58–9, 62, 66, 73–4, 401, 403–4, 409, 429, 443–4, 456–7, 460, 464
 alliance with 118, 446, 464
 see also ambassadors, Henry IV, Rosny, Treaty of Hampton Court
Fry, Cynthia 430
Fuller, Nicholas 288–9, 297, 305, 326–31, 336, 405, 454–5

Galloway, Patrick 46, 61, 92, 157, 167, 349
Garnet, Henry SJ 359–60, 367–72, 374, 377, 537 n.63
gender 26, 111, 179–80, 193–4, 240, 349, *passim*
genealogy 100, 105, 190–1, 213–14, 398–401, 412
Gerard, John SJ 128, 367–8, 374, 536 n.42
Germany 42, 50, 69, 76–7, 430
  Elector-Palatine, Frederick V 189–90, 194, 212–13, 463
  Protestant Union 385–6, 460–3
  see also emperor and Julich-Cleves succession
gifts 160, 232, 243–4, 247–8
  exchanges 46, 196, 199–200, 235–6, 248–51, 445–6, 449
  from and to ambassadors 194, 199, 433, 445–6
  to favourites 220, 224–7, 267, 436
  to and from rulers 385–6, 446
  New Year's 235
Gowrie Day 33–4, 234, 248–9, 408–9, 471–2
Greenwich Palace 118, 127, 142, 186–7, 192–3, 196, 203, 205, 217–18, 234–5, 241, 245–9, 277–8, 313–14, 331
Grey, Thomas Baron Grey of Wilton 3–4, 106–7, 129–32, 142, 144–6, 148, 151–2, 157–61
Gunpowder Plot 6, 29–31, 33–4, 160, 185, 191–2, 218, 252–3, 273–4, 305, 342–3, 360–6, 383, 452–3, 455, 472, 539 n.153
  commemorations 377–9, 471
  executions 369–72
  interrogations 363–4, 366–72, 377–8
  official versions of 372–4
  popular responses to 374–7
  trials 368–70
  see also plays
Guy, John 483 n.13

Ha, Polly 532 n.121
Hakluyt, Richard 422–4
Hampton Court 78–9, 118, 154–5, 162, 167, 187, 192–3, 204, 217–18, 409, 435–6

Hampton Court Conference 161–7, 178–81, 299, 321–2, 336–7, 341, 345–7, 433–4, 468, 472
Harington, Sir James 250–1
Harington, Baron John of Exton 205–6, 363–5
Harington, Lady Anne 120–1, 194
Harington, John 206, 231
Harrison, Stephen 167–8
harvests 77, 79–80, 475
Hastings, earls of Huntingdon 97–8, 121
Hastings, Sir Francis 288–9, 291, 334–6, 532 n.105
Hay, Sir James 224–5
  wedding 245
Hayward, John 401–2
Henry IV, king of France 2, 13, 41–3, 50, 52, 74, 98–9, 193–4, 224–5, 242, 383–4, 418, 430, 434–5, 446–7, 455–8, 460–2
  assassination 243, 252–3, 312–13, 381, 386, 458, 462–3
  see also ambassadors
Henry VII, king of England 1–3, 22, 31–2, 35–6, 52, 54, 72, 96, 100–1, 123, 172–4, 179, 243–4, 315–16, 394
Henry VIII, king of England 1, 14–17, 19, 31, 52, 55, 81, 97, 135–6, 192–3, 217, 221, 315–16, 346–8, 398, 421–2, 469–70, 472
Henry, prince, son of James and Anna 55, 66, 108–9, 119–22, 163–4, 169–70, 175–6, 178, 185, 193–4, 201, 213, 242–4, 246–50, 314, 361–2, 445–6
  baptism 50–4
  and chivalry 123, 207, 243, 472
  death 5, 187–9, 227, 244
  education 68, 211
  household 203–4, 207, 209, 212, 229–34, 267
  investiture as prince of Wales 203, 214, 231, 243, 309, 313–14, 413–14, 462–3, 471–2
  marriage 193–4, 211–12, 242, 430–1
  and music 209
  patronage of the arts 203–5, 232, 472
  portraits of 205–8, 233
  religion 188, 232–4, 350–1
Herbert, Philip 186, 226, 233, 240–1
  as earl of Montgomery 186

Herbert, William, third earl of
  Pembroke 123, 126, 155, 192–3, 227,
  231, 233, 408, 527 n.116
Heywood, Thomas 27–30, 414–15
Hieron, Samuel 324–5, 341–2
high commission, court of 85, 91, 166,
  267–8, 271–2, 326–31, 351
  Cawdrey's Case 1591 327–8, 473
  ex officio oath 85, 87, 91, 327–8
Hildersham, Arthur 90–1, 325–6, 333–4,
  531 n.91
Hoby, Sir Edward 288–9, 291, 438–9,
  544 n.78, 551 n.112
Hodgett, Michael 366–7
Holles, Sir John 229, 232, 551 n.112
Holyrood 38–9, 46–9, 54–5, 95, 107,
  109–10, 120
Home of Spott, Sir George 116, 220–5,
  279–80, 410, 433
  as earl of Dunbar 195, 201, 222–3,
  259–60, 279–80, 282, 408–11, 466
Howard, Charles, earl of
  Nottingham 10–11, 13, 19–20,
  73–4, 123, 249, 272–3, 276–8, 434–5,
  441, 522 n.108
  embassy to Spain 272, 448–50
  family 275
  marriage to Margaret
  Stewart 249, 272
Howard, Frances, daughter of the earl
  and countess of Suffolk 244–5, 279
Howard, Lord Henry 4, 87, 95–6, 116,
  124, 130
  and Cecil 276, 281–2, 523 n.143
  as earl of Northampton 169, 207,
  226–7, 230–1, 261, 278–9, 288, 315,
  361–2, 368–70, 396, 433
  family 275, 279
  reformer 277–8
  relationship with James I 278
  religion 276–7, 281–2, 522 n.127
  rewards 276–8
  at Somerset House Conference 441
  under Elizabeth 276
Howard, Thomas, Baron of Walden 9, 18,
  87, 117, 135–6, 276, 278–9, 522 n.108,
  523 n.143
  and Cecil 274, 282
  as earl of Suffolk 226, 244–6, 361–3, 408
  wife 229–30, 278–9, 282, 369–70

Hudson, Thomas 67–8
Hume of Godscroft, David 401–2
hunting 4, 78, 111, 167, 187, 197–8,
  224–5, 304–5, 364
  see also James VI and I
Hutton, Matthew, archbishop of
  York 356–7, 468
Hyde, Laurence 288–9, 407

impositions 251–2, 271, 287–8, 312–17,
  469–70
  Bate's Case 287–8, 313, 469–70
Ireland 10, 13, 31–2, 60, 74–5, 104–6, 130,
  265–6, 390, 415, 453, 455, 469–70
  flight of the earls 6, 418–19
  'mandates policy' 417–18
  Nine Years' War 74–6, 415–17, 419–21
  O'Doherty, Sir Cahir 418–21
  O'Donnell, Rory, earl of
  Tyrconnell 415–18, 455
  O'Neill, Hugh, earl of Tyrone 4–5,
  10, 74–5, 415–18, 420–1, 432,
  455, 457
  Old English Catholics 416–18
  plantation of Ulster 6, 222, 390, 415,
  419–22, 429, 470
  Scots in Ireland 415, 419–20, 470

Jacob, Henry 324, 338, 532 n.124
James VI of Scotland and I of England
  absolutist ideas 56, 465, 468–9
  access to 114, 154–5, 218–21, 226,
  251–3, 256–8, 313–14
  accession to English throne 3–4,
  11–12, 15–16, 25–6, 30–1, 42, 80,
  87–8, 95–6, 99–100, 103–7, 110,
  124–5, 127, 218, 237, 353–4, 429,
  432, 465
  appearance 37–64, 392
  attitude towards Dutch 431–2, 434,
  437, 448
  attitude towards parliaments 284–7,
  293, 295–301, 303–4, 306–8,
  310–15, 317
  character 5, 12, 187, 260, 294, 357–8,
  362–3, 379, 464
  childhood 35–8
  chivalry 44–5, 53, 233
  clemency 107–8, 111–12, 155–7,
  159–61, 201

James VI of Scotland and I of
  England (*cont.*)
  and conformity in religion 166,
    233–4, 321–6, 334–5, 340,
    350–1, 387
  consultations with privy
    councillors 256–7, 259–60, 282–3,
    292–3, 306–7, 441–2
  see also Elizabeth
  contrasts with Elizabeth 465–8
  coronation 124–5, 127–9, 134–42,
    152–3, 502 n.66
  criticisms of 34, 57–8, 60–3, 66, 72,
    114–16, 160–2, 196, 224–5, 229,
    250–3, 259, 289–90, 303–4, 331–3,
    351–2, 368–9, 388–9, 406, 468
  daughters 32, 54–5, 186–7, 221,
    445, 464
  deaths of children 55, 221
  see also Henry, prince, and Elizabeth,
    princess
  difficulties ruling Scotland 38–41, 153,
    155, 165, 467
  divine right kingship 56, 62–5, 72,
    138–40, 170, 180, 252–3, 286–8,
    310–12, 381, 465, 467–9
  duplicity/political flexibility 42, 50–1,
    58–60, 62–3, 72, 126, 218–19, 384,
    430–1, 435–6, 446
  ecumenism 59–60, 179, 290–1, 384–5
  expenditure 214–15, 239, 241, 251–2,
    267, 269–70, 309–10
  and Fuller's case 328–30
  and French 434–6
  heir to Elizabeth I 1–3, 10, 13,
    96–7, 99, 111
  household in England 4, 76, 214–15,
    217–20, 222–3, 229–30, 251–2, 273,
    278–9, 288, 301–2, 379–80, 391–2
  see also bedchamber
  hunting 11–12, 39, 45, 67–8, 111, 116,
    118, 217, 225–6, 246, 248–50, 252–3,
    255–9, 273, 333–4, 379, 434–5, 446,
    466, 468
  income 231, 250–2, 267, 269–70
  see also impositions and wardship
  language 164
  largesse 111, 114–15, 118–19, 135–6,
    225–7, 229, 251–2, 258, 267
  marriage 42–3

marriage of son 193–4, 211–13
misogyny 163, 190–1
and music 207–9, 350
patronage of the arts 66–9, 203–5, 207
peacemaker 61, 69, 145, 170, 179,
  193–4, 233, 431–3, 436, 455–64, 474
performances 114, 153–70, 175,
  177–80, 354–5, 430–1, 433–5, 471–2
phoenix 25–6, 30, 174–5
poet 55–61, 180
policies 4–5, 40–2, 44–5, 94, 126, 161,
  193–4, 290–1, 296–7, 304, 351–2,
  354–5, 357–9, 381, 388–92, 394–7,
  407–11, 415–17, 420, 429–31, 435–7,
  451, 454, 456, 463–4, 474, 546 n.156
portraits of 37–8, 49, 69–70, 205,
  377–8, 463
privy chamber 3, 160, 162, 165–6,
  210–11, 218–20, 230–1
progress to London 1603 91–3,
  107–17, 124, 286, 354
reformer 94, 167, 263–4, 277–8, 286,
  290–1, 299, 306, 343–7, 354, 357
relationship with Anna 63, 109–10,
  118–20, 186–7, 191–6, 199–201,
  237, 240–1
relationship with Elizabeth I 18, 22,
  31–4, 40–2, 46, 50, 54, 58–9, 62–3,
  111, 430
relationship with Prince Henry
  233–5
see also marriage of son
and religion 348–9, 368–9, 472–4,
  535 n.12
sexuality 38–9, 44–5, 226,
  465–6
and Somerset House
  Conference 441–4
speeches 34, 55, 62–3, 72, 164, 178–9,
  288–91, 304, 306–8, 311–14, 372–4,
  395–8, 467
suitors 87, 107, 118–19, 258, 269–70
summer progresses 192–3, 217, 234,
  246–7, 444–6, 472
title/right to English throne 99–104,
  106, 124–5, 137–8, 143–4, 147,
  152–3, 168–9, 178–9
translations 56, 58
trip to Denmark 43–5, 53
work ethic 257–8, 441–2, 466

INDEX

writings 44–5, 55–66, 72, 103, 124–5, 172–4, 382–6, 466–7
see also proclamations, Basilikon Doron, Trew Law
Jones, Inigo 203–5, 232, 238–9, 243–5, 248
Jones, William 336, 532 n.111
Jonson, Ben 6, 23, 180, 209–10, 222, 277
   The Alchemist 342
   Althorp 121–2
   Catiline 253
   Panegyric 180
   royal entry 167–8, 172, 177
   masques 203, 207–9, 238–9, 242–5, 248
   Sejanus His Fall 251–3
   Volpone 376
judges 15, 260, 284, 293–4, 298–9, 306–8, 329, 406–7, 467–9
Juhala, Amy 219–20
Jülich-Cleves, succession crisis 213–14, 312–13, 460–3

Kauffman, Lucy 534 n.165
Kewes, Paulina 496 nn.23, 28, 554 n.5, 555 n.20
Kip, William 167–8
Kirk 38–42, 46–7, 55, 58–9, 61–2, 67, 72, 86, 165, 167, 390, 395, 405–6, 409–10
knighthoods 110–11, 114–15, 135–6, 169, 220, 262
Knollys, William, Baron Knollys 261, 279, 477
Knyvett, Sir Thomas 186, 363

Lake, Sir Thomas 226–7, 256–8, 466
Lambeth articles 83–4, 350, 472
law 65, 105–7, 115–16, 137–8, 140, 151–2, 199–200, 202, 287, 298–9, 304, 391–2, 401–2, 405–6, 408, 544 n.75
   common law 79, 85, 97, 148, 286–9, 297, 311–12, 326–9, 405–7, 469–70
   courts 89, 217, 271–2
   statute 97, 99, 179, 202, 221, 271–2, 280, 301, 305, 326–8, 395
   writ of prohibitions 271–2, 326–31, 535 n.200
   see also high commission
Lecey, John 355–6
Lepanto, The 58–60

Lewkenor, Sir Lewis 217–18
libels 56, 228, 253, 259, 276–7, 332–3, 341–2, 396–7
localities 3, 254, 260, 283, 289, 301–2, 315, 474–5
   JPs 11, 79, 104, 246, 261–3, 334–5, 349–50, 365, 381–2, 387–9, 405, 474–5, 520 n.46
   lord lieutenants 89, 261–3, 410–11, Appendix 2, 537 n.81
London 2–3, 11, 18–19, 22, 29–30, 76–9, 95, 103–5, 107, 117, 128, 136, 216–17, 256, 347, 363–6, 379–80, 396–7, 401–2, 412, 418, 445
   Bourse 27, 216–17, 411
   City 16, 27, 75–9, 96, 99, 111, 135, 193–4, 216–17, 247–9, 285, 426
   lord mayor 15, 19–20, 78–9, 96, 99, 117, 136, 243, 412
   royal entry 1604 26–7, 60, 154–5, 167–79, 394
   royal entry 1606 248

Macdonald, Alan R. 554 n.7
Magna Carta 326–7
Maitland, John, Baron Thirlestane 47–8, 190–1, 195
Manners, Roger, fifth earl of Rutland 114, 127, 274
Marie de' Medici, wife of Henry IV of France 194, 202–3, 212–13, 463
Markham, Sir Griffin 92–3, 127–32, 142, 145, 147–8, 151, 156–9
Martin, Richard 117, 288–9, 291, 424
Mary I, queen of England 1–3, 24, 29, 32, 81, 104, 185, 241
Mary, Queen of Scots 1, 12, 18, 31–2, 35–9, 42, 48, 55–6, 58, 64–5, 82–3, 92–3, 95, 97, 105, 127, 150–1, 226, 255, 355–6, 392, 399
   tomb 32–3, 189, 278
masques 67, 237, 240–1, 244–5, 250–2, 472, 518 nn.196,198
   Althorp 121–2
   Anna's masques 193–4, 202–3, 214–15, 236–44, 273, 440, 446–7, 517 n.171
   Lennox's masques 221–2, 237
   Prince Henry's masques 203, 243

Matthew, Tobie, bishop of Durham 93, 111, 137, 178, 322–5, 338–9, 355, 522 n.108, 529 n.12
May, Steven 60–1
McCabe, Richard 56
medals 26–7, 34, 49, 69, 207, 286–7, 377–8, 392, 459–60, 463
Melville, Andrew 47–8, 50–1, 66, 409
merchants 43, 79–80, 170–4, 250–2, 256, 258, 269–70, 277–8, 403–4, 423–4, 426, 434, 438–9, 441–4, 446–7, 454–5, 459
  see also commerce
Midlands 121, 246, 299, 360–1, 364, 366–7, 418
  rising 1607 200, 263–4, 475
monopolies 79, 88–9, 112, 116–17, 133, 149, 223–4, 254, 265, 267, 299, 423–4
Montagu, Sir Edward 263–4, 291, 299–300, 334–6
Montagu, James, dean of the chapel royal 331–2, 334, 349, 382–3
Montaigne de, Michel 154, 210–11, 426–8
Montgomerie, Alexander 67–8
Moors 48, 52–4
Mordaunt, Baron Henry 361–2, 366, 536 n.21, 537 n.91
Morrill, John 545 n.114
Mosse, Miles 100
Munday, Anthony 412, 414–15

navy 11, 232, 248–9, 272–3, 277–8, 379–80, 420–1
Neville, Sir Henry 107–8, 404
Newton, Diana 532 n.99
Nicholls, Mark 367
nobility 219–20, 247, 408
  baronet 267, 388–9
  English 11–13, 15, 18–20, 76, 80–1, 96–7, 101, 107–8, 111–12, 123, 135–7, 160, 178, 186, 222, 246–7, 265, 284, 495 n.8
  English Catholic 129, 152, 273–4, 276–7, 354–5, 357–8, 361–2, 366, 387–9
  Scottish 38–40, 42–3, 46, 50, 52, 54–5, 58–9, 61–3, 69, 72, 100, 119–20, 186, 284

Norman Conquest 65, 137, 302–3, 391–2
Northamptonshire 89–93, 121–2, 263–4, 334–6, 338–9, 360, 385, 529 n.21
Norway 45, 53, 203, 394

oath of allegiance 355–6, 380–8, 452–3, 539 n.154, 540 n.157
Oatlands, Surrey 135, 192–3, 241, 247
Oliver, Isaac 197–8, 207–8
Ostend 431–2, 436, 446
Overall, John 84, 164, 347

pamphlets 26–7, 49, 74, 86
  pamphlet war 383–7
Parker, William, Baron Monteagle 361–3, 372, 537 n.63
parliaments, English 4, 11, 65, 79, 90–2, 223–4, 229–31, 265, 289–90, 372–3, 465, 467–8, 524 n.4, 525 n.38
  conflict with monarch 286–8, 291–4, 297–9, 303–4, 310–14, 316–17, 390, 467
  differences from Scottish 284–5, 405–6
  Elizabethan 299–300, 313, 467
  1614 parliament 189–90, 317
  1604 session 154–5, 168, 178, 260, 286, 290–305, 355, 357–8, 372, 396, 438–9
  1606 session 305–6, 379–80, 403, 452–3
  1606–07 session 244–5, 295–6, 306–11, 403–5, 454–5
  1610 session 243, 263, 267, 286, 308–17, 326, 345–6, 381, 462, 467
  speaker, the 285, 291, 294–5, 303–4, 315–16, 336, 387
  taxes 76, 88, 290–1, 305–6, 310–11, 315
Parry, Sir Thomas 202, 281
Peck, Linda Levy 276–7
Percy, Henry, earl of Northumberland 3–4, 80–1, 92–3, 95–6, 106, 274–5, 361–2, 366–7, 434–5, 477
  Under Elizabeth 275
Percy, Thomas 275, 360–6, 377
Persons Robert SJ 64–6, 82–3, 98, 128, 353, 382–4, 467

petitions 87–90, 93–4, 111–12, 116–19, 160, 256, 262, 343–4, 403–4
  poor man's 88–90
  parliamentary 301–4, 306–7, 313–15, 323, 454–5
  see also Catholics and Puritans
Philip III, king of Spain 74–5, 98–9, 132–3, 202–3, 211–13, 241, 244, 272, 354–5, 360, 383–4, 386, 418, 432–3, 436–8, 440–3, 447, 449–51, 453–61
Pickering, Lewis 92, 332–3
piracy 254, 256, 272, 453–5
plague 54–5, 283, 475
  1590s 77, 79
  1603 118, 122, 124–5, 134–5, 145–6, 154–5, 161–2, 168, 177, 290, 437
  1606 248
plays 26–31, 84, 86, 216, 228–9, 240–1, 246, 251–3, 413–15, 470
  at court 236, 248–9, 413–14
  Devil's Charter 375–6
  Dutch Courtesan 228–9
  Eastward Ho 114–15, 209–10, 228–9
  Heywood's *Part 1* and *Part 2* 27–30, 375
  History of King Leir 413
  Isle of Gulls 209–10, 228–9, 253
  Philotas 209–10
  Tragedie of Bonduca 414, 427–8
  Whore of Babylon 30, 375–6
  see also Shakespeare and Jonson
plots 27, 124–5
  Bye and Main Plots 126–34, 142–53, 336, 354–5, 368–9, 372, 436
  executions of plotters 154–9
  see also Gunpowder Plot
poems 23–5, 30–1, 47–51, 56, 66–8, 105, 149–50, 210–11, 289, 375, 377, 393–4, 412
Poland 394, 401, 408–9
poor 76–9, 89–90, 232, 475
pope 12, 41–2, 50–1, 61, 66, 123, 199–201, 233–4, 250, 342–3, 355, 370, 373–4, 377, 384–6, 388–9, 418, 461, 464
  Clement VIII 98–9, 192, 384, 450
  Paul V 382–4, 541 n.198
  power of deposition 81, 84–5, 123, 140, 164–7, 333, 357, 370, 380–1, 388
portraits 26–7, 69, 278–9
  see also VI and I James and Anna

Portugal 2, 400–1, 544 n.67
prayer book 179, 321–2
  of 1559 4–5, 84–6, 137, 163, 166, 327, 339
  of 1604 33–4, 299–300, 322–3, 326–7, 331–4, 336, 338, 350–1, 409, 472
  see also Puritans
predestination 61, 83–4, 164, 232, 343, 349–50, 472
Presbyterians
  anti-Presbyterian 86, 138–9, 164–5, 300–1, 324, 334, 337, 346, 409
  English 84, 86, 90–1, 166, 337–8, 532 n.121
  Scottish 39–41, 46–8, 53–5, 57–9, 61–3, 66, 72, 123, 140, 395, 409, 470
privateering 73–4, 423–4, 434, 439, 441, 453
privy council
  Elizabethan 2–4, 11–13, 16, 19, 254–6, 265, 282–3, 288
  changes under James 255–7, 259–62, 265, 288, 465, 468, 521 n.63
  continuities 261, 283
proclamations 34, 56, 81–2, 87–8, 107–8, 116–18, 259–60, 263–4, 287, 290–2, 306, 311–12, 322–3, 355, 357–8, 372, 387–8, 434
  accession proclamation 11–12, 15–16, 95–7, 99–100, 103–6, 152–3, 175–6
  coronation 127–8, 134–5
  for arrests 128–30, 363
  implementing Anglo-Scottish Union 118, 239, 391–2, 396–9, 467
  right to issue 271–2, 287, 314–15, 391–2, 397
Puritans 84–6, 92, 100, 143, 166–7, 321–2, 347, 472
purveyance 76, 79, 88–9, 94, 116–17, 267, 286, 290–1, 299, 301–4, 306–7, 309–10, 314–17
  anti-Puritan 86, 290, 322, 326, 341–2, 350–2, 384–5
  deprivations 321, 323–8, 333–5, 343–4, 350–1, 473
  in parliament 289, 305, 324, 327–8, 334–5
  nonconforming ministers 286, 299, 314–15, 321–6, 332–4, 337–8, 351
  pamphlets 86, 330, 336–7, 351–2

purveyance (*cont.*)
    petitioning 86, 90–2, 94, 124–5, 130,
        161–2, 179, 333–6, 338, 343–4, 354
    polemical campaign
        against 84, 339–41
    subscription 166–7, 322–7, 331–2, 350–1
    see also Hampton Court Conference,
        high commission, prayer book,
        Presbyterian

Questier, Michael 488 n.38
Quinn, Walter 68

Ralegh, Sir Walter 3–4, 20, 79, 89, 107–8,
    111–12, 130, 132–4, 142–51, 157–60,
    201, 212–13, 224, 226–7, 272, 422–3,
    501 nn.47, 52
Ramsay, Sir John, Viscount
    Haddington 224–6, 280
    wedding 245
Redich, Alexander 325–6, 531 n.91
Reid, Steven 492 n.154
Reynolds, John 163–7, 346–7, 534 n.171
Richmond Palace 9, 96, 188, 203–4,
    231–2, 243
Rickard, Jane 466–7
riots 77–9, 359, 418
Rosny, Maximilien de Béthune, marquis
    de 432, 434–6, 446–7
Rovida, Allesandro, senator of
    Milan 440–4
Royston 167, 235–6, 255–7, 280, 293,
    333–4, 362, 382–3, 462–3
Rudd, Anthony, bishop of St
    David's 115–16, 324
Rudolph II, emperor 232, 460–3
'running at the ring' 51–5, 221, 233–4,
    248–9
Russell, Conrad 292, 526 n.89, 527 n.93
Russell, Lucy, countess of Bedford 120,
    210–11, 229–31, 393–4, 433

Sackville, Thomas, Baron Buckhurst
    19–20, 92, 123, 152–3, 169, 269–70
    as earl of Dorset 169–70, 270–1,
        281, 441
Sandys, Sir Edwin 288–9, 297–9, 302–3,
    307–8, 404, 424, 454–5, 526 n.62
see also 384–5
Savoy 192, 211–13, 237, 385–6, 461

Scotland 2–3, 85, 108, 115–16, 373–4,
    421, 470
    Highlands 41, 405–6, 418, 420
    Iona Statutes 421
    Western Isles 41–2, 405–6, 420–1
    see also Edinburgh and Union
seditious words 79, 124–5, 152–3,
    289–90, 359, 508 n.21
separatism 324–5, 338–9, 532 n.125
sermons 15–16, 26–7, 29–31, 45, 66, 81,
    85–91, 100, 111, 115–16, 124, 157,
    168–9, 178, 187, 289–90, 331,
    348–50, 372–4, 379, 468
    coronation sermon 138–9
    court sermons 233–4, 245–6, 310–11,
        331, 348–9
Seton, Alexander, Lord Fyvie 41, 108–9,
    396, 403
Seymour, Edward, earl of Hertford
    97–8, 447–8
Seymour, Edward, Lord
    Beauchamp 1, 97–9
Seymour, William 189–90, 508 n.27
Shakespeare, William 6, 22–3, 27, 54,
    240–1, 248–9, 375–6, 398,
    548 n.204
    A Midsummer Night's Dream 53–4
    Cymbeline 413–14
    King Lear 413–14
    Macbeth 375–6, 471
    Measure for Measure 180–1, 342,
        507 n.111
    The Tempest 425, 428
    Titus Andronicus 470
    Twelfth Night 86, 234
Sharpe, Kevin 466–7
Smuts, Malcolm 471, 548 n.214,
    554 n.209
Society of Antiquaries 398
Solomon 26, 48, 51, 87, 90, 101, 240–1,
    387, 466–7
Somerset, Edward, fourth earl of
    Worcester 20, 106, 256–8, 273–4,
    276–7, 282, 315, 361–2, 478,
    522 n.113
    and Catholics 273–4, 359
Somerset House 192–3, 199–200,
    203–4, 213–15
    see also peace negotiations 1604
Somerset, Thomas 106

INDEX

Southwell, Elizabeth 10–11, 14–15, 17, 366–7
Sowerby, Tracey 541 n.190
Spain 1–2, 4–5, 11–12, 29–30, 41–2, 50–1, 58–9, 73, 103, 400–1, 417–18, 456–7, 459–61
  armada 1588 6, 22, 24, 27, 31–4, 61–2, 73–4, 375
  debate over peace with 148, 437–9, 474–5
  Elizabethan war against 73–7, 88, 98–9, 174, 211, 305, 398, 423, 431–2, 439
  Inquisition 85, 437–9, 443–4, 450, 454–5
  and New World 160–1
  peace negotiations 1604 29, 192–3, 211, 237–8, 267–8, 272, 281–2, 360, 432–3, 437, 439–44
  see also Treaty of London
  Anglo-Spanish tensions 449–50, 452–5
  see also ambassadors, Philip III, United Provinces
Spelman, Sir Henry 395–6, 405–6
Spencer, Sir Richard 121, 456–7, 459–60
St James's Palace 188, 204–5, 207, 231–2, 243
star chamber 13, 200, 217, 254–5, 264, 271–2, 281, 327, 332–3, 335–6, 349, 358–9, 366–7
Stilma, Astrud 59–60
Stewart, Francis, fifth earl of Bothwell 40, 43–4, 46, 50, 63
Stewart, James, later earl of Arran 39–40, 42, 58–9
Stirling 35–6, 38–9, 51, 108–9, 119–20, 191, 231
Stuart, Arbella 1, 10, 18–19, 97–9, 169–70, 186, 189–90, 201, 369–70, 508 n.27
  and plots 129, 132–4, 142–5, 147, 150–2, 156–7, 503 n.94
Stuart, Esmé, sieur d'Aubigny, first earl and first duke of Lennox 38–9, 56–8, 67, 478, 488 n.11
Stuart, Esmé, Lord Aubigny 222, 241, 408, 415
Stuart, Ludovick, second duke of Lennox 43–4, 46–8, 53–4, 56–7, 69, 116, 119–21, 186, 221–3, 248, 280, 282, 408, 415, 424, 446–7

succession 1–2, 26, 213, 297–8, 400–1
  hereditary principle 12–13, 64–5, 96, 138, 189–90, 355–6, 471
  to Elizabeth 1–3, 11–13, 44–5, 50–5, 57–60, 64–5, 68, 96–8, 111, 126, 185, 192, 353, 393, 470
  to James 26, 42, 44, 185, 189–90, 213, 222
surplice 84–5, 91, 322, 324–6, 331–2, 341
Sweden 66, 211, 385, 394, 408–9, 419, 463

Talbot, Gilbert, seventh earl of Shrewsbury 114, 121, 123
Tassis, Juan de, count of Villamediana 193–4, 237, 432–3, 436–7, 439–40, 443–5
Thames, river 17, 135, 172, 217, 243–4, 248, 412
Theobalds, Hertfordshire 72, 113–14, 116–17, 167, 187, 192–3, 195, 204, 248, 250–1, 268, 315, 384–5
Thornborough, John, bishop of Bristol 289–90, 400
Thrush, Andrew 268
tithes 91
  impropriated 161, 344–6, 534 n.165
tournaments 33–4, 50–2, 186, 203, 221, 224–6, 233–4, 243, 247–9, 472
  see also 'running at the ring'
Tower of London 3–4, 15–16, 26–7, 99, 107–8, 118, 127–36, 142–3, 149, 156, 160–1, 167–9, 200, 218–19, 248–9, 275, 295, 330–3, 335–6, 363, 366–9, 377–8, 405, 409, 508 n.27, 535 n.9
  lieutenant of the 147, 363, 377–8
Treaty of Berwick 1586 40–2
Treaty of Hampton Court 1604 434–6, 446
Treaty of London 1604 199, 207, 423–4, 445–50, 551 n.91
  ratification of 447–50
  frictions after 451–5
  see also Spain
Treaty of Vervins, 1598 2, 74, 432, 435–6, 443–4
Tresham, Francis 361–2, 366, 368
Tresham, Sir Thomas 92–3, 124–5, 354–5, 361, 496 n.39
Trew Law, The 63–6, 259–60, 286–7, 353

630   INDEX

Tyacke, Nicholas 288–9
tyranny 24, 65–6, 115–16, 228, 287–8,
    315–16, 348, 386, 436–7, 468–9, 475

United Provinces 32, 41–2, 66, 74, 230–1,
    429, 434–5, 437, 446–7, 451–2,
    454–5, 460
  Dutch 41–2, 58, 60, 66, 73–4, 130,
    170–1, 173–5, 390–1, 430–1, 433,
    436–7, 440–3, 446, 461–2
  Holland 50–1, 377–8
  negotiations for a peace with
    Spain 453, 456–8
  Treaty with England 1608 458
  1609 truce 459–60
Union 168–70, 172, 179–80, 218–19,
    222–3, 229, 244–5, 260, 266, 294,
    296–7, 328, 390–411, 469–70
  Anglo-Scottish marriages 225, 272,
    279, 407–8
  Anglo-Scottish tensions 121, 123, 390
  anglocentricity of 393, 400–1, 411–12
  anti-Scottish sentiment 72, 97, 105,
    114–15, 124–5, 228–9, 279, 292, 297,
    307, 363–4, 390, 405, 470
  attempts at congruity 408–11, 470,
    545 n.114
  and English parliament 296–9, 305–8,
    403–6, 527 n.125
  'imperfect union' 394
  Instrument, The 305–7, 402–4, 413
  and naturalization 257–8, 286, 289,
    306–8, 400, 402–7, 467, 545 n.102
  'perfect union' 394, 404, 469–70,
    543 n.66
  pro-Union tracts 399–402, 405–6
  Scots' attitudes towards Union 280,
    308, 390, 392–3, 395–404, 543 n.43
  see also James VI and I, policies
universities 23–4, 26–7, 31–2, 79–80,
    161–2, 246, 284, 323, 343–5, 350,
    379–80, 401–2, 472
  of Cambridge 83–4, 331, 347
  of Oxford 246, 249–50, 347
  scholars 23–5
Usher, Roland 530 n.27

Vanson, Adam 47, 69
Vautrollier, Thomas 56–8

Venice 383–6, 446–7, 456
  see also Venetian ambassador
Villiers, George, later earl of
  Buckingham 195, 200, 226, 465–6

Waldegrave, Robert 47–8, 63–4, 399
Wales 150–1, 179, 231, 393, 395, 398, 405,
    411–12, 469–70
  council of 116, 260, 271–2, 314–15,
    381, 540 n.163
  see also Henry, prince
Walsingham Lady Audrey 194–5, 229–30,
    515 n.108
wardship 80, 88–9, 94, 267, 290–1, 299,
    301–4, 309–10, 312, 314–17, 405
  see also great contract
Watson, Anthony, bishop of
  Chichester 13–14, 21–2, 92,
    156–7, 344
Watson, William 92–3, 126–30, 133,
    142–6, 336
Wentworth, Thomas 308–10
Westminster Abbey 18–22, 31–2, 134–7,
    146, 186–9, 191–2, 275, 278,
    299–300, 347
Whitehall Palace 9, 15, 17, 21, 26–7, 106,
    118, 134–6, 141–2, 168–9, 178,
    192–3, 199, 204, 216–18, 221,
    234–5, 238–9, 241–3, 245–6, 248–9,
    256–7, 259–60, 268–9, 271, 284–5,
    292–3, 303, 307–8, 311–13, 361–4,
    379, 445
Whitgift, John, archbishop of
  Canterbury 13–15, 19, 21–2, 83–5,
    137–8, 140–2, 161–4, 166, 322–3,
    332, 344–5, 349–51, 484 n.31,
    484 n.33, 526 n.75
Willet, Andrew 26, 90, 101
Winchester 131, 145–6, 149, 153, 155–6,
    160, 236
  executions 156, 160
  trials 145–6, 153, 155
Windsor 118–19, 121–3, 127, 202, 234–5,
    248–9, 436
  order of the garter 118–19, 123, 130,
    233–5, 248–9, 350, 408, Appendix 3
Winwood, Sir Ralph 451–2, 457, 459–61
witchcraft 63–4, 139, 466–7, 491 n.138
Wormald, Jenny 491 n.138

Wotton, Sir Henry 204–5, 385–6, 446–7, 541 n.188
Wriothesley, Henry, earl of Southampton 15–16, 107–8, 123, 130–1, 135–6, 151–2, 229–31, 274, 424, 435–6, 527 n.116
Wroth, Sir Robert 288–9, 299, 301–3

Yelverton, Sir Henry 288–9, 293
York 109, 111–14, 120–1, 218–19, 285, 401–2
  archbishop of York 285, 338–9, 357
Young, Peter 36–7, 232

Zouche, Edward La, Baron Zouche 116